# Interpersonal
# Communication

*Fourth Edition*

# Interpersonal Communication

## Relating to Others

**Steven A. Beebe**
Texas State University–San Marcos

**Susan J. Beebe**
Texas State University–San Marcos

**Mark V. Redmond**
Iowa State University

PEARSON

Boston   New York   San Francisco
Mexico City   Montreal   Toronto   London   Madrid   Munich
Paris   Hong Kong   Singapore   Tokyo   Cape Town   Sydney

Executive Editor: Karon Bowers
Editor: Brian Wheel
Senior Development Editor: Carol Alper
Editorial Assistant: Jennifer Trebby
Marketing Manager: Mandee Eckersley
Senior Editorial-Production Administrator: Beth Houston
Editorial-Production Service: Lifland et al., Bookmakers
Text Design and Composition: Schneck-DePippo Graphics
Photo Research: Helane Prottas
Composition and Prepress Buyer: Linda Cox
Cover Administrator: Linda Knowles
Manufacturing Buyer: Megan Cochran

For related titles and support materials, visit our online catalog at www.ablongman.com.

**Library of Congress Cataloging-in-Publication Data**

Beebe, Steven A.
    Interpersonal communication : relating to others / Steven A. Beebe, Susan J. Beebe,
  Mark V. Redmond.—4th ed.
      p.    cm.
    Includes bibliographical references and index.
    ISBN 0-205-41792-2
    1. Interpersonal communication. I. Beebe, Susan J. II. Redmond, Mark V., 1949–. III. Title
  BF637.C45 B43 2001
  153.6—dc21                                      00-066388

Printed in the United States of America
10 9 8 7 6 5         08 07 06

Credits appear on page 419, which constitutes a continuation of the copyright page.

## Dedicated to Our Families

Mark and Matthew Beebe

Peggy, Nicholas, and Eric Redmond, and Beth Maroney

# Brief Contents

# List of Features

## Building Your Skills

# Contents

## Chapter 2
## Interpersonal Communication and Self   32

## Chapter 3
## Interpersonal Communication and Perception   66

## Chapter 6
## Verbal Communication Skills    156

## Understanding How Words Work    157

## Recognizing the Power of Words    161

## Chapter 8
## Conflict Management Skills    218

## Part Three
## Interpersonal Communication in Relationships    255

## Chapter 9
## Understanding Interpersonal Relationships    256

# Preface

The secret to effective interpersonal relationships is not really a secret. It's a fundamental principle that transcends both culture and time. Distilled to its three-word essence, the centuries-old "secret" is: Be other-oriented. A focus on others rather than yourself remains the hallmark of every faith movement in the world. Yet this book is not about religion. It's about how you relate verbally and nonverbally to others in interpersonal situations. To be other-oriented, you need not abandon your own thoughts, feelings, and behavior; an other-oriented person is self-aware as well as aware of others. Becoming other-oriented is instead the mindful process of considering the thoughts, needs, feelings, and values of others, rather than an exclusive focus on self. The importance of being other-oriented was the foundation of the first three editions of *Interpersonal Communication: Relating to Others,* and it continues as the central theme of the fourth edition.

This book is designed to be the primary text for college-level courses in interpersonal communication. We've written this book for college students ages 18 to 80 who are seeking research-based principles and skills to enhance their interpersonal relationships. We emphasize *research-based*, because this is not merely a book of "how to" techniques to "win friends and influence people." Our ideas are based on decades of communication research and reflect the latest thinking about how human beings relate to each other. Our balance of principles and skills is designed to help students enhance their own command of communication skills, as well as to give them insights into why people communicate as they do in interpersonal situations.

## Our Approach to Interpersonal Communication

### An Other-Oriented Approach

We believe that considering the thoughts and feelings of others is a fundamental prerequisite for improving interpersonal communication. Becoming other-oriented is not a single skill, but rather a collection of skills and principles that are designed to increase your sensitivity to and understanding of others. Being other-oriented doesn't mean you abandon your own ideas and feelings only to please others; that would not only be unethical, it would be an ineffective approach to developing genuine, honest relationships with others. We repeatedly stress that true empathy, emotional intelligence, and sensitivity are possible only when we feel secure about our own identities.

Becoming other-oriented includes all of the classic skills and principles typically taught in interpersonal communication courses—such as listening, providing feedback, and using conflict management skills and verbal and nonverbal skills—and places additional emphasis on the importance of the perceptions, thoughts, attitudes, beliefs, values, and emotions of others. We also review how relationships are formed and maintained and sometimes are redefined and deteriorate. Toward the end of each chapter we include a feature called "Becoming Other-Oriented," in which we identify a principle or skill to help you become more aware of others. We also use a margin icon, like the one in the margin here, to highlight other-oriented ideas and strategies throughout the book.

## An Emphasis on Diversity

It's impossible to be other-oriented without being willing to acknowledge diversity. Inherent in our other-oriented approach is the theme that people differ in significant ways. It is because of those diverse differences that we need skills and principles that allow us to develop common links so we can establish meaningful interpersonal relationships with others. The body of research about gender- and culture-based differences in communication behavior has continued to grow; the last decade saw a significant leap in our understanding of the role that differences in culture, gender, religion, political perspectives, and other points of view have on people's ability to connect to others. In this book we do more, however, than just point to differences between human beings. Using a competency-based approach, we present practical, research-based strategies for increasing understanding when interacting with those who are different from us.

Communication occurs when people find commonalities in meaning that transcend their differences. In Chapter 4, "Interpersonal Communication and Cultural Diversity: Adapting to Others," we not only identify barriers to competent intercultural communication but also present strategies to bridge the chasm of differences that too often divide rather than unite people. In addition, we distill research conclusions and communication strategies for understanding differences in the "Understanding Diversity" features in every chapter. But our discussion of diversity is not merely window dressing; through examples, illustrations, and research conclusions liberally woven throughout the book, we identify ways to become other-oriented despite differences we encounter in people of the other gender or of other cultures or ideologies.

## An Emphasis on Relationships

Relationships are the ongoing connections we make with others through interpersonal communication. As the book's subtitle, *Relating to Others,* suggests, we highlight the importance of cultivating relationships by developing an increased awareness of and sensitivity to our relationships with others. Our emphasis on relationships is reflected in the wide range of relationship types we discuss, including relationships with friends, lovers, family members, and coworkers, as well as relationships formed and developed over the Internet. In an approach that is new to this edition, we discuss not only positive, affirming relationships but also the "dark side" of relationships—such issues as aggressiveness, argumentativeness, deception, and hurtful messages. Whether emphasizing the positive nature of relationships or providing a glimpse of the darker aspects of relating to others, we rely on the latest communication research so that readers will have access to up-to-the-minute thinking about how relationships can be improved.

## An Emphasis on the Internet and Interpersonal Relationships

Contemporary technology has a profound influence on how we relate to others, not just online but in person as well. In every chapter, we discuss research findings about how our electronic connections affect our face-to-face relationships. A new feature in this edition is the inclusion of "Weblinks" at the end of each chapter, which enrich and enliven chapter content with supplemental readings and activities. Although our primary focus remains on live, face-to-face communication, we believe we cannot and should not ignore the ever-increasing role of technology in interpersonal communication.

# New Features of the Fourth Edition

We are continually grateful for the popularity enjoyed by the first three editions of our book. For this edition we endeavored to retain the elements of the earlier editions that students and instructors like best. Our other-oriented approach, emphasis on diversity, focus on relationships, and expanded coverage of technology, coupled with our balanced discussion of principles and skills, are the essential reasons both students and instructors enthusiastically praise this book.

Because new research about interpersonal communication continues to unfold, and because we wish to continuously refine our approach to presenting both classic and contemporary research, we've made several changes to make this book the best possible resource for learning about interpersonal communication. Here's a summary of some of the key revisions we've made to the fourth edition:

- Expanded the final three chapters from the previous edition into four chapters to capture the relevant aspects of new interpersonal communication research.

- Provided updated research conclusions about interpersonal communication in every chapter.

- Added new examples, illustrations, and cartoons to help students see connections between research conclusions and their own lives.

- Added a new margin icon to highlight other-oriented material.

- Included in every chapter a new feature called "Applying Theory and Research," in which we select a theory or recent research article and apply the information to students' lives in an interesting and meaningful way.

- Included in every chapter a new feature called "Becoming Other-Oriented," in which we spotlight principles and strategies based on our signature concept, to help students focus on the interests and needs of others.

- Developed a new chapter-end feature called "Weblinks," in which we list interesting and useful Web addresses where students can find supplemental information about interpersonal communication. These links are also included and updated on our companion Website www.ablongman.com/beebe.

- Made the following additions and changes to individual chapters:

### Chapter 1:

Added new information about social learning theory to the discussion of interpersonal communication competence.

### Chapter 2:

- Enriched our discussion of symbolic interaction theory.
- Provided new information about understanding cultural differences in self-disclosure.

### Chapter 3:

- Added new information about diversity and perception.
- Included new information about the fundamental attribution error and self-serving bias.
- Added discussion and applications of politeness theory.

### Chapter 4:

- Updated information about the importance of diversity in our lives.
- Expanded our discussion of how to be interculturally competent.

### Chapter 5:

- Provided new information about shifting attention as a barrier to interpersonal listening.
- Included new information about listener apprehension.
- Moved information about confirmation and disconfirmation from Chapter 6 to this chapter's expanded discussion of responding skills.
- Streamlined and fine-tuned our discussion of critical listening skills.

### Chapter 6:

Refined the discussion of developing supportive communication skills.

### Chapter 7:

- Identified the importance of using supportive nonverbal behavior with others.
- Described the characteristics of people who are skilled in interpreting nonverbal communication.
- Added new material about detecting deceitful nonverbal communication.

**Chapter 8:**

- Refined our definition of interpersonal conflict.
- Added new material about cultural differences and preferred conflict management style.
- Revised our discussion of conflict management styles by identifying five rather than three styles.
- Added new information about negotiation skills.

**Chapter 9:**

- Focused the discussion of the nature of interpersonal relationships on intimacy, attraction, and power.
- Consolidated information about the types of interpersonal relationships and included a new discussion on cross-sex friendships.
- Included new information on the principles of power in relationships and the negotiation of relational power.

**Chapter 10:**

- Added information about male and female initiation of date requests.
- Reorganized the discussion of the skills and strategies used in initiating, escalating, and maintaining interpersonal relationships.

**Chapter 11:**

- Included coverage of challenges facing relationships, including failure events, physical separation and distance, and social norms.
- Added new information about the dark side of interpersonal communication that focuses on deception, hurtful messages, aggressiveness, and argumentativeness.
- Included the latest research about what happens to relationships when relationship partners lie.

**Chapter 12:**

- Rearranged and updated the content of this chapter and enhanced the emphasis on interpersonal relationships and the Internet.
- Described the role and impact of family rituals on interpersonal communication.
- Included new information on workplace romances.

## Our Partnership with Instructors

As important as we think a textbook is, it is only one tool that facilitates student learning. In the fourth edition of *Interpersonal Communication: Relating to Others*, we continue our tradition of offering a wide variety of instructional resources to help instructors teach and students learn principles and skills of interpersonal communication.

Built into the book is a vast array of pedagogical features:

- A chapter-opening quotation to provide an initial captivating focal point for the chapter.
- A list of chapter learning objectives.
- A comprehensive chapter-opening outline of key content.

- "Understanding Diversity" features that highlight applications of interpersonal communication in a diverse world.

- "Building Your Skills" features that help students see the connection between knowing and doing.

- New "Becoming Other-Oriented" features that help students understand the signature theme of the book.

- A new other-oriented icon appearing in the margin to highlight material that focuses on the needs and concerns of others.

- Liberal use of "Recap" features to help students distill the essence of key concepts and terms.

- A margin glossary of all boldface terms in the text.

- Chapter-end questions that focus on critical thinking and ethics to spark thought and class discussion.

- Chapter-end "For Your Journal" questions and activities to prompt reflection and application.

- "Learning with Others," chapter-end collaborative learning activities and exercises.

- New end-of-chapter "Weblinks" to supplemental resources and activities.

In addition to the learning resources built into the book, we offer an abundance of valuable instructor and student supplements.

## Instructor's Supplements

### Print Supplements

- *Instructor's Resource Manual.* By Sue Stewart of Texas State University–San Marcos, this comprehensive guide provides a wealth of teaching tips, lecture outlines, sample syllabi, Internet exercises, class assignments, and student activities. This guide also includes the *Companion Website Teaching Tool,* containing activities, teaching suggestions, and test questions to help the instructor integrate the Companion Website into his or her own teaching style and classroom environment.

- *Test Bank.* This test bank by Thomas E. Jewell of Bergen Community College contains multiple-choice, true/false, matching, short answer, essay, midterm, and final exam questions.

- *The Blockbuster Approach: A Guide to Teaching Interpersonal Communication with Video, 3e.* The guide by Thomas E. Jewell of Bergen Community College provides lists and descriptions of commercial videos that can be used in the classroom to illustrate interpersonal concepts and complex interpersonal relationships. Sample activities are also included.

- *VideoWorkshop for Interpersonal Communication Instructor's Teaching Guide.* Written by Lynn M. Disbrow, of Sinclair Community College, this guide provides teaching suggestions, quiz questions and answers, and discussion starters that will help instructors use the VideoWorkshop for Interpersonal Communication CD-ROM in class. A correlation guide helps you relate the materials to your text. The complete CD-ROM and Student Learning Guide are included in the guide. Go to www.ablongman.com/videoworkshop for more details.

### Electronic Supplements

- *Computerized Test Bank.* The questions in the print Test Bank are also available electronically through our computerized testing system, TestGen EQ. The fully networkable test-generating software is now available on a multiplatform CD-ROM. The user-friendly interface enables instructors to view, edit, and add questions, transfer questions to tests, and print tests in a variety of fonts. Search and sort features allow instructors to locate questions quickly and arrange them in a preferred order.

- *PowerPoint Presentation™.* This package by Nan J. Peck of Northern Virginia Community College consists of a collection of text-specific lecture outlines and graphic images keyed to every chapter in the text and is available on the Web at suppscentral.ablongman.com.

- *Allyn and Bacon Digital Media Archive for Communication, Version 2.0 (Windows and Macintosh).* This resource, available on CD-ROM, offers more than 200 still images, video excerpts, Weblinks, and assorted lecture resources that can be incorporated into multimedia presentations in the classroom.

- *Online Course Management.* CourseCompass, powered by Blackboard and hosted nationally, is Allyn and Bacon's own course management system. CourseCompass helps you manage all aspects of teaching your course. It features preloaded content to support the Interpersonal Communication course. (Your sales representative can give you additional information.) Instructors at colleges and universities with WebCT™ and Blackboard™ licenses can have access to special course management packages in these formats as well.

Allyn and Bacon provides a selection of video materials especially tailored for the Interpersonal Communication course. Contact your sales representative for details.

- *Allyn and Bacon Interpersonal Communication Video, Volume II.* This 30-minute video presents a variety of scenarios that portray interpersonal concepts and relationships. A user's guide accompanies the video and contains scripts, discussion questions, and exercises for each episode.

- *Allyn and Bacon Interpersonal Communication Video.* This 30-minute video contains three scenarios illustrating concepts in interpersonal communication including communication fundamentals, perception, the self, listening, conflict, intimacy, and relationships. The video comes with a guide featuring transcripts and teaching activities.

- *Video: Interpersonal Communication.* Eight interpersonal scenarios examine a wide range of interpersonal issues including perception, ethics, self-disclosure, sexual harassment, and dysfunctional relationships. An extensive guide provides a script, class discussion questions, and exercises for each of the episodes.

- *Interpersonal Movie Library.* This collection is available to adopters and contains feature films dealing with a range of interpersonal topics.

- *Allyn and Bacon Communication Video Library.* The library contains a collection of communication videos produced by Film for the Humanities and Sciences.

### Student Supplements

### Print Supplements

- *Skillbuilder Workbook.* This guide by Mark Redmond helps students reinforce and enhance their understanding of the principles and skills of interpersonal communication. Filled with exercises, activities, and study aids, it provides students with a wealth of opportunities to review and apply concepts introduced in the text.

- *Research Navigator Guide for Speech Communication.* By Terrence Doyle of Northern Virginia Community College and Linda R. Barr of the University of the Virgin Islands, this booklet covers the basics of using the Internet, conducting Web searches, and critically evaluating and documenting Internet sources. It also contains Internet activities and URLs specific to the discipline of speech communication.

### Electronic Supplements

- *Companion Website with Online Practice Tests* (www.ablongman.com/beebe). Created by Sue Stewart of Texas State University–San Marcos, this site includes Weblinks and Internet activities to enrich the course. The site also contains on-line learning objectives, practice tests, and interactive discussions.

- *VideoWorkshop for Interpersonal Communication.* By Lynn M. Disbrow, of Sinclair Community College, VideoWorkshop is a new way to bring video into your course for maximized learning. This total teaching and learning system includes quality video footage on an easy-to-use CD-ROM, plus a Student Learning Guide and an Instructor's Teaching Guide—both with textbook-specific Correlation Grids. The result? A program that brings textbook concepts to life with ease and that helps students understand, analyze, and apply the objectives of the course. VideoWorkshop is available for students as a value-pack option with the text.

- *Communication Tutor Center* (access code required). Our Tutor Center provides free, one-on-one tutoring for students who purchase a new copy of participating Allyn and Bacon textbooks. Qualified instructors tutor students on all material covered in the texts. The approach is highly interactive, providing both knowledge of the academic discipline and methods for study of that discipline. Tutoring assistance is offered by phone, fax, Internet, and e-mail during Tutor Center hours. For more details and ordering information, please contact your Allyn and Bacon publisher's representative.

## Acknowledgments

This book is not only a collaboration among the three of us, but also a collaboration with a host of others. Without the research conclusions of the talented, creative scholars who have studied interpersonal communication and published their results, a book of this scope would not be possible. We also thank our students, who are a constant source of questions, ideas, inspiration, and challenges that enrich our teaching and writing.

We are especially thankful for the continuing outstanding editorial support and leadership that kept our multi-author team collaborating with aplomb. Executive editor Karon Bowers, who has worked with us for a decade, continues to be a source of inspiration and unwavering support. Brian Wheel, our new series editor, has proven to be a valuable fount of ideas and information. Senior development editor Carol Alper fits into the author team like a member of the family; we continue to be grateful for her expert guidance.

We also appreciate the dozens of gifted interpersonal communication instructors and scholars who read the manuscript and offered suggestions that have made this a better book. We thank the following people for sharing their information, ideas, and ingenuity with us:

## Reviewers for the Fourth Edition

Scott E. Caplan
*University of Delaware*

Reginald E. Ecarma
*Campbellsville University*

David L. Edwards
*South Central Technical College*

Janie Harden Fritz
*Duquesne University*

Adna G. Howell
*Delta College*

Heidi McGrew
*Sinclair Community College*

Lisa M. Orick
*Albuquerque Technical Vocational Institute*

James R. Pauff
*Bowling Green State University*

Nan Peck
*Northern Virginia Community College*

Vincent Scott Smithson
*Purdue University North Central*

Lori Wisdom-Whitley
*Everett Community College*

## Reviewers for the First, Second, and Third Editions

Rebecca Anderson
*Johnson County Community College*

Leonard Barchak
*McNeese University*

Cameron Smith Basquiat
*Community College of Southern Nevada*

Judyth Betz-Gonzales
*Delta College*

Marion Boyer
*Kalamazoo Community College*

Norman Clark
*Appalachian State University*

Carolyn P. DeLeCour
*Palo Alto College*

Carol Z. Dolphin
*University of Wisconsin–Waukesha*

Terrence Doyle
*Northern Virginia Community College*

Patricia M. Harris-Jenkinson
*Sacramento City College*

Sherry J. Holmen
*Albuquerque Technical Vocational Institute*

David D. Hudson
*Golden West College*

Diana K. Ivy
*Texas A & M University–Corpus Christi*

Thomas E. Jewell
*Marymount College*

Elizabeth R. Lamoureux
*Buena Vista University*

Timothy P. Mottet
*Texas State University–San Marcos*

Nan Peck
*Northern Virginia Community College*

Terry Perkins
*Eastern Illinois University*

Susan Richardson
*Prince George's Community College*

Michael Schliessman
*South Dakota State University*

Cheri Simonds
*Illinois State University*

Anntarie Lanita Sims
*Trenton State College*

Dickie Spurgeon
*Southern Illinois University*

Glen H. Stamp
*Ball State University*

Dick Stine
*Johnson County Community College*

Claire Sullivan
*University of Maine*

James J. Tolhuizen
*Indian University–Northwest*

Sally Vogl-Bauer
*University of Wisconsin–Whitewater*

Sheryl L. Williams
*University of Wisconsin–Whitewater*

Richard L. Wiseman
*California State University–Fullerton*

We are blessed with the support and ideas of our colleagues and friends. Sue and Steve thank Thompson Biggers, a valued friend and colleague who helped conceptualize this book. Mary Jeanette Smythe and Tom Willett are long-time teachers and friends who provided seminal instruction about interpersonal communication. Phil Salem, Lee Williams, Tim Mottet, Cathy Fleuriet, and Maureen Keeley are friends and colleagues at Texas State University–San Marcos who have positively influenced our work. John Masterson, a valued friend and colleague, also greatly influenced our teaching and writing about interpersonal communication. Special thanks go to the late Michael Argyle at Oxford University, Oxford, England, who sponsored Steve as a Visiting Scholar at

Oxford's Wolfson College and generously shared his research findings. Thanks, too, to Peter Collett, friend and colleague from Oxford, for his assistance, support, and friendship. Thayne McCollough, from Gonzaga University, also a colleague whom Steve met in Oxford, provided valuable support for this project.

Over the years Mark has had the opportunity to interact with a number of colleagues who have helped shape his views and understanding of interpersonal communication. Particularly, Mark thanks Kay Mueller, Denise Vrchota, Terry Pickett, David Waggoner, Judith Bunyi, and Steve Ralston for help in the earlier editions. Denise has continued to provide her unique insights for improving the text that can be found woven into the fourth edition. Beth Lamoureux at Buena Vista University continues to be an extraordinary supporter of our text, as well as a supportive friend. Mark's office neighbor and colleague Eric Abbott has provided invaluable advice, counsel, and support during the development of this edition. Mark would also like to acknowledge and thank a group of colleagues he met years ago when they were all graduate students at the University of Denver and with whom he developed enduring and treasured friendships: Rich Arthur, at Slippery Rock University; John Masterson, Texas Lutheran University; Diane Ritzdorf, Arapahoe High School; Marc Routhier, Frostburg State University; Jim Tolhuizen, Indiana University Northwest; and especially Phil Backlund, Central Washington University.

We have had outstanding staff support from many people. Sue Hall, senior administrative assistant in the Department of Communication Studies at Texas State, continues to be an invaluable assistant and friend. Sondra Howe and Bob Hanna are other valued colleagues and staff members who provided skilled support. We thank Kosta Tovstiadi for his skilled research assistance and Ernie Dominguez for his help in tracking down and double-checking our Weblinks.

Finally, our families provide ongoing love and support to each of us. Mark thanks his parents, Jack and Alice Redmond; his brother, Jack; and his sisters, Ruthann, Mary Lynn, and Tina, who helped shape a family environment that planted the seeds for studying and appreciating interpersonal communication. Those seeds have been nurtured into a full-grown fascination with how communication shapes our lives and personal development by his wife, Peggy, his daughter Beth, and his sons, Nicholas and Eric. On a practical level, Mark owes a lot of his understanding of chat rooms and instant messaging to them.

Steve and Sue want especially to thank their parents, Russell and Muriel Beebe and Herb and Jane Dye, their first and finest teachers of interpersonal communication, combining more than 120 years of marriage; both sets of parents model the quintessential skill of being other-oriented. We also thank our son Mark for teaching us that the power of love overcomes life's challenges and our son Matt, who teaches us about the importance of finding music in days filled with both sunshine and clouds.

Steven A. Beebe
Susan J. Beebe
*San Marcos, Texas*

Mark V. Redmond
*Ames, Iowa*

# About the Authors

Steven A. Beebe is Professor and Chair of the Department of Communication Studies and Associate Dean of the College of Fine Arts and Communication at Texas State University–San Marcos. Steve is the author or co-author of nine widely used communication books, most of which have been through multiple editions, as well as of numerous articles, book chapters, and conference presentations. He has been a Visiting Scholar at both Oxford University and Cambridge University in England, has traveled widely in Europe and Asia, and has played a leadership role in establishing new communication curricula in Russian universities. In 1996 he was named Outstanding Communication Professor by the National Speaker's Association. He has also received the President's Award for Research as well as the President's Award for Service at Texas State. His passions in life include his family and a life-long love of music; he is a pianist and organist and is currently struggling to learn the cello.

Susan J. Beebe's professional interests and expertise encompass both oral and written communication. Currently serving as Acting Director of Lower-Division Studies in the Department of English at Texas State University–San Marcos, Sue has co-authored three books and has published a number of articles and teaching materials in both English and communication studies. She has received both the Texas State Presidential Award for Excellence in Service and the College of Liberal Arts Award for Excellence in Scholarly/ Creative Activities. An active volunteer in the community of San Marcos, Texas, Sue was the founding coordinator of the San Marcos Volunteers in Public Schools Program and has served on the San Marcos School Board and the Education Foundation Board. In 1993 she was named the statewide Friend of Education by the Texas Classroom Teachers' Association; in 2000 the San Marcos school district presented her with its Lifetime Achievement Award. Sue enjoys reading, traveling, and caring for the Beebe family pets, a Shih Tzu named Martin and a cat named Alice. Sue and Steve have two sons: Mark, a 2001 graduate of Rice University; and Matt, a senior at Southwestern University.

Mark V. Redmond is an Associate Professor and Coordinator of the Communication Studies program in the Greenlee School of Journalism and Communication at Iowa State University. Besides this book, Mark has authored an introductory communication theory and research text, edited an upper-level text in interpersonal communication, and has a public speaking text forthcoming. His research focuses on social decentering (taking into account another person's thoughts, feelings, perspectives, etc.), one of the themes incorporated in this text. His studies have included an examination of initial interactions between strangers, adaptation in interpersonal interactions, interpersonal influence, and intercultural communication competence. Now that his children are in their late teens and early twenties, he appreciates the personal insights he is gaining into the lives of today's college students. He is a Cyclone sports fan with an avocation for playing basketball at least three times a week (despite an aging hook shot). An unaccomplished piano and guitar player, he loves composing and writing songs and vows to someday complete the musical he's been working on for twenty years.

# Interpersonal
# Communication

# Part One

# Interpersonal Communication Foundations

Chapter 1
Introduction to Interpersonal Communication

Chapter 2
Interpersonal Communication and Self

Chapter 3
Interpersonal Communication and Perception

Chapter 4
Interpersonal Communication and Cultural Diversity:
Adapting to Others

The first four chapters present fundamental concepts that frame our study of interpersonal communication. In Chapter 1 you will learn answers to these questions: What is interpersonal communication? What is the connection between interpersonal communication and interpersonal relationships? Why is it important to study relationships? What can I do to improve my relationships with others? Chapter 2 offers concepts and skills to help you understand more about who you are and how your self-concept and sense of self-worth influence your relationships, as well as how you reveal yourself to others. In Chapter 3 you will learn that perception plays a key role in effective interpersonal communication. By recognizing the factors that influence your perceptions and actively analyzing the meaning of perceptual information, you can become more adept at sharing your sense of the world with others. Chapter 4 explores principles to help you better understand people who are different from you and explains how developing an other-oriented perspective helps bridge cultural differences.

## CHAPTER 1

# Introduction to Interpersonal Communication

## OBJECTIVES

1. Compare and contrast definitions of communication, human communication, and interpersonal communication.

2. Explain why it is useful to study interpersonal communication.

3. Compare and contrast communication as action, interaction, and transaction.

4. Describe the key components of the communication process.

5. Discuss five principles of interpersonal communication.

6. Describe four interpersonal communication myths.

7. Identify strategies that can improve your communication competence.

## OUTLINE

Defining Interpersonal Communication

The Importance of Interpersonal Communication to Our Lives

An Evolving Model for Human and Interpersonal Communication

Mediated Interpersonal Communication: A New Frontier

Principles of Interpersonal Communication

Interpersonal Communication Myths

How to Improve Your Own Interpersonal Communication Competence

*Communication is to a relationship
what breathing is to maintaining life.*

Virginia Satir

Interpersonal communication is like breathing; it is a requirement for life. And, like breathing, interpersonal communication is inescapable. Unless you live in isolation, you communicate interpersonally every day. Listening to your roommate, talking to a teacher, meeting for lunch with a friend, or talking to your parents or your spouse are all examples of interpersonal communication.

It is impossible *not* to communicate with others. Even before we are born, we respond to movement and sound. With our first cry we announce to others that we are here. Once we make contact with others, we communicate, and we continue to do so until we draw our last breath. Even though many of our messages are not verbalized, we nonetheless send messages to others—intentionally and sometimes unintentionally. Whether we intend for them to or not, people draw conclusions from our behavior. Without interpersonal communication, a special form of human communication that occurs as we manage our relationships, people suffer and even die. Recluses, hermits, and people isolated in solitary confinement dream and hallucinate about talking with others face-to-face.

Human communication is at the core of our existence. Think of the number of times you communicated with someone today, as you worked, ate, studied, shopped, or went about your other daily activities. Most people spend between 80 and 90 percent of their waking hours communicating with others.[1] It is through these interactions with others that we develop interpersonal relationships.[2]

Because these relationships are so important to our lives, later chapters will focus on the communication skills and principles that explain and predict how we develop, sustain, and sometimes end relationships. We'll explore such questions as the following: Why do we like some people and not others? How can we interpret other people's unspoken messages with greater accuracy? Why do some relationships blossom and others deteriorate? How can we better manage disagreements with others? How can we better understand our relationships with our family, friends, and coworkers?

This chapter charts the course ahead, addressing key questions about what interpersonal communication is and why it is important. We will begin by seeing how our understanding of the interpersonal communication process has evolved. And we will conclude by examining how we initiate and sustain relationships through interpersonal communication.

# Defining Interpersonal Communication

To understand interpersonal communication, we must begin by understanding how it relates to two broader categories: communication in general and human communication. Scholars have attempted to arrive at a general definition of communication for decades, yet experts cannot agree on a single one. One research team counted more than 126 published definitions;[3] however, in the broadest sense, **communication** is the process of acting on information.[4] Someone does or says something, and others think or do something in response to the action or the words as they understand them.

Communication is not unique to humans. It is possible, for example, for you to act on information from your dog. He barks; you feed him. This definition also suggests that your dog can act on information from you. You head for the cupboard to feed him; he wags his tail and jumps up in the air, anticipating his dinner. Researchers do study communication between species as well as communication systems within single animal species, but these fields of study are beyond the scope of this book. The focus of our study is on a form of human communication: people communicating with other people.[5]

To refine our broad definition, we can say that **human communication** is the process of making sense out of the world and sharing that sense with others by creating meaning through the use of verbal and nonverbal messages.[6] We learn about the world by listening, observing, tasting, touching, and smelling; then we share our conclusions with others. Human communication encompasses many media: speeches, songs, radio and television broadcasts, e-mail, letters, books, articles, poems, and advertisements.

**Interpersonal communication** is a distinctive, transactual form of human communication involving mutual influence, usually for the purpose of managing relationships. Three essential elements of this definition distinguish the unique nature of interpersonal communication from other forms of human communication.[7]

## Interpersonal Communication Is a Distinctive Form of Communication

For years many scholars defined interpersonal communication simply as communication that occurs when two people interact face-to-face. This limited definition suggests that if two people are interacting, then they are communicating. Today, interpersonal communication is defined not just by the number of people who communicate, but also by the quality of the communication. Interpersonal communication occurs not simply when you interact with someone, but when you treat the other as a unique human being.

Think of all human communication as ranging on a continuum from impersonal to interpersonal communication. **Impersonal communication** occurs when you treat people as objects, or when you respond to their roles rather than to who they are as unique people. Philosopher Martin Buber influenced our thinking about human communication when he presented the concept of honest dialogue as the essence of true, authentic communication.[8] He described communication as consisting of two different qualities of relationships. He discussed an "I–It" relationship as an impersonal one; the other person is viewed as an "It" rather than as an authentic, genuine person. When you buy a pair of socks at a clothing store, you have a two-person, face-to-face, relatively brief interaction with someone. You communicate. Yet that interchange could hardly be described as intimate or personal. When you ask a server in a restaurant for a glass of water, you are interacting with the role, not necessarily with the

**communication.** Process of acting on information.

**human communication.** Process of making sense out of the world and attempting to share that sense with others by creating meaning through the use of verbal and nonverbal messages.

**interpersonal communication.** A distinctive, transactual form of human communication involving mutual influence, usually for the purpose of managing relationships.

**impersonal communication.** Communication that occurs when we treat people as objects, or when we respond to their roles rather than to who they are as unique persons.

individual. You know nothing personal about him (or her), and he knows nothing personal about you (unless he eavesdrops by your table).

Interpersonal communication occurs when you interact with another person as a unique, authentic individual rather than as object or "It." Buber calls this kind of relationship an "I–Thou" relationship. In this kind of relationship, there is true dialogue. An "I–Thou" relationship is not self-centered. The communicators have developed an attitude toward each other that is honest, open, spontaneous, nonjudgmental, and based on equality rather than superiority.[9] The exchanges with the sock-seller or server have the potential to become true interpersonal communication, but they only do so if you begin to interact with these people as unique individuals. If, for example, during your conversation with the server, you discover you were born in the same town and develop other personal links, the impersonal, role-oriented communication becomes more personal, and the quality of the communication moves toward the intimate end of the continuum.

We're not suggesting that the goal of every communication transaction is to develop a personal, intimate dialogue. That would be unrealistic and inappropriate. It would be odd to develop close personal relationships with others just because you were talking with them while buying socks or asking for a glass of water at a restaurant. It's possible to go through an entire day communicating with others but not be involved in interpersonal communication. As we noted earlier, interpersonal communication is a distinctive form of communication; it does not occur just because two people are communicating.

Additionally, although interpersonal communication is more intimate and reveals more about the people involved than does impersonal communication, not all interpersonal communication involves sharing closely guarded personal information. As we discuss later in the book, there are degrees of intimacy when interacting with others. Table 1.1 compares and contrasts interpersonal communication and impersonal communication.

*In* face-to-face encounters, we simultaneously exchange both verbal and nonverbal messages that result in shared meanings. Through this kind of interrelation, we build relationships with others.

---

**TABLE *1.1*   The Continuum Between Interpersonal Communication and Impersonal Communication**

| Interpersonal Communication | Impersonal Communication |
|---|---|
| • People are treated as unique individuals. | • People are treated as objects. |
| • People communicate in an "I–Thou" relationship. Each person is special. | • People communicate in an "I–It" relationship. Each person has a role to perform. |
| • There is true dialogue and honest sharing of self with others. | • There is mechanical, stilted interaction, rather than honest sharing of feelings. |
| • Interpersonal communication often involves communicating with someone you care about, such as a good friend or cherished family member. | • Impersonal communication involves communicating with people such as sales clerks and servers—you have no history with them and you expect no future with them. |

## Interpersonal Communication Involves Mutual Influence Between Individuals

Mutual influence means that *all* partners are affected by a transaction, not just one person. Interpersonal communication may or may not involve words. The transaction may be fleeting or enduring. While you are talking and your mother is listening, you are also simultaneously observing your mother's nonverbal expressions. Just because she is not speaking does not mean she is not communicating. She not only hears *what* you have to say, but also observes *how* you say it.

The degree of mutual influence varies a great deal from transaction to transaction. You probably would not be affected a great deal by a brief smile that you received from a traveling companion on a bus, but you would be greatly affected by your lover telling you he or she was leaving you. Every interpersonal communication transaction influences us. Sometimes it changes our lives dramatically, sometimes in small ways. Long-lasting interpersonal relationships are sustained not by one person giving and another taking, but by a spirit of mutual equality. Both you and your partner listen and respond with respect for each other. There is no attempt to manipulate others. True dialogue, says researcher Daniel Yankelovich, involves a collaborative climate. It's not about winning and losing an argument. It's about being understood and accepted.[10]

Buber defines the quality of being fully "present" when communicating with another person as an "I–Thou" relationship.[11] To be present is to give your full attention to the other person. The quality of interpersonal communication is enhanced when both you and your partner are simultaneously present and focused on each other.

## Interpersonal Communication Is the Fundamental Means We Use to Manage Our Relationships

An interpersonal **relationship** is the ongoing connection you make with others through interpersonal communication. Relationships go through a series of developmental stages. The initial stages of relationships often involve sharing less intimate or personal information. Later stages include more intimate conversations and behaviors.

You initiate and form relationships by communicating with others whom you find attractive in some way. You seek to increase your interactions with people with whom you wish to develop relationships, and you continually interpersonally communicate to maintain the relationship. You also use interpersonal communication to end relationships that you have decided are no longer viable.

In this book we define interpersonal communication as a unique form of human communication. There are other forms of communication, as well. **Mass communication** occurs when someone communicates the same message to many people at once, but the creator of the message is usually not physically present, and listeners have virtually no opportunity to respond immediately to the speaker. Messages communicated via radio and TV are examples of mass communication. **Public communication** occurs when a speaker addresses an audience in person. **Small-group communication** occurs when a group of from three to fifteen people meet to interact with a common purpose and mutually influence one another. The purpose of the gathering could be to solve a problem, make a decision, learn, or just have fun. While communicating with others in a small group, it is also possible to communicate with others interpersonally—to communicate to manage a relationship with one or more individuals in the group. Finally, **intrapersonal communication** is communication with yourself. Thinking is perhaps the best example of intrapersonal communication. In our discussion of self and communication in Chapter 2, we discuss the relationships between your thoughts and your interpersonal communication with others.

**relationship.** An ongoing connection made with another person through interpersonal communication.

**mass communication.** Communication that occurs when one person issues the same message to many people at once; the creator of the message is usually not present, and there is virtually no opportunity for listeners to respond to the speaker.

**public communication.** Communication that occurs when a speaker addresses an audience in person.

**small-group communication.** Communication that occurs when a group of from three to fifteen people meet to interact with a common purpose and mutually influence one another.

**intrapersonal communication.** Communication with yourself; thinking.

# $\mathcal{T}$he Importance of Interpersonal Communication to Our Lives

**W**hy learn about interpersonal communication? Because it touches every aspect of our lives. It is not only pleasant or desirable to develop quality interpersonal relationships with others, it is vital for our well-being. We have a strong need to communicate interpersonally with others. Learning how to understand and improve interpersonal communication can improve relationships with family, loved ones, friends, and colleagues and can enhance the quality of physical and emotional health.

1. ***Being skilled in interpersonal communication can improve relationships with family.*** Relating to family members can be a challenge. The divorce statistics in the United States document the difficulties that can occur when people live in relationships with others: About half of all marriages end in divorce. We don't claim that you will avoid all family conflicts or that your family relationships will always be harmonious if you learn principles and skills of interpersonal communication. You can, however, develop more options for responding when family communication challenges come your way. You will be more likely to develop creative, constructive solutions to family conflict if you understand what's happening and can promote true dialogue with your spouse, parent, brother, or sister. Furthermore, family relationships play a major role in determining how you interact with others. Family communication author Virginia Satir calls family communication "the largest single factor determining the kinds of relationships [people make] with others."[12] Being able to have conversations with family members and loved ones is the fundamental way of establishing close, personal relationships with them.

2. ***Being skilled in interpersonal communication can improve relationships with friends and lovers.*** You don't choose your biological family, but you do choose your friends. Friends are people you choose to be with because you like them, and usually they like you. For unmarried people, developing friendships and falling in love are the top-rated sources of satisfaction and happiness in life.[13] Conversely, losing a relationship is among life's most stressful events. Most people between the ages of 19 and 24 report that they have had from five to six romantic relationships and have been "in love" once or twice.[14] Studying interpersonal communication may not unravel all the mysteries of romantic love and friendship, but it can offer insight into behaviors.

3. ***Being skilled in interpersonal communication can improve relationships with colleagues.*** In many ways, colleagues at work are like family members. Although you choose your friends and lovers, you don't always have the same flexibility in choosing those with whom or for whom you work. Understanding how relationships develop on the job can help you avoid conflict and stress and increase your sense of satisfaction. In addition, your success or failure in a job often hinges on how well you get along with supervisors and peers.

    Several surveys document the importance of quality interpersonal relationships in contributing to success at work.[15] The abilities to listen to others, manage conflict, and develop quality interpersonal relationships with others are usually at the top of the list of the skills employers seek in today's job applicants.

4. ***Being skilled in interpersonal communication can improve physical and emotional health.*** Research has shown that the lack or loss of a close relationship can lead to ill health and even death. Physicians have long observed that patients who

*R*esearch shows that effective interpersonal skills can be beneficial to our emotional and physical well-being.

are widowed or divorced experience more medical problems such as heart disease, cancer, pneumonia, and diabetes than do married people.[16] Grief-stricken spouses are more likely than others to die prematurely, especially around the time of the departed spouse's birthday or near their wedding anniversary.[17] Being childless can also shorten one's life. One study found that middle-aged, childless wives were almost two-and-one-half times more likely to die in a given year than those who had at least one child.[18] Terminally ill patients with a limited number of friends or no social support die sooner than those with stronger ties.[19] Without companions and close friends, opportunities for intimacy and stress-minimizing interpersonal communication are diminished. Although being involved in intimate interpersonal relationships can lead to conflict and feelings of anger and frustration, researchers suggest that when all is said and done, having close relationships with others is a major source of personal happiness.[20] Studying how to enhance the quality of your communication with others can make life more enjoyable and enhance your overall well-being.

## *Recap* Comparing Key Definitions

| Term | Definition |
|---|---|
| **Communication** | The process of acting on information |
| **Human communication** | The process of making sense out of the world and sharing that sense with others by creating meaning through verbal and nonverbal messages |
| **Interpersonal communication** | The process of interacting with another and mutually influencing each other, usually for the purpose of managing relationships |

# *A*n Evolving Model for Human and Interpersonal Communication

Interpersonal communication involves more than simply transferring or exchanging messages; it is a complex process of creating meaning in the context of an interpersonal relationship. To understand this process more fully, it is useful to see how our perspectives on the human communication process have evolved over the past half century.[21] We will begin with the simplest and oldest model of the human communication process and then discuss more contemporary models.

## Human Communication as Action: Message Transfer

"Did you get my message?" This simple sentence summarizes the communication-as-action approach to human communication. Communication takes place when a message is sent and received. Period. It is a way of transferring meaning from sender to receiver.

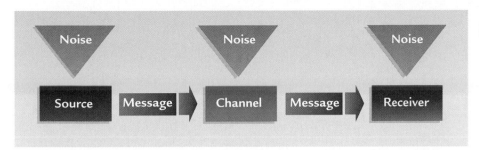

FIGURE *1.1*

A Simple Model of Human
Communication as Action

Figure 1.1 shows a basic model that depicts communication as a linear input/output process. Today, although they view the process as more complicated, researchers still define most of the key components in this model in basically the same way.

## Source

The **source** for communication is the originator of a thought or an emotion, who expresses ideas and feelings as a code that can be understood by a receiver. Translating ideas, feelings, and thoughts into a code is called **encoding.** Vocalizing a word, gesturing, and establishing eye contact are signals that we use to encode our thoughts into a message that can be decoded by someone. **Decoding,** the opposite process of encoding, occurs when the words or unspoken signals are interpreted by the receiver.

## Receiver

The **receiver** is the person who decodes and attempts to make sense of what the source encoded. Think of a radio station as a source broadcasting to a receiver that picks up the station's signal. In human communication, however, there is something in between the source and the receiver: People filter messages through past experiences, attitudes, beliefs, values, prejudices, and biases.

## Message

**Messages** are the written, spoken, and unspoken elements of communication to which people assign meaning. You can send a message intentionally (talking to a professor before class) or unintentionally (falling asleep during class); verbally ("Hi. How are you?"), nonverbally (a smile and a handshake), or in written form (this book).

## Channel

A message is communicated from sender to receiver via some pathway called a **channel.** Channels correspond to your senses. When you call your mother on the telephone, the channel is an auditory one. When you talk with your mother face-to-face, the channels are many. You see her: the visual channel. You hear her: the auditory channel. You may smell her perfume: the olfactory channel. You may hug her: the tactile channel.

## Noise

**Noise** is anything that interferes with a message and keeps it from being understood and achieving its intended effect. Without noise, all messages would be communicated with sublime accuracy. But noise is always present. It can be literal (the obnoxious roar of a neighbor's lawn mower), or it can be psychological (instead of concentrating on your teacher's lecture, you may start thinking about the chores you need to finish before the end of the day). Whichever kind it is, noise gets in the way of the message and may even distort it. Communicating accurate messages involves minimizing both external and psychological noise.

The action approach is simple and straightforward, but it has a key flaw: Human communication rarely, if ever, is as simple and efficient as "what we put in is what we

**source.** Originator of a thought or emotion, who puts it into a code that can be understood by a receiver.

**encode.** To translate ideas, feelings, and thoughts into a code.

**decode.** To interpret ideas, feelings, and thoughts that have been translated into a code.

**receiver.** Person who decodes a message and attempts to make sense of what the source has encoded.

**message.** Written, spoken, and unspoken elements of communication to which people assign meaning.

**channel.** Pathway through which messages are sent.

**noise.** Anything literal or psychological that interferes with accurate reception of the communication of the message.

FIGURE *1.2*

**A Model for Communication as Interaction.**
Interaction models of communication include feedback as a response to a message sent by the communication source and context as the environment for communication.

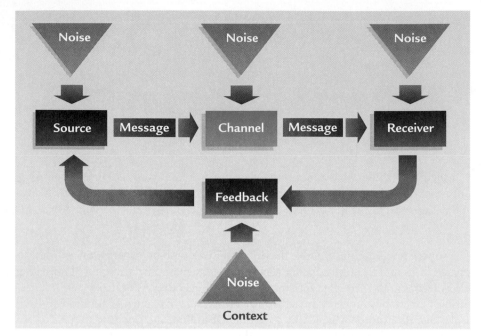

get out." Others cannot automatically know what you mean just because you think you know what you mean. Although by the early 1940s, when the action approach was formulated, communication scholars had already begun identifying an array of key elements in the communication process, the action approach overlooked their complexity.

### Human Communication as Interaction: Message Exchange

The next big leap in understanding human communication came in the late 1940s and early 1950s. The communication-as-interaction perspective used the same elements as the action models but added two new ones: feedback and context.

Think of a Ping-Pong game. Like a Ping-Pong ball, messages bounce back and forth. We talk; someone listens and responds; we listen and respond to this response. This perspective can be summarized using a physical principle: For every action there is a reaction.

**Feedback** is the response to the message. Without feedback, communication is rarely effective. When you order your black olive pizza and the server says in response, "That's a black olive pizza, right?" he has provided feedback to ensure that he decoded the message correctly. Like other messages, feedback can be intentional (your mother gives you a hug when you announce your engagement) or unintentional (you yawn as you listen to your uncle tell his story about bears again); verbal ("That's a black olive pizza, right?") or nonverbal (blushing after being asked to dance).

A second component recognized by the interaction perspective is **context**, the physical and psychological environment for communication. All communication takes place in some context. As the cliche goes, "Everyone has to be somewhere." A conversation with your good friend on the beach would likely differ from one the two of you might have in a funeral home. Context encompasses not only the physical environment but also the number of people present and their relationship with the communicators, the communication goal, and the culture the communicators are part of.[22]

This perspective, as shown in Figure 1.2, is more realistic, but it still has limitations. Although it emphasizes feedback and context, it does not quite capture the com-

**feedback.** Response to a message.

**context.** Physical and psychological environment for communication.

plexity of interpersonal communication, which typically takes place simultaneously. The interaction model of communication still views communication as a linear, step-by-step process. But in interpersonal situations, both the source and the receiver send and receive messages at the same time.

## Recap

### Components of the Human Communication Process

| Term | Definition |
| --- | --- |
| Source | Person who has an idea or emotion and encodes it for a receiver |
| Receiver | Person or group who decodes intentional or unintentional messages from a source |
| Message | Written, spoken, and unspoken elements of communication to which people assign meaning |
| Channel | Pathway through which messages pass between source and receiver |
| Noise | Anything literal or psychological that interferes with the clear reception and interpretation of a message |
| Encode | To translate ideas, feelings, and thoughts into a code |
| Decode | To interpret ideas, feelings, and thoughts that have been translated into a code |
| Context | Physical and psychological environment for communication |
| Feedback | Verbal and nonverbal responses to messages |

## Human Communication as Transaction: Message Creation

The communication-as-transaction perspective, which evolved in the 1960s, acknowledges that when you talk to another, you are constantly reacting to what your partner is saying. Most scholars today view the transaction perspective as the most realistic model for interpersonal communication. Like action and interaction, transaction uses various components to describe communication. However, in this model, all the components are simultaneous. As Figure 1.3 indicates, you send and receive messages concurrently. Even as you talk, you are also interpreting your partner's nonverbal and verbal responses.

Transactional communication also occurs within a context defined more broadly than in the action or interaction models. Transactional communication suggests that your communication is influenced by forces that may not be immediately evident to you or your communication partner. The past experiences and culture of the people involved in the communication, the setting of the communication, and the thoughts and emotions of the communicators are all influencing how messages are being interpreted.

FIGURE *1.3*

**A Model for Communication as Mutual Transaction.**
The source and receiver of a message experience communication simultaneously.

Whereas models of communication as action or interaction view communication as linear—there are specific causes and effects that can explain how messages are interpreted—communication as transaction is much more complicated. An understanding of the relationships you establish changes from moment to moment as the conversation unfolds and your thoughts influence how you are responding to the message. A transactional approach to communication suggests that no single cause explains why you interpret messages the way you do. In fact, it is inappropriate to point to a single factor to explain how you are making sense of the messages of others; communication is messier than that. The meaning of messages in interpersonal relationships evolves from the past, is influenced by the present, and is affected by visions of the future.

One researcher says that interpersonal communication is "the coordinated management of meaning" through **episodes,** during which the message of one person influences the message of another.[23] Technically, only the sender and receiver of those messages can determine where one episode ends and another begins.

## Recap

### An Evolving Model for Interpersonal Communication

| | |
|---|---|
| **Human Communication as Action**  | Human communication is linear, with meaning sent or transferred from source to receiver. |
| **Human Communication as Interaction**  | Human communication occurs as the receiver of the message responds to the source through feedback. This interactive model views communication as a linear action–reaction sequence of events. |
| **Human Communication as Transaction**  | Human communication is mutually interactive. Meaning is created based on a concurrent sharing of ideas and feelings. This transaction model most accurately describes human communication. |

## Mediated Interpersonal Communication: A New Frontier

Today's technology allows us to expand our definition of interpersonal communication. Instead of having to rely on face-to-face contact for our interpersonal exchanges, we can now use various types of media to carry our interpersonal messages: Telephones, faxes, e-mail, and electronic chat rooms are among the sometimes bewildering assortment of devices through which we can interact, exercise mutual influence, and develop interpersonal relationships. When we use one of these media to carry the message, we are using **mediated interpersonal communication.**

At present, the most effective interpersonal communication, especially for expressing feelings, occurs when no media filters interfere with the clarity of the message or delay feedback from the receiver of the message. For this reason, our key focus in this book is on unmediated interaction between people.

But we will also begin to explore the new frontier in interpersonal communication. Can you communicate interpersonally with someone on the Internet? Can relationships be developed with others without meeting them face-to-face? There is evidence that people can and do develop meaningful relationships with others without

**episode.** Sequence of interaction between individuals, during which the message of one person influences the message of another.

**mediated interpersonal communication.** Communication with others established or maintained through media (such as e-mail, telephones, or faxes) rather than through face-to-face encounters.

meeting them in person. Research suggests that some long-distance relationships can be as satisfying as face-to-face relationships.[24] If you are attending a college or university away from family, friends, or loved ones, you may have found that sending e-mail messages can help keep you in touch with others who are important to you. College freshmen and their parents report that e-mail connections reduce homesickness and the sadness parents often feel as their son or daughter leaves home. The past few years have seen an increase in the number of people who meet in chat rooms on the Internet and eventually develop real-time relationships. In 2002, more than 35 million Americans visited online dating sites each month. By 2003, that number had swelled to 45 million users a month, with the numbers continuing to skyrocket.[25]

People have even developed new ways to communicate the feelings, emotions, and other responses that make it possible to communicate nonverbally. You are probably familiar with emoticons (keyboard symbols like :-O). You can also communicate emotions via e-mail by "screaming," TYPING IN ALL CAPITAL LETTERS TO SHOUT THE MESSAGE. In still other situations, you might respond to someone by verbally describing nonverbal behaviors: "I am frowning right now as I read what you are sending me."

Of course, just as not all face-to-face communication is interpersonal communication, not all mediated communication results in unique relationships with others. One of the key characteristics of these mediated communication situations is the reduced level of nonverbal cues. Even if you use emoticons, when you can't see the other person's facial expression, amount of eye contact, or whether he or she seems interested in what you are saying, accurately communicating your meaning, especially your feelings and emotions, can be challenging.

A growing body of research, however, suggests that when you interact with people using computer-mediated communication, you can compensate for the lack of nonverbal cues. If you've been interacting with someone over a period of several weeks or months, you begin to pick up cues about his or her emotions and feelings just from the words he or uses and from what you have learned about that person's behavior.

Communication researcher Joseph Walther and his colleagues have developed a **social information-processing theory** that explains how you can develop quality relationships with others via e-mail and other electronic means.[26] According to this theory, a key difference between face-to-face and computer-mediated communication is the rate at which information reaches you. During live, in-person communication, you process a lot of information quickly; you process the words you hear as well as the myriad of nonverbal cues you see (facial expression and body posture) and hear (tone of voice and use of pauses). During e-mail interactions, there is less information to process, so it takes a bit longer for the relationship to develop—but it does develop as you learn more about your e-mail partner's likes, dislikes, and feelings. Also, if you expect to communicate with your electronic communication partner again, there is evidence that you will pay more attention to the relationship cues that develop. In one study, Joseph Walther and Judee Burgoon found that the relationships that developed between people who met face-to-face differed little from those between people who had computer-mediated interactions.[27] In fact, they found the computer-mediated group actually developed *more* socially rich relationships than the face-to-face groups.

A study by Lisa Tidwell and Joseph Walther investigated how computer-mediated communication affects how much and how quickly people reveal information about themselves and the overall impressions people form of one another.[28] In comparing

**social information-processing theory.** Theory that explains how people use information they receive from others via e-mail and other electronic media to develop relationships with others.

## applying theory and research

### Does Your Level of Communication Apprehension Predict the Type of Relationships You Have with Others Online?

Do people "meet" others online to overcome some of the apprehension they may feel when they communicate with people face-to-face? Michelle Mazur and Ryan Burns wanted to know whether Internet relationships that blossomed online can be explained in part because communicating in cyberspace arouses less communication apprehension, especially for people who are shy or introverted. They administered a survey via the Internet to people who had met their romantic partners online and who used the Internet to maintain their relationships. Participants completed measures to assess their general level of communication apprehension (how anxious or nervous they are when communicating with others), their level of introversion (shyness), and their relational interdependence (how connected or close they are with their partners).

The researchers found out that people who are generally more apprehensive about communicating with other people in face-to-face situations reported that their relationship with their online romantic partner was interdependent or close. Stated another way, people who are highly apprehensive about communicating with others report their online relationships as important to them. Introverts commu-

nicate less with other people in face-to-face communication situations. The researchers found that people who scored high as introverts reported lower levels of connectedness in their online relationships.

### Applying the Research to Your Life

What do the results of this study mean? If you are apprehensive about communicating with other people in live, face-to-face situations, you may be more comfortable communicating with people via the Internet. People who are highly anxious and apprehensive about communicating with others face-to-face can nonetheless satisfy their need to connect with others by relating to others online. This study also suggests that if you are introverted (shy about establishing relationships with others), you will be more likely to "keep to yourself" online; you will perceive your relationship with others as more independent, which suggests more separateness than closeness in a relationship. There's a difference between wanting to keep to yourself and just being apprehensive about communicating with others. If you are communication apprehensive, you be-

come *nervous* when you have to talk to others. If you're an introvert, you generally are *shy* and less comfortable connecting to others. Communication apprehension is more specifically a description of how much anxiety you experience when talking with others. Cyberspace can be liberating for you if you're apprehensive about communicating with others; you may be less anxious about sharing information about yourself if you don't have to look at the other person while you're communicating with him or her. If you're simply introverted or shy, you may reach out to others online but still prefer relationships in which you and your partner are less interlinked or interdependent. Researchers don't yet have all the answers about similarities and differences between communicating online and communicating face-to-face. They do have evidence, however, that if you are apprehensive about communicating in person, you will likely be more comfortable communicating via the Internet.

*Source:* Michelle A. Mazur and Ryan J. Burns, "Perceptions of Relational Interdependence in Online Relationships: The Effects of Communication Apprehension and Introversion," *Communication Research Reports, 17*(4), (2000): 397–406.

computer-mediated exchanges with face-to-face conversations, Tidwell and Walther found that people in computer-mediated "conversations" asked more direct questions, which resulted in people's revealing *more* information about themselves, not less, when online. The pattern of differences between computer-mediated communication and face-to-face communication is still being discovered as computer-mediated communication becomes an even more significant part of modern life.

Because of technology, some electronic interpersonal exchanges may not be simultaneous. Nonetheless, there can be mutual understanding, and the communication can be truly personal rather than impersonal. We suggest that these electronic communication exchanges, even though not as rich in nonverbal and relational information, can mirror characteristics of face-to-face interpersonal communication in the sense that you are developing or maintaining a unique relationship with someone. In addition, electronically mediated relationships can involve mutual influence. And whether you're e-mailing someone that you'd like to get married or just to get together for a cup of coffee, e-messages can alter both lives and relationships. Clearly, not all e-mail correspondence is interpersonal communication; today's technology, however, sometimes makes it possible to emulate in cyberspace the characteristics of interpersonal transactions.

One research team suggests that the richness of a communication channel can be measured by four criteria: (1) the amount of feedback that the communicators can receive; (2) the number of cues that the channel can convey and that can be interpreted by a receiver; (3) the variety of language that communicators use; and (4) the potential for expressing emotions and feelings.[29] Using these four criteria, researchers have developed a continuum of communication channels, from communication-rich to communication-lean. Figure 1.4 illustrates this continuum.

There is some evidence that if we have a negative message to communicate to someone, such as you want to break off a relationship with someone, you may select a less-rich communication message—you may be more likely to send a letter or an

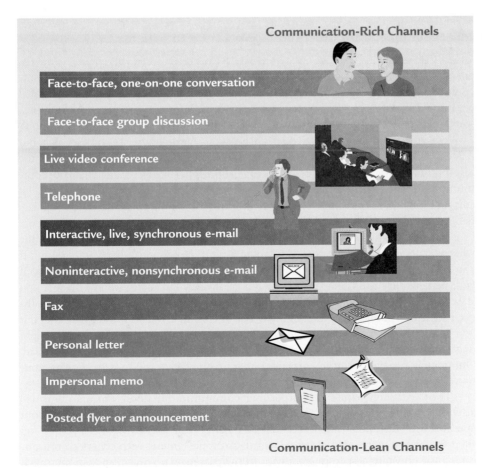

**Communication-Rich Channels**

Face-to-face, one-on-one conversation

Face-to-face group discussion

Live video conference

Telephone

Interactive, live, synchronous e-mail

Noninteractive, nonsynchronous e-mail

Fax

Personal letter

Impersonal memo

Posted flyer or announcement

**Communication-Lean Channels**

FIGURE *1.4*

A Continuum of Communication-Rich and Communication-Lean Channels of Communication.
Adapted from L. K. Trevino, R. L. Draft, and R. H. Lengel, "Understanding Managers' Media Choices: A Symbolic Interactionist Perspective." In *Organizations and Communication Technology,* edited by J. Fulk and C. Steinfield (Newbury Park, CA: Sage, 1990), 71–94.

e-mail rather than share the bad news face-to-face.[30] Similarly, you'll want to share good news in person, when you can enjoy the positive reaction to your message.

In summary, we believe this new frontier of electronic communication makes it possible for people to develop interpersonal relationships with others who are miles away. We agree with Walther and Tidwell that

> The "Information Superhighway" is clearly not just a road for moving data from one place to another, but a roadside where people pass each other, occasionally meet, and decide to travel together. You can't see very much of other drivers at first, unless you do travel together for some time. There are highway bandits, to be sure, who are not as they appear to be—one must drive defensively—and there are conflicts and disagreements on-line as there are off-road, too.[31]

# Principles of Interpersonal Communication

As we introduce the study of interpersonal communication in this chapter, it is useful to present fundamental principles that help explain the nature of interpersonal communication. Underlying our current understanding of interpersonal communication are five principles: Interpersonal communication connects us to others, is irreversible, is complicated, is governed by rules, and involves both content and relationship dimensions.

## Interpersonal Communication Connects Us to Others

Unless you are a living in a cave or have become a cloistered monk, you interact with others every day. Even if you work at home in front of a glowing computer screen, you encounter other people in the course of living your life. The opportunities for interpersonal communication are ubiquitous—they are everywhere. It is through inescapable interpersonal communication with others that we affect and are affected by other human beings.

We agree with author H. D. Duncan, who said, "We do not relate and then talk, but relate in talk." Fundamental to an understanding of interpersonal communication is the assumption that the quality of interpersonal relationships stems from the quality of communication with others. It's been said—and we noted earlier—that people can't *not* communicate. Even though this perspective is debated among communication scholars because people often don't intend to express ideas or feelings, without question interpersonal communication is inescapable in the twenty-first century. Try to think of a time when you are *not* communicating. Hard to do, isn't it? How about when you're asleep? If you fall asleep while reading this book, others who see you may draw conclusions about you; perhaps they will think you attended a great party last night, when in reality you stayed up late studying for a biology exam. In your interpersonal conversations with others, people may similarly draw an unintended conclusion about your interest in them. If you inadvertently yawn while a friend is telling you about the record-size fish he caught on his recent trip to the Ozarks, you don't intend to offend him; you're just exhausted. Our point is that even when you may not be conscious of what you're doing, you are connecting to others through the ever-present process of communication.

The inescapable nature of interpersonal communication doesn't mean others will *accurately* decode your message; it does mean that others are drawing inferences about you and your behavior—inferences that may be right or may be wrong. Even as you silently stand in a crowded elevator, your lack of eye contact with others communicates your unwillingness to interact with fellow passengers. Your unspoken messages,

# *Understanding Diversity*

## The World Is Here

One of our most visionary politicians said that he envisioned a time when the United States could become the brain of the world, by which he meant the repository of all the latest advanced information systems. I thought of that remark when an enterprising poet friend of mine called to say that he had just sold a poem to a computer magazine and that the editors were delighted to get it because they didn't carry fiction or poetry. Is that the kind of world we desire? A humdrum homogenous world of all brains but no heart, no fiction, no poetry; a world of robots with human attendants, bereft of imagination or culture. Or does North America deserve a more exciting destiny? To become a place where the cultures of the world crisscross. This is possible because the United States is unique in the world: The world is here.[32]

These words from Ishmael Reed's essay "The World Is Here" remind us that America is not a one-dimensional culture. You need not travel to far-off places to develop interpersonal relationships with people from other cultures, races, or ethnic backgrounds. America has long been known as a melting pot—a place where people from a variety of cultures and traditions have come together to seek their fortunes. Others think America is more like a tossed salad than a melting pot—in a salad each ingredient retains its essential character rather than melting together to form a united whole. Focusing on communication and diversity means much more than focusing on cultural differences. Culture consists of the learned values, behaviors, and expectations shared by a group of people. You need skill and sensitivity to develop quality interpersonal relationships with others whose religion, race, ethnicity, age, gender, or sexual orientation differs from your own. Throughout the text, we include boxes like this one to help you develop your sensitivity to important issues related to cultural diversity. As you embark on your study of interpersonal communication, consider these questions, either individually or with a group of your classmates:

1. What are the implications of this melting pot or tossed salad culture for your study of interpersonal communication?

2. Is there too much emphasis on being politically correct on college campuses today? Support your answer.

3. What specific interpersonal skills will help you communicate effectively with others from different cultural and ethnic traditions?

---

even when you are asleep, provide cues that others interpret. Remember: *People judge you by your behavior, not your intent.* Your interpersonal communication is how you develop connections to others. Even in well-established interpersonal relationships, you may be evoking an unintended response to your behavior.

## Interpersonal Communication Is Irreversible

"Disregard that last statement made by the witness," instructs the judge. Yet the clever lawyer knows that once her client has told the jury that her husband gave her a black eye during an argument, the client cannot really "take it back." This principle applies to all forms of communication. We may try to modify the meaning of a spoken message by saying something like "Oh, I really didn't mean it." But in most cases, the damage has been done. Once created, communication has the physical property of matter; it can't be uncreated. As the helical model in Figure 1.5 suggests, once interpersonal communication begins, it never loops back on itself. Instead, it continues to be shaped by the events, experiences, and thoughts of the communication partners. A Russian proverb nicely summarizes the point: "Once a word goes out of your mouth, you can never swallow it again."

FIGURE *1.5*

**Interpersonal Communication Is Irreversible.**
This helical model shows that interpersonal communication never loops back on itself. Once it begins, it expands infinitely as the communication partners contribute their thoughts and experiences to the exchange. Copyright © F. E. X. Dance in *Human Communication Theory* (Holt, Rinehart and Winston, 1967), 294. Reprinted with permission.

## Interpersonal Communication Is Complicated

No form of communication is simple. If any were, we would know how to reduce the number of misunderstandings and conflicts in our world. Because of the variables involved in interpersonal exchanges, even simple requests are extremely complex. Communication theorists have noted that whenever you communicate with another person, there are really at least six "people" involved: (1) who you think you are; (2) who you think the other person is; (3) who you think the other person thinks you are; (4) who the other person thinks he or she is; (5) who the other person thinks you are; and (6) who the other person thinks you think he or she is.[33] Whew! And when you add more people to the interaction, it becomes even more involved.

Moreover, when humans communicate, they interpret information from others as symbols. A **symbol** is a word, sound, or visual image that represents something else, such as a thought, concept, or object; it can have various meanings and interpretations. Language is a system of symbols. In English, symbols do not resemble the objects they represent. The word (symbol) for *cow* does not look at all like a cow; someone, somewhere, decided that *cow* should mean a beast that chews a cud and gives milk. The reliance on symbols to communicate poses a communication challenge; you are often misinterpreted. Sometimes you don't know the code. Only if you are up-to-date on contemporary slang will you know that "homeskillet" means a good friend, "circle of death" means a lousy pizza, and "papaflage" is strategy for hiding something from your father.

**THE FAR SIDE®  By GARY LARSON**

"I'm afraid you misunderstood . . .
I said I'd like a mango."

Messages are not always interpreted as we intend them. Osmo Wiio, a Scandinavian communication scholar, points out the messiness of communicating with others when he suggests the following maxims:

If communication can fail, it will.

If a message can be understood in different ways, it will be understood in just that way which does the most harm.

There is always somebody who knows better than you what you meant by your message.

**symbol.** Word, sound, or visual image that represents a thought, concept, or object.

The more communication there is, the more difficult it is for communication to succeed.[34]

Although we are not as pessimistic as Professor Wiio, we do suggest that the task of understanding each other is challenging.

## Interpersonal Communication Is Governed by Rules

When you play Monopoly, you know that there are explicit rules about how to get out of jail, buy Boardwalk, or pass "Go" and get two hundred dollars. The rules are written down. When you play a game with others, there may even be some unwritten rules, such as when you play *Monopoly* with Grandpa, you always let him buy Boardwalk, because he gets grumpy as a bear before breakfast if he doesn't get to buy it. Similar rules govern how you communicate with others. Most of these rules are embedded in your culture or discussed verbally rather than being collected in a written rulebook.

According to communication researcher Susan Shimanoff, a **rule** is a "followable prescription that indicates what behavior is obligated, preferred, or prohibited in certain contexts."[35] The rules that help define appropriate and inappropriate communication in any given situation may be *explicit* or *implicit.* For your interpersonal communication class, explicit rules are probably spelled out in your syllabus. But your instructor has other rules that are more implicit. They are not written or verbalized, because you learned them long ago: Only one person speaks at a time, you raise your hand to be called, you do not pass notes.

Interpersonal communication rules are developed by the people involved in the interaction and by the culture in which the individuals are communicating. Many times we learn communication rules from experience, by observing and interacting with others.

British researcher Michael Argyle and his colleagues asked people to identify general rules for relationship development and maintenance and then rate their importance. Here are the most important rules:[36]

Partners should respect each other's privacy.

Partners should not reveal each other's secrets.

Partners should look the other person in the eye during conversation.

Partners should not criticize the other person publicly.

Although we may modify rules to achieve the goals of our relationships, and although there may be cultural differences, these general rules remain fairly constant. In interpersonal relationships the rules of a relationship are mutually defined and agreed on. Most of us don't like to be told what to do or how to behave all the time. The expectations and rules are continually renegotiated as the relationship unfolds. Few of us learn relationship rules by copying them from a book. Most of us learn these rules from experience, through observing and interacting with family members and friends. Individuals who grow up in environments in which these rules are not observed may not know how to behave in close relationships.

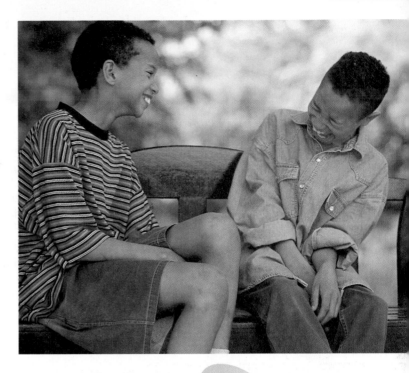

*F*or many of us, friendships are vital to our personal well-being. By improving our interpersonal communication skills, we can learn how to improve our friendships.

**rule.** A followable prescription that indicates what behavior is obligated, preferred, or prohibited in certain communication situations or contexts.

### Interpersonal Communication Involves Both Content and Relationship Dimensions

What you say (your words) and how you say it (your tone of voice, amount of eye contact, facial expression, and posture) can reveal much about the true meaning of your message. If one of your roommates loudly and abruptly bellows, "HEY, DORK! CLEAN THIS ROOM!" and another roommate uses the same verbal message but more gently and playfully suggests, "Hey, dork. Clean this room," both are communicating a message aimed at achieving the same outcome. But the two messages have different relationship cues. The first, shouted message suggests that your roommate may be frustrated that the room is still full of leftovers from last night's pizza party, whereas roommate number two's teasing request suggests he or she may be fondly amused by your untidiness.

The **content** of a communication message consists of the new information, ideas, or suggested actions that the speaker wishes to share. The **relationship dimension** of a communication message is usually more implied; it offers cues about the emotions, attitudes, and amount of power and control the speaker feels toward the other.[37]

Another way of distinguishing between the content and relationship dimensions of communication is to consider that the content of a message refers to *what* is said. Relationship cues refer to *how* it is communicated. This distinction explains why reading a transcript of what someone says can reveal a quite different meaning from actually hearing the person say the message.

## *I*nterpersonal Communication Myths

Several common misconceptions about interpersonal communication can undermine the quality of your interpersonal relationships with others. As we embark on our study of interpersonal communication, it's just as important to unlearn some commonly held misconceptions as it is to learn research conclusions and time-tested principles of interpersonal communication. Don't believe the following myths.

### Myth: "More Words Will Make the Meaning Clearer"

More is not necessarily better. Just as there is a time to talk, there is a time to be silent. Piling on more words when your interpersonal communication partner is already baffled by what you are talking about can make matters worse. If someone is confused, hurt, or angry, continuing to add verbiage may hurt, not help. Maybe you just need to stop and listen rather than talk. Or ask a question and then just silently wait for an answer. Or perhaps, rather than words, your friend needs a nonverbal message of reassurance, a hug, a smile, or a nod of your head in agreement. And just as a picture can be worth a thousand words, so demonstrating to someone what you mean can be more powerful than continuing to pile on the words. When you communicate feelings and attitudes, your nonverbal, unspoken expressions are where the action is.

Are we suggesting that more communication is always bad? No. Just don't fall into the trap of believing that more words will solve all problems, enhance the quality of interpersonal relationships, and make the meaning clearer. There is a time to stop talking and listen.

### Myth: "Meanings Are in Words"

In and of itself, spoken or written, a word has no meaning. It's just a sound, marks on paper, or characters on a computer screen. Our definition of human communication

**content.** New information, ideas, or suggested actions that a speaker wishes to share.

**relationship dimension.** The implied aspect of a communication message, which conveys information about emotions, attitudes, power, and control.

says that meaning is created. It is created in our own and others' minds and hearts when we communicate. Meaning resides in people, not words. Others provide the meaning to "connect the dots" between the words you've spoken and the meaning you intend to create. But sometimes people connect the dots in a way you had not intended. Words are symbols we use to communicate with others. Because a symbol is something that represents something else, a symbol, by its very nature, can have different meanings for different people. And meanings for some words change over time. The word *gay,* for example, probably had a different meaning to your grandmother when she was growing up than it does to you (or to her) today. Even the best wordsmith or professional speechwriter can use words that result in missed meaning and uncertainty. Differences in culture, background, education, and experience often explain why words create different meanings for different people. When you greet your aunt by enthusiastically demanding, "What's up?" she may find such a greeting a bit too informal and think you're being rude. But to your best buddy, "What's up?" is just a normal way of saying "hello." You intended no disrespect to your aunt, but she took your colloquial welcome the wrong way. Our point: Just because you've tossed out some words, don't assume others will always catch what you threw to them. Meanings are in people, not in words.

### Myth: "Information Equals Communication"

"How many times do I have to tell you not to use the copy machine?" "Can't you read? It's in the syllabus." "It's in the policy and procedure manual." "Are you deaf? I've told you that I love you several times." Each of these exasperated communicators seems to have thought that information is the same thing as communication. It's not. Information is not communication. This simple, yet powerful, principle helps combat the myth that if you say it or write it, then communication has taken place.

Earlier in the chapter we defined communication at the most basic level as acting on information. If you say it, but no one hears it—does that mean there has been communication? Like the proverbial tree that falls silently in the forest because no one is there to hear it, the message you thought you sent is not really communication just because you've put your thoughts into a code. Encoding does not always ensure decoding. And as we already discussed, even if someone has decoded the message, it could be different from the one you intended. Information is not communication.

### Myth: "Interpersonal Relationship Problems Are Always Communication Problems"

"You don't understand me!" shouts Paul to his exasperated partner, Pat. "We just can't communicate anymore!" Paul seems to think the problem he and Pat are having is a communication problem. But Paul and Pat may understand each other perfectly; they may simply disagree. Although it's certainly true that conflict and discord in interpersonal relationships can occur because of misunderstandings, not *all* conflict and bumpy relationships stem from misunderstandings. There could be several explanations for why a relationship is experiencing turbulence. Perhaps the communication partners are very clear when communicating, but are so self-centered or self-absorbed

*I*nstead of focusing entirely on the message we want to convey, we can sometimes communicate even more effectively when we take the time to be other-oriented—to listen to what others are saying.

that the quality of the relationship suffers. Or perhaps the communication partners just don't like each other; or, if they do like and understand each other, they just disagree. Their messages are understood but rejected. Although missed meaning may be a contributing factor in interpersonal conflict, it's a myth that all relational discord stems from misunderstanding.

Even though one purpose of this course is to help you enhance the quality of your relationships by becoming a better communicator, we don't claim that *all* interpersonal conflict stems from misunderstanding one another. Nor are we claiming that learning principles and skills of interpersonal communication will solve all your interpersonal relationship problems. One of this book's three authors was approached by a potential client who said, "I understand you are a communication consultant. I need help with my communication skills. *Do something to me* to make me a better communicator." But communication skill development does not work like Harry Potter's magic wand; there's not something that can be "done to" someone to enhance communication ability. And even if there were a wizard's wand to make others perfectly understand all your communication, and you theirs, your interpersonal relationships would undoubtedly still experience stress and conflict.

## How to Improve Your Own Interpersonal Communication Competence

Now that we have previewed the study of interpersonal communication, you may be saying to yourself, "Well, that's all well and good, but is it possible to improve my own interpersonal communication? Aren't some people just born with better interpersonal skills than others?" Just as some people have more musical talent or greater skill at throwing a football, evidence does suggest that some people may have an inborn, biological talent for communicating with others.[38] You probably know people who have never had a course in communication, but who develop sensitive, caring interpersonal relationships with others.

A growing body of research on what is called the **communibiological approach** to communication suggests that some people inherit certain traits or characteristics that affect the way they communicate with others. There may be a genetic basis for why people communicate as they do. For example, perhaps someone you know may have been born to have more stage fright or anxiety when communicating with others.[39] And some people may not be as comfortable interacting in interpersonal situations as others are.

So what are the implications of the communibiological approach to communication? Does this mean you can't improve your interpersonal communication? *Absolutely not!* Some researchers and teachers believe, however, that the communibiological approach gives too much weight to biology and not enough to how we can learn to compensate for what nature did not give us.[40] The underlying premise of our study of interpersonal communication is that you can learn ways to enhance your interpersonal communication competence.

**Social learning theory** suggests that we can learn how to adapt and adjust our behavior toward others; how we behave is not sorely dependent on our genetic makeup. By observing and interacting with others (hence the name *social* learning), we discover that we can adapt and adjust our behavior. Although biology unquestionably plays a key role in how we behave, we can't blame biology for all aspects of our behavior. We believe that people can learn how to enhance their communication competence.

**communibiological approach.** Theoretical perspective that suggests people's communication behavior can be predicted based on personal traits and characteristics that result from their genetic or biological background.

**social learning theory.** Theory of human behavior that suggests we can learn how to adapt and adjust our behavior toward others; how we behave is not solely dependent on our genetic or biological makeup.

To be competent is to communicate in ways that are perceived to be both *effective* and *appropriate*.[41] You communicate effectively when your message is understood by others and achieves its intended effect. For example, if you want your roommate to stop using your hair dryer, and after you talk to your roommate, he stops using your hair dryer, your message has been effective.

Competent communication should also be appropriate. By *appropriate,* we mean that the communicator should consider the time, place, and overall context of the message and should be sensitive to the feelings and attitudes of the listener. If you got your roommate to stop using your hair dryer by saying, "If you don't stop using my hair dryer I'm going to throw your underwear out in the street!" your high-handed tactics would not be perceived as appropriate. Your message might be effective—your roommate might understand you and stop using your hair dryer—but not appropriate; thus, you would not get an award for being a competent communicator. A calm conversation with your roommate that is understood, achieves the intended effect, is appropriate to the time and place, and considers both your needs and the needs of your roommate would be labeled competent. Note that we suggested that your needs as a communicator should be considered when you appropriately communicate with others. Being appropriate does not mean that you abandon your self-respect and always bend to please others.

Although competence may seem like a straightforward concept, there is an important underlying issue: Who determines what is appropriate? Communication scholar Mary Jane Collier suggests that competence is a concept that is based on privilege; to label someone as competent means that another person has made a judgment as to what is appropriate or inappropriate behavior. Collier asks the following questions: ". . . competence and acceptance for whom? Who decides the criteria? Who doesn't? Competent or acceptable on the basis of what social and historical context?"[42] What Collier points out is that we have to be careful not to insist on one approach (our own approach) to interpersonal communication competence. *There is no single best way to communicate with others.* There are, however, avenues that can help you become both more effective and more appropriate when communicating with others. We suggest a six-part strategy for becoming a more competent communicator.

## Become Knowledgeable

By reading this chapter, you have already begun improving your communication skills. Effective communicators are knowledgeable. They know how communication works. They understand the components, principles, and rules of the communication process. As you read further in this book, you will learn theories, principles, concepts, and rules that will help you explain and predict how humans communicate.

Understanding these things is a necessary prerequisite for enhancing your interpersonal effectiveness, but this kind of knowledge alone does not make you an effective communicator. You would not let someone fix your car's carburetor if he or she had only read a book. Knowledge must be coupled with skill. And we acquire skill through practice.

## Become Skilled

Effective communicators know how to translate knowledge into action.[43] You can memorize the characteristics of a good listener but still not listen well. To develop skill requires practice and helpful feedback from others who can confirm the appropriateness of your actions.

It has been suggested that learning a social skill is not much different from learning how to drive a car or operate a computer.[44] To learn any skill, you must break it down into subskills that you can learn and practice. "Hear it, see it, do it, correct it" is the formula that seems to work best for learning any new behaviors. In this book we examine the elements of complex skills (such as listening), offer activities that let you practice the skills, and provide opportunities for you to receive feedback and correct your application of the skills.

## Become Motivated

Practicing skills requires work. You need to be motivated to use your knowledge and skill. You must want to improve, and you must have a genuine desire to connect with others if you wish to become a competent communicator. You may know people who understand how to drive a car and have the skill to drive, yet hesitate to get behind the wheel. Or maybe you know someone who took a course in public speaking but is reluctant to stand in front of a crowd. Similarly, someone may pass a test about interpersonal communication principles with flying colors, but unless that person is motivated to use those newfound skills, his or her interactions with others may not improve.

## Become Flexible

In this book we do not identify tidy lists of sure-fire strategies that you can use to win friends and influence people. The same set of skills is not effective in every situation, so competent communicators do not assume that "one size fits all." Rather, they assess each unique situation and adapt their behavior to achieve the desired outcome. They examine the context, the situation, and the needs, goals, and messages of others to establish and maintain relationships.

## Become Ethical

**Ethics** are the beliefs, values, and moral principles by which we determine what is right or wrong. Ethics and ethical behavior have always been critical components of human interactions. Effective interpersonal communicators are ethical. To be an ethical communicator means to be sensitive to the needs of others, to give people choices rather than forcing them to act a certain way. Unethical communicators believe that they know what other people need, even without asking them for their preferences. As we discuss in Chapter 6, being manipulative and forcing opinions on others usually results in a climate of defensiveness. Effective communicators seek to establish trust and reduce interpersonal barriers, rather than erect them. Ethical communicators keep confidences; they keep private information that others wish to be kept private. They also do not intentionally decrease others' feelings of self-worth. Another key element in being an ethical communicator is honesty. If you intentionally lie or distort the truth, then you are not communicating ethically or effectively. At the end of each chapter, we offer a section called Focus on Ethics, in which we pose ethical questions to help you explore the ethics of interpersonal relationships.

**ethics.** The beliefs, values, and moral principles by which people determine what is right or wrong.

**other-oriented communicator.** One who considers the thoughts, feelings, and perspectives of communication partners while maintaining his or her own integrity.

## Become Other-Oriented

The signature concept for our study of interpersonal communication is the goal of becoming other-oriented in relationships. To be an **other-oriented communicator** is to consider the thoughts, needs, experiences, personality, feelings, motives, desires, culture, and goals of our communication partners, while still maintaining our own integrity. The choices we make in forming our messages, in deciding how to best express those messages, and in deciding when and where to deliver those messages will be more effective when we consider the other person's thoughts and feelings. *To emphasize the importance of being an other-oriented communicator, throughout this book we'll use this margin icon to highlight discussions of being other-oriented.*

Being other-oriented involves a conscious effort to consider the world from the point of view of those with whom you interact. This effort occurs almost automatically when you are communicating with those you like or who are similar to you. Thinking about the thoughts and feelings of those you dislike or who are different from you is more difficult and requires more effort and commitment.

*Ethical communicators are sensitive to the needs of others.*

Think about a person you dislike. Do you truly understand the factors in his or her life that have had an impact on the way he or she behaves? Do you appreciate the emotions he or she feels? If you're not confident you can accurately understand the thoughts and feelings of a person you dislike, it probably signals the need to work on your ability to be other-oriented.

Sometimes we are **egocentric communicators;** we create messages without giving much thought to the person who is listening. To be egocentric is to be self-focused and self-absorbed. Scholars of evolution might argue that our tendency to look out for Number One ensures the continuation of the human species and is therefore a good thing. Yet, it is difficult to communicate effectively when we focus exclusively on ourselves. If we fail to adapt our message to our listener, we may not be successful in achieving our intended communication goal. Other people can often perceive whether we're self-focused or other-oriented (especially if the person we're talking with is a sensitive, other-oriented communicator).

We may find ourselves speaking without considering the thoughts and feelings of our listener when we have a need to purge ourselves emotionally or to confirm our sense of self-importance, but doing so usually undermines our relationships with others. A self-focused communicator often alienates others. Fortunately, research suggests that, almost by necessity, we adapt to our partner in order to carry on a conversation.[45] Such adaptation includes such things as simply asking questions in response to our partner's disclosures, finding topics of mutual interest to discuss, selecting words and examples that are meaningful to our partner, and avoiding topics that we don't feel comfortable discussing with another person.

Adapting messages to others does *not* mean that we tell them only what they want to hear; that would be unethical. Nor does being considerate of others mean abandoning all concern for our own interests; that would be unwise. Other-oriented communicators maintain their own personal integrity while simultaneously being aware of the thoughts and feelings of others. Being other-oriented is more than just being "nice."[46] It involves being principled enough to be considerate of others, but making mindful choices about how and when to adapt interpersonal messages to others.

**egocentric communicator.** A person who creates messages without giving much thought to the person who is listening; a person who is self-focused and self-absorbed.

## *Becoming Other-Oriented*

### Consider Others' Needs and Perspectives Without Abandoning Your Own Integrity

*A*t the heart of our study of interpersonal communication is the principle of becoming other-oriented. To be other-oriented means that you become aware of others' thoughts, feelings, goals, and needs and respond appropriately in ways that offer personal support. It does not mean that you abandon your own needs and interests or that you diminish your self-respect. To have integrity is to behave in a thoughtful, integrated way toward others while being true to your core beliefs and values. To be other-oriented is to have integrity; you don't just agree with others or give in to the demands of others in encounters with them.

Do you know a sycophant? A *sycophant* is a person who praises others only to manipulate emotions so that

his or her needs are met. Sycophants may look as though they are focused on others, but their behavior is merely self-serving. A sycophant is not other-oriented. A person who is truly other-oriented is aware of the thoughts, feelings, and needs of others and then mindfully and honestly chooses to respond to those needs. To enhance your other-oriented awareness and skill takes practice. Throughout the book we will offer both principles and opportunities to practice the skill and mind-set of being other-oriented.

To develop an awareness of being other-oriented with a communication partner, role-play the following interpersonal situations in two ways. First, role-play the scene as a communicator who is not other-oriented but rather self-focused. Then reenact the same scene as a communicator who is other-oriented—someone who considers the thoughts and feelings of the other person while maintaining his or her own integrity.

Suggested situations:

- Return a broken DVD player to a department store salesperson

- Correct a grocery store cashier who has scanned an item at the wrong price

- Meet with a teacher who gave your son or daughter a failing grade

- Ask your professor for a one-day extension on a paper that is due tomorrow

- Ask someone for a donation to a worthy cause

- Ask a professor for permission to get into a class that has reached its maximum enrollment

- Accept an unappealing compact disc as a gift from a friend

- Remind your son or daughter that he or she needs to practice the cello

How do you become other-oriented? Being other-oriented is really a collection of skills rather than a single skill. We devote considerable discussion throughout the book to developing this collection of essential communication skills.[47]

Focusing on others begins with an accurate understanding of your self-concept and self-esteem; we discuss these foundation principles in the next chapter. As you will learn in Chapter 3, developing an accurate perception of both yourself and others is an important element of relating to others effectively.

Becoming other-oriented also involves adapting to those who may be considerably different from you. Your communication partner may have a different cultural background, be of the opposite sex, or be older or younger than you. In Chapter 4 we explore some of these differences, especially cultural differences, that can sometimes challenge effective and appropriate communication with others; we also suggest specific strategies to help you adapt to others who differ from you.

Being other-oriented is more than just having a set of skills or behaviors. It also includes developing positive, healthy attitudes about others. In 1951 Carl Rogers wrote a pioneering book called *Client-Centered Therapy,* which transformed the field of psychotherapy. In it Rogers explains how genuine positive regard for another person and an open and supportive communication climate lay the foundation for trusting relationships. Rogers emphasizes the importance of listening in forging a connection to another human being. We explore this topic in depth in Chapter 5.

People gain insight into others' feelings by being sensitive to nonverbal messages as well as the explicit verbal statements they make. We discuss verbal communication skills in Chapter 6 and nonverbal communication skills in Chapter 7. The skills and principles of managing conflict presented in Chapter 8 provide tools and ideas for understanding others when you disagree.

Chapters 9, 10, and 11 build on the principles of interpersonal relationships introduced in this chapter to help you understand how relationships evolve, are maintained, and sometimes end. The final chapter applies our discussion of other-oriented interpersonal communication to various contexts such as families, friends, and colleagues. Our goals are to help you understand better how you relate to others and to help you develop enhanced interpersonal skill.

### Recap   How Can You Improve Your Communication Competence?

| | |
|---|---|
| **Become Knowledgeable** | Learn principles, concepts, and ideas. |
| **Become Skilled** | Translate knowledge into action. |
| **Become Motivated** | Resolve to use your knowledge and skill. |
| **Become Flexible** | Select the right behavior; one size does not fit all. |
| **Become Ethical** | Offer choices, establish trust, and reduce barriers to interpersonal communication. |
| **Become Other-Oriented** | Focus on others rather than only on your needs. |

# Summary

At the most basic level, communication is the process of acting on information. Human communication is the process of making sense of the world and sharing that sense with others. Interpersonal communication is the process of developing a unique relationship with another person by interacting and sharing mutual influence. Early models of human communication viewed it as a simple message-transfer process. Later models viewed communication as interaction and then as transaction. Contemporary approaches to interpersonal communication emphasize the simultaneous nature of the process. They identify seven key components in the interpersonal communication process:

source, receiver, message, channel, noise, context, and feedback. Electronic media may encourage further evolution of our models for interpersonal communication.

The goal of this book is to help you improve your interpersonal skills and relationships. Interpersonal relationships range from impersonal to intimate, are governed by rules, and involve both content and relationship dimensions. The most effective interpersonal communicators are not swayed by common myths about communication. Rather, they are knowledgeable, skilled, motivated, flexible, ethical, and other-oriented. Learning to connect with others is the key to establishing satisfying relationships.

# For Discussion and Review

## Focus on Critical Thinking

1. Analyze a recent interpersonal exchange that did not go well. Write down some of the dialogue. Did the other person understand you? Did your communication have the intended effect? Was your message ethical?

2. Make a relationship scale on a piece of paper, and label it "impersonal" at one end and "intimate" at the other. Place your family members and closest friends on the scale; then compare and discuss your entries with your classmates.

3. What rules govern your relationship with your mother? Your father? Your communication teacher? Your roommate? Your spouse?

## Focus on Ethics

4. Think about your primary goal for this course. Is it to develop strategies to achieve your own personal goals? Is it to develop sensitivity to the needs of others? What is behind your desire to achieve your goal? Is your purpose ethical?

5. Your parents want you to visit them for the holidays. You would rather spend the time with a friend. You don't want to hurt your parents' feelings, so you tell them that you have an important project that you are working on; you won't be able to come home for the holidays. Your message is understood. It achieves the intended effect: Your parents don't seem to have hurt feelings, and you don't go home. Explain whether your message is ethical or unethical.

# For Your Journal

1. Try to identify at least three personal goals for improving your interpersonal relationships. Write several specific objectives that you hope to accomplish by the end of this course.

2. Briefly describe a recent communication exchange that was not effective. Perhaps you or your communication partner did not understand the message, or the message may not have achieved its intended goal, or it may have been unethical. Analyze the communication exchange, applying the components of communication discussed

in this chapter. For example, what was the communication context? What were sources of internal and external noise? Did you have problems encoding and decoding? Were there problems with the communication channel?

3. Keep a one-day log of your electronically mediated interactions, such as phone calls, e-mail messages, fax messages. Describe each one, noting whether there was a greater emphasis on the content or on the emotional elements of the messages you exchanged during the interaction.

# Learning with Others

1. Working with a group of your classmates, develop a five-minute lesson to teach one of the following concepts to your class:

    a. How interpersonal relationships range from impersonal to intimate
    b. Human communication as action
    c. Human communication as interaction
    d. Human communication as transaction
    e. How interpersonal relationships are governed by rules
    f. How to improve communication effectiveness

2. Working with a group of your classmates, develop your own model of interpersonal communication. Include all of the components that are necessary to describe how communication between people works. Your model could be a drawing or an object (such as a Slinky toy) that symbolizes the communication process. Share your model with the class, describing the decisions your group made in developing it. Illustrate your model with a conversation between two people, pointing out how elements of the conversation relate to the model.

http://www.coopcomm.org/ This site provides self-help information, encouragement, and teaching materials for better communication at work, with family and friends, and in the community. It also offers free books, essays, and exercises to help you improve your interpersonal skills.

http://www.queendom.com/tests/health/social_anxiety_r_access.html Take this social anxiety test to assess how comfortable you are when interacting with other people.

http://www.changedynamics.com/samples/commun.htm View brief articles and selected information about the human communication process.

http://ilc2.doshisha.ac.jp/users/kkitao/organi/wca/ This web site of the World Communication Association provides links to a host of communication associations throughout the world.

http://natcom.org The National Communication Association is the largest association of communication scholars and professionals in the world. This site provides a wealth of information about the study of human communication.

http://www.queendom.com/tests/relationships/communication_skills_r_access.html Communicating with others is an essential skill in business dealings, friendships, family affairs, and romantic relationships. Find out your own level of interpersonal communication skills with the Communication Skills Test.

http://www.hostingtech.com/news/2003/4/25/St_Nitf_What_Is_The_Impact_Of_Email_On_p0424045.6rw.html What is the impact of e-mail on interpersonal communication? A new study by Earthlink explores this question.

# 2 Interpersonal Communication and Self

*Sometimes I think we're alone. Sometimes I think we're not. In either case, the thought is staggering.*

R. Buckminster Fuller

Philosophers suggest that there are three basic questions to which all people seek answers: (1) "Who am I?" (2) "Why am I here?" and (3) "Who are all these others?" In this chapter we focus on these essential questions about the self. We view them as progressive. Grappling with the question of who you are and seeking to define a purpose for your life are essential to understanding others and becoming other-oriented in your interpersonal communication and relationships.

Fundamentally, all your communication starts or ends with you. When you are the communicator, you intentionally or unintentionally code your thoughts and emotions to be interpreted by another. When you receive a message, you interpret the information through your own frame of reference. Your self-image and self-worth, as well as your needs, values, beliefs, and attitudes, serve as filters for your communication with others. As you establish and develop relationships, you may become more aware of these filters, and perhaps want to alter them. A close relationship often provides the impetus for change.

To understand the role that self-concept plays in interpersonal communication, we will explore the first two basic questions—"Who am I?" and "Why am I here?"—in an effort to discover the meaning of self. We will examine the multifaceted dimensions of self-concept, learn how it develops, and compare self-concept to self-esteem. Then we will move to the third basic question, "Who are all these others?" What you choose to tell and not tell others about yourself reveals important clues about who you are, what you value, and how you relate to another person. We will explore the process of self-disclosure—purposefully revealing information about yourself—later in this chapter.

## Self-Concept: Who Are You?

You can begin your journey of self-discovery by doing the exercise in Building Your Skills: Who Are You?

How did you answer the question "Who are you?" Perhaps you listed activities in which you participate, or groups and organizations to which you belong. You may have listed some of the roles you assume, such as student, child, or parent. All these things are indeed a part of your self, the sum total of who you are. Psychologist Karen Horney defines **self** as "that central inner force, common to all human beings and yet unique in each, which is the deep source of growth."[1]

Your answers are also part of your **self-concept.** Your self-concept is your subjective description of who you *think* you are—it is filtered through your own perceptions. For example, you may have great musical talent, but you may not believe in it enough to think of yourself as a musician. You can view self-concept as the labels you consistently use to describe yourself to others.

Who you are is also reflected in the attitudes, beliefs, and values that you hold. These are learned constructs that shape your behavior and self-image. An **attitude** is a learned predisposition to respond to a person, object, or idea in a favorable or unfavorable way. Attitudes reflect what you like and what you don't like. If you like school, butter pecan ice cream, and your brother, you hold positive attitudes toward these things. You were not born with a fondness for butter pecan ice cream; you learned to like it just as some people learn to enjoy the taste of snails, raw fish, or pureed turnips.

**self.** Sum total of who a person is; a person's central inner force.

**self-concept.** A person's subjective description of who he or she is.

**attitude.** Learned predisposition to respond to a person, object, or idea in a favorable or unfavorable way.

---

## *Building Your Skills*

### Who Are You?

Consider this question: Who are you? More specifically, ask yourself this question ten times. Write your responses in the spaces provided here or on a separate piece of paper. It may be challenging to identify ten aspects of yourself. The Spanish writer Cervantes said, "To know thyself . . . is the most difficult lesson in the world." Your answers will help you begin to explore your self-concept and self-esteem in this chapter.

I am _____

I am _____

I am _____

I am _____

I am _____

I am _____

I am _____

I am _____

I am _____

I am _____

**Beliefs** are the way in which you structure your understanding of reality—what is true and what is false. Most of your beliefs are based on previous experience. You believe that the sun will rise in the morning and that you will get burned if you put your hand on a hot stove.

How are attitudes and beliefs related? They often function quite independently of each other. You may have a favorable attitude toward something and still believe negative things about it. You may believe, for example, that your school football team will not win the national championship this year, although you may be a big fan. Or you may believe that God exists, yet not always like what God does. Beliefs have to do with what is true or not true, whereas attitudes reflect likes and dislikes.

**Values** are enduring concepts of good and bad, right and wrong. Your values are more resistant to change than either your attitudes or your beliefs. They are also more difficult for most people to identify. Values are so central to who you are that it is difficult to isolate them. For example, when you go to the supermarket, you may spend a few minutes deciding whether to buy regular or cream-style corn, but you probably do not spend much time deciding whether you will steal the corn or pay for it. Our values are instilled in us by our earliest interpersonal relationships; for almost all of us, our parents shape our values. The model in Figure 2.1 illustrates that values are central to our behavior and concept of self, and that what we believe to be true or false stems from our values. Attitudes are at the outer edge of the circle because they are the most likely to change. You may like your coworker today but not tomorrow, even though you *believe* the person will come to work every day and you still *value* the concept of friendship.

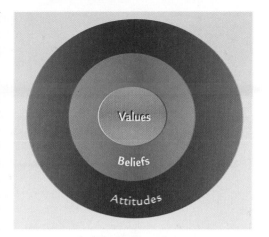

FIGURE *2.1*

Values, Beliefs, and Attitudes in Relation to Self

 **Recap**

## Who You Are Is Reflected in Your Attitudes, Beliefs, and Values

| | Definition | Dimensions | Example |
|---|---|---|---|
| **Attitude** | Learned predisposition to respond favorably or unfavorably to something | Likes–Dislikes | You like ice cream, incense, and cats. |
| **Belief** | The way in which you structure reality | True–False | You believe your parents love you. |
| **Value** | Enduring concepts of what is right and wrong | Good–Bad | You value honesty and truth. |

## One or Many Selves?

Shakespeare's famous line "To thine own self be true" suggests that you have a single self to which you can be true. But do you have just one self? Or is there a more "real you" buried somewhere within? "I'm just not myself this morning," sighs Sandy, as she drags herself out the front door to head for her office. If she is not herself, then *who is she*? Most scholars conclude that we have a core set of behaviors, attitudes, beliefs, and values that constitutes our self—the sum total of who we are. But our *concept* of self can and does change, depending on circumstances and influences.

In addition, our self-concepts are often different from the way others see us. We almost always behave differently in public than we do in private. Sociologist Erving Goffman suggests that, like actors and actresses, we have "on-stage" behaviors when others are watching and "backstage" behaviors when they are not.[2] Goffman writes that "often what talkers undertake to do is not to provide information to a recipient but to

**belief.** Way in which you structure your understanding of reality—what is true and what is false.

**value.** Enduring concept of good and bad, right and wrong.

eter Blake sought to explore his self-dimensions by painting his self-portrait. What qualities does this self-portrait reveal about the artist?

present dramas to an audience. Indeed, it seems that we spend most of our time not engaged in giving information but in giving shows."[3] With an audience present, whether it's one person or several, you adapt and "perform."

Perhaps the most enduring and widely accepted framework for describing who we are was developed by the philosopher William James. He identified three components of the self: the material self, the social self, and the spiritual self. We will continue our exploration by examining these components.

### The Material Self

Perhaps you've heard the statement "You are what you eat." The concept of the **material self** goes a step further by suggesting that "You are what you have." The material self is a total of all the tangible things you own: your body, your possessions, your home. As you examine your list of responses to the question "Who are you?" note whether any of your statements refers to one of your physical attributes or something you own.

One element of the material self gets considerable attention in this culture: the body. Do you like the way you look? Most of us, if we're honest, would like to change something about our appearance. When there is a discrepancy between our desired material self and our self-concept, we may respond to eliminate the discrepancy. We may try to lose weight, change nose shape, or acquire more hair. The multibillion-dollar diet industry is just one of many that profit from our collective desire to change our appearance. We also attempt to keep up with the proverbial Joneses by acquiring more expensive clothes, cars, and homes. By extension, what we own becomes who we are. The bigger, better, and more luxurious our possessions, we may subconsciously conclude, the better we are.

### The Social Self

Look at your "Who are you?" list once more. How many of your responses relate to your **social self,** the part of you that interacts with others? William James believed that you have many social selves—that, depending on the friend, family member, colleague,

## Building Your Skills

### Dimensions of Your Self

ake another look at your responses to the question "Who are you?" Divide your list according to James's categories of material, social, and spiritual selves. If, for example, nothing on your original list relates to your spiritual self, make an entry here so that you have a response for each of the three "selves."

**Material Self**
References to physical elements that reflect who you are. *Example:* I collect antiques.

_____

_____

_____

_____

**Social Self**
References to interactions with others that reflect who you are. *Example:* I am a member of the Chess Club.

_____

_____

_____

_____

**Spiritual Self**
References to values, morals, and beliefs. *Example:* I believe the *Book of Mormon* is an inspired book.

_____

_____

_____

_____

or acquaintance with whom you are interacting, you change the way you are. A person has, said James, as many social selves as there are people who recognize him or her.

For example, when you talk to your best friend, you are willing to "let down your hair" and reveal more thoughts and feelings than you would in a conversation with your communication professor, or even your parents. We discuss this process of self-disclosure later in the chapter. Each relationship that you have with another person is unique because you bring to it a unique social self.

### The Spiritual Self

Your **spiritual self** consists of all your internal thoughts and introspections about your values and moral standards. It does not depend on what you own or with whom you talk; it is the essence of who you *think* you are, and of your *feelings* about yourself, apart from external evaluations. It is an amalgam of your religious beliefs and your sense of who you are in relationship to other forces in the universe. Your spiritual self is the part of you that answers the question "Why am I here?"

*Recap*

## William James's Dimensions of Self

|  | Definition | Examples |
|---|---|---|
| **Material Self** | All the physical elements that reflect who you are | Body, clothes, car, home |
| **Social Self** | The self as reflected through your interactions with others; actually, a variety of selves that respond to changes in situations and roles | Your informal self interacting with your best friend; your formal self interacting with your professors |
| **Spiritual Self** | Introspections about values, morals, and beliefs | Belief or disbelief in God; regard for life in all its forms |

## How Your Self-Concept Develops

James's three elements define the dimensions of the self, but they do not tell us where responses to the question "Who are you?" come from. In truth, we can only speculate about their origins. But some psychologists and sociologists have advanced theories that suggest you learn who you are through five basic means: (1) interactions with other individuals, (2) association with groups, (3) roles you assume, (4) your own labels, and (5) your personality. Like James's framework, this one does not cover every base in the study of self, but its constructs can provide some clues about how your own self-concept develops.

### Interaction with Individuals

In 1902, Charles Horton Cooley first advanced the concept of the **looking-glass self,** which was his term for the notion that we form our self-concepts by seeing ourselves in a kind of figurative looking glass: We learn who we are by interacting with others, much as we look into a mirror and see our reflection.[4] Like Cooley, George Herbert Mead also believed that our sense of who we are is a consequence of our relationship with others.[5] And Harry Stack Sullivan theorized that from birth to death our self changes primarily because of how people respond to us.[6] One sage noted, "We are not only our brother's keeper; we are our brother's maker."

**material self.** Your concept of self as reflected in a total of all the tangible things you own.

**social self.** Your concept of self as reflected in your social interactions with others.

**spiritual self.** Your concept of self based on your thoughts and introspections about your values, moral standards, and beliefs.

**looking-glass self.** Concept that suggests you learn who you are based on your interactions with others, who reflect your self back to you.

The process begins at birth. Our names, one of the primary ways we identify ourselves, are given to us by someone else. During the early years of our lives, our parents are the key individuals who reflect who we are. If our parents encouraged us to play the piano, we probably play now. As we become less dependent on our parents, our friends become highly influential in shaping our attitudes, beliefs, and values. And friends continue to provide feedback on how well we perform certain tasks. This, in turn, helps us shape our sense of identity as adults—we must acknowledge our talents in math, language, or art in our own minds before we say that we are mathematicians, linguists, or artists.

Fortunately, not *every* comment affects our sense of who we think we are. We are likely to incorporate the comments of others into our self-concept under three conditions.

First, we are more likely to believe another's statement if he or she repeats something we have heard several times. If one person casually tells you that you have a good singing voice, you are not likely to launch a search for an agent and a recording contract. But if several individuals tell you on many different occasions that you have a talent for singing, you may decide to do something about it.

Second, we are more likely to value another's statements if we perceive him or her to be credible. If we believe the individual is competent, trustworthy, and qualified to make a judgment about us, then we are more likely to believe the person's assessment. You would be more likely to think you were a talented singer if you heard it from opera star Luciano Pavarotti rather than from your Aunt Sally. Again, while we are very young, our parents are the dominant voices of credibility and authority. If they tell us repeatedly that we are spoiled and sloppy, then we will probably come to view ourselves that way. If they tell us we are loving, gifted, and charming, we are likely to believe it.

Third, we are likely to incorporate another's comments into our own concept of self if the comments are consistent with other comments and our own experience. If your boss tells you that you work too slowly, but for years people have been urging you to slow down, then your previous experience will probably encourage you to challenge your boss's evaluation.

### Association with Groups

I'm a Democrat. I'm a Girl Scout. I'm a rabbi. I'm a coach. I'm a member of the Marching Mules Band. Each of these self-descriptive statements has something in common. Each one answers the "Who are you?" question by providing identification with a group or organization. Reflect once more on your responses to the "Who are you?" question. How many responses associate you with a group? Religious groups, political groups, ethnic groups, social groups, study groups, and occupational and professional groups play important roles in determining your self-concept. Some of these groups you are born into; others you choose on your own. Either way, these group associations are significant parts of your identity.

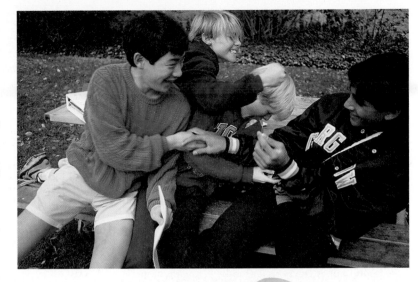

As we noted, peer pressure—"keeping up with the Joneses"—is a powerful force in shaping attitudes and behavior, and adolescents are particularly susceptible to it. But adolescents are not alone in allowing the attitudes, beliefs, and values of others to shape their expectations and behavior. Most adults, to varying degrees, ask themselves, "What will the neighbors think? What will my family think?" when they are making choices.

*In American culture, rough-and-tumble, aggressive behavior among boys when they interact with one another is often accepted, or even encouraged.*

Associating with groups is especially important for people who are not part of the dominant culture. Gays and lesbians, for example, find the support provided by associating with other gays and lesbians to be beneficial to their well-being. The groups you associate with not only provide information about your identity, but also provide needed social support.

### Roles You Assume

Look again at your answers to the "Who are you?" question. Perhaps you see words or phrases that signify a role you often assume. Father, aunt, sister, uncle, manager, salesperson, teacher, and student are labels that imply certain expectations for behavior, and they are important in shaping self-concept. Couples who live together before they marry often report that marriage alters their relationship. Before, they may have shared domestic duties such as doing dishes and laundry. But when they assume the labels of "husband" and "wife," they slip into traditional roles. Husbands don't do laundry. Wives don't mow the grass. These stereotypical role expectations that they learned long ago may require extensive discussion and negotiation. Couples who report the highest satisfaction with marriage agree on their expectations regarding roles ("We agree that I'll do laundry and you'll mow the grass").[7]

One reason we assume traditional roles automatically is that our gender group asserts a powerful influence from birth on. As soon as parents know the sex of their child, many begin placing their children in the group by following cultural rules. They paint the nursery pink for a girl, blue for a boy. Boys get catcher's mitts, train sets, or footballs for their birthdays; girls get dolls, frilly dresses, and tea sets. These cultural conventions and expectations play a major role in shaping our self-concept and our behavior. People often describe male babies as strong, solid, and independent; little girls are cute, cuddly, and sweet.[8] Recent research suggests that up until the age of 3, children themselves are not acutely aware of sex roles. Between the ages of 3 and 5, however, masculine and feminine roles begin to emerge,[9] and they are usually solidified between the ages of 5 and 7.

## *applying theory and research*

### Symbolic Interaction Theory

We defined human communication as the way we make sense of the world and share that sense with others by creating meaning through verbal and nonverbal messages. **Symbolic interaction theory** is based on the assumption that we each make sense of the world based upon our interactions with others. We interpret what a word, symbol, or experience means based, in part, on how other people react to our use of words and symbols. Even our own understanding of who we think we are (our self-concept) is influenced by who others tell us we are. Central to understanding ourselves is understanding the importance of other people in shaping our self-understanding. Symbolic interaction theory has had a major influence on communication theory because of the pervasive way our communication with others influences our attitudes, beliefs, values, and self-concept.

George Herbert Mead is credited with the development of symbolic interaction theory, although Mead did not write extensively about his theory.[10] One of Mead's students, Herbert

Blumer, actually coined the term *symbolic interaction* to describe the process through which our interactions with others influence our thoughts about others, our life experiences, and ourselves. Mead believed that we cannot have a concept of our own self-identity without interactions with other people.

### APPLYING
#### the Research to Your Life

Symbolic interaction theory suggests that you make sense out of your world and your life experiences based on the influence of your family, friends, and other people with whom you communicate. Because of the far-reaching influence of others on your life, it's sometimes hard to be consciously aware of how other people shape your thoughts about yourself and others. Consider the following questions to explore how other people have shaped your understanding of your self-concept and attitudes you hold.

1. How have other people helped shape your own sense of your skills and talents? Identify specific people and recall things they have said to you that have either reinforced or contradicted your understanding of your own abilities and skills.

2. How do you and your friends and family members talk about your attitudes toward the college or university you now attend? How do other people, especially your family and friends, describe your school, either positively or negatively? How do their comments influence your own attitudes about your school?

3. Has your own concept of who you are undergone dramatic changes? What role did the comments and expressed attitudes of your family, friends, and coworkers have on how you changed your self-concept?

*Source:* George Herbert Mead, *Mind, Self, and Society* (Chicago: University of Chicago Press, 1934).

**symbolic interaction theory.** The theory that people make sense of the world on the basis of their interactions with other people.

**androgynous role.** Gender role that includes both masculine and feminine qualities.

Although it is changing, American culture is still male-dominated. What we consider appropriate and inappropriate behavior is often different for males and for females. For example, in group and team meetings, task-oriented, male-dominated roles are valued more than feminine, relationship-building roles.[11] We applaud fathers who work sixty hours a week as "diligent and hard-working," but criticize mothers who do the same as "neglectful and selfish."

Although our culture defines certain roles as masculine or feminine, we still exercise individual choices about our gender roles. One researcher developed an inventory designed to assess whether we play traditional masculine, feminine, or androgynous roles.[12] Because an **androgynous role** is both masculine and feminine, such a role encompasses a greater repertoire of actions and behaviors.

### Self-Labels

Although our self-concept is deeply affected by others, we are not blank slates for them to write on. The labels we use to describe our own attitudes, beliefs, values, and actions also play a role in shaping our self-concept.

Where do our labels come from? We interpret what we experience; we are self-reflexive. **Self-reflexiveness** is the human ability to think about what we are doing while we are doing it. We talk to ourselves about ourselves. We are both participants and observers in all that we do. This dual role encourages us to use labels to describe who we are.

When you were younger, perhaps you dreamed of becoming an all-star basketball player or a movie star. Your coach may have told you that you were a great player or a terrific actor, but as you matured, you probably began observing yourself more critically. You scored no points; you did not get the starring role in the local production of *Annie.* So you self-reflexively decided that you were not, deep down, a basketball player or an actor, even though others may have labeled you as "talented." But sometimes, through this self-observation, people discover strengths that encourage them to assume new labels. One woman we know never thought of herself as "heroic" until she went through seventy-two hours of labor before giving birth!

### Your Personality

The concept of personality is central to **psychology,** the study of how your thinking influences how you behave. According to psychologist Lester Lefton, your **personality** consists of a set of enduring internal predispositions and behavioral characteristics that describe how you react to your environment.[13] Understanding the forces that shape your personality is central to increasing your awareness of your self-concept and how you relate to others. Your personality influences whether you are outgoing or shy, humorous or serious, mellow or nervous, and a host of other descriptions that could be used to describe general traits or characteristics about you. There remains a considerable debate as to how much of your personality is influenced by genetics—traits you inherit from your ancestors—and how much is learned behavior. Does nature or nurturing play the predominant role in your personality? As we noted in Chapter 1, the **communibiological approach** to communication suggests that a major factor affecting how people communicate with others is genetic makeup.[14] Others argue that although it's true that communication behavior is influenced by genes, we should not forget that humans can learn to adjust and adapt.[15]

One personality characteristic that communication researchers have spent considerable time studying is whether you are comfortable or uncomfortable interacting with other people. Some people just don't like to talk with others.[16] We may say such a person is shy. **Shyness** is the behavioral tendency not to talk with others. One study found that about 40 percent of adults reported they were shy.[17] In public-speaking situations we say a person has stage fright; a better term to describe this feeling is *communication apprehension.* **Communication apprehension,** according to communication experts James McCroskey and Virginia Richmond, is "the fear or anxiety associated with either real or anticipated communication with another person or persons."[18] One study found that up to 80 percent of the population experiences some degree of nervousness or apprehension when they speak in public.[19] Another study found that about 20 percent of people are considerably anxious when they give a speech.[20] What makes some people apprehensive about communicating with others? Again, we get back to the nature–nurture issue. Heredity plays an important role in whether you are going to feel nervous or anxious when communicating with someone

**self-reflexiveness.** Human ability to think about what you are doing while you are doing it.

**psychology.** Study of how thinking influences behavior.

**personality.** Set of enduring internal predispositions and behavioral characteristics that describe how people react to their environment.

**communibiological approach.** Perspective that suggests that genetics and biological influences play a major role in influencing communication behavior.

**shyness.** Behavioral tendency not to talk or interact with other people.

**communication apprehension.** Fear or anxiety associated with either real or anticipated communication with other people.

# Building Your Skills

## Assessing Your Willingness to Communicate

### Willingness-to-Communicate Scale

**Directions:** In the following 20 situations, a person might choose to communicate or not to communicate. Assume that you have **completely free choice**. Indicate in the space at the left the percentage of times you would **choose to initiate communication** in each type of situation. Choose any numbers between 0 and 100.

_____  1.  Talk with a service station attendant.

_____  2.  Talk with a physician.

_____  3.  Present a talk to a group of strangers.

_____  4.  Talk with an acquaintance while standing in line.

_____  5.  Talk with a salesperson in a store.

_____  6.  Talk in a large meeting of friends.

_____  7.  Talk with a police officer.

_____  8.  Talk in a small group of strangers.

_____  9.  Talk with a friend while standing in line.

_____  10.  Talk with a waiter/waitress in a restaurant.

_____  11.  Talk in a large meeting of acquaintances.

_____  12.  Talk with a stranger while standing in line.

_____  13.  Talk with a secretary.

_____  14.  Present a talk to a group of friends.

_____  15.  Talk in a small group of acquaintances.

_____  16.  Talk with a garbage collector.

_____  17.  Talk in a large meeting of strangers.

_____  18.  Talk with a spouse (or girlfriend/boyfriend).

_____  19.  Talk in a small group of friends.

_____  20.  Present a talk to a group of acquaintances.

## Computing Scores on the Willingness-to-Communicate Scale

**Scoring:** The WTC permits computation of one total score and seven subscores. The range for all scores is 0–100. Follow the procedures outlined below.

1.  Group discussion—add scores for items 8, 15, and 19; divide sum by 3. Scores 89 or above = high WTC, scores below 57 = low WTC in this context.

2.  Meetings—add scores for items 6, 11, and 17; divide sum by 3. Scores 80 or above = high WTC, scores below 39 = low WTC in this context.

3.  Interpersonal—add scores for items 4, 9, and 12; divide sum by 3. Scores 94 or above = high WTC, scores below 64 = low WTC in this context.

4.  Public speaking—add scores for items 3, 14, and 20; divide sum by 3. Scores 78 or above = high WTC, scores below 33 = low WTC in this context.

5.  Stranger—add scores for items 3, 8, 12, and 17; divide sum by 4. Scores 63 or above = high WTC, scores below 18 = low WTC with these receivers.

6.  Acquaintance—add scores for items 4, 11, 15, and 20; divide sum by 4. Scores 92 or above = high WTC, scores below 57 = low WTC with these receivers.

7.  Friends—add scores for items 6, 9, 14, and 19; divide sum by 4. Scores 99 or above = high WTC, scores below 71 = low WTC with these receivers.

To compute the total score for the WTC, add the totals for stranger, friend, and acquaintance; then divide by 3. Scores above 82 = high WTC, below 52 = low WTC.

*Source:* James C. McCloskey and Virginia P. Richmond, *Fundamentals of Human Communication: An Interpersonal Perspective* (Prospect Heights, IL: Waveland Press, 1996), p. 53.

---

**willingness to communicate.** General term for an individual's tendency to be shy or apprehensive about communicating with others.

else. But so does whether you were reinforced for talking with others as a child, as well as other experiences that are part of your culture and learning.

Your overall **willingness to communicate** with others is a general way of summarizing the shyness or apprehension that you feel when talking with others in a variety of situations, including interpersonal conversations. If you are unwilling to communicate with others, you will be less comfortable in a career that forces you to interact with others. To assess your willingness to communicate, take the self-test developed by McCroskey and Richmond in the Building Your Skills box. The test will give you an overall score as well as a score in specific communication situations such as meetings, interpersonal conversations, communicating with strangers, and communicating with friends.

Understanding the factors that influence your self-concept—such as your interactions with individuals and groups, the roles you assume, your self-labels, and your personality, including your overall comfort level in communicating with others—can help you understand who you are and why you interact (or don't interact) with others. But it's not only who you are that influences your communication, it's your overall sense of self-esteem or self-worth that affects how you express yourself and respond to others.

## $\mathcal{S}$elf-Esteem: Your Self-Worth

$\mathbf{Y}$our self-esteem is closely related to your self-concept. Your self-concept is a *description* of who you are. Your self-esteem is an *evaluation* of who you are. The term **self-worth** is often used interchangeably with *self-esteem*. Several researchers have sought to determine whether men or women have higher levels of self-esteem. The results are mixed. No clear-cut pattern emerges.[21]

People derive their sense of self-worth from comparing themselves to others, a process called *social comparison.* **Social comparison** helps people measure how well they think they are doing compared to others. I'm good at playing soccer (because I beat others); I can't cook (because others cook better than I do); I'm not good at meeting people (most people I know seem to be more comfortable interacting with others); I'm not handy (but my brothers and sisters can fix a leaky faucet). Each of these statements implies a judgment about how well or badly you can perform certain tasks, with implied references to how well others perform the same tasks. A belief that you cannot fix a leaky faucet or cook like a chef may not in itself lower your self-esteem. But if there are *several* things you can't do well, or *many* important tasks that you cannot seem to master, these shortcomings may begin to color your overall sense of worth.

In the 1960s psychologist Eric Berne developed the concept of a **life position** to describe people's overall sense of their own worth and that of others.[22] He identified four life positions: (1) "I'm OK, you're OK," or positive regard for self and others; (2) "I'm OK, you're not OK," or positive regard for self and low regard for others; (3) "I'm not OK, you're OK," or low self-regard and positive regard for others; and (4) "I'm not OK, you're not OK," or low regard for both self and others. Your life position is a driving force in your relationships with others. People in the "I'm OK, you're OK" position have the best chance for healthy relationships because they have discovered their own talents and also recognize that others have been given talents different from their own.

Another way communication researchers talk about being "OK" is by referring to what is called *face.* **Face** is a person's positive perception of himself or herself in interactions with others.[23] **Facework** is the use of communication to maintain one's own positive self-perception (self-face) or to support, reinforce, or even challenge someone else's self-perception (other-face).[24] You are involved in facework, for example, when you announce to your parents that you made the dean's list during your most recent semester in college. By telling them the good news about your academic success, you're using communication to maintain your parents' positive image of you and thus reinforce your own positive self-image. The effort you expend to save face (protect your positive image) reflects the kind of perception you want others to have of you. You may also engage in facework to maintain the esteem of others. When your roommate's mother calls and you tell her that your roommate is studying in the library when she's actually at a party, you're also engaging in facework.

**self-worth (self-esteem).** Your evaluation of your worth or value based on your perception of such things as your skills, abilities, talents, and appearance.

**social comparison.** Process of comparing yourself to others who are similar to you to measure your worth and value.

**life position.** Your feelings of regard for yourself and others, as reflected in your sense of worth and self-esteem.

**face.** A person's positive perception of himself or herself in interactions with others.

**facework.** Using communication to maintain your own positive self-perception (self-face) or to support, reinforce, or challenge someone else's self-perception (other-face).

# How to Improve Your Self-Esteem

We have mentioned that low self-esteem can affect our own communication and interactions. In recent years teachers, psychologists, ministers, rabbis, social workers, and even politicians have suggested that many societal problems also stem from collective feelings of low self-esteem. Feelings of low self-worth may contribute to choosing the wrong partners; to becoming dependent on drugs, alcohol, or other substances; or to experiencing problems with eating or other vital activities. So people owe it to society, as well as to themselves, to maintain or develop a healthy sense of self-esteem.

Although no simple list of tricks can easily transform low self-esteem into feelings of being valued and appreciated, you can improve how you think about yourself and interact with others. We'll explore seven proven techniques that have helped others.

## Engage in Self-Talk

*Although positive self-talk will never be able to make all of us become champion cyclists like Lance Armstrong, it can help us focus on our own goals and improve our performance levels.*

Cycling champion Lance Armstrong is also a cancer survivor. When he got sick, he told a friend, "Cancer picked the wrong guy. When it looked around for a body to hang out in, it made a big mistake when it chose mine. Big mistake."[25] The positive self-talk reflected in his words undoubtedly helped Armstrong to overcome the challenge of cancer and go on to win the Tour de France several times.

**Intrapersonal communication** is communication within yourself—self-talk. Realistic, positive self-talk can have a reassuring effect on your level of self-worth and on your interactions with others. Conversely, repeating negative messages about your lack of skill and ability can keep you from trying and achieving. Sports psychologist Karlene Sugarman claims, "Positive self-talk will help your performance, negative self-talk will make matters worse. Positive self-talk helps you to develop secure attitudes toward your performance and validates your capabilities."[26]

Of course, blind faith without hard work won't succeed. Self-talk is not a substitute for effort; it can, however, keep you on track and help you ultimately to achieve your goal.

### Visualize a Positive Image of Yourself

**Visualization** takes the notion of self-talk one step further. Besides just telling yourself that you can achieve your goal, you can actually try to "see" yourself conversing effectively with others, performing well on a project, or exhibiting some other desirable behavior. Recent research suggests that an apprehensive public speaker can manage his or her fears not only by developing skill in public speaking, but also by visualizing positive results when speaking to an audience.[27] If you are one of the many people who fear speaking in public, try visualizing yourself walking to the lectern, taking out your well-prepared notes, and delivering an interesting, well-received speech. This visualization of positive results enhances confidence and speaking skill. The same technique can be used to boost your sense of self-worth about other tasks or skills. If, for example, you tend to get nervous when meeting people at a party, imagine yourself in a room full of people, glibly introducing yourself to others with ease. Visualizing yourself performing well can yield positive results in changing long-standing feelings of inadequacy. Of course, your visualization should be realistic and coupled with a plan to achieve your goal.

BALLARD STREET copyright © Van Amarongen. Reprinted with permission of Creators Syndicate.

Michael continually measures himself against others.

### Avoid Comparing Yourself with Others

Even before we were born, we were compared with others. The latest medical technology lets us see sonograms of fetuses still in the womb, so parents may begin comparing children with other babies before birth. For the rest of our lives we are compared with others, and rather than celebrating our uniqueness, comparisons usually point up who is bigger, brighter, and more beautiful. Many of us have had the experience of being chosen last to play on a sports team, passed over for promotion, or standing unchosen against the wall at a dance.

In North American culture we may be tempted to judge our self-worth by our material possessions and personal appearance. If we know someone who has a newer car (or simply a car, if we rely on public transportation), a smaller waistline, or a higher grade point average, we may feel diminished. Comparisons such as "He has more money than I have" or "She looks better than I look" are likely to deflate our self-worth. Sisters and centenarians Sadie and Bessie Delaney inspired many by their refusal to let what they didn't have deter their sense of personal accomplishment. In their bestseller, *Having Our Say,* these two family matriarchs write of the value of emphasizing what we have, rather than comparing our lack of resources with the abundance of others who have more.

Rather than finding others who seemingly are better off, focus on the unique attributes that make you who you are. Avoid judging your own value by comparing yourself with others. A healthy, positive self-concept is fueled not by judgments of others, but by a genuine sense of worth that you recognize in yourself.

**intrapersonal communication.** Communication within yourself; self-talk.

**visualization.** Technique of imagining that you are performing a particular task in a certain way. Positive visualization can enhance your self-esteem.

# *All the Good Things*

He was in the first third-grade class I taught at Saint Mary's School in Morris, Minnesota. All thirty-four of my students were dear to me, but Mark Eklund was one in a million. Very neat in appearance, he had that happy-to-be-alive attitude that made even his occasional mischievousness delightful.

Mark also talked incessantly. I had to remind him again and again that talking without permission was not acceptable. What impressed me so much, though, was his sincere response every time I had to correct him for misbehaving—"Thank you for correcting me, Sister!" I didn't know what to make of it at first, but before long I became accustomed to hearing it many times a day.

One morning my patience was growing thin when Mark talked once too often, and then I made a novice-teacher's mistake. I looked at Mark and said, "If you say one more word, I am going to tape your mouth shut!"

It wasn't ten seconds later when Chuck blurted out, "Mark is talking again." I hadn't asked any of the students to help me watch Mark, but since I had stated the punishment in front of the class, I had to act on it.

I remember the scene as if it had occurred this morning. I walked to my desk, very deliberately opened the drawer and took out a roll of masking tape. Without saying a word, I proceeded to Mark's desk, tore off two pieces of tape and made a big X with them over his mouth. I then returned to the front of the room.

As I glanced at Mark to see how he was doing, he winked at me. That did it! I started laughing. The entire class cheered as I walked back to Mark's desk, removed the tape, and shrugged my shoulders. His first words were, "Thank you for correcting me, Sister."

At the end of the year I was asked to teach junior-high math. The years flew by, and before I knew it Mark was in my classroom again. He was more handsome than ever and just as polite. Since he had to listen carefully to my instruction in the "new math," he did not talk as much in ninth grade as he had in third.

One Friday, things just didn't feel right. We had worked hard on a new concept all week, and I sensed that the students were growing frustrated with themselves—and edgy with one another. I had to stop this crankiness before it got out of hand. So I asked them to list the names of the other students in the room on two sheets of paper, leaving a space between each name. Then I told them to think of the nicest thing they could say about each of their classmates and write it down.

It took the remainder of the class period to finish the assignment, but as the students left the room, each one handed me the papers. Charlie smiled. Mark said, "Thank you for teaching me, Sister. Have a good weekend."

That Saturday, I wrote down the name of each student on a separate sheet of paper, and I listed what everyone else had said about that individual. On Monday I gave each student his or her list. Some of them ran two pages. Before long, the entire class was smiling. "Really?" I heard whispered. "I never knew that meant anything to anyone!" "I didn't know others liked me so much!"

No one ever mentioned those papers in class again. I never knew if they discussed them after class or

## Reframe Appropriately

**Reframing** is the process of redefining events and experiences from a different point of view. Just as reframing a work of art can give the picture a whole new look, reframing events that cause you to devalue your self-worth can change your perspective. Research suggests that in times of family stress, individuals who can engage in self-talk and describe the event from someone else's perspective manage stress more successfully. For example, if you get a report from your supervisor that says you should improve one area of your performance, instead of listening to the self-talk that says you're bad at your job, reframe the event within a larger context: Tell yourself that one negative comment does not mean you are hopeless as a worker.

Of course, not all negative experiences should be lightly tossed off and left unexamined, because you can learn and profit from your mistakes. But it is important to remember that your worth as a human being does not depend on a single exam grade, a single response from a prospective employer, or a single play in a football game. Looking at the big picture—what effect this small event will have on your whole life, on society, on history—places negative experiences, which all people have, in a realistic context.

**reframing.** Process of redefining events and experiences from a different point of view.

with their parents, but it didn't matter. The exercise had accomplished its purpose. The students were happy with themselves and one another again.

That group of students moved on. Several years later, after I returned from a vacation, my parents met me at the airport. As we were driving home, Mother asked the usual questions about the trip—the weather, my experiences in general. There was a slight lull in the conversation. Mother gave Dad a sideways glance and simply said, "Dad?" My father cleared his throat as he usually did before saying something important. "The Eklunds called last night," he began.

"Really?" I said. "I haven't heard from them for several years. I wonder how Mark is."

Dad responded quietly. "Mark was killed in Vietnam," he said. "The funeral is tomorrow, and his parents would like it if you could attend." To this day I can still point to the exact spot on I-494 where Dad told me about Mark.

I had never seen a serviceman in a military coffin before. Mark looked so handsome, so mature. All I could think at that moment was, *Mark, I would give all the masking tape in the world if only you could talk to me.*

The church was packed with Mark's friends. Chuck's sister sang "The Battle Hymn of the Republic." Why did it have to rain on the day of the funeral? It was difficult enough at the graveside. The pastor said the usual prayers, and the bugler played taps. One by one those who loved Mark took a last walk by the coffin and sprinkled it with holy water.

I was the last one to bless the coffin. As I stood there, one of the soldiers who had acted as a pallbearer came up to me. "Were you Mark's math teacher?" he asked. I nodded as I continued to stare at the coffin. "Mark talked about you a lot," he said.

After the funeral, most of Mark's former classmates headed to Chuck's farmhouse for lunch. Mark's mother and father were there, obviously waiting for me. "We want to show you something," his father said, taking a wallet out of his pocket. "They found this on Mark when he was killed. We thought you might recognize it."

Opening the billfold, he carefully removed two worn pieces of notebook paper that had obviously been taped, folded and refolded many times. I knew without looking that the papers were the ones on which I had listed all the good things each of Mark's classmates had said about him. "Thank you so much for doing that," Mark's mother said. "As you can see, Mark treasured it."

Mark's classmates started to gather around us. Charlie smiled rather sheepishly and said, "I still have my list. It's in the top drawer of my desk at home." Chuck's wife said, "Chuck asked me to put his in our wedding album." "I have mine too," Marilyn said. "It's in my diary." Then Vicki, another classmate, reached into her pocketbook, took out her wallet and showed her worn and frazzled list to the group. "I carry this with me at all times," Vicki said without batting an eyelash. "I think we all saved our lists."

That was when I finally sat down and cried. I cried for Mark and for all his friends who would never see him again.

*Source:* Helen P. Mrosla © *Proteus*, Shippensburg University.

## Develop Honest Relationships

Having at least one other person who can help you objectively and honestly reflect on your virtues and vices can be extremely beneficial in fostering a healthy, positive self-image. As we noted earlier, other people play a major role in shaping your self-concept and self-esteem. The more credible the source of information, the more likely you are to believe it. Having a trusted friend, colleague, minister, or counselor who can listen without judging you and give you the straight scoop about yourself can help you avoid "pity parties." Prolonged periods of self-pity left unchecked and unconfirmed can lead to feelings of inferiority. Later in the chapter we discuss how honest relationships are developed through the process of self-disclosure. As the author of the essay "All the Good Things" learned, honest, positive support can provide encouragement for a lifetime.

## Let Go of the Past

Your self-concept is not a fixed construct. It was not implanted at birth to remain constant for the rest of your life. Things change. You change. Others change. Individuals with low self-esteem may be locking on to events and experiences that happened years ago and tenaciously refusing to let go of them. Someone once wrote, "The lightning bug is brilliant, but it hasn't much of a mind; it blunders through existence with its headlight on behind." Looking back at what we can't change only reinforces a sense of helplessness. Constantly replaying negative experiences in our mental DVD player only serves to make our sense of worth more difficult to change. Becoming aware of the changes that have occurred and can occur in your life can help you develop a more realistic assessment of your value. If you were overweight as a child, you may have a difficult time accepting that your worth does not hinge on pounds you carried years ago. Being open and receptive to change in self-worth is important to developing a healthy self-concept. Longfellow's advice to let go of the past remains wise advice today: "Look not mournfully into the past. It comes not back again. Wisely improve the present. It is thine. Go forth to meet the shadowy future, without fear...." Abraham Lincoln is considered one of the best presidents of the United States. He had many skills, including the ability to appropriately reframe past defeats, coupled with talent and perseverance. He lost seven elections, including a race for the U.S. Senate two years before being elected president. He had several businesses that failed, lost several jobs, became bankrupt, and spent six months in bed because of a nervous breakdown. Despite these many setbacks, he looked to future possibilities rather than past losses.[28]

### Seek Support

Some of your self-image problems may be so ingrained that you need professional help. A trained counselor, clergy member, or therapist can help you sort through them. Therapists traditionally take a psychoanalytic approach, inviting you to search for experiences in your past that may help you first to understand your feelings and then to change them. Other counselors use different techniques. If you are not sure to whom to turn for a referral, you can start with your school counseling services. Or, if you are near a medical-school teaching hospital, you can contact the counseling or psychotherapy office there for a referral.

Because you have spent your whole lifetime developing your self-esteem, it is not easy to make big changes. But talking through problems can make a difference. As communication researchers Frank E. X. Dance and Carl Larson see it, "Speech communication empowers each of us to share in the development of our own self-concept and the fulfillment of that self-concept."[29]

### Recap

## Strategies for Improving Your Self-Esteem

| | |
|---|---|
| **Engage in Self-Talk** | If you're having a bad hair day, tell yourself that you have beautiful eyes and lots of friends who like you anyway. |
| **Visualize** | If you feel nervous before a meeting, visualize everyone in the room congratulating you on your great ideas. |
| **Avoid Comparison** | Focus on your positive qualities and on what you can do to enhance your own talents and abilities. |
| **Reframe Appropriately** | If you experience one failure, keep the larger picture in mind, rather than focusing on that isolated incident. |
| **Develop Honest Relationships** | Cultivate friends in whom you can confide and who will give you honest feedback for improving your skills and abilities. |
| **Let Go of the Past** | Talk yourself out of your "old tapes"; focus on ways to enhance your abilities in the future. |
| **Seek Support** | Talk with professional counselors who can help you identify your gifts and talents. |

PEANUTS reprinted by permission of Newspaper Enterprise Association.

# $\mathcal{H}$ow Self-Concept and Self-Esteem Affect Interpersonal Communication and Relationships

**Y**our self-concept and self-esteem filter every interaction with others. They determine how you approach, respond to, and interpret messages. Specifically, your self-concept and self-esteem affect your ability to be sensitive to others, your self-fulfilling prophecies, your interpretation of messages, your own social needs, and your typical communication style.

## Self and Others

We have suggested the importance of becoming other-oriented—being sensitive to the thoughts and feelings of others—as a requisite for developing quality interpersonal relationships with others.

Becoming other-oriented involves recognizing that your "self" is different from others. As the Peanuts cartoon reminds us, the world does not revolve around our solitary selves. Others influence our actions and our self-image. Mead suggests that we develop an "I," which is based on our own perspective of ourselves, and a "Me," which is an image of ourselves based on the collective responses we receive and interpret from others. Being aware of how your concept of self ("I") differs from the perceptions others have of you ("Me") is an important first step in developing an other-orientation.

When you begin the **social decentering** process—taking into account what others may be thinking and feeling—you often interpret your assumptions about others using your own self as a frame of reference, especially if you do not know the other person well.[30] For example, if you are nervous and frightened when you have to take a test, you might assume that your friend will react the same way. You may need to remind yourself that the other person is separate from you and may have a different set of responses.

When you use a **specific-other perspective,** you rely on information that you have observed or that you can imagine about a particular person to predict his or her reactions. For example, if you know firsthand that your sister hates to have someone take food from her plate during dinner, you may use that experience to conclude that she would dislike sharing a bag of popcorn at the movies.

Sometimes a **generalized-other perspective** will be more useful. When you think about and respond to others, you can apply knowledge and personal theories that you have about people in general or about specific subgroups to the person with whom

**social decentering.** Cognitive process in which you take into account another person's thoughts, feelings, values, background, and perspective.

**specific-other perspective.** A perspective that uses information that one can observe or imagine about another person to predict that person's behavior.

**generalized-other perspective.** A perspective that uses observed or imagined information about many people, or people in general, to predict a person's behavior.

you are interacting. For example, you might think that your economics professor, who holds a Ph.D., would prefer to be addressed as "Doctor" rather than as "Mister" because almost all your other professors with doctorates prefer to be called "Doctor."

Your ability to predict how others will respond to you is based on your ability to understand how your sense of the world is similar to and different from theirs. First you must know yourself well. Then you can know and understand others. One of the best ways to improve your ability to be other-oriented is to notice how others respond when you act on the predictions and assumptions you have made about them. You may discover that you have not moved out of your own frame of reference enough to make an accurate prediction about another person.

### Self-Fulfilling Prophecy

What people believe about themselves often comes true because they expect it to come true. Their expectations become a **self-fulfilling prophecy.** If you think you will fail the math quiz because you have labeled yourself inept at math, then you must overcome not only your math deficiency, but also your low expectations of yourself. The theme of George Bernard Shaw's *Pygmalion* is "If you treat a girl like a flower girl, that's all she will ever be. If you treat her like a princess, she may be one." Your attitudes, beliefs, and general expectations about your performance have a powerful and profound effect on your behavior.

The medical profession is learning the power that attitudes and expectations have over healing. Physician Howard Brody's research suggests that in many instances, just giving patients a placebo—a pill with no medicine in it—or telling patients that they have been operated on when they haven't had an operation can yield positive medical results. In his book *The Placebo Response,* Brody tells of a woman with debilitating Parkinson's disease who made a miraculous recovery; her only treatment was the doctors' telling her that they had completed a medical procedure.[31] They hadn't. Yet before the "treatment" she could barely walk; now she can easily pace around the room. There is a clear link, suggests Dr. Brody, between mental state and physical health. Patients who believe they will improve are more likely to improve.

### Self and Interpretation of Messages

Although it may have been several years since you've read A. A. Milne's classic children's stories about Winnie-the-Pooh, you probably remember Eeyore, the donkey friend of Winnie-the-Pooh and his friends. Eeyore lives in the gloomiest part of the Hundred Acre Wood and has a self-image to match. In one story all the animals congregate on a stormy night to check on Eeyore:

> . . . they all came to the part of the forest known as Eeyore's gloomy place. On this stormy night it was terribly gloomy indeed—or it would have been were it not for Christopher Robin. He was there with a big umbrella.
>
> "I've invited Eeyore to come and stay with me until the storm is over," said Christopher Robin.
>
> "If it ever is," said Eeyore, "which doesn't seem likely. Not that anybody asked me, you understand. But then, they hardly ever do."[32]

Perhaps you know or have known an Eeyore—someone whose low self-esteem colors how he or she interprets messages and interacts with others. According to research, such people are more likely to

- Be more sensitive to criticism and negative feedback from others.

- Be more critical of others.

**self-fulfilling prophecy.** A prediction about your future actions that is likely to come true because you believe that it will come true.

- Believe they are not popular or respected by others.

- Expect to be rejected by others.

- Prefer not to be observed when performing.

- Feel threatened by people who they feel are superior.

- Expect to lose when competing with others.

- Be overly responsive to praise and compliments.

- Evaluate their overall behavior as inferior to that of others.[33]

The Pooh stories offer an antidote to Eeyore's gloom in the character of the optimistic Tigger, who assumes that everyone shares his exuberance for life:

> . . . when Owl reached Piglet's house, Tigger was there. He was bouncing on his tail, as Tiggers do, and shouting to Piglet. "Come on," he cried. "You can do it! It's fun!"[34]

If, like Tigger, your sense of self-worth is high, research suggests you will

- Have higher expectations for solving problems.

- Think more highly of others.

- Be more likely to accept praise and accolades from others without feeling embarrassed.

- Be more comfortable having others observe you when you perform.

- Be more likely to admit you have both strengths and weaknesses.

- Prefer to interact with others who view themselves as highly competent.

- Expect other people to accept you for who you are.

- Be more likely to seek opportunities to improve skills that need improving.

- Evaluate your overall behavior more positively than would people with lower self-esteem.[35]

Reflecting the assumption that self-concept influences behavior is the principle of **selective exposure,** which suggests that people tend to place themselves in situations consistent with who they think they are. Whom do you usually find at a Baptist church on Sunday morning? Baptists. Who are the attendees at a Democratic convention? Democrats. If you view yourself as a good student who wants an A in the class, where are you likely to be during class time? People's interpretation of messages and their behavior both reinforce their perceptions of self.

## Self and Interpersonal Needs

According to social psychologist Will Schutz, our concept of who we are, coupled with our need to interact with others, profoundly influences how we communicate with others. Schutz identifies three primary social needs that affect the degree of communication we have with others: the need for inclusion, the need for control, and the need for affection.[36] Each of us has a **need for inclusion**—the need to be included in the activities of others and to experience human contact and fellowship. We need to be invited to join others, and perhaps we need to invite others to join us. Of course, the level and intensity of this need differ from person to person, but even loners desire some social contact. Our need to include others and be included in activities may stem, in part, from our concept of ourselves as either a "party person" or a loner.

**selective exposure.** Principle that suggests people tend to place themselves in situations that are consistent with their self-concept and self-esteem.

**need for inclusion.** Interpersonal need to be included and to include others in social activities.

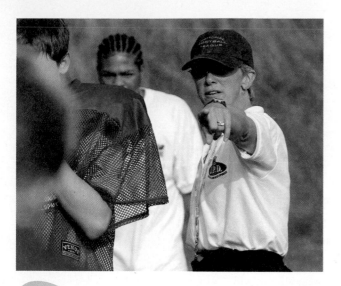

We also have a **need for control:** We need some degree of influence over the relationships we establish with others. We may also have a need to *be* controlled because we desire some level of stability and comfort in our interactions with others. If we view ourselves as people who are comfortable being in charge, we are more likely to give orders to others rather than take orders from them.

And finally, we each have a **need for affection.** We need to give and receive love, support, warmth, and intimacy, although the amounts we need vary enormously from person to person. If we have a high need for affection, we will more likely place ourselves in situations where that need can be met. The greater our needs for inclusion, control, and affection, the more likely it is that we will actively seek others as friends and initiate communication with them.

*A*lthough assertiveness is often thought of as a masculine trait, anyone can use an assertive communication style.

## Self and Communication Style

Our self-concept and self-esteem ultimately affect how we treat other people. One dimension of the self that is particularly relevant to our interactions with others is communication style. Each of us has a **communication style,** sometimes called *social style,* that is identifiable by the habitual ways we behave toward others. The style we adopt helps others interpret our messages and predict how we will behave. As they get to know us, other people begin to expect us to communicate in a certain way, based on previous associations with us.

How do we develop our communication style? Many communication researchers, sociologists, and psychologists believe that we have certain underlying traits or personality characteristics that influence how we interact with others. Some scholars believe these traits stem from genetics—we are born with certain personality characteristics. We are who we are because that's the way we are made.[37] As discussed in Chapter 1, others emphasize the social learning approach—we communicate with others as we do because of our interactions with others such as our parents and friends. The truth is that researchers cannot yet explain exactly how we come to communicate as we do.

Even though we don't know the precise role of nature or nurture in determining how we communicate, most inventories of personality or communication style focus on two primary dimensions that underlie how we interact with others—assertiveness and responsiveness.[38] **Assertiveness** is the tendency to make requests, ask for information, and generally pursue our own rights and best interests. An assertive style is sometimes called a "masculine" style. By masculine, we don't mean that only males can be assertive, but that in many cultures being assertive is synonymous with being masculine. You are assertive when you seek information if you are confused, or direct others to help you get what you need.

**Responsiveness** is the tendency to be sensitive to the needs of others. Being other-oriented and sympathetic to the feelings of others, and placing others' feelings above your own are examples of being responsive. Researchers sometimes label responsiveness a "feminine" quality. Again, this does not mean only women are or should be responsive, only that many cultures stereotype being responsive as a traditional behavior of females.

**need for control.** Interpersonal need for some degree of domination in our relationships, as well as the need to be controlled.

**need for affection.** Interpersonal need to give and receive love, personal support, warmth, and intimacy.

**communication style.** Identifiable or habitual way in which you communicate to other people.

**assertiveness.** Tendency to make requests, ask for information, and generally pursue your own rights and best interests.

**responsiveness.** Tendency to be sensitive to the needs of others, including being sympathetic to others' feelings and placing the feelings of others above your own feelings.

What is your communication style? To assess your style of communication on the assertiveness and responsiveness dimensions, take the "Sociocommunicative Orientation" test by James McCroskey and Virginia Richmond in the Building Your Skills box. You may discover that you test higher on one dimension than on the others. It's also possible to be high on both or low on both. Assertiveness and responsiveness are two different dimensions; you need not have just one or the other.

What many people want to know is, "What's the best communication style? Should I be assertive or responsive?" The truth is, there is no one best style for every situation. Sometimes the appropriate thing to do is to assert yourself—to ask or even demand that you receive what you need and have a right to receive. In other situations, it may be more appropriate to be less confrontational. Maintaining the quality of the relationship by simply listening and being thoughtfully responsive to others may be best. The appropriateness of your communication style involves issues we will discuss in future chapters, such as how you adapt to culture and gender differences, your needs, the needs and rights of others, and the goal of your communication.

## *Building Your Skills*

## Sociocommunicative Orientation

**Directions:** The following questionnaire lists 20 personality characteristics. Please indicate the degree to which you believe each of these characteristics applies to you, as you normally communicate with others, by marking whether you (5) strongly agree that it applies, (4) agree that it applies, (3) are undecided, (2) disagree that it applies, or (1) strongly disagree that it applies. There are no right or wrong answers. Work quickly; record your first impression.

_____ 1. helpful

_____ 2. defends own beliefs

_____ 3. independent

_____ 4. responsive to others

_____ 5. forceful

_____ 6. has strong personality

_____ 7. sympathetic

_____ 8. compassionate

_____ 9. assertive

_____ 10. sensitive to the needs of others

_____ 11. dominant

_____ 12. sincere

_____ 13. gentle

_____ 14. willing to take a stand

_____ 15. warm

_____ 16. tender

_____ 17. friendly

_____ 18. acts as a leader

_____ 19. aggressive

_____ 20. competitive

**Scoring:** Items 2, 3, 5, 6, 9, 11, 14, 18, 19, and 20 measure assertiveness. Add the scores on these items to get your assertiveness score. Items 1, 4, 7, 8, 10, 12, 13, 15, 16, and 17 measure responsiveness. Add the scores on these items to get your responsiveness score. Scores range from 50 to 10. The higher your score, the higher your orientation as assertive and responsive.

_Source:_ James C. McCroskey and Virginia P. Richmond, _Fundamentals of Human Communication: An Interpersonal Perspective_ (Prospect Heights, IL: Waveland Press, 1996), p. 91.

## Recap

### How Self-Concept and Self-Esteem Affect Interpersonal Communication and Relationships

| | Definition | Examples |
|---|---|---|
| **Message Interpretation and Interaction** | Feelings of high or low self-esteem affect how you understand and react to messages. | If you have high self-esteem, you are more likely to accept praise without embarrassment. |
| **Self-Fulfilling Prophecy** | What you believe about yourself will come true because you expect it to come true. | You expect to have a rotten time at a party so you behave in ways that guarantee you won't enjoy the party. |
| **Communication Style** | Your self-concept and self-esteem contribute to habitual ways of responding to others. | Your image of yourself influences your responsive or assertive behavior toward others. |

# Self-Disclosure: Connecting Self to Others Through Talk

One important way people develop and revise their self-concept is through other people's reactions to their self-disclosure. **Self-disclosure** occurs when you purposefully provide information to others about yourself that they would not learn if you did not tell them. People can learn your approximate age, height, and weight by just observing you. But they can't learn your *exact* age, height, or weight unless you tell them. Self-disclosure ranges from revealing innocuous information about who you are to admitting your deepest fears and most private fantasies. Disclosing personal information not only provides a basis for another person to understand you better, it conveys your level of trust and acceptance of the other person. Because others self-disclose, you are able to learn information about them and deepen your interpersonal relationships with them.[39] To help explore the relationships among self-concept, self-esteem, and self-disclosure, we will describe how self-disclosure occurs, note how people become aware of who they are through self-disclosure, and identify general characteristics of self-disclosure.

Interpersonal relationships cannot achieve intimacy without self-disclosure. Without true self-disclosure, you form only superficial relationships. You can confirm another person's self-concept, and have your self-concept confirmed, only if both you and your partner have revealed yourselves to each other.

### Understanding the Depth and Breadth of Self-Disclosure: The Social Penetration Model of Self-Disclosure

**self-disclosure.** Purposefully providing information to others that they would not learn if you did not tell them.

**social penetration model.** Model of self-disclosure and relational development that reflects both depth and breadth of shared information.

What makes your best friend your best friend? Undoubtedly, one characteristic is that you have shared your most personal information with him or her. You share more personal information over a broader range of topics with people you know well and who know you, than you do with people you know only superficially. Researchers Irwin Altman and Dalmas Taylor developed a model called **social penetration** that illustrates how much and what kinds of information people reveal in various stages of a relationship.[40] Their model starts with a circle that represents all the potential information about yourself that you could disclose to someone (see Figure 2.2, circle A). This circle is divided into many pieces like a pie, with each piece of pie representing a

FIGURE 2.2

Social Penetration Models

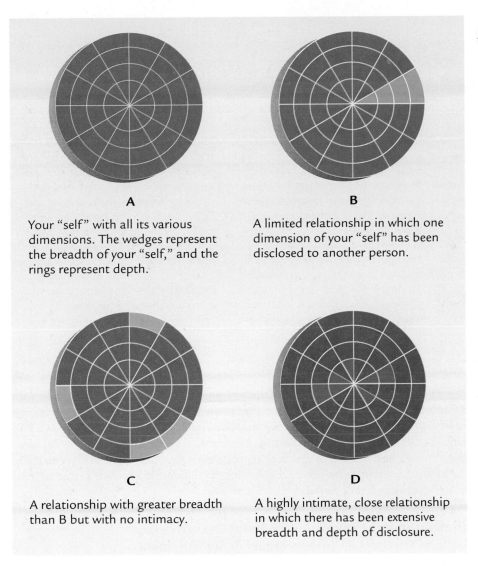

**A**

Your "self" with all its various dimensions. The wedges represent the breadth of your "self," and the rings represent depth.

**B**

A limited relationship in which one dimension of your "self" has been disclosed to another person.

**C**

A relationship with greater breadth than B but with no intimacy.

**D**

A highly intimate, close relationship in which there has been extensive breadth and depth of disclosure.

particular aspect of yourself. For instance, some pieces in your pie might relate to athletic activities, religious beliefs, family, school, recreational activities, political interests, and fears. These pieces of pie represent the breadth of topics or information available about you.

In addition, the concentric circles in the pie represent the depth of information you could disclose. By depth, we mean how personal or intimate the information is; telling your friend about your fear of elevators is more intimate than telling someone that your favorite ice cream is homemade vanilla. The smallest circle represents the most personal information. Each of your relationships represents a degree of social penetration, or the extent to which the other person has penetrated your concentric circles (depth) and shared pieces of your pie (breadth). For example, the shading on circle B shows a relationship that involves a high degree of penetration, but of only one aspect of yourself. Perhaps you have a good friend with whom you study and go to the library, but you don't spend much time socializing with your friend; it's all work and no play with this friend. You might have disclosed some personal or intimate information to your friend about your study skills and weaknesses, but little about your family, hobbies, political views, or other aspects of who you are.

# *Understanding Diversity*

## Cultural Differences in Self-Disclosure

*T*he social penetration model of self-disclosure, as described on page 54, suggests that self-disclosure can be described by both breadth—the number of topics we discuss—and depth—the level of intimacy we establish with others. Do cultural differences affect how much we disclose to one another? Several researchers suggest that the answer is yes. People's cultural backgrounds affect both the kinds of things they reveal and the intimacy of the information about themselves they share with others. Intercultural communication scholar William Gudykunst found that North Americans are more likely than Japanese to reveal more personal and intimate information about themselves with people whom they consider to be close friends.[41] Americans were more likely than the Japanese to talk about their sex lives, dating patterns, and love interests and to reveal their emotions. A researcher investigating Korean communication pat- terns found that North Americans tend to disclose more than Koreans about their marital status, sexual morality, and use of birth control.[42] But Koreans were more likely than Americans to talk about issues related to education and family rules. What are the larger impli- cations of these studies? Simply this: The amount of self-disclosure that is considered appropriate is learned; the level of self-disclosure with which we are comfortable varies from culture to culture. Cultural norms influence how much we reveal about our selves.

---

Your relationships with your instructors probably look a little like circle B, with its limited breadth. In circle C, more pieces of the pie are shaded, but the information is all fairly safe, superficial information about yourself, such as where you went to school, your hometown, or your major. These would be the kind of disclosures associated with a new friendship. Circle D represents almost complete social penetration, the kind achieved in an intimate, well-developed relationship in which a large amount of self-disclosure has occurred.

## Understanding How We Learn About Ourselves from Others: The Johari Window Model of Self-Disclosure

To disclose information to others, you must first be aware of who you are. Your **self-awareness** is your understanding of who you are. In addition to just thinking about who you are, asking others for information about yourself and then listening to what they tell you can enhance your self-awareness. There are a variety of personality tests, such as the Myers-Briggs personality inventory, that may give you additional insight into your interests, style, and ways of relating to others. Most colleges and universities have a career services office where you can take vocational aptitude tests to help you identify careers that fit who you are.

The **Johari Window model** nicely summarizes how your awareness of who you are is influenced by your own level of disclosure, as well as by how much others share information *about* yourself *with* you. (The name "Johari Window" sounds somewhat mystical and exotic, but it is simply a combination of the first names of the creators of the model, Joseph Luft and Harry Ingham.[43]) As Figure 2.3 shows, the model looks like a window. Like the circles in the social penetration model, the window represents your self. This self includes everything about you, including things even you don't yet see or realize. One axis is divided into what you have come to know about yourself and what you don't yet know about who you are. The other axis represents what someone

**self-awareness.** A person's conscious understanding of who he or she is.

**Johari Window model.** Model of self-disclosure that reflects the movement of information about yourself from Blind and Unknown quadrants to Hidden and Open ones.

else may know about you and not know about you. The intersection of these categories creates a four-panel, or four-quadrant, window.

Quadrant 1 is an *open area*. The open area contains information that others know about you and that you are also aware of—such as your age, your occupation, and other things you might mention about yourself. At first glance, all four quadrants in the window appear to be the same size. But that may not be the case (in fact, it probably isn't). In the case of quadrant 1, the more information that you reveal about yourself, the larger this quadrant will be. Put another way, the more you open up to others, the larger the open area will be.

Quadrant 2 is a *blind area*. This part of the window contains information that other people know about you, but that you do not know. Perhaps when you were in grade school, someone put a sign on your back that said, "Kick me." Everyone was aware of the sign but you. The blind area of the Johari Window represents much the same situation. For example, you may see yourself as generous, but others may see you as a tightwad. As you learn how others see you, the blind area of the Johari Window gets smaller. Generally, the more accurately you know yourself and perceive how others see you, the better your chances to establish open and honest relationships with others.

Quadrant 3 is a *hidden area*. This area contains information that you know about yourself, but that others do not know about you. You can probably think of many facts, thoughts, feelings, and fantasies that you would not want anyone else to know. They may be feelings you have about another person or something you've done privately in the past that you'd be embarrassed to share with others. The point here is not to suggest you should share all information in the hidden area with others. It is useful to know, however, that part of who you are is known by some people, but remains hidden from others.

Quadrant 4 in an *unknown area*. This area contains information that is unknown to both you and others. These are things you do not know about yourself *yet*. Perhaps you do not know how you will react under certain stressful situations. Maybe you are not sure what stand you will take on a certain issue next year or even next week. Other people may also not be aware of how you would respond or behave under certain conditions. Your personal potential, your untapped physical and mental resources, are unknown. You can assume that this area exists, because eventually some (though not necessarily all) of these things become known to you, to others, or to both you and others. Because you can never know yourself completely, the unknown quadrant will always exist; you can only guess at its current size, because the information it contains is unavailable to you.

As we did with the social penetration model, we can draw Johari Windows to represent each of our relationships (see Figure 2.4 on page 58). Window A shows a new or restricted relationship for someone who knows himself or herself very well. The open and blind quadrants are small, but the unknown quadrant is also small. Window B shows a very intimate relationship, in which both individuals are open and disclosing.

We've discussed what self-disclosure is and described two models that explain how self-disclosure works and affects your understanding of who you think you are. Next we will describe characteristics of self-disclosure and discuss how disclosure, both appropriate and inappropriate, can affect our interpersonal relationships with others.

FIGURE *2.3*

Johari Window

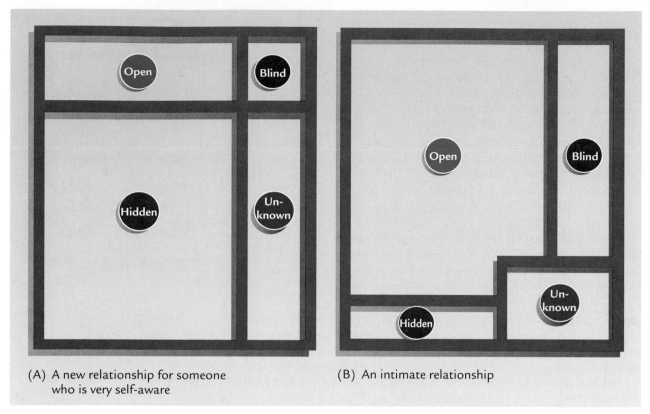

(A) A new relationship for someone
     who is very self-aware

(B) An intimate relationship

FIGURE 2.4

Variations on Johari Windows

# Characteristics of Self-Disclosure

**M**ike was sitting alone at the counter at his neighborhood diner enjoying his favorite meatloaf sandwich. Just as he was reaching for the catsup bottle, a young woman on the stool next to him struck up a conversation with him. Within ten minutes, Mike not only learned where this woman was from, but also whom she dated, how much money she made last year, and how embarrassed she was when her parents found her in a compromising position with her boyfriend on the front porch (which she described in vivid detail, complete with sound effects). Have you had the experience of meeting someone who told you more than you wanted to know about himself or herself? Although self-disclosure is a means of establishing relationships with others, revealing too much too soon or making the disclosure only a one-way stream of revelatory information violates self-disclosure norms for most North Americans. It is by revealing who we are in the normal course of conversations that others come to know us and (we often hope) grow to like us.[44]

Researchers have found that we self-disclose in predictable ways. For example, there is some evidence that women are slightly more likely to self-disclose than are men.[45] The following discussion describes other characteristics of appropriate self-disclosure.

### Self-Disclosure Usually Moves in Small Increments

What made Mike so uncomfortable during his meeting with his dining neighbor was how much information he learned about his companion in such a short period of time. Most people usually reveal information about themselves a little bit at a time, rather than delivering a condensed version of their autobiography all at once. Most North Americans would share Mike's discomfort at learning too much too soon. Monitor your own self-disclosure. Are you revealing information at a greater depth sooner than you should? If you do, others may find your disclosure disquieting. Appropriate self-disclosure should be well timed to suit the occasion and the expectations of the individuals involved.

## Self-Disclosure Moves from Less Personal to More Personal Information

As the social penetration model illustrates, we can describe the depth of our self-disclosure by the intimacy level of the information we share. If we move too quickly to more intimate information before we've developed a history with someone, we violate social norms or expectations our partner may have. John Powell, author of the book *Why Am I Afraid to Tell You Who I Am?* notes that the information we reveal about ourselves often progresses through the following predictable levels.[46]

Level 5: *Cliché communication.* We first establish verbal contact with others by saying something that lets the other person know we acknowledge his or her presence. Standard phrases such as "Hello" or "Hi, how are you?" or the more contemporary "What's up?" signal the desire to initiate a relationship, even if it is a brief, superficial one.

Level 4: *Facts and biographical information.* After using cliché phrases and responses to establish contact, we typically next reveal nonthreatening information about ourselves, such as our names, hometowns, or majors.

Level 3: *Attitudes and personal ideas.* After noting our name and other basic information, we often begin talking about more personal information such as our attitudes about work or school, or other relatively safe topics. At this level, the information is not too threatening or revealing, but we do begin to talk about our likes and dislikes or about what we assume are noncontroversial topics.

Level 2: *Personal feelings.* At this level, we discuss topics and issues that are exceedingly more personal. After we've developed rapport with someone, we then share more intimate fears, secrets, and attitudes. Increasingly, we take risks when we share this information. It requires trust to share these personal feelings.

Level 1: *Peak communication.* Powell calls this the ultimate level of self-disclosure that is seldom reached; his other name for level 1 communication is "gut level" communication. Only with our most intimate friends do we reveal such personal information. And it's possible, says Powell, that we may not reach this level of intimacy with our life partners, parents, or children. Peak communication is rare because of the risk and trust involved in being so open and revealing.

## Self-Disclosure Is Reciprocal

In mainstream U.S. culture, when people share information about themselves, they expect the other person to share similar information about herself or himself. If you introduce yourself by name to someone, you expect that person to respond by telling you his or her name. This cultural rule allows people to use disclosure as a strategy for gaining information and reducing uncertainty. The reciprocal nature of self-disclosure is called the **dyadic effect:** You disclose to me, and I'll disclose to you.

## Self-Disclosure Involves Risk

Although self-disclosure is a building block for establishing intimacy with others, it can be risky. Once you disclose something to someone, that person can now share the information with others; that person has additional power if the information is something you'd rather not have others know.

There is also the risk of rejection when you tell someone something that is personal. As Powell comments, "If I tell you who I am, and you do not like who I am, that is all that I have."[47] Once you reveal what you believe is your true nature or personal feeling and you are rejected or rebuffed, you can't explain your rejection away by saying, "Oh, they don't know the real me." If you've revealed what you honestly believe is "the real you," experiencing disapproval from your partner can hurt worse than if your partner did not know "the real you."

There is evidence that people are more likely to disclose more personal information about themselves when they communicate online than they would when communicating with others face-to-face. Communication researchers Lisa Tidwell and Joseph Walther wanted to know whether there are differences between face-to-face conversations and e-mail conversations in amount of self-disclosure, perceptions of confidence, and effectiveness of communication. They found that when people communicate via e-mail, they exchange information more directly with each other and perceive themselves and others to be more "conversationally effective" because they are more direct. E-mail conversation partners also reported that they were more confident when communicating online than they were in their face-to-face encounters.[48] Although researchers still have much to learn about communicating via e-mail and the Internet, the more structured nature of this context of communication is helping them learn more about the nature of self-disclosure and interpersonal communication patterns.

## Self-Disclosure Involves Trust

As we have already noted, to know something personal about someone is to have power over that person. If someone has shared information with you, you have the power to reveal that information to others. To reveal personal information about someone that was shared with you in confidence is unethical. If you've made a promise not to reveal something, you should keep it. Using personal information against others to manipulate and control is a misuse of the trust that was placed in you.[49] According to British social psychologists Michael Argyle, Monica Henderson, and Adrian Furnham, one of the most fundamental expectations people have of their friends is that they will not reveal confidences. When you say, "Oh, I won't tell anyone. Your secret's safe with me," mean it.

Perhaps the most intimate secrets are known by family members; our parents and siblings know quite a few things about us that we'd rather others not know. Interpersonal communication researchers Anita Vangelisti, John Caughlin, and Lindsay Timmerman found several factors that may help predict whether we do or don't disclose family secrets. For example, we would be *more* likely to share a family secret under certain conditions:

**dyadic effect.** The reciprocal nature of self-disclosure: "You disclose to me, and I'll disclose to you."

- During an intimate conversation with another person we found out that this person had a similar problem, or we thought revealing the secret would help the other person.

- We thought the secret would eventually come to light even if we didn't reveal the secret.

- There was some urgency or importance in revealing the secret; if we didn't reveal the secret, the concealment would create more problems than revealing the secret would cause.

- We thought the family member wouldn't mind if the secret were told; the family member would still accept us.

- It seemed like a normal and natural thing to reveal, given the topic of conversation; if the topic came up, we might disclose the secret.[50]

You might read this list and become worried that your family members might tell things they know about you that you'd rather others not know. Not to worry (too much). The researchers also found that there were some secrets that people would never disclose.

### Self-Disclosure Over Time: Enhancing Intimacy

Self-disclosure is often associated with relationship development, because it is through the process of revealing information about yourself that it becomes possible for relationships to become more intimate. However, simply disclosing information about yourself is no guarantee that your relationship will become intimate.[51] (Note that when we talk about intimacy and self-disclosure, we're not just talking about sex; rather, we're talking about both greater depth and breadth of self-disclosure.) In an intimate friendship, we become aware of things about our friend that few if any other people may know. Intimacy occurs through the process of self-disclosure.

As relationships move toward intimacy, they typically include periods of high self-disclosure early in the relationship. However, the *amount* of information that is disclosed decreases as the relationship becomes more and more intimate. In other words, there is generally more self-disclosing activity earlier in a relationship than later. As a relationship proceeds, we begin sharing low-risk information fairly rapidly, move on to share higher-risk information, and then finally, to share our most personal disclosures. The more intimate the relationship becomes, the more intimate the information that is disclosed. The sculpture in the photo represents the way we reveal ourselves when we

*As* we develop a relationship, we reveal more of ourselves, removing the masks that we routinely use with strangers.

are with close friends; with our best friends, we may reveal what is behind our "masks." Holding back from sharing intimate information signals a reluctance to escalate the relationship. The amount of information that we have to share about ourselves is finite, so we slow down as we have less left to disclose.

Graph A in Figure 2.5 on page 62 illustrates a typical disclosure pattern over the course of a long and intimate relationship. The peaks and valleys represent periods of variable disclosure. Note that most of the disclosure takes place in the beginning of the relationship. Not all relationships progress this way, however. The relationship in graph B represents two individuals who started to get to know each other but were interrupted before they

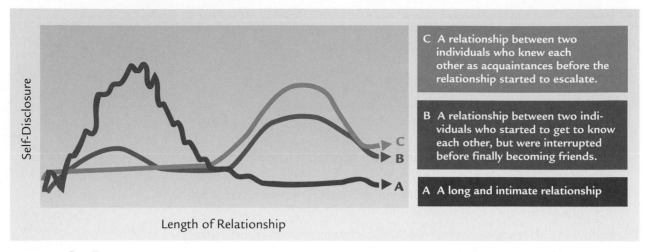

C A relationship between two individuals who knew each other as acquaintances before the relationship started to escalate.

B A relationship between two individuals who started to get to know each other, but were interrupted before finally becoming friends.

A A long and intimate relationship

FIGURE *2.5*

Self-Disclosure and Relational Development

became close friends. They might have stopped because of some conflict, indecisiveness about pursuing the relationship, or external circumstances that limited opportunities for interacting. When the disclosure resumed, it became more intense. Graph C represents two individuals who probably knew each other as acquaintances for some time but never really had the opportunity or inclination to self-disclose. Once they did begin to escalate the relationship, however, there was a steep rise in self-disclosure. This graph might represent two coworkers who eventually start dating, or two students who have shared a class or two together before striking up a friendship.

Generally, a dramatic increase or decrease in self-disclosure reflects some significant change in the relationship. Even long-term relationships have significant increases and decreases in disclosure that signify changes. Before the birth of a first child, for example, both parents might disclose their fears and expectations about child rearing, and the information might have a profound effect on the relationship.

*Interpersonal relationships cannot achieve intimacy without self-disclosure.* Without true self-disclosure, we form only superficial relationships. You can confirm another person's self-concept, and have your self-concept confirmed, only if both you and your partner have revealed yourselves to each other.

Future chapters will discuss the essential other-oriented skills of perceiving others accurately, using and understanding verbal and nonverbal messages, and listening empathetically.

 *Building Your Skills*

## Self-Disclosure Patterns

Think about two of your current relationships and draw a graph like those in Figure 2.5 to show how the self-disclosure has progressed in each of them. How do the patterns compare? What do the differences or similarities reflect about the two relationships? What caused the peaks and valleys? Were there times when one person tried to increase the rate of self-disclosure, and the other person rejected that attempt? What happened?

## Becoming Other-Oriented

### A World View

It is sometimes a challenge to avoid becoming self absorbed—focusing exclusively on yourself and not others. There is evidence that the challenge of becoming other-oriented rather than self-absorbed is not new. Most world religions emphasize a common spiritual theme, known in Christianity as the Golden Rule: Do unto others as you would have others do unto you. This "rule" is the basis for most ethical codes throughout the world and has been the foundation of ideas about how we should treat others for centuries. The following excerpts from various religious traditions emphasize the importance of becoming other-oriented.

| | |
|---|---|
| **Hinduism** | This is the sum of duty: Do nothing to others that would cause pain if done to you. |
| **Buddhism** | One should seek for others the happiness one desires for one's self. |
| **Taoism** | Regard your neighbor's gain as your own gain, and your neighbor's loss as your loss. |
| **Confucianism** | Is there one principle that ought to be acted on throughout one's whole life? Surely it is the principle of loving-kindness: do not unto others what you would not have them do unto you. |
| **Zoroastrianism** | The nature alone is good that refrains from doing unto another whatsoever is not good for itself. |
| **Judaism** | What is hateful to you, do not do to others. That is the entire law: all the rest is but commentary. |
| **Islam** | No one of you is a believer until he desires for his brother that which he desires for himself. |
| **Christianity** | Do unto others what you would have others do unto you. |

*Source:* Adapted from Wayne Ham, *Man's Living Religions* (Independence, MO: Herald Publishing House, 1966), 39–40.

---

### Recap

## Characteristics of Appropriate Self-Disclosure

| | |
|---|---|
| **Self-disclosure usually moves in small increments.** | Don't be in a hurry to tell someone too much about yourself too quickly. |
| **Self-disclosure moves from less personal to more personal information.** | Revealing personal feelings and intimate information without establishing a foundation of sharing less personal information is likely to make your partner feel uncomfortable. |
| **Self-disclosure is reciprocal.** | Appropriate self-disclosure involves dyadic interaction; it should not be a one-way monologue. |
| **Self-disclosure involves risk.** | "But if I tell you who I am, you may not like who I am, and that is all that I have." You run the risk of being rejected by others when you disclose to them. |
| **Self-disclosure involves trust.** | Disclosing to others means you trust them not to reveal your secrets to others or use the personal information against you. When others self-disclose, you have an ethical responsibility to keep confidential what you've learned. |
| **Self-disclosure has the potential to enhance the quality of our interpersonal relationships.** | Revealing information about yourself makes it possible for relationships to become more intimate. |

# Summary

We all seek answers to three questions: "Who am I?" "Why am I here?" "Who are all these others?" William James answered the first question by dividing the self into three parts. The material self includes our bodies and those tangible possessions that give us identity. The social self is the part that engages in interaction with others. The spiritual self consists of thoughts and assumptions about values and moral standards and beliefs about forces that influence our lives. Other theorists conclude that our self-concept develops through interaction with other people. The groups we belong to also give us identity. Our roles as sisters, brothers, students, and parents are important in how we view who we are; the roles we assume provide labels for who we are. We also make our own observations about ourselves apart from others, and about groups or roles we assume. Our gender plays a key part in affecting our view of who we are in relationship to others.

Given the importance of developing a positive sense of self-esteem, we identified strategies that can enhance your self-worth. Those strategies include engaging in self-talk, using positive visualization, avoiding comparisons with others, reframing, developing honest relationships, letting go of the past, and seeking support when needed.

Our sense of self relates to self-disclosure. Self-disclosure occurs when we purposefully provide information to others that they would not learn if we did not tell them. The social penetration model of self-disclosure describes how the depth and breadth of our disclosure can affect our relationships. The Johari Window model of self-disclosure provides an explanation of the relationship between our self-awareness and self-disclosure. The four quadrants in the Johari Window (Open, Hidden, Unknown, and Blind) reflect how much information we and others know about ourselves. As we develop relationships, the sizes of these windows change relative to one another. Appropriate self-disclosure (1) moves in small increments, (2) moves from less to more personal information, (3) is reciprocal, (4) involves risk, and (5) involves trust.

Finally, self-disclosure has the potential to enhance the quality of our interpersonal relationships. The amount of information we disclose decreases as a relationship becomes more intimate. We first are likely to share low-risk information; as the relationship matures, we typically disclose more personal, high-risk information.

# For Discussion and Review

## Focus on Critical Thinking

1. Joel, who is 30 years old, married, and the father of two children, suffers from feelings of low self-esteem. Although he has many friends and a wife who loves him, he feels that others perform much better than he does at work. What strategies would help Joel enhance his self-esteem?

2. Make a list of all the groups, clubs, and organizations to which you belong. Rank them from most important to least important. What does your ranking tell you about these groups in reference to your self-concept?

3. Provide an original example of how visualization might help you enhance your self-esteem. Describe the positive scene.

4. Provide an example from your own experiences that illustrates the Johari Window model of self-disclosure.

## Focus on Ethics

5. Discuss the ethical implications of using untrue flattery to enhance a friend's self-esteem.

6. Many self-help books on the market claim to enrich your social life by providing sure-fire techniques for enhancing self-esteem. Do you think these claims are ethical? Why or why not?

7. Aelish has long planned to attend a top-notch Ivy League college. Her grades, however, are only in the C and B range. Her SAT scores are average. Should she try to reframe this factual information or deal with her problem in another way?

8. Carmelita would like to become better friends with Hector. She decides to disclose some personal information to Hector, hoping that this self-disclosure will increase feelings of intimacy between them. Is it ethical to self-disclose to others as a strategy to enhance intimacy in a relationship?

# For Your Journal

1. Record goals for your self-talk and note your self-talk messages day by day. You might want to organize your journal around specific topics such as academic achievement, personal appearance, or social skills. Under academic achievement you might write, "I will monitor my self-talk messages to keep myself on track while I study for two hours each day." Your personal appearance self-talk goal may be to tell yourself something positive about your appearance, instead of thinking only about what you don't like.

2. In your journal, write the ten responses you wrote for Building Your Skills: Who Are You? at the beginning of this chapter. At the end of the course, again write ten responses to the "Who are you?" question, without looking at your earlier responses. What are the differences in your responses? How do you explain them?

3. If someone were to walk into one of your favorite rooms in your home, dorm, or apartment, what conclusions might he or she draw about your social style? Are you neat and well organized? Or does your room have the characteristics of an expressive personality? Write a brief description of who you are from a social-style perspective, based on the clues in your room.

# Learning with Others

1. Rank the following list of values from 1 to 12. In a group with other students, compare your answers. Discuss how your personal ranking of these values influences your interaction with others.

| | |
|---|---|
| _____ Honesty | _____ Justice |
| _____ Salvation | _____ Wealth |
| _____ Comfort | _____ Beauty |
| _____ Good health | _____ Equality |
| _____ Human rights | _____ Freedom |
| _____ Peace | _____ Mercy |

2. Make a shield of your life (like a coat of arms): Draw a large outline of a shield that fills up an entire sheet of paper. Divide your shield into four equal sections. In the upper right-hand section of your shield, draw or symbolize something for which you have skill or talent. In the upper left-hand section, draw or symbolize something you are trying to improve or a new skill you are learning. In the lower right-hand section, draw or symbolize your most prized material possession. Finally, in the lower left-hand section, write three words that you hope someone would use to describe you.

    Share your shield with other students. Tell your classmates why you drew what you did. Discuss how your shield reflects your attitudes, beliefs, and values.

3. Go through your personal music library of tapes or CDs and identify a selection that best symbolizes you. Your selection may be based on either the lyrics or the music. Bring your selection to class and play it for your classmates. (Your instructor will bring a tape or CD player.) Tell why this music symbolizes you. Discuss with classmates how your choice of music provides a glimpse of your culture and a vehicle for self-expression.

## weblinks

http://yesterday.indstate.edu/gdc_commself/gdc_commself.htm This self-assessment instrument includes a quiz that assesses your understanding of fundamental concepts about interpersonal communication.

http://www.social-anxiety.com Go to this site to learn more about shyness and social phobias; case studies are also provided.

http://www.shyness.com The *Encyclopedia of Mental Health* discusses symptoms, causes, consequences, and treatment of shyness.

http://www.queendom.com Assess your personality and other communication-related variables.

http://www.abacon.com/commstudies/interpersonal/dindisclosure.html Want to learn more about the Johari Window? This site about self-disclosure helps explain the Johari Window and gives you an opportunity to complete an interactive activity and take a short quiz to test your understanding of the concept.

http://www.winnning-solutions.com/Trainings/interpersonal.html Check out this site to assess your personality type. Explore relationships between your personality and interpersonal communication.

http://users.rcn.com/zang.interport/personality.html Take this online personality test to find out more about yourself and how you can better understand those around you.

http://rateyourself.com To better understand yourself, go to this site to take several surveys and tests to assess your personal strengths and weaknesses.

# 3

# Interpersonal Communication and Perception

## OBJECTIVES

1. Define perception and interpersonal perception.

2. Identify and explain the three stages of interpersonal perception.

3. Describe the relationship between interpersonal communication and interpersonal perception.

4. Explain how we form impressions of others, describe others, and interpret others' behavior.

5. Identify the eight factors that distort the accuracy of our interpersonal perceptions.

6. Offer five suggestions for improving interpersonal perceptions.

## OUTLINE

Understanding Interpersonal Perception

Perception and Interpersonal Communication

Perceiving Others

Identifying Barriers to Accurate Perception

Improving Your Perception Skills

*What you see and what you hear depends a good deal on where you are standing. It also depends on what sort of person you are.*

C. S. Lewis

---

*L*ook at the Norman Rockwell painting on the next page. What is happening, and what has happened? What is the relationship among the individuals in the painting? You probably have deduced that the boy was running away from home, the policeman found him, and then he took the boy into the local coffee shop for ice cream or some other treat. Perhaps you think that the man behind the counter is wistfully recalling his own days of running away as a child. What are your feelings about the policeman? Do you see him as a friendly and caring person who has a good understanding of kids?

In Chapter 1 we defined human communication as the process of making sense of the world and sharing that sense with others by creating meaning through the use of verbal and nonverbal messages. In this chapter we discuss the first half of that definition—the process of making sense of our world. How we make sense out of what we experience is the starting point for what we share with others. As human beings, we interpret and attribute meaning to what we observe or experience, particularly if what we are observing is other people. We tend to make inferences about their motives, personalities, and other traits based on their physical qualities and behaviors. Those who are skilled at making observations and interpretations have a head start in developing effective interpersonal relationships.

Most of the time, we are unaware of our own perception process. For example, you may not have realized that you were drawing conclusions about the painting until you read the questions above. But we may become aware of the process when differences in perception cause a conflict or disagreement. In truth, no two individuals ever perceive the same thing in exactly the same way. Fortunately, communication tools such as conversation allow us to create shared meanings despite the differences in our perceptions.

Your perceptions are influenced by who you are, including the accumulation of your experiences. If you have had several bad experiences with the police, for example, you may not view the policeman in the painting as friendly. Or if you know something about the life and work of Norman Rockwell, who painted the picture, you may view all his works as representations of an idyllic American culture and society that existed only in his mind. As we noted in Chapter 2, everything people perceive is filtered through their self-concept.[1] It is important to recognize and examine factors that might

$\mathcal{S}$aturday *Evening Post* cover, September 20, 1958. Old Corner House Collection, Stockbridge, Massachusetts.

distort the accuracy of your interpretations. You can also reduce inaccuracies by applying an other-oriented approach as you interact with people. By focusing on how others perceive the world, you can reduce the amount of distortion that your own self-concepts impose on your perceptions.

Before we turn to the role that perception plays in interpersonal communication, let's first take a closer look at the interpersonal perception process itself.

## $\mathcal{U}$nderstanding Interpersonal Perception

**W**hat is perception? **Perception** is the process of experiencing your world and then making sense out of what you experience. You experience your world through your five senses. For example, a sound travels through the air and causes your eardrum to vibrate, which activates the nerves and sends a signal to the brain. A similar sequence of events takes place when you see, smell, feel, or taste something. The process of perception also includes organizing and interpreting information provided by the senses. You come out of a building and see wet pavement and puddles of water, hear thunder, smell a distinct odor caused by ions, and observe drops of water falling in front of you. You integrate all those bits of information and conclude that it is raining, and has been for a while.

Your perceptions of people, however, include analysis and interpretation that goes beyond simple interpretation of sensory information. **Interpersonal perception** is the process by which you decide what people are like and give meaning to their actions. It includes making judgments about personality and drawing inferences from what you observe.[2] When you meet someone new, you *select* certain information to attend to: You note whether the person is male or female, has an accent, smiles, and uses

**perception.** Experiencing your world and making sense out of what you experience.

**interpersonal perception.** Selecting, organizing, and interpreting your observations of other people.

a friendly tone of voice, as well as particular personal information (she is from Boone, Iowa). You then *organize* the information under some category that is recognizable to you, such as "a friendly Midwesterner." Then you *interpret* the organized perceptions: This person is trustworthy, honest, hardworking, and likable.

In our discussion we focus on this kind of interpersonal perception, which relates to understanding our observations of other people. We begin by examining the three stages of the interpersonal perception process that we have already described: selecting, organizing, and interpreting what we observe.

### Stage 1: Selecting

Sit for a minute after you read this passage and tune in to all the sensory input you are receiving: Consider the feel of your socks against your feet, the pressure of the floor on your heels, the pressure of the piece of furniture against your body as you sit, the buzzing sounds from various sources around you—"white noise" from a refrigerator, personal computer, fluorescent lights, water in pipes, voices, passing traffic, or your own heartbeat or churning stomach. What do you smell? What do you see? Without moving your eyes, turn your awareness to the images you see in the corner of your vision. What colors do you see? What shapes? What taste is in your mouth? How do the pages of this book feel against your fingertips? Now stop reading and consider all these sensations. Try to focus on all of them at the same time. You can't.

The number of sensations people can attend to at any given time is limited. Therefore, you are selective about which sensations make it through to the level of awareness. Perhaps you close your eyes or sit in the dark as you listen to music. This allows you to select more auditory sensations because you are eliminating visual ones.

During the selection stage, you attempt to simplify the stimuli that flood in through your senses, using various techniques. You use perceptual filters to screen out constant sensations that you have learned are unimportant, such as the sensations of your clothes against your skin and the surrounding white noise and smells. However, you do attend to the sensation of the elastic in your underwear if it pulls too tight, because a threshold of arousal is crossed, forcing the brain to attend to that stimulus. Each of your senses has such a threshold.

Directing your attention to specific stimuli and consequently ignoring others is called **selective perception.** Your eye and your brain do not work like a camera, which records everything in the picture. When you develop film, you capture what was in the viewfinder. Your brain doesn't necessarily process *everything* you see through your "viewfinder." Similarly, your ear is not a microphone that consciously picks up every sound. Although the sounds are there, your brain selects sounds that are significant or important to you in some way.

In a court of law, eyewitness testimony often determines whether someone is innocent or guilty of a crime. Recent research suggests, however, that a witness's powers of observation are not flawless. In fact, scientists have discovered several perceptual errors in eyewitness testimony. Many innocent people have been convicted because of what a witness thought he or she saw or heard.[3] As this evidence documents, the eye is not a camera; the ear is not a microphone.

### Stage 2: Organizing

Look at the four items in Figure 3.1 on page 70. What does each of them mean to you? If you are like most people, you will perceive item A as a rabbit, item B as a telephone number, item C as the word *interpersonal,* and item D as a circle. Strictly speaking, none of those perceptions is correct. We'll discuss why after we explore the second stage of perception: organizing.

**selective perception.** Directing your attention to specific stimuli and consequently ignoring other stimuli.

A.

B. **5 5 5  4 4 3 3**

C. **N T R P R S N L**

D.

FIGURE *3.1*

What Do You See?

After we select certain stimuli, we organize them into convenient, understandable, and efficient patterns that let us make sense of what we have observed. Organizing makes it easier for us to process complex information because it lets us impose the familiar onto the unfamiliar, and because we can easily store and recall simple patterns. For example, when you looked at item A in Figure 3.1, you saw the pattern of dots as a rabbit because "rabbit" is a concept you know and to which you attach various meanings. The set of dots would not have meaning for you in and of itself, nor would it be meaningful for you to attend to each particular dot or to the dots' relationships to one another. It would be possible to create a mathematical model of the dots indicating their placement on an X–Y grid, but such a model would be extremely complex and difficult to observe and remember. It's much easier to organize the dots in a way that refers to something stored in your memory: a rabbit. For similar reasons, people organize patterns of stars in the sky into the various constellations and give them names that reflect their shapes, like the bear, the crab, and the Big and Little Dippers. People also search for and apply patterns to their perceptions of other people. You might have a friend who jogs and works out at a gym. You put these together and label the friend "athletic." That label represents a pattern of qualities you use in relating to your friend, a pattern that will be discussed later in the chapter.

The way people organize information depends partly on the way they punctuate it. **Punctuation** is the process of making sense out of stimuli by grouping, dividing, organizing, separating, and categorizing information when communicating with others.[4] Just as punctuation marks on this page tell you when a sentence ends, punctuation in the perception process makes it possible for you to see patterns in information. To many Americans, Item B in Figure 3.1 looks like a telephone number because it has three numbers followed by four numbers. You might also remember that 555 is the prefix you use for calling Directory Assistance. However, the digits could just as easily represent two totally independent numbers: five hundred fifty-five followed by the number four thousand, four hundred thirty-three. How we interpret the numbers depends on how we punctuate or separate them. When we record information, we use commas, periods, dashes, and colons to signal meanings and interpretations. In our minds we sometimes impose punctuation marks where we believe they should be. For example, perhaps you mentally put a dash between 555 and 4433, even though no dash appears there.

When it comes to punctuating relational events and behaviors, people develop their own separate sets of standards. You will sometimes experience difficulties and disagreements because of differences in how you and your partner choose to punctuate a conversational exchange or a shared sequence of events.[5] One classic example of relational problems resulting from differences in punctuation involves a husband who withdraws and a wife who nags.[6] The husband punctuates their interactions in such a way that he sees his withdrawing as a reaction to her nagging. The wife, in contrast, sees herself as nagging her husband because he keeps withdrawing. The husband and wife punctuate their perceptions differently because they each perceive different starting points for their interactions. Resolving such conflicts involves having the parties describe how they have punctuated the event and agree on a common punctuation.

In addition to punctuating, you also **superimpose,** or place a familiar structure on information you select. Looking again at Figure 3.1, you can see that people's inclination to superimpose structure and consistency on what they observe also leads them to create a familiar word from the meaningless assemblage of letters in item C,

**punctuation.** Making sense out of stimuli by grouping, dividing, organizing, separating, and categorizing information.

**superimpose.** To place a familiar structure on information you select.

and to label the figure in item D a circle, even though circles are continuous lines without gaps. This process of filling in missing information is called **closure.** We apply the same principles in our interactions with people. When we have an incomplete picture of another human being, we impose a pattern or structure, classify the person on the basis of the information we do have, and fill in gaps. For example, when meeting someone for the first time who looks and acts like someone you already know, you may make assumptions about your new acquaintance based upon the characteristics of the person you already know well. You superimpose attributes of the person whom you already know upon the stranger. Many of us are uncomfortable with uncertainty; providing closure and superimposing our assumptions upon a new acquaintance help us make better sense out of what is new and unfamiliar.

## Stage 3: Interpreting

You see your best friend across a crowded room at a party. Your friend waves to you, and you say to yourself, "He wants to talk with me." Or you nervously wait as your British literature teacher hands back the results of the last exam. When the professor calls your name, she frowns ever so slightly; your heart sinks. You think, "I must have bombed on the test." Or, while you were out, your administrative assistant left you a note that your sister called. You're worried. You reflect, "My tightwad sister never uses her daytime cell phone minutes to call during the day. There must be something wrong." In each of these situations, you're trying to make sense out of the information you hear or see. You're attempting to interpret the meaning of the verbal and nonverbal cues you experience.

Once you have selected and organized stimuli, you next typically interpret the stimuli. We attach meaning to what we observe, hear, taste, smell, and touch. Our interpretations may not be accurate, but we make them nonetheless. We learn through socialization (what we learn from others) and our own recurring experiences to attribute meaning to particular stimuli. In some cases the meanings are fairly standard, as with language, for example. You read the word *computer,* and you have some sense of what that word means. But other instances are much more personal.

If you shake someone's hand and it feels like a wet, dead fish, what is your reaction and interpretation? If you notice someone you don't know winking at you in one of your classes, what do you think? If a toddler is crying in a room full of people and a woman comes over and picks the child up, what do you assume about the woman? In each instance you probably impose meaning on what you observe to complete the perceptual process. We'll discuss how the process of selecting, organizing, and interpreting affects our perceptions of others and influences our interpersonal relationships.

**closure.** The filling in of missing information.

### Recap

### The Interpersonal Perception Process

| Term | Explanation | Examples |
|---|---|---|
| **Selecting** | The first stage in the perceptual process, in which we select certain sensations to focus awareness on | Sitting in your apartment where you hear lots of traffic sounds and car horns, but attending to a particular rhythmic car honking that seems to be right outside your door. |
| **Organizing** | The second stage in the perceptual process, in which we assemble stimuli into convenient and efficient patterns | Putting together the car honking with your anticipation of a friend's arrival to pick you up in her car to drive to a movie that starts in five minutes. |
| **Interpreting** | The final stage in perception, in which we assign meaning to what we have observed | Deciding the car honking must be your friend signaling you to come out to the car quickly because she's running late. |

# Perception and Interpersonal Communication

Interpersonal perception is a two-way street. Our perceptions of others affect the ways in which we communicate with them, and their perceptions of us affect the way they communicate with us. We continually modify the topics, the language, and the manner in which we communicate according to the perceptions we have of others.

The way that others talk and behave also tells us a great deal about how they perceive us. Maybe you can remember the first time someone younger than you called you Mr., Ms., Mrs., or Miss (if it hasn't happened yet, it will). It probably surprised you to realize that someone perceived you as "old," or as someone with authority. We analyze others' reactions to us for clues about their perceptions of who we are. For example, suppose your new college friends go out to play basketball, your favorite sport, but do not invite you. When you later ask them why, they say they always thought of you as the unathletic, studious type. Sometimes others' perceptions of us are surprising. If we never ask, we may never discover that they are inaccurate. The degree to which others have a conception of us that differs from our own is often a measure of the quality of the relationship. The stronger the interpersonal relationship, the closer our self-perceptions are to the perceptions others have of us.[7]

How much we notice about another person's communication behavior relates to our level of interest and need. Perception can be either a passive or an active process. **Passive perception** occurs simply because our senses are in operation. We see, hear, smell, taste, and feel things around us without any conscious attempt to do so.

**Active perception** is the process of seeking out specific information by intentionally observing and questioning; we make a conscious effort to figure out what we are experiencing. We actively perceive information when we are uncertain about what we are seeing or hearing. We've all heard noises that startle us and make us wonder, "What was that?" We then try to recall the sound and identify it, or we might investigate—seek out additional information.

If you can gain information and reduce your uncertainty about others, then you can predict their reactions and behaviors, adapt your behaviors and strategies, and therefore maximize the likelihood of fulfilling your social needs.[8] Although this might sound calculating, it really isn't. If you enjoy outdoor activities such as camping and hiking, one of your goals in establishing social relationships is probably to find others who share your interest. So observing, questioning, and processing information to determine a potential friend's interests can help you assess whether the relationship will meet your goals. In Chapter 5 we discuss ways to improve your ability to gain information through more effective listening.

**passive perception.** Perception that occurs because your senses are in operation.

**active perception.** Perception that occurs because you seek out specific information through intentional observation and questioning.

# Perceiving Others

As we collect information about others, we organize and interpret that information in various ways. Interpersonal perception involves three processes: forming impressions of others; applying implicit personality theories and mental constructs, which we use to organize information about people; and finally, developing attribution theories, which help us explain why people behave the way they do.

## How We Form Impressions of Others

**Impressions** are collections of perceptions about others that we maintain and use to interpret their behaviors. Impressions tend to be very general: "She seemed nice," "He was very friendly," or "What a nerd!" According to **impression formation theory,** we form these impressions through perceptions of physical qualities and behavior, information people disclose about themselves, and information that third parties tell us. We tend to form these impressions readily and part with them reluctantly. When we first meet someone, we form a first impression without having much information, and we often hold on to this impression throughout the relationship.

In one famous study conducted by Solomon Asch, individuals were asked to evaluate two people based on two lists of adjectives.[9] The list for the first person had the following adjectives: *intelligent, industrious, impulsive, critical, stubborn,* and *envious.* The list for the other person had the same adjectives, but in reverse order. Although the content was identical, respondents gave the first person a more positive evaluation than the second. One explanation for this is that the first words in each list created a first impression that respondents used to interpret the remaining adjectives. In a similar manner, the first impressions we form about someone often affect our interpretation of subsequent perceptions of that person.

This effect of attending to the first pieces of information that we observe is called the **primacy effect.** We also tend to put a lot of stock in the last thing we observed, which is called the **recency effect.**[10] For example, if you have thought for years that your friend is honest, but today you discover that she lied to you about something important, that lie will have a greater impact on your impression of her than the honest behavior she has displayed for years.

We also attempt to manage the impressions others form of us. We make guesses about how other people will interpret our own physical displays and behaviors; as a result, we attempt to manipulate those displays and behaviors to our advantage. Think about the first day of classes this semester. Did you think about what clothes you were going to wear to classes? Did you worry about how your hair looked, or your breath smelled? Most of us choose clothes that we think will create a positive statement and reflect who we are. In this way we attempt to manage the impressions others form of us. Our ability to manage such impressions effectively depends on our ability to *decenter* socially (as discussed in the next chapter) by looking at ourselves from other people's perspectives. The more accurately you can determine how others will react to people's looks and behaviors, the more potential you have for adapting your own looks and behaviors.

## How We Describe Others

Do you like to "people watch"? If you have some time on your hands while waiting for a friend, you may just start looking at people and making guesses about what these strangers may do for a living, or whether they are friendly or grumpy, peaceful or petulant, kind or mean. You make assumptions about their personalities. Even when we know people well, we don't know everything about them. Most of us have developed an **implicit personality theory,** a pattern of associated qualities that we attribute to people, which allows us to understand them—whether we've met them 10 minutes ago or 10 years ago. We make guesses about who they are, based on the information we already have about them. Implicit personality theory provides a way of organizing the vast array of information we have about people's personalities.[11] Implicit personality theories are essentially stereotypes that we apply to people in general. We accomplish perceptual closure through the use of implicit personality theory; that is, we are

**impression.** A collection of perceptions about others that you maintain and use to interpret their behaviors.

**impression formation theory.** Theory that explains how you develop perceptions about people and how you maintain and use those perceptions to interpret their behaviors.

**primacy effect.** Placing heavy emphasis on the first pieces of information that you observe about another, to form an impression.

**recency effect.** Placing heavy emphasis on the most recent information that you observe about another, to form or modify an impression.

**implicit personality theory.** Your unique set of beliefs and hypotheses about what people are like.

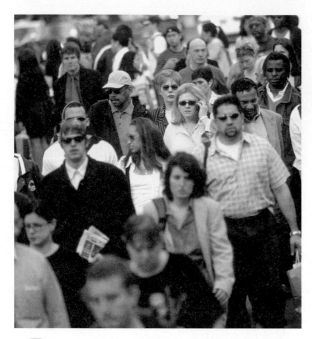

*E*ffective people watching can give us the information we need to understand others.

able to fill in the blanks about a person's personality without actually having to observe additional qualities. Once you have determined that someone is a "warm" person, you automatically associate other related terms. Your implicit personality theory may be similar to that held by others in your culture, but each person forms his or her own individual theory. There is more consistency between the personality frameworks you would use to judge two strangers than there is between the personality framework you use and the one another person uses to describe the same stranger.

Implicit personality theories allow us to manage a lot of information effectively, but they also can lead us to incorrect conclusions about other people. How accurately does "happy" actually describe a "warm" person? There are probably unhappy warm people. In assuming a connection between these two concepts, you might have reached an erroneous conclusion about the other person. When you assume the warm person is happy, you might not perceive the person's need for support and nurturing. As a result, your responses will be inappropriate and lead to ineffective interpersonal communication.

One feature common to most of our implicit personality theories is the tendency to put people into one of two categories: people we like and people we don't like. Categorizing people as those we "like" often creates a **halo effect,** in which we attribute a variety of positive qualities to them without personally confirming the existence of these qualities. If you like me, you will put a halo around your impression of me and then apply those qualities from your implicit personality theory that apply to people you like, such as being considerate of other people, warm, caring, and fun to be with and having a great sense of humor. However, if you don't like me, you might think of me more as a devil, attributing a variety of negative qualities from your implicit personality theory. This is called the **horn effect.** Research suggests that during periods of conflict in our relationships, we are more likely to attribute negative behaviors to our feuding partner than we are to ourselves.[12]

In support of the premise underlying the horn effect, researchers Dominic Infante and Andrew Rancer observed that some people have a tendency to see the worst in others, which causes them to lash out and be verbally aggressive.[13] There is also evidence that some people interpret any negative feedback they receive as a personal attack, no matter how carefully the feedback is worded.[14] For many people, there is no such thing as "constructive criticism." Like a sunburned sunbather, such people perceive even a mild suggestion presented with a light touch as a stinging rebuke.

Although implicit personality theory describes how we organize and interpret our perceptions of people's personalities in general, we develop categories for people, called *constructs,* that help us explain our perceptions of a specific person. According to psychologist George Kelly, a **construct** is a bipolar quality (that is, a quality with two opposite categories) that we use to classify people.[15] We may pronounce someone as good or bad, athletic or nonathletic, warm or cold, funny or humorless, selfish or generous, and so on.

### How We Interpret the Behavior of Others

"I know why Alice didn't come to our meeting. She just doesn't like me," says Cathy. "She also just wants people to think she's too busy to be bothered with our little

**halo effect.** Attributing a variety of positive qualities to those you like.

**horn effect.** Attributing a variety of negative qualities to those you dislike.

**construct.** A bipolar quality that you associate with people as you conceptualize them.

**attribution theory.** Theory that explains how you generate explanations for people's behaviors.

**causal attribution theory.** Theory of attribution that is based on determining whether a person's actions are caused by circumstance, a stimulus, or the person.

group." Cathy seems not only to have formed a negative impression of Alice, but also to harbor a hunch as to why Alice didn't come to the meeting. Cathy is attributing meaning to Alice's behavior. Even though Alice could have just forgotten about the meeting, Cathy thinks Alice's absence is caused by feelings of superiority and contempt. Cathy's assumptions about Alice can be explained by attribution theory.

**Attribution theory** explains how we ascribe specific motives and causes to the behaviors of others. It helps us interpret what people do. For example, suppose the student sitting next to you in class gets up in the middle of the lecture and walks out. Why did the student leave? Did the student become angry at something the instructor said? No, the lecturer was simply describing types of cloud formations. Was the student sick? You remember noticing that the student looked a little flushed and occasionally winced. Maybe the student has an upset stomach. Or maybe the student is just a bit of a rebel and often does strange things like leaving in the middle of a class.

Social psychologist Fritz Heider says that we are "naive psychologists,"[16] because we all seek to explain people's motives for their actions. We are naive because we do not create these explanations in a systematic or scientific manner, but rather by applying common sense to our observations. Developing the most credible explanation for the behavior of others is the goal of the attribution process.

**Causal attribution theory** identifies three potential causes for any person's action: circumstance, a stimulus, or the person herself or himself.[17] Attributing behavior to *circumstance* means that you believe a person acts in a certain way because the situation leaves no choice. This way of thinking places responsibility for the action outside of the person. You would be attributing to circumstance if you believed the student quickly left the classroom because of an upset stomach. Concluding that the student left because the instructor said something inappropriate would be attributing the student's action to the *stimulus* (the instructor). But if you knew the instructor hadn't said anything out of line, and that the student was perfectly healthy, you would place the responsibility for the action on the student. Attributing to the *person* means that you believe there is some quality about the person that caused the observed behavior.

*To* help us understand the people we know, we develop a set of constructs for each person. A highly perceptive person may see a whole array of constructs for this woman: whimsical, warm, dependable, friendly, generous, and kind. A person with a less developed set of constructs may see only her whimsical side.

## *Understanding Diversity*

### The Power of Perspective

*A*s noted in our discussion of standpoint theory, where you stand makes a difference in what you see and how you interpret human behavior. Following the September 11, 2001, terrorist attacks on the United States, discussions about the perceptions of the power and influence of different cultural groups and countries became more common.

Men and women, blacks and whites, Jews and Christians, Muslims and Hindus, Hispanics and Asians, gay and straight individuals, all experience life from their own cultural standpoint, which means they all have perceptions about their influence on others. To become more other-oriented is to become aware of your own perceived place in society and to be more sensitive to how that position of power or lack of power affects how you perceive others with a different standpoint.

To explore applications of standpoint theory in your life, consider the following questions:

1. How would you describe your standpoint in terms of power and influence in your school or at work, or in your family? Have you ever experienced rejection, alienation, or discrimination based on how others perceived you?

2. How would other people in your life (parents, siblings, children, coworkers, employer, or friends) describe your power and influence on them?

3. How does your standpoint influence your relationship with others? Identify a specific relationship with a teacher, coworker, or family member in which different standpoints influence the quality of the relationship in either positive or negative ways.

4. What can you do to become more aware of how your standpoint influences your interactions with others? How can your increased awareness enhance the quality of your interpersonal communication with others?

---

To explore how attributions to a person affect us, interpersonal communication researchers Anita Vangelisti and Stacy Young wanted to know whether intentionally hurtful words inflict more pain than unintentionally hurtful comments.[18] As you might suspect, if we think someone intends to hurt us, spiteful words have more sting and bite than if we believe someone does not intend to hurt our feelings. Our attributions are factors in our impressions.

**Standpoint theory** is yet another framework that seeks to explain how we interpret the behavior of others. The theory is relatively simple: We each see the world differently because we're each viewing it from a different position. Some people have positions of power, and others do not; the resources we have to help us make our way through life provide a lens through which we view the world and the people in it. The quotation by C. S. Lewis that opens this chapter points to the power of perspective: Where you stand makes a difference in what you see.

Standpoint theory explains why people with differing cultural backgrounds have different perceptions of others' behavior. In the early nineteenth century, German philosopher Georg Hegel noted this simple but powerful explanation of why people see and experience the world differently.[19] Hegel was especially interested in how one's standpoint was determined in part by one's power and influence. For example, people who have greater power and more influence in a particular culture may not be aware of their power and influence and how this power affects their perceptions of others. A person with less power (which in many cultures includes women and people of color) may be acutely aware of the power he or she doesn't have.

A number of factors affect the accuracy of our attributions: our ability to make effective and complete observations; the degree to which we are able to observe directly

**standpoint theory.** The theory that a person's social position, power, or cultural background, influences how the person perceives the behavior of others; where you stand makes a difference in what you see.

the cause and the effect; the completeness of our information; our position or stand-point; and our ability to rule out other causes. It is also helpful to know how unique a person's response is to the particular stimulus, to compare the person's response to how other people typically respond, and to know whether the person usually responds each time in the same way to the stimulus. Even with the most complete information, however, we can never completely understand another person's action because we cannot become the other person. Fortunately, we can improve our level of under-standing by becoming more sensitive to the assumptions or theories we use to make attributions.

## How We Organize and Interpret Interpersonal Perceptions

| Theory | Description | Examples |
|---|---|---|
| **Impression Formation Theory** | We form general impressions of others based on general physical qualities, behaviors, and disclosed information. | Categorizing people as nice, friendly, shy, or handsome |
| **Implicit Personality Theory** | We develop a set of relationships among personality characteristics. | "If she is intelligent, then she must be caring, too." |
| **Attribution Theory** | We develop reasons to explain the behaviors of others. | "I guess she didn't return my call because she doesn't like me." "He's just letting off steam because he had a bad week of exams." |
| **Causal Attribution Theory** | We ascribe a person's actions to circumstance, a stimulus, or the person himself or herself. | "He didn't go to class because his alarm didn't go off." "He didn't go to class because it was a makeup session." "He didn't go to class because he is bored by it." |
| **Standpoint Theory** | We interpret the behavior of others through the lens of our own social position, power, or cultural background. | "He won't join the fraternity because he doesn't understand how important that network can be to his professional career." |

# Identifying Barriers to Accurate Perception

Think about the most recent interaction you had with a stranger. Do you re-member the person's age, sex, race, or body size? Did the person have any dis-tinguishing features, such as a beard, tattoos, or a loud voice? The qualities you recall will most likely serve as the basis for attributions you make about that person's be-havior. But these attributions, based on your first impressions, might be wrong. Each person sees the world from his or her own unique perspective. That perspective is clouded by a number of distortions and barriers that contribute to inaccurate inter-personal perception. We'll examine these barriers next.

## Ignoring Information

*People sometimes don't focus on important information, because they give too much weight to information that is obvious and superficial.*[20] Why do we ignore important information that may be staring us in the face? It's because, as you learned in the discussion about at-tribution theory, we tend to explain the motives for a person's actions on the basis of the most obvious information rather than on in-depth information we might have. When meeting someone new, we perceive his or her physical qualities first: color of skin, body size and shape, age, sex, and other obvious characteristics. We overattribute to these qualities, because they are so vivid and available, and ignore other details. We have all been victims of these kinds of attributions, some of us more than others. Often we are unaware that others are making biased attributions, because they do not express them openly. But sometimes we can tell by the way others react to us and treat us.

One female student described a job interview in which the male interviewer talked at her for fifteen minutes and then abruptly dismissed her without asking a single question. One of her male friends with less distinguished academic qualifications and work experience spent forty minutes fielding questions from this same interviewer. Did the interviewer have a sex bias? Probably. Looking only at the female student's gender, he attributed qualities to her that he decided would make her unsuitable for the job. Instead of looking at the more specific information her résumé provided, he simply disregarded it. This tendency reflects our desire to simplify stimuli, but it can be dangerous and unfair.

### Overgeneralizing

*People treat small amounts of information as if they were highly representative.*[21] This tendency also leads people to draw inaccurate, prejudicial conclusions.[22] For example, a professor may talk to two students and then generalize the impression he or she develops of those two students to the entire student population. In a similar way, most people tend to assume that the small sampling of another person's behavior is a valid representation of who that person is. As you saw in Figure 3.1, you might create a rabbit even when you have only a few dots on which to base your perception.

### Oversimplifying

*People prefer simple explanations to complex ones.* When Imelda picks you up late to go to a movie, she says, "Sorry, I lost track of the time." The next day, Mary also picks you up late to go to a movie. She says, "Sorry. You wouldn't believe how busy I've been. I ran out of hot water when I was showering, and my hair dryer must be busted. It kept shutting off. Then I stopped to get something to eat, and it took forever to get my order. And then it turned out they had it all messed up and had to redo it." Whose explanation can you accept more easily, Imelda's or Mary's?

Usually people prefer simple explanations; they tend to be more believable and easier to use in making sense of another's actions. But in reality our behaviors are affected by a multitude of factors, as Mary's explanation indicates. Unfortunately, it takes a lot of effort to understand what makes another person do what he or she does—more effort than we are typically willing to give.

### Stereotyping

*Preconceived notions about what they expect to find may keep people from seeing what's before their eyes and ears.* We see what we want to see, hear what we want to hear. We stereotype others. To **stereotype** someone is to place someone in a rigid category and then interpret all the person's behavior from the framework of that category. The word *stereotype* was originally a printing term, referring to a metal plate that was cast from type set by a printer. The plate would print the same page of type over and over again. When we stereotype people, we place them into inflexible, all-compassing categories. We "print" the same judgments on anyone placed in a given category. We may even choose to ignore contradictory information that we receive directly from the other per-

**stereotype.** To attribute a set of qualities to a person because of the person's membership in some category.

son. Instead of adjusting our conception of that person, we adjust our perception. The halo and horn effects discussed earlier reflect this tendency. For example, if an instructor gets an excellent paper from a student who she has concluded is not particularly bright or motivated, she may tend to find errors and shortcomings that are not really there, or she may even accuse the student of plagiarism.

Stereotyping others is apparently widespread. It's not limited to one cultural group. In a study investigating whether people from a variety of cultural backgrounds make stereotypical judgments of others, researchers found that stereotyping is rampant in many cultures.[23] In this study, participants from Australia, Botswana, Canada, Kenya, Nigeria, South Africa, Zambia, Zimbabwe, and the United States all consistently formed stereotypes of others.

*S*tereotypes can help us make sense out of the wide range of stimuli we encounter every day. But we also need to be sure that we don't overuse stereotypes and fail to see people as individuals.

Categorizing individuals is not an inherently bad thing to do, but it is harmful to hang on to an inflexible image of another person in the face of contradictory information. For example, not all mothers are responsible or loving. But because American culture reveres motherhood, we may not easily process our perceptions of a mother who is abusive or negligent.

### Imposing Consistency

*People overestimate the consistency and constancy of others' behaviors.* When we organize our perceptions, we also tend to ignore fluctuation in people's behaviors and instead see them as consistent. We believe that if someone acted a certain way one day,

## *Understanding Diversity*

### Moving Beyond a First Impression

*B*ecause of the stereotypes that abound, many of us tend to form inaccurate impressions about people of other races. But as this brief story from an article about interracial friendships shows, we can use conver-

sation skills to check out our perceptions directly and move beyond inaccurate first impressions.

Janet, twenty-five, and Eleanor, thirty-three, politely tiptoed around their differences at first, pretending they were both "just people." But when they became roommates on the verge of closeness, they confronted each other: "Why do you

play only black music?" "How is your family going to react to me?" "Is it true that whites . . . ?" "Is it true that blacks . . . ?" They found that when they detached themselves from the stereotypes, they became friends despite their differences; in fact, they saluted their differences as part of their interest in each other.

*Source:* Bebe Moore Campbell, *Ms.*

## Building Your Skills

### Preconceived Explanations

Think about your own preconceptions about cause–effect relationships. For each of the following, think about what your first explanation of the cause would be.

- A person not calling back after a first date

- A waitress giving you lousy service

- Your car not being repaired after you paid a high service fee

- A teacher being late for class

- A child beating up other kids

- A student copying test answers from the student next to him

- A mother refusing to let her teenage son drive the car on Friday nights

Now go back and generate as many alternative explanations for each behavior as you can. How can you be sure which explanation is correct?

---

he or she will continue to act that way in the future. Perhaps you have embarrassed yourself in front of a new acquaintance by acting foolish and silly. At another encounter with this new acquaintance, you realize that the person is continuing to see your behavior as foolish, even though you don't intend it to be seen that way. The other person is imposing consistency on your inconsistent behavior.

In fact, everyone's behavior varies from day to day. Some days we are in a bad mood, and our behavior on those days does not represent what we are generally like. As intimacy develops in relationships, we interact with our partners in a variety of activities that provide a more complete picture of our true nature.

### Focusing on the Negative

*People give more weight to negative information than to positive information.*[24] Job interviewers often ask you to describe your strengths and weaknesses. If you describe five great strengths and one weakness, it is likely that the interviewer will attend more to the one weakness you mention than to the strengths. We seem to recognize this bias and compensate for it when we first meet someone by sharing only positive information about ourselves.

In another of the Solomon Asch experiments on impression formation, participants heard one of the following two lists of terms describing a person: (1) *intelligent, skillful, industrious, warm, determined, practical, cautious;* or (2) *intelligent, skillful, industrious, cold, determined, practical, cautious.*[25] The only difference in these two lists is the use of *warm* in the first list and *cold* in the second. Despite the presence of six other terms, those with the "cold" list had a much more negative impression of the person than those with the "warm" list. One piece of negative information can have a disproportionate effect on our impressions and negate the effect of several positive pieces of information.

### Making a Fundamental Attribution Error

*People are more likely to believe that others are to blame when things go wrong than to believe that the problem was beyond their control.* Your parents were looking forward to celebrating their twenty-fifth wedding anniversary. They planned a quiet family celebration at a restaurant. You set your personal digital assistant to remind you one week before the anniversary dinner to buy them a present to give to them at the dinner. You

## applying theory and research

### Politeness Theory

Social psychologists Penelope Brown and Stephen Levinson suggest that people from all cultures have a universal need to be treated with politeness.[26] Politeness theory predicts that we will have a positive perception of people who treat us politely and respectfully. Although people from different cultures have varying levels of need to be treated politely, what seems clear is that everyone needs to be valued and appreciated.

A concept related to politeness theory is the need to project a positive image or to have a positive face. Sociologist Erving Goffman suggests that saving face is important for most people.[27] As we discussed in Chapter 2, by "face" we mean more than just our physical face; we're talking about an overall projection of a positive image to other people. Because of our need to be treated politely, our perceptions of others are affected when people violate our expectations and do or say things that are impolite or cause us to lose face. It is polite to help others save face and protect their positive self-image. We behave in ways to help us present the best possible image of ourselves to others.

To have a positive face is to be approved of and liked by others. When people treat us with politeness, they help contribute to a positive face. Providing compliments, behaving respectfully, and showing concern for others are all ways of using positive politeness to help others project a positive face.

All would be well and good if we could always provide positive, confirming comments to others, but that simply is not realistic or possible. We engage in face-threatening acts when we communicate in a way that undermines someone's positive face. According to politeness theory, people can communicate in a variety of ways that are face-threatening. The following list is arranged from most to least face-threatening.

1. Bluntly communicate a negative message. ("Your office is a mess.")

2. Deliver the negative message but also communicate a positive face-saving message. ("Your office is a mess, but perhaps messy is the look you want.")

3. Deliver the negative message but offer a counter explanation to help the person save face. ("Your office is a mess, but that's understandable given how much work you do around here.")

4. Communicate the negative message but do so "off the record" or in such an indirect way that the other person saves face. ("I'm not supposed to tell you this, but even though your office is a mess, the boss is impressed with how well you seem to find everything.")

5. Don't communicate any message that would cause someone to lose face.

### APPLYING

#### the Research to Your Life

How is politeness theory of value to you? By being aware of people's need for politeness to help them save face, you can try to be more aware of how you communicate negative messages to others. You can help others maintain a positive face by consciously trying to be more indirect or to offer a counter explanation when you deliver a negative message.

Consider the following questions as you apply politeness theory to your own relationships:

1. If you have a face-threatening message for a friend or loved one, what would be a way of expressing yourself while also letting the other person save face?

2. How are your perceptions of others influenced by the manner in which they help you save face? Provide an example of when someone helped you save face and that effort had a positive effect on how you perceived the person.

3. Is being polite and trying to help someone save face merely a way to manipulate others so that they perceive you in a favorable way?

*Source:* P. Brown and S. Levinson, *Politeness: Some Universals in Language Usage* (Cambridge, England: Cambridge University Press, 1987).

hadn't anticipated, however, that you'd lose your Palm Pilot. When the phone rang and your mom asked, "Where are you?" it all came jarringly back to you: Today was their anniversary, and you'd forgotten it! Not only did you forget to buy them a present, you forgot to attend the dinner. Your parents were hurt. Your mother's quivering "How could you forget?" still sears your conscience. Your parents' hurt feelings evolved into anger. They think you just didn't care enough about them to remember such an important day. Rather than thinking that there might be an explanation for why you forgot their important day, they blame you for your thoughtlessness. Although they certainly have a right to be upset, their assuming that you don't care about them is an example of what researchers call a fundamental attribution error.

A **fundamental attribution error** occurs when a person believes that the cause of a problem is something personally controllable (such as forgetting an important date because you don't care about your parents) rather than something uncontrollable (losing your personal digital assistant and having no back-up system to remind you of the event).[28] As summarized by communication researcher Kory Floyd, fundamental attribution error "predicts that, all other things being equal, people are more likely to attribute others' behavior to internal, controllable causes than to external uncontrollable causes."[29] For example, fundamental attribution error would predict that you're more likely to assume that the person who cuts you off in traffic is a jerk rather than that he's trying to get out of the way of the truck that's tailgating him. If you assume another person made a conscious choice to hurt you instead of considering that there may be other reasons for the person's behavior that are beyond the person's control, you've made a fundamental attribution error.

### Exhibiting Self-Serving Bias

*People are more likely to save face by believing that they are not the cause of a problem; people assume that other people or events are more than likely the source of problems or events that may put them in an unfavorable light.* In one classic episode of *The Simpsons*, Bart Simpson created a popular catch phrase by saying, "I didn't do it" when he clearly was the cause of a calamity. Whether it was lighting Lisa's hair on fire, calling Moe's tavern asking for Al Coholic, or putting baby Maggie on the roof, Bart would simply say, "I didn't do it." We chuckle at Bart's antics and would never stoop to such juvenile pranks. Yet there is evidence that when we do cause a problem or make a mistake, we are more likely to blame someone else rather than ourselves. Bart's "I didn't do it" approach to life represents self-serving bias.

**Self-serving bias** is the tendency to perceive our own behavior as more positive than others' behavior. Sociologist Erving Goffman was one of the first to note this tendency when he wrote his classic book *The Preservation of Self in Everyday Life*.[30] We are likely, for example, to attribute our own personal success to our hard work and effort rather than any to external, uncontrollable causes. You get an A on your anthropology paper because, you think, "I'm smart." When you get an F on your history paper, it's because your neighbor's loud party kept you up all night and you couldn't study. Self-serving bias is the tendency to take credit for the good things that happen to you and to say "I didn't do it" or "It's not my fault" when bad things happen to you.[31] Research has consistently found that we try to make sense out of the world by first protecting our own sense of positive self-regard.[32] The self-serving bias in the way we attribute meaning to what others do and the events that occur in our lives is one of the obstacles to becoming other-oriented. Blaming others and blaming external causes rather than owning up to our own foibles can keep us from taking an honest look at ourselves. Of course, there are many times when, in fact, you "didn't do it." The challenge is in sorting out when you are at fault and when you're not. Self-serving bias makes it difficult to make that decision objectively. Simply being aware of the self-serving bias may help you become more objective and accurate in identifying the cause of calamities in your own life.

**fundamental attribution error.** Attributing another person's behavior to internal, controllable causes rather than to external, uncontrollable causes.

**self-serving bias.** The tendency to perceive our own behavior as more positive than others' behavior.

## Recap

**Barriers to Accurate Perception**

| | |
|---|---|
| **Ignoring information** | We don't focus on important information because we give too much weight to obvious and superficial information. |
| **Overgeneralizing** | We treat small amounts of information as if they were highly representative. |
| **Oversimplifying** | We prefer simple explanations to complex ones. |
| **Stereotyping** | We allow our pre-existing rigid expectations about others to influence our perceptions. |
| **Imposing consistency** | We overestimate the consistency and constancy of others' behavior. |
| **Focusing on the negative** | We give more weight to negative information than to positive information. |
| **Making a fundamental attribution error** | We are more likely to believe that others are to blame when things go wrong than to assume that the cause of the problem was beyond their control. |
| **Exhibiting self-serving bias** | We save face by believing that other people, not ourselves, are the cause of problems; when things go right, it's because of our own skills and abilities rather than help from others. |

# Improving Your Perception Skills

With so many barriers to perceiving and interpreting other people's behavior accurately, what can you do to improve your perceptual skills? Increasing your awareness of the factors that lead to inaccuracy will help initially, and you will find further suggestions in this section. Ultimately, your improvement will depend on your willingness to expand your experiences, to communicate about your perceptions with others, and to seek out and consider others' perceptions of you. Realize that you have had a lifetime to develop these barriers and that it will take time, commitment, and effort to overcome their effects.

And just by reading this chapter you've gained greater understanding of how the perception process affects your relationships with others. Use your knowledge of the perceptual process to sharpen your own perceptions and conclusions. Here are additional strategies to help you become a more accurate perceiver.

### Link Details with the Big Picture

Any skilled detective knows how to take a small piece of information or evidence and use it to reach a broader conclusion. Skilled perceivers keep the big picture in mind as they look for clues about a person. In this chapter we have encouraged you to become more sensitive to details when observing others. But be cautious of taking one scrap of evidence and spinning out inaccurate conclusions about a person. Just because someone may dress differently from you, or have a pronounced accent, don't rush to judgment about the person's competence based on such few snatches of information. Look and listen for other cues about your new acquaintance that can help you develop a more accurate understanding of who that person is. As we noted in this chapter, what we see first (primacy) or last (recency) may have the most powerful effect on our overall conclusion. Try not to use the early information to form a quick or rigid judgment that may be inaccurate. Look at all the details you've gathered.

### Become Aware of Others' Perceptions of You

The best athletes don't avoid hearing criticisms and observations from their coaches. Instead, they seek out as much feedback as they can about what they are doing right and wrong. Olympic training often involves the use of videotaped replays and computer analysis so that athletes can see themselves as others see them and use that perspective to improve their performance. It is difficult to be objective about our own behavior, so feedback from others can help us with our self-perceptions. The strongest relationships are those in which the partners are willing both to share their perceptions and to be receptive of the perceptions of the other.

### Increase Your Awareness

Your senses are constantly bombarding you with information, much of which you ignore. You can increase the amount of information you process from your senses by consciously attending to the input. When you interact with others, try to identify one new thing to focus on and observe each time. Watch gestures, eyes, the wrinkles around eyes, foot movements; listen to tone of voice. Each observation will provide information that potentially can improve the quality of your interactions. You may create additional problems, however, if you focus so narrowly on one element that you miss others or overestimate the meaning of irrelevant information. Try to notice as much detail as possible, but keep the entire picture in view.

### Become Other-Oriented

Effective interpersonal perception depends on the ability to understand where others are coming from, to get inside their heads, to see things from their perspectives.

Becoming other-oriented involves a two-step process: social decentering (consciously *thinking* about another's thoughts and feelings) and empathizing (*responding emotionally* to another's feelings).[33] What does your boss think and feel when you ar-

## *Becoming Other-Oriented*

### Ten Questions That Can Help You Become Other-Oriented

1. What factors or circumstances are affecting the person?

2. How can I determine whether there are factors I don't know about or don't fully understand?

3. What do I know about this person that explains his or her behaviors and feelings?

4. What is going through the other person's mind at this time?

5. What are the other person's feelings at this time?

6. What other explanations could there be for the person's actions?

7. What would I think if I were in the same situation?

8. How would I feel if I were in the same situation?

9. What would other people think if they were in that situation?

10. How would other people feel if they were in that situation?

LUANN reprinted by permission of Newspaper Enterprise Association, Inc.

rive late for work? What would your spouse think and feel if you brought a dog home as a surprise gift? Throughout this book we offer suggestions for becoming other-oriented, for reminding yourself that the world does not revolve around you. Being other-oriented enables you to increase your understanding of others and improve your ability to predict and adapt to what others do and say.

To improve your ability to socially decenter and to empathize, strive for two key goals: (1) Gather as much information as possible about the circumstances that are affecting the other person; and (2) gather as much information as possible about the other person. In the next chapter we expand on these ideas as we discuss in more detail how to adapt to others by decentering and empathizing. As we've emphasized before, being other-oriented is not a single skill, but a family of related communication skills (such as socially decentering, empathizing, listening, responding, interpreting verbal and nonverbal messages, appropriately adapting to others, and managing conflict).

**indirect perception checking.**
Seeking additional information to confirm or refute interpretations you are making through passive perception such as observing and listening.

**direct perception checking.**
Asking for confirmation from the observed person of an interpretation or a perception about him or her.

## Check Your Perceptions

You can check out the accuracy of your perceptions and attributions indirectly and directly. **Indirect perception checking** involves seeking additional information through passive perception, either to confirm or to refute your interpretations. If you suspect someone is angry at you but is not admitting it, for example, you could look for more cues in his or her tone of voice, eye contact, and body movements to confirm your suspicion. You could also listen more intently to the person's words and language.

**Direct perception checking** involves asking straight out whether your interpretations of a perception are correct. This often is not easy to do, for several reasons: You don't like to admit uncertainty or suspicions to others; you might not trust that they will respond honestly; if your interpretations are wrong, you might suffer embarrassment

or anger. But asking someone to confirm a perception shows that you are committed to understanding his or her behavior. If your friend's voice sounds weary and her posture is sagging, you may assume that she is depressed or upset. If you ask, "I get the feeling from your tone of voice and the way you're acting that you are kind of down

Do you think these people are using direct or indirect perception checking, or a combination of the two styles?

and depressed; what's wrong?" your friend can then either provide another interpretation: "I'm just tired; I had a busy week"; or expand on your interpretation: "Yeah, things haven't been going very well. . . ." Your observation might also trigger a revelation: "Really? I didn't realize I was acting that way. I guess I am a little down."

## Summary

Interpersonal perception is a fundamental element of interpersonal communication. Our communication and interpersonal relationships are affected by the ways we perceive those with whom we interact. Interpersonal perception involves more than just the arousal of the senses; it also involves selecting, organizing, and interpreting what we observe in order to decide what people are like and to give meaning to their actions.

Our perceptions of others affect how we communicate, and how others perceive us affects how they communicate with us. Interpersonal perception can be a passive or an active process. It is passive when only our senses are in operation; it is active when we feel a need for information and intentionally seek it. We are motivated to seek information in situations that have high amounts of uncertainty. Perception of information helps reduce uncertainty and provides us with more control of the situation.

Interpersonal perception affects and is affected by the development of impressions, our own implicit personality theories, and attributions. Our general impressions of individuals are often affected by primacy and recency effects; we pay particular attention to the first things we notice and the most recent things we notice about others. In our interactions with others, we all seem to operate as "naive psychologists," developing and applying our own implicit personality theories. These implicit personality theories represent the general way we believe people behave. We develop specific personal constructs that represent the qualities we associate with specific people we know. Finally, we try to explain the actions and behaviors of others through the process of attribution. According to attribution theorists, we seek to find out the intent and cause of a person's action; for example, we see a person's action as a response to a given circumstance, a particular stimulus, or the person's own personality. To make rational and accurate attributions, we must overcome perceptual barriers. There are a number of tendencies that distort the accuracy of our attributions, such as focusing on obvious or negative information.

The following suggestions can help you to improve your interpersonal perception: (1) link details with the big picture; (2) increase your awareness skills; (3) increase your awareness of others' perceptions of you; (4) become other-oriented; and (5) check your perceptions.

## For Discussion and Review

### Focus on Critical Thinking

1. Think about some of your recent interpersonal conflicts. How would you describe your perception of the problem in each conflict? How do you think the others would describe their perceptions of it? What role did perception play in contributing to or resolving the conflict?

2. What do you think contributes to the development of the tendency to perceive others inaccurately? How might the effects of those factors be minimized or eliminated?

### Focus on Ethics

3. Do you have a right in an intimate relationship to expect your partner to share his or her perceptions of you, whether those perceptions are positive or negative? Explain your reasoning.

4. If you are aware of how you are distorting your own perceptions and attributions, should you try to change them? Is it a moral obligation? Explain your reasoning.

# For Your Journal

1. As you interact with a friend, try to assess your awareness level of the cues that are being communicated. Ask your friend to confirm your interpretation of the cues you have observed. How effective and accurate were you at picking up information?

2. Consult the list of barriers to accurate perception and analyze yourself. Which barriers influence your perceptions the most? What problems do those distortions create in your interactions with others?

3. Choose two of the suggestions for improving your perceptions. Develop a plan for applying those suggestions in your next interaction with one of your friends. Try the suggestions; then write an evaluation of how well you applied them, how well they worked, and how you might modify your plan to apply the suggestions in the future.

# Learning with Others

1. Choose a magazine ad or illustration, a photograph, or a painting that shows a group of people, and bring it to class. In groups of four or five, pass around the pictures. For each picture, write down a few words to describe your perceptions of what you see. What are the people doing? What is their relationship to one another? What is each one like? How is each one feeling? Why are they doing what they are doing? After you have finished, share with one another what you wrote down. Try to determine why there were differences. What factors influenced your perceptions?

2. Pair up with someone in class whom you do not know and have not interacted with before. Without saying anything to each other, write down the words from the following list that you think apply to the other person. Now chat together for five minutes. In a separate section of your paper, write down any additional words that you believe apply to the person; you can also go back and put a line through any of the words in the first list that you now think are inaccurate. Share with your partner what words you put down before and during the conversation, and what words you changed. Have your partner share his or her perceptions of you. Discuss, as best you can, the reasons you chose each word.

| intelligent | athletic | artistic | studious |
| nice | funny | conceited | friendly |
| introvert | extrovert | hard worker | shy |
| talented | popular | inquisitive | moody |
| emotional | happy | brave | responsible |
| leader | follower | uncertain | confused |

http://www.selfgrowth.com/index.html This is a site devoted to personal growth, self-improvement, and self-help. You can also sign up to receive a free newsletter.

http://novaonline.nv.cc.va.us/eli/spd110td/interper/siteindex.html Learn more about the perception process at this site; explore how the way you make sense out of the world affects the way you communicate with others.

http://www.carroll.cc.md.us/library/coursepages/communication.htm Visit this site to discover a collection of Internet links that present brief articles about perception relating to families and parenting.

## CHAPTER 4

# Interpersonal Communication and Cultural Diversity: Adapting to Others

*Every tale can be told in a different way.*

Greek proverb

One student overheard before class exclaimed, "I've had it with all this cultural diversity stuff. It seems like every textbook in every class is obsessed with it. My history textbook talks about all these obscure people I've never heard of before. In English lit all we're reading is stuff by people from different cultures. I'm tired of all this politically correct nonsense. I mean, we're all Americans. We're not all going off and live in China. Why don't they just teach us what we need to know and cut all this diversity garbage?"

Perhaps you've encountered this kind of "diversity backlash" among some of your classmates—or maybe you hold this attitude yourself. It may seem unsettling that textbooks are changing and that educators are concerned with cultural diversity. But these changes are not motivated by an irrational desire to be politically correct. They are taking place because the United States is changing. As suggested by the statistics in Understanding Diversity: A Diversity Almanac, the United States is becoming increasingly culturally diverse. With this diversity comes a growing awareness that learning about cultural differences can affect every aspect of people's lives in positive ways. You may not plan to travel the world, but the world is traveling to you. A central goal of your study of interpersonal communication is to learn how to better relate to others. Some of the differences that contribute to diversity and that may interfere with developing relationships include differences in age, learning style, gender, religion, ethnicity, sexual orientation, social class, race, and culture.

In the first three chapters, we acknowledged the influence of diversity on interpersonal relationships. In this chapter we examine in more detail the impact that people's differences have on their lives and suggest some communication strategies for bridging those differences in interpersonal relationships. Specifically, we focus on the nature of cultural difference, identify barriers that result from those differences, and suggest strategies that can help you better understand, appreciate, and adapt to people who are different from you. Our premise for this discussion of diversity is that in order to live comfortably in the 21st century, people must learn ways to

A goal in our study of interpersonal communication is to learn how we can put aside differences in age, gender, race, or ability that might cause a barrier to effective communication.

89

# *Understanding Diversity*

## A Diversity Almanac

1. Two-thirds of the immigrants on this planet come to the United States.[1]

2. In the United States there are "minority majorities" (where minorities outnumber traditional European Americans) in Miami, Laredo, Gary, Detroit, Washington, DC, Oakland, Atlanta, San Antonio, Los Angeles, Chicago, Baltimore, Houston, New York, Memphis, San Francisco, Fresno, and San Jose.[2]

3. It is estimated that more than 40 million U.S. residents have a non-English first language, including 18 million people whose first language is Spanish.[3]

4. Almost one-third of U.S. residents under age 35 are members of minority groups, compared with one-fifth of those age 35 or older. According to U.S. Bureau of the Census population projections, by the year 2025 nearly half of all young adults in this country will come from minority groups.[4]

5. If the current trend continues, by the year 2050 the percentage of the U.S. population that is white will decrease to 53 percent, down from a current 79 percent. Asians will increase to 16 percent, up from 1.6 percent; Latinos will more than triple their numbers to over 25 percent, up from just over 7.5 percent; and African Americans will increase their proportion slightly from the current 12 percent.[5]

6. It is estimated that during the first ten years of the 21st century, Vermont's Asian population will grow by 80 percent, Arizona's will increase by 52 percent, and the state of Delaware's will grow by 56 percent.[6]

7. During the 1990s the U.S. foreign-born population increased four times faster than the native-born population.[7]

8. At the end of the 20th century, one in ten U.S. residents was born outside the country.[8]

9. One out of every eight U.S. residents speaks a language other than English at home, and one-third of children in urban U.S. public schools speak a first language other than English.[9]

10. To capture the United States's increasing complexity of racial diversity, the 2000 U.S. Census forms allowed respondents to mark one or more of fourteen categories of race. Because respondents could check more than one box, there were sixty-three racial possibilities. The five primary race categories are American Indian or Alaska Native, Asian, Black or African American, native Hawaiian or Other Pacific Islander, and White. The new multi-race categories include American Indian or Alaska Native and White; Asian and White; Black or African American and White; and American Indian or Alaska Native and Black or African American.[10]

11. During the past decade, the combined population of African Americans, Native Americans, Asians, Pacific Islanders, and Latinos grew 13 times faster than the non-Hispanic white population.[11]

12. According to 2001 U.S. Census figures, there are more than 35 million people of Hispanic origin in the United States—a 58 percent gain of 13 million people since 1990—making Latinos the largest cultural minority group in the United States.[12]

13. According to the most recent census, 56 million Americans, or 20 percent of the population, were either born outside of the United States or had at least one parent who was born outside of the United States.[13]

14. Over 25 percent of residents of California were born outside of the United States.[14]

appreciate and understand cultural differences instead of ignoring them, suffering because of them, or wishing that they would disappear.

Researchers Carley Dodd and John Baldwin argue that, because of the pervasive nature of culture, virtually every interaction we have with another person has intercultural overtones.[15] To interact with other people is to be touched by the influence of culture and cultural differences. Textbooks and courses are reflecting the change, not initiating it.

# The Nature of Culture

Exactly what is culture? **Culture** is a learned system of knowledge, behaviors, attitudes, beliefs, values, and norms that is shared by a group of people.[16] In the broadest sense, culture includes how people think, what they do, and how they use things to sustain their lives. Researcher Geert Hofstede describes culture as the "mental software" that touches every aspect of how we make sense out of the world and share that sense with others.[17] Cultural diversity results from the unique nature of each culture. The elements, values, and context of each culture distinguish it from all others.

Sometimes when we speak of culture, we may be referring to a co-culture. A **co-culture** is a distinct cultural group within a larger culture. For example, about 80 percent of the population of the United States are classified as White, European American, or Caucasian. Members of minority groups such as African Americans, Latinos, and Asians develop a co-culture, or what is sometimes called a *microculture.* Many communication researchers consider gender one of the most important co-cultures that significantly affect our communication with others. Gays and lesbians constitute another important co-culture in our society. The Amish, Mennonite, Mormon, and Jewish religious groups are examples of important religious co-cultures. The elderly are yet another example of a co-culture.[18] Understanding Diversity: Our Range of Differences on page 92 describes both cultural and co-cultural variables that affect our interpersonal relationships with others.

## Cultural Elements

Categories of things and ideas that identify the most profound aspects of cultural influence are known as **cultural elements.** According to one research team, cultural elements include the following:

- *Material culture:* things and ideas
- *Social institutions:* schools, governments, religious organizations

**culture.** Learned system of knowledge, behavior, attitudes, beliefs, values, and norms that is shared by a group of people.

**co-culture.** A microculture; a distinct cultural group that exists within a larger cultural context (such as the gay and lesbian culture).

**cultural element.** Category of things and ideas that identify the most profound aspects of cultural influence (such as schools, governments, music, theater, language).

---

## *Building Your Skills*

### Assessing Your Communication with Strangers

Your comfort level in communicating with strangers is related to your ability to communicate with people from other cultures. Respond to each statement with a number that indicates the degree to which it is true of your communication with strangers: (1) Always False, (2) Usually False, (3) Sometimes True and Sometimes False, (4) Usually True, or (5) Always True.

_____ 1. I accept strangers as they are.

_____ 2. I express my feelings when I communicate with strangers.

_____ 3. I avoid negative stereotyping when I communicate with strangers.

_____ 4. I find similarities between myself and strangers when we communicate.

_____ 5. I accommodate my behavior to strangers when we communicate.

To find your score, add the numbers you wrote next to each statement. Scores range from 5 to 25. The higher your score, the greater your potential for developing a strong relationship with someone from a different background.

*Source:* William B. Gudykunst, *Bridging Differences: Effective Intergroup Communication* (Newbury Park, CA: Sage, 1998), 143.

# *Understanding Diversity*

## Our Range of Differences

Cultural diversity includes more than differences in ethnic background or gender. To become other-oriented is to consider a range of differences that affect how we communicate and respond to others. Note the following differences that affect our interactions with others.

**Age**  Different generations, because they experience different cultural and historical events, often view life differently. If your grandparents experienced the Great Depression of the 1930s, they may have different attitudes about savings accounts than you or even your parents do. Today's explicit song lyrics may shock older Americans who grew up with such racy lyrics as "makin' whoopee." The generation gap is real.

**Religion**  Eating habits and attitudes toward abortion and use of alcohol are just a few of the aspects of a person's religious beliefs and traditions that can affect relationships. Although most people in the United States are Christians, there is great diversity in the beliefs and practices of different denominations. Here is a breakdown of the top ten denominations by percentage of total U.S. population:

1. Roman Catholic            26.2%
2. Baptist                   19.4%
3. Protestant
   (nondenominational)        9.8%
4. Methodist                  8.0%
5. Lutheran                   5.2%
6. Christian
   (Disciples of Christ)      4.8%
7. Presbyterian               2.8%
8. Pentecostal                1.8%
9. Episcopalian/Anglican      1.7%
10. Mormon/Latter Day Saint   1.4%

The top five other religions in the United States by percentage of the population are the following:

1. Judaism                   1.8%
2. Islam                      .5%
3. Buddhism                   .4%
4. Hinduism                   .2%
5. Bahaism                    .01%

**Disability**  Although you may not think of the disabled as part of the cultural diversity equation, there is evidence that we unconsciously alter our communication style when we converse with disabled people. For example, we make less eye contact with people who are in wheelchairs; we also afford them more personal space when conversing. We often speak more loudly and more slowly to those who are blind. Many disabled people find these behaviors insulting.

**Social Class**  The U.S. Constitution declares that all people are created equal, but there is dramatic evidence that class differences exist and affect communication patterns. Social psychologist Michael Argyle reports that the cues we use to make class distinctions are (1) way of life, (2) family, (3) job, (4) money, and (5) education. Class differences influence whom we talk with, whether we are likely to invite our neighbors over for coffee, and whom we choose as our friends and lovers. Most of us must make a conscious effort if we want to expand beyond our class boundaries.

**Gender**  In this book we emphasize how gender affects the way we listen, use words, and send and interpret nonverbal messages. Sex differences are biological differences between males and females: only men can impregnate; only women can menstruate, gestate, and lactate. But gender differences focus on learned behavior that is culturally associated with being a man or a woman. Gender role definitions are flexible: a man can adopt behavior that is associated with a female role definition in a given culture and vice versa.

**Sexual Orientation**  During the past two decades gays and lesbians have become more assertive in expressing their rights within American society. Issues such as whether gays belong in the military, in the clergy, and in the teaching professions have stirred the passions of many. Being gay has become a source of pride for some, but it is still a social stigma for others. The incidence of suicide among gay teenagers is significantly higher than among non-gay teens. Although gay people are gaining legal rights and protections, they are still subject to discriminatory laws and social intolerance. The gay and lesbian community functions as a co-culture or a micro-culture within the larger U.S. culture.

**Race**  According to the dictionary, race is based on the genetically transmitted physical characteristics of a group of people who are also classified together on the basis of a common history, nationality, or geographical location. Skin color and other physical characteristics affect our responses and influence the way people of different races interact. Racial prejudice still has a devastating effect on interpersonal communication patterns and relationships.

**Ethnicity**  Ethnicity is a social classification based on a variety of factors such as nationality, religion, language, or ancestral heritage. Nationality and geographical location are especially important in defining an ethnic group. Those of Irish ancestry are usually referred to as an ethnic group rather than as a race. The same could be said of Britons, Norwegians, and Spaniards. Ethnicity, like race, fosters common bonds that affect communication patterns. On the positive side, ethnic groups bring vitality and variety to American society. On the negative side, members of these groups may experience persecution or rejection by members of other groups in our society.

- *Belief systems:* ideas about individuals and the universe

- *Aesthetics:* music, theater, art, dance

- *Language:* verbal and nonverbal communication system[19]

As we grow, we learn to value these cultural elements. You were not born with a certain taste in music, clothes, and automobiles. Through **enculturation,** the process of communicating a group's culture from generation to generation, you learned what you liked by choosing from among the elements available within your culture. Your friends, colleagues, the media, and most importantly, your family, communicate information about these elements and advocate choices for you to make.

Cultures are not static; they change as new information and new influences penetrate their stores of knowledge. We no longer believe that bathing is unhealthy, or that we can safely use makeup containing lead. These changes resulted from scientific discoveries. But other changes take place through **acculturation;** we acquire other approaches, beliefs, and values by coming into contact with other cultures. Today, acupuncture, yoga, t'ai chi, and karate studios are commonplace in most cities across America. Taco shells are available in every supermarket; salsa sales now surpass ketchup sales; and Dunkin' Donuts sells bagels. In less obvious ways, "new" perspectives from other cultures have also influenced our thoughts, actions, and relationships.

## Cultural Values

Identifying what a given group of people values or appreciates can provide insight into the behavior of an individual raised within that group. Although there are great differences among the world's **cultural values,** Geert Hofstede identified four variables for measuring values that are significant in almost every culture[20] (see Table 4.1 on page 94). According to Hofstede, each culture places varying degrees of value on masculine and feminine perspectives, avoidance of uncertainty, distribution of power, and individualism. Hofstede's research conclusions have been widely summarized to describe differences among these four key cultural values. Although his research has been criticized as dated (his information is now more than thirty years old) and based primarily on males who worked at IBM (the primary source for much of his information), his research remains one of the most comprehensive, data-based studies of cultural values.[21] He surveyed more than 100,000 employees in more than 50 countries; his research effort has yet to be duplicated or surpassed.

### Masculine versus Feminine Perspectives

Some cultures emphasize traditional male values, whereas others place greater value on female perspectives. These values are not really about biological sex differences but about overarching approaches to interacting with others.

People from **masculine cultures** tend to value more traditional roles for both men and women. Masculine cultures also value achievement, assertiveness, heroism, and material wealth. Research reveals that men tend to approach communication from a content orientation, meaning that they view communication as functioning primarily for information exchange. Men talk when they have something to say. This is also consistent with the tendency for men to base their relationships, especially their male friendships, on sharing activities rather than talking.

Men and women from **feminine cultures** tend to value such things as caring for the less fortunate, being sensitive toward others, and enhancing the overall quality of life.[22] Women, as research suggests, tend to approach communication for the purpose of relating or connecting to others, of extending themselves to other people in order

**enculturation.** Process of communicating a group's culture from generation to generation.

**acculturation.** Process through which an individual acquires new approaches, beliefs, and values by coming into contact with other cultures.

**cultural values.** What a given group of people values or appreciates.

**masculine culture.** Culture that emphasizes achievement, assertiveness, heroism, and material wealth.

**feminine culture.** Culture that emphasizes relationships, caring for the less fortunate, and overall quality of life.

TABLE *4.1*    **Examples of Countries That Illustrate Four Cultural Values**

| Cultural Value | Examples of Countries That Scored Higher on This Cultural Value | Examples of Countries That Scored Lower on This Cultural Value |
|---|---|---|
| **Masculinity:** People from countries with higher masculinity scores prefer high achievement, men being in more assertive roles, and more clearly differentiated sex roles than do people from countries with lower scores on this cultural dimension. | Japan, Australia, Venezuela, Italy, Switzerland, Mexico, Ireland, Jamaica, Great Britain | Sweden, Norway, Netherlands, Denmark, Yugoslavia, Costa Rica, Finland, Chile, Portugal, Thailand |
| **Uncertainty Avoidance:** People from countries with higher uncertainty avoidance scores generally prefer to avoid uncertainty; they like to know what will happen next. People from countries with lower scores are more comfortable with uncertainty. | Greece, Portugal, Guatemala, Uruguay, Belgium, Japan, Yugoslavia, Peru, France, Argentina, Chile | Singapore, Jamaica, Denmark, Sweden, Hong Kong, Ireland, Great Britain, Malaysia, India, Philippines, United States, Canada |
| **Power Distribution:** People from countries with higher power distribution scores generally prefer greater power differences between people; they are generally more accepting of someone having authority and power than are people from countries with lower scores on this cultural dimension. | Malaysia, Guatemala, Panama, Philippines, Mexico, Venezuela, Arab countries, Ecuador, Indonesia, India | Austria, Israel, Denmark, New Zealand, Ireland, Sweden, Norway, Finland, Switzerland, Great Britain |
| **Individualism:** People from countries with higher individualism scores generally prefer individual accomplishment rather than collective or collaborative achievement. | United States, Australia, Great Britain, Canada, Netherlands, New Zealand, Italy, Belgium, Denmark, Sweden, France | Guatemala, Ecuador, Panama, Venezuela, Colombia, Indonesia, Pakistan, Costa Rica, Peru, Taiwan, South Korea |

*Source:* Adapted from Geert Hofstede, *Cultures and Organizations: Software of the Mind* (London: McGraw-Hill, 1991).

to know them and be known by them.[23] What women talk about is less important than the fact that they're talking, because talking implies relationship.

Here's a short way of summarizing this difference: *Men often communicate to report; women often communicate to establish rapport.*[24] So the point of difference isn't in the way the sexes actually communicate, but in their motivations for communicating. The *how* may not be that different; the *why* may be very different.[25]

Of course, rarely is a culture on the extreme end of the continuum; many are somewhere in between. For centuries, most countries in Europe, Asia, and the Americas have had masculine cultures. Men and their conquests dominate history books; men have been more prominent in leadership and decision making than women. But today many of these cultures are moving slowly toward the middle—legal and social rules are encouraging more gender balance and greater equality between masculine and feminine roles.

### Tolerance of Uncertainty versus Avoidance of Uncertainty

Sven works for a phone company in the United States as a customer service representative. He grew up in Finland, where many people have a higher tolerance for bureaucratic uncertainty than do people in the United States. Jake is from Long Island, New York; he expects (sometimes demands) that his problems be resolved quickly. Sven's higher tolerance for uncertainty and Jake's desire for straight, prompt answers to questions created an oil-and-water confrontation. Jake phoned Sven to complain about the slow response to his request to have a new phone line installed for his fax machine. Sven tried to be reassuring, but Jake got the distinct impression that Sven was not sympathetic and thought that a week's wait for a new line was perfectly reasonable. Jake expected his new line within twenty-four hours. Both had difficulty tuning in to the cultural difference in their expectations about how quickly a bureaucracy should respond to an individual request.

Some cultures tolerate more ambiguity and uncertainty than others. Cultures in which people need certainty to feel secure are more likely to have and enforce rigid rules for behavior and develop more elaborate codes of conduct. People from cultures with a greater tolerance for uncertainty have more relaxed, informal expectations for others. "Go with the flow" and "It will sort itself out" are phrases that describe their attitudes. Sven and Jake's experience is explained by a study showing that people from Portugal, Greece, Peru, Belgium, and Japan have high certainty needs, but people from Scandinavian countries tend to tolerate uncertainty.[26]

*A*sian cultures have traditionally put a high value on masculine domination of women, but today there is a gradual trend toward greater equality between masculine and feminine roles.

### Concentrated versus Decentralized Distribution of Power

Some cultures value an equal or decentralized distribution of power, whereas others accept a concentration of hierarchical power in a centralized government and other organizations. In cultures in which people prefer a more centralized approach to power, hierarchical bureaucracies are common, and people expect some individuals to have more power than others. Russia, France, and China are all high on the concentrated power scale. Those that often strive for greater equality and distribution of power and control include many (but not all) citizens of Australia, Denmark, New Zealand, and Israel. People from these latter countries tend to minimize differences in power between people.

### Individual versus Group Achievement

*Cealy:* We've got this group project to do. Let's divvy up the work and then meet back here next week to see what each of us has done.

*Ayako:* Wait a minute, Cealy. It might seem to be more efficient to divide up the work into little separate pieces, but in the end we'll have a better report if we all work on every section.

*Cealy:* Are you kidding? We'll be here all night! Josh, you take the history of the problem. Bert, you look at problem causes and effects. Ayako, why don't you do a literature search on the Internet and start looking up articles.

*Ayako:* All right. But I still think it would be better to go to the library together. I think we'd have better luck if we worked on each aspect of the problem as a team.

Cealy and Ayako clearly have different strategies for working together. Cealy approaches the project from an individualistic perspective; Ayako prefers a collective or

# applying theory and research

## Uncertainty Reduction Theory

Uncertainty reduction theory, developed by Charles Berger and Richard Calabrese, helps explain how we seek to reduce our uncertainty during an initial meeting with strangers or when we find ourselves in a new situation.[27] In some respects, each of us is different from everyone else. The more different we are from others and the less we know about them, the more uncertainty and sometimes anxiety and fear we may have about other people.

Uncertainty reduction theory describes how we strategically interact with others to enhance our understanding of others so that strangers seem less strange to us. The theory predicts that high levels of uncertainty will increase information-seeking behavior, such as asking questions or doing research about a new place we may be visiting. As we become less uncertain and more certain, we use fewer information-seeking strategies because we have a better understanding of how to predict what will happen to us.[28]

When we are uncertain about someone else, we could use a passive strategy and just observe the person to see if we can learn more about him or her and thus reduce our uncertainty. Another strategy to reduce our uncertainty of others is more active: We could ask others for information about the person who is unfamiliar to us. Or we could use an interactive strategy to try to reduce our uncertainty about someone by asking questions, self disclosing, and listening for self disclosures from the other person.

As we noted in Table 4.1, people in some cultures (such as people from Argentina, Chile, and Peru) prefer to avoid uncertainty. They would rather have straight answers and know whom they are talking to; they are uncomfortable with uncertainty. People in other cultures (like Canadians, the British, and Jamaicans) are more comfortable with uncertainty. They feel that eventually things will get sorted out and they can be patient and wait for things to be resolved. Although we caution that these are broad generalizations and are not true in each situation, we can nonetheless use such generalizations to test our assumptions and help unravel our uncertainty. Geert Hofstede suggests that people who dodge uncertainty by avoiding people who are different from themselves, and who are also more likely to visit places that are in their comfort zone rather than to seek new places to visit, operate from the framework that "What is different is dangerous."[29] Hofstede suspects that people in cultures with a low need to avoid uncertainty, people who are more comfortable with uncertainty, would agree with the phrase, "What is different is interesting."

## Applying
### the Research to Your Life

Your comfort level with strangers and people who are different from you may stem from your personal tolerance for uncertainty. If you generally prefer to avoid new places, especially places that are different from your current surroundings, you may also be someone who likes certainty and dislikes uncertainty. If you prefer certainty and you don't prefer ambiguity, you may be more likely to use communication strategies to manage the uncertainty, or to avoid situations that create uncertainty. You'll be less likely to strike up a conversation with people who are different from yourself. If you are comfortable with uncertainty, you will be not quite as anxious, nervous, or upset if you don't have all of the answers; you'll likely be more patient finding out information about a stranger. The goal of inviting you to consider your own approach to uncertainty is not to change your tolerance for uncertainty, but to help you understand why and how you behave toward others who are different from you. Consider the following questions to help you apply uncertainty reduction theory to your interactions with others:

1. On a scale of 1 to 10 (with 10 being very comfortable with uncertainty and 1 being very uncomfortable with uncertainty), how would you rate your own level of comfort with uncertainty about others?

2. Do you actively try to reduce your uncertainty level, or do you just live with not knowing information about others, especially others who are different from you?

3. What strategies do you use to learn about others who are different from you? Do you prefer to use passive, active, or interactive strategies to reduce your uncertainty?

4. Do you actively avoid people who are different from you?

5. Would you rather visit new places or return to surroundings that are comfortable and familiar?

*Source:* C. R. Berger and R. J. Calabrese, "Some Explorations in Initial Interactions and Beyond: Toward a Developmental Theory of Interpersonal Communication," *Human Communication Research,* 1 (1975): 99–112.

group strategy to achieve the goal. Traditionally, North Americans champion individual accomplishments and achievements. People from Asian backgrounds often value collective or group achievement more highly. One researcher summed up the American goal system this way:

> Chief among the virtues claimed . . . is self-realization. Each person is viewed as having a unique set of talents and potentials. The translation of these potentials into actuality is concurred the highest purpose to which one can devote one's life.[30]

In a collectivistic culture, conversely, people strive to attain goals for all members of the family, group, or community. In Kenyan tribes, for example,

> [N]obody is an isolated individual. Rather, his [or her] uniqueness is a secondary fact. . . . In this new system group activities are dominant, responsibility is shared, and accountability is collective. . . . Because of the emphasis on collectivity, harmony and cooperation among the group tends to be emphasized more than individual function and responsibility.[31]

Individualistic cultures tend to be more loosely knit socially; individuals feel responsible for taking care of themselves and their immediate families.[32] In collectivistic cultures, individuals expect more support from others; they also experience more loyalty to and from the community. Because collectivistic cultures place more value on "we" than "I," teamwork approaches usually succeed better in their workplaces. U.S. businesses have tried to adopt some of Japan's successful team strategies for achieving high productivity.

## Recap
### Cultural Values

| | |
|---|---|
| **Masculine and Feminine** | • Masculine cultures value achievement, assertiveness, heroism, material wealth, and more traditional sex roles. |
| | • Feminine cultures value relationships, caring for the less fortunate, overall quality of life, and less traditional distinctions between sex roles. |
| **Uncertainty and Certainty** | • Cultures that value certainty do not like ambiguity and value feeling secure. |
| | • Cultures that value uncertainty are comfortable with ambiguity and less information. |
| **Decentralized and Centralized Power** | • Centralized power cultures value having power in the hands of a small number of people. |
| | • Decentralized power cultures favor equality and an even distribution of power in government and organizations. |
| **Individualistic and Collectivistic** | • Individualistic cultures value individual achievement and accomplishments. |
| | • Collectivistic cultures value group and team collaboration. |

## Cultural Contexts

Individuals from different cultures use cues from the **cultural context** to varying degrees to enhance messages and meaning. This insight led anthropologist Edward T. Hall to

**cultural context.** Information not explicitly communicated through language but through environmental or nonverbal cues.

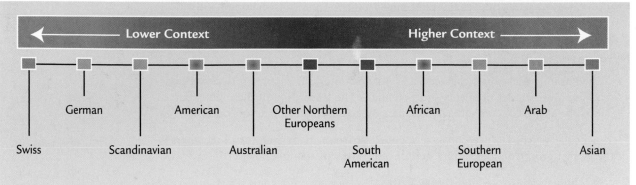

←———— **Lower Context**                              **Higher Context** ————→

| German | | American | | Other Northern Europeans | | African | | Arab |

Swiss          Scandinavian          Australian          South American          Southern European          Asian

**Low-Context Cultures**
Prefer information to be provided explicitly, usually in words
- Are less aware of nonverbal cues, environment, and situation
- Need detailed background information
- Tend to segment and compartmentalize information
- Control information on a "need to know" basis
- Prefer explicit and careful directions from someone who "knows"
- Consider knowledge a commodity
- Ask questions more directly

**High-Context Cultures**
Prefer information to be drawn from the surroundings rather than explicitly expressed
- Consider nonverbal cues important
- Rely on physical context for information
- Take environment, situation, gestures, and mood into account when interpreting messages
- Maintain extensive information networks
- Ask questions or ask for specific information less directly
- Maintain more reserve during initial conversations

*Source:* Based on research by Edward T. Hall, *Beyond Culture* (Garden City, NY: Doubleday, 1976) and adapted from Donald W. Klopf, *Intercultural Encounters: The Fundamentals of Intercultural Communication* (Englewood, CO: Morton Publishing 1998), 33.

FIGURE *4.1*

High/Low Contexts: Where Different Cultures Fall on the Context Scale

categorize cultures as either high- or low-context.[33] As shown in Figure 4.1, in **high-context cultures,** nonverbal cues are extremely important in interpreting messages. **Low-context cultures** rely more explicitly on language and use fewer contextual cues to send and interpret information. Individuals from high-context cultures may perceive people from low-context cultures as less attractive, knowledgeable, and trustworthy, because they violate unspoken rules of dress, conduct, and communication. Individuals from low-context cultures often are not skilled in interpreting unspoken, contextual messages.[34]

*Recap*   **The Nature of Culture**

| | |
|---|---|
| **Cultural Elements** | Things and ideas that represent profound aspects of cultural influence, such as art, music, schools, and belief systems |
| **Cultural Values** | What a culture reveres and holds important |
| **Cultural Contexts** | Information not explicitly communicated through language but gleaned from environmental or nonverbal cues. High-context cultures (such as Japanese, Chinese, Korean) derive much information from these cues. Low-context cultures (such as North American, Western European) rely more heavily on words. |

**high-context culture.** Culture that derives much information from nonverbal and environmental cues.

**low-context culture.** Culture that derives much information from the words of a message and less information from nonverbal and environmental cues.

# Barriers to Effective Intercultural Communication

Sari, who had recently moved from New York to New Orleans, couldn't understand it. The dinner party was supposed to start at 7 P.M., but when she drove up, hers was the only car in front of the house. She was astonished that guests could be so discourteous. Finally, after about 20 minutes, another guest arrived. Then another. Not until 7:45 was everyone present who had been invited. What Sari didn't understand was that most of the guests came from a cultural background where a half-hour delay in the starting time for social events was normal. Sari expected punctuality, but most of the other guests assumed that the dinner party would just start when everyone was ready.

**Intercultural communication** occurs when individuals or groups from different cultures communicate. The transactional process of listening and responding to people from different cultural backgrounds can be challenging. The greater the difference in culture between two people, the greater the potential for misunderstanding and mistrust.

Misunderstanding and miscommunication occur between people from different cultures because of different coding rules and cultural norms, which play a major role in shaping patterns of interaction. The greater the difference between the cultures, the more likely it is that they will use different verbal and nonverbal codes. When you encounter a culture that has little in common with your own, you may experience **culture shock,** or a sense of confusion, anxiety, stress, and loss. If you are visiting or actually living in the new culture, your uncertainty and stress may take time to subside as you learn the values and codes that characterize the culture. But if you are simply trying to communicate with someone from a background very different from your own—even on your home turf— you may find the suggestions in this section helpful in closing the communication gap.[35]

The first step to bridging differences between cultures is to find out what hampers effective communication. What keeps people from connecting with others from other cultures? Sometimes it is different meanings created by different languages or by different interpretations of nonverbal messages. Sometimes it is the inability to stop focusing on oneself and begin focusing on the other. We'll examine some of these barriers first, then discuss strategies and skills for overcoming them.

## Ethnocentrism

Marilyn had always been intrigued by Russia. Her dream was to travel the country by train, spending time in small villages as well as exploring the cultural riches of Moscow, Pyatigorsk, and St. Petersburg. Her first day in Russia was a disappointment, however. When she arrived in Moscow, she joined a tour touting the cultural traditions of Russia. When the tour bus stopped at Sparrow Hills, affording the visitors a breathtaking hilltop view of the Moscow skyline, she was perplexed and mildly shocked to see women dressed in elegant wedding gowns mounted on horseback and galloping through the parking lot. Men in suits were cheering them on as a crowd of tipsy revelers set off fireworks and danced wildly to a brass band. "What kind of people are these?" sniffed Marilyn.

"Oh," said the tour guide, "it is our custom to come here to celebrate immediately following the wedding ceremony."

"But in public with such raucousness?" queried Marilyn.

"It is our tradition," said the guide.

"What a backward culture. They're nothing but a bunch of peasants!" pronounced Marilyn, who was used to more refined nuptial celebrations at a country club or an exclusive hotel.

**intercultural communication.** Communication between or among people who have different cultural traditions.

**culture shock.** Feeling of stress and anxiety a person experiences when encountering a culture different from his or her own.

*C*olorful celebrations like this ritual purification ceremony in Bali can reinforce healthy ethnic pride. When this pride is taken to the extreme through ethnocentric feelings, barriers between groups may result.

For the rest of the tour Marilyn judged every Russian behavior as inferior to that of Westerners. That first experience colored her perceptions, and her ethnocentric view served as a barrier to effective interpersonal communication with the Russian people she met.

**Ethnocentrism** stems from a conviction that our own cultural traditions and assumptions are superior to those of others. In short, it is the opposite of an other-orientation that embraces and appreciates the elements that give another culture meaning. This kind of cultural snobbism is one of the fastest ways to create a barrier that inhibits rather than enhances communication.

The concept of ethnocentrism is not new. Almost 100 years ago W. G. Sumner defined it as "the technical name of this view of things in which one's own group is the center of everything and all others are scaled and rated with reference to it."[36] Many scholars have found that virtually all cultural groups are ethnocentric to some degree.[37] Some even argue that it's not always bad to see one's own cultural group as superior; ethnocentric tendency enhances group pride and patriotism and encourages cultural traditions.[38] A problem occurs, however, when a group views its own preferences as *always* the best way. Extreme ethnocentrism creates a barrier between the group and others.

### Different Communication Codes

You are on your first trip to Los Angeles. As you step off the bus and look around for Hollywood Boulevard, you realize you have gotten off at the wrong stop. You see what looks like an old-fashioned corner grocery store with "Bodega" painted on a red sign.

## *Understanding Diversity*

### Ethnocentric Thinking

*All good people agree,*
*And all good people say,*
*All nice people like Us, are We,*
*And everyone else is They.*

*I*n a few short lines, Rudyard Kipling captured the essence of what sociologists and anthropologists call ethnocentric thinking. Members of all societies tend to believe that "All nice people like Us, are We . . . ." They find comfort in the familiar and often denigrate or distrust others. Of course, with training and experience in other climes, they may learn to transcend their provincialism, placing themselves in others' shoes. Or, as Kipling put it,

*. . . if you cross over the sea,*
*Instead of over the way,*
*You may end by (think of it!)*
*    looking on We*
*As only a sort of They.*

In a real sense, a main lesson of the sociology of intergroup relations is to begin to "cross over the sea," to learn to understand why other people think and act as they do and to be able to empathize with their perspectives.

*Source:* Adapted from Faun B. Evans, Barbara Gleason, and Mark Wiley, *Cultural Tapestry: Readings for a Pluralistic Society* (New York: HarperCollins, 1992).

## Building Your Skills

### Assessing Your Ethnocentrism

The following measure of ethnocentrism was developed by communication researchers James Neuliep and James McCroskey. Answer the following questions honestly.

This instrument is composed of 24 statements concerning your feelings about your culture and other cultures. In the space provided to the left of each item indicate the degree to which the statement applies to you by marking whether you (5) strongly agree, (4) agree, (3) are neutral, (2) disagree, or (1) strongly disagree with the statement. There are no right or wrong answers. Work quickly and record your first response.

_____ 1. Most other cultures are backward compared with my culture.

_____ 2. People in other cultures have a better lifestyle than we do in my culture.

_____ 3. Most people would be happier if they didn't live like people do in my culture.

_____ 4. My culture should be the role model for other cultures.

_____ 5. Lifestyles in other cultures are just as valid as those in my culture.

_____ 6. Other cultures should try to be more like my culture.

_____ 7. I'm not interested in the values and customs of other cultures.

_____ 8. It is not wise for other cultures to look up to my culture.

_____ 9. People in my culture could learn a lot from people in other cultures.

_____ 10. Most people from other cultures just don't know what's good for them.

_____ 11. People from my culture act strange and unusual when they go into other cultures.

_____ 12. I have little respect for the values and customs of other cultures.

_____ 13. Most people would be happier if they lived like people in my culture.

_____ 14. People in my culture have just about the best lifestyles of anywhere.

_____ 15. My culture is backward compared with most other cultures.

_____ 16. My culture is a poor role model for other cultures.

_____ 17. Lifestyles in other cultures are not as valid as those in my culture.

_____ 18. My culture should try to be more like other cultures.

_____ 19. I'm very interested in the values and customs of other cultures.

_____ 20. Most people in my culture just don't know what is good for them.

_____ 21. People in other cultures could learn a lot from people in my culture.

_____ 22. Other cultures are smart to look up to my culture.

_____ 23. I respect the values and customs of other cultures.

_____ 24. People from other cultures act strange and unusual when they come into my culture.

To determine your ethnocentrism, **reverse** your score for items 2, 3, 5, 8, 9, 11, 15, 16, 18, 19, 20, and 23. For these items, 5 = 1, 4 = 2, 3 = 3, 2 = 4, and 1 = 5. That is, if your original score was a 5, change it to a 1. If your original score was a 4, change it to a 2, and so forth. Once you have reversed your score for these 12 items, add up all 24 scores. This is your generalized ethnocentrism score. Scores greater than 80 indicate high ethnocentrism. Scores of 50 and below indicate low ethnocentrism.

_Source:_ J. W. Neuliep and J. C. McCroskey, "The Development of a U.S. and Generalized Ethnocentrism Scale," _Communication Research Reports,_ 14 (1997): 393.

So you walk in and ask the man behind the counter, "How do I get to Hollywood Boulevard, please?"

"_No hablo inglés,_" says the man, smiling and shrugging his shoulders. But he points to a transit map pasted onto the wall behind the counter.

Today, even when you travel within the United States, you are likely to encounter people who do not speak your language. Obviously, this kind of intercultural difference poses a formidable communication challenge. And even when you do speak the

**ethnocentrism.** Belief that your cultural traditions and assumptions are superior to those of others.

same tongue as someone else, he or she may come from a place where the words and gestures have different meanings. Your ability to communicate will depend on whether you can understand each other's verbal and nonverbal codes.

In the preceding example, although the man behind the counter did not understand your exact words, he noted the cut of your clothing, your backpack, and your anxiety, and he deduced that you were asking directions. And you could understand what his gesture toward the transit map meant. Unfortunately, not every communication between speakers of two different languages is this successful.

Even when language is translated, meaning can be missed or mangled. Note the following examples of mistranslated advertisements:

- "Body by Fisher" in a General Motors auto ad became "Corpse by Fisher" in Flemish.

- A Colgate-Palmolive toothpaste named "Cue" was advertised in France before anyone realized that *Cue* also happened to be the name of a widely circulated pornographic book about oral sex.

- Pepsi-Cola's "Come Alive with Pepsi" campaign, when it was translated for the Taiwanese market, conveyed the unsettling news that "Pepsi brings your ancestors back from the grave."

- Parker Pen could not advertise its famous "Jotter" ballpoint pen in some languages because the translation sounded like "jockstrap" pen.

- One American airline operating in Brazil advertised that it had plush "rendezvous lounges" on its jets, unaware that in Portuguese (the language of Brazil), *rendezvous* implies a special room for making love.[39]

### Stereotyping and Prejudice

All Europeans dress fashionably.

All Asians are good at math.

All Americans like to drive big cars.

These statements are stereotypes. They are all inaccurate. As we discussed in Chapter 3, to **stereotype** someone is to push him or her into an inflexible, all-encompassing category. Our tendency to simplify sensory stimuli can lead us to adopt stereotypes as we interpret and label the behavior of others.[40] Stereotypes become a barrier to effective intercultural communication when we fail to consider the uniqueness of individuals, groups, or events. Two anthropologists suggest that every person is, in some

**stereotype.** To place a person or group of persons into an inflexible, all-encompassing category.

respects, (1) like all other people, (2) like some other people, and (3) like no other people.[41] The challenge when meeting others is to sort out how they are alike and how they are unique.

Can stereotypes play any useful role in interpersonal communication? It may sometimes be appropriate to draw on stereotypes, or generalizations drawn from limited instances. If, for example, you are alone and lost in a large city at two o'clock in the morning and another car repeatedly taps your rear bumper, it would be prudent to try to drive away as quickly as possible, rather than to hop out of your car to make a new acquaintance. You would be wise to prejudge that the other driver might have some malicious intent. In most situations, however, **prejudice**—a judgment or opinion of someone formed on the basis of stereotypes or before you know all the facts—inhibits effective communication, especially if your labels are inaccurate or assume superiority on your part.

Certain prejudices are widespread. Although there are more females than males in the world, one study found that even when a male and a female hold the same type of job, the male's job is considered more prestigious than the female's.[42] Today, gender and racial discrimination in hiring and promotion is illegal in the United States. But some people's opinions have not kept pace with the law.

### Assuming Similarity

Just as it is inaccurate to assume that all people who belong to another social group or class are worlds apart from you, it is usually erroneous to assume that others act and think just as you do. Even if they appear to be like you, all people are not alike. Although this statement is not profound, it has profound implications. Like Sari, who *assumed* that others would value punctuality as she did, people often make the mistake of assuming that others value the same things they do, maintaining a self-focused perspective instead of an other-oriented one. As you saw in Chapter 3, focusing on superficial factors such as appearance, clothing, and even a person's occupation can lead to false impressions. Instead, you must take the time to explore a person's background and cultural values before you can determine what you really have in common.

# Improving Intercultural Competence

**E**leanor Roosevelt once said, "We have to face the fact that either all of us are going to die together or we are going to live together, and if we are to live together we have to talk."[43] In essence, she was saying that to overcome differences people need effective communication skills. It is not enough just to point to the barriers to effective intercultural communication and say, "Don't do that." Although identifying the causes of misunderstanding is a good first step to becoming interculturally competent, most people need help with specific strategies to help them overcome these barriers. In this book and in this chapter, we want to focus attention on the interpersonal communication strategies that can lead to intercultural communication competence.

The remaining portion of this chapter presents three sets of strategies to help you bridge differences between yourself and people who come from different cultural

**prejudice.** A judgment or opinion of someone formed before you know all of the facts or the background of that person.

backgrounds. These three strategy sets—developing appropriate knowledge, developing motivation, and developing skill—are based on our understanding of how to be a competent communicator.[44]

Our suggestion to enhance your understanding or **knowledge** of others is based on the assumption that knowing more about others is important in quality relationships. One of the barriers to effective intercultural communication is having different communication codes. Improving your knowledge of how others communicate can reduce the impact of this barrier. We offer strategies to help you learn more about other cultures by actively pursuing information about others.

A second set of strategies focuses on becoming motivated to improve your intercultural communication knowledge and skills. **Motivation** is an internal state of readiness to respond to something. A competent communicator wants to learn and improve; an incompetent communicator is not motivated to develop new skills. Technically, no one can motivate you to do something; motivation comes from within. But developing strategies to appreciate others who are different from you may help you appreciate different cultural approaches to communication and relationships. We suggest you endeavor to be tolerant of uncertainty and to avoid knee-jerk negative evaluations of others.

The final set of strategies, developing **skill** in adapting to others, focuses on specific behaviors that can help overcome the barriers and cultural differences we have discussed. To address the barrier of ethnocentrism, we will identify the advantages of becoming a more flexible communicator. We will also describe the essential competences of becoming other-oriented—focusing on the needs, goals, and values of others, instead of only on yourself—and of adapting your communication to others. As we discussed in Chapter 1, becoming other-oriented is critical to the process of relating to others.

### Developing Knowledge: Strategies to Understand Others Who Differ from Us

Knowledge is power. To increase your knowledge of others who are different from you, we suggest that you actively seek information about others, ask questions and listen for the answers, and establish common ground. Let's discuss these strategies in more detail.

### Seek Information

Seeking information about a culture or even about a specific communication situation can be a useful strategy to enhance the quality of intercultural communication. Why? Because seeking information helps manage uncertainty and anxiety that we may feel when we interact with people who are different from us.[45] Sometimes we feel uncomfortable in intercultural communication situations because we just don't know how to behave. We aren't sure what our role should be; we can't quite predict what will happen when we communicate with others because we're in a new or strange situation. Actively seeking information about a culture or about people from a culture other than your own can help you manage some of the anxiety and uncertainty you may experience when you communicate in new cultural contexts. Seeking new information can also help counter inaccurate information and prejudice.

Every person has a **world view** based on cultural beliefs about the universe and key issues such as death, God, and the meaning of life.[46] According to communication scholar Carley Dodd, "A culture's world view involves finding out how the culture perceives the role of various forces in explaining why events occur as they do in a social setting."[47] These beliefs shape our thoughts, language, and behavior. Only through intercultural communication can we hope to understand how each individual views

**knowledge.** Information that enhances understanding of others; one of the elements necessary to becoming a competent communicator.

**motivation.** Internal state of readiness to respond to something; an element of interpersonal competence.

**skill.** Behavior that improves the effectiveness or quality of communication with others.

**world view.** Perception shared by a culture or group of people about key beliefs and issues, such as death, God, and the meaning of life, which influences interaction with others.

the world. As you speak to a person from another culture, think of yourself as a detective watching for implied, often unspoken messages that provide information about the values, norms, roles, and rules of that person's culture.

You can also prepare yourself by studying the culture. If you are going to another country, courses in the history, anthropology, art, or geography of that place can give you a head start on communicating with understanding. Learn not only from books and magazines, but also from individuals whenever possible.

Intercultural scholar William Gudykunst has discovered some patterns in the way people seek new information to manage the uncertainty they experience when communicating with people from an unfamiliar culture.[48] He's found that people in high-context cultures (who place an emphasis on nonverbal messages) are typically more cautious when communicating in initial conversations than are people from low-context cultures (who emphasize the verbal content of a message). If you're from a low-context culture (such as the United States), you are more likely to pay attention to overt, obvious nonverbal expressions; people from high-context cultures are more likely to focus on more subtle nonverbal cues for their information. Gudykunst has also found that people from high-context cultures are more likely to make assumptions about others than are people from low-context cultures. People from low-context cultures are more likely to use self-disclosure and to be more direct in asking for information to manage uncertainty than are people from high-context cultures.

Even in a high-context culture, no one will fault you for asking directly for help if you show a sincere desire to learn. If you are trying to communicate with someone closer to home who is from a different background, you can study magazines, music, food, and other readily available sources of information about his or her culture. Or visit each other's homes or hangouts to observe and learn more about each other.

Given the inextricable link between language and culture, the more you learn about another language, the more you will understand the traditions and customs of the culture. Politicians have long known the value of using even a few words of their constituents' language. President Kennedy impressed and excited a crowd in Berlin by proclaiming, "Ich bin ein Berliner" ("I am a Berliner"). Even though his diction was less than perfect, he conveyed the message that he identified with his listeners. Speaking even a few words can signify your interest in learning about the language and culture of others.

As we noted at the beginning of this chapter, when we speak of culture, we are also referring to co-cultures. A co-culture is a cultural group within a larger culture. Learning how men and women, each a separate co-culture, communicate differently can help us improve our communication with the opposite gender. Men, for example, are more likely to develop friendships through participating in common activities with other men (playing on a baseball team, working together).[49] Women are more likely to develop friendships through talking together rather than working together.

Reading books about differences between the way men and women communicate is one strategy to help both sexes improve understanding and develop insight into different approaches to communication. Deborah Tannen's *You Just Don't Understand* is a popular book that can help create a dialogue between men and women about communication differences and thus promote greater knowledge about how to improve communication.

As you read about other cultures or co-cultures, it is important not to develop rigid categories or stereotypes for the way others may talk or behave. Proclaiming "Oh, you're just saying that because you're a man" or "You women always say things like that" can increase rather than decrease communication barriers. Throughout this book we discuss research-based gender differences in the way men and women communicate to enhance your understanding and improve communication with members of the opposite sex. But we don't recommend that you treat men and women as completely separate species from different planets or automatically assume you will immediately misunderstand the opposite sex.

### Ask Questions and Listen Effectively

When you encounter a person from another background, asking questions, then pausing to listen, is a simple technique for gathering information and also for confirming the accuracy of your expectations and assumptions. For example, some cultures, such as the Japanese, have rigid expectations regarding gift giving. It is better to ask what these expectations are than to assume that your good old down-home manners will see you through.

When you ask questions, be prepared to share information about yourself, too. Otherwise, your partner may feel as if you are interrogating him or her as a way to gain power and dominance rather than from a sincere desire to learn about cultural rules and norms.

Communication helps to reduce the uncertainty that is present in any relationship.[50] When you meet people for the first time, you may be uncertain about who they are and what they like and dislike. When you communicate with someone from another culture, the uncertainty level is particularly high. As you begin to interact, you exchange information that helps you develop greater understanding. If you continue to ask questions, eventually you will feel less uncertain about how the person is likely to behave.

Just asking questions and sharing information about yourself are not sufficient to bridge differences in culture and background. It is equally important to listen to what others share. In the next chapter we provide specific strategies for improving your listening skills.

### Develop a "Third Culture"

Several researchers suggest that one of the best ways to enhance understanding when communicating with someone from a different cultural background is to develop a **third culture.** This is created when the communication partners join aspects of separate cultures to create a third, "new" culture that is more comprehensive and inclusive than either of the two separate cultures.[51]

According to one intercultural communication researcher, F. L. Casmir, a third-culture approach to enhancing the quality of intercultural communication occurs when the people involved in the conversation construct "a mutually beneficial interactive environment in which individuals from two different cultures can function in a way beneficial to all involved."[52]

How do you go about developing a third culture? In a word: talk. Developing a third culture does not just happen all at once; it evolves from dialogue. The communicators construct a third culture *together*. After they realize that cultural differences may divide them, they may develop a third culture by making a conscious effort to develop common assumptions and common perspectives for the relationship. Dialogue, negotiation, conversation, interaction, and a willingness to let go of old ways and experiment with new frameworks are the keys to developing a third culture as a basis for a new relationship.

Developing a third-culture mentality can reduce our tendency to approach cultural differences from an "us versus them" point of view. Rather than trying to eliminate communication barriers stemming from two different sets of experiences, adopting a third-culture framework creates a new understanding of the other on the part of both participants.[53]

**third culture.** Common ground established when people from separate cultures create a third, "new," more comprehensive and inclusive culture.

Consider the example of Marsha, a businesswoman from Lincoln, Nebraska, and Tomiko, a businesswoman from Tokyo, Japan. In the context of their business relationship, it would be difficult for them to develop a comprehensive understanding of each other's cultural traditions. However, if they openly acknowledged the most significant of these differences and sought to create a third culture by identifying explicit rules and norms for their interaction, they might be able to develop a more comfortable relationship with each other.

As described by communication researcher Benjamin Broome, the third culture "is characterized by unique values and norms that may not have existed prior to the dyadic [two-person] relationship."[54] Broome labels the essence of this new relationship **relational empathy,** which permits varying degrees of understanding, rather than requiring complete comprehension of another's culture or emotions.

One of the barriers to effective intercultural communication is having different communication codes. In seeking a third culture, you are seeking a way to develop a common code or framework to enhance understanding. Developing such a code that both individuals can understand may include each party's learning the language of the other. It can also include discussing meanings of nonverbal communication so that misunderstandings can be reduced. Further, it involves using the skill of checking your perceptions that we discussed in the previous chapter.

The cultural context includes all the elements of the culture (learned behaviors and rules, or "mental software") that affect the interaction. Do you come from a culture that takes a tea break each afternoon at 4 P.M.? Does your culture value hard work and achievement, or relaxation and enjoyment? Creating a third culture acknowledges the different cultural contexts and interactions participants have experienced and seeks to develop a new context for future interaction.

*I*n families with members from different cultures, creating a third culture that is more inclusive than the separate cultures the family members belong to can eliminate some communication barriers.

## Develop Knowledge to Enhance Understanding

| Seek Information About the Culture | Learn about a culture's world view. |
| --- | --- |
| Ask Questions and Listen | Reduce uncertainty by asking for clarification and listening to the answer. |
| Develop a Third Culture | Create common ground. |

## Developing Motivation: Strategies to Accept Others Who Differ from Us

Competent communicators want to learn and improve. They are motivated to enhance their ability to relate to others and to accept others as they are. A key to accepting others is to develop a positive attitude of tolerance and acceptance of those who are different from you. We suggest three strategies to help improve your acceptance and appreciation of others who differ from you: Tolerate ambiguity, develop mindfulness, and avoid negative judgments of others.

**relational empathy.** Essence of a relationship that permits varying degrees of understanding, rather than requiring complete comprehension of another's culture or emotions.

## Building Your Skills

### Can You Tolerate Ambiguity?

Respond to each statement with a number from 1 to 5: (1) Always False, (2) Usually False, (3) Sometimes False and Sometimes True, (4) Usually True, or (5) Always True.

_____ 1. I am comfortable in new situations.

_____ 2. I deal with unforeseen problems successfully.

_____ 3. I experience little discomfort in ambiguous situations.

_____ 4. I am relaxed in unfamiliar situations.

_____ 5. I am not frustrated when things do not go the way I expected.

To find your score, add the numbers you wrote next to each statement. Scores range from 5 to 25. The higher your score, the greater your tolerance for ambiguity.

_Source:_ William B. Gudykunst, _Bridging Differences: Effective Intergroup Communication_ (Newbury Park, CA: Sage, 1998), 121.

### Tolerate Ambiguity

Communicating with someone from another culture produces uncertainty. It may take time and several exchanges to clarify a message. Be patient and try to expand your capacity to tolerate ambiguity if you are speaking to someone with a markedly different world view.

When Ken and Rita visited Miami, they asked their hotel concierge to direct them to a church of their faith, and they wound up at one with a predominantly Haitian congregation. They were not prepared for the exuberant chanting and verbal interchanges with the minister during the sermon. They weren't certain whether they should join in or simply sit quietly and observe. Ken whispered to Rita, "I'm not sure what to do. Let's just watch and see what is expected of us." In the end, they chose to sit and clap along with the chanting rather than to become actively involved in the worship. Rita felt uncomfortable and conspicuous, though, and had to fight the urge to bolt. But after the service, several members of the congregation came up to greet Ken and Rita, invited them to lunch, and expressed great happiness in their visit. "You know," said Rita later in the day, "I'm so grateful that we sat through our discomfort. We might never have met those terrific people. Now I understand why their worship is so noisy—they're just brimming with joy."

### Develop Mindfulness

"Our life is what our thoughts make it," said Marcus Aurelius in _Meditations_. To be **mindful** is to be consciously aware of cultural differences, to acknowledge that there is a connection between thoughts and deeds when you interact with a person from a background different from your own. William Gudykunst suggests that being mindful is one of the best ways to approach any new cultural encounter.[55] Remember that there are and will be cultural differences, and try to keep them in your consciousness. Also try to consider the other individual's frame of reference or world view and to use his or her cultural priorities and assumptions when you are communicating.[56] Adapt your behavior to minimize cultural noise and distortion.

If you have seen the movie _My Big Fat Greek Wedding_, you remember that the lead characters in the movie, who decide to get married, are from different cultural traditions. They make a mindful, conscious effort to be aware of their differences yet relate to each other in positive, supportive ways. Not only the married couple, but their parents and family members, eventually develop the skill of being mindful of differences as a way of enhancing the quality of their relationships with one another.

**mindful.** Aware of cultural differences and the connection between thoughts and deeds in one's interactions with someone from a background different from one's own.

# *Understanding Diversity*

## Tao: A Universal Moral Code

*I*t's clear that there are cultural differences among the world's people and that these differences have existed since there have been people. Anthropologists and communication scholars who study intercultural communication teach us the value of adapting to cultural differences in order to understand others better. But are there any universal values that are or have been embraced by all humans? The question is not a new one; scholars, theologians, and many others have debated for millennia whether there are any universal underpinnings for all human societies. In Chapter 3 we noted that social psychologists Penelope Brown and Stephen Levison suggest that people from all cultures have a universal need to be treated with politeness.[57] Are there other needs and values that all humans share? To uncover such commonalities is to develop a truly human communication theory rather than a theory that applies to a specific cultural context.

C. S. Lewis, a British scholar, author, and educator who taught at both Oxford University and Cambridge University, argued that there are universal ethical and moral principles that under-gird all societies of civilized people, regardless of their religious beliefs, cultural background, or government structure.[58] He suggested that the existence of Natural Laws, or what he called a *Tao*—a universal moral code—informs human ethical decisions. In his book *The Abolition of Man*, Lewis presented eight universal principles, or laws. He did not claim that all societies have followed these laws—many of them have been clearly violated and continue to be violated today—but he did suggest they provide a bedrock of values against which all societies may be measured. Here are his eight laws:

1. The Law of General Beneficence: Do not murder, be dishonest, or take from others what does not belong to us.

2. The Law of Special Beneficence: Value your family members.

3. Duties to Parents, Elders, and Ancestors: Especially hold your parents, those who are a generation older than you, and your ancestors with special honor and esteem.

4. Duties to Children and Posterity: We have a special obligation to respect the rights of the young and to value those who will come after us.

5. The Law of Justice: Honor the basic human rights of others; each person is of worth.

6. The Law of Good Faith and Veracity: Keep your promises and do not lie.

7. The Law of Mercy: Be compassionate to those less fortunate than you are.

8. The Law of Magnanimity: Avoid unnecessary violence against other people.

To support his argument that these are universal values, Lewis offered quotations from several well-known sources, including religious, historical, and political writings, both contemporary and centuries-old. Lewis implied that these eight laws may be viewed as a universal Bill of Rights, and that they constitute an underlying set of principles that either implicitly or explicitly guide all civilized society. Do you agree? Is it useful to search for underlying principles of humanness? Despite cultural differences, are there underlying values or principles that should inform our interactions with others? Is there truly a universal human theory of communication? Or might it do more harm than good to suggest that universal principles underlie what it means to behave and communicate appropriately and effectively?

---

You can become more mindful through self-talk, something we discussed in Chapter 2. Self-talk consists of rational messages you tell yourself to help you manage your emotions or discomfort with a certain situation. Imagine that you are working on a group project with several of your classmates. One classmate, Suji, was born in Iran. When interacting with you, he consistently stands about a foot away from you, whereas you are more comfortable with three or four feet between you. When Suji encroaches on your space, you could be mindful of the reason for this behavior by mentally noting, "Suji sure likes to get close to people when he talks to them. This may represent a practice in his culture." This self-talk message makes you consciously aware that there may be a difference in your interaction styles. If you still feel uncomfortable,

# Building Your Skills

## Measuring Mindfulness

Respond to each statement with a number from 1 to 5: (1) Always False, (2) Usually False, (3) Sometimes False and Sometimes True, (4) Usually True, or (5) Always True.

_____ 1. I pay attention to the situation and context when I communicate.

_____ 2. I can describe others with whom I communicate in great detail.

_____ 3. I seek out new information about the people with whom I communicate.

_____ 4. I try to find rational reasons why others may behave in a way I perceive negatively.

_____ 5. I recognize that the person with whom I am communicating has a different point of view than I do.

To find your score, add the numbers you wrote next to each statement. Scores range from 5 to 25. The higher your score, the more mindful you are when you communicate.

_Source:_ William B. Gudykunst, _Bridging Differences: Effective Intergroup Communication_ (Newbury Park, CA: Sage, 1998), 120.

instead of blurting out, "Hey, man, why so close?" you could express your own preferences with an "I" message: "Suji, I'd prefer a bit more space between us when we talk."

### Avoid Negative Judgments about Another Culture

| | |
|---|---|
| _American tourist on her first visit to France:_ | Can you believe it? How repulsive! These people actually eat horse meat and think it's a delicacy. |
| _Black teenager watching his white classmates dance:_ | Man, they don't know anything about good music! And those dances are so dumb. I don't call this a party. |
| _Japanese businessperson visiting Argentina:_ | These people are never on time. No wonder they can never catch up to us. |
| _German student, after watching a documentary about life in Japan:_ | No wonder they work so hard. They have dinky little houses. I'd work long hours too if I had to live like that. |

The kind of ethnocentrism that underlies judgments like these is a communication barrier. It is also an underlying cause of suspicion and mistrust and, in extreme cases, a spark that ignites violence. Instead of making judgments about another culture, try simply to acknowledge differences and to view them as interesting challenges rather than as obstacles to be eradicated.

## Develop Motivation to Accept Others

| | |
|---|---|
| **Tolerate Ambiguity** | Take your time and expect some uncertainty. |
| **Develop Mindfulness** | Be conscious of cultural differences, rather than ignoring the differences. |
| **Avoid Negative Judgments** | Resist thinking that your culture has all the answers. |

## Developing Skill: Strategies to Adapt to Others Who Differ from Us

To be skilled is to be capable of putting into action what you know and want to achieve. The underlying skill in being interculturally competent is the ability to be flexible, to be other-oriented, and to adapt your communication to others. We discuss these crucial skills here as an introduction to the communication skills that we present in the next four chapters.

### Develop Flexibility

When you interact with someone from another background, your responding skills are crucial. You can only learn so much from books; you must be willing to learn as you communicate. Every individual is unique, so cultural generalizations that you learn from research may not always apply. It is not accurate to assume, for example, that *all* French people are preoccupied with food and fashion. Many members of minority groups in the United States find it draining to correct these generalizations in their encounters with others. Pay close attention to the other person's nonverbal cues when you begin conversing; then adjust your communication style and language if necessary to put the person at ease. And avoid asking questions or making statements based on generalizations.

### Become Other-Oriented

Throughout the book we have emphasized the importance of becoming other-oriented—focusing on others rather than yourself—as an important way to enhance your interpersonal competence.[59] We have also discussed the problems ethnocentrism can create when you attempt to communicate with others, especially with those whose culture differs from yours. We now offer two specific ways to increase your other-orientedness: social decentering and empathy.

Although our focus in this discussion is on how to increase other-orientation in intercultural interactions, the principles apply to *all* interpersonal interactions. The major difference between intercultural interactions and those that occur within your own culture is primarily the obviousness of the differences between you and the other person.

1. *Social Decentering.* **Social decentering,** the first strategy, is a *cognitive process* in which you take into account the other person's thoughts, feelings, values, background, and perspectives. This process involves viewing the world from the other person's point of view. The greater the difference between you and the other person, the more difficult it is to accomplish social decentering. In doing the exercise in Building Your Skills: Predicting How Others Feel on page 112, you may find it easier to predict the reaction of your close friend than those of any of the other people described. The rest of your rankings will depend on the various experiences you have had. You've no doubt had interactions with members of the opposite sex and with someone of a different age, and you may have had interactions with someone of a different race, so these are probably the next highest ranked. Interactions with people from other cultures are probably the most difficult because your experiences with such interactions are often limited. It is easier to socially decenter about someone whose culture and background are similar to yours.

   There are three ways to socially decenter, or take another's perspective: (1) Develop an understanding of another, based on how you have responded when something similar has happened to you; (2) base your understanding of others on the knowledge you have about a specific person; or (3) make generalizations about someone, based on your understanding of how you think most people would feel or behave.[60]

**social decentering.** Cognitive process in which we take into account another person's thoughts, feelings, values, background, and perspectives.

# *Building Your Skills*

## Predicting How Others Feel

How well do you think you could predict someone's reactions to finding out his or her mother or other close relative has just died? Rank-order each of the following from 1 (the person whose reaction you could predict most confidently) to 6 (the person whose reaction you'd be least confident about predicting).

_____ A.  A close friend of the same sex, age, race, and culture

_____ B.  A 60-year-old male Chinese farmer

_____ C.  A college student who is twenty years older than you but of the same race, sex, and culture

_____ D.  A 10-year-old California girl who is the child of Asian and Latino parents

_____ E.  A college student of a different race but the same age, culture, and sex as you

_____ F.  A college student of the opposite sex but of the same age, race, and culture

What qualities do you feel provide you the best information on which to base your judgments? Why? What would you need to know about each person to feel comfortable in making a prediction? How can you get that information?

First, when you draw on your direct experience, you use your knowledge of what happened to you in the past to help you guess how someone else may feel. To the degree that the other person is similar to you, your reactions and theirs will match. For example, suppose you are talking to a student who has just failed a midterm exam in an important course. You have also had this experience. Your reaction was to discount it because you had confidence you could still earn a passing grade. You might use this self-understanding to predict your classmate's reactions. To the degree that you are similar to the classmate, your prediction will be accurate. But suppose your classmate comes from a culture with high expectations for success. Your classmate might feel upset over having dishonored his family by his poor performance. In this situation, your understanding of your own reaction needs to be tempered by your awareness of how similar or dissimilar the other person is to you. Recognition of differences should lead you to recognize the need to socially decenter in another way.

*Grief for the loss of a loved one is a universal emotion experienced by people in all cultures.*

The second way we socially decenter—or take the perspective of another—is based on specific knowledge we have of the person with whom we are interacting. Drawing on your memory of how your classmate reacted to a previous failed midterm gives you a basis to more accurately predict his reaction. Even if you have not observed your classmate's reaction to the same situation, you project how you think he would feel based on similar instances. As relationships become more intimate, you gain more information to allow you to socially decenter more readily. Your accuracy in predicting and understanding your partners usually increases as relationships become more intimate. In intercultural interactions, the more opportunity you have to interact with the same person and learn more about the person and his or her culture, the more your ability to socially decenter will increase.

The third way to socially decenter is to apply your understanding of people in general, or of categories of people from whom you have gained some knowledge. Each of us develops implicit personality theories, constructs, and attributions of how people act, as discussed in Chapter 3. You might have a general theory to explain the behavior of men and another for women. You might have general theories about Mexicans, Japanese, Canadians, Slovenians, Texans, or Iowans. As you meet someone who falls into one of your categories, you draw on that conceptualization to socially decenter. The more you can learn about a given culture, the stronger your general theories can be, and the more effectively you can use this method of socially decentering. The key, however, is to avoid developing inaccurate, inflexible stereotypes of others and basing your perceptions of others only on those generalizations.

2. *Empathy.* Besides *thinking* about how another may feel (socially decentering), you can have an *emotional* reaction to what others do or tell you. A second skill for becoming other-oriented is learning to feel empathy for another. **Empathy** is an *emotional reaction* that is similar to the one being experienced by another person (as compared to social decentering, which is a *cognitive reaction*). Empathy is feeling what another person feels. Our emotional reaction may or may not be of the same intensity as the emotions the other person is experiencing. You may experience mild pity for your classmate who has failed the midterm, in contrast to his stronger feeling of anguish and dishonor. Or you may share his same feelings of anguish and dishonor.

Some emotional reactions are almost universal and cut across cultural boundaries. You may experience empathy when seeing photos or videos depicting emotional scenes occurring in other countries. Seeing a mother crying while holding her sick or dying child in a refugee camp might move you to cry and feel a deep sense of sadness or loss. You empathize with the woman. You might also experience empathy for your brother, who has just received the devastating news that his best friend has been killed in an automobile accident. As tears come to your eyes, you grieve with him. Empathy can enhance interpersonal interactions in a number of ways: It can provide a bond between you and the other person; it is confirming; it is comforting and supportive; it can increase your understanding of others; and it can strengthen the relationship. People can empathize most easily with those who are similar, and in situations in which they have had a similar emotional experience.

Developing empathy is different from sympathizing with others. When you offer **sympathy,** you tell someone you are sorry he or she feels what he or she is feeling: "I'm sorry your Uncle Joe died" or "I'm sorry to hear you failed your test." When you sympathize with others, you acknowledge their feelings. But when you empathize, you experience an emotional reaction that is similar to the other person's; you, too, feel grief or sadness. We discuss strategies for developing empathic listening skills in the next chapter.

### Appropriately Adapt Your Communication to Others

The logical extension of being flexible and becoming other-oriented is to adapt your communication to enhance the quality and effectiveness of your interpersonal communication. To **adapt** means to adjust your behavior to others to accommodate differences and expectations. Appropriate adaptation occurs in the context of the relationship you have with the other person and what is happening in the communication environment. **Communication accommodation theory** suggests that all people adapt their behavior to others to some extent. Those who adapt to others appropriately and sensitively are more likely to experience more positive communication.[61] Adapting to

**empathy.** An emotional reaction that is similar to the reaction being experienced by another person; empathizing is feeling what another person is feeling.

**sympathy.** Acknowledgment that someone may be feeling bad; compassion toward someone.

**adapt.** To adjust one's behavior in accord with what someone else does. We can adapt based on the individual, the relationship, and the situation.

**communication accommodation theory.** Theory that all people adapt their behavior to others to some extent.

## Becoming Other-Oriented

### The Platinum Rule

*T*he ultimate goal of becoming other-oriented goes beyond having sympathy for others. Being other-oriented may even go beyond what is typically labeled as the "Golden Rule": Do to others as you would have them do to you. Or, as stated by the Buddha: Consider others as yourself. In Chapter 2 (page 63) we identified additional interpretations of the same principle from a variety of religious traditions. Communication researcher Milton Bennett calls the ultimate other-oriented principle "the Platinum Rule": *Do to others as they themselves would like to be treated.*[62] Rather than treating people as *you* would like to be treated, interact with others the way you think and feel *they* would like to be treated. For example, when ordering a pizza for your friends, the golden rule would suggest you order a pizza with toppings you would like; the platinum rule is to order what you think your dining partners would like. Or, if you've decided to buy your friend a book for her birthday, buy a book not because you like it, but because you think your friend will like it. According to Bennett, at its essence, empathy is "the imaginative, intellectual and emotional participation in another person's experience."[63] The goal, according to Bennett, is to attempt to think and feel what another person thinks and feels and to go beyond trying to feel what the other person feels and take positive action toward others in response to your empathic feelings.

As you ponder the virtues and challenges of becoming other-oriented, consider the following questions:

1. Is the Platinum Rule always useful, desirable, or even possible? Explain your answer.

2. What are some of the obstacles to applying the Platinum Rule during your everyday interactions with others?

3. How can the Platinum Rule be useful when you are having a disagreement or conflict with another person?

4. Think about a time when you used the Platinum Rule. What was the effect on the person with whom you were communicating?

---

others doesn't mean you only tell others what they want to hear and do what others want you to do. Such spineless, placating behavior is not wise, effective, or ethical. Nor are we suggesting that you adapt your behavior only so that you can get your way; the goal is effective communication, not manipulation. We are suggesting, however, that you be aware of what your communication partner is doing and saying, especially if there are cultural differences between you, so that your message is understood and you don't unwittingly offend others. Although it may seem common sense, being sensitive to others and adapting behaviors to others are not as common as you might think.

Sometimes people adapt their behavior based on what they think someone will like. At other times they adapt their communication after realizing they have done something wrong. When you modify your behavior in anticipation of an event, you **adapt predictively.** For example, you might decide to buy a friend flowers to soften the news about breaking a date because you know how much your friend likes flowers. When you modify your behavior after an event, you **adapt reactively.** For example, you might buy your friend flowers to apologize for a fight.

There are a number of reasons people adapt their communication with another person. People often adapt messages in an attempt to make them more understandable. For instance, in talking to someone with limited understanding of English, you would probably choose simple words and phrases. People also adapt messages in order to accomplish goals more effectively. In intercultural interactions, people frequently adapt communication behavior in response to the feedback or reactions they are receiving. Table 4.2 lists a variety of ways to adapt verbal messages to others.

**adapt predictively.** To modify or change behavior in anticipation of an event.

**adapt reactively.** To modify or change behavior after an event.

TABLE *4.2*    **Communication Adaptation Behaviors**

| Type | Examples |
|---|---|
| *Topical:* Choosing a topic or issue to discuss because you know it will interest the other person. | Talking about a mutual friend or a party you both went to, asking if he or she saw a particular play that was in town. |
| *Explanatory/Elaboration:* Providing additional information or detail because you recognize that the other person does not know it. | Explaining your mother's eating habits to a new friend, explaining to a neighbor how to keep squirrels away from bean plants. |
| *Withholding Explanation or Information:* Not providing an explanation because your partner already knows the information, because it might hurt or anger your partner, because you fear the other person might misuse it, or because you wish to avoid violating confidentiality. | Not elaborating on the parts of an auto engine when you describe a car problem because you know the listener is knowledgeable about cars, not telling a friend you saw his or her lover with another person because the friend would be hurt, not telling someone about your interest in a mutual friend because you are afraid that person would tell the mutual friend. |
| *Examples/Comparisons/Analogies:* Choosing examples that you know your partner will find relevant. | Explaining in-line skating by comparing it to ice skating, something your partner knows how to do. |
| *Personal Referencing:* Referring to your partner's specific attitudes, interests, personality, traits, or ethnic background. | "I've got something to tell you I think you'll find funny." "Could you help me balance my checkbook? You're so good at math." "That's a behavior I'd expect from you, given the way your parents raised you." |
| *Vernacular/Language:* Choosing or avoiding certain words because of their potential effect on the listener. Using words that have a unique meaning for you and your partner. Using words that you think are appropriate to the other person's level of understanding. | A wife asking her husband whether he was "catching flies" during a movie, meaning he was asleep with his mouth wide open. A father telling his child that a criminal is someone who does bad things. Two computer jocks talking about "bytes," "RAM," and "chips." |
| *Disclosure:* Consciously deciding to share information about yourself that the other person does not know. | Telling your lover about your sexual fantasies. Telling your instructor about family problems. |
| *Immediate Follow-Up Questioning:* Seeking additional information from the other person about information he or she shares during the interaction. | "So, what was it like growing up in small-town Iowa?" "Tell me more about your vacation in Florida." "Where are you going on your date?" |
| *Delayed Follow-Up Questioning:* Seeking additional information from the other person about previous information he or she shared. | "How's your mother doing after her operation yesterday?" "How was your date Saturday night?" |
| *Adapting to Immediate Reaction/Feedback:* Modifying your words or behavior because of your partner's reaction. | Quickly changing the topic when your friend starts to cry when you talk about her mother's death. |

*Source:* © Mark V. Redmond, 1994. Used by permission.

Conversants also adapt to nonverbal cues. Many times they raise or lower voice volume in response to the volume of a partner, or lean toward people in response to their leaning toward the speaker. We talk more about such nonverbal cues in Chapter 7.

Adaptation across intercultural contexts is usually more difficult than adapting within your own culture. Imagine shaking hands with a stranger and having the stranger hold on to your hand as you continue to talk. In the United States, hand-holding between strangers violates nonverbal norms. But in some cultures, maintaining physical contact while talking is expected. Pulling your hand away from this person would be rude. What may be mannerly in one culture is not always acceptable in another. Adapting to these cultural differences means developing that "third culture" that we talked about earlier in the chapter.

Taking an other-oriented approach to communication means considering the thoughts, feelings, background, perspectives, attitudes, and values of your partners and adjusting your interaction with them accordingly. Other-orientation leads to more effective interpersonal communication, regardless of whether you are dealing with someone in your family or a person from another country.

By careful analysis of the factors that affect communication partners, you can develop understanding and empathy. That understanding and empathy can then help you make the most effective strategic communication choices as you adapt your messages and responses.

In an effective interpersonal relationship, your partner is also orienting himself or herself to you. A competent communicator has knowledge of others, is motivated to enhance the quality of communication, and possesses the skill of being other-oriented.

If you learn the skills and principles we have presented here, will it really make a difference in your ability to relate to others? Recent evidence suggests the answer is yes. A study by communication researcher Lori Carell found that students who had been exposed to lessons in empathy linked to a study of interpersonal and intercultural communication improved their ability to empathize with others.[64] There is evidence that if you master these principles and skills, you will be rewarded with greater insight and ability to relate to others who are different from you.

## *Recap*  Develop Skill to Adapt to Others

| | |
|---|---|
| **Develop flexibility.** | Learn to "go with the flow." |
| **Become other-oriented.** | Put yourself in the other person's mental and emotional mindset; listen and respond appropriately. |
| **Adapt your communication to others.** | Adjust your behavior to others to accommodate differences and expectations. |

## *S*ummary

A culture is a system of knowledge that is shared by a group of people. It includes cultural elements, values, goals, and contexts. Cultural elements are categories of things and ideas that identify key aspects of cultural influence. Cultural values reflect how individuals regard masculine and feminine behaviors and individual and collective achievements. They also reflect whether individuals can tolerate ambiguity or need a high degree of certainty, and whether they prefer concentrated or decentralized power structures. The goals of a culture depend on the way it values individual versus group achievement. In high-context cultures, the meaning of messages depends heavily on nonverbal information;

people in low-context cultures rely more heavily on words than on context for deriving meaning.

Intercultural communication occurs when individuals or groups from different cultures communicate. Several barriers inhibit effective intercultural communication. Ethnocentrism is the belief that one's own cultural traditions and assumptions are superior to those of others. Differences in language and the way people interpret nonverbal messages also interfere with effective intercultural communication. People stereotype by placing a group or a person into an inflexible, all-encompassing category. A related barrier is prejudice—people often prejudge someone before they know all the facts. Stereotyping and prejudice can keep people from viewing others as unique individuals and therefore hamper effective, honest communication. Finally, assuming that one is similar to others can also be a barrier to intercultural communication. All humans have some similarities, but their cultures have taught them to process the world differently.

Although it is reasonably easy to identify cultural differences, it is more challenging to bridge those differences. To enhance understanding between cultures, we suggest the following: Develop knowledge by seeking information about the culture, ask questions and listen, and develop a "third culture." Increase your motivation to appreciate others who are different from you by tolerating ambiguity, developing mindfulness, and avoiding negative judgments about another culture. Finally, enhance your skill by becoming flexible. Be other-oriented by socially decentering and becoming more empathic. And adapt your verbal and nonverbal communication to others.

# For Discussion and Review

## Focus on Critical Thinking

1. Jonna, an American, has just been accepted as a foreign exchange student in Germany. What potential cultural barriers may she face? How should she manage these potential barriers?

2. What's the problem in assuming that other people are like us? How does this create a barrier to effective intercultural communication?

3. If you were to design a lesson plan for elementary age students about how to deal with racial and ethnic stereotypes, what would you include?

4. What are appropriate ways to deal with someone who consistently utters racial slurs and evidences prejudice toward racial or ethnic groups?

## Focus on Ethics

5. Marla is the director of the campus multicultural studies program. She wants to require all students in a four-year degree program to take at least four courses that focus on multicultural issues. Is it appropriate to force students to take such a concentration of courses?

6. When Wayne, a Catholic Polish American, went to visit Dave, who was from an old Southern Baptist family, Dave's dad made a bigoted statement about African Americans. This upset Wayne, and he wondered whether Dave's father was prejudiced against Catholics, too. Should Wayne have spoken up and told Dave's dad that he did not like the remark?

7. Is it ethical or appropriate for someone from one culture to attempt to change the cultural values of someone from a different culture? For example, culture A practices polygamy: one husband can be married to several wives. Culture B practices monogamy: one husband can be married to only one wife. Should a person from culture B attempt to make someone from culture A change his or her ways?

# For Your Journal

1. Describe your perceptions of your own cultural values, based on the discussion of cultural values in this chapter. On a scale of 1 to 10, rate yourself in terms of masculine versus feminine perspective, individual versus group achievement, tolerance of uncertainty versus need for certainty, and centralized versus decentralized power. Provide an example of one of your own interpersonal communication experiences to illustrate each of these values.

2. Write a journal entry discussing how you have experienced one of the barriers to effective intercultural communication described in this chapter. Have you been ethnocentric in your thoughts or behavior or a victim of ethnocentrism? Describe a situation in which communication was difficult because you and your communication partner spoke different languages. Have you been a victim of stereotyping or prejudice? Have you assumed someone was similar to you and later found that there were more differences than you had suspected?

# Learning with Others

1. Get better acquainted with the international and inter-cultural experiences of your classmates by playing Diversity Bingo.[65]

   **Diversity Bingo** Your assignment is to locate people who either have done or know about the things listed in the boxes below, and then to obtain their autographs. You must first introduce yourself and share two personal things not listed in any of the boxes. After the introduction, the person may autograph the appropriate boxes for you. The person who collects the most autographs wins. You may not go back to the same person twice.

2. Bring to class a fable, folktale, or children's story from a culture other than your own. As a group, analyze the cultural values implied by the story or characters in the story.

3. In small groups, identify examples from your own experiences for each barrier to effective intercultural communication discussed in the text. Use one of the examples to develop a skit to perform for the rest of the class. See whether the class can identify which intercultural barrier your group is depicting. Also suggest how the skills and principles discussed in the chapter might have improved the communication in the situation you role-play.

| Was born outside the United States | Has attended a Native American powwow | Knows the significance of Angel Island | Is a morning person | Is a vegetarian | Has worked outside the United States |
|---|---|---|---|---|---|
| Has been to Australia | Can communicate in American Sign Language | Has attended a Cinco de Mayo celebration | Likes 20th-century classical music | Knows the significance of the Stonewall Riots | Knows which country's government the U.S. Constitution was modeled after |
| Has traveled outside the United States | Celebrates Hanukkah | Has had his or her last name mispronounced | Is a late-night person | Knows who Rosa Parks is | Knows the opening date of deer season or fishing season |
| Can name at least two traditionally black U.S. colleges | Has been a student for more than five years | Has a lesbian, gay, or bisexual friend | Has a Native American ancestor | Worked while going to high school | Has been to Europe |
| Is bilingual or multilingual | Knows what Kwanzaa is | Knows the meaning of Juneteenth | Knows the meaning of Jeri Curl | Has danced to Tex-Mex music | Can name the books of the Old or New Testament |
| Is an avid country music fan | Has been to a longhouse | Knows his or her Chinese birth sign | Has danced to zydeco music | Knows why many Irish people immigrated to the United States in the 1880s | Is an avid Dilbert fan |

## Diversity Bingo, Answers

| | | | | |
|---|---|---|---|---|
| | | American Sign is used by the hearing impaired to communicate. | Cinco de Mayo celebrates the Mexican victory over the French in 1862. | A 1969 police raid on a NY bar started the gay rights movement. |
| | A powwow is a Native American celebration. | Angel Island is where Chinese immigrants disembarked to enter the United States. | | |
| | Hanukkah is a Jewish holiday celebrating rededication of the Temple in 165 B.C. | | | Rosa Parks is a Black woman who refused to sit down in the back of a bus in Montgomery, Ala. |
| Howard, Hampton, Tuskegee, and Spelman are among notable African American colleges. | | | | |
| | Kwanzaa is an African American holiday. | Juneteenth celebrates the freeing of slaves in Texas in 1865. | Jeri Curl is hair treatment used by African Americans. | Tex-Mex music is a country swing style that originated in southern Texas. |
| | A longhouse is a Native American meeting place. | Chinese birth signs: Rat, Ox, Tiger, Rabbit, Dragon, Snake, Horse, Goat, Monkey, Rooster, Dog, Pig | Zydeco is a style of Cajun dance music popular in southern Louisiana. | There was a devastating potato famine in Ireland in the 1880s. |

### weblinks

http://www.cal.org/pubs/ncrcpubs.html  This site offers a wealth of information for people who teach and learn languages of other cultures.

http://www.thesurvivorproject.org  This site is maintained by a nonprofit organization that promotes understanding and acceptance of human diversity and human rights through education, oral history, and the arts.

http://community-2.webtv.net/SoundBehavior/ DIVERSITYFORSOUND/  This page highlights excellent links related to multicultural awareness and diversity. It also provides useful resource links for understanding the power of human differences.

http://www.inform.umd.edu/EdRes/Topic/WomensStudies/ Click on the link to "Gender Issues" to learn more about the development of women's studies at U.S. colleges and universities.

http://www.britsoc.org.uk/about/antirace.htm  Learn how social scientists use words and phrases when referring to ethnicity.

http://www.yforum.com  Visitors to the National Forum on People's Differences can ask questions about others and their religion, culture, gender, ethnicity, sexual preferences, or other topic that may be too personal or embarrassing to ask in person.

*CHURCH PICNIC*, 1988; 72 × 72, acrylic on canvas. Faith Ringgold © 1988. High Museum.

# Part Two

# Interpersonal Communication Skills

People judge you by your behavior, not by your intentions. The following four chapters focus on research-based communication skills that can help you monitor and shape your behavior to improve the quality of your relationships. Chapter 5 offers tips and strategies for listening to others and confirming your understanding of what you hear. Chapter 6 explores how the words people use and misuse affect relationships with others. Becoming other-oriented involves both listening to the words and reading the behavior cues of others. Chapter 7 focuses on the scope and importance of unspoken messages. We will explore the implications of the adage "Actions speak louder than words." Chapter 8 presents principles and skills to help you manage conflict and disagreements with others.

# Listening and Responding Skills

## OBJECTIVES

1. Describe five elements of the listening process.
2. Identify characteristics of four listening styles.
3. Understand why we listen, and list several important barriers to effective listening.
4. Identify ways to improve your other-orientation and listening skills.
5. Identify responding skills and understand strategies for improving them.

## OUTLINE

# I never learned anything while I was talking.

Larry King

*T*hink about your best friend. What are some of the qualities you most admire in your friend? Many people would respond that one of the most valued qualities in a friend is his or her just being there—supporting, comforting, and listening. As theologian Henri Nouwen so eloquently put it,

> Listening is much more than allowing another to talk while waiting for a chance to respond. Listening is paying full attention to others and welcoming them into our very beings. . . . Listening is a form of spiritual hospitality by which you invite strangers to become friends, to get to know their inner selves more fully, and even dare to be silent with you.[1]

Simply stated, friends listen. They listen even if we sometimes say foolish things. Again, Nouwen describes it well: "True listeners no longer have an inner need to make their presence known. They are free to receive, to welcome, to accept."[2] As we consider the essential skills of interpersonal communication, the skill of listening to others would be at or near the top of the list in terms of importance.[3] Skilled communicators do more than impassively listen—they appropriately respond to what we say. They confirm that they understand and care for us by providing both verbal and nonverbal feedback. In this chapter we explore the interpersonal communication skills of listening and responding.

You spend more time listening than participating in any other communication activity. In fact, you spend more time listening to others than doing almost anything else. Typical Americans spend more than 80 percent of an average day communicating with other people, and, as the pie chart in Figure 5.1 shows, they spend 45 percent of that communication time listening to others.[4] Ironically, most people's formal communication training focuses on writing, the activity to which they devote the least amount of communication time. Chances are that until now you have had no formal training in listening. In this chapter, we focus on this often neglected, yet quintessential, skill for developing quality interpersonal relationships. Listening is the process by which people learn the most about others. In addition, we explore ways to respond appropriately to others.

FIGURE *5.1*

**What You Do with Your Communication Time**

123

# Listening Defined

"**D**id you hear what I said?" demanded a father who had been lecturing his teenage son on the importance of hanging up his clothes. In fact, his son did *hear* him, but he may not have been *listening*. **Listening** is a complex process of selecting, attending to, constructing meaning from, remembering, and responding to verbal and nonverbal messages.[5] When we listen, we hear words and try to make sense out of what we hear. **Hearing** is the physiological process of decoding sounds. You hear when sound vibrations reach your eardrum and cause the middle ear bones—the hammer, anvil, and stirrup—to move. Eventually, these sound vibrations are translated into electrical impulses that reach the brain. In order to listen to something, you must first select that sound from competing sounds. Then you must attend to it, understand it, and remember it. A fifth activity—responding—confirms that listening has occurred.[6]

## Selecting

**Selecting** a sound is choosing one sound as you sort through the various sounds competing for your attention. As you listen to someone in an interpersonal context, you focus on the words and nonverbal messages of your partner. Even now, as you are reading this book, there are undoubtedly countless noises within earshot. Stop reading for a moment and sort through the various sounds around you. Do you hear music? Is there noise from outside? How about the murmur of voices, the tick of a clock, the hum of a computer, the whoosh of an air conditioner or furnace? To listen, you must select which of these sounds will receive your attention.

## Attending

After selecting a sound, you then **attend** to or focus on it. Attention can be fleeting. You may attend to the sound for a moment and then move on or return to other thoughts or other sounds. Typically, you attend to those sounds and messages that meet your needs or are consistent with what you think you should be focusing on. If you are hungry, you may select and then attend to a commercial for a sizzling burger or a crispy-crust pizza. Information that is novel or intense, or that somehow relates to you, also may capture your attention. And conflict, humor, new ideas, and real or concrete things command your attention more easily than abstract theories that do not relate to your interests or needs.

## Understanding

Whereas hearing is a physiological phenomenon, **understanding** is the process of assigning meaning to the sounds you select and to which you attend; to understand a

**listening.** Selecting, attending to, creating meaning from, remembering, and responding to verbal and nonverbal messages.

**hearing.** Physiological process of decoding sounds.

**selecting.** Sorting through various sounds competing for your attention.

**attending.** Focusing on a particular sound or message.

**understanding.** Assigning meaning to sounds.

message is to construct meaning from what you hear and see There are several theories about how you assign meaning to words you hear, but there is no universally accepted notion of how this process works. We know that people understand best if they can relate what they are hearing to something they already know. A well-advertised series of commercial foreign language tapes bases its guarantees of success on this principle, claiming that speakers of English can quickly learn to speak Spanish like a native by using mnemonic devices—for example, using the word *S-O-C-K-S* to remember the Spanish phrase *"Eso si, que es?"*

A second basic principle about how people understand others is this: The greater the similarity between individuals, the greater the likelihood for more accurate understanding. Individuals from different cultures who have substantially different religions, family lifestyles, values, and attitudes often have difficulty understanding each other, particularly in the early phases of a relationship.

You understand best that which you also experience. Perhaps you have heard the Montessori school philosophy: I hear, I forget; I see, I remember; I experience, I understand. Hearing alone does not create understanding. People hear over one billion words each year, but understand only a fraction of that number. They may not be attending to the words coming their way, or they may simply not know what some words mean. In Chapter 3 we discussed the processes involved in perception and observed that different people can reach dramatically different conclusions about the same events and messages, based on their previous experiences. A key to establishing relationships with others is trying to understand those differences in experience in order to arrive at a common meaning for the messages exchanged.

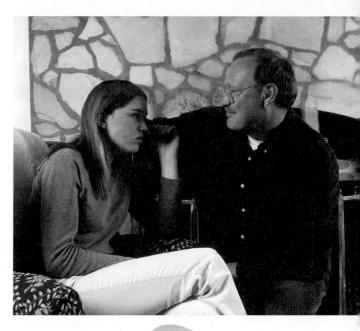

*H*ealthy family relations result when parents and children are able to develop people-oriented listening styles.

## Remembering

**Remembering** is recalling information. Some researchers theorize that you store every detail you have ever heard or witnessed; your mind operates like a video camera. But you cannot retrieve or remember all the tapes. Sometimes you were present, yet have no recollection of what occurred.

Human brains have both short-term and long-term memory storage systems. Short-term memory is where you store almost all the information you hear. You look up a phone number in the telephone book, mumble the number to yourself, then dial the number, only to discover that the line is busy. Three minutes later you have to look up the number again because it did not get stored in your long-term memory. Short-term storage is very limited. Just as airports have just a few short-term parking spaces, but lots of spaces for long-term parking, brains can accommodate a few things of fleeting significance, but acres of important information. Most of us forget hundreds of bits of insignificant information that pass through our brains each day.

The information stored in long-term memory includes events, conversations, and other data that are significant. People tend to remember dramatic and vital information, as well as seemingly inconsequential details connected with such information. Most people over the age of 45 today know exactly where they were on November 22, 1963, the day President Kennedy was assassinated. Many over the age of 65 can also recall where they were on December 7, 1941, when Japanese bombers attacked Pearl

**remembering.** Recalling information.

Harbor. Do you recall the day in April 1999, when students were indiscriminately shot at Columbine High School in Colorado? What were you doing on the morning of September 11, 2001, when you first heard that a plane had flown into the World Trade Center in New York? Information makes it to long-term memory because of its significance to us.

### Responding

Interpersonal communication is transactive; it involves both talking and responding. You are **responding** to people when you let them know you understand their messages. Responses can be nonverbal; direct eye contact and head nods let your partner know you're tuned in. Or you can respond verbally by asking questions to confirm the content of the message: "Are you saying you don't want us to spend as much time together as we once did?" or by making statements that reflect the feelings of the speaker: "So you are frustrated that you have to wait for someone to drive you where you want to go." We discuss responding skills in more detail later in the chapter.

**Recap**

### What Is Listening?

| | |
|---|---|
| **Selecting** | Sorting through various sounds that compete for your attention |
| **Attending** | Focusing on a particular sound or message |
| **Understanding** | Assigning meaning to sounds |
| **Remembering** | Recalling information |
| **Responding** | Confirming your understanding of a message |

## ℒistening Styles

What's your listening style? Do you focus more on the content of the message than on the feelings being expressed by the speaker? Or do you prefer brief sound bites of information? Your **listening style** is your preferred way of making sense out of the spoken messages you hear. Listening researchers Kitty Watson, Larry Barker, and James Weaver found that listeners tend to fall into one of four listening styles: people-oriented, action-oriented, content-oriented, or time-oriented.[7]

### People-Oriented Listeners

As you might suspect from the label, **people-oriented listeners** tend to be comfortable with and skilled at listening to people's feelings and emotions. They are likely to empathize and search for common areas of interest. People-oriented listeners embody many of the attributes of being other-oriented that we've discussed throughout the book—they seek strong interpersonal connections when listening to others. Preliminary evidence suggests that people-oriented listeners may be less apprehensive when interacting with others in small-group and interpersonal interactions.[8]

**responding.** Confirming your understanding of a message.

**listening style.** Preferred way of making sense out of spoken messages.

**people-oriented listener.** Listener who is comfortable with and skilled at listening to people's feelings and emotions.

## Action-Oriented Listeners

An **action-oriented listener** prefers information that is well organized, brief, and error-free. An action-oriented listener doesn't like the speaker to tell lengthy stories and digress. The action-oriented listener may think "Get to the point" or "What am I supposed to do with this information?" when hearing a message filled with too many anecdotes or rambling, disorganized bits of information. Whereas a people-oriented listener would be more likely to focus on the feelings of the person telling the story, the action-oriented listener wants to know the point or the punch line. There is new evidence to suggest that action-oriented listeners are more likely to be more skeptical when listening to information. Researchers call this skepticism **second-guessing**—questioning the ideas and assumptions underlying a message. Rather than taking the information they hear at face value, action-oriented listeners are more likely to reinterpret or evaluate the literal message to determine whether it is true or false—they make another guess (hence the term *second-guessing*) as to whether the information they are listening to is accurate.[9]

*"Are you listening to me?"*

## Content-Oriented Listeners

If you are a **content-oriented listener,** you are more comfortable listening to complex, detailed information than are people with other listening styles. A content-oriented listener hones in on the facts, details, and evidence in a message. In fact, if a message does not include ample supporting evidence and specific details, the content-oriented listener is more likely to reject the message. Like the action-oriented listener, content-oriented listeners are likely to make second guesses about the messages they hear. Content-oriented listeners are also less apprehensive when communicating with others in group and interpersonal situations.[10] Content-oriented listeners would make good judges or lawyers; they focus on issues and arguments and listen to see whether a speaker's conclusion is accurate or credible.

## Time-Oriented Listeners

You're a **time-oriented listener** if you like your messages delivered succinctly. Time-oriented listeners are keenly aware of how much time they have to listen. They have many things on their "to do" list; their "in basket" often overflows, so they want messages delivered quickly and briefly. Whereas a people-oriented listener might enjoy spending time over a cup of coffee catching up on the day's activities, a time-oriented listener is more like a drive-by listener—a time-oriented listener may think, "Give me what I need so I can keep on moving to my next task or hear my next message. Don't ramble, don't digress, just get to the point quickly."

Knowing your listening style can help you better understand how to adapt to various listening situations. If, for example, you know that you are a time-oriented or action-oriented listener and your friend or companion is a people-oriented listener, you and your friend will need to adjust your speaking and listening styles. When speaking to an action-oriented listener, give the listener a brief preview of what you will be talking about. You could say, "Phil, there are three things I'd like to share with you." Stick to that structure. When speaking to a people-oriented listener, realize that he or she will feel rushed or hurried if you skip information about feelings or relationships. A people-oriented listener prefers to spend more time talking about emotions than do

**action-oriented listener.** Listener who prefers information that is well-organized, brief, and error-free.

**second-guessing.** Questioning the ideas and assumptions underlying a message; assessing whether the message is true or false.

**content-oriented listener.** Listener who is more comfortable listening to complex, detailed information than are those with other listening styles.

**time-oriented listener.** Listener who likes messages delivered succinctly.

those with other listening styles. A time-oriented listener would like information summarized as in a concisely written business memo punctuated with bullets and lists of essential information.

What is the best listening style? It depends on the listening situation and the communication context and objectives. In a high-pressure, fast-paced job such as stock trading, you don't have time to listen to stories about clients' families or the latest TV show; you need information delivered quickly and efficiently. A father listening to a daughter talk about her rotten day at school, would find a people-oriented listening style better for listening to his daughter pour her heart out. Being aware of your own preferred listening style and the needs of your communication partner can help you adopt a listening style that best suits the situation.

## Listening Barriers

E ven though people spend so much of their communication time listening, most don't listen as well as they should. Twenty-four hours after you hear a speech, a class lecture, or a sermon, you have forgotten more than half of what was said. And it gets worse. In another twenty-four hours you have forgotten half of what you remembered, so you really remember only a quarter of the lecture.

Interpersonal listening skills are not much better. If anything, they may be worse. When you listen to a speech or lecture, you have a clearly defined listening role; one person talks, and you are expected to listen. But in interpersonal situations, you may have to alternate quickly between speaking and listening. This takes considerable skill and concentration. Often you are thinking of what you want to say next, rather than listening.

One surprising study found that we sometimes pay more attention to strangers than to intimate friends or partners. Married couples in the study tended to interrupt each other more often and were generally less polite to each other than were strangers involved in a decision-making task.[11] Apparently, we take listening shortcuts when communicating with others in close relationships. As Understanding Diversity: Who Listens Better, Men or Women? suggests, often the problem is gender related.

Most interpersonal listening problems can be traced to a single source—ourselves. While listening to others, we also "talk" to ourselves. Our internal thoughts are like a play-by-play sportscast. We mentally comment on the words and sights that we select and to which we attend. If we keep those comments focused on the message, they may be useful. But we often attend to our own internal dialogues instead of others' messages. Then our listening effectiveness plummets.

## *Understanding Diversity*

### Who Listens Better, Men or Women?

Research provides no definitive answer to the question "Who listens better, men or women?" There is evidence that men and women listen somewhat differently and have different expectations about the role of listening and talking. Deborah Tannen suggests that one of the most common complaints wives have about their husbands is "He doesn't listen to me anymore" along with "He doesn't talk to me anymore." Another scholar noted that complaints about lack of communication were usually at the top of women's lists of reasons for divorce but were mentioned much less often by men. Why are women more often dissatisfied with the listening and talking process than men? Tannen's explanation: Women expect different things from conversations than men expect.

One researcher suggests that men and women may have different atten-tion styles. When men listen, they may be looking for a new structure or organizational pattern, or trying to separate bits of information they hear. They continually shape, form, observe, inquire, and direct energy toward a chosen goal. Men's attention style is reported to be more emotionally controlled than women's attention style. Women are described as more subjective, empathic, and emotionally involved as they listen. They are more likely to search for relationships among parts of a pattern and to rely on more intuitive perceptions of feelings. They are also more easily distracted by competing details. Females may hear more of the message because they reject less of it. These differences in attention styles and the way men and women process information can potentially affect listening, even though we have no direct evidence linking attention style to listening skill.

Another researcher suggests that when men listen, they listen to solve a problem; men are more instrumental and task-oriented. Women listen to seek new information to enhance understanding. What are the implications of these research studies? They may mean that men and women focus on different parts of messages and have different listening objectives. These differences can affect relationship development. Males may need to recognize that while they are attending to a message and looking for new structure to solve a problem or achieve a goal, they may hear less of the message and therefore listen less effectively. And even though many females may hear more of the message, they may need to make connections between the parts of the information they hear to look for major ideas, rather than just focusing on the details. In any case, gender-based differences in attention style and information processing may account for some of the relational problems that husbands and wives, lovers, siblings, and male and female friends experience.[12]

---

Inattentive listening is a bit like channel surfing when we watch TV—pushing the remote control button to switch from channel to channel, avoiding commercials and focusing for brief periods on attention-grabbing programs. When we listen to others, we may fleetingly tune in to the conversation for a moment, decide that the content is uninteresting, and then focus on a personal thought. These thoughts are barriers to communication, and they come in a variety of forms.

Are we more attentive listeners to TV? Apparently not. One research team phoned TV viewers as soon as the evening news program was over. On average, most people remembered only about 17 percent of what they heard. And even when they were reminded of some of the news coverage, most averaged no better than 25 percent recall.[13] Even though more highly educated viewers did a little better, the overall conclusion is not good: We often don't "catch" what we hear, even a few moments after hearing it.

### Being Self-Absorbed

You're in your local grocery store during "rush hour." It appears that most of your community has also decided to forage for food at the same time. You are trying to get in and out of the store quickly, but many of the harried shoppers are oblivious to those around them. They stop in the aisle, blocking the path for others (including you). They elbow their way into crowded checkout stands. And the "express lane" that limits customers to ten items or fewer is backed up because more than one shopper has difficulty counting to ten. You find yourself becoming tense—not just because you are hungry, but because it seems the grocery store is filled with people who are self-absorbed; they are focused on getting their needs met and are oblivious the needs of others.

Self-absorbed listeners are focused on their needs rather than yours; the message is about *them,* not *you.* During conversations with a self-absorbed communicator, you have difficulty sustaining the conversation about anything except your self-absorbed partner's ideas, experiences, and stories. This problem is also called **conversational narcissism.** To be narcissistic is to be in love with oneself, like the mythical Greek character Narcissus, who became enamored with his reflection in a pool of water.[14]

The self-absorbed listener is actively involved in doing several things other than listening. The self-absorbed person is much more likely to interrupt others in mid-sentence. He or she is seeking ways to focus the attention on himself or herself.

The self-absorbed listener is also not focusing on his or her partner's message but thinking about what he or she is going to say next. This focus on an internal message can keep a listener from selecting and attending to the other person's message. If you are supposed to be listening to Aunt Mae tell about her recent trip to the Buckner County Fair, but you are eager to hit her up for a loan, your personal agenda will serve as a barrier to your listening ability. Or you may simply decide that Aunt Mae's monologue is boring and unimportant and give yourself permission to tune out as she drones on. Like humorist James Thurber's famous daydreamer, Walter Mitty, you may eventually find yourself unable to respond cogently, lost in your own world.[15]

How do you short-circuit this listening problem? First, diagnose it. Note consciously when you find yourself drifting off, thinking about your agenda rather than concentrating on the speaker. Second, throttle up your powers of concentration when you find your internal messages are distracting you from listening well. If you notice that you are telling yourself that Aunt Mae's anecdote is boring, you can also mentally remind yourself to listen with greater energy and focus.

### Unchecked Emotions

Words are powerful symbols that affect people's attitudes, behavior, and even blood pressure. Words arouse people emotionally. **Emotional noise** occurs when emotional

**conversational narcissism.** Focusing on personal agendas and being self-absorbed rather than focusing on the needs and ideas of others.

**emotional noise.** Form of communication interference caused by emotional arousal.

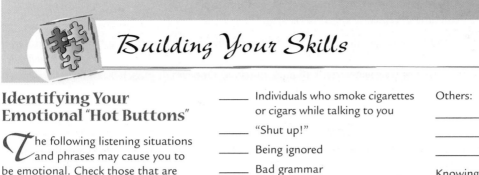

## Building Your Skills

### Identifying Your Emotional "Hot Buttons"

*T*he following listening situations and phrases may cause you to be emotional. Check those that are "hot buttons" for you as a listener, and add others that strongly affect you, positively or negatively.

_____ "You never/always . . ."

_____ Know-it-all attitudes

_____ Individuals who smoke cigarettes or cigars while talking to you

_____ "Shut up!"

_____ Being ignored

_____ Bad grammar

_____ "You never listen."

_____ Obscene language

_____ Whining

_____ "What you should do is . . ."

_____ Being interrupted

Others:

_____

_____

_____

Knowing what your emotional hot buttons are can help prevent your overreacting when they are pushed.

*Source:* Adapted from Diane Bone, *The Business of Listening* (Los Altos, CA: Crisp Publications, 1995), 52.

---

arousal interferes with communication effectiveness. If you grew up in a home in which R-rated language was never used, then four-letter words may be distracting to you. Words that insult your religious or ethnic heritage can be fighting words. Most people respond to certain trigger words like a bull to a waving cape; they want to charge in to correct the speaker or perhaps even do battle with him or her.

Sometimes it is not specific words, but rather concepts or ideas that cause an emotional eruption. Some talk-radio hosts try to boost their ratings by purposely using demagogic language that elicits passionate responses. Although listening to such conflict can be interesting and entertaining, when your own emotions become aroused, you may lose your ability to converse effectively. Unchecked emotions can interfere with focusing on the message of another.

The emotional state of the speaker may also affect your ability to understand and evaluate what you hear. If you are listening to someone who is emotionally distraught, you will be more likely to focus on his or her emotions than on the content of the message.[16] Communication author R. G. Owens advises that when you are communicating with someone who is emotionally excited, you should remain calm and focused and try simply to communicate your interest in the other person.[17]

Your listening challenge is to avoid emotional sidetracks and keep your attention focused on the message. When you find yourself distracted by emotional noise brought on by objectionable words or concepts, or by an emotional speaker, make an effort to quiet the noise and steer back to the subject at hand.

### Criticizing the Speaker

The late Mother Teresa once said, "If you judge people, you have no time to love them." Being critical of the speaker may distract a listener from focusing on the message. As you learned in Chapter 3, most people are distracted by appearances, forming impressions of others based solely on nonverbal information. Superficial factors such as clothing, body size and shape, age, and ethnicity all affect our interpretation of a message. In his essay "Black Men and Public Space," journalist Brent Staples provides this account of an incident that made communication impossible because of the way a woman reacted to his appearance:

> On assignment for a local paper and killing time before an interview, I entered a jewelry store on the city's affluent Near North Side. The proprietor excused herself and returned with an enormous red Doberman pinscher straining at the end of a leash. She stood, the dog extended toward me, silent to my questions, her eyes bulging nearly out of her head.[18]

Again, it is important to monitor your internal dialogue to make sure you are focusing on the message rather than criticizing the messenger. Good listeners say to themselves, "While it may be distracting, I am simply not going to let the appearance of this speaker keep my attention from the message."

### Differing Speech Rate and Thought Rate

Your ability to think faster than people speak is another listening pitfall. The average person speaks at a rate of 125 words a minute. Some folks talk a bit faster, others more slowly. In contrast, you have the ability to process up to 600 or 800 words a minute. The difference between your mental ability to handle words and the speed at which they arrive at your cortical centers can cause trouble, giving you time to daydream and to tune the speaker in and out, and giving you the illusion that you are concentrating more attentively than you actually are.[19]

You can turn your listening speed into an advantage if you use the extra time instead to summarize what a speaker is saying. By periodically sprinkling in mental summaries during a conversation, you can dramatically increase your listening ability and make the speech-rate/thought-rate difference work to your advantage.

### Shifting Attention

Some people can do two things at once, and some people can't. To be able to multitask—work on several tasks simultaneously—is a valued skill for administrative assistants, but some people have more difficulty multitasking than others. When it comes to listening to more than one message at a time, research suggests that men are more likely to have difficulty attending to multiple messages; when they are focused on a message, they may have more difficulty than women in carrying on a conversation with another person.[20] Men have a tendency to lock on to a message, while women seem more adept at shifting between two or more simultaneous messages. When many men watch a TV program, they may seem lost in their video world—oblivious to other voices around them. Women, on the other hand, are more likely to be carrying on a conversation with one person and also focusing on a message they may hear nearby. No, this difference doesn't mean that women are more likely to eavesdrop intentionally—simply that some women have greater potential to listen to two things at once.

What are the implications of this research? It may be especially important for women to stop and focus on the message of others, rather than on either internal or external competing messages. And men may need to be sensitive to others who may want to speak to them, rather than becoming oblivious to their surroundings and fixated on their own internal message or on a single external message such as sports, news, opera, or a movie on TV. Being able to stop competing thoughts and focus on a single message can enhance comprehension of the message on which you are focused.[21] It's useful, however, to make sure this message is the most important one to which you should be attending.

## Information Overload

We live in an information-rich age. We are all constantly bombarded with sights and sounds, and experts suggest that the volume of information competing for our attention is likely to become even greater in the future. Fax machines, car phones, audio feautures on computers, and other technological devices can interrupt conversations and distract us from listening to others.

Be on the alert for these information interruptions when you are talking with others. Don't assume that because you are ready to talk, the other person is ready to listen. If your message is particularly sensitive or important, you may want to ask your listening partner, "Is this a good time to talk?" Even if he or she says yes, look for eye contact and a responsive facial expression to make sure the positive response is genuine.

*I*nformation overload can prevent us from being able to communicate effectively with people around us.

## External Noise

As you will recall, all the communication models in Chapter 1 include the element of noise—distractions that take your focus away from the message. Many households seem to be addicted to noise. Often there is a TV on (sometimes more than one), a computer game beeping, and music emanating from another room. These and other sounds compete for your attention when you are listening to others.

Besides literal noise, there are other potential distractors. A headline in your evening paper about a lurid sex scandal may "shout" for your attention just when your son wants to talk with you about his latest science fiction story. A desire to listen to your new compact disk of "Pacific Overtures" may drown out your spouse's overtures to a heart-to-heart about your family's budget problems. The lure of music, TV, books, or your computer can all distract you from your listening task.

Distractions make it difficult to sustain attention to a message. You have a choice to make. You can attempt to listen through the labyrinth of competing distractions, or you can modify the environment to reduce them. Turning off the stereo, setting down the paper, and establishing eye contact with the speaker can help minimize the noise barrier.

## Listener Apprehension

Not only do some people become nervous and apprehensive about speaking to others, but some are anxious about listening to others. Listener apprehension is the fear of misunderstanding or misinterpreting, or of not being able to adjust psychologically to messages spoken by others.[22] Because some people are nervous or worried about missing the message, they *do* misunderstand the message; their fear and apprehension keep them from absorbing it. President Franklin Roosevelt's admonition that "The only thing we have to fear is fear itself" implies correctly that fear can become "noise" and keep people from listening to messages accurately. If you are one of those people who are nervous when listening, you may experience difficulty understanding all you hear.

If you're an apprehensive listener, you will have to work harder when you listen to others. When listening to a public speech, it may acceptable to use a tape or digital recorder or to start taking notes; it's not appropriate or even always possible to have a recorder or paper and pencil to take notes during interpersonal conversations. If you're on the phone, you can take notes when you listen to help you remember the message content, but taping phone conversations without the other speaker's consent is not ethical. Whether you're face-to-face with the speaker or on the phone, what you can do is try to mentally summarize the message as you're listening to it. Concentrating on the message by mentally summarizing what you hear can help take your mind off your anxiety and help you focus on the message.

## Recap

### Overcoming Barriers to Listening

| Listening Barrier | To Overcome the Barrier |
|---|---|
| **Being Self-Absorbed** | Consciously become aware of the self-focus and shift attention. |
| **Unchecked Emotions** | Use self-talk to manage emotions. |
| **Criticizing the Speaker** | Focus on the message, not the messenger. |
| **Differing Speech and Thought Rate** | Use the time difference between speech rate and thought rate to mentally summarize the message. |
| **Shifting Attention** | Focus on the most important message vying for your attention. |
| **Information Overload** | Realize when you or your partner is tired or distracted and not ready to listen. |
| **External Noise** | Take charge of the listening environment by eliminating distractions. |
| **Listener Apprehension** | Concentrate on the message as you mentally summarize what you hear. |

# Improving Listening, Comprehension, and Responding Skills

Many of the listening problems that we have identified stem from focusing on oneself rather than on the messages of others. Dale Carnegie, in his classic book *How to Win Friends and Influence People,* offered this tip to enhance interpersonal relationships: "Focus first on being interested, not interesting."[23] In essence, he was affirming the importance of being other-oriented when listening to others.

You can become a more other-oriented listener by following three steps you probably first encountered in elementary school: (1) stop, (2) look, and (3) listen; then (4) ask questions, and (5) reflect content by paraphrasing. Although these steps may seem simplistic, they can provide the necessary structure to help you refocus your mental energies and improve your listening power. These steps to improved listening are supported by a considerable body of listening research. Let's consider each step separately.

## Stop

Stop what? What should you *not* do in order to be a better listener? As noted earlier, while you are "listening" you may also be "talking" to yourself. Many of the barriers to improved listening skills relate to the focus people place on themselves and their own messages rather than on others. Your internal, self-generated messages may distract you from giving your undivided attention to what others are saying.

It boils down to this: When you listen, you are either on task or off task. When you are on task, you are concentrating on the message; when you're off task, your mind may be a thousand miles away. What's important is to be aware of what you are doing. A four-stage model of how people learn any skill, often attributed to psychologist Abraham Maslow, suggests that as people practice and develop the skill of decentering, they operate at one of four levels of competence:

- Unconscious incompetence

- Conscious incompetence

- Conscious competence

- Unconscious competence

The first level—*unconscious incompetence*—means you are unaware of your own incompetence. You don't know what you don't know. In this case, before you read this chapter, you may simply not have been aware that you can be distracted by your internal dialogue when you interact with others.

*In a noisy environment, listeners must carefully select the sounds of a conversation from an array of other sounds they are hearing.*

The second level is *conscious incompetence.* At this level you become aware or conscious that you are not competent; you know what you don't know. You may now be aware that you are an easily distracted listener, but you do not know how to solve the problem.

The third level is *conscious competence:* You are aware that you know something, but applying it has not yet become a habit. You might have to work at decentering when you first begin using it.

The final level of skill is *unconscious competence.* At this level your skills become second nature to you. After the age of six, most people are unconsciously competent at tying their shoes; it is automatic. In the same way, you may become so skilled in the decentering process that you do it as the rule rather than as an exception. At this level you will also probably have the capacity to empathize with others as you listen.

Two researchers studied how to enhance the performance of "professional listeners" who work in call centers, places where customers call to order products, make product suggestions, or even offer complaints.[24] They found that customers preferred listeners who were focused and communicated that they were devoting their full attention to the caller. Training listeners to avoid distractions, hone in on the essence of a caller's message, and stop and focus on what the callers were telling them increased customers' confidence and satisfaction in the speaker-listener relationship. The researchers also concluded that the ability to stop and focus on the comments of others can be taught. People who learn how to stop mental distractions can improve their listening comprehension.

## Look

Nonverbal messages are powerful. As the primary ways we communicate feelings, emotions, and attitudes, they play a major role in the total communication process, particularly in the development of relationships. Facial expressions and vocal cues, as well as eye contact, posture, and use of gestures and movement, can dramatically color the meaning of a message. When the nonverbal message contradicts the verbal message, people almost always believe the nonverbal message. In listening to others, it is vital that you focus not only on the words, but also on the nonverbal messages. Listen with your eyes as well as your ears.

Another reason to look at another person is to establish eye contact, which signals that you are focusing your interest and attention on him or her. If your eyes are darting over your partner's head, looking for someone else, or if you are constantly peeking at your watch, your partner will rightly get the message that you're not really listening. Researcher J. Harrigan found that people telegraph desire to change roles from listener to speaker by increasing eye contact, using gestures such as a raised finger, and shifting posture.[25] So it is important to maintain eye contact and monitor your partner's non-verbal signals when you are listening as well as when you are speaking.

It is important, however, not to be distracted by nonverbal cues that may prevent you from interpreting the message correctly. A research team asked one group of college students to listen to a counselor, and another group both to watch the counselor and to listen.[26] The students then rated the counselor's effectiveness. Students who both saw and heard the counselor perceived him as *less* effective, because his distracting nonverbal behaviors affected their evaluations. In Chapter 7, we provide more information about how to enhance your skill in interpreting the nonverbal messages of others.

## Listen

After making a concerted effort to stop distracting internal dialogue and to look for nonverbal cues, you will be in a better position to understand the verbal messages of others. To listen is to do more than focus on facts and message details; it is to search for the essence of the speaker's thoughts. We recommend the following strategies to help you improve your listening skill:

1. *Determine your listening goal.* You listen to other people for several reasons—to learn, to enjoy yourself, to evaluate, or to provide empathic support. With so many potential listening goals and options, it is useful to decide consciously what your listening objective is.

   If you are listening to someone give you directions to the city park, then your mental summaries should focus on the details of when to turn left and how many streets past the courthouse you go before you turn right. The details are crucial to achieving your objective. If, in contrast, your neighbor is telling you about her father's triple bypass operation, then your goal is to empathize. It is probably not important that you be able to recall when her father checked into the hospital or other details. Your job is to listen patiently and to provide emotional support. Clarifying your listening objective in your own mind can help you use appropriate skills to maximize your listening effectiveness.

2. *Transform listening barriers into listening goals.* If you can transform into listening goals the listening barriers you read about earlier, you will be well on your way to improving your listening skill. Make it a goal not to focus on your personal agenda. Make it a goal to use self-talk to manage emotional noise. Set a goal not to criticize the speaker. Remind yourself before each conversation to create mental summaries that capitalize on the differences between your information processing rate and the speaker's verbal delivery rate. And make it your business to choose a communication environment that is free of distraction from other incoming information or noise.

3. *When your listening goal is to remember a message, mentally summarize the details of the message.* This suggestion may seem to contradict the suggestion to avoid focusing only on facts; but if your goal is to be able to recall information, it is

important to grasp the details your partner provides. As we noted earlier, you can process words much more quickly than a person speaks. So periodically summarize the names, dates, and locations in the message. Organize the speaker's factual information into appropriate categories or try to place events in chronological order. Without a full understanding of the details, you will likely miss the speaker's major point.

4. *Mentally weave these summaries into a focused major point or series of major ideas.* Facts usually make the most sense when you can use them to help support an idea or major point. So, as you summarize, try to link the facts you have organized in your mind with key ideas and principles. Use facts to enhance your critical thinking as you analyze, synthesize, evaluate, and finally summarize the key points or ideas your listening partner is making.[27]

5. *Practice listening to challenging material.* To improve or even maintain any skill, you need to practice it. Listening experts suggest that listening skills deteriorate if people do not practice what they know. Listening to difficult, challenging material can sharpen listening skills, so good listeners practice by listening to documentaries, debates, and other challenging material rather than to material that entertains but does not engage them mentally.

## Ask Questions

Sometimes when someone has something momentous to share, the story tumbles out in a rambling, disorganized way. You can help sort through the story if you ask questions to identify the sequence of events. "What happened first?" and "Then what happened?" can help both you and your partner clarify what happened.

If your partner is using words or phrases that you don't understand, ask for definitions. "He's just so lackadaisical!" moans Mariko. "What do you mean by lackadaisical? Could you give me an example?" asks Reggie. Sometimes asking for an example helps the speaker sort through the events as well.

Of course, if you are trying to understand another's feelings, you can ask how he or she is feeling, or how the event or situation made him or her feel. Often, however, nonverbal cues are more revealing than a verbal disclosure about feelings and emotions.

## Reflect Content by Paraphrasing

The only way to know whether you understand a message is to check your understanding of the facts and ideas by paraphrasing your understanding. Verbally reflecting what you understood the speaker to say can dramatically minimize misunderstanding. Respond with a statement such as

"Are you saying . . ."

"You seem to be describing . . ."

"So the point you are making seems to be . . ."

"Here is what I understand you to mean . . ."

"So here's what seems to have happened . . ."

Then summarize the events, details, or key points you think the speaker is trying to convey. Your summary need not be a word-for-word repetition of what the speaker

# *Becoming Other-Oriented*

## Identifying Message Details and Major Ideas

How skilled are you at noting both the details of a message and its major ideas? To become a skilled listener, it's important to know how to identify both of these aspects of what someone is telling you. Here's a chance to practice your skill in identifying and remembering bits of information, as well as the main meaning of a message.

Read each of the following statements. After you have read each statement, cover it with your hand or a piece of paper. First, list as many of the details as you can recall from the message. Second, summarize your understanding of the major idea or key point of the message. As a variation on this activity, rather than reading the statement, have

someone read the statement to you and then identify the details and major idea.

*Statement 1:* "I'm very confused. I reserved our conference room for 1 P.M. today for an important meeting. We all know that conference space is tight. I reserved the room last week with the administrative assistant. Now I learn that you are planning to use the conference room at noon for a two-hour meeting. It's now 11 a.m. We need to solve this problem soon. I have no other option for holding my meeting. And if I don't hold my meeting today, the boss is going to be upset."

*Statement 2:* "Hello, Marcia? I'm calling on my cell phone. Where are you? I thought you were supposed to meet me at the circle drive 45 minutes ago. You know I can't be late for my seminar this evening. What do you mean, you're waiting at the circle drive? I don't see

you. No, I'm at Switzler Hall circle drive. You're where? No, that's not the circle drive I meant. I thought you'd know where I meant. Don't you ever listen? If you hurry, I can just make it to the seminar."

*Statement 3:* "Oh, Mary, I just don't know what to do. My daughter announced that when she turns 18 next week she's going to shave her head, get a large tattoo, and put a ring in her nose and eyebrow. She said it's something she's always wanted to do and now she can do it without my permission. She's always been such a sweet, compliant girl, but she seems to have turned wacky. I've tried talking with her. And her father isn't much help. He thinks it may look 'cool.' I just don't want her to look like a freak when she has her senior picture taken next month."

---

has said, nor do you need to summarize the content of *each* phrase or minor detail. Rather, you will **paraphrase** to check the accuracy of your understanding. Here is an example:

*Juan:*   This week I have so much extra work to do. I'm sorry if I haven't been able to help keep this place clean. I know it's my turn to do the dishes tonight, but I have to get back to work. Could you do the dishes tonight?

*Brigid:*   So you want me to do the dishes tonight and for the rest of the week. Right?

*Juan:*   Well, I'd like you to help with the dishes tonight. But I think I can handle it for the rest of the week.

*Brigid:*   OK. So I'll do them tonight and you take over tomorrow.

*Juan:*   Yes.

Research conducted in clinical counseling settings found that when a listener paraphrases the content and feelings of a speaker, the speaker is more likely to trust and value the listener.[28] Paraphrasing to check understanding is also a vital skill to use when you are trying to reconcile a difference of opinion. Chapter 8 shows you how to use it in that context.

**paraphrase.** A verbal summary of the key ideas of your partner's message that helps you check the accuracy of your understanding.

## Recap    How to Improve Your Listening Skills

| Step | Listening Skill | Action |
|---|---|---|
| **Stop** | Tune out distracting competing messages. | Become conscious of being distracted; use self-talk to remain focused. |
| **Look** | Become aware of the speaker's nonverbal cues; monitor your own nonverbal cues to communicate your interest in the speaker. | Establish eye contact; avoid fidgeting or performing other tasks when someone is speaking to you. Listen with your eyes. |
| **Listen** | Create meaning from your partner's verbal and nonverbal messages. | Mentally summarize details; link these details with main ideas. |
| **Ask questions** | Clarify the message by questioning the speaker. | Ask for definitions and examples; clarify feelings and sequences of events. |
| **Reflect content by paraphrasing when appropriate** | Briefly state the essence of what the speaker has said to ensure the accuracy of your understanding. | Summarize the key details, or points of what the speaker has said. |

## Improving Empathic Listening and Responding Skills

When your friends have "one of those days," perhaps they seek you out to talk about it. They may not have any real problems to solve—perhaps it was just a day filled with miscommunication and squabbles with their partners or coworkers. But they want to tell you the details. Your friends are seeking a listener who focuses attention on them and understands what they are saying. As we discussed in Chapter 4, at the heart of being other-oriented is cultivating **empathy**—feeling what someone else is feeling. The word *empathy* comes from a Greek word for "passion" and is related to the German word *Einfuhling*, which means "to feel with."

Developing empathy is not a single skill but a collection of skills that help you predict how others will respond. Daniel Goleman's book *Emotional Intelligence* is an outstanding resource that discusses the role and importance of our emotions in developing empathy with others.[29] Goleman has found evidence that people who are emotionally intelligent—sensitive to others, empathic, and other-oriented—have better interpersonal relationships. Goleman summarizes the centrality of emotions in developing empathy by quoting Antoine De Saint-Exupery: "It is with the heart that one sees rightly; what is essential is invisible to the eye."[30]

Good listening, especially listening to empathize with another, is active, not passive. To listen passively is to avoid displaying any behavior that lets the speaker know you are listening.[31] Passive listeners sit with a blank stare or a frozen facial expression. Their thoughts and feelings could be anywhere, for all the speaker knows. Those who engage in **active listening,** in contrast, respond mentally, verbally, and nonverbally to a speaker's message. Responding serves several specific functions. First, it can be a measure of how accurately you understood the message. If you burst out laughing as your friend tells you about losing his house in a flood, he'll know you misunderstood what he was saying. Second, your responses indicate whether you agree or disagree

**empathy.** Feeling what others are feeling, rather than just acknowledging that they are feeling a certain way.

**active listening.** Interactive process of responding mentally, verbally, and nonverbally to a speaker's message.

with the comments others make. If you tell your friend that you do not approve of her comments on abortion, she'll know your position on the information she shared. Finally, your responses tell speakers how they are affecting you. When you get tears in your eyes as you listen to your friend describe how lonely he has felt since his father died, he will know that you are affected by the pain he is feeling. Like radar that guides high-tech weapons, your feedback provides information to help others decide whether or not to correct the course of their messages.

Of course, listening to empathize is only one of the possible listening goals you may have. We are not suggesting that ferreting out someone's emotions is the goal of every listening encounter. That would be tedious for both you and your listening partners. But when you do want to listen empathically and respond, you must shift the focus to your partner and try to understand the message from his or her perspective.[32] Psychologist and counselor Carl Rogers summarized the value of empathy when he said, "A high degree of empathy in a relationship is possibly the most potent factor in bringing about change and learning."[33]

The quiz in Building Your Skills: Test Your Empathy Ability can help you determine how effectively you empathize with others. We then discuss strategies you can use to enhance your empathy skills.

# Building Your Skills

## Test Your Empathy Ability

Empathy is an emotional capability that often grows out of a conscious decentering process. It is the ability to move away from yourself enough to "feel with" another person. But feeling empathy does not mean abandoning your own self. On the contrary, empathic people often have a strong self-concept and high self-esteem, which enable them to be generous with others. Take this short test to assess your empathy. Respond to each statement by indicating the degree to which the statement is true regarding the way you typically communicate with others. When you think of how you communicate, is the statement (1) Always false, (2) Usually false, (3) Sometimes false and sometimes true, (4) Usually true, or (5) Always true?

_____  1. I try to understand others' experiences from their perspectives.

_____  2. I follow the Golden Rule ("Do unto others as you would have them do unto you") when communicating with others.

_____  3. I can "tune in" to emotions others are experiencing when we communicate.

_____  4. When trying to understand how others feel, I imagine how I would feel in their situation.

_____  5. I am able to tell what others are feeling without being told.

_____  6. Others experience the same feelings I do in any given situation.

_____  7. When others are having problems, I can imagine how they feel.

_____  8. I find it hard to understand the emotions others experience.

_____  9. I try to see others as they want me to.

_____ 10. I never seem to know what others are thinking when we communicate.

To find your score, first reverse the responses for the even-numbered items (if you wrote 1, make it 5; if you wrote 2, make it 4; if you wrote 3, leave it as 3; if you wrote 4, make it 2; if you wrote 5, make it 1). Next, add the numbers next to each statement. Scores range from 10 to 50. The higher your score, the more you are able to empathize.

_Source:_ William Gudykunst, _Bridging Differences_, 3rd ed. (Thousand Oaks, CA: Sage, 1998), 234.

### Understand Your Partner's Feelings: Imagine How You Would Feel

When your goal is to empathize with your partner, you might begin by imagining how you would feel under the same circumstances. If your spouse comes home dejected from being hassled at work, try to recall how you felt when that happened to you. If a friend calls to tell you his mother is ill, try to imagine how you would feel if the situation were reversed. Of course, your reaction to these events might be different from your spouse's or your friend's. You may need to decenter and remember how your partner felt in other similar situations, to understand how he or she is feeling now.

### Paraphrase Emotions

The bottom line in empathic responding is to make certain that you accurately understand how the other person is feeling. You can paraphrase, beginning with such phrases as

"So you are feeling . . ."

"You must feel . . ."

"So now you feel ..."

"Emotionally, you must be feeling . . ."

In the following example of empathic responding, the listener asks questions, summarizes content, and summarizes feelings.

*David:* I think I'm in over my head. My boss gave me a job to do, and I just don't know how to do it. I'm afraid I've bitten off more than I can chew.

*Mike:* (Thinks how he would feel if he were given an important task at work but did not know how to complete the task, then asks for more information.) What job did she ask you to do?

*David:* I'm supposed to do an inventory of all the items in the warehouse on the new computer system and have it finished by the end of the week. I don't have the foggiest notion of how to start. I've never even used that system.

*Mike:* (Summarizes feelings.) So you feel panicked because you may not have enough time to learn the system *and* do the inventory.

*David:* Well, I'm not only panicked, I'm afraid I may be fired.

*Mike:* (Summarizes feelings.) So your fear that you might lose your job is getting in the way of just focusing on the task and seeing what you can get done. It's making you feel like you made a mistake in taking this job.

*David:* That's exactly how I feel.

Note that toward the end of the dialogue Mike has to make a couple of tries to summarize David's feelings accurately. Also note that Mike does a good job of listening and responding without giving advice. Just by being an active listener, you can help your partner clarify a problem.

Researcher John Gottman summarizes several specific ways to make listening active rather than passive:[34]

- Start by asking questions.

- Ask questions about people's goals and visions of the future.

*Building Your Skills*

## Sympathy versus Empathy

Most card shops have a sympathy card section. Such cards let people know you realize they are feeling bad about something—perhaps the death of someone close to them. To offer **sympathy** is to offer your support and acknowledge that someone is feeling bad. Empathy goes one step further than sympathy. Empathy means that you try to perceive the world from another's perspective; you attempt to feel what someone else feels.

Respond to these sample situations with sympathy and with empathy.

1. A good friend just phoned to tell you that her well-loved fourteen-year-old dog has just died.

   Respond with sympathy: _____

   _____

   Respond with empathy: _____

   _____

   _____

2. Your older brother comes to visit you and tells you that he and his wife are getting a divorce after twenty years of marriage.

   Respond with sympathy: _____

   _____

   Respond with empathy: _____

   _____

   _____

*Source:* Adapted from William Gudykunst, *Bridging Differences,* 3rd ed. (Thousand Oaks, CA: Sage, 1998). Reprinted by permission of Sage Publications, Inc.

- Look for commonalities.
- Tune in with all your attention.
- Respond with an occasional brief nod or sound.
- From time to time, paraphrase what the speaker says.
- Maintain the right amount of eye contact.
- Let go of your own agenda.

We have discussed responding and active listening using a tidy step-by-step text-book approach. In practice, you may have to back up and clarify content, ask more questions, and rethink how you would feel before you attempt to summarize how someone else feels. Conversely, you may be able to summarize feelings *without* asking questions or summarizing content if the message is clear and it relates to a situation with which you are very familiar. Overusing paraphrasing can slow down a conversation and make the other person uncomfortable or irritated. But if you use it judiciously, paraphrasing can help both you and your partner keep focused on the issues and ideas at hand.

Reflecting content or feeling through paraphrasing can be especially useful in the following situations:

- Before you take an important action
- Before you argue or criticize
- When your partner has strong feelings or wants to talk over a problem
- When your partner is speaking "in code" or using unclear abbreviations
- When your partner wants to understand your feelings and thoughts

**sympathy.** Acknowledgment that someone is feeling bad.

- When you are talking to yourself
- When you encounter new ideas[35]

Sometimes, however, you truly don't understand how another person really feels. At times like this, be cautious of telling others, "I know just how you feel." It may be more important simply to let others know that you care about them than to grill them about their feelings.

If you do decide to use paraphrasing skills, keep the following guidelines in mind:

- Use your own words.

- Don't go beyond the information communicated by the speaker.

- Be concise.

- Be specific.

- Be accurate.

Do *not* use paraphrasing skills if you aren't able to be open and accepting, if you do not trust the other person to find his or her own solution, if you are using these skills as a way of hiding yourself from another, or if you feel pressured, hassled, or tired. And as we have already discussed, overuse of paraphrasing can be distracting and unnatural.

Don't be discouraged if your initial attempts to use these skills seem awkward and uncomfortable. Any new skill takes time to learn and use well. The instructions and samples you have read should serve as guides, rather than as hard-and-fast prescriptions to follow during each conversation.

## *Building Your Skills*

### Listening and Paraphrasing Content and Emotion

*W*orking in groups of three, ask person A to briefly identify a problem or conflict that he or she is having (or has had) with another person (coworker, supervisor, spouse, or family member). Person B should use questioning, content paraphrasing, and emotion paraphrasing skills to explore the problem. Person C should observe the discussion and evaluate person B's listening and paraphrasing skills, using the Observer Checklist. Make a check mark next to all of the skills that person B uses effectively.

### Observer Checklist

**Nonverbal Skills**

_____ Direct eye contact

_____ Open, relaxed body posture

_____ Uncrossed arms

_____ Uncrossed legs

_____ Appropriate hand gestures

_____ Reinforcing head nods

_____ Responsive facial expression

_____ Responsive tone of voice

_____ Appropriate volume

**Verbal Skills**

_____ Effective and appropriate questions

_____ Accurate paraphrase of content

_____ Accurate paraphrase of emotion

_____ Timely paraphrase

_____ No interruptions

# applying theory and research

## *Listening to Others' Stories as Co-Storyteller*

A study conducted by communication researchers Janet Bavelas, Linda Coates, and Trudy Johnson sought to investigate what kinds of responses listeners make when listening to a personal story and how those responses affect the speaker. To investigate the effect of listeners' responses to a storyteller, they had one person listen and another person tell a story about a time when she or he had experienced a close call—such as narrowly missing being hurt or injured. In one condition the listener was just to listen and make no comments. In the second condition, the listener was to listen and summarize the gist of what the speaker was saying in a sentence or two. The third condition had the listener actively paraphrase what the speaker was saying. For the fourth condition, the listeners were to listen while mentally counting how many days it was until Christmas. Although this last condition sounds like a bizarre task, the purpose was to explore the effects of having a listener supposedly listening but not paying attention to what the speaker was saying. The researchers wanted to know whether how a listener responded to what a speaker was saying had an impact on how the speaker told the story.

## Applying
### the Research to Your Life

The researchers found out that when the listener made no responses

to the speaker, the speaker told the story less effectively. When speakers had a listener who made specific responses and responded in meaningful ways, the speakers were better at telling their story. The researchers also discovered that listeners are more likely to make specific rather than general comments later in the narrative. This observation makes sense; more specific comments are more likely to occur later in a story because the listener has had time to learn about the major elements in the story he or she is listening to. The results suggest that an effective listener is really a "co-narrator," or active participant in the communication process, rather than merely a passive listener. It's not that specific comments are better than general comments; what's important is that the responses the listener makes should be appropriate—comments that fit the story can actually help the speaker gauge how effectively he or she is telling the story. And without any responses, the speaker may think the listener isn't really interested in the story. The kinds of responses a listener makes during an effective conversation are different than those a listener makes if a speaker is delivering a monologue. Because communication is transactive, a dynamic process in which meaning is created between speaker and listener, the kinds of responses a listener makes should be authentic, not "canned" or stilted.

What do these results mean to you? If, while your friend is pouring

her heart out about the exasperating experience of having a flat tire in the rain, you respond with a vacant look and periodically grunt, "Uh-uh," or "OK," or " Ah," your mumbles may lead your friend to believe you aren't really listening all that closely. And if your friend thinks you aren't interested or listening to her story, she may either cut the story short or try to throttle up the drama of the story to get your attention. On the other hand, if you appropriately paraphrase the worst parts of her experience, or provide well-timed responses that fit with what she is saying, she's more likely to believe that you are really listening and that you care about her ordeal.

Empathic listeners respond at appropriate times, with appropriate words and phrases; they don't just mumble responses here and there. Responding to a speaker is, in some respects, like being a co-storyteller or co-narrator of the story; your listening and responding help shape the story. So if you're listening to someone tell a boring story, it may be partially your fault. A good listener can help bring out the best in a speaker.

*Source:* J. B. Bavelas, L. Coates, and T. Johnson, "Listeners as Co-Narrators," *Journal of Personality and Social Psychology,* 79, 6 (2000): 941–952.

## Listen

When I ask you to listen to me and you start giving advice,
    you have not done what I asked.
When I ask you to listen to me and you begin to tell me why I shouldn't feel that way,
    you are trampling on my feelings.
When I ask you to listen to me and you feel you have to do something
    to solve my problems, you have failed me, strange as that may seem.
Listen! All I asked, was that you listen. Not talk or do—just hear me.
Advice is cheap: 50 cents will get you both Dear Abby and Billy Graham
    in the same newspaper.
And I can do for myself; I'm not helpless. Maybe discouraged and faltering,
    but not helpless.
When you do something for me that I can and need to do for myself,
    you contribute to my fear and weakness.
But when you accept as a simple fact that I do feel what I feel,
    no matter how irrational, then I quit trying to convince you and
    can get about the business of understanding what's behind this irrational feeling.
And when that's clear, the answers are obvious and I don't need advice.
Irrational feelings make sense when we understand what's behind them.
Perhaps that's why prayer works, sometimes, for some people—
    because God is mute, and doesn't give advice or try to fix things,
    God just listens and lets you work it out for yourself.
So, please listen and just hear me, and, if you want to talk,
    wait a minute for your turn, and I'll listen to you.

Anonymous

## Responding to Confirm or Disconfirm Others

**Couple A:**

*Wife to husband:* "I just don't feel appreciated anymore."

*Husband to wife:* "Margaret, I'm so very sorry. I love you. You're the most important person in the world to me."

**Couple B:**

*Wife to husband:* "I just don't feel appreciated anymore."

*Husband to wife:* "Well, what about my feelings? Don't my feelings count? You'll have to do what you have to do. What's for dinner?"

It doesn't take an expert in interpersonal communication to know that Couple B's relationship is not warm and confirming. Researchers have studied the specific kinds of responses people offer to others.[36] Some responses are confirming; other responses are disconfirming. A **confirming response** is an other-oriented statement that causes others to value themselves more; Wife A is likely to value herself more after her husband's confirming response. A **disconfirming response** is a statement that causes others to value themselves less. Wife B knows first-hand what it's like to have her feelings ignored and disconfirmed. Are you aware of whether your responses to others confirm

**confirming response.** Statement that causes another person to value himself or herself more.

**disconfirming response.** Statement that causes another person to value himself or herself less.

them or disconfirm them? To help you be more aware of the kinds of responses you make to others, we'll review the results of studies that identify both confirming and disconfirming responses.[37]

### Provide Confirming Responses

The adage "People judge us by our words and behavior rather than by our intent" summarizes the underlying principle of confirming responses. Those who receive your messages determine whether they have the effect you intended. Formulating confirming responses requires careful listening and attention to the other person. Does it really matter whether we confirm others? Marriage researcher John Gottman used video cameras and microphones to observe couples interacting in an apartment over an extended period of time. He found that a significant predictor of divorce was neglecting to confirm or affirm one's marriage partner during typical, everyday conversation—even though couples who were less likely to divorce spent only a few seconds more confirming their partner than couples who eventually did divorce. His research conclusion has powerful implications: Long-lasting relationships are characterized by supportive, confirming messages.[38] We will describe several kinds of confirming responses in this section.

### Direct Acknowledgment

When you respond directly to something another person says to you, you are acknowledging not only the statement, but also that the person is worth responding to.

*Joan:*    It certainly is a nice day for a canoe trip.

*Mariko:*  Yes, Joan, it's a great day to be outside.

### Agreement About Judgments

When you confirm someone's evaluation of something, you are also affirming that person's sense of taste and judgment.

*Nancy:*  I think the steel guitar player's riff was fantastic.

*Victor:*  Yes, I think it was the best part of the performance.

### Supportive Response

When you express reassurance and understanding, you are confirming a person's right to his or her feelings.

*Lionel:*  I'm disappointed that I only scored 60 on my interpersonal communication test.

*Sarah:*   I'm sorry to see you so frustrated, Lionel. I know that test was important to you.

### Clarifying Response

When you seek greater understanding of another person's message, you are confirming that he or she is worth your time and trouble. Clarifying responses also encourage the other person to talk in order to explore his or her feelings.

*Larry:*   I'm not feeling very good about my family situation these days.

*Tyrone:*  Is it tough with you and Margo working different shifts?

### Expression of Positive Feeling

We feel confirmed or valued when someone else agrees with our expression of joy or excitement.

*Lorraine:*  I'm so excited! I was just promoted to associate professor.

*Dorette:*   Congratulations! I'm so proud of you! Heaven knows you deserve it.

## Compliment

When you tell people you like what they have done or said, what they are wearing, or how they look, you are confirming their sense of worth.

*Jean-Christophe:* Did you get the invitation to my party?

*Manny:* Yes! It looked so professional. I didn't know you could do calligraphy. You're a talented guy.

In each of these examples, note how the responder provides comments that confirm the worth or value of the other person. But keep in mind that confirming responses should be sincere. Offering false praise is manipulative, and your communication partner will probably sniff out your phoniness.

## Avoid Disconfirming Responses

Some statements and responses can undermine another person's self-worth. We offer these categories so that you can avoid using them and also recognize them when someone uses them to chip away at your self-image and self-esteem.

### Impervious Response

When a person fails to acknowledge your statement or attempt to communicate, even though you know he or she heard you, you may feel a sense of awkwardness or embarrassment.

*Rosa:* I loved your speech, Harvey.

*Harvey:* (No response, verbal or nonverbal.)

### Interrupting Response

When people interrupt you, they are implying that what they have to say is more important than what you have to say. In effect, they could also be implying that they are more important than you are.

*Anna:* I just heard on the news that . . .

*Sharon:* Oh yes. The stock market just went down 100 points.

### Irrelevant Response

An irrelevant response is one that has nothing at all to do with what you were saying. Chances are your partner is not listening to you at all.

*Arnold:* First we're flying down to Rio, and then to Quito. I can hardly wait to . . .

*Peter:* They're predicting a hard freeze tonight.

The real message Peter is sending is "I have more important things on my mind."

### Tangential Response

A tangential response is one that acknowledges you, but that is only minimally related to what you are talking about. Again, it indicates that the other person isn't really attending to your message.

*Richard:* This new program will help us stay within our budget.

*Samantha:* Yeah. I think I'll save some bucks and send this letter by regular mail.

### Impersonal Response

A response that intellectualizes and uses the third person distances the other person from you and has the effect of trivializing what you say.

*Diana:* Hey, Bill. I'd like to talk with you for a minute about getting your permission to take my vacation in July.

*Bill:* One tends to become interested in recreational pursuits about this time of year, doesn't one?

### Incoherent Response

When a speaker mumbles, rambles, or makes some unintelligible effort to respond, you may end up wondering if what you said was of any value or use to the listener.

*Paolo:* George, here's my suggestion for the merger deal with Techstar. Let's make them an offer of forty-eight dollars a share and see how they respond.

*George:* Huh? Well . . . so . . . well . . . hmmm . . . I'm not sure.

### Incongruous Response

When a verbal message is inconsistent with nonverbal behavior, people usually believe the nonverbal message, but they usually feel confused as well. An incongruous response is like a malfunctioning traffic light with red and green lights flashing simultaneously—you're just not sure whether the speaker wants you to go or stay.

*Sue:* Honey, do you want me to go grocery shopping with you?

*Steve:* (Shouting) OF COURSE I DO! WHY ARE YOU ASKING?

Although it may be impossible to eliminate all disconfirming responses from your repertoire, becoming aware of the power of your words and monitoring your conversation for offensive phrases may help you avoid unexpected and perhaps devastating consequences.

 *Recap*

## How to Respond with Empathy

| Responding with Empathy | Action |
| --- | --- |
| Understand Your Partner's Feelings | Ask yourself how you would feel if you had experienced a similar situation, or recall how you did feel under similar circumstances. Or recall how your partner felt under similar circumstances. |
| Paraphrase Emotions | When appropriate, try to summarize what you think your partner may be feeling. |
| Provide Confirming Responses | Acknowledge what others say to you, confirm others' judgments, offer supportive responses, seek to clarify others' messages, affirm others' positive feelings, and pay sincere compliments. |
| Avoid Disconfirming Responses | Provide some acknowledgment of others' attempts to communicate; do not interrupt; avoid irrelevant, tangential, impersonal, incoherent, or incongruous responses. |

# Improving Critical Listening and Responding Skills

After putting it off for several months, you've decided to buy a mobile phone. As you begin to talk to your friends, you're surprised to find a bewildering number of factors to consider: Do you want digital? Cellular? Voice mail? Do you want your phone to take photos? How many weekend minutes, evening minutes, or daily minutes of calling time do you need? You decide to head to a store to see if a salesperson can help you sort through the maze of options. The salesperson is friendly enough, but you become even more overwhelmed with the number of options, bells, and whistles to consider. As you try to make this decision, your listening goal is not to empathize with those who extol the virtues of mobile phones. Nor do you need to take a multiple-choice test on the information they share. To sort through the information, you need to listen critically.

Critical listening involves listening to evaluate the quality, appropriateness, value, or importance of the information you hear. *The goal of a critical listener is to use information to make a choice.* Whether you're selecting a new phone, deciding whom to vote for, choosing a potential date, or evaluating a new business plan, you will be faced with many opportunities to use your critical listening skills in interpersonal situations.

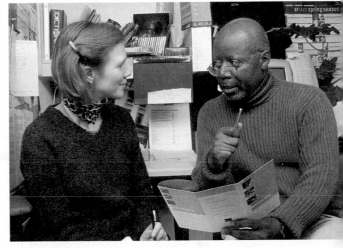

*Effective critical listening skills are crucial in a business environment.*

## Identify Useful and Flawed Information

A critical listener does not necessarily offer negative comments. A critical listener seeks to identify both good information and information that is flawed or less helpful. We call this process *information triage*. *Triage* is a French term that usually describes the process used by emergency medical personnel to determine which of several patients is the most severely ill or injured and needs immediate medical attention. **Information triage** is a process of evaluating and sorting out information. An effective critical listener performs information triage; he or she is able to distinguish useful and accurate information and conclusions from information that is less useful, as well as conclusions that are inaccurate or invalid.

How do you develop the ability to perform information triage? Initially, listening critically involves the same strategies as listening to comprehend, we discussed earlier. Before you evaluate information, it's vital that you first *understand* the information. Second, examine the logic or reasoning used in the message. And finally, be mindful of whether you are basing your evaluations on facts (something observed or verifiable) or inference (a conclusion based on partial information). Although courses in logic, argumentation, and public speaking often present skills to help you evaluate information, it's also important to listen critically during interpersonal conversations.

## Avoid Jumping to Conclusions

Imagine that you are a detective investigating a death. You are given the following information: (1) Leo and Moshia are found lying together on the floor; (2) Leo and Moshia are both dead; (3) Leo and Moshia are surrounded by water and broken glass; (4) on the sofa near Leo and Moshia is a cat with its back arched, apparently ready to defend itself.

**critical listening.** Listening to evaluate and assess the quality, appropriateness, value, or importance of information.

**information triage.** Process of evaluating information to sort good information from less useful or valid information.

Given these sketchy details, do you, the detective assigned to the case, have any theories about the cause of Leo and Moshia's demise? Perhaps they slipped on the water, crashed into a table, broke a vase, and died (that would explain the water and broken glass). Or maybe their attacker recently left the scene, and the cat is still distressed by the commotion. Clearly, you could make several inferences (conclusions based on partial information) as to the probable cause of death. Oh yes, there is one detail we forgot to mention: Leo and Moshia are fish. Does that help?

People often spin grand explanations and hypotheses based on sketchy details. Acting on inferences, people may act as though the "facts" clearly point to a specific conclusion. Determining the difference between a fact and an inference can help you more accurately use language to reach valid conclusions about what you see and experience.

What makes a fact a fact? Most students, when asked this question, respond by saying, "A fact is something that has been proven true." If that is the case, *how* has something been proven true? In a court of law, a **fact** is something that has been observed or witnessed. Anything else is speculation or inference.

> "Did you see my client in your house, taking your jewelry?" asks the wise attorney.
> "No," says the plaintiff.
> "Then you do not know for a fact that my client is a thief."
> "I guess not," the plaintiff admits.

Problems occur when we respond to something as if it were a fact (something observed), when in reality it is an **inference** (a conclusion based upon speculation):

> "It's a fact that your mother doesn't like me."
> "It's a fact that you will be poor all of your life."
> "It's a fact that you will fail this course."

Each of these statements, although it might very well be true, misuses the term *fact*. If you cannot recognize when you are making an inference instead of stating a fact, you may give your judgments more credibility than they deserve. Being sensitive to the differences between facts and inferences can improve both critical listening and responding skills.

## ♪mproving Your Responding Skills

**W**e've offered several strategies for responding to others when your goal is to comprehend information, empathize with others, or evaluate messages. Regardless of your communication goal, you can use several additional strategies to enhance your skill in responding to others. The timing of the response, usefulness of the information, amount of detail, and descriptiveness of the response are important to consider when responding to others.

### Provide Well-Timed Responses

Feedback is usually most effective when you offer it at the earliest opportunity, particularly if your objective is to teach someone a skill. For example, if you are teaching your friend how to make your famous egg rolls, you provide a step-by-step commentary as you watch your pupil. If he makes a mistake, you don't wait until the egg rolls are finished to tell him that he left out the cabbage. He needs immediate feedback to finish the rest of the sequence successfully.

**fact.** Something that has been directly observed to be true and thus has been proven to be true.

**inference.** Conclusion based on speculation.

Sometimes, however, if a person is already sensitive and upset about something, delaying feedback can be wise. Use your critical thinking skills to analyze when feedback will do the most good. Rather than automatically offering immediate correction, use the just-in-time (JIT) approach and provide feedback just before the person might make another mistake. If, for example, your daughter typically rushes through math tests and fails to check her work, remind her right before her next test to double-check her answers, not immediately after the one she just failed. To provide feedback about a relationship, select a mutually agreeable place and time when both of you are rested and relaxed; avoid hurling feedback at someone "for his own good" immediately after he offends you.

*When* you are teaching someone a new skill, the timing of your feedback is just as important as what you say. When should this grownup tell the child he is helping how to improve his handstand?

## Provide Usable Information

Perhaps you've heard this advice: Never try to teach a pig to sing. It wastes your time. It doesn't sound pretty. And it annoys the pig. When you provide information to someone, be certain that it is useful and relevant. How can you make sure your partner can use the information you share? Put yourself in your partner's mind-set. Ask yourself, "If I were this person, how would I respond to this information? Is it information I can act on? Or is it information that may make matters worse?" Under the guise of providing effective feedback, you may be tempted to tell others your complete range of feelings and emotions. But research suggests that selective feedback is best. In one study, married couples who practiced selective self-disclosure were more satisfied than couples who told everything they knew or were feeling.[39] Immersing your partner in information that is irrelevant or that may be damaging to the relationship may be cathartic, but it may not enhance the quality of your relationship or improve understanding.

## Avoid Unnecessary Details

When you are selecting meaningful information, also try to cut down on the volume of information. Don't overwhelm your listener with details that obscure the key point of your feedback. Hit only the high points that will benefit the listener. Be brief.

## Be Descriptive Rather Than Evaluative

"You're an awful driver!" shouts Doris to her husband, Frank. Although Doris may feel she has provided simple feedback to her spouse about his skills, Frank will probably not respond warmly or even listen closely to her feedback. If Doris were to be more descriptive and less evaluative, then he might be inclined to listen: "Frank, you are traveling 70 miles an hour in a 50 miles an hour zone" or "Frank, I get very nervous when you zigzag so fast through the freeway traffic" is a less offensive comment. It describes Frank's behavior rather than rendering judgments about him that are likely to trigger a defensive response.

# Building Your Skills

## Practicing Your Responding Skills

The purpose of this exercise is to help you practice your responding skills. Read each of the following situations and then write each of the four types of responses, just as if you were talking to someone:

1. *Ask questions:* Probe for more information.

2. *Paraphrase content:* What is the essence of the message?

3. *Provide a decentering response:* What is the other person thinking?

4. *Provide an empathic response:* What is the other person feeling?

Now pair up with another person and compare your responses. If necessary, revise one or more of your responses to make sure it is appropriate.

*Situation 1:* "I'm not sure what to do. My life seems consumed with work. I'm trying to go to school, I work more than 20 hours a week, and when I get home I have the kids to take care of. I'm exhausted. But I can't quit my job; I need the money. And if I drop out of school, it just means I'll be stuck with a minimum-wage job longer. I have to take care of my kids—I can't just stop meeting their needs. But what about me? I'm exhausted, and I know I can't keep going on like this."

*Situation 2:* "I'm really struggling with what to do about my religion. When I was growing up, my family and I would always attend a very liberal church; there were few rules and no list of do's and don'ts. As I've grown older, my beliefs have changed. I need more structure in my life. I've started worshiping with another group that offers more fundamental views toward religion. The problem is that my parents, family, and even many of my friends believe I'm betraying them and my own heritage; my change in worship habits is affecting my relationship with them. I just don't feel comfortable worshiping as I used to, but I also don't want to create conflict with my family and friends."

*Situation 3:* "I'm really not sure what to do about my relationship with Ben. We've been together for about a year now. I moved in with him a couple of months ago. But lately we've had more friction between us; we seem to disagree about more things. It seems to me that we want different things out of our relationship. I'm comfortable with just keeping things as they are, but Ben would like to make a more serious commitment. The increased conflict we're having makes me question whether our relationship will work out long term."

*Source:* Adapted from David W. Johnson, *Reaching Out: Interpersonal Effectiveness and Self-Actualization* (Boston: Allyn & Bacon, 2000), 234.

---

 **Recap**

## Suggestions for Improving Responding Skills

| | |
|---|---|
| **Provide Well-Timed Responses** | Sometimes immediate feedback is best; at other times provide a just-in-time (JIT) response when it will do the most good. |
| **Provide Meaningful Information** | Select information that your partner can act on, rather than making vague comments or suggestions that are beyond his or her capabilities. |
| **Avoid Unnecessary Details** | Avoid information overload; be brief. |
| **Be Descriptive** | Don't evaluate your listening partner; focus on behavior rather than on personality. |

# Summary

Listening effectively to others is the quintessential skill required for establishing other-oriented relationships. Listening—a complex process of receiving, constructing meaning from, and responding to verbal and nonverbal messages—involves selecting, attending, understanding, remembering, and responding. Preferred listening styles vary. Some of us are people-oriented listeners; some are action-oriented; others are content-oriented; and still others are time-oriented.

Most of us don't listen effectively because we are self-oriented instead of other-oriented. Barriers to effective listening include being self-absorbed, being distracted by unchecked emotions, criticizing the speaker, not taking advantage of the difference between speech rate and thought rate, shifting attention, being distracted by information overload and external noise, and experiencing listener apprehension.

To become better listeners, we can pursue three seemingly simple steps: Stop, look, and listen. To stop means to avoid tuning in to our own distracting messages and to become mindful of what others are saying. To look is to observe and interpret unspoken messages. Nonverbal communication skills and principles are discussed in greater detail in Chapter 7. After stopping and looking, we can then listen more effectively to others by focusing on details and the speaker's key ideas. Being other-oriented does not mean we should abandon our own convictions or values, but that we should make a conscious effort to pay attention to the needs and concerns of others. After we complete these three steps, we should ask questions and reflect content by paraphrasing.

We can further improve our ability to listen and respond empathically by seeking to understand our partner's feelings, paraphrasing his or her emotions, and providing confirming responses. We can further improve our ability to listen and respond critically by looking for faulty logic and becoming competent at distinguishing facts from inferences. And we can improve our skills at responding, regardless of the communication objective, by providing well-timed responses, providing usable information, avoiding unnecessary details, and being descriptive rather than evaluative.

# For Discussion and Review

## Focus on Critical Thinking

1. Identify two situations during the past twenty-four hours in which you were an effective or ineffective listener. What factors contributed to your listening skill (or lack of skill)?

2. Miranda and Salvador often disagree about who should handle some of the child-rearing tasks in their home. When they have discussions about these issues, what are some effective listening skills and strategies that they could use to make sure they understand each other?

3. Jason and Chris are roommates. They both work hard each day and come home exhausted. What suggestions would you offer to help them listen effectively even when they are tired?

## Focus on Ethics

4. Is it possible for paraphrasing and active listening to become a way to manipulate others? Support your answer.

5. Your friend asks you how you like her new dress. You really feel it is a bit too revealing and may embarrass her. But it is time to leave for an appointment. Should you respond honestly, even though it may mean that you and your friend will be late for important engagements?

6. Your roommate wants to tell you about his day. You are tired and really don't want to hear all the details. Should you fake attention so that you won't hurt his feelings, or simply tell your roommate you are tired and would rather not hear the details?

# For Your Journal

1. Use the following checklist, first published in the *International Listening Association Newsletter,* to monitor your listening problems for one full day.

   ### A Checklist for Listeners

   Today I . . .

   Interrupted other people _____ times.

   Misunderstood other people _____ times.

   Lost track of a conversation _____ times.

   Stopped making eye contact with a speaker _____ times.

   Asked someone to repeat himself/herself _____ times.

   Let my mind wander while listening to someone _____ times.

   Changed the subject in the middle of a conversation _____ times.

   Jumped to a conclusion about what someone was going to say _____ times.

   Reacted emotionally to what someone was saying before he or she finished _____ times.

   After keeping track of your personal listening statistics, what changes would you like to make in your listening behavior?

2. Monitor and then jot down notes about your own self-talk during a conversation with another person. What competing thoughts and ideas occurred to you while you were conversing with your partner? What did you do to refocus on the message?

# Learning with Others

1. **Charting Your Listening Cycle**
   Are you a morning person or an evening person? Use the chart shown here to plot your listening energy cycle. Draw a line starting at 6 A.M. showing the highs and lows of your potential listening effectiveness. For example, if you are usually still asleep at 6 A.M., your line will be at 0 and start upward when you awake. If you are a morning person, your line will peak in the morning. Or perhaps your line will indicate that you listen best in the evening.

   After you have charted your typical daily listening cycle, gather in small groups with your classmates to compare listening cycles. Identify listening strategies that can help you capitalize on your listening "up" periods. Also, based on the chapter and your own experiences, identify ways to enhance your listening when you traditionally have low listening energy.

2. Assign one student from your group to speak very slowly on a difficult subject. The other members of the group should write down short summaries during pauses in the speech. Compare summaries with others in the group.

3. Make a list of "red-flag" words that have derailed your listening ability in the past. Ask another student to make up a paragraph about an important issue, using these words, and read it aloud to you. Monitor your reactions to the words and see whether you can steer your internal conversations back to the issue. Also, notice how you begin to feel about the speaker and what you do about those feelings.

http://www.bethanymurray.com/emotcomp.htm Interpersonal communication skills require a healthy emotional intelligence quotient (IQ) and emotional awareness, the ability to recognize one's emotions and their impact on others. Find out more about your emotional IQ at this site.

http://www.seorf.ohiou.edu/~af313/Brian/EmotionalQ/eq.htm Here's another site where you can assess your emotional IQ.

http://facstaff.bloomu.edu/jtomlins/stress.htm Stress affects your ability to listen and concentrate. Take a stress test provided by *Newsweek* magazine.

http://www.selfgrowth.com/test.html Visit this site and take a short, ten-question quiz to assess your ability to manage your emotions and be empathic toward others.

http://www.ihhp.com/sasqtest.htm This is another site that provides a short quiz to assess your skill in being sensitive to your own and others' emotions.

http://www-ai.ijs.si/eliza/eliza.html Can computers listen and respond to human communication? At this site you'll meet "Eliza," who "listens" and then responds to you. Ask Eliza questions, and she will answer.

# Verbal Communication Skills

*Words can destroy. What we call each other ultimately becomes what we think of each other, and it matters.*

Jeanne J. Kirkpatrick

---

**W**ords are powerful. Those who use them skillfully can exert great influence with just a few of them. Consider these notable achievements:

Lincoln set the course for a nation in a 267-word speech: the Gettysburg Address.

Shakespeare expressed the quintessence of the human condition in Hamlet's famous "To be, or not to be" soliloquy—363 words long.

Two billion people adhere to a comprehensive moral code expressed in a mere 297 words: the Ten Commandments.

Words have great power in private life as well. In this chapter we will examine ways to use them more effectively in interpersonal relationships. We'll investigate how to harness the power that words have to affect emotions, thoughts, and actions, and we'll describe links between language and culture. We will also identify communication barriers that may keep you from using words effectively and note strategies and skills for managing those barriers. Finally, we will examine the role of speech in establishing supportive relationships with others.

According to one study, a person's ability to use words—more specifically, to participate in conversation with others—is one of the best predictors of communication competence.[1] People who simply didn't talk much were perceived as being less interpersonally skilled than people who spent an appropriate amount of time engaged in conversation with others. This chapter is designed to help you better understand the power of words and to use them with greater skill and confidence.

## Understanding How Words Work

**A**s you read the printed words on this page, how are you able to make sense out of these black marks? When you hear words spoken by others, how are you able to interpret those sounds? Although several theories attempt to explain how people learn language and ascribe meaning to both printed and uttered words, there is no single universally held view that neatly clarifies the mystery.

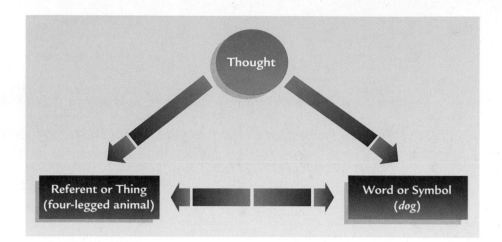

FIGURE *6.1*

Triangle of Meaning

Here's one thing that *is* known about words and meaning: *Meanings are in people, not in words.* As we noted in Chapter 1, one of the myths about communication is that words contain meaning. They don't. Meaning is created because words, which are arbitrary symbols, are used within a specific context and interpreted within a cultural framework to yield both denotative and connotative meaning. It's inaccurate to assume that a word means the same thing to everyone. The transactional nature of interpersonal communication suggests that meaning is co-created through the process of using and making sense out of words. People construct their reality based on how they use words to make sense of the world. Words don't mean anything until someone interprets them and creates meaning. Now let's unpack that last sentence to gain a fuller appreciation of the transactional nature of words and meaning.

### Words Are Symbols

As we noted in Chapter 1, words are **symbols** that represent something else. A printed or spoken word represents an image, sound, concept, or experience. Take the word *cat,* for instance. The word may conjure up in your mind's eye a hissing creature with bared claws and fangs. Or perhaps you envision a cherished pet curled up by a fireplace.

The classic model in Figure 6.1 was developed by Charles K. Ogden and Ivor Richards to explain the relationships between *referents, thought,* and *symbols.*[2] **Referents** are the things the symbols (words) represent. **Thought** is the mental process of creating an image, sound, concept, or experience triggered by the referent or the symbol. So the three elements—referents, thought, and symbols—are inextricably linked. Although some scholars find this model too simplistic to explain how people link all words to meaning, it does illustrate the process for most concepts, people, and tangible things.

### Words Are Arbitrary

**symbol.** Word, sound, or visual device that represents an image, sound, concept, or experience.

**referent.** Thing that a symbol represents.

**thought.** Mental process of creating an image, sound, concept, or experience triggered by a referent or symbol.

American linguist (a person who studies the origin and nature of language) Charles Hockett suggested that words are, for the most part, arbitrary.[3] There's not an obvious reason many words represent what they refer to. The word *dog,* for example, does not look like a dog or sound like a dog. Yet there is a clear connection in your mind between your pet pooch and the symbol *dog.* The words we use have agreed-upon general meaning, but there is not typically a logical connection between a word and what it represents. Yes, some words, such as *buzz, hum, snort,* and *giggle,* do recreate the sounds they represent. And many words can trace their origin to other languages. But most of the time words have an arbitrary meaning. A linguistic group, such as all the people who speak the English language, has agreed that the word *tree,* for example, will represent the thing with bark, branches, and leaves growing in your yard or a nearby park. The arbitrary nature of most words means that there is no inherent meaning in a word. Therefore, unless we develop a common meaning for a word, misunderstanding and miscommunication may occur.

## Words Are Context Bound

Your English or speech communication teacher has undoubtedly cautioned you that taking something out of context changes its meaning. Symbols derive their meaning from the situation in which they are used. The phrase *old man* could refer to a male over the age of seventy, your father, your teacher, your principal, or your boss. You need to know the context of the phrase in order to decipher its specific meaning. The transactional nature of communication emphasizes how meaning is created through discussion.

## Words Are Culturally Bound

As you learned in Chapter 4, culture consists of the rules, norms, values, and mores of a group of people, which have been learned and shaped by successive generations. The meaning of a symbol such as a word can change from culture to culture. To a European, for example, a "Yankee" is someone from the United States; to a player on the Boston Red Sox, a "Yankee" is an opponent; and to someone from the American South, a "Yankee" is someone from the American North. A few years ago, General Motors sold a car called a Nova. In English, *nova* means bright star—an appropriate name for a car. In Spanish, however, the spoken word *nova* sounds like the words "no va," which translate, "It does not go." As you can imagine, this name was not a great sales tool for the Spanish-speaking market.

One way to measure how words reflect culture is to consider the new words that become new entries in dictionaries. Here are some of the recent additions to *Webster's New World College Dictionary,* published at the start of the twenty-first century.

*Bubba:* A slang term that means *brother*

*Pumped:* Enthusiastic, confident

*Viewbook:* Richly illustrated booklet produced by a college or university for prospective students

*Slamming:* Switching someone's long-distance phone service without a person's knowledge

*Megaplex:* Many movie screens in a single place, which show different features

*Racial profiling:* Alleged to be a policy of police who stop vehicles that are driven by people from a particular racial or ethnic group

*Face time:* Time spent in the presence of someone

*Hat hair:* Hair that becomes matted after wearing a hat

The study of words and meaning is called *semantics.* One important body of semantic theory known as **symbolic interaction theory** suggests that a society is bound together by the common use of symbols. Originally developed by sociologists as a way of making sense out of how societies and groups are linked together,[4] the theory of symbolic interaction also illuminates how we use our common understanding of symbols to form interpersonal relationships. Common symbols foster links in understanding and therefore lead to satisfying relationships. Of course, even within a given culture people misunderstand each other's messages. But the more similar the cultures of the communication partners, the greater the chance for a meeting of meanings.

Some researchers, such as linguist Deborah Tannen, suggest that gender plays a major role in how we interpret certain verbal messages.[5] Women tend to interpret messages based on how personally supportive they perceive the message to be. Men, according to Tannen, are more likely to interpret messages based on issues related to dominance and power. Research confirms that psychological gender is a better predictor than biological sex of the general framework we use to interpret messages.[6] Clearly, our life experiences help us interpret the words we hear.

## Words Communicate Denotative and Connotative Meaning

Language is the vehicle through which we share our sense of the world with others. Through language people translate experience into symbols and then use the symbols to share the experience. But as you learned in Chapter 1, symbol sharing through language is not just a simple linear process of uttering a word and having its meaning clearly understood by another. Messages create both content and feelings. So language creates meaning on two levels: the denotative and the connotative.

The **denotative meaning** of a word creates content. The denotation of a word is its restrictive or literal meaning. For example, here is one dictionary definition for the word *school*:

> An institution for the instruction of children; an institution for instruction in a skill or business; a college or a university.[7]

This definition is the literal, or denotative, definition of the word *school;* it describes what the word means in American culture.

The **connotative meaning** of a word creates feelings. Words have personal and subjective meanings. To you, the word *school* might mean a wonderful, exciting place where you meet your friends, have a good time, and occasionally take tests and perform other tasks that keep you from enjoying your social life. To others, *school* could be a restrictive, burdensome obligation that stands in the way of making money and getting on with life. The connotative meaning of a word is more individualized. Whereas the denotative, or objective, meaning of the word *school* can be found in your *Webster's New World Dictionary* or the *Oxford English Dictionary,* your subjective, personal response to the word is probably not contained there.

**symbolic interaction theory.** Theory that members of a society are bound together through common use of symbols.

**denotative meaning.** Restrictive or literal meaning of a word.

**connotative meaning.** Personal and subjective meaning of a word.

## Recap

### Denotative and Connotative Meaning

| Meaning | Definition | Examples |
|---|---|---|
| Denotative | Literal, restrictive definition of a word | Mother: the female person who gave birth to you |
| Connotative | Personal, subjective reaction to a word | Mother: the warm, caring woman who nurtured and loved you; or the cold, distant woman who always implied that you were not measuring up to her standards |

## Words Communicate Concrete or Abstract Meaning

Words can be placed along a continuum from abstract to concrete. People call a word *concrete* if they can experience its referent with one of their senses; if you can see it, touch it, smell it, taste it, or hear it, then it's concrete. If you cannot do these things with the referent, then the word is abstract. You can visualize the continuum from abstract to concrete as a ladder:

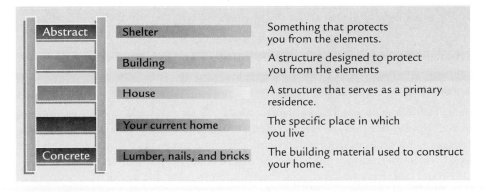

| | |
|---|---|
| **Abstract** | |
| Shelter | Something that protects you from the elements. |
| Building | A structure designed to protect you from the elements |
| House | A structure that serves as a primary residence. |
| Your current home | The specific place in which you live |
| **Concrete** | |
| Lumber, nails, and bricks | The building material used to construct your home. |

In general, the more concrete the language, the easier it is for others to understand.

## Recognizing the Power of Words

> Sticks and stones may break my bones,
> But words can never hurt me.

This old schoolyard chant may provide a ready retort for the desperate victim of name-calling, but it is hardly convincing. With more insight, the poet Robert Browning wrote, "Words break no bones; hearts though sometimes." And in his book *Science and Sanity*, mathematician and engineer Alfred Korzybski argued that the words we use (and misuse) have tremendous effects on our thoughts and actions.[8] Browning and Korzybski were right. As we said at the beginning of this chapter, words have power.

### Words Have Power to Create

"To name is to call into existence—to call out of nothingness," wrote French philosopher Georges Gusdorff.[9] Words give you a tool to create the world by naming and labeling what you experience. You undoubtedly learned in your elementary science class that Sir Isaac Newton discovered gravity. It would be more accurate to say that he *labeled* rather than discovered it. His use of the word *gravity* gave us a cognitive category; we now converse about the pull of the earth's forces that keeps us from flying into space. Words give us the symbolic vehicles to communicate our creations and discoveries to others.

When you label something as "good" or "bad," you are using language to create your own vision of how you experience the world. If you tell a friend that the movie you saw last night was vulgar and obscene, you are not only providing your friend with a critique of the movie; you are also communicating your sense of what is appropriate and inappropriate.

As we noted in Chapter 2, you create your self-worth largely with self-talk and with the labels you apply to yourself. Psychologist Albert Ellis believes that you also create your moods and emotional state with the words you use to label your feelings.[10] If you get fired from a job, you might say that you feel angry and helpless, or you might declare that you feel liberated and excited. The first response might lead to depression, and the second to happiness. One fascinating study conducted over a thirty-five-year period found that people who described the world in pessimistic terms when they were younger were in poorer health during middle age than those who had been optimistic.[11] Your words and corresponding outlook have the power to affect your health. The concept of reframing, discussed in Chapter 2 as a way to improve self-concept, is based on the power of words to "call into existence" whatever we describe with them.

### Words Have Power to Affect Thoughts and Actions

How about some horse meat for supper tonight? Most of us find such a question disgusting. Why? Horse meat is not something we typically eat. Perhaps the reason horse meat is not a featured delicacy at the local supermarket is simply that we have no other word for it. Your butcher does not advertise pig meat or cow meat; labeling the meat as pork chops, ham, and sausage, or as steak and ribs, makes it sound more appetizing. Advertisers have long known that the way a product is labeled affects our propensity to purchase it.

Words also have power to affect policy and procedures. Consider the unsubstantiated story about a young FBI man who was put in charge of the supply department. In an effort to save money, he reduced the size of memo paper. One of the smaller sheets ended up on J. Edgar Hoover's desk. The director didn't like the small size and wrote on the narrow margin of the paper, "Watch the borders." For the next six weeks, it was extremely difficult to enter the United States from Canada or Mexico.

In the late 1960s a California sociology professor conducted an experiment to demonstrate that words have power to affect behavior.[12] He divided his class into two groups. To one group, he distributed a bumper sticker that boldly displayed the words "I support the Black Panthers." At that time, many members of the students' local community thought the Panthers were using unnecessary force to promote their agenda. Students in this first group had to drive around for a week with the stickers on their cars. The other group drove around as usual, without stickers.

It took only a few hours to prove the professor's point: Words do affect attitudes and behavior.

*Most of us can agree on the denotative meaning for the word* school. *But the connotative meaning will be different for everybody.*

Students who had the stickers were harassed by other motorists and issued traffic tickets at an alarming rate. The other group had no increase in hassles. By the end of the study, seventeen days later, the "Panther" group had received thirty-three traffic citations.

## Words Have Power to Affect and Reflect Culture

In the early part of the twentieth century, anthropologists Edward Sapir and his student Benjamin Whorf worked simultaneously to refine a theory called **linguistic determinism.**[13] The essence of linguistic determinism is that language shapes the way we think. Our words also reflect our thoughts and our culture. A related principle, called **linguistic relativity,** states that each language has unique elements embedded within it. Together these two principles form the underlying elements in the **Sapir-Whorf hypothesis,** which suggests that language shapes our culture and culture shapes our language. To prove the theory, Benjamin Whorf studied the languages of several cultures, particularly that of Hopi Native Americans. He discovered that in Hopi, one word (the word *masa'ytaka*) is used for every creature that flies, except for birds. While this seems odd to an English-speaker, because the English language has many different words for different flying creatures (and things such as airplanes, balloons, and rockets), for the Hopi, flying creatures (or objects) constitute a single category. Whorf saw this as proof of his hypothesis that the words we use reflect our culture and our culture influences our words. Similarly, today's highly developed technological culture has given rise to many new words that reflect the importance we place on technology; terms such as *PC, hard drive,* and *gigabytes* weren't part of your grandparents' language. And the fact that a certain type of behavior is now labeled Attention-Deficit/ Hyperactivity Disorder (ADHD) is an example of how words can create a reality in a culture. Grandpa might argue that there weren't any ADHD kids in his day—some kids were just "rowdy."[14] Although today most linguists don't support the Sapir-Whorf hypothesis in its most extreme interpretation, there is nonetheless evidence to suggest that the words we use do, to some extent, reflect our culture; they reflect our thoughts and how we view the world. To understand your culture as well as your thoughts, the Sapir-Whorf hypothesis suggests that you study the words you use to gain insight about yourself and your culture.

If an impartial investigator from another culture were to study a transcript of all of your spoken utterances last week, what would he or she learn about you and the culture in which you live? If you frequently used words like *MP3* and *download,* the investigator would know that these things are important to you. But he or she might not know what they mean if they are not also part of his or her culture. Linguists have identified how the September 11, 2001, terrorist attacks have affected language. Linguist David Barnhart, who tracks new words, points out that the short-hand reference to *9/11* is a way of referring not simply to a date but to an entire national experience.[15]

Words not only reflect your culture; there is evidence that they mold it. When Wendell Johnson, a speech therapist, noticed that very few Native Americans in a certain tribe stuttered, he also found that their language had no word for stuttering.[16] He concluded that few people had this affliction because it never entered their minds as a

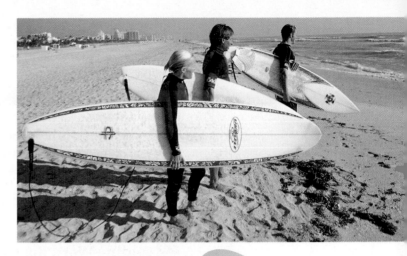

*S*urfers have created their own special language as part of the culture they share.

**linguistic determinism.** Theory that describes how use of language determines or influences thoughts and perceptions.

**linguistic relativity.** The theory that each language includes some unique features that are not found in other languages.

**Sapir-Whorf hypothesis.** Based on the principles of linguistic determinism and linguistic relativity, the hypothesis that language shapes our thoughts and culture, and our culture and thoughts affect the language we use to describe our world.

possibility. Perhaps you've heard that Eskimos have twenty-three different words for snow. Even though they really don't have quite that many, there is evidence that they have more words for snow than someone native to Miami, Florida.[17]

These examples also show that the words people use affect their **world view**—how they interpret what they experience. If you were to don someone else's prescription glasses, the world would literally look different to you, and the glasses would either enhance or inhibit your ability to see the world around you. In a sense, your world view is your own set of prescription glasses, which you formulate over time, based on your experiences, attitudes, beliefs, values, and needs. The words you use to describe your view of the world reflect and further shape your perspective. And you, in turn, help to shape your culture's collective world view through your use of language.

## Avoiding Word Barriers

According to theologian and educator Ruel Howe, a communication barrier is "something that keeps meaning from meeting."[18] Words have the power to create monumental misunderstandings as well as deep connections. Although it is true that meanings are in people, not in words, sometimes assumptions or inaccurate use of words hinders understanding. Let's identify some of the specific barriers to understanding that people sometimes create through language.

### Bypassing: One Word, Two Thoughts

A student pilot was on his first solo flight. When he called the tower for flight instructions, the control tower asked, "Would you please give us your altitude and position?" The pilot replied, "I'm five feet ten inches, and I'm sitting up front."

**Bypassing** occurs when the same words mean different things to different people. Meaning is fragile. And the English language is imprecise in many areas. One researcher estimated that the 500 words used most often in daily conversations have more than 14,000 different dictionary definitions. And this number does not take into account personal connotations. So it is no wonder that bypassing is a common communication problem.

Pavlov's dog salivated when he heard the bell that he had learned to associate with food. Sometimes we respond to symbols the way Pavlov's dog did to the bell, forgetting that symbols (words) can have more than one meaning.

**world view.** Culturally acquired perspective for interpreting experiences.

**bypassing.** Confusion caused by the same words' meaning different things to different people.

© Zits partnership. Reprinted with special Permission of King Features Syndicate.

# Building Your Skills

## The Talkaholic Scale

Are you a "talkaholic," or do you know someone who is? The simple description of a "talkaholic" is someone who talks more than most people. Being other-oriented means not only being a good listener, as we discussed in Chapter 5, but also being sensitive to how much you talk. "Talkaholics" often oververbalize. They are sometimes insensitive to others' need for information. We're not suggesting that you should not contribute to the conversation, and at times it is appropriate for you to talk and others to listen. But consider whether you may be a conversation dominator. Take the following test developed by communication researchers James McCroskey and Virginia Richmond to determine your "talkaholic" quotient. The higher your score, the higher your tendency to be a "talkaholic" when relating to others.

### Directions

The questionnaire below includes sixteen statements about talking behavior. Please indicate the degree to which you believe each of these characteristics applies to you by marking, on the line before each item, whether you (5) strongly agree that it applies, (4) agree that it applies, (3) are undecided, (2) disagree that it applies, or (1) strongly disagree that it applies. There are no right or wrong answers. Work quickly; record your first impression.

_____ 1. Often I keep quiet when I know I should talk.

_____ 2. I talk more than I should sometimes.

_____ 3. Often I talk when I know I should keep quiet.

_____ 4. Sometimes I keep quiet when I know it would be to my advantage to talk.

_____ 5. I am a "talkaholic."

_____ 6. Sometimes I feel compelled to keep quiet.

_____ 7. In general, I talk more than I should.

_____ 8. I am a compulsive talker.

_____ 9. I am not a talker; rarely do I talk in communication situations.

_____ 10. Quite a few people have said I talk too much.

_____ 11. I just can't stop talking too much.

_____ 12. In general, I talk less than I should.

_____ 13. I am not a "talkaholic."

_____ 14. Sometimes I talk when I know it would be to my advantage to keep quiet.

_____ 15. I talk less than I should sometimes.

_____ 16. I am not a compulsive talker.

Scoring: To determine your score on this scale, complete the following steps:

Step 1. Add the scores for items 2, 3, 5, 7, 8, 10, 11, and 14.

Step 2. Add the scores for items 13 and 16.

Step 3. Complete the following formula: Talkaholic score = 12 + total from step 1 – total from step 2.

A score of 40 or above suggests that you are a talkaholic.

*Source:* James C. McCroskey and Virginia P. Richmond, *Fundamentals of Human Communication: An Interpersonal Perspective* (Prospect Heights, IL: Waveland Press, 1996), 66. Reprinted with permission of James C. McCroskey and Virginia P. Richmond.

---

## Lack of Precision: Uncertain Meaning

Alice Roosevelt Longworth writes about a merchant seaman who was being investigated under the McCarran Act. "Do you," asked the interrogator, "have any pornographic literature?"

"Pornographic literature!" the sailor burst out indignantly. "I don't even have a pornograph!"

At a ceremony in the Princeton University chapel, an old lady buttonholed an usher and commanded, "Be sure you get me a seat up front, young man. I understand they've always had trouble with the agnostics in the chapel!"

Each of these examples, along with the Far Side cartoon on page 166, illustrates a **malapropism**—a confusion of one word or phrase for another that sounds similar to it. You have probably heard people confuse such word pairs as *construction* and *instruction,* and *subscription* and *prescription.* Although this confusion may at times be

**malapropism.** Confusion of one word or phrase for another that sounds similar to it.

*THE FAR SIDE*   BY GARY LARSON

© 1985 FarWorks, Inc. All Rights Reserved/Dist. by Creators Syndicate

The Far Side® by Gary Larson © 1985 FarWorks, Inc. All Rights Reserved. Used with permission.

Ha ha ha, Biff. Guess what? After we go to the drugstore and the post office, I'm going to the vet's to get tutored.

humorous, it may also result in failure to communicate clearly. So, too, can using words out of context, using inappropriate grammar, or putting words in the wrong order. Confusion is the inevitable result, as these sentences taken from a letter to the Philadelphia welfare department illustrate:

> I want my money as quickly as I can get it. I've been in bed with the doctor for two weeks, and it didn't do me any good. If things don't improve, I will have to send for another doctor.

The following statements appeared in church bulletins:

> The eighth-graders will be presenting Shakespeare's *Hamlet* in the church basement on Friday at 7 P.M. The congregation is invited to attend this tragedy.

> This afternoon there will be meetings in the north and south ends of the church. Children will be baptized on both ends.

And here are portions of letters written to a landlord:

> The toilet is blocked and we cannot bathe the children until it is cleared.

> Will you please send someone to mend our cracked sidewalk? Yesterday my wife tripped on it and is now pregnant.

These are funny examples, but in fact, incorrect or unclear language can launch a war or sink a ship. It is vital to remember that *meanings are in people, not in words.* We give symbols meaning; we do not receive inherent meaning *from* symbols. If you are other-oriented, you will assess how someone else will respond to your message and try to select those symbols that he or she is most likely to interpret as you intend.

For most communication, the object is to be as correct, specific, and concrete as possible. Vague language creates confusion and frustration. Consider this example:

*Derrick:*   Where's the aluminum foil?

*Pam:*   In the drawer.

*Derrick:*   What drawer?

*Pam:*   In the kitchen.

*Derrick:*   But where in the kitchen?

*Pam:*   By the fridge.

*Derrick:*   But which one? There are five drawers.

*Pam:*   Oh, the second one from the top.

*Derrick:*   Why didn't you say so in the first place?

But is it possible to be too precise? It is if you use a restricted code that has a meaning your listener does not know. A **restricted code** is a set of words that have a particular meaning to a subgroup or culture. Sometimes we develop abbreviations or specialized terms that make sense and save time when we speak to others in our group. Musicians, for example, use special terms that relate to reading and performing music. Most computer hackers know that "a screamer" is someone who sends e-mail messages typed in ALL CAPITAL LETTERS. Ham radio operators use codes to communicate

**restricted code.** A set of words that have particular meaning to a person, group, or culture.

over the airwaves. Yet in each instance this shorthand language would make little sense to an outsider. In fact, groups that rely on restricted codes may have greater cohesiveness because of this shared "secret" language, or **jargon**. Whatever your line of work, guard against lapsing into phrases that can only be interpreted by a few.

When people have known one another for a long time, they may also use restricted codes for their exchanges. Often married couples communicate using shorthand speech that no outsider could ever interpret.

## Allness: The Language of Generalization

The tendency to use language to make unqualified, often untrue generalizations is called **allness**. Allness statements deny individual differences or variations. Statements such as "All women are poor drivers" and "People from the South love iced tea" are generalizations that imply that the person making the pronouncement has examined all the information and has reached a definitive conclusion. Although the world would be much simpler if we *could* make such statements, reality rarely, if ever, provides evidence to support sweeping generalizations.

For example, although research documents differences in the ways men and women communicate, it is inaccurate to say that all women are more emotional and that all men are task-oriented. Empathic, other-oriented speakers avoid making judgments of others based only on conventional wisdom or traditionally held attitudes and beliefs. If you respond to someone of a different gender, sexual orientation, or ethnicity based on stereotypical concepts, you will diminish your understanding and the quality of the relationship.

One way to avoid untrue generalizations is to remind yourself that your use and interpretation of a word are unique. Saying the words "to me" either to yourself or out loud before you offer an opinion or make a pronouncement can help communicate to others (and remind yourself) that your view is uniquely yours. Rather than announcing, "Curfews for teenagers are ridiculous," you could say, "To me, curfews for teenagers are ridiculous."

**Indexing** your comments and remarks is another way to avoid generalizing. To index is to acknowledge that each individual is unique. Rather than announcing that all doctors are abrupt, you could say, "My child's pediatrician spends a lot of time with me, but my internist never answers my questions." This helps you remember that doctor number one is not the same as doctor number two.

## Static Evaluation: The Language of Rigidity

You change. Your world changes. An ancient Greek philosopher said it best: "You can never step in the same river twice." A **static evaluation** is a statement that fails to recognize change; labels in particular have a tendency to freeze-frame our awareness. Ruby, known as the class nerd in high school, is today a successful and polished businessperson; the old label does not fit.

In addition, some people suffer from "hardening of the categories." Their world view is so rigid that they can never change or expand their perspective. But the world is a technicolor moving target. Just about the time you think you have things neatly figured out and categorized, something moves. Your labels may not reflect the buzzing, booming, zipping process of change. It is important to acknowledge that perception is a process, and to avoid trying to nail things down permanently into all-inclusive categories.

General semanticists use the metaphorical expression "the map is not the territory" to illustrate the concept of static evaluation. Like a word, a map symbolizes or represents reality. Yet the road system is constantly changing. New roads are built, old ones are

**jargon.** Another name for restricted code: specialized terms or abbreviations whose meanings are known only to members of a specific group.

**allness.** Tendency to use language to make unqualified, often untrue generalizations.

**indexing.** Avoiding generalizations by using statements that separate one situation, person, or example from another.

**static evaluation.** A pronouncement that does not take the possibility of change into consideration.

closed. If you were to use a 1949 map to guide you on your cross-country trip from Washington, D.C., to Kansas City, Missouri, you would probably lose your way because the interstate highway system would not even be on it. Similarly, if you use old labels and do not adjust your thinking to accommodate change, you will get lost semantically.

Perhaps you have a parent who still uses "old maps" when you come home to visit, expecting that you will be there for dinner each night and will still eat four helpings at every meal. Your parent may not understand that you have changed and that his or her old map does not function well in your new territory. You may have to help construct a new one.

To avoid static evaluation yourself, try dating your observations and indicate to others the time period from which you are drawing your conclusion. For example, if your second cousin comes to town for a visit, say, "When I last saw you, you loved to listen to The Dixie Chicks." This allows for the possibility that your cousin's tastes may have changed during the last few years. But most importantly, try to observe and acknowledge changes in others. If you are practicing what you know about becoming other-oriented, you are unlikely to erect this barrier.

## Polarization: The Language of Extremes

Describing and evaluating what you observe in terms of extremes, such as good or bad, old or new, beautiful or ugly, brilliant or stupid, is known as **polarization.** General semanticists remind us that the world comes not in black and white but in a variety of colors, hues, and shades. If you describe things in extremes, leaving out the middle ground, then your language does not accurately reflect reality. And because of the power of words to create, you may believe your own pronouncements.

"You either love me or you don't love me," says Jerome.

"You're either for me or against me," replies Lisa.

Both people are overstating the case, using language to polarize their perceptions of the experience.

Family counselors who listen to family feuds find that the tendency to see things from an either/or point of view is a classic symptom of a troubled relationship. Placing the entire blame on your partner for a problem in your relationship is an example of polarizing. Few relational difficulties are exclusively one-sided.

## Biased Language: Insensitivity Toward Others

Using words that reflect your biases toward other cultures or ethnic groups, the other gender, people with a different sexual orientation, or people who are different from you in some other way can create a barrier for your listeners. Because words, including the words used to describe people, have power to create and affect thoughts and behavior, they can affect the quality of relationships with others. Although TV and radio shows and magazine articles may debate the merits of political correctness, it is clear that sexist or racially stereotypical language can offend others. We'll address three issues in language use that can reflect poorly on the speaker and affect interpersonal relationships with others: sexist language, ethnic or racially biased language, and elitist language—language that assumes superiority.

### Avoid Sexist Language

Sexist language is the use of words that reflect stereotypical attitudes or that describe roles in exclusively male or female terms.

**polarization.** Describing and evaluating what you observe in terms of extremes such as good or bad, old or new, beautiful or ugly.

Words such as congress*man,* mail*man,* and *man*kind ignore the fact that women are part of the workforce and the human race. Contrast these with *member of Congress, letter carrier,* and *humankind,* which are gender-neutral and allow for the inclusion of both men and women. Or, rather than eliminating the word *man* from your vocabulary, try to use appropriate labels when you know the gender of the subject. A male police officer is a *policeman;* a female police officer is a *policewoman.* Rather than *salesperson,* you could say *salesman* or *saleswoman,* depending on the gender of the seller.

O'Donnell found that even dictionaries fall into the trap of describing men and women with discriminatory language.[19] Included in the *Oxford English Dictionary* definition for *woman* are (1) an adult female being, (2) a female servant, (3) a lady-love or mistress, and (4) a wife. Men are described in more positive and distinguished terms: (1) a human being, (2) the human creation regarded abstractly, (3) an adult male endowed with many qualities, and (4) a person of importance of position.

Many of our social conventions also diminish or ignore the importance of women:

| Sexist | Unbiased |
|---|---|
| I'd like you to meet Dr. and Mrs. John Chao. | I'd like you to meet Dr. Sue Ho and Dr. John Chao. They are husband and wife. |
| | or |
| | I'd like you to meet John Chao and Sue Ho. They're both doctors at Mercy Hospital. |
| Let me introduce Mr. Tom Bertolone and his wife, Beverly. | Let me introduce Beverly and Tom Bertolone. |

Language has, however, made more substantial progress in reflecting changes and changed attitudes toward women in the professional arena. Compare the terms used to describe workers now with those used in the 1950s:

*T*he term *policeman* fails to accurately describe the person shown here. A more inclusive term would be *police officer.*

| Terms Used Today | Terms Used in 1950s |
|---|---|
| Flight attendant | Stewardess |
| Firefighter | Fireman |
| Police officer | Policeman |
| Physician | Female doctor |
| Women at the office | Girls at work |
| Ms. | Miss/Mrs. |
| People/humans | Mankind |

Consciously remembering to use nonsexist language will result in several benefits.[20] First, nonsexist language reflects nonsexist attitudes. Your attitudes are reflected in your speech, and your speech affects your attitudes. Monitoring your speech for sexist remarks can help you monitor your attitudes about sexist assumptions you may hold. Second, using nonsexist language will help you become more other-oriented. Monitoring your language for sexist remarks will reflect your sensitivity to others. Third, nonsexist language will make your speech more contemporary and unambiguous. By substituting the word *humankind* for *mankind,* for example, you can communicate that you are including all people, not just men, in your observation or statement. And finally, your nonsexist language will empower others. By eliminating sexist bias from your speech, you will help confirm the value of all the individuals with whom you interact.

In addition to the debate over language that refers to gender, there is considerable and controversial discussion about the way people talk about sexual orientation. Regardless of your personal view about sexual orientation, the principle of being other-oriented suggests that you can be sensitive in the way you speak of it. Your approval or disapproval of someone's sexual preferences should not undermine your goal of being an effective communicator. Labeling someone a *fag, queer,* or *dyke* not only may be offensive and hurtful to the person being labeled, but may also reflect on the sensitivity of the person doing the labeling. In most circles, the preferred terms for people who are homosexual are *gay* for men and *lesbian* for women. We're not suggesting that certain words be expunged from dictionaries or never uttered; we are suggesting that when describing others, people should be sensitive to how they wish to be addressed and discussed.

### Avoid Ethnic or Racially Biased Language

In addition to monitoring your language for sexual stereotypes, avoid racial and ethnic stereotypes. Using phrases such as "She's an Indian giver," or "I jewed him down" (to negotiate a price for goods or services), or "He doesn't have a Chinaman's chance" demonstrates an insensitivity to members of other cultural groups. Monitor your speech so that you are not, even unconsciously, using phrases that depict a racial group or ethnic group in a negative, stereotypical fashion.

Is Supreme Court Justice Clarence Thomas Black or African American? Is labor leader Dolores Huerta Hispanic or Latina? Given the power of words, the terms we use to label ethnic groups reflect perceptions of culture and identity. Using the wrong word can result in your being labeled "politically incorrect," or worse, a "bigot." In 1995, the U.S. Bureau of Labor Statistics surveyed 60,000 households, asking what ethnic label they liked best. More than 44 percent of households then called "Black" by the government preferred the term "Black," and 28 percent preferred "African American." Twelve percent preferred "Afro-American" and a little more than 9 percent had no preference. In another ethnic category, "Hispanic" was the choice of 58 percent of those currently labeled "Hispanics," rather than terms such as "Latino" or the generic "of Spanish origin." More than 10 percent had no preference. The survey also reported that the label "American Indian" was the term of choice for slightly fewer than half of the respondents, whereas 37 percent preferred "Native American." Most of those currently designated "White" preferred that term, although 16 percent liked the term "Caucasian" and a very small percentage liked the term "European American."[21] Some of these preferences may surprise you, in that they may have changed since this survey was conducted. A sensitive, other-oriented communicator keeps abreast of such changes and adopts the designations currently preferred by members of the ethnic groups themselves.

### Avoid Language That Demeans Someone's Age, Ability, or Social Class

Language barriers are created not only when a speaker uses sexist or racially biased language, but also when a speaker disparages a person's age, mental or physical ability, or social standing. Calling someone a "geezer," "retard," or "trailer trash" may seem to some harmless or humorous, but may be perceived by others as disparaging.[22]

Discrimination based on age is a growing problem in the workplace. In some occupations, as a worker moves into his or her fifties, it may be difficult to change jobs or find work. Despite laws designed to guard against age discrimination, such discrimination clearly exists. As we have noted, the language that people use has power to affect attitudes and behavior. That's why using negative terms to describe the elderly can be a subtle—or sometimes not-so-subtle—way of expressing disrespect toward the older generation.

Similarly, the way someone describes people with disabilities can negatively affect how they may be perceived. A study by researcher John Seiter and his colleagues found that when people with a disability were called demeaning or disparaging names, they were perceived as less trustworthy, competent, persuasive, and sociable than when the same people were described in more positive or heroic terms.[23] At the end of their study, the authors note, "communicators who want to be effective should avoid using derogatory language." Guard against calling attention to someone as a "cripple," "retarded," "dim-witted," or "mental"; these terms are offensive. As suggested by communication researcher Dawn Braithwaite, the preferred terms are "disabled people" or "people with disabilities."[24]

Also monitor the way you talk about someone's social class. Although some societies and cultures make considerable distinctions among classes, it is nonetheless offensive today to use words that are intended to demean someone's social class. Terms such as "welfare recipient," "manual laborer," and "blue-collar worker" are often used derogatorily. Avoid labeling someone in such a way that shows disrespect toward the person's social standing, education, or socioeconomic status.

## Recap

### Word Barriers

| Barrier | Definition | Examples |
| --- | --- | --- |
| Bypassing | Confusion caused by the fact that the same word may evoke different meanings for different people | *W.C.* might mean *wayside chapel* to a Swiss and *water closet* to someone from England. |
| Lack of clarity | Using words inappropriately or in imprecise ways | Sign in Acapulco hotel: "The manager has personally passed all the water served here." |
| Allness | Lumping things or people into all-encompassing categories | All Texans drive pickup trucks and hang a rifle in their back windows. |
| Static evaluation | Labeling people, objects, and events without considering change | You still call your twenty-eight-year-old nephew a juvenile delinquent because he spray-painted your fence when he was eleven. |
| Polarization | Using either/or terms—good or bad, right or wrong | You're either for me or against me. |
| Biased language | Using language that reflects gender, racial, ethnic, age, ability, or class biases | My mom is a mailman. |

## Using Words to Establish Supportive Relationships

"I'm going to win this argument."
"You're wrong and I'm right. It's as simple as that."
"You're going to do it my way or else!"

None of these statements is likely to result in a positive communication climate. All three are likely to lead to debate rather than true dialogue. The words you hear and use are central to your establishing a quality or positive relationship with others.

TABLE *6.1*    **Debate and Dialogue Compared**

| Debate | Dialogue |
|---|---|
| There is one right answer, and you assume that you have it. | Many people have pieces of the answer; together you can find the best solution. |
| The goal is to win. | The goal is to seek common ground and agreement. |
| The focus is on combat; you try to prove that you are right and the other person is wrong. | The focus is on collaboration and seeking common understanding. |
| You search for weakness and errors in others' positions. | You search for strengths and value the truth in what others say. |
| You defend your views. | You use the contributions of others to improve your thinking. |

*Source:* Adapted from Daniel Yankelovich, *The Magic of Dialogue: Transforming Conflict into Cooperation* (New York: Simon & Schuster, 1999), 39–40.

Author and researcher Daniel Yankelovich suggests that the goal of conversations with others should be to establish a genuine dialogue rather than to verbally arm-wrestle a partner in order to win the argument.[25] A true dialogue involves establishing a climate of equality, listening with empathy, and trying to bring assumptions into the open. Expressing equality, empathy, and openness is more likely to occur if you approach conversations as dialogue rather than debate. As shown in Table 6.1, in true dialogue people look for common ground rather than using a war of words to defend a position.

For more than three decades, Jack Gibb's observational research has been used as a framework for both describing and prescribing verbal behaviors that contribute to feelings of either supportiveness or defensiveness. His research, one of the most cited studies in communication textbooks in the past century, is so popular because he's identified practical strategies for developing supportive relationships with others—dialogue rather than debate—through the way we talk to each other.[26] Gibb spent several years listening to and observing groups of people in meetings and conversations, noting that some exchanges seem to create a supportive climate, whereas others create a defensive one. Words and actions, he concluded, are tools we use to let someone know whether we support them or not. Now let's consider how you can use words to create a supportive climate rather than an antagonistic or defensive one.

### Describe Your Own Feelings, Rather Than Evaluate the Behavior of Others

Most people don't like to be judged or evaluated. Criticizing and name-calling obviously can create relational problems, but so can attempts to diagnose others' problems or win their affection with insincere praise. In fact, any form of evaluation creates a climate of defensiveness. As British statesman Winston Churchill declared, "I am always ready to learn, although I do not always like being taught." Correcting others, even when we are doing it "for their own good," can raise their hackles.

# Building Your Skills

## Practice Using "I" Language

An essential skill in being supportive rather than creating defensiveness is describing what you want with "I" language rather than "you" language. Rephrase the following "you" statements into "I" statements.

| "You" Language | "I" Language |
| --- | --- |
| _____ 1. You are messy when you cook. | _____ |
| _____ 2. Your driving is terrible. | _____ |
| _____ 3. You never listen to me. | _____ |
| _____ 4. You just lie on the couch and never offer to help me. | _____ |
| _____ 5. You always decide what movie we see. | _____ |

One way to avoid evaluating others is to eliminate the accusatory *you* from your language. Statements such as "You always come in late for supper" or "You need to pick up the dirty clothes in your room" attack a person's sense of self-worth and usually result in a defensive reaction.

Instead, use the word *I* to describe your own feelings and thoughts about a situation or event: "I find it hard to keep your supper warm when you're late," or "I don't enjoy the extra work of picking up your dirty clothes." When you describe your own feelings instead of berating the receiver of the message, you are in essence taking ownership of the problem. This approach leads to greater openness and trust because your listener is less likely to feel rejected or as if you are trying to control him or her. Also, when you express your emotions, make sure you choose the right words to communicate your feelings. Building Your Skills: Practice Using "I" Language will help you practice accurately expressing your feelings.

A climate of defensiveness can stall communication. Long before your interaction passes from defensiveness to stony silence, try using "I" language.

### Solve Problems Rather Than Try to Control Others

When you were younger, your parents gave you rules to keep you safe. Even though you may have resented their control, you needed to know what was hot, when not to cross the street, and not to stick your finger in a light socket. Now that you are an adult, people who treat you like a child may be trying to control your behavior, to take away your options. In truth, people have little or no control over someone else's behavior.

## *Building Your Skills*

### Supportive/Defensive Communication Role-Play

*D*ivide into groups of two to four people. Each team or group should prepare a short play depicting one of the supportive or defensive communication responses described in this chapter. Perform your play for the class or another team to see whether they can identify the type of supportive or defensive communication behavior your team is portraying. Consider one of the following situations or develop one of your own:

Speaking with a professor about a grade

Returning a broken item to a store

Talking with your child about his or her grades

Responding to a telemarketer who calls you during dinner

Talking with one of your employees who made a work-related mistake

Rebooking a flight because your flight was canceled by the airline

Taking an order from a customer at a fast-food restaurant

Receiving a complaint from a customer about poor service

Talking with someone who has knocked on your door to invite you to his or her church

Asking someone to turn down the stereo or TV while you are trying to study

*Variation:* Instead of illustrating supportive and defensive communication, role-play an example of one of the confirming or disconfirming communication behaviors discussed in Chapter 5.

---

Most of us don't like others' attempts to control us. Someone who presumes to tell us what's good for us, instead of helping us puzzle through issues and problems, is likely to engender defensiveness. Open-ended questions, such as "What seems to be the problem?" or "How can we deal with the issue?" create a more supportive climate than critical comments, such as, "Here's where you are wrong" or commands such as "Don't do that!"

### Be Genuine Rather Than Manipulative

To be genuine means that you honestly seek to be yourself rather than someone you are not. It also means taking an honest interest in others and considering the uniqueness of each individual and situation, avoiding generalizations or strategies that focus only on your own needs and desires. A manipulative person has hidden agendas; a genuine person discusses issues and problems openly and honestly.

Carl Rogers, the founder of person-centered counseling, suggests that true understanding and dialogue occur when people adopt a genuine or honest positive regard for others.[27] If your goal is to look out only for your own interests, your language will reflect your self-focus. At the heart of being genuine is being other-oriented—being sincerely interested in those with whom you communicate. Although it's unrealistic to assume you will become best friends with everyone you meet, you can, suggests Rogers, work to develop an unselfish interest, or what he called an unconditional positive regard for others. That's hard to do. But the effort will be rewarded with a more positive communication climate.

### Empathize Rather Than Remain Detached from Others

Empathy is one of the hallmarks of supportive relationships. As you learned earlier, empathy is the ability to understand the feelings of others and to predict the emotional

## applying theory and research

### The Power of a Kind Word

*C*omforting messages are those intended to help reduce the amount of stress people feel during times of turbulence, personal change, and anxiety. Amy Bippus wanted to find out what types of comforting messages people consider truly helpful. She also wanted to analyze the general categories of messages of comfort and to consider whether the skill with which a comfort message was presented influenced how the receiver felt about being comforted.

She first interviewed people about their experiences of talking with a friend about something that "stressed out" the friend. People who had offered such messages of comfort thought that talking with a friend who was under stress helped improve the friend's mood, helped the friend adopt a positive attitude, and helped distract the friend from the problem.

Bippus then conducted another study in which people completed a questionnaire about their experiences of having a friend offer comfort and try to reduce stress. She wanted to know whether there were general categories or types of comments that were helpful when pro-

viding comfort to someone. The analysis of the data identified five categories of skilled comforting behavior. The most important category was Other-Orientation, followed by Problem Solving, Relating, Refraining from General Negativity, and Different Perspective. The positive outcomes that resulted from the comforting messages were Positive Mood, Empowerment, and Stopped Rumination.

### *A*PPLYING
#### the Research to Your Life

The results of this study provide the good news that talking to people who offer comfort and support can help you manage stress and anxiety. One of the most important things you can do to offer helpful and comforting comments echoes a theme we have stressed throughout this book: Be other-oriented. When providing comfort to someone else, don't focus on your own problems and concerns; focus on the concerns and needs of the other person. Helping to sort through

the problem and relating and listening positively to the other person are also valuable kinds of supportive behavior. Finally, avoiding being negative—emphasizing what's positive—and simply helping the other person to gain a new perspective are also especially helpful types of comforting behavior.

Providing comforting messages helps enhance a person's mood, empowers the person so he or she feels renewed or energized, and also helps the other person to stop wallowing in the problem and reframe the situation in a new, positive way. Although people sometimes need professional counselors during times of stress and change, this study suggests that being a good listener and offering positive, comforting messages can also help others during their times of anxiety and stress.

*Source:* Amy M. Bippus, "Recipients' Criteria for Evaluating the Skillfulness of Comforting Communication and the Outcomes of Comforting Interactions," *Communication Monographs,* 68, 3 (September 2001): 301–313.

responses they will have to different situations. Being empathic is the essence of being other-oriented. The opposite of empathy is neutrality. To be neutral is to be indifferent or apathetic toward another. Even when you express anger or irritation toward another, you are investing some energy in the relationship.

Suppose that after an unsuccessful attempt to persuade his family to take a trip to Yellowstone National Park, Preston declares, "I don't care what you think; that's where we're going." His proclamation reflects a disregard for the feelings of others in his family. This insensitivity is self-defeating. The defensive climate Preston creates with his words will probably prevent the whole family from enjoying the vacation.

# Building Your Skills

## Expressing Your Emotions

Communication is enhanced if you can clearly express the emotions you are feeling. One way to communicate your emotions is to describe how you are feeling with a well-chosen word or phrase. The following list gives you several options for expressing your feelings in positive, neutral, or negative terms. Categorizing these terms as positive, neutral, or negative doesn't mean that you should only use positive or neutral terms and avoid negative terms. What's important is that you select a word that accurately helps you communicate your emotions to others.

| Positive | | Neutral | Negative | |
|---|---|---|---|---|
| calm | hopeful | amazed | afraid | helpless |
| cheerful | hysterical | ambivalent | alone | horrible |
| comfortable | interested | apathetic | angry | humiliated |
| confident | joyful | bashful | annoyed | intimidated |
| content | loving | bored | bitter | listless |
| delighted | optimistic | detached | confused | mad |
| ecstatic | passionate | hurried | defeated | mean |
| elated | peaceful | lukewarm | defensive | miserable |
| enthusiastic | playful | numb | depressed | paranoid |
| excited | pleased | possessive | devastated | rebellious |
| flattered | refreshed | sentimental | disappointed | regretful |
| free | romantic | vulnerable | disgusted | resentful |
| friendly | sexy | | disturbed | restless |
| glad | tender | | empty | sad |
| grateful | warm | | exhausted | shocked |
| happy | willing | | fearful | suspicious |
| high | wonderful | | frustrated | terrified |
| | | | furious | ugly |
| | | | guilty | |

To practice expressing your emotions, imagine yourself in each of the following situations, and use some of the words listed here to write a response for each situation. Describe your response using either a single word or a short phrase, such as "I feel angry," or express your feelings in terms of what you'd like to do, such as "I'd be so embarrassed I would sink through the floor" or "I would feel like leaving and never coming back to this house."

- You have several thousand dollars charged to your credit cards, and you get fired from your job.

- Your best friend, with whom you spend a lot of time, is moving to another country.

- You have just learned that your adored aunt has died and left you a $35,000 inheritance.

- Even though you do your best to keep your room clean, your roommate is complaining again that you are a slob.

- You have brought your two-year-old son to a worship service, but he talks and runs around during the service and will not sit still. Other worshipers are looking at you with disapproval.

- You arrive at your vacation hotel only to discover that they do not have a reservation for you, and you do not have your room confirmation number.

## Be Flexible Rather Than Rigid Toward Others

Most people don't like someone who always seems certain that he or she is right. A "you're wrong, I'm right" attitude creates a defensive climate. This does not mean that you should have no opinions and go through life blithely agreeing to everything. And it doesn't mean that there is *never* one answer that is right and others that are wrong. But instead of making rigid pronouncements, you can use phrases such as "I may be wrong, but it seems to me . . ." or "Here's one way to look at this problem." This manner of speaking gives your opinions a softer edge that allows room for others to express a point of view.

## Building Your Skills

### Using Word Pictures to Express Your Feelings

A word picture is a short statement or story that dramatizes an emotion you experience. Using a visual image can add extra power in expressing your feelings when a simple descriptive word may not suffice. Word pictures can be used to clarify how you feel, to offer praise or correction, and to create greater intimacy. A key goal of a word picture is to communicate your feelings and emotions. An effective way to express your emotions through a word picture is to use a simile. A simile, as you may remember from your English class, is a compar-

ison that uses the word *like* or *as* to clarify the image you want to communicate. "When you forgot my birthday, I felt like crumbs swept from the table," exclaimed Marge to her forgetful husband. Or, after a hard day's work, Jeff told his family, "I feel like a worn-out punching bag—I've been pounded time and time again, and now I feel torn and scuffed. I need a few minutes of peace and quiet before I join in the family conversation." His visual image helped communicate how exhausted he really felt. The best word pictures use an experience or image to which the listener can relate. To practice your skill, try to develop word pictures to express in a

powerful and memorable way the feelings you might have in the following situations.

● You have just learned that a cherished family pet has died.

● You want to tell your friends how happy you are when you learn you received an A in a difficult course.

● You've asked your sister not to leave empty milk cartons in the refrigerator, but you discover another empty carton in the fridge.

● Your family is planning a vacation but didn't ask you to be involved in the planning.

### Present Yourself as Equal Rather Than Superior

You can antagonize others by letting them know that you view yourself as better than they are. You may be gifted and intelligent, but it's not necessary to announce it. And although some people have the responsibility and authority to manage others, "pulling rank" does not usually produce a cooperative climate. With phrases such as "Let's work on this together" or "We each have a valid perspective," you can avoid erecting walls of resentment and suspicion.

Also, avoid using abstract language to impress others. Keep your messages short and clear, and use informal language. When you communicate with someone from another culture, you may need to use an **elaborated code** to get your message across. This means that your messages will have to be more explicit, but they should not be condescending. For example, two of this book's authors vividly remember trying to explain to a French exchange student what a fire ant was. First, we had to translate *ant* into French, and then we had to provide scientific, descriptive, and narrative evidence to help the student understand how these tiny biting insects terrorize people in the southern part of the United States.

Underlying the goal of creating a supportive rather than a defensive communication climate is the importance of providing emotional support when communicating with others. A basic principle of all healthy interpersonal relationships is the importance of communicating positive, supportive messages that communicate liking or affection.[28] Several researchers have documented that providing verbal messages of comfort and support, not surprisingly, enhances the quality of a relationship.[29] As a relationship develops over time and the communication partners gain more credibility and influence, messages of comfort play an even more important role in maintaining

**word picture.** Short statement or story that illustrates or describes an emotion; word pictures often use a simile (a comparison using the word *like* or *as*) to clarify the image.

**elaborated code.** Conversation that uses many words and various ways of describing an idea or concept to communicate its meaning.

**Using Supportive Communication and Avoiding Defensive Communication**

| Supportive Communication Is . . . | Defensive Communication Is . . . |
|---|---|
| **Descriptive:** Use "I" language that describes your own feelings and ideas. | **Evaluative:** Avoid using "You" language that attacks the worth of another person. |
| **Problem Oriented:** Aim communication at solving problems and generating multiple options. | **Controlling:** Don't attempt to get others to do *only* what you want them to do in order to control the outcome. |
| **Spontaneously Genuine:** Develop a here-and-now orientation. Be honest and authentic rather than fake and phony. | **Strategically Manipulative:** Avoid planning your conversation in advance to get what you want. Don't develop a script to manipulate and accomplish your goal. |
| **Empathic:** Be emotionally involved in the conversation; attempt to understand what your partner is thinking and feeling. | **Neutrally Detached:** Avoid being emotionally indifferent or creating the impression that you don't care how another person is feeling. |
| **Provisionally Flexible:** Be open to receive new information; demonstrate flexibility in the positions you take. | **Certain and Rigid:** Don't take a dogmatic, entrenched, or rigid position on issues; be willing to listen to others. |
| **Equal:** Adopt a communication style based on mutual respect and assume each person has a right to express ideas and share information. | **Superior:** Avoid assuming an attitude or mind-set that you and your ideas are better than others. |

the quality of the interpersonal relationship.[30] We use not only words of comfort but, as you will learn in Chapter 7, nonverbal expressions of comfort as well.[31]

Communication researchers have documented the power of humor in helping to turn a tense, potentially conflict-producing confrontation into a more supportive, positive conversation. A study by communication researcher Amy Bippus found that most people report using humor as a way of providing comfort to others.[32] Humor also was perceived as a productive way to help a distressed person better cope with problems and stress.

# *U*sing Words to Be Appropriately Assertive

**S**ometimes people aren't other-oriented. As discussed in this chapter, some people may communicate in a way that creates a defensive climate that may increase feelings of mistrust and even anger. At times you run across people who are verbally aggressive, obnoxious, or worse—they may try to coerce or intimidate you into doing things you'd rather not do. Should the other-oriented person just politely accept obnoxious verbal assaults? No—being other-oriented doesn't mean you should ignore such boorish behavior. Nor do you have to respond in the same way you were treated. Rather than return mean-spirited aggressiveness with an equally inappropriate stream of aggressive words or rude behavior, consider using your verbal skills to be appropriately assertive. To be **assertive** is to make requests, ask for information, stand up for your rights, and generally pursue your own best interests without denying your partner's rights.

**assertive.** Able to pursue one's own best interests without denying a partner's rights.

# Building Your Skills

## How to Assert Yourself If You Are Sexually Harassed

### What Is Sexual Harassment?

Any unwelcome sexual advances, requests for sexual favors, or other inappropriate verbal or physical behavior of a sexual nature may be classified as sexual harassment. Examples include

- Repeated and unwanted requests for dates, sexual flirtations, or propositions of a sexual nature

- Unwanted sexual remarks or questions about a person's clothing, body, or sexual activity

- Unnecessary touching, patting, hugging, or brushing against a person's body

- Direct or implied threats that failure to submit to sexual advances will affect employment, work status, grades, letters of recommendation, or residential choice

- Physical assault

- A pattern of conduct that causes humiliation or discomfort, such as inappropriate terms of greeting; sexually explicit or sexist comments, questions, or jokes; or leering at a person's body

*Source:* Information adapted from Texas State University policy and procedure statement on sexual harassment and Vicki West, "Sexual Harassment: Identify, Stop, and Prevent" seminar.

### What to Do If You Are Sexually Harassed

- Be direct and candid with the person.

- Use "I" messages (for example, "I don't like those kinds of jokes made about me").

- Avoid being overly dramatic; remain confident that the incident will be dealt with.

- If the incident happens at school or work, use the grievance procedure.

- Report the harasser to your supervisor, department chair, or dean.

- If the harasser is your supervisor or an administrative official, report the incident to his or her supervisor.

- Report the harassment immediately after it occurs. The longer you wait, the less credible your story will be.

- When the harassment occurs, write down important facts.

- Report the incident as if you were a journalist: give the who, what, when, where, and how. Keep to the facts.

- Be prepared to give the interviewer names of witnesses.

- Put aside your anger and be thorough when telling the story.

---

Each individual has rights. You have the right to refuse a request someone makes of you, the right to express your feelings as long as you don't trample on the feelings of others, and the right to have your personal needs met if this doesn't infringe on the rights of others. Assertive people let their communication partners know when a message or behavior is infringing on their rights.

Some people confuse the terms *assertive* and *aggressive*. Being **aggressive** means pursuing your interests by denying the rights of others. Assertiveness is other-oriented; aggressiveness is exclusively self-oriented. Aggressive people blame, judge, and evaluate to get what they want. We'll expand on our discussion of aggressive behavior when we discuss relationship challenges in Chapter 11. Aggressive communicators use defensive communication tactics, including such intimidating nonverbal cues as steely stares, a bombastic voice, and flailing gestures. Assertive people can ask for what they want without judging or evaluating their partners.

When presenting the do's and don'ts of appropriate verbal communication in this chapter, we've often emphasized strategies for initiating communication with others.

**aggressive.** Expressing one's interests while denying the rights of others by blaming, judging, and evaluating other people.

### Recap

## Assertiveness versus Aggressiveness

| Assertiveness | Aggressiveness |
| --- | --- |
| Expresses your interests without denying the rights of others | Expresses your interests and denies the rights of others |
| Is other-oriented | Is self-oriented |
| Describes what you want | Evaluates the other person |
| Discloses your needs using "I" messages | Discloses your needs using "you" messages |

Sometimes what's most challenging is to respond appropriately when another person (who has not taken a course in interpersonal communication) comes at you with an inappropriately aggressive, argumentative, or defensive message, especially if the inappropriate message that's hurled at you takes you by surprise. You do not have to be passive when you are on the receiving end of such messages. We suggest instead that an effective communicator is appropriately assertive.

One approach to responding to aggressive or other inappropriate communication that we've already discussed is to use "I" messages to express your thoughts and feelings rather than "you" messages. "You creep! You ate the last breakfast taco" is an aggressive, defensive "you" statement. In contrast, "I haven't had breakfast yet. I asked you to save one taco for me; now I won't have anything to eat for breakfast" is an assertive statement of your rights and describes the consequences of violating them.

## Behaving Assertively: Five Steps

Many people have a tendency to withdraw in the face of controversy, even when their rights are being violated or denied. But you can develop skill in asserting yourself by practicing five key suggestions.[33]

### Describe

*Describe how you view the situation.* To assert your position, you first need to describe how you view the situation. You need to be assertive because the other person has not been other-oriented. For example, Doug is growing increasingly frustrated with Maria's tardiness for weekly staff meetings. He approaches the problem by first describing his observation: "I have noticed that you are usually fifteen minutes late to our weekly staff meetings." A key to communicating your assertive message is to monitor your nonverbal message, especially your voice. Avoid sarcasm or excessive vocal intensity. Calmly yet confidently describe the problem.

### Disclose

*Disclose your feelings.* After describing the situation from your perspective, let the other person know how you feel.[34] Disclosing your feelings will help to build empathy and avoid lengthy harangues about the other person's unjust treatment. "I feel you don't take our weekly meetings seriously," continues Doug as he asserts his desire for Maria to be on time to the meeting. Note that Doug does not talk about how others are feeling ("Every member of our group is tired of your coming in late"); he describes how *he* feels.

THE BORN LOSER reprinted by permission of Newspaper Enterprise Association, Inc.

### Identify Effects

*Identify effects.* Next, you can identify the *effects* of the other person's behavior on you or others. "When you are late, it disrupts our meeting," says Doug.

### Be Silent

*Wait.* After taking the first three steps, simply wait for a response. Some people find this step hard. Again, be sure to monitor your nonverbal cues. Make sure your facial expression does not contradict your verbal message. Delivering an assertive message with a broad grin might create a double bind for your listener, who may not be sure what the primary message is—the verbal one or the nonverbal one.

## Becoming Other-Oriented

### Bumper Sticker Slogans

The key to shared understanding is to focus on the needs, goals, and mind-set of your communication partner. Throughout this chapter we have emphasized how to develop an other-oriented approach when communicating verbally. To help you remember some of the essential principles of being other-oriented, consider the following "bumper sticker" slogans:

**Meanings are in people, not in words.**

Words are arbitrary, contextually and culturally bound symbols that can have denotative and connotative, concrete or abstract meaning. Focus on what the words may mean to your partner.

*Think before you speak.*

Words have tremendous power in our lives. They create and affect people's emotions and actions, as well as affecting and reflecting culture. Before you speak, consider the impact your words will have on others. Remember that words can hurt—and once spoken, words cannot be taken back.

**SAY WHAT YOU MEAN; MEAN WHAT YOU SAY**

Chose your words with care. Be mindful of the potential for miscommunication and misunderstanding. The spoken word belongs half to the person who speaks and half to the person who understands.

**Speak to others as you think they'd like to be spoken to.**

Words can engender a supportive communication climate or create defensiveness, which can lead to misunderstandings. Try to put yourself in your partner's place when you're conversing with others.

### Paraphrase

*Paraphrase content and feelings.* After the other person responds, paraphrase both the content and the feelings of the message. Suppose Maria says, "Oh, I'm sorry. I didn't realize I was creating a problem. I have another meeting that usually goes overtime. It's difficult for me to arrive at the start of our meeting on time." Doug could respond, "So the key problem is a time conflict with another meeting. It must make you feel frustrated to try to do two things at once."

If the other person is evasive, unresponsive, or aggressive, you'll need to cycle through the steps again: Clearly describe what the other person is doing that is not acceptable; disclose how you feel; identify the effects; wait; then paraphrase and clarify as needed. A key goal of an assertive response is to seek an empathic connection between you and your partner. Paraphrasing feelings is a way of ensuring that both parties are connecting.

If you tend to withdraw from conflict, how can you become assertive? Visualizing can help. Think of a past situation in which you wished you had been more assertive and then mentally replay the situation, imagining what you might have said. Also practice verbalizing assertive statements. When you are able to be appropriately assertive, consciously congratulate yourself for sticking up for your rights. To sharpen your assertiveness skills, try Building Your Skills: How to Assert Yourself.

# Building Your Skills

## How to Assert Yourself

**W**orking with a partner, describe a situation in which you could have been more assertive. Ask your partner to assume the role of the person toward whom you should have been more assertive. Now replay the situation, using the following skills:

1. *Describe:* Tell the other person that what he or she is doing bothers you. Describe rather than evaluate.

2. *Disclose:* Then tell the other person how you feel. For example, "I feel *X,* when you do *Y.*"

3. *Identify effects:* Tell the other person the effects of his or her behavior on you or your group. Be as clear and descriptive as you can.

4. *Wait:* After you have described, disclosed, and identified the effects, wait for a response.

5. *Paraphrase:* Use reflective listening skills: Question, paraphrase content, paraphrase feelings.

## Observation of Assertiveness Skills

**A**sk your classmates to observe your role play and provide feedback, using the following checklist. When you have finished asserting your point of view, reverse roles.

_____ Clearly describes what the problem was

_____ Effectively discloses how he or she felt

_____ Clearly describes the effects of the behavior

_____ Pauses or waits after describing the effects

_____ Uses effective questions to promote understanding

_____ Accurately paraphrases content

_____ Accurately paraphrases feelings

_____ Has good eye contact

_____ Leans forward while speaking

_____ Has an open body posture

_____ Has appropriate voice tone and quality

### How to Assert Yourself

| Step | Example |
|------|---------|
| 1. Describe. | "I see you haven't completed the report yet." |
| 2. Disclose. | "I feel the work I ask you to do is not a priority with you." |
| 3. Identify effects. | "Without that report, our team will not achieve our goal." |
| 4. Be silent. | Wait for a response. |
| 5. Use reflective listening: | |
|     Question. | "Do you understand how I feel?" |
|     Paraphrase content. | "So you were not aware the report was late." |
|     Paraphrase feelings. | "Perhaps you feel embarrassed." |

# Summary

The words we use have great power to affect our self-image and to influence the relationships we establish with others. Words are symbols that refer to objects, events, people, and ideas. They are arbitrary. We interpret their meaning through the context and culture to which they belong. Communication is complex because most words create both denotative (literal) meanings and connotative (subjective) meanings, and because words range from concrete to abstract.

The power of words stems from their ability to create images and to influence our thoughts, feelings, and actions. There is also an important link between the words we use and our culture. Language shapes culture and culture shapes language. Our view of the world is influenced by our vocabulary and the categories we have created with words.

Several word barriers can contribute to misunderstanding in interpersonal communication. Bypassing occurs when a word means one thing to one person and another to someone else. Our verbal expressions may lack clarity, either because we make language errors or because the meaning we want to convey is not clear to us. Allness statements can mislead and alienate listeners because the speaker falsely implies that he or she knows all there is to know about something. Another barrier, static evaluation, fails to take changes into account and uses outdated labels and categories. Polarization is the language of extremes; when someone thinks in black and white, many shades of meaning disappear. Finally, biased language that is insensitive to others creates noise that interferes with the meaning of a message. Being verbally aggressive attacks another person's self-worth. Finally, being overly argumentative is also inappropriate.

The words you use can ultimately enhance or detract from the quality of relationships you establish with others. Supportive communication is descriptive rather than evaluative, problem-oriented rather than control-oriented, genuine rather than contrived or strategically manipulative, empathic rather than neutral, flexible rather than rigid, and assumes equality rather than superiority.

When you become the victim of inappropriate, non–other-oriented verbal attacks or intimidating behavior, we suggest that you respond assertively. To be assertive involves five steps: describe, disclose, identify effects, silently wait, then paraphrase what your communication partner has said. Being a competent communicator involves listening and then appropriately responding to enhance, rather than detract from, the quality of interpersonal communication.

# For Discussion and Review

## Focus on Critical Thinking

1. Marge and Paul are having an argument. Paul shouts, "You're constantly criticizing me! You don't let me make any important decisions!" How could Paul communicate how he feels in a more supportive way?

2. Alan asked Jessie to pick him up after work at the parking garage at 5:30 P.M. Jessie waited patiently at the parking garage on the other side of campus and finally went home at 6:30 P.M., having seen no sign of Alan. Alan was waiting at the parking garage behind his office rather than at the one on the other side of the campus. What word barriers do you think led to this misunderstanding?

3. Rephrase the following statements to use less biased language:

   a. I'd like to introduce Mr. Russell Browne and his wife, Muriel.

   b. In an office memo: "Several gals have been leaving their purses at their desks."

4. Rephrase the following statements, using the skill of indexing.

   a. All politicians want power and control over others.

   b. All teachers are underpaid.

   c. All Texans like to brag about how great their state is.

## Focus on Ethics

5. If you really don't want to listen to your coworker go into detail about her latest vacation trip or provide details about the recent escapades of her children or grandchildren, is it appropriate to tell her that you'd rather not hear her "news"? Support your response.

6. Is it ethical to correct someone when he or she uses sexist language or makes a stereotyping remark about someone's race, gender, or sexual orientation? What if that person is your boss or your teacher? Explain your answer.

7. Is it ethical to mask your true feelings of anger and irritation with someone by using supportive statements or confirming statements when what you really want to do is tell him or her "the truth" in no uncertain terms?

# For Your Journal

1. Keep a log of examples of word barriers you experience or encounter. Note examples of bypassing, lack of precision in language, and other uses of words that inhibit communication. The examples could come from your own verbal exchanges or those that you observe in the conversations of others.

2. Make a list of words that are in your vocabulary today that were not in your vocabulary five years ago. Include new vocabulary words that you may have learned in school as well as words or phrases that were not generally used or that have been coined in the last half-decade (for example, *eBay, Googled*).

3. Record a sample dialogue between you and a good friend that illustrates some of the confirming responses described in Chapter 5.

# Learning with Others

1. Think of a bypass miscommunication that you've experienced. Share your recollection with a small group, and compare your feelings and responses with those of others.

2. In your group, choose one person to play someone who is recently divorced and whose spouse is not abiding by a child custody agreement and insists on seeing the children at odd hours. Another person should play the role of a trusted friend who only listens and responds. Ask the trusted friend to use the skills he or she learned in this chapter along with effective listening skills presented in Chapter 4. Then do a group evaluation of his or her response.

http://www.vandruff.com/art_converse.html  Are you a conversational terrorist, or do you know someone who is? In the article *Conversational Terrorism: How NOT to Talk,* you'll discover dos and don'ts for conversing with others and learn how to avoid terrorizing others when you talk with them.

http://www.sayitwell.com/article_10.html  Find out more about the meaning of words and determine whether you use powerful or weak language by reading the article *Communicating Verbally* by Candice M. Coleman. She reminds us that the meaning isn't in the words themselves, but in our perception of a word's meaning.

http://family.go.com/raisingkids/child/skills/feature/dony108scwords/dony108scwords.html  In the article *Words That Hurt: What You Should Never Say to Your Kids* by Charles E. Schaefer, you will discover how words can indeed wound children more deeply than a physical blow.

http://www.pitt.edu/~uclid/tips.htm  At this site you'll learn tips about language and examples of good and bad uses of language. You'll be reminded that language reflects, reinforces, and shapes our perceptions of others.

http://www.cwu.edu/~cwuchci/washoebio.html  This site gives a biography of Washoe, a chimpanzee who was the first nonhuman to acquire a human language, American Sign Language.

http://www.pcwebopaedia.com/  Uncertain of the meaning of a word that you find on the Internet? Look it up on the "Webopaedia." This site will help you interpret words you don't understand.

http://info.astrian.net/jargon/  This site can help you communicate with clarity, especially about technology-related issues. Here you'll find a comprehensive dictionary of technical jargon, especially computer jargon that appears on the web.

http://linguistlist.org/~ask-ling/  Ask-a-Linguist is a service provided by The Linguist List, an Internet network for professional linguists. This site is designed to allow anyone interested in language or linguistics to ask a question and get a response from a panel of professional linguists.

## CHAPTER 7

# Nonverbal Communication Skills

## OBJECTIVES

1. Explain why nonverbal communication is an important and challenging area of study.
2. Describe the functions of nonverbal communication in interpersonal relationships.
3. Summarize research findings that describe codes of nonverbal communication behavior.
4. Describe three bases for interpreting nonverbal behavior.
5. Formulate a strategy for improving your ability to interpret nonverbal messages accurately.

## OUTLINE

Why Learn About Nonverbal Communication?

The Challenge of Interpreting Nonverbal Messages

Nonverbal Communication Codes

Interpreting Nonverbal Communication

Improving Your Ability to Interpret Nonverbal Messages

*What you are speaks so loudly that*
*I cannot hear what you say.*

Ralph Waldo Emerson

---

*Eddie:* Lisa, will you get the telephone?

*Lisa:* Get it yourself!

*Eddie:* Hey! Why so testy? All I asked you
to do was answer the phone!

If you could view a videotape of Eddie and Lisa's interaction, perhaps you could see the source of the conflict. Eddie's tone of voice and his scowling facial expression might make his simple request seem more like an order.

As we noted in Chapter 1, communication has both content and relationship dimensions. Tone of voice, eye contact, facial expressions, posture, movement, vocal cues, appearance, use of personal space, manipulation of the communication environment, and other nonverbal clues reveal how people feel toward others. We can define **nonverbal communication** as behavior other than written or spoken language that creates meaning for someone. In this chapter we focus on how nonverbal communication affects the quality of our interpersonal relationships. As we identify the functions and codes of nonverbal cues, we will also explore ways to improve skill in interpreting the nonverbal messages of others.

## Why Learn About Nonverbal Communication?

When you are sitting in a public place such as a shopping mall, airport, or bus stop, do you make assumptions about what other people might be like, as you observe their nonverbal behavior? Most of us are people watchers, and we rely on nonverbal communication clues to predict how others may feel about and react to us. Nonverbal communication plays a major role in relationship development because it is also the main channel we use to communicate our feelings and attitudes toward others. But because much of our nonverbal communication behavior is subconscious, most of us have only a limited awareness or understanding of it. We can begin examining nonverbal communication by looking at the ways we use it.

**nonverbal communication.** Behavior other than written or spoken language that creates meaning for someone.

### Nonverbal Messages Communicate
### Our Feelings and Attitudes

Daryl knew that he was in trouble the moment he walked into the room. His wife, Sandra, gave him a steely stare. Her brow was furrowed, and her arms were crossed. On the table was a dish of cold lobster Newburg, extinguished candles burnt to nubs, and dirty dishes in all but one spot: his. Daryl was in the doghouse for forgetting the special meal his wife had prepared, and he needed no words to sense the depth of her displeasure.

Psychologist Albert Mehrabian concluded that as little as 7 percent of the emotional meaning of a message is communicated through explicit verbal channels.[1] The most significant source of emotional communication is our face—according to Mehrabian's study, it channels as much as 55 percent of our meaning. Vocal cues such as volume, pitch, and intensity communicate another 38 percent of our emotional meaning. In all, we communicate approximately 93 percent of the emotional meaning of our messages nonverbally. Although these percentages do not apply to every communication situation, the results of Mehrabian's investigation do illustrate the potential power of nonverbal cues in communicating emotion.[2] Researchers are continuing to find new ways to measure the impact and power of nonverbal messages in the communication of emotions.[3]

When we interact with another person, we base our feelings and emotional responses not on what our partner says, but rather on what he or she does. We also alter our nonverbal communication to suit different relationships. With good friends you let down your guard; you may slouch, scratch, and take off your shoes—all of which show you trust them. But if you were interviewing for a job or meeting your fiancé's parents for the first time, your posture would probably be stiffer and your smiles more carefully controlled as you tried to convey the impression that you are mature, competent, and respectable.

### Nonverbal Messages Are More Believable

"Honey, do you love me?" asks Brenda.

"OF COURSE I LOVE YOU! HAVEN'T I ALWAYS TOLD YOU THAT I LOVE YOU? I LOVE YOU!" shouts Jim, keeping his eyes glued to his morning newspaper.

Brenda will probably not be that reassured by Jim's pledge of affection. The contradiction between his spoken message of love and his nonverbal message of irritation and disinterest will leave her wondering about his true feelings.

Actions speak louder than words. This cliché became a cliché because nonverbal communication is more believable than verbal communication. Nonverbal messages are more difficult to fake. One research team concluded that North Americans use the following cues, listed in order from most to least important, to help them discern when a person is lying.[4]

- Greater time lag in response to a question
- Reduced eye contact
- Increased shifts in posture
- Unfilled pauses
- Less smiling
- Slower speech
- Higher pitch in voice
- More deliberate pronunciation and articulation of words

Because it is difficult to manipulate an array of nonverbal cues, a skilled other-oriented observer can see when a person's true feelings leak out. Social psychologists Paul Ekman and Wallace Friesen have identified the face, hands, and feet as key sources of nonverbal cues.[5] Are you aware of what your fingers and toes are doing as you are reading this book? Even if you become expert at masking and manipulating your face, you may first signal disinterest or boredom with another person by finger wiggling or toe wagging. Or you may twiddle a pen or pencil. When you become emotionally aroused, the pupils of your eyes dilate, and you may blush, sweat, or change breathing patterns.[6] Lie detectors rely on these unconscious clues. A polygraph measures a person's heart and breathing rate, as well as the electrical resistance of the skin (called *galvanic skin response*), to determine whether he or she is giving truthful verbal responses.

## Nonverbal Messages Work with Verbal Messages to Create Meaning

Although we rely heavily on nonverbal messages, they do not operate independently of spoken messages in our relationships. Instead, verbal and nonverbal cues work together in two primary ways to help us make sense of others' messages.

1. *Nonverbal cues substitute for, repeat, contradict, or regulate verbal messages.* An extended thumb signals that a hitchhiker would like a ride. A circle formed by the thumb and index finger can either signal that everything is A-OK or convey an obscene message. When someone asks, "Which way did he go?" you can silently point to the back door. In these instances, you are substituting nonverbal cues for a verbal message.

   You can also use nonverbal cues to repeat or reinforce your words. "Where is the personnel department?" asks a job applicant. "Three flights up. Take the elevator," says the security guard, pointing to the elevator. The guard's pointing gesture repeats her verbal instruction and clarifies the message.

   "Sure, this is a good time to talk about the Henrikson merger," says the business executive, nervously looking at her watch, stuffing papers into her attaché case, and avoiding eye contact with her coworker. In this instance, the nonverbal cues contradict the verbal ones. And as you learned earlier, the nonverbal message is almost always the one we believe.

   We also use nonverbal cues to regulate our participation in verbal exchanges. In most informal meetings it is not appropriate or necessary to signal your desire to speak by raising your hand. Yet somehow you are able to signal to others when you'd like to speak and when you'd rather not talk. How does this happen? You use eye contact, raised eyebrows, an open mouth, or perhaps a single raised index finger to signal that you would like to make a point. If your colleagues do not see these signals, especially the eye contact, they may think you are not interested in talking.[7]

2. *Nonverbal cues accent and complement verbal messages.* "Unless we vote to increase our tax base," bellows Mr. Coddlington, "we will not have enough classroom space to educate our children." While delivering his impassioned plea to the school board, Mr. Coddlington also loudly slaps the lectern to accent his message and reinforce its intensity. A scolding mother's wagging finger and an angry supervisor's raised voice are other nonverbal cues that accent verbal messages.

   Simultaneous and complementary verbal and nonverbal messages can also help to color the emotion we are expressing or the attitude we are conveying.

The length of a hug while you tell your son you are proud of him provides additional information about the intensity of your pride. The firmness of your handshake when you greet a job interviewer can confirm your verbal claim that you are eager for employment.

### People Respond and Adapt to Others Through Nonverbal Messages

Even though we discuss verbal messages and nonverbal messages in separate chapters in this book, verbal and nonverbal cues often work together to create meaning. Also keep in mind that interpersonal communication, especially the expression of nonverbal messages, is a transactional process. Meaning is created simultaneously between those communicating. **Interaction adaptation theory** describes the transactive process of how people adapt to the communication behavior of others.

Based on interaction adaptation theory, Judee Burgoon and her colleagues have concluded that nonverbal cues play a key role in how people adapt to others.[8] If, for example, your friend leans forward to tell a story, you may lean forward to listen. Or if during a meeting you sit with folded arms, unconvinced of what you are hearing, you may look around the conference table and find others with similarly folded arms. As if we are part of an intricate dance, when we communicate, we relate to others by responding to their movements, eye contact, gestures, and other nonverbal cues.

Sometimes we relate by mirroring the posture or behavior of others. Or we may find ourselves gesturing in sync with someone's vocal pattern. At times you are conscious of such mirroring of behavior, which is called **interactional synchrony.** At other times you may not be aware that when your friend folds her arms while talking with you, you also fold your arms across your chest in a similar way. One researcher found that people evaluate such synchrony as positive; somewhat synchronized behavior (but not so synchronized that it feels as though someone is purposefully imitating you) communicates partners' mutual interest and positive regard.[9]

*P*ortrait artists pay close attention to nonverbal cues such as posture, facial expression, and gesture to capture their subjects' personalities. What do the nonverbal cues reveal about this Spanish dancer?

### Nonverbal Messages Play a Major Role in Interpersonal Relationships

As you learned in Chapter 1, because of the ubiquitous nature of nonverbal communication, you cannot *not* communicate; psychologist Raymond Birdwhistell suggests that as much as 65 percent of the social, or relational, meaning in messages is based on nonverbal communication.[10] Of course, the meaning that others interpret from your behavior may not be the one you intended, and the inferences they draw based on nonverbal information may be right or wrong.

You learned in Chapter 3 that people begin making judgments about strangers just a fraction of a second after meeting them, based on nonverbal information. Within the first four minutes of interaction, you scope the other person out and draw conclusions about him or her.[11] Another research team found that you may decide whether a date is going to be pleasant or dull during the first thirty seconds of meeting your partner, before your partner has had time to utter more than "Hello."[12] Nonverbal cues, accurate or not, affect first impressions.

**interaction adaptation theory.** Theory suggesting that people interact with others by adapting to what others are doing.

**interactional synchrony.** The mirroring of each other's nonverbal behavior by communication partners.

# applying theory and research

## Adapting to Intimacy

Interaction adaptation theory, discussed on page 190, suggests that we adapt to the behavior of people around us. Researchers in one study wanted to find out how different levels of intimacy affect how one partner will adapt or respond to the other. There were four different levels of intimacy in this study: very low intimacy, low intimacy, high intimacy, and very high intimacy. There was also a control group in which there was no expression of intimacy between the two partners.

First, the experimenters had two people interact in a small apartment. After the couple's short conversation, the researchers asked one person to come into another room to fill out a questionnaire while the other person, the target of the study, stayed in the first room to complete a questionnaire. The person who left the room was then instructed to be either intimate or highly intimate, or to exhibit a low or a very low level of intimacy with the other person when they had a second conversation. In the high or very high intimacy group, the second member of the couple was told to increase his or her nonverbal intimacy toward the partner by "moving somewhat closer to [the] partner, smiling more, using more eye contact and perhaps touching the partner." The subjects were

also told to be "warmer and more flirtatious with their partner." Those in the very high intimacy condition were given the same instructions but were told to be dramatically intimate. People who had the low intimacy conversation were told to "act colder and more disinterested" toward their partner. In the very low intimacy condition, the subjects were told to move far away from their partners, smile much less, use much less eye contact, and act extremely bored.

What the researchers were really looking at was how the target person adapted to the person who came back in the room. Targets in the two intimacy treatments (intimate and highly intimate) responded by also being *more* intimate—smiling, moving closer to their partners, and being more pleasant and engaging. Targets in the two low intimacy conditions also mirrored what their partners were doing and became *less* nonverbally pleasant—defined in part by having less eye contact and not smiling—as well as becoming more verbally hostile. The researchers reported that the targets also used "verbal repair strategies," meaning that they asked what was wrong and attempted to understand why the other person was acting less intimate. In summary, people adapted by mirroring the behavior of the

other person; in the low intimacy condition, the target used conversation to try to understand what was happening.

## Applying the Research to Your Life

This study suggests that people are likely to adapt their nonverbal behavior to mirror what their partner does. If a friend or another person you know increases nonverbal intimacy, there is the likelihood that you will also increase your nonverbal intimacy. If an acquaintance is not intimate or is standoffish, you're also likely to be less open and responsive to that person. When people disconfirm you in obvious ways, such as by saying negative things about you or not looking at you or frowning at you when talking to you, you're likely not only to reciprocate but also to compensate for such disconfirming behavior.

*Source:* Laura K. Guerrero, Susanne M. Jones, and Judee K. Burgoon, "Responses to Nonverbal Intimacy Change in Romantic Dyads: Effects of Behavioral Valence and Degree of Behavioral Change on Nonverbal and Verbal Reactions," *Communication Monographs,* 67 (December 2000): 325–46.

Nonverbal expressions of support also are important when providing comforting messages to others during times of stress and anxiety. Communication researchers Susanne Jones and Laura Guerrero found that being nonverbally expressive and supportive is important in helping people cope with stress.[13] Providing empathic, supportive facial expressions and vocal cues, hugs, and positive touch helps reduce stress and enhance a person's overall well-being.

Nonverbal cues are important not only when people initiate relationships, but also as they maintain and develop mature relationships with others. In fact, the more intimate the relationship, the more people use and understand the nonverbal cues of their partners. Communication researchers Ascan Koerner and Mary Anne Fitzpatrick have found that a spouse's ability to interpret nonverbal cues accurately significantly enhances marital satisfaction on the part of the other spouse.[14] It seems that if you can accurately identify your partner's moods and emotions, your partner is more satisfied with the quality of the relationship.

Long-married couples spend less time verbalizing their feelings and emotions to each other than they did when they were first dating; each learns how to interpret the other's subtle nonverbal cues. If your spouse is silent during dinner, you may know that the day was a tough one and you should give her a wide berth. And if, when you put on your new Kelly green pants, your husband grimaces as he asks, "New pants?" you may understand that he does not love them. In fact, all of us are more likely to use nonverbal cues to convey negative messages than to announce explicitly our dislike of something or someone. People also use nonverbal cues to signal changes in the level of satisfaction with a relationship. When we want to cool things off, we may start using a less vibrant tone of voice and cut back on eye contact and physical contact with our partner.

## Reasons to Study Nonverbal Communication

1. Nonverbal messages communicate our feelings and attitudes.

2. Nonverbal messages are usually more believable than verbal messages.

3. Nonverbal messages work with verbal messages to create meaning.

   - Nonverbal cues substitute for, repeat, contradict, or regulate verbal messages.

   - Nonverbal cues accent and complement emotional messages.

4. People respond and adapt to others through nonverbal messages.

5. Nonverbal messages play a major role in initiating, maintaining, and developing interpersonal relationships.

# The Challenge of Interpreting Nonverbal Messages

Even though we have made great claims for the value of studying nonverbal behaviors, it is not always easy to decipher unspoken messages.[15] You have dictionaries to help interpret words, but there is no handy reference book to help decode nonverbal cues. Although the phrase "body language" is often used in casual conversation, there is no universal or agreed-on interpretation for body movements or gestures. To help you with the decoding process, we will classify some common types of nonverbal behaviors. But first you should be aware of some of the difficulties that hinder classification.

## Nonverbal Messages Are Often Ambiguous

Most words carry a meaning that everyone who speaks the same language can recognize. But the meaning of nonverbal messages may be known only to the person displaying them. Perhaps even more importantly, that person may not intend for the behavior to have any meaning at all. And some people have difficulty expressing their emotions nonverbally. They may have a frozen facial expression or a monotone voice. Or they may be teasing you, but their deadpan expressions lead you to believe that their negative comments are heartfelt. Often it is difficult to draw meaningful conclusions about another person's behavior, even if you know him or her quite well.

### Nonverbal Messages Are Continuous

Words are discrete entities; they have a beginning and an end. You can circle the first word in this sentence and underline the last one. Nonverbal behaviors are not as easily dissected. Like the sweep of a second hand on a watch, nonverbal behaviors are continuous. Some, such as a slap or a hand clap, have definite beginnings and endings. But more often than not, nonverbal behavior unfolds without clearly defined starting and stopping points. Gestures, facial expressions, and even eye contact can flow from one situation to the next with seamless ease. Researchers have difficulty studying nonverbal cues because of this continuous stream, so trying to categorize and interpret them will be challenging for us as well.

### Nonverbal Cues Are Multichanneled

Have you ever tried to watch two or more TV programs at once? Some televisions let you see as many as eight programs simultaneously so that you can keep up with three ball games and two soap operas and view commercials on the three other channels. Like the programs on a multichannel TV, nonverbal cues come at us from a variety of sources simultaneously. And just as you can really only pay attention to one channel at a time on your multichannel television—although you can move among them very rapidly—so too can you actually attend to only one nonverbal cue at a time.[16] Social psychologist Michael Argyle suspects that negative nonverbal messages (frowns, grimaces, lack of eye contact) command attention before positive messages when the two compete.[17] Moreover, if the nonverbal message contradicts the verbal message, then you may have trouble interpreting either one correctly.[18]

### Nonverbal Interpretation Is Culture Based

There is some evidence that humans from every culture smile when they are happy and frown when they are unhappy.[19] We also all raise, or flash, our eyebrows when

# *Understanding Diversity*

## Cultural Differences in Interpreting Nonverbal Messages

*R*esearch investigating nonverbal communication in a variety of cultures confirms that individuals interpret nonverbal messages from their unique cultural perspective. Note the following conclusions:[20]

### Facial Expressions
One research team found that some facial expressions, such as those conveying happiness, sadness, anger, disgust, and surprise, were the same in 68 to 92 percent of the cultures examined. All humans probably share the same neurophysiological basis for expressing emotions, but learn different rules for displaying and interpreting the expressions. For example, the Japanese culture does not reinforce the show of negative emotions; it is important for Japanese to "save face" and to help others save face as well.

### Eye Contact
There seems to be more eye contact in interpersonal interactions between Arabs, South Americans, and Greeks than between people from other cultures. There is evidence that some African Americans look at others less than do Whites when sending and receiving messages. One of the most universal expressions appears to be the eyebrow flash (the sudden raising of the eyebrows when meeting someone or interacting with others).

### Gestures
Hand and body gestures with the most shared meaning among Africans, North Americans, and South Americans include pointing, shrugging, nodding the head, clapping, pointing the thumb down, waving hello, and beckoning. There are, however, regional variations within cultures; it is not wise to assume that all people in a given culture share the same meaning for certain gestures. The "okay" gesture made by forming a circle with the thumb and finger has

sexual connotations for some South American and Caribbean countries. In France the "okay" sign means "worthless."

### Space
Arabs, Latin Americans, and Southern Europeans seem to stand closer to others than do people from Asia, India, Pakistan, and northern Europe. If you have been to Britain, you know that people queue or wait for buses in orderly straight lines. In France, however, queuing is less orderly, and individuals are more likely to push forward to be the next customer or get the next seat on the bus. As with gestures, however, there are regional variations in spatial preferences.

For a look at a comparison between White American and African American nonverbal communication, visit the following Web site: www.nwsel.org/cnorse/booklets/ccc/table4.html

---

meeting or greeting others, and young children in many cultures wave to signal that they want their mothers, raise their arms to be picked up, and suck their thumbs for comfort.[21] All this suggests that there is some underlying basis for expressing emotion. Yet each culture may develop unique rules for displaying and interpreting these gestures and expressions.

Consider the case of the Muslim woman who was detained by police officers as she strolled through downtown St. Paul, Minnesota. She attracted their attention because she was wearing a veil. Revealing her face in public would violate her religious beliefs. Or consider another example: Unless you grew up there, you might be startled when on a visit to New Orleans you stumble on a handkerchief-waving, dancing, exuberantly singing crowd and discover that it is an African American jazz funeral. What to the uninformed may seem like disrespect for the dead, others recognize as a joyous send-off to a better world. An American tourist in Russia might be puzzled to hear an audience break out in synchronized rhythmic hand clapping to express its appreciation of an act at the Moscow Circus—but rhythmic (rather than random) hand clapping is the norm for Russian audiences.

**kinesics.** Study of human movement and gesture.

# Nonverbal Communication Codes

**K**eeping in mind all the challenges to our understanding that we've just discussed, we can begin looking at the categories of nonverbal information that researchers have studied: movement and gestures, eye contact, facial expressions, use of space and territory, touch, and personal appearance. Although we will concentrate on the codes that fall within these categories in mainstream Western culture, we will also look at codes for other cultures and subcultures.

## Body Movement, Posture, and Gestures

In 1771, when English explorer Captain Cook arrived in the New Hebrides, he didn't speak the language of the natives. His only way of communicating was sign language. Through gestures, pointing, and hand waving, he established contact with the natives. There is evidence that people have used gestures to communicate since ancient times—especially to bridge cultural and language differences. The first record of the use of sign language to communicate is found in Xenophon's *The March Up Country,* in which he describes unspoken gestures used to help the Greeks cross Asia Minor around 400 B.C. Even when we do speak the same language as others, we use gestures to help us make our point.[22]

**Kinesics** is the study of human movement and gesture. Francis Bacon once noted, "As the tongue speaketh to the ear, so the hand speaketh to the eye." People have long recognized that movement and gestures provide valuable information to others. Various scholars and researchers have proposed paradigms for analyzing and coding these movements and gestures, just as grammarians have codified spoken or written language.[23]

One paradigm identifies four stages of "quasi-courtship behavior."[24] The first stage is *courtship readiness.* When you are attracted to someone, you may suck in your stomach, tense your muscles, and stand up straight. The second stage includes *preening behaviors:* You manipulate your appearance by combing your hair, applying makeup, straightening your tie, pulling up your socks, and double-checking your appearance in the mirror. In stage three you demonstrate *positional cues,* using your posture and body orientation to ensure that you will be seen and noticed by others.

One researcher found 52 gestures and nonverbal behaviors that women use to signal an interest in men. Among the top unspoken flirting cues were smiling and surveying a crowded room with the eyes, and moving closer to the object of affection.[25] People intensify these cues in the fourth stage, *appeals to invitation,* using close proximity, exposed skin, open body positions (uncrossed arms and legs), and eye contact to signal availability and interest. The classic Norman Rockwell painting here shows teenagers illustrating typical appeals to invitation. Subjects in one study reported that they were aware of using all these techniques to promote an intimate relationship. In fact, people use these

*C*an you identify the quasi-courtship behavior in this painting?

## Building Your Skills

### Communicating Interest

Nonverbally play the roles of both a good listener and a bad listener. First, imagine that you are listening to someone talk. As a good lis-

tener, how would you communicate your interest in what the person is saying, without uttering a word? Note your posture, eye contact, presence or lack of hand movement. Are your arms and legs crossed?

Now role-play a poor listener—someone who appears to be bored or even irritated by what a speaker is saying. What are the differences in the cues you use?

---

quasi-courtship behaviors to some extent in almost any situation in which they are trying to gain favorable attention from another.

Another team of researchers focused on nonverbal behaviors that prompt people to label someone warm and friendly, or cold and distant.[26] The team found that "warm" people face their communication partners directly, smile more, make more direct eye contact, fidget less, and generally make fewer unnecessary hand movements. "Cold" people make less eye contact, smile less, fidget more, and turn away from their partners.

Posture and body orientation reveal important information. Open body posture communicates that you are receptive and a responsive listener. When you are trying to decrease your contact with someone, say, at a party or family gathering, you are likely to turn away from the individual you want to avoid. Your body orientation and posture provide important cues to your interest and willingness to continue or end communication with someone.

Mehrabian has identified the nonverbal cues that contribute to perceptions of liking.[27] He found that an open body and arm position, a forward lean, and a relaxed posture communicate liking. When you are attempting to persuade someone, you typically have more eye contact and a more face-to-face body orientation; you are more likely to lean forward and closer to others.

Ekman and Friesen classified movement and gestures according to their function. They identified five categories: emblems, illustrators, affect displays, regulators, and adaptors.[28]

### Emblems

**emblems.** Nonverbal cues that have specific, generally understood meanings in a given culture and may substitute for a word or phrase.

Nonverbal cues that have specific, generally understood meanings in a given culture and may actually substitute for a word or phrase are called **emblems.** When you are busy typing a report that is due tomorrow and your young son bounces in to ask for permission to buy a new computer game, you turn from your computer and hold up an open palm to indicate your desire for uninterrupted quiet. To communicate your enthusiastic enjoyment of a violin soloist at a concert, you applaud wildly. You want your children to stop talking in the library, so you put an index finger up to your pursed lips.

### Illustrators

**illustrators.** Nonverbal behaviors that accompany a verbal message and either contradict, accent, or complement it.

People frequently accompany a verbal message with **illustrators** that either contradict, accent, or complement the message. Slamming a book closed while announcing, "I don't want to read this anymore" or pounding a lectern while proclaiming, "This point is important!" are two examples of nonverbal behaviors that illustrate the verbal message. Typically, English-speakers use nonverbal illustrators at the beginning of clauses or phrases.[29] TV newscasters, for example, turn a page to signal that they are moving to a new story or topic. Most of us use illustrators to help us communicate information about the size, shape, and spatial relationships of objects. You probably even use them when you talk on the phone, although probably not as many as you use in face-to-face conversation.[30]

### Affect Displays

Nonverbal movements and postures used to communicate emotion are called **affect displays.** As early as 1872, when Charles Darwin systematically studied the expression of emotion in both humans and animals,[31] people recognized that nonverbal cues are the primary ways to communicate emotion. Facial expressions, vocal cues, posture, and gestures convey the intensity of your emotions.[32] If you are happy, for example, your face will telegraph your joy to others. The movement of your hands, the openness of your posture, and the speed with which you move will tell others *how* happy you are. Similarly, if you are feeling depressed, your face will probably reveal your sadness or dejection, while your slumped shoulders and lowered head will indicate the intensity of your despair. When you are feeling friendly, you use a soft tone of voice, an open smile, and a relaxed posture.[33] When you feel neutral about an issue, you signal it by putting little expression on your face or in your voice. When you feel hostile, you use a harsh voice, frown with your teeth showing, and keep your posture tense and rigid.

### Regulators

People use **regulators** to control the interaction or flow of communication between themselves and another person. When you are eager to respond to a message, you make eye contact, raise your eyebrows, open your mouth, raise an index finger, and lean forward slightly. In a classroom, you may raise your hand to signal overtly that you want to talk. When you do not want to be part of the conversation, you do the opposite: avert your eyes, close your mouth, cross your arms, and lean back in your seat or away from the verbal action as attempts to regulate the interaction.

### Adaptors

When you are cold, you reach for a sweater or wrap your arms around your chest to keep warm. When it's 102 degrees Fahrenheit in the shade without a breeze, you may reach for a fan to make your own breeze. These behaviors are examples of **adaptors**—nonverbal behaviors that help you satisfy a personal need and adapt to the immediate situation. When you adjust your glasses, scratch a mosquito bite, or comb your hair, you are using movement to help you manage your personal needs and adapt to your surroundings—and you're communicating something about yourself to whoever may be present.

### The Five Categories and Interpersonal Communication

Understanding these five categories of nonverbal behavior can help you understand interpersonal communication by giving you a new and more precise way to think about your own behavior. By noting how often you use emblems instead of words to communicate a message, you can recognize how important emblems are in your relationships with others. The more you rely on emblems that have unique meanings for you and your partner, the more intimate the interpersonal relationship. Also, start to notice whether your nonverbal behavior contradicts what you say. Monitoring your use of illustrators can help you determine whether you are sending mixed signals to

**affect display.** Nonverbal behavior that communicates emotions.

**regulators.** Nonverbal messages that help to control the interaction or flow of communication between people.

**adaptors.** Nonverbal behaviors that satisfy a personal need and help a person adapt or respond to the immediate situation.

others. Be aware of how you display affect. Knowing that your face and voice communicate emotion, and that posture and gesture indicate the intensity of your feelings, can help you understand how others make inferences about your feelings and attitudes. If other people have difficulty interpreting your emotional state, you may not be projecting your feelings nonverbally. And finally, notice how you use adaptors. Individuals who do not learn the cultural norms of displaying adaptors can have a difficult time socially. For example, if you were never taught not to comb your hair or belch at the table, you may find you receive few dinner invitations.

Since nonverbal cues are ambiguous, it may not be a good idea to use them to achieve a specific objective. But as you have seen, people are more likely to respond in predictable ways if you use behaviors they can recognize and interpret easily.

## Categories of Movement and Gestures

| Category | Definition | Example |
|---|---|---|
| Emblems | Behaviors that have specific, generally understood meaning | Raising a hitchhiking thumb. |
| Illustrators | Cues that accompany verbal messages and add meaning to the message | Pounding the lectern to emphasize a point. |
| Affect displays | Expressions of emotion | Hugging someone to express love. |
| Regulators | Cues that control and manage the flow of communication between people | Looking at someone when you wish to speak. |
| Adaptors | Behaviors that help you adapt to your environment | Scratching, combing your hair. |

### Eye Contact

Whether you choose to look at someone or avert your gaze has an enormous impact on your relationship with that person.[34] Researcher Adam Kendon has identified four functions of eye contact in interpersonal interactions.[35]

First, eye contact serves a *cognitive* function because it gives you information about another person's thought processes. For example, if your partner breaks eye contact after you ask him or her a question, you will know that he or she is probably thinking of something to say.

Second, people use eye contact to *monitor* the behavior of others. You receive a major portion of the information you obtain through your eyes. You look at others to determine whether they are receptive to your messages. In fact, this search for feedback is implicit in the word for the center part of the eye, *pupil,* which comes from the Latin word *pupilla* or "little doll." When you look into someone's eyes, you can see a miniature reflection of yourself.[36]

Third, eye contact is one of the most powerful *regulatory* cues you use to signal when you want to talk and when you don't. We have noticed that when we ask questions such as "Who can tell me the four functions of eye contact?" students quickly yet unobtrusively avert their eyes to signal, "Don't call on me." When you do want to communicate with others, you make eye contact—as, for example, when standing in line at the bakery, you fix your eyes on the clerk to signal, "My turn next. Please wait on me."

Finally, the area around your eyes serves an *expressive* function. The eyes have been called the "mirror of the soul" because they reveal emotions to others. You may cry, blink, and widen or narrow your gaze to express your feelings.

As shown in Table 7.1, researchers Mark Knapp and Judith Hall have summarized conclusions on nonverbal communication that predict when you are most and least likely to have eye contact with someone.[37]

---

**TABLE 7.1   When Are You Most and Least Likely to Make Eye Contact with Someone?**

| You are more likely to make eye contact when you | You are less likely to make eye contact when you |
| --- | --- |
| • Like or love your partner | • Do not like your partner |
| • Are physically distant from him or her | • Are physically near your partner |
| • Are discussing easy, impersonal topics | • Are discussing difficult, intimate topics |
| • Have nothing else to look at | • Have other things to look at |
| • Are interested in your partner's reactions | • Are not interested in your partner's reactions |
| • Are trying to dominate or persuade your partner | • Are not trying to dominate or persuade your partner |
| • Are from a culture that emphasizes eye contact | • Are from a culture that de-emphasizes eye contact |
| • Are an extrovert | • Are an introvert |
| • Have a high need to affiliate or to be included | • Have a low need to affiliate or to be included |
| • Are dependent on your partner (and your partner is not responsive) | • Are more independent of your partner (and your partner is responsive to you) |
| • Are listening rather than talking | • Are talking rather than listening |
| • Are female | • Are male |

*Source:* Adapted from Mark L. Knapp and Judith A. Hall, *Nonverbal Communication in Human Interaction* (Fort Worth, Texas: Harcourt Brace, 1997), 390–391.

When people do establish eye contact with others, it may seem that their gaze is constant. Yet research suggests that they actually spend the majority of their time looking at something other than the person's eyes. One research team found that people focus on something else, including their partner's mouth, 57 percent of the time.[38] Not surprisingly then, facial expressions are another rich source of information in your communication with others.

### Facial Expression

The Palo Alto, California, city council may well have the distinction of being the first legislative body to try to regulate facial expression. They proposed a code of conduct banning facial expressions that show "disagreement or disgust."[39] The controversy generated by the proposal attests to the importance of facial expressions in the communication process. So, too, does our reliance on *emoticons,* the "smiley faces" and other symbols created with combinations of keyboard characters to communicate facial expression via e-mail. The face is the exhibit gallery for emotional displays.

To interpret a partner's facial expressions accurately, you need to put your other-orientation skills to work, focusing on what the other person may be thinking or feeling. It helps if you know the person well, can see his or her whole face, have plenty of time to watch it, and understand the situation that prompted the emotion.[40] But it is also helpful to know the cues for "reading" facial expressions.

Your face is versatile. According to Ekman and Friesen, it is capable of producing over 250,000 different expressions.[41] Research suggests that women have greater variety in their emotional expressions and spend more time smiling than men.[42] But all facial expression can be grouped in six primary emotional categories; the following list describes the changes that occur on your face for each one.[43]

*Surprise:*    Wide-open eyes; raised and wrinkled brow; open mouth.

*Fear:*    Open mouth; tense skin under the eyes; wrinkles in the center of the forehead.

*Disgust:*    Raised or curled upper lip; wrinkled nose; raised cheeks; lowered brow; lowered upper eyelid.

*Anger:*    Tensed lower eyelid; either pursed lips or open mouth; lowered and wrinkled brow; staring eyes.

## *Building Your Skills*

### Facial Expression Quiz

*S*tudents should divide into teams of two people. Person A selects one of the six primary emotions communicated by the face and attempts to display the emotion to person B. The six primary emotions are happiness, sadness, surprise, disgust, anger, and fear. Communicate all six emotions *in random order.*

Person B attempts to identify the emotions expressed by person A. When person A has communicated all six emotions, reverse roles.

*Happiness:*   Smiling; mouth may be open or closed; raised cheeks; wrinkles around lower eyelids.

*Sadness:*   Lip may tremble; corners of the lips turn downward; corners of the upper eyelid may be raised.

The face can shift between the six categories rapidly, as is evident on the NASA videotape of activity inside Mission Control at the Johnson Space Center during the final minutes of the doomed flight of the space shuttle Columbia in February 2003. *New York Times* reporter John Schwartz describes how

> though the voices of the mission controllers remained steady, their faces and body language showed a marked transition from the cool professionalism to wide-eyed alertness to dread and, finally, tears.[44]

How accurately do people interpret emotions expressed on the face? Several studies have attempted to measure subjects' skill in identifying emotional expressions of others. They have found that reading facial expression is a tricky business. According to Ekman and Friesen, even though faces provide a great deal of information about emotions, people have learned how to control facial expressions.[45] In addition, facial expressions seem to be contagious. One researcher who showed his subjects video clips of President Reagan giving speeches discovered that they were likely to smile when Reagan smiled and frown when Reagan appeared angry or threatening.[46] Another study found that people were better able to judge the accuracy of facial expressions when the expressions were more complex.[47] The distinctiveness of a facial expression with compound meanings may be what makes it easier to interpret. It is also probable that people have more practice interpreting facial expressions with compound meanings than they do those that communicate a single emotion such as sadness or happiness.

At the opposite end of the spectrum from complex facial expressions are what Ekman calls "microexpressions," fleeting facial expressions that may last only .05 of a second. Most of Ekman's test groups, including policemen and judges, have difficulty detecting microexpressions. On the other hand, Buddhists, whom Ekman calls "gymnasts of the mind," were surprisingly sensitive to microexpressions.[48]

## Vocal Cues

A Spanish electronics engineer recently devoted four years to studying the cries of his baby son and approximately 100 other infants. His work resulted in the production of a calculator-size translator called WhyCry. Its inventor claims that the machine can translate a baby's cry into one of five icons ("hungry," "sleepy," "uncomfortable," "stressed," or "bored") with 87 percent accuracy, a figure that rises to 98 percent when parents use a "symptom table" of body language.[49]

Whether you are an infant or an adult, your voice is a major vehicle for communicating your emotions and a primary tool for communicating information about the nature of relationships between you and others. As an adult, you use your voice to present one message on the surface (with words) and usually a more accurate expression of your feelings with your vocal quality. Say the following sentence out loud, as if you really mean it: "This looks great." Now say it sarcastically, as if you really don't think it looks great. Clearly, your vocal cues provide the real meaning.

Some vocal expressions of emotion are easier to identify than others. Expressions of joy and anger are obvious ones, whereas shame and love are the most difficult emotions to identify based on vocal cues alone.[50] People are also likely to confuse fear with nervousness, love with sadness, and pride with satisfaction.

Your voice also provides information about your self-confidence and your knowledge of the subject matter in your messages. Most of us would conclude that a speaker who mumbles, speaks slowly, consistently mispronounces words, and uses "uhs" and "ums" is less credible and persuasive than one who speaks clearly, rapidly, and fluently.[51] Even though mispronunciations and vocalized pauses ("ums" and "ahs") seem to have a negative effect on credibility, they do not seem to be a major impediment to attitude change. People may, for example, think that you are less knowledgeable if you stammer, but you may still be able to get your persuasive message across.

In addition to providing information about emotions, self-confidence, and knowledge, vocal cues, known as **backchannel cues,** can serve a regulatory function in interpersonal situations, signaling when we want to talk and when we don't. When we are finished talking, we may lower the pitch of our final word. When we want to talk, we may start by interjecting sounds such as "I . . . I . . . I . . ." or "Ah . . . Ah . . . Ah . . ." to interrupt the speaker and grab the verbal ball. We also may use more cues such as "Sure," "I understand," "Uh-huh," or "Okay" to signal that we understand the message of the other person and now we want to talk or end the conversation. These backchannel cues are particularly useful in telephone conversations when we have no other nonverbal cues to help us signal that we would like to get off the phone.

Not only "ums" and "ahs" but also speaking rate influences our perception of others. One team of researchers found that North Americans evaluated speakers with a moderate to slightly faster speaking rate as more "socially attractive" than speakers who had a slow rate of speech.[52] North American listeners also seem to prefer a speaking rate that is equal to or slightly faster than their own speaking rate.

Sometimes it is not what we say, or even how we say it, that communicates our feelings. Being silent may communicate volumes. One researcher, in commenting about the importance of silence in speech, said, "Silence is to speech as white paper is to this print. . . . The entire system of spoken language would fail without [people's] ability to both tolerate and create sign sequences of silence–sound–silence units."[53]

Would you be comfortable just sitting silently with a good friend? Sidney Baker's theory of silence suggests that the more at ease you are when you share a silence with a close friend, the more comfortable you are with just being together and enjoying each other's companionship. People need to talk until there is nothing left to say; by that point, the uncertainty has been managed. In most long-term relationships, partners may not feel a need to fill the air with sound. Just being together to enjoy each other's company may be most fulfilling. Baker calls such moments "positive silence."[54] While watching a sunset with a close friend, for example, there may be no need to narrate what you are seeing—it's enough just to experience it.

### Personal Space

Imagine that you are sitting alone in a booth at your local pizza parlor. As you sit munching your thin-and-crispy pepperoni pizza, you are startled when a complete stranger sits down in your booth directly across from you. With several empty tables and booths in the restaurant, you feel very uncomfortable that this unknown individual has invaded "your" area.

Normally, people do not think much about the rules of personal space, but in fact every culture has fairly rigid ways of regulating space in social interactions. Violations of these rules can be alarming and, as in the preceding scenario, even threatening. How close you are willing to get to others relates to how well you know them and to considerations of power and status.

**backchannel cues.** Nonverbal cues, typically vocal cues, that signal your wish to begin or end a conversation.

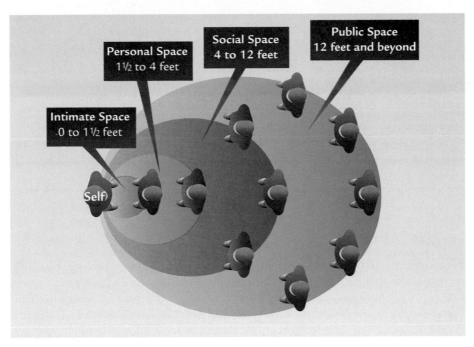

FIGURE *7·1*

Edwin T. Hall's Four Zones of Space

One pioneer in helping people understand the silent language of personal space was Edward T. Hall. His study of **proxemics** investigated how close or how far away from people and things we arrange ourselves.[55] Hall identified four spatial zones that speakers in Western cultures unconsciously define for themselves, as shown in Figure 7.1. When we are between 0 and 1½ feet from someone, we are occupying **intimate space.** This is the zone in which the most intimate interpersonal communication occurs. It is open only to those with whom we are well acquainted, unless we are forced to stand in an elevator, a fast-food line, or some other crowded space.

The second zone, which ranges from 1½ to 4 feet from each person, is called **personal space.** Most conversations with family and friends occur in this zone. If someone you don't know well invades this space on purpose, you may feel uncomfortable.

Zone three, called **social space,** ranges from 4 to 12 feet from a person. Most group interaction, as well as many professional relationships, take place in this zone. The interaction tends to be more formal than that in the first two zones.

**Public space,** the fourth zone, begins 12 feet from a person. Interpersonal communication does not usually occur in this zone, and many public speakers and teachers position themselves even more than 12 feet from their audience.

The specific space that you and others choose depends on several variables.[56] The more you like someone, the closer you will stand to the person. We allow individuals with high status to surround themselves with more space than we allow for people with lower status. Large people also usually have more space around them than smaller people do, and women stand closer to others than men do.[57] All of us tend to stand closer to others in a large room than we do in a small room.

In a group, who's in charge, who's important, and who talks to whom are reflected by the spatial arrangement people select. The more dominant group members tend to select seats at the head of a table, while shyer individuals often select a corner seat at a rectangular table.[58]

**proxemics.** Study of how close or far away from people and objects people position themselves.

**intimate space.** Zone of personal space most often used for very personal or intimate interactions, ranging from 0 to 1½ feet from the individual.

**personal space.** Zone of personal space most often used for conversation, ranging from 1½ to 4 feet from the individual.

**social space.** Zone of personal space most often used for group interactions, ranging from 4 to 12 feet from the individual.

**public space.** Zone of interactions most often used by public speakers or anyone speaking to many people, ranging beyond 12 feet from the individual.

## Edward T. Hall's Classification of Spatial Zones

|  | Distance from the Individual | Examples |
| --- | --- | --- |
| **Zone One** | 0 to 1½ feet | Communicating with our most intimate acquaintances |
| **Zone Two** | 1½ feet to 4 feet | Conversing with good friends and family members |
| **Zone Three** | 4 feet to 12 feet | Working with others in small groups and in professional situations |
| **Zone Four** | 12 feet and beyond | Public-speaking situations |

### Territory

**Territoriality** is the study of how animals (including humans) use space and objects to communicate occupancy or ownership of space. Earlier we gave the example of a stranger sitting down with you in a pizza parlor. In that case, you had assumed "ownership" of the booth in the pizza parlor and the accompanying "right" to determine who sat with you, because you and your pizza were occupying the booth. In addition to invading your personal space, the intrusive stranger broke the rules that govern territoriality.

People announce ownership of space with territorial markers—things that signify the area has been claimed—much as explorers once planted flags claiming uncharted land for their kings. When you are studying at the library, for example, and need to hop up and check a reference at the computerized card catalog, you might leave behind a notebook or a pencil. In rural areas, landowners post signs at the borders of their property to keep hunters off their territory. Signs, locks, electronic security systems, and other devices secure home and office territories.

You also use markers to indicate where your space stops and someone else's starts. "Good fences make good neighbors," wrote the poet Robert Frost. When someone sits too close, you may try to erect a physical barrier, such as a stack of books or a napkin

**territoriality.** Study of how animals and humans use space and objects to communicate occupancy or ownership of space.

When you sit down at one end of a park bench, how much of the bench do you consider to be your territory? When someone sits at the other end, is that an invasion of your space?

holder, or you might use your body as a shield by turning away. If the intruder does not get the hint that "this land is my land," you may ultimately resort to words to announce that the space is occupied.

## Touch

Standing elbow to elbow in a crowded elevator, you may find yourself in physical contact with total strangers. As you stiffen your body and avert your eyes, a baffling sense of shame floods over you. If you are sitting at a conference table and you accidentally brush the toes of your shoes against your colleague's ankle, you may jerk away and even blush or apologize. Why do people react this way to unpremeditated touching? Normally, you touch to express intimacy. When intimacy is not your intended message, you instinctively react to modify the impression.

Countless studies have shown that intimate touching is vital to your personal development and well-being.[59] Infants and children need to be touched to confirm that they are valued and loved. Many hospitals invite volunteers in to hold and rock newborns whose mothers cannot do it themselves. Advocates of breastfeeding argue that the intimate touching it entails strengthens the bond between mother and child.[60]

The amount of touch you need, tolerate, receive, and initiate depends on many factors. The amount and kind of touching you receive in your family is one big influence. If your mom or dad greets you with hugs, caresses, and kisses, then you probably do this to others. If your family is less demonstrative, you may be restrained yourself. Studies by researcher Nancy Henley show that most of us are more likely to touch people when we are feeling friendly, or happy, or under some of the following other specific circumstances:[61]

- When we ask someone to do something for us
- When we share rather than ask for information
- When we try to persuade someone to do something
- When we are talking about intimate topics
- When we are in social settings that we choose rather than in professional settings that are part of our job
- When we are thrilled and excited to share good news
- When we listen to a troubled or worried friend

## Appearance

In all interactions with others, appearance counts. American culture places a high value on how much you weigh, the style of your hair, and the clothes you wear; these things are particularly important in the early stages of relationship development. Attractive females have an easier time persuading others than do those who are perceived as less

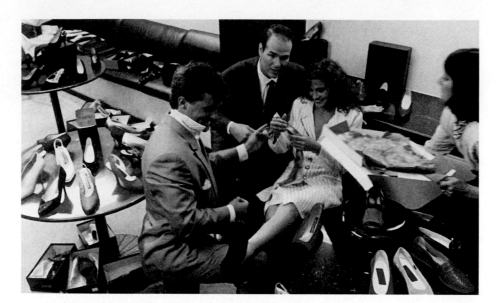

*D*oes your experience support research that shows that attractive people are more credible, happier, more popular, and more sociable than less attractive people?

attractive. In general, Americans think attractive people are more credible, happier, more popular, more sociable, and even more prosperous than less attractive people.[62]

There is also evidence that if you believe that others think a person is attractive, you'll be more likely to evaluate that person as attractive as well.[63] To test this self-fulfilling prophecy effect, researchers had subjects conduct interviews with people. Some subjects were told they were meeting a person others had rated as attractive. Other subjects interviewed a person they were led to believe had been evaluated as less attractive by others. If they thought they were interviewing someone whom others evaluated as attractive, then research subjects, too, were more likely to evaluate the person as attractive. Similarly, if they thought they were interviewing someone rated less attractive by others, then the interviewers evaluated the person they were interviewing as less attractive. Rather than supporting the adage "What you see is what you get," the study found "What you expect to see is what you think you got."

In Chapter 2 we discussed the link between self-concept and personal appearance. The shape and size of your body also affects how others perceive you. Heavier and rounder individuals are often perceived to be older, more old-fashioned, less good-looking, more talkative, and more good-natured than thin people, who are perceived to be more ambitious, more suspicious of others, more uptight and tense, more negative, and less talkative. Muscular and athletically fit folks are seen as better looking, taller, and more adventurous. These perceptions are, in fact, so common that they have become easily recognizable stereotypes on which casting directors for movies, TV shows, and plays rely in selecting actors and actresses.

Aside from keeping you warm and within the legal bounds of decency, your clothes also affect how others perceive you. The clothes you wear are a way of communicating to others how you want to be treated. One classic study found that a man who jaywalked while dressed in nice clothes attracted more fellow violators than he could when he was shabbily attired.[64] Although studies have attempted to identify a "power" look, and magazines are constantly giving prescriptions for ways to be attractive and stylish, there is no formula for dressing for success.[65] Styles and expectations about appearances change. You have only to look at the clothing norms of the 1950s, 1960s, or 1970s to note how they differ from those of today.

**immediacy.** Feelings of liking, pleasure, and closeness communicated by such nonverbal cues as eye contact, forward lean, touch, and open body orientation.

## Recap Codes of Nonverbal Communication

| | |
|---|---|
| **Movements and Gestures** | Communicate information, status, warmth, credibility, interest in others, attitudes, liking |
| **Eye Contact** | Serves cognitive, monitoring, regulatory, and expressive functions |
| **Facial Expressions** | Express emotions |
| **Vocal Cues** | Communicate emotion through pitch, rate, volume, and quality; modify the meaning of messages |
| **Personal Space** | Provides information about status, power, and intimacy |
| **Territory** | Provides cues to use, ownership, or occupancy of space |
| **Touch** | Communicates intimacy, affection, or rejection |
| **Appearance** | Influences perceptions of credibility and attraction |

# Interpreting Nonverbal Communication

So what does it all mean? How do you make sense out of the postures, movements, gestures, eye contact, facial expressions, uses of space and territory, touch, and appearance of others? Albert Mehrabian has found that people synthesize and interpret nonverbal cues along three primary dimensions: *immediacy, arousal,* and *dominance.*[66] These three dimensions provide a useful way to summarize how nonverbal cues may be interpreted.

## Immediacy

Sometimes we cannot put a finger on the precise reason we find a person likable or unlikable. Mehrabian believes that immediacy cues are a likely explanation. Immediacy cues are behaviors that communicate liking and engender feelings of pleasure. The principle underlying the communication of our feelings of **immediacy** is simple: We move toward persons and things we like and avoid or move away from those we dislike. Immediacy cues increase our sensory awareness of others. Use of space and territory is not the only cue that contributes to positive or negative feelings. Mehrabian has noted several other nonverbal cues that increase immediacy. One of the most powerful is touch; others include a forward lean, increased eye contact, and an open body orientation. The meaning of these behaviors is usually implied rather than explicitly spelled out in words.

Not surprisingly, communication researcher Lois Hinkle found that spouses who reported high feelings of affection for their mates reported that their mates responded by expressing more immediacy cues toward them.[67] There is also evidence that when someone expresses immediate or pleasant nonverbal messages toward us, we reciprocate by responding in a pleasant manner. Researchers Judee

MY KEEN SENSE OF READING BODY LANGUAGE TELLS ME THAT YOU MIGHT ALREADY HAVE ONE FOOT OUT THE DOOR OF THE RELATIONSHIP, MIRIAM...

# *Understanding Diversity*

## Gender Differences and Nonverbal Communication

*T*here is evidence that men and women display and interpret nonverbal cues differently.[68]

### Eye Contact

Women usually use a more prolonged gaze than do men. Women, however, are less likely just to stare at someone; they break eye contact more frequently than men. In general, women receive more eye contact from others than do men.

### Space

Men tend to require more space around them than do women. Women both approach and are approached more closely than men. And when conversing with others, women seem to prefer side-by-side interactions.

### Facial Expression

Research suggests that women smile more than men. It is also reported that women tend to be more emotionally expressive with their faces than men; this is perhaps related to the conclusion that women are more skilled at both displaying and interpreting facial expressions.

### Gesture and Posture

Overall, women appear to use fewer and less expansive gestures than men. Women are more likely, for example, to rest their hands on the arms of a chair while seated; men are more likely to use gestures. Men and women cross their legs differently: women cross their legs at the knees or ankles while men are more likely to sit with their legs apart.

### Touch

Men are more likely to initiate touch with others than are women. Women are touched more than men. Men and women also attribute different meaning to touch; women are more likely to associate touch with warmth and expressiveness than are men.

### Vocal Cues

Vocal patterns may be more related to biological differences in the vocal register than other nonverbal behaviors. Women speak in both higher and softer tones than do men. Women use their voices to communicate a greater range of emotions than do men. Women are also more likely to raise their pitch when making statements; some people interpret the rising pattern (as in asking a question) as an indication of greater uncertainty.

---

Burgoon and Beth Le Poire found that people adapt their nonverbal messages to others.[69] When people express immediacy or liking toward you, you are more likely to reciprocate and express a similar sentiment toward them. Immediacy is contagious. Yet another research study found that expressions of nonverbal immediacy on the part of someone trying to offer support and comfort to another person, such as closer personal distance, touching, and forward lean, helped reduce the other person's stress and tension.[70]

In brief, to communicate that we like someone, we use these cues:[71]

| | |
|---|---|
| *Proximity:* | Close, forward lean |
| *Body orientation:* | Typically face-to-face, but could be side-by-side |
| *Eye contact:* | Mutual eye contact |
| *Facial expression:* | Smiling |
| *Gestures:* | Head nods, movement |
| *Posture:* | Open, arms oriented toward others |
| *Touch:* | Cultural- and context-appropriate touch |
| *Voice:* | Higher pitch, upward pitch |

## Arousal

The face, voice, and movement are primary indicators of **arousal.** If we sense arousal cues, we conclude that another person is responsive to and interested in us. If the person acts passive or dull, we conclude that he or she is uninterested.

When you approach someone and ask whether he or she has a minute or two to talk, that person may signal interest with a change in facial expression and more animated vocal cues. People who are aroused and interested in you show animation in their face, voice, and gestures. Forward lean, a flash of the eyebrows, and a nod of the head are other cues that implicitly communicate arousal. Someone who says, "Sure, I have time to talk with you," in a monotone and with a flat, expressionless face is communicating the opposite. Think of arousal as an on-off switch. Sleeping is the ultimate switched-off state.

## Dominance

The third dimension of Mehrabian's framework for implicit cues communicates the balance of power in a relationship. **Dominance** cues communicate status, position, and importance.[72] A person of high status tends to have a relaxed body posture when interacting with a person of lower status.[73] When you talk to a professor, he may lean back in his chair, put his feet on the desk, and fold his hands behind his head during the conversation. But unless your professor is a colleague or a friend, you will maintain a relatively formal posture during your interaction in his office.

Another dominance cue is the use of space. High-status individuals usually have more space around them; they have bigger offices and more "barriers" protecting them. A receptionist in an office is usually easily accessible, but to reach the president of the company you may have to navigate through several corridors, past several secretaries and administrative assistants who are "guarding" the door.

Other power cues that communicate dominance include use of furniture, clothing, and locations. You study with others at a table in the library; the college president has a large private desk. You may wear jeans and a T-shirt to class; the head of the university wears a business suit. Your dorm may be surrounded by other dorms; the president's residence may be a large house surrounded by a lush, landscaped garden in a prestigious neighborhood. People use space, territory, posture, and artifacts such as clothing and furniture to signal feelings of dominance or submissiveness in the presence of others.

British social psychologist Michael Argyle summarizes the nonverbal cues that communicate dominance:[74]

| | |
|---|---|
| *Use of space:* | Height (on a platform or standing) |
| | Facing a group |
| | More space surrounding a person |
| *Eye contact:* | More when initially establishing dominance |
| | More when staring to establish power |
| | More when talking |
| *Face:* | Frown, no smile |
| *Touch:* | Initiating touch |
| *Voice:* | Loud, low pitch, greater pitch range |
| | Slow, more interruptions, more talk |
| | Slight hesitation before speaking |
| *Gesture:* | Pointing at the other or at his or her property |
| *Posture:* | Standing, hands on hips, expanded chest, more relaxed |

**arousal.** Feelings of interest and excitement communicated by such nonverbal cues as vocal expression, facial expressions, and gestures.

**dominance.** Power, status, and control communicated by such nonverbal cues as a relaxed posture, greater personal space, and protected personal space.

**Recap**

## Dimensions for Interpreting Nonverbal Behavior

| Dimension | Definition | Nonverbal Cues |
|-----------|------------|----------------|
| Immediacy | Cues that communicate liking and pleasure | Eye contact, touch, forward lean, closeness to partner |
| Arousal | Cues that communicate active interest and emotional involvement | Eye contact, varied vocal cues, animated facial expressions, forward lean, movement |
| Dominance | Cues that communicate status and power | Protected space, relaxed posture, status symbols |

# *I*mproving Your Ability to Interpret Nonverbal Messages

A s we have already cautioned, there are no dictionaries to which you can turn for help in interpreting specific nonverbal behaviors. People interpret the messages of others based on their own experiences and cultural perspective. One theory that helps explain how to interpret nonverbal messages is called **expectancy violation theory.** Developed by Burgoon and several of her colleagues, this theory suggests that each of us enters a relationship with certain preconceived expectations for others' behavior.[75] For example, when meeting a business colleague for the first time, most North Americans would expect someone to smile, extend his or her hand, and say, "Hello, I'm Steve Beebe" (or whatever the name is). If, instead, the person clasps two hands together and bows demurely without uttering a word, the nonverbal behavior is not what we expect. This violation of our expectation would result in our thinking about what the "violator" of our expectations might mean by bowing instead of offering to shake our hand. When our expectations are violated, we may feel uncomfortable. Research by communication researchers Beth Le Poire and Stephen Yoshimura found that people tend to adapt to the behavior of others, even when the behavior of others is not what we expected.[76] If someone behaves in a pleasant way by smiling, establishing eye contact, and maintaining an open body posture, we are more likely to reciprocate by displaying equally pleasant nonverbal messages. We interpret the messages of others by considering how we *expect* others to behave and by adapting to others.

Some people are simply better at interpreting nonverbal cues than others. The ability to interpret nonverbal cues is *not* related to a person's race, amount of education, or intelligence, but it *is* related to certain personality traits. Research offers some clues as to who is the most skilled at encoding nonverbal messages.[77]

1. People who are better at accurately expressing their feelings and emotions are also better able to interpret nonverbal expressions from others.

2. People who are skilled in interpreting one channel of information (for example, facial expression or vocal cues) are likely to be more accurate at interpreting nonverbal messages from other channels (such as posture or use of space).

3. People with certain personality characteristics have been found to interpret nonverbal messages more accurately. For instance, people who are extroverted, have high self-esteem, are nondogmatic, are not shy, and are expressive typically do a better job of interpreting nonverbal messages than do people who do not have these personality characteristics.

**expectancy violation theory.**
Theory that you interpret the
messages of others based on how
you expect others to behave.

4. People who select such people-oriented jobs as teachers, salespersons, and nurses often have more skill in interpreting nonverbal messages.

Even if you don't have a natural talent for interpreting nonverbal cues, with training and practice, you can enhance your sensitivity and accuracy in interpreting them. Several principles and key skills can help you to interpret others' nonverbal messages.

## Consider Nonverbal Cues in Context

Just as quoting someone out of context can change the meaning of a statement, trying to draw conclusions from an isolated snatch of behavior or a single cue can lead to misinterpretations. Beware of looking at someone's folded arms and concluding that he or she does not like you or is not interested in what you are saying. It could be that the air conditioner is set too low and the person is just trying to keep warm.

## Look for Clusters of Nonverbal Cues

Instead of focusing on a specific cue, look for corroborating cues that can lead you to a more accurate conclusion about the meaning of a behavior. Is the person making eye contact? Is he or she facing you? How far away is he or she standing from you? Always consider nonverbal behaviors in conjunction with other nonverbal cues, the environment, and the person's verbal message.

## Consider Past Experiences When Interpreting Nonverbal Cues

It may be that "familiarity breeds contempt," as the old saying goes, but familiarity with another person also increases your ability to interpret his or her nonverbal behavior. You may have learned, for example, that when your mother started crying when you played the piano, it signaled pride, not melancholy. Family members can probably interpret each other's nonverbal cues more accurately than can those from outside the family. But after knowing someone over a period of time, you begin to increase your sensitivity to certain glances, silences, movements, and vocal cues that might be overlooked or misunderstood by others.

## Check Your Perceptions with Others

You judge others by their behavior, not by their intent. As we discussed in Chapter 3, the only way to know what people intend is to ask them whether you have interpreted their behavior correctly. But before you blurt out a hunch, first consider the context and confirming cues and think about this person's previous behavior. Then, if you are still confused or uncertain about the meaning of a behavior, ask for clarification.

For example, if you receive a fabulous job offer that requires you to move to a new state, and your spouse greets your enthusiastic announcement with silence, you could ask, "Does your silence mean that you're opposed to the move, or are you speechless with excitement?" Then wait for a response.

Or suppose you work in the kitchen all day to make fish stew for your friend from Iowa. After her first bite, you see her eyes open wide and her lips purse up. So you ask, "Does that mean you don't like it, or did you taste something new and different?"

This key skill is called **perception checking**. We discussed this skill in Chapter 3. You can follow three steps to check your perception of someone's nonverbal behavior. First, observe the nonverbal cues, making a point to note such variables as eye

**perception checking.** Asking someone whether your interpretation of his or her nonverbal behavior is accurate.

contact, posture, use of gestures, facial expression, and tone of voice. Second, try to interpret what the individual is expressing through his or her nonverbal behavior. Finally, check your perception by asking him or her if it is accurate. Of course, we are not suggesting that you need to go through life constantly checking everyone's nonverbal cues. Overusing this skill would be irritating to most people. We are suggesting, however, that when you are uncertain of how someone feels, and it is important to know, a perception check may be in order. Consider this example:

*Deonna:* Hi, Mom. I'm sorry Erik and I missed the family reunion last week. It's been a hectic week. The kids had something goin' on every night, and we just needed to rest.

*Muriel:* (Frowns, makes little eye contact, folds her arms, and uses a flat voice.) Oh, don't worry about it.

*Deonna:* I know you said don't worry about it, Mom, but it looks like you are still upset. I know that look of yours. I also hear in your voice that you are not really pleased. Is it really OK, or are you still a little miffed?

*Muriel:* Well, yes, to be honest, Dad and I were really looking forward to getting all the kids together.

*Deonna:* I'm sorry, Mom. We will make an effort to be at the next one. Thanks for admitting how you really feel.

Asking about a specific nonverbal cue will help you interpret your partner's behavior in future interactions as well. As we noted earlier, evidence suggests that the longer couples are married, the more they rely on nonverbal behavior to communicate. One study claims that most couples spend less than eleven minutes a week in sustained conversation.[78] Even in marriages of fifty years, however, conversation is still required occasionally to clarify nonverbal responses.

## *Recap*
## How to Check Your Perceptions of Others' Nonverbal Cues

| Steps | Consider . . . |
|---|---|
| 1. Observe their nonverbal behavior. | Are they frowning? |
| | Do they make eye contact? |
| | Are their arms crossed? |
| | What is their tone of voice? |
| | What is their posture? |
| 2. Form a mental impression of what you think they mean. | Are they happy, sad, angry? |
| | Is the nonverbal message contradicting the verbal message? |
| 3. Ask questions to check whether your perception is accurate. | "Are you upset? You look angry." |
| | "Your expression and your voice suggest you don't believe me. Do you think I'm lying?" |
| | "The look on your face tells me you really like it. Do you?" |

## Becoming Other-Oriented

### Checking Perceptions

*W*e have identified several strategies to improve your skill at interpreting the nonverbal messages of others, including being able to check your perceptions of others. Accurately perceiving others gets to the heart of becoming other-oriented.

Look at the photographs. First, note the nonverbal behavior of the target person in the picture. Next, form a mental impression of what you think the person is thinking and feeling. Finally, compose a perception-checking question that the other person in the photo could ask to confirm the target person's thoughts and feelings.

**Photo 1**

A. Describe the student's nonverbal behavior.

B. What do you think the student is thinking and feeling?

C. What is a perception-checking question the teacher could ask her student?

**Photo 2**

A. Describe the customer's nonverbal behavior.

B. What do you think the customer is thinking and feeling?

C. What is a perception-checking question the salesman could ask the customer?

## Be Aware That the Nonverbal Expression of Emotion Is Contagious

Have you ever noticed that when you watch a funny movie, you are more likely to laugh out loud if other people around you are laughing? That when you are around people who are sad or remorseful, you are more likely to feel and express sadness? There's a reason this happens. Nonverbal emotional expressions are contagious. People often display the same emotions that a communication partner is displaying. **Emotional contagion theory** suggests that people tend to "catch" the emotions of others.[79] Interpersonal interactions with others can affect your nonverbal expression of emotions.[80] The ancient Roman orator Cicero knew this when he gave advice to public speakers. He said if you want your audience to experience joy, you must be a joyful speaker. Or, if you want to communicate fear, then you should express fear when you speak. Knowing that you tend to catch or imitate the emotions of others can help you interpret your own nonverbal messages and those of others; you may be imitating the emotional expression of others around you.

## Look for Cues That May Communicate Lying

"Look at me, young man. I know you're not telling the truth." Sometimes parents just seem to know whether kids are telling the truth or lying. How do they know? It may

**emotional contagion theory.**
Theory that emotional expression is contagious; people can "catch" emotions just by observing each other's emotional expressions.

TABLE *7.2*    **Who's Telling the Truth? Differences Between Honest and Dishonest Communicators**

| Nonverbal Cue | Honest Communicators | Dishonest Communicators |
|---|---|---|
| **Voice** | Use fewer pauses when they talk | Pause more; they are thinking about what "story" they want to give |
| | Speak fluently, smoothly | Use more nonfluencies ("ah," "er," "um") |
| | Speak at a normal speaking rate | Speak a bit faster than normal |
| **Facial Expression** | Smile genuinely and sincerely | Display a plastered-on, phony smile |
| | | May smile a bit too long |
| **Gestures** | Are less likely to play with objects as they speak | Are more likely to play with objects (for example, twiddle a pencil) |
| | Use fewer gestures | Use more gestures, more self-adaptors, touching their face and body, shrugging shoulders |
| | Are not likely to shift body weight | Are more likely to shift their posture |
| | Generally display less nervousness | Display increased nervousness |
| **Eye Contact** | Maintain normal eye contact—a steady, natural gaze | May look away, maintain less direct eye contact |
| | Have a normal eye-blink rate | Have an increased eye-blink rate, a sign of increased anxiety |

not be the "story" but the nonverbal message that gives the kids away. Several researchers have been interested in identifying those nonverbal cues that indicate deceit.[81] As we've emphasized several times, because of the transactional nature of interpersonal communication, meaning is created as people communicate with others; behaviors do not have a fixed interpretation. Also, remember not to place too much emphasis on a single cue. As we've just noted, look for clusters of cues rather than pointing your finger when someone has less eye contact and saying, "Ah ha! Now I know you're a liar!" Table 7.2 summarizes research conclusions about nonverbal messages, comparing liars and those who are telling the truth.[82]

It would be easier if we each had a nose like Pinocchio's, which would grow just a bit whenever we told a lie. But we don't. Apparently, among the best ways to detect whether someone is telling the truth is to (1) look for nonverbal clues, (2) listen to the content of what the person says, and (3) measure such physiological responses as heart rate, breathing and other factors.[83] Although nonverbal cues (such as hand and finger movements, pauses, and increased use of illustrators) can be important in helping judges sort out truth-tellers from liars, ultimately it's better to listen to the message and monitor physiological responses (which, of course, may not always be practical).

Unless you have a portable lie detector, which measures physiological responses such as heart rate, blood pressure, and breathing rate, the best approach may be to ask other people for corroborating information.[84] Or you can do your own investigation to ferret out whether someone is really telling the truth. Nonverbal cues may be important in giving us an *initial* hunch as to whether someone is telling the truth, but personal detective work may be the real way we ultimately confirm our hunches.

## *S*ummary

Unspoken messages have a major effect on interpersonal relationships. The primary way in which you communicate feelings, emotions, and attitudes is through nonverbal cues. When there is a contradiction between your verbal and nonverbal messages, others almost always believe the nonverbal one. But nonverbal messages usually work with verbal messages to create meaning. It is primarily through nonverbal messages that people respond and adapt to others and initiate, maintain, and develop interpersonal relationships. Important as they are, nonverbal messages can also be challenging. They are usually more ambiguous than verbal messages. Although some nonverbal messages have a definite beginning and ending, most are part of a seamless flow of movement, gestures, glances, and inflections. Also, there are culture-based differences in the way people express and interpret unspoken messages.

Nonverbal cues can be categorized and studied to reveal the codes to our unspoken communication. Movement, posture, and gestures communicate both content and expressive information when we use them as emblems, illustrators, affect displays, regulators, and adaptors. Eye contact is an important code for regulating interaction in interpersonal exchanges. Facial expressions and vocal cues provide a wealth of information about our emotions. Our use of personal space and territory communicates a

variety of messages relating to power, status, and other relational concerns. Touch is one of the most powerful cues to communicate liking; and our appearance telegraphs to others how we wish to be treated and how we perceive our role in relation to them.

One of the most fascinating aspects of nonverbal messages is the potential to reveal hidden meaning communicated through unspoken codes. It is not as easy to read nonverbal cues as it is to read the words on this page, but there is a general framework that can help you assess the nonverbal messages of others, as well as your own nonverbal expressions. Researchers have identified three primary dimensions for interpreting nonverbal messages: Immediacy cues provide information about liking and disliking. Arousal cues tip others off as to your interest and level of engagement with them. And position, power, and status are often communicated through dominance cues.

To enhance your skill in interpreting nonverbal messages, always consider the context in which you observed the cues, and look for clusters of nonverbal behaviors. The longer you have known someone, the easier it is to interpret his or her unspoken messages. But to verify whether you understand someone's nonverbal behavior, ask whether your interpretation is accurate or do your own investigation into the truth.

# For Discussion and Review

## Focus on Critical Thinking

1. Sasha has had difficulty getting hired as a manager. One of her best friends suggests that she ought to pay more attention to her nonverbal behavior when she is interviewed for a job. What advice would you give Sasha to help her monitor her nonverbal interview behavior?

2. Greg has been told that he sometimes comes across as cold, aloof, and standoffish. What could Greg do to communicate his sincere desire to be warm and approachable?

## Focus on Ethics

3. Donald really wants to be hired as a salesperson. He hires a fashion consultant to recommend what he should wear and determine how he should look when he interviews for a job. In general, is it ethical to manipulate your appearance so that you can impress others?

4. Is it appropriate to draw definitive conclusions about another's personality and attitudes based only on a "reading" of his or her other nonverbal cues? Support your answer.

5. Is it ethical for salespeople, politicians, and others who wish to make favorable impressions to alter their nonverbal messages to get you to like them, vote for them, or buy their products? Explain your answer.

# For Your Journal

1. Videotape fifteen minutes of a TV drama or situation comedy. Watch the tape with the sound turned off. Using the four principles of interpreting nonverbal messages, describe the meaning of the nonverbal behaviors you see. After you have made written observations in your journal, watch the program with the sound on and determine how accurate your interpretations were.

2. Mehrabian has suggested that people convey 55 percent of their emotional meaning through facial expressions, 38 percent through vocal cues, and only 7 percent through verbal statements. Spend thirty minutes observing four or five people in a public place, such as a mall, airport, or student center, and attempt to prove or disprove Mehrabian's conclusions. Before you begin your people-watching, design a method for recording your observations in your journal.

# Learning with Others

1. Go on a nonverbal communication scavenger hunt. Your instructor will ask you to observe your family members and friends to find one or more of the following sets of nonverbal communicators:

   a. Examples of emblems, illustrators, affect displays, regulators, and adaptors.

   b. Examples of how people use the four zones of personal space.

   c. Examples of immediacy, arousal, and dominance cues.

   d. Examples of the cognitive, monitoring, regulatory, and expressive functions of eye contact.

   e. Examples of clothing that reveals intentions or personality traits.

2. Spend some time observing people in a public place, such as a restaurant, airport terminal, student center, or bar, and note examples of quasi-courtship behavior as discussed in this chapter on pages 195–196. List the four phases we described (courtship readiness, preening, positional cues, appeals to invitation) on a sheet of paper, and describe several examples to illustrate each of these phases.

http://anthro.palomar.edu/language/language_6.htm
Communication is far more than spoken or written words.
Read the article *Language and Culture: Hidden Aspects of Communication* at this site.

http://www.virginia.edu/career/handouts/interview2.html
Learn the important role nonverbal communication plays
during employment interviews. Visit this site to help you
prepare for an interview.

http://www.culture-at-work.com/nvcnegotiation.html  At
this site you'll learn about the importance of nonverbal
communication when negotiating with others.

http://zzyx.ucsc.edu/~archer/intro.html  This site will help
you sharpen your skills in identifying the meaning of nonverbal messages.

# Conflict Management Skills

## OBJECTIVES

1. Define conflict.

2. Identify commonly held myths about interpersonal conflict.

3. Compare and contrast three types of interpersonal conflict.

4. Describe differences between destructive and constructive approaches to managing conflict.

5. List and describe five stages of conflict.

6. Describe five conflict management styles.

7. Identify and describe six win–lose and six win–win negotiation strategies.

8. Identify and use conflict management skills to help manage emotions, information, goals, and problems when attempting to resolve interpersonal differences.

## OUTLINE

*Outside noisy, inside empty.*

Chinese Proverb

*T*his house stinks," said Paolo, wrinkling up his nose. "It smells like day-old garbage."

"Take it out yourself. It's your job," said Anya, turning her back on him to scrub furiously at an imaginary morsel of food on a frying pan that was already polished clean.

"Hey, hey," said Paolo, holding up both hands in front of him, "I wasn't accusing you. I just said it smelled bad in here. Don't be so touchy."

"Oh, no? Well, you're always criticizing me. You think just because you have a big important job that you can come in here and say anything you like. And I come home from work feeling tired, too, you know, but you don't do anything to help, not even the things you agree to!" shouted Anya, turning around to confront her mate, planting her soapy hands on her hips.

"Well, you're always getting on my case for no reason. I'm not putting up with this stuff from you anymore," snarled Paolo. As he turned on his heel to stalk out of the kitchen, Anya burst into tears.

Why have Paolo and Anya reached an impasse in their attempt to communicate? Paolo and Anya's exchange is complicated, seething with conflicting goals and underlying resentments. Eventually, all relationships experience conflict. How can you avoid the same kind of outcome in your own complicated exchanges?

Conflict management is not a single skill but a set of skills. But to manage conflict effectively involves more than learning simple techniques. The best route to success in resolving conflict effectively is acquiring knowledge about what conflict is, what makes it happen, and what we can do about it. We will begin by defining conflict, then examine some of the myths about it and focus on some of its constructive functions. We will also discuss the relationship among conflict, power, and conflict management styles.

In addition, we will discuss how learning about your typical style of managing conflict can give you insight into managing interpersonal differences. And finally, we will build on our discussions of listening skills and verbal and nonverbal communication in the previous chapters to help you learn to manage the inevitable interpersonal conflicts that arise in the best of relationships.

FIGURE *8.1*

The Struggle Spectrum.
Used by permission of the
National Communication
Association.

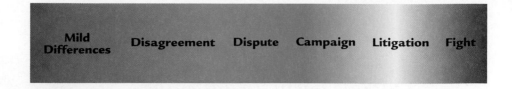

| Mild Differences | Disagreement | Dispute | Campaign | Litigation | Fight |
|---|---|---|---|---|---|

# *W*hat Is Conflict?

**I**nterpersonal conflict is an expressed struggle that occurs when people cannot agree on a way to meet their needs and achieve their goals. If the needs are incompatible, if there are too few resources to accomplish the goals, or if the individuals opt to compete rather than to cooperate to meet needs and achieve goals, then interpersonal conflict occurs. People involved in such a conflict are **interdependent**; this means that what one person does or says affects others.[1] Unresolved and poorly managed interpersonal conflict is a significant predictor of an unsatisfactory relationship, and the opposite is also true: Partners in relationships with effectively managed conflict report being more satisfied with the relationship.[2]

You typically don't know that someone is upset with you until conflict is expressed by a remark or by nonverbal behavior such as a glare, steely facial expression, or emotion-laden tone of voice. The intensity level of a conflict (expressed through the intensity of nonverbal expressions of emotion) usually relates to the intensity of the unmet needs or goals. Conflict sometimes escalates into physical abuse. One research team estimated that 50–60 percent of U.S. households have experienced at least minor forms of violence; there's evidence that in one out of every six romantic relationships, one partner has stalked the other.[3] Experts surmise that one reason violence is so prevalent in many relationships is that people don't have the skills to manage conflict and disagreement.[4] Sam Keltner developed the "struggle spectrum," shown in Figure 8.1, to describe conflicts ranging from mild differences to fights.[5] At the bedrock of all conflict are differences—in goals, needs, and experiences.

**interpersonal conflict.**
Expressed struggle that occurs when people cannot agree on a way to meet their needs or goals.

**interdependent.** Dependent on each other; one person's actions affect the other person.

**O**f course, if Wile E. Coyote and Roadrunner ever found a way to resolve their conflicts, we'd stop watching their cartoons. But humans are better off finding ways to resolve their conflicts.

# Myths About Conflict

Although not all conflict is destructive to relationships, many cultures have taboos against displaying it in public. The prime experiences in life that shape how we learn to express and manage conflict occur in our families of origin—the families in which we grew up. It's in our families that we learn life lessons about relationships that remain with us throughout our days.[6] According to one researcher, many of us were raised with five myths that contribute to our negative feelings about conflict.[7] As you read the following sections, you may shake your head and say, "That's not where I came from." In some American families, conflict is expressed openly and often. But even if your experience has been different, reading about these prevailing myths may help you understand your or your partner's emotional responses to conflict.

### Myth 1: "Conflict Is Always a Sign of a Poor Interpersonal Relationship"

It is an oversimplification to assume that all conflict is rooted in underlying relational problems. Conflict is a normal part of any interpersonal relationship. Although it is true that constant bickering and sniping can be symptomatic of deeper problems, disagreements do not necessarily signal that the relationship is on the rocks. All relationships experience conflict. In fact, overly polite, stilted conversation is more likely to signal a problem than periodic disagreements. The free expression of honest disagreement is often a hallmark of healthy relationships. Assertively and honestly expressing ideas may mean that a person feels safe and comfortable enough with his or her partner to disagree. As we will discuss later, conflict in interpersonal relationships can play a constructive role in leading the couple to focus on issues that may need attention. The ebb and flow of interpersonal psychological intimacy and separation inevitably lead to some degree of conflict in any relationship. When conflict happens in your relationships, don't immediately assume that the relationship is doomed.

### Myth 2: "Conflict Can Always Be Avoided"

"If you can't say anything nice, don't say anything at all." Many of us were taught early in our lives that conflict is undesirable and that we should eliminate it from our conversations and relationships. Yet evidence suggests that conflict arises in virtually every relationship.[8] Because each of us has a unique perspective on our world, it would be extraordinary for us *always* to see eye-to-eye with another person. One study found

© Zits Partnership. Reprinted with special Permission of King Features Syndicate.

that most romantic couples have some kind of disagreement or conflict, on average, about twice a week. Although such conflicts may not be intense, many differences of opinion punctuate our relationships with people we care about.[9]

Research suggests that contentment in marriage relates not to the amount of conflict, but to the way in which partners manage it.[10] Conflict is also a normal and productive part of interaction in group deliberations.[11] It is a myth that conflict is inherently unproductive and something to be avoided. It happens, even in the best of relationships.

### Myth 3: "Conflict Always Occurs Because of Misunderstandings"

"You just don't understand what my days are like. I need to go to sleep!" shouts Janice as she scoops up a pillow and blanket and stalks off to the living room. "Oh, yeah? Well, you don't understand what will happen if I don't get this budget in!" responds Ron, who is hunched over the desk in their bedroom. It is clear that Ron and Janice are having a conflict. They have identified the cause of their problem as a lack of understanding between them, but in reality they *do* understand each other. Ron knows that Janice wants to sleep; Janice knows he wants to stay up and work. Their problem is that they disagree about whose goal is most important. This disagreement, not lack of understanding, is the source of the conflict.

### Myth 4: "Conflict Can Always Be Resolved"

Consultants, corporate training experts, and authors of self-help books often offer advice about how to resolve conflicts so that all will be well and harmony will prevail. Some people claim that with the application of a few skills and how-to techniques, conflicts can disappear like a stain from a shirt laundered with the right kind of detergent. This is simply not true. Not all differences can be resolved by listening harder or paraphrasing your partner's message. Some disagreements are so intense and the perceptions so fixed that individuals may have to agree to disagree and live with it.

### Myth 5: "Conflict Is Always Bad"

It's a common fantasy to dream of eliminating all interpersonal conflict from relationships. It would be bliss, we think, if we could live without disagreement, hassle, haggling, and tension. But conflict is a healthy component of relationships. In fact, if a relationship is conflict-free, the individuals are probably not being honest with each other. Although it can be destructive, conflict can also help us identify issues that need further discussion and lead to negotiations that give us fresh insights into the relationship.

### Conflict Myths

Myth 1:    "Conflict is always a sign of a poor interpersonal relationship."
Myth 2:    "Conflict can always be avoided."
Myth 3:    "Conflict always occurs because of a misunderstanding."
Myth 4:    "Conflict can always be resolved."
Myth 5:    "Conflict is always bad."

# Types of Conflict

At some time or another, many close relationships go through a conflict phase. "We're always fighting," complains a newlywed. But if she were to analyze these fights, she would discover important differences among them. According to communication researchers Gerald Miller and Mark Steinberg, most conflicts fit into one of three different categories: (1) **pseudoconflict**—triggered by a lack of understanding; (2) **simple conflict**—stemming from different ideas, definitions, perceptions, or goals; and (3) **ego conflict**—which occurs when conflict gets personal.[12]

## Pseudoconflict: Misunderstandings

*Will:*   Let's walk to the store.

*Sean:*   No, it's too far. Let's drive.

*Will:*   But the store is close.

*Sean:*   No, it's not.

*Will:*   Yes, it is. It's just off Market Street.

*Sean:*   Oh, you mean the convenience store.

*Will:*   Sure, that's exactly what I mean.

*Sean:*   Oh, no problem. I thought you meant the supermarket.

*Pseudo* means false or fake. Pseudoconflict occurs when we simply miss the meaning in a message. But unless we clear up the misunderstanding by asking for more information, a real conflict might ensue. Note that in this example, Will offers helpful information ("It's just off Market Street") and Sean checks it with feedback ("Oh, you mean the convenience store").

How can you avoid pseudoconflict? A key strategy is to clarify the meaning of words and expressions that you don't understand. Keep the following strategies in mind to minimize misunderstandings before they occur:

- *Check your perceptions:* Ask for clarification of anything you don't understand; seek to determine whether your interpretation is the same as your partner's.

- *Listen between the lines:* Look for puzzled or quizzical facial expressions from your partner. People may not voice their misunderstanding but express their uncertainty nonverbally.

- *Establish a supportive rather than a defensive climate for conversation:* Avoid evaluating, controlling, using manipulative strategies, being aloof, acting superior, or rigidly asserting that you're always right. These classic behaviors are like pushing the button to increase defensiveness and misunderstanding.

## Simple Conflict: Different Stands on the Issues

Simple conflict stems from differences in ideas, definitions, perceptions, or goals. You want to go to Disney World for your vacation; your spouse wants to go to Washington, D.C. Your spouse wants to fly; you would rather take the train. You understand each other, but you disagree.

Pseudoconflict is simply a misunderstanding. Your partner may communicate confusion by facial expressions or other nonverbal behavior. Pseudoconflict can be resolved if partners ask for clarification, listen between the lines, and work to establish a supportive climate.

**pseudoconflict.** Conflict triggered by a lack of understanding and miscommunication.

**simple conflict.** Conflict that stems from different ideas, definitions, perceptions, or goals.

**ego conflict.** Conflict that is based on personal issues; conflicting partners attack each other's self-esteem.

# Understanding Diversity

## Gender, Culture, and Conflict

Research suggests that there are distinctions between feminine and masculine styles of responding to conflict. The feminine style is more likely to focus on relationship issues, whereas the masculine style typically focuses on tasks.[13] Those with the feminine style often interact with others to achieve intimacy and closeness, but those with the masculine style interact to get something done or to accomplish something apart from the relationship. Those employing a masculine style are often more aggressive and assertive than those employing a feminine style when pursuing a goal.[14] The following list summarizes key differences that researchers have observed between feminine and masculine styles of responding to conflict. Note that individuals of either sex may employ some characteristics of both feminine and masculine gender styles.

## Perceived Gender Differences in Responding to Conflict[15]

| Feminine Styles | Masculine Styles |
|---|---|
| Concerned with equity and caring; connect with and feel responsible to others | Concerned with equality of rights and fairness; adhere to abstract principles, rules |
| Interact to achieve closeness and interdependence | Interact for instrumental purposes; seek autonomy and distance |
| Attend to interpersonal dynamics to assess relationship's health | Are less aware of interpersonal dynamics |
| Encourage mutual involvement | Protect self-interest |
| Attribute crises to problems in the relationship | Attribute crises to problems external to the relationship |
| Are concerned with the impact of the relationship on personal identity | Are neither self- nor relationship-centered |
| Respond to conflict by often focusing mainly on the relationship | Respond to conflict by often focusing on rules and being evasive until a unilateral decision is reached |

Although these findings provide a starting point for analyzing our conflicts with members of the opposite sex, we caution against lapsing into

A key to unraveling a simple conflict is to keep the conversation focused on the issues at hand so that the expression of differences does not deteriorate into a battle focusing on personalities.

The following exchange between Jason and Nick illustrates a conflict over a simple difference of opinion; notice how both partners stick to the issues and figure out a way to resolve their differences.

*Jason:*  I want to watch *The Simpsons* tonight. It's their Christmas show.

*Nick:*  No way, man. I have to watch a documentary about textiles for my history class. It's an assignment.

*Jason:*  But I've worked all weekend. I'm beat. The last thing I want to watch is some stuffy old documentary on the history of weaving.

*Nick:*  Tell you what. Go ahead and watch *The Simpsons.* I'll videotape the documentary and watch it later. Deal?

*Jason:*  Okay. Thanks. And I'll grill some burgers so we can have supper together first.

"allness" statements such as "Oh, you're just like all women. That's why you disagree with me." Or "You're just like all men. You never want to focus on how I feel." Even thinking in these ways can prevent you from listening to what your partner is saying. Also, although research has identified some gender-based differences in the way we manage conflict, some research studies suggest that the differences can, at times, be quite small. The context for the argument or the specific conflict trigger may be a more important factor than gender in shaping how we respond to and manage interpersonal conflict.[16]

The most recent perspective on analyzing gender differences is called the *partnership perspective*. Rather than viewing gender differences as a gulf between people who live on different planets, this perspective suggests that men and women are not locked into particular styles or approaches.[17] The partnership approach emphasizes the importance of keeping channels open and avoiding the tendency to stereotype communication styles by gender.

An individual's culturally learned assumptions influence his or her conflict behavior. In some cultures, most conflict is **expressive;** it focuses on the quality of relationships, and on managing interpersonal tension and hostility. In other cultures, conflict is more **instrumental.** It centers less on relationships and more on achieving a specific goal or objective.[18] One researcher noted that for people from low-context cultures (those who derive more meaning from words than from the surrounding context), conflicts are most often instrumental.[19] Most North Americans come from low-context cultures. Many Asian cultures, in contrast, are high-context cultures. They are also collectivist: they value group effort over individual achievement. For people from these cultures, conflicts often center on expressive, relational concerns. Keeping peace in the group or saving face is often a higher priority than achieving a goal.

Managing culture-based conflict requires a strong other-orientation. One research team suggests that Anglo-Americans of European descent receive little training in how to develop solutions to problems that are acceptable to an entire group.[20] They are often socialized to stick up for their own rights at any cost, and they approach conflict as a win–lose situation. In contrast, people from collectivist cultures approach conflict management situations from a win–win perspective; it is important that both sides save face and avoid ridicule. Such differences in approaches provide a double challenge. In addition to disagreeing over the issue at hand, people from different cultures may also have different strategies for reaching agreement.

This next exchange between Sue and Nadiya is a bumpier one. What starts as a simple conflict deteriorates into a series of personal attacks.

*Nadiya:* Sue, can I borrow your skirt? I have a date tonight. It would look great with my new jacket.

*Sue:* Sorry, Nadiya. I'm going to wear it tonight. I've got to give a presentation to the school board about our new mentor program.

*Nadiya:* In case you don't remember, when you brought it home, you said I could borrow it any time. Besides, you haven't paid back the twenty bucks I loaned you to buy it.

*Sue:* Yes, but I bought the skirt especially for this occasion.

*Nadiya:* Well, don't ask to borrow anything from me ever again. You're just plain selfish.

*Sue:* Oh, yeah? Well *you're* the one who hogs all the space in the refrigerator. Talk about someone who's selfish. If that's not the pot calling the kettle black!

**expressive conflict.** Conflict that focuses on issues about the quality of the relationship and managing interpersonal tension and hostility.

**instrumental conflict.** Conflict that centers on achieving a particular goal or task and less on relational issues.

*Nadiya:*  All right, now that we're being honest about who hogs what, *you're* the one who monopolizes the bathroom in the morning.

And so it escalates. The original disagreement about the skirt is forgotten, and egos become attacked and bruised.

To keep simple conflict from escalating into personal vendettas, consider the following strategies:

- *Clarify your and your partner's understanding* of the issues and your partner's understanding of the source of the disagreement.

- *Keep the discussion focused* on facts and the issue at hand, rather than drifting back to past battles and unrelated personal grievances.

- *Look for more than just the initial solutions* that you and your partner bring to the discussion; generate many options.

- *Don't try to tackle too many issues at once.* Perform "issue triage"—identify the important issues and work on those.

- *Find the kernel of truth in what your partner is saying.* Find agreement where you can.

- *If tempers begin to flare and conflict is escalating, cool off.* Come back to the discussion when you and your partner are fresh.

## Ego Conflict: Conflict Gets Personal

As you can see from the preceding exchange between Sue and Nadiya, a personal attack puts your partner on the defensive, and many people behave according to the adage "The best defense is a good offense." When you launch a personal attack, you are "picking a fight." And as Sue and Nadiya's exchange illustrates, fights that begin as pseudo- or simple conflicts can easily lapse into more vicious ego conflicts. Here's another example:

*Shasta:*  I've told you before. I think we should split the expenses 50–50. You never listen to me. You always want everything to go your way. I'm tired of you trying to boss me around.

*Carol:*  Face it, Shasta, you just can't take constructive criticism. You've never liked me since I moved in here to help you out by sharing some expenses.

*Shasta:*   It's just that I don't like a bully. You try to dictate what we're supposed to have for dinner, what TV show to watch, and what music to hear. Well, you're not the boss of me!

*Carol:*   What an ungrateful attitude! After all I've done to help you out, and now you're complaining about such petty stuff. You're a real piece of work, Shasta.

Note that as each person in the conflict becomes more defensive about his or her position, the issues become more tangled.

Remember Paolo and Anya's argument about taking out the garbage at the beginning of this chapter? It started with what was probably an offhand remark and escalated into a major argument because both participants began attacking each other and bringing up other sensitive issues instead of focusing on the original comment.

If you find yourself involved in ego conflict, try to refrain from hurling personal attacks and emotional epithets back and forth. Instead, take turns expressing your feelings without interrupting each other, then take time to cool off. It is difficult to use effective listening skills when your emotions are at a high pitch.

Here are additional strategies to consider when conflict becomes personal:

- *Try to steer the ego conflict back to simple conflict:* Stay focused on issues rather than personalities.

- *Make the issue a problem to be solved rather than a battle to be won.*

- *Write down what you want to say:* It may help you clarify your point, and you and your partner can develop your ideas without interruption. A note of caution: Don't put angry personal attacks in writing. Make your written summary rational, logical, and brief rather than emotion-laden.

- *When things get personal, make a vow not to reciprocate:* Use "I" messages that we talked about in Chapter 5 ("I feel uncomfortable and threatened when we yell at each other" rather than "you" messages ("You're such a creep. You never listen.") to express how you are feeling.

 **Types of Conflict**

|  | Pseudoconflict | Simple Conflict | Ego Conflict |
|---|---|---|---|
| **What It Is** | Individuals misunderstand each other. | Individuals disagree over which action to pursue to achieve their goals. | Individuals feel personally attacked. |
| **What to Do** | Check your perceptions. | Clarify understanding. | Return to issues rather than personal attacks. |
|  | Listen between the lines; look for nonverbal expressions of puzzlement. | Stay focused on facts and issues. | Talk about a problem to be solved rather than a fight to be won. |
|  | Be supportive rather than defensive. | Generate many options rather than arguing over one or two options. | Write down rational arguments to support your position. |
|  | Listen actively. | Find the kernel of truth in what your partner is saying; emphasize where you agree. | Use "I" messages rather than "You" messages. |

# Conflict as a Process

Cathy was reading the Sunday paper, enjoying a second cup of coffee, and listening to her favorite classical music station. All seemed well. Suddenly, for no apparent reason, her roommate Barb brusquely stormed into the room and shouted, "I can't stand it anymore! We have to talk about who does what around here." Cathy was taken completely off guard. She had no idea her roommate was upset about the division of household chores. To her, this outburst seemed to come out of the blue; in reality, however, several events had led up to it.

Most relational disagreements have a source, a beginning, a middle, an end, and an aftermath.[21] Let's find out about these stages.

### Source: Prior Conditions

The first phase in the conflict process is the one that sets the stage for disagreement; it begins when you become aware that there are differences between you and another person. The differences may stem from role expectations, perceptions, goals, or resources. In the previous example, Barb perceived that she and Cathy played different roles in caring for the household.

In interpersonal relationships, *many* potential sources of conflict may be smoldering below the surface. It may take some time before they flare up into overt conflict. Moreover, they may be compounded with other concerns, making them difficult to sort out. And it may not be just one conversation or issue that triggers conflict; multiple conflict "trip wires" may contribute to a conflict episode.[22]

### Beginning: Frustration Awareness

At this stage, at least one of you becomes aware that the differences in the relationship are increasingly problematic. You may begin to engage in self-talk, noting that something is wrong and creating frustration. Perhaps you realize that you won't be able to achieve an important goal or that someone else has resources you need to achieve it. Or you may become aware of differences in perceptions. Barb knew that Cathy's family always spent their weekends relaxing. All the members of Barb's family, in contrast, pitched in on weekends to get household chores done for the week. Barb may have recognized that difference, even as her frustration level rose.

Becoming aware of differences in perception does not always lead to increased frustration. But when the differences interfere with something you want to accomplish, then your frustration level rises. Barb wanted to get the house clean so she could turn her attention to studying for a test she had the next day. Cathy's apparent indifference to helping Barb achieve that goal was a conflict trigger.

### Middle: Active Conflict

When you bring your frustration to the attention of others, a conflict becomes an active, *expressed struggle*.[23] If frustrations remain only as thoughts, the conflict is passive, not active. Active conflict does not necessarily mean that the differences are expressed with shouting or emotional intensity. An expression of disagreement may be either verbal or nonverbal. Calmly asking someone to change an attitude or behavior to help you achieve your goal is a form of active conflict; so is kicking your brother under the table when he starts to reveal your secret to the rest of the family.

Cathy was not aware of the division of labor problem until Barb stormed into the room demanding a renegotiation of roles. Barb had been aware of her frustration for some time, yet had not acted on it. Many experts advocate not waiting until your frustration level escalates to peak intensity before you approach someone with your conflict. Unexpressed frustration tends to erupt like soda in a can that has just been shaken. Intense emotions can add to the difficulty of managing a conflict.

## End: Resolution

When you begin to try to manage the conflict, it has progressed to the resolution stage. Of course, not all conflicts can be neatly resolved. Couples who divorce, business partners who dissolve their corporation, or roommates who go their separate ways have all found solutions, even though they may not be amicable ones.

After Barb's outburst, she and Cathy were able to reach a workable compromise about the division of their household labor. Cathy agreed to clean the house every other week; Barb promised not to expect her to do it on weekends.

## Aftermath: Follow-Up

As Yogi Berra once said, "It ain't over 'til it's over." After a conflict has been resolved, the follow-up stage involves dealing with hurt feelings or managing simmering grudges, and checking with the other person to confirm that the conflict has not retreated into the frustration awareness stage. As we noted in Chapter 1, interpersonal relationships operate as transactive processes rather than as linear, step-by-step ones. Conflict does progress in stages, but you may need to resolve the same conflict again unless you confirm your understanding of the issues with your partner.

The Friday after their discussion, Cathy proudly showed off a spotless apartment to Barb when she came home from class. Barb responded with a grin and a quick hug and privately resolved to get up early on Sunday morning so that she could go out to get Cathy pastries and the Sunday papers before she awoke. This kind of mutual thoughtfulness exemplifies a successful follow-up in a conflict.

## Recap — Understanding Conflict as a Process

| | |
|---|---|
| **Prior Conditions Stage** | The stage is set for conflict because of differences in the individuals' actions or attitudes. |
| **Frustration Awareness Stage** | One individual becomes aware that the differences are problematic and becomes frustrated and angry. |
| **Active Conflict Stage** | The individuals communicate with each other about the differences; the conflict becomes an expressed struggle. |
| **Resolution Stage** | The individuals begin seeking ways to manage the conflict. |
| **Follow-Up Stage** | The individuals examine their own feelings and check with each other to monitor whether both are satisfied with the resolution. |

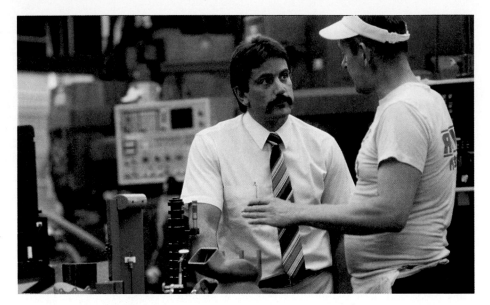

*B*y focusing on the problem at hand rather than assuming a defensive attitude, this machinist and his foreman may reach a constructive solution to their conflict.

Understanding the stages of conflict can help you better manage the process. You'll also be in a better position to make the conflict a constructive rather than a destructive experience. Conflict is **constructive** if it helps build new insights and establishes new patterns in a relationship. Airing differences can lead to a more satisfying relationship in the long run. David W. Johnson lists the following as benefits of conflict in interpersonal relationships. Interpersonal conflict

- Focuses attention on problems that may have to be solved
- Clarifies what may need to be changed
- Focuses attention on what is important to you and your partner
- Clarifies who you are and what your values are
- Helps you learn more about your partner
- Keeps relationships interesting
- Strengthens relationships by increasing your confidence that you can manage disagreements[24]

Although conflict can be constructive, we don't want to oversell the value or function of conflict in relationships with others. Conflict can also be **destructive.** The hallmark of destructive conflict is a lack of flexibility in responding to others.[25] Conflict can become destructive when people view their differences from a win–lose perspective, rather than looking for solutions that allow both individuals to gain. If the combatants assume that one person will lose, the resulting competitive climate precludes cooperation and flexibility.

One way to minimize destructive conflict cycles is to understand the sequence of conflict-triggering causes so that you can address them at an early stage. It's important to perceive interpersonal conflict not just as something you react to once an issue has surfaced; becoming aware of underlying frustrations before they blossom into active expressions of conflict can help maintain both honesty and trust in a relationship. Also, diagnosing whether the conflict is a misunderstanding, a simple disagreement, or a personal vendetta can give you insight into managing disagreements before they move closer to a fight on the struggle spectrum.

**constructive conflict.** Conflict that helps build new insights and establishes new patterns in a relationship.

**destructive conflict.** Conflict that dismantles rather than strengthens relationships.

# Conflict Management Styles

What's your approach to managing interpersonal conflict: fight or flight? Do you tackle conflict head-on or seek ways to remove yourself from it? Most of us do not have a single way of dealing with differences, but we do have a tendency to manage conflict by following patterns that we have used before. The pattern we choose depends on several factors: our personality, the individuals with whom we are in conflict, the time and place of the confrontation, and other situational factors. For example, if your boss gives you an order, you respond differently from the way you do if your spouse gives you an order. Virginia Satir, author of *Peoplemaking,* a book about family communication, suggests that we learn conflict response patterns early in life.[26]

One of several classifications of **conflict styles** is a five-style model based on the work of K. W. Thomas and R. H. Kilmann that includes two primary dimensions: concern for others and concern for self.[27] These two dimensions result in five conflict management styles, shown in Figure 8.2. The five styles are (1) avoidance, (2) accommodation, (3) competition, (4) compromise, and (5) collaboration. Before you read the following sections, try Building Your Skills: Identifying Your Conflict Management Style (pages 232–233), to see what style you typically use in managing conflict.

FIGURE *8.2*

Conflict Management Styles. The five conflict management styles in relation to concern for others and concern for self.

## Avoidance

One approach to managing conflict is to back off and try to side-step the conflict. Typical responses from someone who uses this style are "I don't want to talk about it," "It's not my problem," "Don't bother me with that now," or "I'm not interested in that." The **avoidance** style might indicate that a person has low concern for others as well as for himself or herself. This is sometimes called the "lose–lose" approach to conflict. The person using the avoiding conflict style wishes the problem or conflict would go away by itself and appears uninterested in managing the conflict or in meeting the needs of the other person involved in the disagreement. People who avoid conflict may also just not like the hassle of dealing with a difficult, uncomfortable situation. Not dealing directly with conflict may also stem from being unassertive and unable to stand up for one's own rights.

Other times people avoid conflict because they don't want to hurt the feelings of others. There may be times when avoiding a major blowup with someone is a wise strategy, but hoping the conflict will go away on its own may not always be the best plan.

Evidence suggests that husbands are more likely to avoid confrontation as a way of managing conflict with their wives. One research team argues that males are likely to avoid conflict because of the way they process information, especially emotions.[28] Avoiding conflict is viewed by husbands as the most comfortable way of managing the uncertainty that is a byproduct of conflict. Avoiding becomes a defense mechanism to avoid dissonance that could occur if the conflict were dealt with in a more direct way. In short, husbands may implicitly reason that it's better to keep quiet and avoid conflict than to speak up and try to sort things out; for them, the dissonance that results from speaking up is not worth the effort.

In some respects, avoiding conflict could be perceived as uncooperative. However, although it may not be cooperative, there are some advantages to avoiding

**conflict style.** The consistent pattern or approach you use to manage disagreement with others.

**avoidance.** Managing conflict by backing off and trying to side-step it.

*Building Your Skills*

## Identifying Your Conflict Management Style

We each learn to manage conflict in different ways. This exercise helps you increase your awareness of your conflict management style.

Complete the following questionnaire, "What Would I Do in a Conflict?" After you've completed and scored the questionnaire, rank-order the five conflict strategies, from the one you use most to the one you use least. Your instructor may ask you to discuss your results with another person or with a group of your classmates. Think of examples that illustrate each of the conflict styles.

### What Would I Do in a Conflict?

1. You and a classmate both want to use the only available computer at the same time.
   a. I would give up wanting it and give up on the classmate as a friend.
   b. I would try to force the classmate to let me use the computer first.

2. You and a classmate both want the same library book at the same time.
   a. I would give up on wanting it and give up on the classmate as a friend.
   b. I would listen carefully to why my classmate needed the book,

and if his reasons were more important than mine, I would let him have it. because a good friend is important.

3. You and a classmate both want to sharpen your pencil at the same time.
   a. I would let the classmate go first and give up on her as a friend.
   b. I would suggest that we solve the problem by one person sharpening both pencils so both of us have to wait an equal amount of time.

4. You and a classmate both want to be first in the lunch line.
   a. I would let the classmate go first and give up on him as a friend.
   b. I would collaborate by proposing to alternate who goes first each day.

5. You and a classmate both want the same chair at your favorite table in the library.
   a. I would try to force the classmate to let me have the chair, not caring if she was angry or upset with me.
   b. I would listen carefully to why my classmate wanted the chair, and if her reasons were more important than mine, I would

let her have it, because a good friend is important.

6. You and a classmate are working on a group project. Both of you want to draw the illustrations, and neither wants to write the report.
   a. I would try to force the classmate to let me draw the illustrations, not caring if he was angry or upset with me.
   b. I would compromise by agreeing for each of us to draw half of the illustrations and write half of the report.

7. You and a classmate have been playing ball. Neither of you wants to put the equipment away.
   a. I would try to force the classmate to do it, not caring if she was angry or upset with me.
   b. I would suggest that we solve the problem by putting the equipment away together.

8. You and a classmate are making a video. Both of you want to run the camera, and neither wants to narrate.
   a. I would listen carefully to why my classmate wanted to do the filming, and if his reasons were more important than mine, I would let him do it, because a good friend is important.

conflict. It provides time for each person in the conflict to think about the issues, cool down, and ponder other approaches to dealing with the issues. If the conflict issue really is trivial or silly, it may also be advantageous not to throttle up the tension to make a mountain out of a molehill.

There are also several disadvantages of avoiding conflict. If you avoid the conflict, you may be sending a message that you really don't care about the other person's feelings; you're more concerned about your own needs. Avoiding the conflict may also just make things worse. A conflict that was simply simmering may boil over if it's not

b. I would ask the classmate to compromise so that each of us filmed half of the time and each narrated half of the time.

9. You told a classmate a secret, and she told it to several other people.

   a. I would listen carefully to why my classmate told my secret, and if her reasons were more important than mine, I would forgive her, because a good friend is important.

   b. I would try to solve the problem by asking my classmate what happened and by working out an agreement about keeping secrets in the future.

10. You and a classmate both believe you did most of the work on a joint report.

   a. I would compromise by agreeing that we both did half.

   b. I would try to solve the problem by reviewing each aspect of the paper and deciding who did how much on each aspect.

### Scoring Procedure

Circle the letters below to indicate how you answered each question. Then total the number of letters circled in each column.

| Question | Avoiding | Competing | Accommodating | Compromising | Collaborating |
|---|---|---|---|---|---|
| **1.** | a | b | | | |
| **2.** | a | | b | | |
| **3.** | a | | | b | |
| **4.** | a | | | | b |
| **5.** | | a | b | | |
| **6.** | | a | | b | |
| **7.** | | a | | | b |
| **8.** | | | a | b | |
| **9.** | | | a | | b |
| **10.** | | | | a | b |
| **Total** | _____ | _____ | _____ | _____ | _____ |

The column with the greatest total indicates your predominant conflict management style. Remember: There is no one best style to use all of the time. Although the collaborating or compromising approaches are more likely to result in dialogue, there are times when it may be better to avoid, compete, or accommodate.

tended to. And of course another disadvantage is that the issue remains unresolved. Like a lump in the throat, the conflict just sits there.

## Accommodation

To accommodate is to give in to the demands of others. Someone who accommodates believes it's OK if the other person gets what he or she wants. People may sometimes adopt an **accommodation** style because they fear rejection if they rock the boat. They

**accommodation.** Managing conflict by giving in to the demands of others.

may be seeking approval or trying to avoid threats to their self-worth; to avoid creating a scene, they just do what the other person wants. Or they may be interested in meeting the other person's needs by abandoning their own interests. Sometimes people who accommodate don't seem to get angry or upset; they just do what others want them to do. But, in reality, they also accommodate to serve their own interests—to get people to like them. This conflict management style is sometimes called the "lose–win" approach. If you consistently accommodate, you sacrifice your own needs so that someone else can win the argument.

Using the accommodation style has several advantages. For one thing, it shows that you're reasonable and you want to help. If the issue is a minor or trivial one, you may gain some credibility by just letting it slide. Of course, if you are wrong or have made a mistake, accommodation is an appropriate response.

There are disadvantages to accommodating, just as there are disadvantages to any conflict style. Throughout this book we've stressed the importance of becoming other-oriented. But we've also noted that being other-oriented means considering the needs and position of the other person, without necessarily doing what the other person wants. Sometimes a person may accommodate for self-protection rather than because he or she is genuinely interested in others. In the following exchange, note Luke's accommodation response to Martin:

*Martin:*　Luke, I'm not in agreement with you on the QCN merger. I think the merger should be called off.

*Luke:*　OK. Whatever you think is best. I just want you to feel good about your decision.

To accommodate can give the accommodator a false sense of security by producing a "pseudosolution"—one that doesn't really solve anything, but just postpones the effort of seeking a solution to the problem. Also, if you consistently accommodate, you may diminish your power to the extent that others take advantage of you; the next time a conflict arises, the expectation may be that you'll give in and the other person will get his or her way again. In addition, if you accommodate too quickly, you short-circuit the possibility of finding a creative solution that is to everyone's liking.

### Competition

"You're wrong!" shouts Ed. "Here's how to get our project in on time. We can't waste time in the library. We just have to write up what we have."

"But Ed," suggests Derrick, "the assignment calls for us to have three library sources."

"No. We don't have time. Just do it," Ed insists.

Ed sees the issue as a competition that he must win.

Each of us has some need to control and also some need to be controlled by others. But people who have a **competition** conflict management style have a win–lose philosophy. They want to win at the expense of the other person, to claim victory over their opponents. They want to control others. They are typically not other-oriented; instead, they are focused on themselves.

People who compete often resort to blaming, or seeking a scapegoat, rather than assuming responsibility for a conflict. "I didn't do it," "Don't look at me," and "He made me do it" are typical blaming statements.

If these strategies do not work, people with a competitive style may try threats and warnings. Threats refer to actions that people can actually carry out.[29] Warnings are negative prophecies they cannot actually control. The boyfriend who says, "If you

**competition.** A conflict management style that stresses winning a conflict at the expense of the other person involved.

don't stop calling me names, I'm going to leave you," has issued a threat; he has the power to leave. If he were to say, "Don't call your parents names or they'll write you out of their will," that would be a warning. In reality, he has no control over his partner's parents.

Obviously, threats are more powerful than warnings in changing behavior, and then only if the other person would genuinely find the threatened actions punishing or disruptive. If a parent threatens to ground a child, the child will take the threat seriously only if he or she knows the parent will carry it out. If the parent has backed down in the past, the child will probably not pay much attention to the threat.

Is it ever appropriate to compete with others? Yes, if you believe that your position is clearly the best approach and that anything short of achieving your goal would be harmful to you and to others. In an election, someone will win and someone will lose. At the conclusion of a judicial trial, someone typically wins and someone loses. But even hard-fought elections and controversial trials have rules designed to maintain fairness for all involved in the conflict or decision. During often emotional periods of competition, those involved nonetheless need to maintain an ethical concern for others.

### Compromise

To compromise is to attempt to find a middle ground—a solution that somewhat meets the needs of all concerned. The word *somewhat* is important. Often when people compromise, no one gets precisely what he or she wants; each has to give up a bit of what he or she had hoped to get. When trying to craft a compromise, you're really expecting to lose something and win something simultaneously; you also expect your partner to lose and win. That's why the **compromise** style is called "a lose/win–lose/win" approach to conflict. As shown in Figure 8.2, when you compromise, you have some concern for others as well as some concern for yourself.

Compromise has some advantages. It can be a good thing if a quick resolution to the conflict is needed. To compromise reinforces the notion that all parties involved share in equal power. Compromise can also be useful if what is needed is a temporary solution. And it has the advantage of helping everyone save face, because everyone wins at least something.

But if compromising results in each person giving in but no person feeling pleased with the compromise, then a more collaborative approach to managing the conflict may be appropriate. Compromise can be tempting because it's easy. And while it's true that each party in the conflict may win with a compromise, the flip side is that each party also loses a bit. Finally, to compromise just to make the conflict go away can be another way of avoiding underlying issues that may need to be discussed.

### Collaboration

To collaborate is to have a high concern for both yourself and others. People who use a **collaboration** style of conflict management are more likely to view conflict as a set of problems to be solved rather than a game in which one person wins and another loses. Collaboration, which requires other-oriented strategies that foster a win–win climate, is based on the following principles offered by Harvard researchers Roger Fisher and William Ury:[30]

*Separate the people from the problem.* People who take a collaborative approach leave personal grievances out of the discussion, describing problems without making judgmental or evaluative statements about personalities.

**compromise.** To attempt to find the middle ground in a conflict.

**collaboration.** Use of other-oriented strategies to manage a conflict so as to achieve a positive solution for all involved.

*Focus on shared interests.* Collaborators ask questions such as "What do we both want? What do we both value? Where are we already agreeing?" to emphasize common interests, values, and goals.

*Generate many options to solve the problem.* People who collaborate use brainstorming and other techniques to generate alternative solutions. (You will learn more about problem-solving techniques later in this chapter.)

*Base decisions on objective criteria.* People who collaborate try to establish standards for an acceptable solution to a problem—these standards may involve cost, timing, and other factors. Suppose, for example, that you and your neighbor are discussing possible ways to stop a nearby dog from barking throughout the night. You decide on these criteria: The solution must not harm the dog; it must be easy for the owner to implement; the owner must agree to it; it should not cost more than fifty dollars; and it must keep the dog from disturbing the sleep of others. Your neighbor says, "Maybe the dog can sleep in the owner's garage at night." This solution meets all but one of your criteria, so you call the owner, who agrees to put the dog in the garage by 10 P.M. Now everyone wins, because the solution meets a sound, well-considered set of objective criteria.

The collaboration conflict management style is best used when those on all sides of the conflict need some new, fresh ideas. Using a collaborative approach also enhances commitment to the resolution of the conflict because all are involved in shaping the outcome. Collaborative approaches to managing conflict build rapport because everyone's concerns are at least noted, if not fully addressed. Finally, collaboration considers feelings and affirms the value of the interpersonal relationship.

It may sound as though collaboration is always the best approach to managing conflict. However, there are times when its disadvantages may outweigh the advantages.[31] One of the biggest disadvantages is the time, skill, patience, and energy required to manage conflict collaboratively. If a solution is needed quickly, other approaches such as compromise may be best. Also, some people use the appearance of collaboration as a pretense to compete; a person who is skilled in negotiation and who uses words well can manipulate a collaborative conflict approach to accomplish his or her goals. What may, on the surface, look like collaboration is really competition with a pleasant face and smooth words.

So which style of managing conflict is best? The short answer to this question is "It depends." It depends on the outcome you seek, the amount of time you have, the quality of the relationship you have with the other people involved, and the amount of perceived power you and others have.[32] Each style has advantages and disadvantages; no style has an inherent advantage all of the time. The competent, other-oriented communicator consciously decides whether to compete, avoid, compromise, accommodate, or collaborate. Although collaboration seems to be the style preferred by most people, it, too, may not always be appropriate. Research suggests that what most people find most uncomfortable is either (1) no clear resolution to a conflict, (2) a conflict management process that is poorly managed, or (3) the avoidance of issues that they would like to discuss.[33] *There is no single conflict management style that "works" in all situations.* We do, however, strongly suggest that, when time and other factors permit, a collaborative (win–win) conflict management style is worth exploring.[34] But because, as the saying goes, "it takes two to tango," it's hard to be collaborative if your partner in the conflict is avoiding or competing. Nonetheless, it's best to be conscious of and competent in the use of strategies and approaches for managing the inevitable disagreements that arise in any interpersonal relationship. The conflict management skills presented at the end of this chapter are anchored in a collaborative approach to managing conflict.

**Conflict Management Styles**

| | **The person who uses this style . . .** |
|---|---|
| **Avoidance** | Withdraws from conflict; tries to side-step confrontation; finds conflict uncomfortable. A lose–lose approach to conflict. |
| **Accommodation** | Easily gives in to the demands of others; typically wants to be liked by others. A lose–win approach to conflict. |
| **Competition** | Dominates the discussion and wants to accomplish the goal even at the expense of others. A win–lose approach to conflict. |
| **Compromise** | Seeks the middle ground; will give up something to get something. A lose/win–lose/win approach to conflict. |
| **Collaboration** | Views conflict as a problem to be solved; negotiates to achieve a positive solution for all involved in the conflict. A win–win approach to conflict. |

# Negotiation Strategies

**N**egotiation is a communication process in which individuals or groups exchange proposals and interact with each other to create understanding and agreement or to achieve a goal.[35] Negotiation implies that there is a conflict that one or both parties would like to resolve or manage. To agree to negotiate is often the first step toward managing a conflict productively.

Does research offer suggestions for effectively negotiating with others? Yes, but as in many areas of communication research, there is no list of sure-fire strategies and skills that are guaranteed to be effective in all negotiation situations. Researchers who study how best to negotiate with others have considered two different types of negotiation goals: (1) one of the negotiators wants to achieve his or her goal but is not interested in the other person's achieving his or hers (win–lose), and (2) both negotiators seek the best solution for each person involved in the negotiation (win–win).[36]

## Win-Lose Negotiation Strategies

A win–lose negotiation strategy has many of the same characteristics of the competition conflict style. This is not a negotiation style we recommend using as your primary negotiation style. A win–lose posture is typically not other-oriented. Because we acknowledge that there may be situations in which it is appropriate for one person to win and the other person to lose (if, for example, you know the other person is out to destroy you), we describe the win–lose strategies here so that you can recognize these strategies when others employ them when negotiating with you.

- *Win–lose negotiators are typically tough bargainers;* they use a "take it or leave it" approach, or say that their offer is only good for a limited time.

- *Win–lose negotiators often argue loudly rather than calmly seek consensus.*

**negotiation.** A communication process in which individuals or groups exchange proposals and interact with each other to create understanding and agreement, or to achieve a goal.

## *applying theory and research*

## *Cultural Differences and Preferred Conflict Management Style*

$\mathcal{C}$an cultural differences explain why people have a preference for using a specific conflict management style? That was a question that researchers Deborah Cai and Edward Fink wanted to explore. More specifically, do people from an individualistic culture (people who prefer establishing and maintaining their individual rights) have different preferences for ways of managing conflict than people from a collectivistic culture (where the tendency to work for the good of the group is often stronger than the tendency to achieve individual goals)? The researchers also wanted to know whether there are general trends in preferences for conflict management style.

To address these two issues, the researchers gave people from more than thirty different countries a questionnaire to complete. Some questions were designed to determine whether subjects were from a primarily individualistic or primarily collectivistic culture; other questions assessed subjects' preferred style of managing conflict. The five conflict styles that Cai and Fink defined were similar to the five styles we describe in this chapter: (1) obliging (accommodating), (2) avoiding, (3) domineering (competing), (4) compromising, and (5) integrating (collaborating).

Overall, the researchers found that the integrating (collaborating) style was the most preferred conflict style, regardless of cultural background, followed by obliging (accommodating), compromising, and domineering (competing). People from individualistic cultures preferred the avoiding style more than did people from collectivistic cultures. People from collectivist cultures

seemed to prefer compromising and integrating (collaborating) more than did people from individualistic cultures. Another interesting finding was that people from different cultures actually interpreted four of the five conflict styles slightly differently. In other words, people from collectivistic cultures had a different interpretation of what compromising really involved, compared to people from individualistic cultures. Dominating (competing) was the only conflict management style that was interpreted similarly by people in different cultural groups.

## $\mathcal{A}$PPLYING
### the Research to Your Life

What do these results mean to you? Although one survey does not let us draw conclusions that refer to everyone, the results nonetheless suggest some trends.

- As noted above, collaboration (or integration, as it was called in this study) was the most preferred conflict management style, regardless of cultural background. So, if you're uncertain of another person's cultural background, collaboration may be a good "default" approach to managing conflict.

- People from individualistic cultures (such as individuals from the United States) are more likely to avoid conflict than are people from collectivistic cultures. Although this is a preference, it doesn't mean that it's always best to avoid conflict; it just means that people from individual-

istic cultures tend to reach for that style first. If you're from an individualistic culture, you shouldn't be surprised if others from the same cultural background have a tendency to avoid conflict. Of course, avoidance of conflict does have its advantages, but also, as we noted on pages 231–233, disadvantages.

- Because people from collectivistic cultures prefer compromising and integrative collaboration, styles that take time, it may be wise to not rush the conflict management process if you're interacting with someone from a collectivistic culture. In fact, taking your time in managing conflict is probably a good idea no matter whom you're interacting with, unless finding a resolution quickly is important.

- Finally, because someone from a culture other than your own may have a different understanding of what a conflict management style entails, you may think you're being collaborative, but the person from the other culture may not interpret your behavior as collaborative. The competencies and strategies for enhancing the quality of communication with people from other cultures that we presented in Chapter 4 are especially useful when managing conflict.

*Source:* Deborah A. Cai and Edward L. Fink, "Conflict Style Differences Between Individualists and Collectivists," *Communication Monographs,* 69 (March 2002): 67–87.

- *Win–lose negotiators use things the other person values to their own advantage;* they figure out what the other person wants and then skillfully use that to motivate the other person to give in.

- *Win–lose negotiators have other alternatives in mind before starting the negotiation;* negotiation experts call this the Best Alternative to a Negotiated Agreement, more commonly known by the acronym **BATNA;**[37] it's a "hip-pocket" way for negotiators to achieve their goal without negotiation.[38]

- *Win–lose negotiators sometimes bluff and mislead their opponent,* although there is research that suggests bluffing can backfire if your negotiation partner calls your bluff.[39]

- *Win–lose negotiators may communicate that they want to reach agreement but may really want to prolong the negotiation* in the hope that the other person will finally just give in.

## Win–Win Negotiation Strategies

If your goal is to be collaborative so that all parties involved in the negotiation achieve a benefit, consider the following negotiation strategies.

- *Win–win negotiators identify specific, clear, and reasonably high goals for themselves.* International peace negotiator Bill Richardson suggests that making friends, defining your goals, keeping your eyes "on the prize," and shrugging off insults are among the most important elements in any negotiation process.[40]

- *Win–win negotiators are reluctant to lower their goals;* they stand firm while seeking creative ways to achieve what they want.

- *Win–win negotiators know and discuss their priorities;* they make tradeoffs on issues of less importance to them.

- *Win–win negotiators are good problem solvers.*

- *Win–win negotiators know when to hold firm to what is important to them;* they are "selectively contentious," which means they express their passion when the issue or idea under discussion is important to them.[41]

- *Win–win negotiators express a genuine interest in their opponent's needs, interests, and goals* without offering phony support or fake flattery.

## *C*onflict Management Skills

**F**or many people, at the heart of enhancing the quality of interpersonal relationships is learning to manage conflict. Managing conflict, especially emotion-charged ego conflict, is not easy. The more stress and anxiety you feel at any given time, the more likely you are to experience conflict in your relationships with others. When you are under stress, it's more likely that conflict will become personal and degenerate into ego conflict. And just the opposite is true: When you're rested and relaxed, you're less likely to experience conflict. But even while relaxed and with a fully developed set of skills, don't expect to avoid conflict. Conflict happens. The following skills, previewed in our discussion of a collaborative approach to conflict, can help you generate options that promote understanding and provide a framework for collaboration.[42]

**BATNA.** Best Alternative to a Negotiated Agreement; a solution to a conflict that can be achieved without negotiation.

## Manage Your Emotions

For weeks you have been working on a brochure with a tight deadline. You turned it over to the production department with instructions two weeks ago. Today you call to check on its progress, and you discover that it is still sitting on the production coordinator's desk. You feel your anger begin to erupt. You're tempted to march into the production coordinator's office and scream at her, or to shout at her supervisor.

Try to avoid taking action when you are in such a state. You may regret what you say, and you will probably escalate the conflict.

Often the first sign that we are in a conflict situation is a feeling of anger, frustration, fear, or even sadness, which sweeps over us like an ocean wave. If we feel powerless to control our own emotions, we will have difficulty taking a logical or rational approach to managing the conflict. Expressing our feelings in an emotional outburst may make us feel better for the moment, but it may close the door to logical, rational negotiation.

When we are emotionally charged, we experience physical changes as well. One researcher found that

> . . . our adrenaline flows faster and our strength increases by about 20 percent. The liver, pumping sugar into the bloodstream, demands more oxygen from the heart and lungs. The veins become enlarged and the cortical centers where thinking takes place do not perform nearly as well. . . . The blood supply to the problem-solving part of the brain is severely decreased because, under stress, a greater portion of blood is diverted to the body's extremities.[43]

Such changes fuel our fight–flight responses. If we choose to stay, verbal or physical violence may erupt; if we flee from the conflict, we cannot resolve it. Until we can tone down (not eliminate) our emotions, we will find it difficult to apply other skills. Let's look at some specific strategies that you can draw on when an intense emotional response to conflict clouds your judgment and decision-making skills.[44]

### Be Aware That You Are Becoming Angry and Emotionally Volatile

One characteristic of people who "lose it" is that they let their emotions get the best of them. Before they know it, they are saying and doing things that they later regret. Unbridled and uncensored emotional outbursts rarely enhance the quality of an interpersonal relationship. An emotional purge may make you feel better, but your partner is likely to reciprocate, which will only escalate the conflict spiral.

Before that happens, become aware of what is happening to you. As we described earlier, your body will start to react to your emotions with an increased heart rate. Be sensitive to what is happening to you physically.

### Seek to Understand Why You Are Angry and Emotional

Understanding what's behind your anger can help you manage it. Realize that it is normal and natural to be angry. It's a feeling everyone experiences. You need not feel guilty about it. Anger is often expressed as a defense when you feel violated or when you are fearful of losing something that is important to you. Two powerful anger triggers are (1) feeling that you have not been treated fairly, and (2) feeling entitled to something that you are being denied. Think about the last time you became very angry. Chances are your angry outburst stemmed from a sense that you were not treated fairly or that someone denied you something you were entitled to. Often there is a sense of righteous indignation when you are angry. You are being denied something you feel you should have.

### Make a Conscious Decision About Whether to Express Your Anger

Rather than just letting anger and frustration build and erupt out of control, make a conscious choice about whether you should express your frustration and irritation. We're not denying that there are valid reasons for you to express anger and frustration, or suggesting that you should not express your feelings. Sometimes there is no way to let someone know how important an issue is to you other than by forcefully expressing your irritation or anger. As these lines from William Blake illustrate, sometimes the wisest strategy is to be honest with others and express how you feel.

> I was angry with my friend:
>
> I told my wrath, my wrath did end.
>
> I was angry with my foe:
>
> I told it not, my wrath did grow.

If you do decide to express your anger, don't lose control. Be direct and descriptive. The guidelines for listening and responding that we provided in Chapter 5 can serve you well. Keep your anger focused on issues rather than personalities.

### Select a Mutually Acceptable Time and Place to Discuss a Conflict

If you are upset, or even tired, you risk becoming involved in an emotion-charged shouting match. If you ambush someone with an angry attack, don't expect him or her to be in a receptive frame of mind. Instead, give yourself time to cool off before you try to resolve a conflict. In the case of the lapsed deadline mentioned earlier, you could call both the production coordinator and her boss and schedule an appointment to meet with them later in the day. By that time, you could gain control of your feelings and also think the issue through. Of course, issues sometimes need to be discussed on the spot; you may not have the luxury of waiting. But whenever practical, make sure the other person is ready to receive you and your message.

### Plan Your Message

If you are approaching someone to discuss a disagreement, take care to organize your message. Identify your goal and determine what outcome you would like; do not barge in and pour out your emotions.

### Breathe

One of the simplest yet most effective ways to avoid overheating is to breathe. As you become aware that your emotions are starting to erupt, take a slow, deep breath. Then breathe again. This can help calm you and manage the physiological changes that adrenaline creates. Deep breathing—the prime strategy women use to manage the pain of childbirth—can be a powerful way to restore calmness to your spirit. Focusing on your breathing is also one of the primary methods of meditation. We're not suggesting that you hyperventilate. But taking deep, slow breaths that not only fill your upper lungs but move your diaphragm—the muscle that moves as your lungs expand and contract—is an active strategy to help you regain rational control.

### Monitor Nonverbal Messages

As you learned in Chapter 7, your actions play a key role in establishing the emotional climate in any relationship. Monitoring your nonverbal messages can help to de-escalate an emotion-charged situation. Speaking calmly, using direct eye contact, and maintaining a calm, nonthreatening facial expression will signal that you wish to collaborate rather than control. Your nonverbal message should also support your

## *Becoming Other-Oriented*

### Tips for Managing Anger

One of the biggest obstacles to being other-oriented during conflict is the anger we often experience when we feel we're not being listened to or our rights are being violated.[45] Anger is an emotional response to fear. Stated another way, anger is an outward response to an inward feeling of fear. And fear is often about losing something or not getting something we believe is rightfully ours. We may become angry, for example, if we fear we may lose our job or if we sense a relationship that is important to us may be dissolving or becoming less important to the other person. Anger also occurs when we feel someone is keeping us from what we want and have a right to have, someone is unjustly blaming us for something, or someone is attacking us. Some people may tell you it is a good idea to express your anger to the person who is making you angry; get your anger out; don't keep it bottled up. There are times when expressing your anger is appropriate. Being assertive in expressing what bothers you is appropriate when the other person is not aware of what is bothering you. But

uncensored angry words can escalate the anger you feel and also increase others' anger.[46] One research team offers these prescriptions for managing your own anger or coping with someone else's anger during conflict.[47]

- *Be determined not to get angry yourself.* If you know you are going to face someone who is likely to tick you off, prepare yourself before you meet with him or her. Assertively express your feelings, but make a promise to yourself not to "lose it" and allow the encounter to degenerate into a shout fest.

- *Get on the same physical level as the other person.* One person should not be standing and the other sitting. Try to face each other eye-to-eye. You can also build rapport by trying to mirror the posture of the other person. We're not suggesting that you mimic your partner (this would probably make him or her more angry), but try to adopt a similar communication position.

- *Be silent.* If you are angry and afraid you might say something you'll regret, just be quiet and listen.

- *Express your concern nonverbally.* Because much of an emotional

message is communicated nonverbally, use your facial expression and eyes to let the other person know you care about him or her. Your communication partner will believe what you do, more than what you say.

- *Make an appropriate empathic statement.* Saying "I would probably feel angry if I had experienced what you experienced" or "I think I can see why you are so upset" may help. But be careful not to say, "I know just how you feel" or "I know where you're coming from." For many people, those statements can seem patronizing.

- *Remind yourself that you control your own emotions.* Even though others may do and say things that can upset you, you are the only person who can control yourself and your response to others. Try to respond mindfully to others rather than just reacting emotionally to them.

- *Recognize that angry emotional outbursts rarely change someone's mind.* Exploding in an angry tirade may make you feel better for a moment by getting it "off your chest," but it usually does little to advance understanding and manage the issues at hand.

verbal response. If you say you are listening to someone, but you continue to read the paper or work on a report, you are communicating a lack of interest in the speaker and the message.

### Avoid Personal Attacks, Name-Calling, and Emotional Overstatement

Using threats and derogatory names can turn a simple conflict into an ego conflict. When people feel attacked, they respond by protecting themselves. Also try to avoid exaggerating your emotions. If you say you are irritated or annoyed rather than furious, you can still communicate your feelings, but you take the sting out of your description.

Avoid the bad habit of **gunny-sacking.** This occurs when you dredge up old problems and issues from the past, like pulling them out of an old bag or gunny sack, to use against your partner. Keep your focus on the issues at hand, not on old hurts. Gunny-sacking usually succeeds only in increasing tension, escalating emotions and reducing listening effectiveness.

### Take Time to Establish Rapport

Evidence suggests that you'll be more successful in managing conflict if you don't immediately dive in and attempt to sort out the issues with your partner.[48] Taking time to establish a positive emotional climate can pay big dividends; this is especially important if you're not well acquainted with the person you're having the conflict with. One study compared how effectively conflict was managed in two different groups.[49] In one group, the conflict negotiators spent time face-to-face, "schmoozing" and getting to know one another, before trying to negotiate a solution to a conflict. In the other group, the negotiators exchanged information via e-mail but did not meet face-to-face. The negotiators who spent time establishing a positive relationship in person were more successful in managing the conflict to everyone's satisfaction. Schmoozing is important in building rapport and establishing a positive communication climate.

Even if you know the other person well, take some time to build rapport. Chatting about such seemingly innocuous topics as the weather or local events can help break the ice and provide a basis for a more positive conversational climate. A positive emotional climate is especially important when trying to sort through vexing, conflict-producing issues.

Several researchers also note how important it is to help the other person in the conflict save face—to not leave the conversation feeling demoralized and humiliated.

### Use Self-Talk

Kosta was chairing the committee meeting when Monique accused him of falsifying the attendance numbers at the last fine arts festival. Instead of lashing back at Monique, he paused, took a slow, deep breath, and thought, "I'm tired. If I snarl back, all we will do is escalate this issue out of proportion. I'll talk with Monique later after we have both cooled down." Perhaps you think that talking to yourself is an eccentricity. Nothing could be further from the truth. As you saw in Chapter 2, thoughts are directly linked to feelings,[50] and the messages we tell ourselves play a major role in how we feel and respond to others. Ask yourself whether an emotional tirade and an escalating conflict will produce the results you want. When Eleanor Roosevelt noted that "No one can make you feel inferior without your consent," she was acknowledging the power of self-talk to affect your emotional response to what others say and do.

### Manage Information

Because uncertainty, misinformation, and misunderstanding are often byproducts of conflict and disagreement, skills that promote mutual understanding are an important

*What strategies do this mother and daughter seem to have drawn on to manage their conflicts?*

**gunny-sacking.** Dredging up old problems and issues from the past, like pulling them out of an old bag or gunny sack, to use against your partner.

component of cooperative conflict management. Based on the listening and responding skills discussed in Chapter 5, the following specific suggestions can help you reduce uncertainty and enhance the quality of communication during conflict.

### Clearly Describe the Conflict-Producing Events

Instead of just blurting out your complaints in random order, think of delivering a
brief, well-organized minispeech. Offer your perspective on what created the conflict,
sequencing the events like a well-organized story. Describe the events dispassionately
so that the other person shares your understanding of the problem.

When Marsha almost had a car accident, she came home and told her husband, "Last
week you said you would get the brakes fixed on the car. On Monday, when you still
hadn't taken the car in, you said you would do it on Wednesday. Now it's Friday, and the
brakes are in even worse shape. I had a close call this afternoon when the car almost
wouldn't stop. We've got to get those brakes fixed before anyone drives that car again."

### "Own" Your Statements by Using Descriptive "I" Language

"I feel upset when you post the week's volunteer schedule without first consulting with
me," reveals Katrina. Her statement is an example of the **"I" language** that we have
discussed several times in this book. "I" language expresses how a speaker is feeling.
The use of the word "I" conveys a willingness to "own" one's feelings and statements
about them.

If Katrina had said, "You always prepare a schedule without telling anyone first.
All of us who volunteer are mad about that," her statement would have had an accusatory sting. Beginning the statement with "you" sets the listener up for a defensive response. Also, notice that the speaker does not take responsibility for the anger; she
suggests that it belongs to several unidentified people as well. If you instead narrow the
issue down to a conflict between you and the other person, you put the conflict into a
more manageable framework.

### Use Effective Listening Skills

Managing information is a two-way process. Whether you are describing a conflict
situation to someone, or that individual is bringing a conflict to your attention, good
listening skills will be invaluable.

Give your full attention to the speaker and make a conscious point of tuning out
your internal messages. Sometimes the best thing to do after describing the conflict-
producing events is simply to wait for a response. If you don't stop talking and give
the other person a chance to respond, he or she will feel frustrated, the emotional pitch
will go up a notch, and it will become more difficult to reach an understanding.

Finally, remember to not only focus on the facts or details, but also analyze them
so you can understand the major point the speaker is making. Try to use your understanding of the details to interpret the speaker's major ideas. Remember to stay other-
oriented, and "seek to understand rather than to be understood."[51]

### Check Your Understanding of What Others Say and Do

Respond clearly and appropriately. Your response and that of your conflict partner
will confirm that you have understood each other. Checking perceptions is vital when
emotions run high.

If you are genuinely unsure about facts, issues, or major ideas addressed during a
conflict, ask questions to help you sort through them instead of barging ahead with solutions. Then summarize your understanding of the information; do not parrot the
speaker's words or paraphrase every statement, but check key points to ensure that

**"I" language.** Statements that
use the word "I" to express how
a speaker is feeling.

you have understood the message. Note how Ted adeptly paraphrases to check his understanding:

*Maggie:* I don't like the conclusion you've written to the conference report. It doesn't mention anything about the ideas suggested at the symposium. I think you have also misinterpreted the CEO's key message.

*Ted:* So, if I understand you, Maggie, you're saying the report missed some key information and may also include an inaccurate summary of the CEO's speech.

*Maggie:* Yes, Ted. Those are my concerns.

### Be Empathic

Understand others not only with your head, but also with your heart. To truly understand another person, you need to do more than catch the meaning of his or her words; you need to put yourself in the person's place emotionally. Ask yourself these questions: What emotions is the other person feeling? Why is he or she experiencing these emotions? Throughout this book we have stressed the importance of becoming other-oriented. It's especially important to be other-oriented when you disagree with another person. Trying to understand what's behind your partner's emotions may give you the insight you need to reframe the conflict from your partner's point of view. And with this other-oriented perspective you may see new possibilities for managing the conflict.

How do you become empathic? Use the collection of skills that we've discussed in several previous chapters as well as in this chapter. Here's a brief summary of how to be empathic.

- *Stop:* Stop making your arguments and concentrate on your partner's points. Socially decenter by taking into account the other person's thoughts, feelings, values, culture, and perspective. How is your partner "making sense" out of what has happened to him or her? Don't keep hammering at your own ideas; think about how the other person got to the conclusion he or she has arrived at.

- *Look:* Monitor your partner's emotions by observing his or her nonverbal messages. Look for emotional cues in your partner's face; listen for the tone of voice; observe posture and gestures to gauge the intensity of the feelings being expressed. Mentally summarize what emotions you think your partner is experiencing.

- *Listen:* Concentrate on what the other person is saying. Listen both for the details and for the main points the other person is making. Focus on the overall story he or she is telling. Mentally summarize the key ideas your partner is making.

- *Imagine:* Based on your understanding of what your conflict partner has experienced and is feeling, imagine how you would feel if *you* were in your partner's place. True empathy is feeling what your partner is feeling, or at least trying to imagine as best you can the emotions your partner is experiencing.

- *Question:* If you need more information about what your partner has experienced or if there is something you don't understand, gently ask appropriate questions. Don't blast your partner with accusing or negative questions. Just calmly ask for more background information if you need it.

- *Paraphrase:* To confirm your understanding of your partner's point of view, briefly summarize what you think your partner is thinking or feeling. Statements such as, "You're upset with me because you believe I lied to you," "You're feeling frustrated," or "You're angry at me" are examples of paraphrasing statements.

No checklist of skills will magically melt tensions resulting from long-standing or entrenched conflict. But trying honestly to understand both a person's position and the emotion behind it is a good beginning to developing understanding. Realize that it will be difficult to stop, look, listen, imagine, question, and paraphrase if both you and your partner are emotionally agitated. In fact, it's likely you won't use a rational approach to managing conflict until emotional outbursts and intense feelings are toned down a bit. Unchecked emotions are a formidable barrier to understanding others or empathizing with another person's feelings.

*W*hat conflict management techniques could be used instead of the in-your-face confrontation shown here?

### Manage Goals

As you've seen, conflict is goal-driven. Both individuals involved in an interpersonal conflict want something. And for some reason, be it competition, scarce resources, or lack of understanding, the goals appear to be in conflict. To manage conflict, it is important to seek an accurate understanding of these goals and to identify where they overlap.

### Identify Your Goal and Your Partner's Goal

After you describe, listen, and respond, your next task should be to identify what you would like to have happen. What is your goal? Most goal statements can be phrased in terms of wants or desires. Consider the following examples:

| Problem | Goals |
|---|---|
| Your boss wants you to work overtime; you need to pick up your son from day care. | You want to leave work on time; your boss wants the work completed ASAP. |
| Your spouse wants to sleep with the window open; you like a warm room and sleep better with the window closed. | You want a good night's rest; your spouse wants a good night's rest. |
| Your six-year-old son wants to go to a swim party where there will be no lifeguards. | You want your son to be safe; your son wants to have a good time. |

Often in conflicts you will face balancing your goal against the goal of maintaining the relationship that you have with your partner. Eventually, you may decide that the latter goal is more important than the substantive conflict issue.

Research by Charles Pavitt and Bradley Kemp confirms the significant role of relationships in conflict and negotiation situations.[52] If you're negotiating with someone you like, you will expect your negotiation partner to use more supportive approaches to achieve the goal. Conversely, if you're negotiating with someone you don't like, you will expect that person to use more threats and demands, and be more obstinate.

Next, it is useful to identify your partner's goal. In order to manage conflict, you need to know what the other person wants. Use effective listening and responding skills to determine what each of you wants and to verbalize your goals. Obviously, if you both keep your goals hidden, it will be difficult to manage the conflict.

### Identify Where Your Goals and Your Partner's Goals Overlap

The authors of the best-selling book *Getting to Yes,* Roger Fisher and William Ury, stress the importance of focusing on shared interests when seeking to manage differences.[53] Armed with an understanding of what you want and what your partner wants, you can then determine whether the goals overlap. In the conflict over whether the window should be open or closed, the goal of both parties is the same: Each wants a good night's sleep. Framing the problem as "How can we achieve our mutual goal?" rather than arguing over whether the window should be up or down moves the discussion to a more productive level.

If you focus on shared interests (common goals) and develop objective, rather than subjective, criteria for the solution, there is hope for finding a resolution that will satisfy both parties.

### Manage the Problem

If you can structure conflicts as problems to be solved rather than as battles to be won or lost, you are well on your way to seeking strategies to manage the issues that confront you and your partner. Of course, as we have stressed earlier, not all conflicts can be resolved. However, approaching the core of a conflict as a problem to be managed can provide a constructive way of seeking resolution. Structuring a conflict as a problem also helps to manage the emotion and keeps the conversation focused on issues (simple conflict) rather than personalities (ego conflict). The problem-solving structure we suggest here is straightforward: Define the problem, analyze the problem's causes and effects, determine the goal you and your partner seek, generate many possible options, then select the option that best achieves the goals of both you and your partner.

TABLE **8.1**   **Solving Problems: One Method of Organizing Problem-Solving Discussions**

| | |
|---|---|
| 1. Define the problem. | Determine the issue you disagree about. |
| 2. Analyze the problem. | Determine the causes, symptoms, effects, and obstacles. |
| 3. Determine the goals. | Determine what you want. Determine what your partner wants. How do the goals overlap? |
| 4. Generate many solutions. | List many options, rather than debating one or two strategies for achieving the goal. |
| 5. Select the best solution and try it. | Eliminate options that are not mutually agreeable. If possible, take the best ideas among those generated to reach an amicable resolution. |

### Define the Problem

You can apply all the skills described so far to pursue a proven method for problem solving, which is shown in Table 8.1. First, *define the problem.* Most problems boil down to something you want more or less of.

Cara and Vaughn have been going together for over a year. Lately they have been fighting over small issues, so they decide to spend some time talking about what is wrong and trying to understand one another. At the root of their conflicts, they discover, is a basic problem: Cara wants to get married to Vaughn now. Vaughn wants to stay with Cara, but he doesn't want to get married until he feels ready. He also wants to feel financially secure before he marries.

### Analyze the Problem

Next, *analyze the problem.* To analyze is to break something down into its components. With your partner, begin by describing the conflict-producing events in chronological order (see page 244). Then decide whether you're facing a pseudoconflict, a simple conflict, or an ego conflict (see pages 223–227). Attempt to ferret out symptoms, effects, and obstacles; decide whether the conflict stems from several subproblems or from one major issue. As you proceed with your analysis, you and your partner may decide that you need more information to help clarify the issues.

After some discussion, Cara and Vaughn analyze the problem. They realize they come from different family backgrounds and have different expectations about marriage. Cara's folks were high school sweethearts and got married when they were 18. Vaughn's parents are older; they met after each of them had been divorced, and they married after a long, slow-paced relationship. Cara and Vaughn's different frames of reference help explain their feelings about the timing of marriage.

### Determine the Goals

The next step in managing the problem is to *determine your own and your partner's goals,* following the suggestions on pages 246–247. Also, generate objective criteria for a solution (see page 236). The more measurable, verifiable, and objective the criteria, the greater the likelihood that you and your partner will be able to agree when the criteria have been met. Cara and Vaughn decide that, ultimately, they have the same goal: to get married. The issue boils down to timing. So they decide to seek a course of action that will make them both feel secure.

### Generate Multiple Solutions

The next step is to *generate multiple solutions.* Simply understanding the issues and the causes, effects, symptoms, and history of a problem will not enable you to manage a conflict. It takes time and creativity to find mutually satisfactory solutions to most problems. It stands to reason that the more solutions you generate, the greater the probability that you can manage the conflict constructively. One way to generate options is through brainstorming. To use brainstorming, try the following suggestions:

1. Make sure the problem and the goals are clear to both of you.

2. Try to suspend judgment and evaluation temporarily; do not censor your thoughts.

3. Specify a certain time period for brainstorming.

4. Consider brainstorming ideas separately before a meeting with your partner, or write ideas down before verbalizing solutions.

5. Try to develop at least one unique or far-out idea. You can always tame wild ideas down later.

6. Piggyback your ideas onto those of your partner. Encourage your partner to use or modify your ideas.

7. Write down all the ideas suggested.

8. Review all ideas, noting ways to combine, eliminate, or extend them.

If the goal is to find the best way to manage the difficulty, it may take only one good idea to help move the conflict forward to a constructive resolution.

When they brainstorm, Cara and Vaughn generate the following options: Save money for a year and then get married; take turns going to college; take turns working to support each other while the other gets a degree; get married now, get jobs, and postpone college; get married now and take out college loans.

### Select the Best Solution

Finally, Cara and Vaughn decide to *select the best solution.* Sometimes it may take several attempts at defining, analyzing, goal setting, and generating multiple ideas before a mutually agreeable solution emerges. It is always appropriate to recheck your understanding of the issues and goals. Cara and Vaughn decide to combine the best of several ideas. They agree to get engaged, but not to set a date. Instead, they set a financial goal of $5,000 in savings. When they hit that goal, they will set a wedding date. If they are both attending college, they will get part-time jobs so that they have income, and they will also apply for college loans.

If, after repeated attempts, you cannot arrive at a mutually acceptable solution, you may decide to keep trying. Or you may agree to take the issue to an impartial person who can help you identify conflict management strategies and solutions. At work, your immediate superior may be called in to help settle the matter. Or, occasionally, you may agree to disagree and drop it.

The goal of managing conflict is not just to solve a problem, but to help manage relational issues with your partner, especially if your partner thinks he or she has "lost" the conflict. When seeking a solution to interpersonal problems, try to find ways for your partner to "win" while you also achieve your goal. Help your partner save face. The concept of **face,** first introduced in Chapter 2, refers to the self-image or self-respect that you and your partner seek to maintain.[54] Communication researcher Stella Ting-Toomey has conducted studies that emphasize the importance of face-saving or

**face.** Self-image or self-respect that you and your partner seek to maintain.

maintaining a positive image, especially in collectivist cultures such as those in Asia, where maintaining face is especially important.[55] How do you help someone save face and avoid embarrassment? Sometimes you can offer genuine forgiveness. Or you can offer explanations that help reframe the differences, perhaps suggesting that it was really just a misunderstanding that led to the disagreement. After a tough-fought football game, a victorious, well-mannered coach may say, "They were great opponents. I have much admiration for the way they played." Such face-restoring comments can help mend bruised egos. Such is also the case during interpersonal conflict. Finding ways to be gracious or allow your partner to save face is an important other-oriented approach to dealing with people.

Even though we have presented these conflict management steps as prescriptive suggestions, it is important to remember that *conflict is rarely a linear, step-by-step sequence of events.* These skills are designed to serve as a general framework for collaboratively managing differences. But if your partner does not want to collaborate, your job will be more challenging.

In reality, you don't simply manage your emotions and then move neatly on to developing greater understanding with another person. Sorting out your goals and your partner's goals is not something you do once and then put behind you. It will take time and patience to balance your immediate goal with the goal of maintaining a relationship with your partner. In fact, as you try to manage a conflict, you will more than likely bounce forward and backward from one step to another. The framework we've described gives you an overarching perspective for understanding and actively managing disagreements, but the nature of interpersonal relationships means that you and your partner will respond—sometimes in unpredictable ways—to a variety of cues (psychological, sociological, physical) when communicating. Think of the skills you have learned as options to consider, rather than as hard-and-fast rules to follow in every situation.

## *S*ummary

Interpersonal conflict is an expressed struggle that occurs when two people cannot agree on a way to meet their needs or goals. At the root of all conflicts are our individual perspectives, needs, and experiences.

Many people believe myths about the conflict management process, such as that conflict should always be avoided, that conflict always occurs because of misunderstandings, that conflict always occurs because of a poor interpersonal relationship, and that conflict can always be resolved. But conflict in interpersonal relationships is inevitable and is not always destructive. It can actually play a constructive role by identifying areas that need attention and transformation.

Conflict can result from misunderstanding someone (pseudoconflict), or it can stem from a simple difference of opinion or viewpoint (simple conflict). Ego conflict occurs when personalities clash; the conflict becomes personal and you may feel a need to defend your self-image.

Although conflict seems to erupt suddenly, it often originates in events that occur long before the conflict manifests itself. It evolves from these prior conditions into frustration awareness, active conflict, solution, and follow-up stages. Understanding conflict as a process also involves recognizing how people seek and are given control over others.

People develop patterns or styles of managing conflict. We identified five conflict management styles in this chapter: (1) avoidance, (2) accommodation, (3) competition, (4) compromise, and (5) collaboration. A person using the avoidance style simply seeks to withdraw from conflict. The accommodation style involves easily giving in to the demands of others. To compete is to dominate the discussion in order to achieve the desired goal, typically at the expense of another person's achieving his or her goal. The compromiser seeks a middle ground and is willing to give up something in order to gain something. Finally, the collaborator views conflict as a problem to be solved and seeks a solution that allows all parties to win.

Closely related to conflict management styles are styles of negotiating disagreements. To negotiate is to exchange proposals and interact with others to create understanding or agreement or achieve a goal. We described both win–lose negotiation strategies and win–win strategies.

We concluded the chapter by presenting a summary of conflict management skills. Specifically, we addressed how to manage emotions, manage information, manage goals, and manage the problem. It's usually best to focus on the partners' needs before attempting to resolve the underlying cause of your conflict.

# For Discussion and Review

## Focus on Critical Thinking

1. Richard has an explosive temper. He consistently receives poor performance evaluations at work because he lashes out at those who disagree with him. What strategies might help him manage his emotional outbursts?

2. Melissa and Jake always seem to end up making personal attacks and calling each other names when they get into a disagreement. What type of conflict are they experiencing when they do this, and how can they avoid it?

3. Analyze the opening dialogue in this chapter. What are Anya and Paolo doing wrong in managing their differences? Are they doing anything right?

## Focus on Ethics

4. Is it ethical to mask your true emotions in order to get along with others? Is honesty in a relationship always the best policy? Explain your response.

5. Are certain types of power more ethical to use during a conflict than others? Explain your answer, describing conditions that would justify the use of certain types of power.

6. Are there situations in which you should *not* assert your point of view? Provide an example to support your answer.

# For Your Journal

1. Analyze several recent conversations in which you were trying to convince someone to do something. Discuss the types of power you used in your efforts.

2. Consider a recent conflict you have had with someone. Determine whether it was a pseudoconflict, a simple conflict, or an ego conflict. Describe the strategies you used to manage the conflict. Now that you have read this chapter, discuss the other strategies you could have used to help manage the disagreement.

3. Identify a current conflict you are having (or a conflict you had recently) with a friend or acquaintance. Use the problem-solving steps presented in this chapter to seek a solution to the problem that is creating the conflict. Define the problem: Identify the issues. Analyze the

problem: What are the causes, symptoms, effects, and obstacles that keep you from achieving your goal? Determine your goal: What do you want? What does your partner want? Generate many possible solutions to the problem. Finally, select the solution(s) that would permit each person to achieve his or her goal.

4. Briefly describe a conflict during which you did not do a good job of managing your emotions—that is, one in which you became angry and upset and lost your cool. Why did you lose control of your emotions? If you could go back in time, what would you do differently to better manage your emotions before and during the conflict? Consider incorporating some of the suggestions discussed in this chapter.

# $\mathcal{L}$earning with Others

1. Win as Much as You Can[56]

   This activity is designed to explore the effects of trust and conflict on communication. You will be paired with a partner. There will be four partner teams working in a cluster.

   | 4 Xs: Lose $1 each |
   | --- |
   | 3 Xs: Win $1 each<br>1 Y: Lose $3 |
   | 2 Xs: Win $2 each<br>2 Ys: Lose $2 each |
   | 1 X: Win $3 |
   | 3 Ys: Lose $1 each |
   | 4 Ys: Win $1 each |

   *Directions:* Your instructor will provide detailed instructions for playing this game. For ten successive rounds, you and your partner will choose either an X or a Y. Your instructor will tell all partner teams to reveal their choices at the same time. Each round's payoff will de-

pend on the decision made by others in your cluster. For example, according to the scoring chart shown above, if all four partner teams choose X for round one of this game, each partner team loses $1. You are to confer with your partner on each round to make a joint decision. Before rounds 5, 8, and 10, your instructor will permit you to confer with the other pairs in your cluster; in these three rounds, what you win or lose will be multiplied by either 3, 5, or 10. Keep track of your choices and winnings on the score sheet below. When you finish the game, compare your cluster's results with those of others. Discuss the factors that affected your balances. There are three rules:

   - Do not confer with the other members of your cluster unless you are given specific permission to do so. This applies to nonverbal and verbal communication.

   - Each pair must agree on a single choice for each round.

   - Make sure that the other members of your cluster do not know your pair's choice until you are instructed to reveal it.

| Round | Time Allowed | Confer with | Choice | $ Won | $ Lost | $ Balance | |
| --- | --- | --- | --- | --- | --- | --- | --- |
| 1 | 2 min. | Partner | _____ | _____ | _____ | _____ | |
| 2 | 1 min. | Partner | _____ | _____ | _____ | _____ | |
| 3 | 1 min. | Partner | _____ | _____ | _____ | _____ | |
| 4 | 1 min. | Partner | _____ | _____ | _____ | _____ | |
| 5 | 3 min. | Cluster | | | | | Bonus Round: |
| | 1 min. | Partner | _____ | _____ | _____ | _____ | Pay × 3 |
| 6 | 1 min. | Partner | _____ | _____ | _____ | _____ | |
| 7 | 1 min. | Partner | _____ | _____ | _____ | _____ | |
| 8 | 3 min. | Cluster | | | | | |
| | 1 min. | Partner | _____ | _____ | _____ | _____ | Pay × 5 |
| 9 | 1 min. | Partner | _____ | _____ | _____ | _____ | |
| 10 | 3 min. | Cluster | | | | | |
| | 1 min. | Partner | _____ | _____ | _____ | _____ | Pay × 10 |

2. Statements About Conflict

Read each statement once and mark whether you agree (A) or disagree (D) with it. Take five or six minutes to do this.

_____ 1. Most people find an argument interesting and exciting.

_____ 2. In most conflicts someone must win and someone must lose. That's the way conflict is.

_____ 3. The best way to handle a conflict is simply to let everyone cool off.

_____ 4. Most people get upset at a person who disagrees with them.

_____ 5. If people spend enough time together, they will find something to disagree about and will eventually become upset with each other.

_____ 6. Conflicts can be solved if people just take the time to listen to one another.

_____ 7. If you disagree with someone, it is usually better to keep quiet than to express your personal opinion.

_____ 8. To compromise is to take the easy way out of conflict.

_____ 9. Some people produce more conflict and tension than others. These people should be restricted from working with others.

After you have marked the preceding statements, break up into small groups and try to come to a unanimous opinion about each statement. Especially try to find reasons for differences of opinion. If your group cannot reach a unanimous opinion, you may change the wording in any statement to promote consensus. Assign one group member to observe your group interactions. After your group has attempted to reach consensus, the observer should report how effectively the group used the guidelines suggested in this chapter.

http://www.sybilevans.com/quizzes_3.asp  How good are your conflict management skills? Fill out this brief assessment form and find out.

http://learn.lincoln.ac.nz/groupwork/fail/conflict_.htm This site discusses common problems that students encounter when communicating in small groups and how to enhance the quality of interpersonal relationships when conflict occurs.

http://occawlonline.pearsoned.com/bookbind/pubbooks/devito_awl/chapter1/custom26/deluxe-content.html Visit this site to read a brief dialogue that illustrates unproductive conflict strategies (avoidance, force, blame, silencers, gunnysacking, fighting below the belt, face-detracting, verbal aggressiveness, and verbal abuse). You'll want to be able to identify these often unproductive conflict management strategies so that you can increase your skill in managing conflict with others.

http://www.mapnp.org/library/intrpsnl/conflict.htm  At this site, you'll find numerous links to other sites that address interpersonal conflict, including sites that will allow you to assess your conflict management skill.

http://www.coopcomm.org/  This is the home page of the Cooperative Communication Skills Extended Learning Community. You can access free books, essays, and exercises to help you communicate more creatively, resolve conflicts, and work with your family members to become more cooperative.

http://www.cyberparent.com/talk/negotiations.htm  Visit this site to learn tips and strategies for controlling your emotions during negotiations and when experiencing conflict.

# *Part Three*

# Interpersonal Communication in Relationships

The next four chapters focus specifically on interpersonal communication within the context of relationships. In the previous chapters you have learned about some of the fundamental skills of interpersonal communication; now you will see how these skills can be used to initiate, develop, maintain, and terminate relationships with other people. Chapter 9 explores the nature of relationships, focusing on intimacy, attraction, and power and the nature of our relationships with friends, lovers, and family members. Chapter 10 presents a model of relational development, theories to explain the forces that move you through relationships, and skills and strategies specific to developing relationships. Chapter 11 examines the challenges we face in developing and sustaining relationships, some of the darker aspects of interpersonal communication, and finally, relational de-escalation and termination. Chapter 12 applies interpersonal communication principles and skills to interactions with family, in computer-mediated relationships, and with coworkers.

# CHAPTER 9

# Understanding Interpersonal Relationships

## OBJECTIVES

1. Explain how relationships are both systems and processes.

2. Differentiate between relationships of choice and relationships of circumstance.

3. Explain what it means to have an intimate relationship.

4. Describe the elements that contribute to interpersonal attraction.

5. Identify the principles of interpersonal power.

6. Describe the types of power and how to negotiate power in a relationship.

7. Explain how friendships change during our lifetimes.

8. Explain the triangular theory of love and identify the six types of love.

9. Discuss differences among the relationships found in families.

## OUTLINE

An Interpersonal Relationship as a System and a Process

Relationships of Circumstance and Relationships of Choice

Intimacy and Attraction in Relationships

Interpersonal Power in Relationships

Relationships with Friends, Lovers, and Family

*You can hardly make a friend in a year, but you can lose one in an hour.*

---

*Pat:*   Hi, aren't you in my communication course?

*Chris:*   Oh, yeah, I've seen you across the room.

*Pat:*   What do you think about the course so far?

*Chris:*   It's okay, but I feel a little intimidated by some of the class activities.

*Pat:*   I know what you mean. It gets kind of scary to talk about yourself in front of everyone else.

*Chris:*   Yeah. Plus some of the stuff you hear. I was paired up with this one student the other day who started talking about being arrested last year on a drug charge. It made me feel uncomfortable.

*Pat:*   Really? I bet I know who that is. I don't think you have to worry about it.

*Chris:*   Don't mention that I said anything.

*Pat:*   It's okay. I know that guy, and he just likes to act big.

This interaction between Pat and Chris illustrates the reciprocal nature of interpersonal communication and interpersonal relationships. As you learned in Chapter 1, **interpersonal relationships** are connections that we develop with other people as a direct result of our interpersonal communication with them. The character and quality of interpersonal communication are affected, in turn, by the nature of the relationship.

The conversation between Pat and Chris begins with a casual acknowledgment but quickly proceeds to a higher level of intimacy. Chris confides in Pat. Pat, an other-oriented listener, offers confirmation and support; this response encourages Chris to confide even more. In this brief encounter, Pat and Chris have laid the groundwork for transforming their casual acquaintanceship into an intimate relationship.

In this chapter we examine the nature of interpersonal relationships, particularly in terms of intimacy, attraction, and power. In addition, we examine the various types of interpersonal relationships.

**interpersonal relationship.** A connection between two people that is based on their interpersonal communication.

257

# An Interpersonal Relationship as a System and a Process

Interpersonal relationships are transactional, just like interpersonal communication. This means that each person in a relationship affects the other person. Actually, relationships are affected by a wide range of factors that can best be understood by thinking of a relationship as a system. Systems theory was created originally to explain changes that occur in plant life,[1] but it also has proven valuable in explaining a variety of other phenomena, including interpersonal relationships.

A **system** is a set of interconnected elements often described in terms of their relationships as *inputs, throughputs* (or *process*), and *outputs.* The most fundamental notion in systems theory is that a change in any system element affects all the other elements. A relationship can be thought of as a kind of system, which means that a change in one element of the relationship affects the other elements. For example, a change in your best friend's mood or behavior affects your mood and behavior as well. The more interdependent we are, the more impact each partner has on the other partner, and the more a change in one affects the other. Married couples can be classified according to how interdependent their relationship is (as we'll discuss in more detail in Chapter 12) and thus how much it is like a system.

One difficulty in analyzing a relationship as a system is deciding what elements are part of the system; that is, what are its boundaries. Is your job, your relationship with your father, your boss's mood, or your communication teacher an element of your relationship with your best friend? Certainly each of these can affect you, and thus can affect your relationship. If your communication instructor acts particularly nasty to you in class one day (hypothetically, of course—we know how great communication instructors are), that might affect how you feel about yourself and influence your interaction with your best friend. As you read this text, you don't need to worry about deciding what is or is not part of the system; simply recognize that lots of factors affect your relationships, including some of which you are unaware.

**system.** A set of interconnected elements in which a change in one element affects all the other elements.

*In an intimate, trusting relationship, we can feel safe in telling our deepest secrets to another person.*

As a process, a relationship is constantly changing, evolving, and dynamic. They are always moving to a new level and being redefined. The changes might not be enormous, but because you are part of the relationship system, you change too. Part of the change is simply due to the fact that relationships are ongoing—they exist over a period of time. Existing over time means that relationships develop a history; they are accumulative. As you interact with a person, you gain a history together that becomes part of the relationship and affects each subsequent interaction. In the movie *As Good as It Gets,* Helen Hunt plays Carol, a waitress who develops a particular impression of and way of interacting with Jack Nicholson's character, Melvin. When Melvin begins to visit Carol and help her son, she is confused because she still sees him as a diner customer; their previous interactions affect subsequent ones. The accumulation of each succeeding event fosters a romantic relationship.

One last principle of a process is its irreversibility: Once something is done, it can't be undone. Melvin's help with her son continues to affect Carol positively, despite his tactless and irritating manner. Consider how your own relationships are ongoing processes, continually building on each interaction.

## Relationships of Circumstance and Relationships of Choice

In Chapter 1 we pointed out that an interpersonal relationship is an ongoing connection with another person that we carry in our minds (and, metaphorically, in our hearts), whether the other person is present or not. These ongoing connections can be formed either because of circumstances or because of intentional choice. **Relationships of circumstance** form not because we choose them, but simply because our lives overlap with others' in some way. Relationships with family members, teachers, classmates, and coworkers fall into this category. In contrast, relationships that we seek out and intentionally develop are **relationships of choice.** These relationships might include those with friends, lovers, spouses, and counselors. As German poet Emmanuel Von Geibel wrote,

"It is chance that makes brothers but hearts that make friends."

We act and communicate differently in the two types of relationships because the stakes are different. The effect of the same interpersonal communication behavior on different relationships can be dramatic. If we act in foolish or inappropriate ways, our friends might end the relationships. If we act the same way within the confines of our family, our relatives may not like us much, but we will still remain family.

Of course, these categories are not mutually exclusive. Relationships of circumstance can also be relationships of choice: Your brother or sister can also be your best friend. You can break off contact with family members or quit your job to sever your relationships with fellow employees. In addition, the other individual can define and redefine the relationship. Your boss might fire you, a relative might cut you off, or a lover might desert you.

## Intimacy and Attraction in Relationships

One of the most significant aspects of any relationship is its level of intimacy. In everyday usage, the word *intimacy* is often associated with sexual activity; however, interpersonal or psychological intimacy has a broader meaning that applies to

**relationship of circumstance.** Interpersonal relationship that exists because of life circumstances (who your family members are, where you work or study, and so on).

**relationship of choice.** Interpersonal relationship you choose to initiate, maintain, and terminate.

nonsexual relationships as well. What qualities (aside from sexual ones) do you associate with relationships that you think of as close or intimate? Here are some qualities that are commonly associated with interpersonal intimacy:

- Feelings of closeness

- Sharing one's innermost thoughts and feelings

- Mutual appreciation

- Confidence that the partner will provide nurturance/support

- Emotional bonding

- Unconditional support

- Openness and honesty

- Affection and warmth

Ultimately, what seems to make relationships the most intimate is our ability to be ourselves with another person, which means being able to be open and feeling accepted and loved. Thus, we define **interpersonal intimacy** as the degree to which each person's sense of self is confirmed and accepted by his or her partner in a relationship. You can measure the intimacy of relationships by the extent to which other people let you know that they see you the same way you see yourself while expressing positive feelings toward you. In essence, they love you in spite of your flaws and you don't have to hide those flaws from them.

We depend on intimate relationships to provide us with information about ourselves (as exemplified in the Johari window) and to bolster our self-confidence. The more intimate the relationship, the more we depend upon others for acceptance and confirmation of our self-image.[3] During periods when we might not have very intimate relationships, it is sometimes hard to maintain a strong positive self-image. Research confirms that having strong social support networks is related to subjective well-being.[4]

Your self-image can only be confirmed when another person really knows who you are. That is one reason some theorists see self-disclosure as the most significant factor in moving people toward intimate relationships.[5] Chapter 2 discussed how self-disclosure is necessary to develop an intimate relationship. Figure 9.1 orders the labels generally associated with interpersonal relationships according to their relative intimacy.

Going from being strangers to being best friends involves moving through a number of relational stages that are associated with sharing information about ourselves. (Chapter 10 covers more on relationship stages.) Our communication behaviors and strategies are directly linked to the level of relational intimacy—we communicate differently depending on the level of intimacy in a relationship. Interpersonal communication scholars Denise Solomon and Leanne Knobloch hypothesize that in more intimate relationships, people exhibit direct information-seeking behavior to reduce uncertainties, while those in less intimate relationships exhibit indirect behaviors.[6] For example, if a close friend uncharacteristically began binge drinking, you would ask him or her about it. On the other hand, you would be less inclined to ask an acquaintance so directly about his or her drinking. Solomon and Knobloch also speculate that direct information seeking creates greater clarity and understanding, thus increasing the solidarity of intimate relationships.

We communicate our sense of intimacy to others both directly, through our words, and indirectly, through actions. We might tell another person how we feel about him or her and how much we value the relationship. On the other hand, being open and

**interpersonal intimacy.** The degree to which a person's sense of self is accepted and confirmed by another person in a relationship.

Non-Intimate    Highly Intimate

Stranger ←→ Acquaintance ←→ Casual Friend ←→ Friend ←→ Close Friend ←→ Best Friend/Spouse

FIGURE **9.1**

Continuum of Interpersonal
Intimacy and Relationships

honest by disclosing highly personal information is an indirect way of expressing interpersonal intimacy. We also might use nonverbal cues, such as close physical proximity, eye contact, tone of voice, touch, and time spent interacting.

The process of developing an intimate relationship usually begins and is sustained because of your attraction toward another person. Attraction exists whenever you have a positive regard for another person, or when you like someone. **Interpersonal attraction** is the degree to which you want to form or maintain an interpersonal relationship. You might find yourself attracted to an acquaintance, which motivates you to increase your interactions, which in turn increase, decrease, or sustain your attraction.

## Short-Term Initial Attraction and Long-Term Maintenance Attraction

Interpersonal attraction occurs in the early stages of relational development as short-term initial attraction, and in the later stages of relational development as long-term maintenance attraction. You can understand the difference between the two by looking at your own relationships. Think of the dozens of people whom you initially found attractive but with whom you never developed an intimate relationship. **Short-term initial attraction** is the degree to which we sense a *potential* for developing an interpersonal relationship. For instance, you might find one of your classmates to be physically attractive, but never move to introduce yourself. The information you gather in your first interaction with someone can also generate a short-term initial attraction for a relationship, which you may or may not pursue, depending upon the circumstances. **Long-term maintenance attraction,** in contrast, is the type that sustains relationships like your best friendships. It refers to a level of liking or positive feeling that motivates us to maintain or escalate a relationship. Short-term attraction gives way to long-term attraction as a relationship develops through the stages presented in Chapter 10.

Think about your best friend. How did that relationship start? Perhaps it was because he or she was physically attractive, or perhaps you observed your friend laughing and joking with others and found that quality attractive. Why are you still friends with this person? Rarely (except in some movies or TV shows) do we commit to, and maintain, a long-term intimate relationship such as marriage or enduring friendship solely because we find another person physically attractive.[7] Perhaps you have discovered that you and your friend have a lot in common or that your personalities are complementary. For instance, your friend's calm, even disposition might balance your fiery temper.

In a study of initial and maintenance attraction, students were to think about a person with whom they had a close personal relationship and were given a list of reasons for attraction.[8] One group was asked to identify reasons for their initial attraction, while another group was asked to explain their current attraction. The number-one

**interpersonal attraction.** The degree to which you are motivated to form or maintain an interpersonal relationship.

**short-term initial attraction.** Degree to which you sense a potential for an interpersonal relationship.

**long-term maintenance attraction.** A liking or positive feeling that motivates you to sustain a relationship.

reason for initial attraction was the other person's desirable personality, followed by the person's warmth and kindness. The number-one reason for maintenance of attraction was warmth and kindness, followed by desirable personality.

## Elements of Interpersonal Attraction

Why do you feel attracted to some people and not to others? The explanations are complex, but researchers have identified seven elements that influence our feelings of attraction. As you read about them, try to analyze your own feelings about people you find attractive.

### Physical Attraction

The degree to which you find another person's physical appearance appealing represents your **physical attraction** to him or her. That appeal might be based on size, height, clothing, hairstyle, makeup, jewelry, vocal qualities, gestures, and so forth. The old adage "Beauty is in the eye of the beholder" is particularly true in terms of explaining physical attraction. Each culture has its own definition of the physical ideal, which it teaches and perpetuates. In the United States, for instance, advertisements and TV programs promote an ideal of slenderness for both males and females. This certainly contributes to the American fixation on losing weight and staying fit. However, in some cultures, and at various times throughout history, physical attractiveness was synonymous with bulkiness.

**physical attraction.** The degree to which you find another person's physical appearance appealing.

Physical attractiveness has been found to be more important for initial attraction than for maintenance attraction.[9] It acts as a convenient filter to reduce relationship possibilities.[10] In general, people tend to seek out individuals who have the same level of physical attractiveness as they do. Suppose you are really into physical conditioning and that good eating habits, exercising, avoiding drugs, and not smoking are all very important to you. You will probably seek out and attract a physically fit person to be your partner. To a certain degree, the physical image a person presents can reflect more substantive qualities. For example, there is a good possibility that a physically fit individual's philosophy about eating and exercise would be similar to yours. That similarity might serve as the basis for a long-term maintenance attraction. As you learned in Chapter 3, people use superficial information to make inferences about personality with varying degrees of accuracy, but whether they decide to escalate a relationship depends on what happens in the initial interaction and subsequent interactions.

LIZ AND MONTY TRIED TO HIDE IT FROM THEIR COWORKERS, BUT IT WAS QUITE APPARENT THERE WAS A THING BETWEEN THEM.

### Credibility, Competence, and Charisma

Most of us are also attracted to individuals who seem competent. We like those who are sure of themselves, but not full of themselves. We assume they are competent if they seem skilled, knowledgeable, and experienced. Intelligence/competence is a more important predictor of initial attraction in eventual romantic relationships than in friendships.[11] We find people credible if they display a blend of enthusiasm, trustworthiness, competence, and power. Competence, credibility, and sometimes physical attractiveness are all important elements in the composite quality called *charisma,* which inspires strong attraction and allegiance. Political and other types of leaders often depend on their charisma to attract supporters who are motivated to form relationships with them and willing to devote themselves to a cause.

### Proximity

People are more likely to be attracted to people who are physically close than to those who are farther away. You are more likely to form relationships with classmates sitting on either side of you than with someone seated at the opposite end of the room. This is partly because physical **proximity** increases communication opportunities. We tend to talk casually with someone who is right next to us. We are more likely to talk, and therefore to feel attracted to, neighbors who live right next door than to those who live down the block. Any circumstance that increases the possibilities for interacting is also likely to increase attraction; proximity has been found to be a more important factor in initial attraction than in maintenance attraction.[11]

In impromptu surveys of students in our classes over the years, we have found a high percentage form close friendships with dormitory roommates who were randomly assigned. There is a good chance that two individuals will become good friends simply because they share living accommodations.

### Similarity

In general, we are attracted to people on the basis of **similarity**—we like people whose personality, values, upbringing, personal experiences, attitudes, and interests are similar to ours. We seek them out through shared activities. For example, you may join a folk dance group because you know the members share your interest in dance. Within the group, you would be especially attracted to those who have a similar sense of humor, who share the same attitudes on certain issues, or who enjoy some of the other activities that you do. As we interact, we discover both similarities and differences between ourselves and others. We assess the relative weight of those similarities and differences and arrive at a level of attraction that may change over time as we continue to discover more information.

In the initial stages of a relationship, we try to emphasize positive information about ourselves to create a positive and attractive image. We reveal those aspects of ourselves that we believe we have in common with the other person, and the other person does the same.[13] Think about your initial interactions with strangers; typically, you spend the first few minutes trying to find topics of mutual interest. You may discover that the person is from a place near your hometown, has the same musical tastes, likes the same sports, frequents the same restaurants, and on and on. But the depth of this information is limited. You save your revelations about important attitudes and issues for a later stage in the relational development process.[14] Attitude similarity is more likely to be a source of long-term maintenance attraction than of short-term initial attraction. Similarity of interests and leisure activities appears more important in same-sex friendships than opposite-sex relationships.[15]

### Complementary Needs

You have heard the adage "Opposites attract." Although we like people with whom we have much in common, most of us wouldn't find it very exciting to be stuck for the rest of our lives with someone who had identical attitudes, needs, values, and interests. Most of us look instead for someone with **complementary needs**; essentially, people seek a matching of needs such that one partner contributes something to the relationship that

**proximity.** Physical nearness to another.

**similarity.** Having comparable personalities, values, upbringing, personal experiences, attitudes, and interests.

**complementary needs.** Needs that match, such that one partner contributes something to the relationship the other partner needs.

# Building Your Skills

## Are Your Needs Complementary?

*E*valuate your level of interpersonal needs by putting your first initial in the appropriate spot on the rating scale.

1. How much do you like to include others in the activities you do?

   Very little  1———2———3———4———5———6———7———8———9———10  A great deal

2. How much do you like to be included by others when they are involved in activities?

   Very little  1———2———3———4———5———6———7———8———9———10  A great deal

3. How much do you like to take responsibility for decision making?

   Very little  1———2———3———4———5———6———7———8———9———10  A great deal

4. How much do you like to let others make decisions for you?

   Very little  1———2———3———4———5———6———7———8———9———10  A great deal

5. How much do you feel a need to be accepted and loved by others?

   Very little  1———2———3———4———5———6———7———8———9———10  A great deal

6. How much do you feel a need to accept others and to give love to others?

   Very little  1———2———3———4———5———6———7———8———9———10  A great deal

Now think of two close friends. Go back and place their first initials along each rating scale to indicate how much each item applies to them. Or ask your friends to initial the scale for themselves. Compare your ratings with those of your friends. Are there areas where you are similar? Complementary? Are there differences that cause difficulties in the relationship—for example, you both want to make decisions rather than accept others' decisions?

---

the other partner needs. As we discuss in Chapter 2, Schutz identified three interpersonal needs that motivate us to form and maintain relationships with others: inclusion, control, and affection.[16] *Inclusion* represents the need to include others in our activities, or to be included in theirs. *Control* represents the need to make decisions and take responsibility, or the willingness to accept others' decision making. *Affection* represents the need to be loved and accepted by others, or the willingness to give love and acceptance to others.

If you have a high need to control and make decisions, and little respect for others' decision making, you will be more compatible with someone who does not have a similar need—instead, you'll be more comfortable with someone who wants others to make decisions. In essence, we can view a pair of individuals as a team in which each person complements the other. If you're not very good at keeping track of your bills and balancing your checkbook, you might pair up with someone who is good at maintaining a budget to create a strong personal finance team. In reality, there are no "perfect" matches, only degrees of compatibility relative to needs.

## Understanding Diversity

### Dating Customs Around the World

The development of relationships varies from culture to culture. The following list describes some dating behaviors from cultures throughout the world.

### Afghanistan
Dating is rare because most marriages are arranged by parents, and schools are separate for boys and girls. Opportunities to meet are rare. Girls have a 7 P.M. curfew, whereas boys have an 11 P.M. curfew.

### Australia
Most teens go out in large groups and don't pair off until they are 18 or 19 years old. Girls often ask boys out, and pay for the date, too. Couples often go to dinner parties, barbecues, or the beach.

### Central and South America
Dating is not allowed until the age of 15. When of age, most boys and girls date in large groups, going out together to weekend dance parties. When not dancing, teens gather at local clubs to eat and talk.

### Europe
Dating is usually a group event. In Finland, as many as thirty teens may attend a movie together. Slumber parties are common in Italy and Switzerland, where teens gather for parties at a home and sleep there when the party is over.

In Spain, teens join a *pandilla,* a club or a group of friends with the same interests, such as cycling or hiking. Dating is done one-to-one, and both girls and boys ask each other out and split the cost of the evening's entertainment.

In Russia, dates take place at dances or at clubs where teens eat or chat with friends. In small towns, teens meet in the streets downtown or gather around a fountain.

### Iran
It is against the law to date. Teens are separated until they are of marrying age; then their families introduce them to each other and sometimes a courtship follows.

### Japan and Korea
Most high school students don't date or go to parties, but spend their time studying instead. Dating begins in college, when only boys do the asking and pay for the dates.

*Source:* "Dating Customs Around the World." http://www.factmonster.com/ipka/A0767654.htm. Infoplease.com, 2003. Pearson Education: http://www.infoplease.com

In Russian small towns, teens often meet in the streets downtown to socialize together. How does this compare with your experiences?

## Relationship Potential

We need interpersonal relationships to confirm our self-image. **Predicted outcome value theory** claims that we assess the potential for any given relationship to meet this relational need and then weigh that assessment against the potential costs.[17] We are attracted to others with whom a relationship may yield a high outcome value (the rewards might exceed the costs). Over time, our assessments may change. In the romantic comedy *Two Weeks' Notice,* the liberal activist attorney, played by Sandra

**predicted outcome value theory.** Theory that people are most attracted to those relationships that potentially have greater rewards or benefits than costs.

Bullock, initially thought that working for the capitalist, played by Hugh Grant, would do little to meet either of their needs. Over time, the two developed a working relationship that did meet certain needs. At a certain point, they both thought the relationship had gone as far as it could. In the end, however, they discovered that they could have a more intimate relationship with a high outcome value for them both.

Like these film characters, most of us begin predicting outcome values in initial interactions and continually modify our predictions as we learn more about the other person. We pursue attractions beyond the initial interaction stage if we think they can yield positive outcomes, and generally avoid or terminate relationships for which we predict negative outcomes.[18]

### Reciprocation of Liking

**Reciprocation of liking** simply means that we like people who like us. One way to get other people to reciprocate, particularly in romantic relationships, is to show that we like them.[19] However, in initial interactions we are often reluctant to let other people know that we are attracted to them. We may hold back from showing our interest because we fear rejection or fear that we may give the other person a certain amount of power over us.

A study conducted by Mark Redmond and Denise Vrchota found that we often underestimate how much a new acquaintance is attracted to us.[20] Pairs of male and female college students interacted for the first time and then indicated their level of attraction for their partner, as well as their perception of how attracted their partner was to them. Most of the students significantly underestimated the amount of attraction the other person felt for them. It is unclear whether we underestimate because we don't have much confidence that others will like us as much as we like them, or because in general we do not communicate effectively our level of attraction for others. Even in long-term relationships, people sometimes repress their continued attraction for their friends or mates. As you interact with new acquaintances, keep in mind that they probably are more attracted to you than you realize, so you might want to adapt your decision making accordingly.

# Interpersonal Power in Relationships

As relationships move toward intimacy, partners often struggle with the question of who makes the decisions or with the problem of one partner dominating the other. These are issues of power, and they play a significant role in the development, maintenance, and health of a relationship. **Interpersonal power** is the ability in an interpersonal relationship to influence another person in the direction you desire—to get another person to do what you want. As relationships develop, interpersonal interactions reflect changes in the interpersonal power between the partners. The ability of partners to reach a mutually acceptable understanding of their interpersonal power is a determining factor in achieving and maintaining intimate relationships.

### Principles of Interpersonal Power

Think about the people with whom you have interpersonal relationships: friends, coworkers, family members, classmates, and teachers. The people in each of these relationships inevitably have some power over you, and you have power over them. Most of us don't like to think that other people have power over us, but interpersonal

**reciprocation of liking.** We like people who like us.

**interpersonal power.** Ability in an interpersonal relationship to influence another person in the direction one desires.

power is a fundamental element of all our personal relationships. Understanding the following five principles will enable you to more effectively manage power in your day-to-day interactions and on-going relationships.

1. *Power exists in all interactions and all relationships.* Influence is one of the defining qualities of interpersonal communication presented in Chapter 1. When you talk, you are attempting to exert power over other people, if for no other purpose than to get them to listen to you. Have you ever tried to talk to someone who didn't want to listen? This situation can be frustrating because you are exerting power but meeting resistance; the other person's refusal to listen is an exertion of power against you. Most of the time our interactions flow fairly easily as the participants share power, taking turns speaking and listening. By definition, being in a relationship means letting someone have some influence on you.

2. *Power primarily derives from an individual's ability to meet another person's needs within a given relationship.* The degree to which one person can satisfy another person's interpersonal needs (for inclusion, control, and affection) and/or other needs (for food, clothing, safety, sex, money) represents the amount of power that person has. In a **dependent relationship,** one person has a greater need for the partner to satisfy his or her needs. One study of heterosexual romantic couples found that the partner with less emotional involvement in the relationship had more power, and this was generally the man.[21] Maybe you've wanted to continue a relationship that lost its value for your partner, and as a result of this power imbalance, you agreed to requests that you normally would have rejected. The more we depend on one person to satisfy our needs, the more power that person has over us. On the other hand, the more people who are available to meet our needs, the less power any one individual has.

   In the classic movie *Back to the Future*, Marty McFly's dad, George, initially appears powerless against Biff, his supervisor. George lets Biff walk all over him, much to Marty's dismay. Later, George's position changes as he gains confidence and gains power over Biff. Just as George's becoming a successful author makes him no longer dependent on Biff, your ability to satisfy your own needs without reliance on another person reduces the amount of power another person has over you.

3. *Both partners in an ongoing relationship have some degree of power.* In some relationships it might appear as though one person has all the power and his or her partner is powerless. You might have felt that imbalance in your relationship with your parents as you were growing up. However, children do have power in their relationships with their parents. Parents want their children's love, they want to protect their children, they want their children to be happy. These parental wants and needs give children some foundation for influencing their parents.

   When two individuals are mutually satisfying each other's needs, they create an **interdependent relationship;** each person in the relationship has a similar amount of power over the other. The more intimate and exclusive a given relationship, the more we turn to that one person to satisfy a broader spectrum of our needs. You've probably had friends reduce their interactions with you when they turned to their romantic partners to fill the needs you once met.

4. *Power is circumstantial.* Because our needs change, so does power. As you were growing up, you were very dependent on your parents and other adults. However, as you grew and developed skills, you no longer needed your parents to meet certain needs, and thus their power diminished. This change isn't always without some tension as parents begin to realize they don't have the degree of control

**dependent relationship.** A relationship in which one partner has a greater need for the other to meet his or her needs.

**interdependent relationship.** A relationship in which each person has a similar amount of power over the other.

over their children that they used to. One of the authors vividly remembers that sending a young son to his room for "time out" was easy when the son could be carried to his room if he refused to go. However, during the teen years, when the son was as large and strong as his parent, physical power was no longer an option. As you grow even older, your parents might become dependent on you to meet their needs for care. The circumstantiality of power can lead to a feeling of being used when we have been meeting another person's needs, only to have the relationship discarded when those needs no longer exist. For example, you might develop a friendship in which you provide rides to your friend all the time, but once that friend gets her own car, the relationship comes to an end.

5. *Relational development involves a negotiation of each partner's power.* In developing interpersonal relationships, we decide who will have power over us and what type of power they will have. Your relational partners make similar decisions. In Chapter 10 you will read about the tension that is created in deciding to give up some of your autonomy in order to forge a more intimate relationship. Partners often negotiate which individual will have decision making responsibility over what issues. The process often involves tension, conflict, and negotiation. The ability to reach a point at which both partners are content with how power is shared in the relationship is one factor that can affect relational success and satisfaction. Relational stability occurs when partners reach agreement about power in their relationship. In a four-year study of forty-one romantic couples, most of whom got married during that time, each couple's reported balance of power remained stable.[22]

## Types of Power Relationships

In the discussion of attraction, you read about complementary needs; for example, one person who likes to make decisions would make a good partner with another person who likes other people to make decisions for him or her. Complementarity also characterizes relationship power. In **complementary relationships,** one partner usually dominates and the other usually submits: One likes to talk, the other to listen; one likes to lead, the other to follow. You might find such a relationship undesirable for yourself, but for many people such a relationship works to the satisfaction of both partners.

What happens when both partners want to call the shots and make the decision? In **symmetric relationships,** both partners behave in similar ways.[23] Sometimes both partners want to dominate, and sometimes both want to be submissive. A **competitive symmetric relationship** exists when both partners are vying for control or dominance over the other person. For example, each might try to control which TV program they watch or might insist on participating in every spending decision. Competition in such relationships often increases the amount of conflict and negotiation associated with decision making. In some relationships, neither partner wants to take control or make a decision, and this creates a **submissive symmetric relationship.** The following is an example of submissive symmetry (does it sound familiar to you?):

*Bea:* What movie do you want to rent?

*Vic:* Oh, I don't care. You decide.

*Bea:* No, you decide. I don't care either.

Most relationships, however, are neither purely complementary nor purely symmetrical; they are parallel. **Parallel relationships** involve a shifting back and forth of

**complementary relationship.** Relationship in which power is divided unevenly, with one partner dominating and the other person submitting.

**symmetric relationship.** Relationship in which both partners attempt to have the same level of power.

**competitive symmetric relationship.** Relationship in which both partners vie for control or dominance of the other.

**submissive symmetric relationship.** Relationship in which neither partner wants to take control or make decisions.

**parallel relationship.** Relationship in which power shifts back and forth between the partners, depending on the situation.

the power between the partners, depending on the situation. For example, if Janene knows more about computers than her husband, Justin, then he might defer to her the decision about what new computer to purchase. However, Janene might defer to her husband to plan their upcoming vacation, because of his experience planning business trips. Establishing who has power in various situations is a point of contention in developing relationships and takes time for the parties involved to resolve. Power in any relationship changes as individuals change. As Justin gains computer savvy, he might want more say in purchasing a new system. Having knowledge or expertise is one way we hold power over another person.

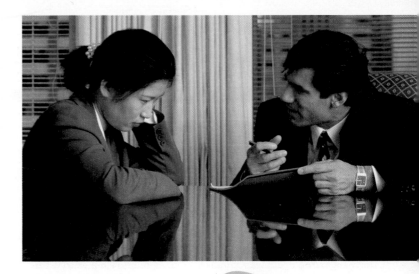

### Types of Power

Why does one person in a relationship have power over the other? There are many explanations; one that works well identifies five sources of power: legitimate (or position) power, referent power, expert power, reward power, and coercive power.[24]

**Legitimate power** is power that is based on respect for a position that a person holds. Teachers, parents, law officers, store managers, and company presidents all have power because of the position they hold relative to other people. When a police officer tells you to pull off to the side of the road, you respond to this enactment of power by obeying the officer's command.

**Referent power** is power that comes from our attraction to another person, or the charisma a person possesses. We let people we like influence us. We change our behavior to meet their demands or desires because we are attracted to them.

**Expert power** is based on a person's knowledge and experience. We grant power to those who know more than we do, or have some expertise we don't possess. This expertise can even include knowledge about how to manage a relationship effectively. We grant power to partners who have more experience in relationships. In many episodes of the *Seinfeld* TV series, the characters deferred to the expertise of their friends when it came to how to handle various relational crises.

**Reward power** is based on another person's ability to satisfy your needs. There are obvious rewards, such as money and gifts, but most rewards are more interpersonal in nature. Reward power is probably the most common form of power in interpersonal relationships. Withholding rewards is actually a form of punishment, or what is called *coercive power.*

**Coercive power** involves the use of sanctions or punishment to influence others. Sanctions include holding back or removing rewards. If you have a high need for physical affection, your partner might withhold that affection if you do not comply with a given request. Punishment involves imposing something on another person that he or she does not want.

### Negotiating Power in Interpersonal Relationships

You decide how much control another person has over you, but the decision is usually the result of weighing the costs of compliance against the costs of noncompliance. Defining who has power can be a source of conflict in interpersonal relationships,

*W*ho appears to have more power in this interaction? What do you think are the sources of each person's power?

**legitimate power.** Power that that is based on respect for a person's position.

**referent power.** Power that comes from our attraction to another person, or the charisma a person possesses.

**expert power.** Power based on a person's knowledge and experience.

**reward power.** Power based on a person's ability to satisfy our needs.

**coercive power.** Power based on the use of sanctions or punishments to influence others.

# *applying theory and research*

## *Power in Marital Relationships*

*M*uch of the research on the types of power presented so far has been done in the context of organizations; however, Virginia Richmond, James McCroskey, and David Roach examined power in the context of marriage. One hundred and thirty-six married couples voluntarily completed instruments that assessed their marital satisfaction, perceptions of the types of power used by their spouses, and their own use of power. When power was used, referent power was used most widely (40 percent of respondents using it themselves; 45 percent of respondents reported their spouse using it), followed by expert power (21 percent of respondents; 28 percent of spouses), reward power (11 percent of respondents; 13 percent of spouses), legitimate power (11 percent of respondents; 12 percent of spouses), and finally, coercive power (6 percent of respondents; 11 percent of spouses).

In examining the impact on satisfaction, the researchers found that use of coercive power related to dissatisfaction in the marriage for both husbands and wives. Further analysis led the research-ers to suggest that dissatisfaction (particularly for wives) seemed likely to lead to the use of coercion, rather than the use of coercion leading to dissatisfaction. The use of referent power was related to satisfaction (though it was not as strong a relationship as that between coercive power and satisfaction). The researchers concluded their study by offering the following advice: In attempting to influence your spouse and still maintain your spouse's satisfaction, the best course of action would be to use referent power and avoid using coercive power.

## *A*PPLYING
### the Research to Your Life

The use of power is probably different in marital relationships than it is in other types of relationships. Married couples are more likely to have established particular roles, foundations for power, and patterns for decision making. The type of power used in less intimate relationships might be a determining factor in their maintenance or escalation. As the study suggests, the type of power you exert may influence your partner's satisfaction, and the level of satisfaction can affect the type of power used. For each of the relationships listed below, think of a particular person and divide the use of power up among the five types to indicate what percentage of the time each type of power is used (the percentages should total 100).

How do your relationships differ in terms of the types of power you and the other person use to influence each other? What do the differences reveal about power and about your relationships? In what ways have the types of power used changed over the course of the relationships? Answering these questions should help you appreciate the role that power plays in your relationships, whether they are casual relationships or marriage.

*Source:* Virginia P. Richmond, James C. McCroskey, and K. David Roach, "Communication and Decision-Making Styles, Power Base Usage, and Satisfaction in Marital Dyads," *Communication Quarterly,* 45 (Fall 1997): 410–426.

| Type of Power | Example | Relationship with a Friend | | Relationship with a Best Friend | | Relationship with a Parent/Relative | |
| --- | --- | --- | --- | --- | --- | --- | --- |
| | | Your Power | Your Friend's Power | Your Power | Your Best Friend's Power | Your Power | Your Parent's Power |
| Reward | 25% | _____ | _____ | _____ | _____ | _____ | _____ |
| Coercive | 10% | _____ | _____ | _____ | _____ | _____ | _____ |
| Referent | 35% | _____ | _____ | _____ | _____ | _____ | _____ |
| Legitimate | 10% | _____ | _____ | _____ | _____ | _____ | _____ |
| Expert | 20% | _____ | _____ | _____ | _____ | _____ | _____ |

potentially bringing about the end of a relationship. When a partner abuses power, then ending the relationship may be warranted. Ideally, partners establish a mutually acceptable and rewarding power relationship.

### Assess Needs

The first step to negotiating a satisfactory balance of power is to identify your needs and those of your partner. What are you looking for from your relationships? Remember that needs can include everything from financial rewards to confirmation of your self-concept.

Your assessment should include both needs that are being satisfied and those that are unsatisfied. You friendships could be meeting your interpersonal needs but leave unmet your desire to start a family. Unmet needs affect both the development of other relationships and the power that other people have over you.

You also should strive to understand the needs of those with whom you have relationships. Identifying your best friends' needs helps you to understand what motivates them as well as appreciate the basis of power that you might have over them. Changes in their needs will also change your ability to influence them. For example, some people have a need to control and dominate other people, and there are others who are perfectly happy to let them do so. If you are not one of those, then you need to decide whether you wish to develop or maintain a relationship with this type of person.

### Assess Need Fulfillment in Relationships

Examine how well a given relationship meets your needs and how well you meet the needs of your relationship partners. The degree to which others satisfy your needs reflects the amount of power those people have. The more needs that are met by one relationship, the more likely you are to sustain that relationship. You might know a person with whom you enjoy jogging (meeting a need for your physical well-being), but with whom you have no other real connection. It would be easier to give up the jogging relationship than to replace a best friend who is meeting many of your needs.

### Identify Need-Based Conflicts and Tensions

Examine your interpersonal conflicts for unresolved power issues. For example, in the first year of marriage, couples often argue about balancing job and family, about financial problems (including who spends money and on what), about the frequency of sexual relations, and about the division of household tasks.[25] These problems involve issues of power, control, responsibility, and decision making. Such issues exist in other relationships as well. Examine your relationships for recurring patterns of conflict, and try to determine the role that power is playing. Conflicts can result from unacceptable imbalances of power (feeling that one or the other partner has too much), from equal amounts of power (with each partner attempting to influence the other), or as a reaction to attempts to exert control or to dominate.

### Directly Discuss Power Issues

Everyday conversation helps engaged and married couples work toward equality of power and task responsibilities and ultimately affects their relational satisfaction.[26] In some instances, your partner might be unaware that he or she is exerting power over you in a manner you dislike. Simply pointing out this problem might be enough to remedy the situation. On the other hand you might need to adopt a more active conflict management style. For example, describe the power problem without evaluation, describe your feelings about the power situation, solicit information from your partner in an active and open manner, and engage in a cooperative approach to negotiating power.

## Interpersonal Power in Relationships

**Principles of Power**

1. Power primarily derives from an individual's ability to meet another person's needs within a given relationship.

2. Both partners in an ongoing relationship have some degree of power.

3. Power exists in all interactions and all relationships.

4. Power is circumstantial.

5. Relational development involves a negotiation of each partner's power.

**Types of Power Relationships**

| | |
|---|---|
| Complementary relationship | One partner dominates and the other submits |
| Symmetric relationship | Both partners attempt to have the same level of power |
|     Competitive Symmetric | Both partners want power and control |
|     Submissive Symmetric | Neither partner wants power or control |
| Parallel relationship | Power shifts back and forth between the partners |

| **Types of Power** | **Basis for the Power** |
|---|---|
| Legitimate power | Power based on respect for the position a person holds |
| Referent power | Power based on attraction to another person or his or her charisma |
| Expert power | Power based on a person's knowledge or experience |
| Reward power | Power based on a person's ability to satisfy our needs |
| Coercive power | Power based on the use of sanctions or punishment to influence others |

**Negotiating Power in Interpersonal Relationships**

1. Assess needs. What needs do you and your partner have?

2. Assess need fulfillment in the relationship. How well is the relationship meeting needs?

3. Identify need-based conflicts and tensions. To what degree is power a factor in relational conflicts?

4. Directly discuss power issues. What issues about power need to be discussed?

# Relationships with Friends, Lovers, and Family

The dimensions of power and intimacy provide a foundation for understanding interpersonal relationships, including the three types that are most important to us: relationships with friends, with lovers (romantic relationships), and with family (including spouses). These three types of relationships share similarities, but they also have significant differences. Not only do they differ in terms of intimacy and power, they also differ in terms of the needs they meet.

Friendships provide us with valuable support. In a survey of more than 100,000 men and women, single women rated friends and social life as the most important source of happiness in their lives, while single men rated friends second only to their job duties.[27]

Generally, in relationships between lovers there is a high degree of intimacy and attachment, as well as sexual activity and/or attraction.[28] Historically, marriage was considered the most intimate relationship, rooted in the goal of procreation and forming a family.[29] Today, gay and lesbian relationships also reflect a form of intimate romantic relationship with relational dynamics similar to heterosexual relationships, including marriage and child rearing.

Families include a variety of relationships: between wife and husband, between parents and children, between siblings, and among other relatives. The relationship between spouses is primarily one of choice (though it can shift to being based solely on circumstance); the other relationships are more circumstantial. Familial relationships provide nurture and support, affect the development of self-concept, exert lifetime and cross-generational influence, and in general represent complex systems of relationships.[30] In this chapter you will read about the types of family relationships, and in Chapter 12 you will read about family communication in general.

## Friends

Friendship is a relationship that exists over time between people who share a common history.[31] A friend is someone we like and who likes us. We trust our friends. We share good and bad times with them. We want to be with them and we make time for that purpose. Or, as one armchair philosopher observed, a real friend is one who will continue to talk to you over the back fence even though he knows he's missing his favorite television program.

Here's a list of some of the qualities of friendship identified in a variety of research studies.[32] Which ones do you feel match your idea of what makes a friend?

Self-disclosure/feeling free to express intimate information

Openness/honesty/authenticity

Compatibility/similarity

Ego-reinforcement/self-concept support

Acceptance of one's individuality

Respect

Helping behavior

Positive evaluation

Trust

Concern and empathy

We each have our own expectations of friendship that include some of the items from this list, as well as additional qualities. How well a given person meets these expectations is one factor that we use in making a choice about whether to establish a friendship. As we noted earlier, friends represent relationships of choice. Friendship develops naturally into an interdependent relationship that is different from other interpersonal relationships with friends; we have no external constraints that keep us together, such as a job, school, or family, even though we often make friends with people in these situations. Usually we form friendships with our equals, whereas we often form other types of relationships with people of different ages or social backgrounds.[33]

Besides helping us enjoy a healthy life, friends help us cope with stress and take care of physical needs, and even help in the development of our personality. Friends also help shape our attitudes and beliefs. Especially during periods of change and crisis in our lives, such as adolescence and retirement, friends help us cope with uncertainty and have a profound influence on our behavior.[34]

One of the most important functions that friends perform is to help us manage the mundane. Most friendships are not based on unusual activities. On the contrary, most of us seek out friends just to talk, to share a meal, or be entertained together.

How many friends do we need? Typically, people have up to five close friends, fifteen other friends, twenty or more members in a social network (which could include family members), and many more people who are simply acquaintances.[35] In all our social interactions, we are happiest when we are in the company of our friends. Perhaps the ancient Roman orator Cicero said it best: A friend multiplies our joys and divides our sorrows.

Friends also perform other functions, such as bolstering our self-esteem. Most of us need people who provide encouragement and tell us that we are decent and likable. It is confirming to have a friend become indignant on our behalf when we have experienced an injustice. Friends can help keep a stream of positive acceptance flowing to counteract the numerous nicks and bruises that our self-worth suffers in the course of daily living.

Friends also provide material help when we need it. When you are away on vacation, you might ask a friend to feed your cat and water your plants. If you run out of gas, you might call a friend to bring you some or pick you up.

### Friendships at Different Stages in Life

Establishing intimacy with another person takes time, so most of us have a limited number of intimate relationships. We also have different needs for intimacy at various stages of our lives. Relationship scholars W. J. Dickens and D. Perlman examined the differences among friendships at four stages in life: childhood, adolescence, adulthood, and old age.[36]

*Childhood Friendships*  At about the age of two, when we start to talk, we begin parallel play with others. As toddlers we perceive our playmates as people who can help meet our needs. Our first friendships are usually superficial and self-centered. Childhood friendships can be categorized into five sometimes overlapping stages.[37] From ages three to seven, we have *momentary playmates*—we interact with those in our presence. From ages four to nine, our friendships involve *one-way assistance*. We still view friendships from a "take" perspective, as instruments to help meet our needs, rather than from a "give" or "give-and-take" perspective.

The third stage, ages six to twelve, is the *fair-weather friend* stage. There is more give and take in friendships, but the reciprocity occurs when things are going well; the relationship is likely to end if problems and conflicts develop. The fourth stage, ages nine to fifteen, is called *mutual intimacy*. With the closeness that develops, relationships become more possessive. The last stage (beginning at about age twelve and continuing through adulthood) allows for more *independence* in friendships, as well as deepening interdependence with friends that permits greater levels of intimacy and sharing.

*Adolescent Friendships*  During adolescence, beginning with the onset of puberty around age twelve, we move away from relationships with parents and other adults and toward greater intimacy with our peers. During adolescence, peer relationships are the most important social influence on our behavior. We develop cliques of friends and form friendship networks. Boys are more likely to join either socially acceptable groups such as a sports or debate team, or less socially desirable groups bent on violence and destruction of property. Girls are more likely to develop intimate relationships with one or two good friends. During adolescence boys seem to have more friends, whereas girls appear to develop closer, more intensive and intimate relationships. Friendship relationships usually peak in late adolescence and early adulthood, before we select a mate.[38]

***Adult Friendships*** Adult friendships are among our most valued relationships. Typically, they provide emotional support, partners for activities, and opportunities to socialize.[39] Women friends are more likely than men friends to routinely engage in the communication of sharing, supporting, and venting.[40] Often, neighbors, relatives, or coworkers become our adult friends after we leave college. These sources of friendships mean that many of them are temporary relationships. We move or take a new job and make friends with the new neighbors or new coworkers while the previous friendships usually fade away. In addition, adult friendships are affected by marriage and usually become secondary to the spousal relationship. Marriage usually lessens the likelihood of having cross-sex friendships, so most adult friendships are with people of one's own sex. Sometimes we are fortunate enough to have special friendships that last throughout our adulthood despite moving, marriage, or new jobs.

***The Elderly and Friendships*** Although the elderly make new friends, they value old ones most. During retirement, when people have more time for socializing, friendships become increasingly important; but older adults form fewer new friendships. Instead, they tend to maintain a small, highly valued network of friends.

Psychologist Howard Markman and his colleagues found that self-disclosure, one of the most important components of friendship, did not seem to change in either depth or amount from young adulthood through age ninety-one.[41] They did report, however, that as friends get older, they engaged in more negative self-disclosure; apparently, as we age, we are more willing to tell our friends less positive things about ourselves, rather than limiting our disclosures to information that makes us "look good."

*E*lderly people may make new friends, but they usually rely most on their spouses and oldest friends to fulfill their need for companionship.

**Recap**

### Friendships at Different Life Stages

| | |
|---|---|
| **Childhood Friendships** | Self-focused and often superficial. |
| **Adolescent Friendships** | Peers influence social behavior. Boys often associate with others in groups, whereas girls develop deep friendships with a smaller circle of friends. |
| **Adult Friendships** | Other relationships may change once a person chooses a lifelong mate. |
| **Elderly Friendships** | Old friends are valued, and friendship networks often shrink. |

### Intergenerational, Intercultural, Interracial, and Cross-Sex Friendships

Most of our friendships are with people who are fairly similar to us. Similarity makes it easier to communicate effectively and to reach mutual understanding. The more we differ from other people, the greater the challenges that must be overcome to maintain a relationship, as is discussed in Chapter 4. However, both friendships and romantic relationships do develop between people who differ in terms of culture, age, and race. Part of the success of these relationships depends on whether the difference is more superficial than profound. For example, the impact of a ten-year age difference between you and another person is likely to be minimal if you both have the same interests in activities and similar values. However, someone forty years older might have a very different outlook on life from yours. Usually, the older people become, the less impact age differences have on them.[42] A fifteen-year-old interacting with a thirty-year-old is a very different kind of relationship than a thirty-year-old talking to a forty-five-year-old.

Think about your relationships with people older or younger than you. How do these relationships differ from relationships with people close to your age? How many close relationships do you have with anyone significantly older or younger? Developing and sustaining such relationships often requires special effort. We are probably more likely to have casual intergenerational relationships. One study compared close friendships between peers of similar age and between friends who were at least ten years different in age.[43] The sample included participants who ranged from eighteen to seventy-six. Close relationships with peers, as compared to relationships with those who were of a different age, were seen as providing more companionship, satisfaction, intimacy, and nurturance, and being more likely to continue in the future. Casual relationships between those who were similar in age and between those who were different in age did not differ on these qualities. The only difference in the casual relationships was that casual friends who differed in age admired each other more than casual friends of similar ages did.

Age is only one of the differences that can affect relationships. Cultural, ethnic, and racial differences also come into play. One of the major elements affecting these friendships is that the qualities and expectations associated with being a friend differ from group to group. In other words, you might engage in behavior that you think is appropriate in your friendship with a person from another culture, only to find that you have offended your friend by violating his or her culturally based expectations. In fact, one study that examined the qualities associated with friendship in various ethnic groups in the United States found that "Latinos emphasized relational support, Asian Americans emphasized a caring, positive exchange of ideas, African Americans emphasized respect and acceptance, and Anglo Americans emphasized recognizing the needs of the individual."[44] Realize, of course, that such generalities may not be valid for a particular member of an ethnic group. However, the study also found that in developing interethnic relationships, individuals seemed unaware of cultural or ethnic differences; in essence, they developed a unique relationship defined by their own relational rules rather than by cultural rules.[45] This is similar to the notion of developing a third culture discussed in Chapter 4.

The development of male–female friendships between heterosexuals is sometimes a challenge because of underlying sexual attraction. In the movie *When Harry Met Sally,* Harry proclaims that "... men and women can't be friends. The sex part always gets in the way." Fortunately, research and your own experiences might indicate that Harry wasn't totally correct. We can develop cross-sex friendships with minimal sexual attraction or redefine romantic relationships as friendships. Heidi Reeder, a communication researcher, conducted two studies on cross-sex relationships: one in which she interviewed twenty pairs of cross-sex friends, and the other in which 231 students completed questionnaires.[46] Both studies found that romantic attraction and physical/sexual attraction diminished as the relationship progressed over time, while friendship attraction increased. While sexual attraction might indeed be an issue within cross-sex relationships, it is reduced when there is a commitment to developing and maintaining the relationship as friends.

Cross-sex friendships can be important relationships because, as with the other relationships that have just been discussed, you can gain insights into how other people think. In this case, your friends can help you better understand the opposite sex. On the basis of interviews with 300 men and women, psychotherapist and author Lillian Rubin found that the men reported feeling a higher level of intimacy and friendship than their female counterparts (some women were surprised to find out they were even considered a friend).[47] Men seemed to gain more from their friendships with women than women did from men. Men valued their friendships with women for providing more nurturance and intimacy than their male friendships. Women did not feel their male friendships were as intimate or rewarding as their female friendships. However, women did enjoy the "masculine" interaction style, the fun activities, and learning about the male perspective.

You probably have your own views about what is important in a friendship that may or may not be in concert with those of your racial or ethnic group. In interacting with people, you should primarily focus on working toward a mutual understanding and acceptance of what your expectations are for your friendship. There is great value in forming relationships with individuals who are different from you; not only can you learn about other people, but you can also gain a better sense of yourself. Learning how another person's age, race, ethnicity, or sex affects his or her values, thoughts, and behaviors can increase your awareness of how those factors have influenced you.

## Lovers: Romantic Relationships

We use the term *lovers* to describe people who are involved in a romantic relationship. Certainly we can love our friends, but that type of love is different from a romantic attachment. Romantic relationships fill particular needs that differ from those friendships fill. People usually think of their lovers as also being their best friends, but romantic, loving relationships differ in quality from friendships. One pair of researchers suggests that love differs from friendship "in the identity of interest that the partners share. Love exists to the extent that the outcomes enjoyed or suffered by each are enjoyed or suffered by both."[48]

Another key difference between friends and lovers lies in how they talk about their relationship. Friends are less likely to talk about what attracted them to each other. Friends are also less likely to celebrate anniversaries and mark the passage of time in formal ways, such as with a card or a special dinner. Love involves an increase in a sense of "we-ness," of passionate solidarity and identification with the other.

Zick Rubin, a lawyer and social psychologist, attempted to identify differences between love and friendship by developing two scales—one to measure love and the other to measure liking.[49] He found that people do make distinctions between love and liking. Love relationships are more passionate and intimate than friendships, but interestingly, people like their lovers only slightly more than they like their friends. And women make greater distinctions between loving and liking than do men.

The closest relationship you develop with another human being will probably be a romantic one. When one research team asked a group of students, "With whom do you have the closest relationship?" 47 percent said it was with a romantic partner.[50] (Thirty-six percent said they were closest to their friends, 14 percent said they were closest to a family member, and 3 percent reported "other.")

Sexual orientation is another factor in how people think about romantic relationships. Romantic relationships can exist between opposite-sex couples as well as same-sex couples. Gay and lesbian romantic relationships share many of the same qualities as heterosexual relationships, though homosexual couples often face the added pressures of social mores, restrictive laws, and condemning attitudes. Conducting research comparing heterosexual and homosexual relationships is difficult, since homosexual couples can't legally marry. Nonetheless, one study found that gay and lesbian couples displayed patterns similar to married heterosexual couples in terms of change in satisfaction over a five-year period.[51] However, same-sex couples were more likely than opposite-sex married couples to end their relationship within those five years, perhaps because of a lack of social acceptance.

The **triangular theory of love** identifies three dimensions that can be used to describe variations in loving relationships: intimacy, commitment, and passion.[52] In this model, intimacy includes such attributes as trust, caring, honesty, supportiveness, understanding, and openness (many of the qualities of intimacy discussed earlier). The second dimension, commitment, includes loyalty, devotion, putting the other first, and needing each other. The final dimension, passion, includes excitement, sexual interest and activity, and extreme longing. Passion has been identified as the most important dimension for developing romantic relationships.[53] Despite controversy over how valid this theory is, recent research has found relationship satisfaction to be related to variations among the three dimensions.[54] These dimensions provide a valu-

**triangular theory of love.**
Theory that suggests that all loving relationships can be described according to three dimensions: intimacy, commitment, and passion.

## *Understanding Diversity*

### Improved Attitudes Toward Interracial Dating

*W*hile blacks and whites may not see eye to eye on many racial issues, one area on which a sizable majority of both races have come to agree is interracial dating and, to a slightly lesser extent, interracial marriage.

That's the finding of a 1999 survey by the Pew Research Center for the People and the Press, based in Washington, D.C.

Pew has documented a gradual shift in racial tolerance since the 1980s in value issues such as interracial dating, said Carroll Doherty, editor of the center.

The survey, done in September and October of 1999, found 70 percent of whites and 82 percent of African Americans approve of interracial dating. In the general population, 73 percent approve, a figure that is up from 48 percent when a 1987 survey was conducted.

The survey polled Americans on a variety of issues including race. In an-

other part of the survey, there also was strong support for interracial marriage, with 77 percent of nonwhites and 60 percent of whites voicing approval. In the general public, including blacks, whites and other minorities, 63 percent said interracial marriages are good because they break down racial barriers.

Tolerance for interracial dating and marriage is what Doherty calls a value issue, and when it comes to such value issues, there seems to a larger degree of consensus between blacks and whites. When asked to respond to the statement "I don't have much in common with other races," 12 percent in the general population said they agree and 85 percent said they don't agree. By contrast, in May 1987, 23 percent agreed.

On the other hand, the survey found more divergent views when it came to public policy issues. Several of those questions have to do with perceptions of racial progress and the role of government. For example, 67 percent of African Americans said there has not been much real improvement in their position in society, while only 34 percent of whites voiced the same view.

When asked whether the government should make every effort to help minorities, 62 percent of blacks agreed with government intervention and 69 percent of whites opposed it.

People do tend to compartmentalize their views on race relations, separating racial progress and government intervention from value issues such as interracial dating and marriage, Doherty said.

Part of the reason the tide may be turning on interracial dating and marriage may be young adults, the under-30 crowd, Doherty said. People staunchly opposed to the races mixing when it comes to dating and marriage are not around anymore.

Doherty said it's likely the center will do another survey about racial issues next year.

*Source:* Lynda Guydon Taylor, "A View from the Experts: Survey Finds Interracial Relationships Well Accepted," *Pittsburgh Post-Gazette,* December 22, 2002, http://www.post-gazette.com/neigh_washington/20021222waexpert4.asp

---

able way of thinking about how love might manifest itself in relationships. According to the triangular theory of love, the presence and strength of each of these three dimensions varies from relationship to relationship, with each combination defining a style of love.

Sociologist John Alan Lee created a similar scheme that defined six types of love found in both romantic and nonromantic relationships: eros, ludis, storge, mania, pragma, and agape.[55] As you read the descriptions of these types, see which best describes the types of love you find in your relationships.

**Eros** is sexual love based on the pursuit of beauty and pleasure. The physical need for sex brings many couples together. Erotic lovers crave sexual intimacy and passionately seek sexual activity to satisfy their need. Sexual attraction brings special needs and emotions to a relationship, sometimes obscuring other concerns. Shakespeare described this phenomenon when he wrote, "But love is blind, and lovers cannot see the petty folly that themselves commit."

**eros.** Sexual, erotic love based on the pursuit of physical beauty and pleasure.

**Ludis** describes love as a game, something to pass the time. Ludic lovers are not seeking long-term relationships; rather, they seek immediate gratification and to win their partner's affection. Their goal is to be in love and to enjoy their partner rather than to achieve a sexual victory.

Early dating relationships are often of the ludic type. Going on a date to a junior high dance is a casual pleasure, not a prelude to a lifelong commitment. Ludis lasts as long as the couple has fun and finds the relationship mutually satisfying.

**Storge** is the sort of love found in most friendships and in relationships with siblings and other family members. Sexual consummation is not a factor in this sort of love, although sexual attraction may be present. A storgic relationship usually develops over a long period of time, and it is solid and more resistant to change than erotic love. Trust, caring, and compassion are high; selfishness is low.

**Mania** describes a relationship that swings wildly between extreme highs and lows. A manic lover is one who is obsessed with the relationship with the other person. Each of the lovers may have an insatiable need for attention, often fueled by a low self-concept.

**Pragma** is the root word for *pragmatic*. This kind of relationship works because the partners' personal requirements, personalities, backgrounds, likes, and dislikes are compatible. In some cultures, parents prearrange marriages because of pragmatic concerns, and if the couple is lucky, passion develops later on, as the relationship takes its course.

**Agape** love is based on a spiritual ideal of love. It involves giving of yourself and expecting nothing in return. This kind of "pure" love may characterize the relationship between a parent and a child, or the relationship between a spiritual leader and his or her followers.

## Family Relationships

Most of you will get married at some point in your life, and many of you will become parents. Most of you had a relationship with your parents or other adult that greatly influenced your development through childhood. And many of you grew up with at least one younger or older sibling. These relationships are the most common ones that constitute family relationships. One feature you probably recognize about your own family relationships is how they have changed and continue to change. Your relationships with your parents and siblings are considerably different than they were when you were a pre-adolescent. Your relationship with your spouse will also change over the course of your marriage, as will your relationships with your own children. All of our family relationships are important to us because, among other things, they affect our self-concept and sense of self-worth.

## Husbands and Wives

You've already read about the nature of intimate and loving relationships, information that obviously applies to married couples. Formal recognition and approval by a culture through the ritual of marriage adds additional meaning and challenges to a relationship. This is one reason some gay and lesbian couples seek the right to marry and thereby gain public and legal recognition of their relationships. Most of us take the commitment of marriage very seriously (despite a few TV executives who have turned marrying a millionaire into a game). When two people enter into marriage, they spend a lot of time defining their roles and working through the trials of cohabitation. The nature of their relationship depends on a variety of factors, such as how they distribute power and make decisions (symmetric, complementary, or parallel) and what roles they each assume. Despite the variety of differences, couples can be classified according to how the partners communicate with one another.

**ludis.** Game-playing love based on the enjoyment of another.

**storge.** Solid love found in friendships and family, based on trust and caring.

**mania.** Obsessive love driven by mutual needs.

**pragma.** Practical love based on mutual benefits.

**agape.** Selfless love based on giving of yourself for others.

Researcher Mary Anne Fitzpatrick has identified four types of married couples that she believes can be found in American society: traditional, independent, separate, and mixed.[56] According to Fitzpatrick, **traditional couples** are interdependent, exhibit a lot of sharing and companionship, follow a daily schedule, are not assertive, have conflicts, emphasize stability over spontaneity, and follow traditional community customs (such as the wife taking the husband's last name). **Independent couples** share and exhibit companionship but allow each other individual space; they believe the relationship should not limit their individual freedoms. They are psychologically interdependent but have a hard time matching schedules, and also engage in conflict. **Separate couples** hold somewhat opposing values; on the one hand, they support traditional marriage and family values; on the other hand, they stress the individual over the couple. They have low interdependence and avoid conflict. This means that by maintaining their autonomy, they display less companionship and sharing than the other couple types, but they still try to keep a daily schedule. In each of the preceding three types of married couples, both the wife and the husband share the same perspective about the nature of their relationship. When the husband and the wife have divergent perspectives on their roles, they are a **mixed couple** (the fourth type). There are six possible combinations of the three other types that make up the mixed category:

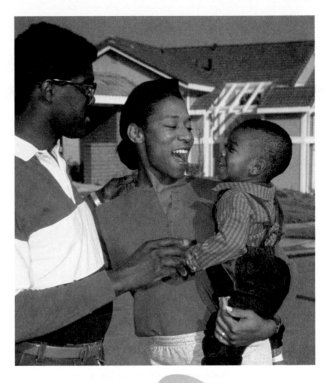

*Research* shows that "traditional" married couples are the most satisfied.

Husband independent and wife traditional

Husband separate and wife traditional

Husband traditional and wife independent

Husband independent and wife separate

Husband separate and wife independent

Husband traditional and wife separate

Before you decide that the separate style sounds appealing, you should know that research shows traditional couples are the most satisfied, while separate couples are the least.[57] One explanation for this is that traditional partners are the most likely to meet each other's relational expectations.[58] In a survey of more than 700 couples, Fitzpatrick and her colleagues found the following percentages of couple types: traditionals, 20 percent; independents, 22 percent; separates, 17 percent; and mixed, 30 percent (among which, the six types were fairly equally distributed at 6–9 percent each).[59] These data are from the late 1970s and early 1980s and therefore may not reflect marriage types today. What types do you think may have increased or decreased in the last twenty years? What type would you most prefer?

### Parents and Children

A great deal of study has been done on the nature of the interaction between parents and their children. Most studies focus on identifying the most effective ways for parents to communicate with their children or describing the nature of parent–child interactions. And some studies have examined the impact of a parent's communication with the child on the development of the child's communication skills as an adult.

**traditional couples.** Married partners who are interdependent and who exhibit a lot of sharing and companionship.

**independent couples.** Married partners who exhibit sharing and companionship and are psychologically interdependent but allow each other individual space.

**separate couples.** Married partners who support the notion of marriage and family but stress the individual over the couple.

**mixed couples.** Married couples in which the husband and wife each adopt a different perspective (traditional, independent, separate) on the marriage.

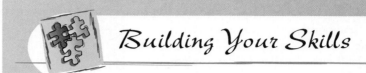

## Origins of Your Interpersonal Communication Skills

*T*hroughout this book you have had the opportunity to assess your interpersonal communication skills. Take a moment now to think about the role your parents or other adult relatives have played in the development of those skills. Does the way you interact with others match your mother or father's style? What skills have you developed by modeling your parents' behavior? What skills are the result of adapting or accommodating to your parents' communication style (for example, your father was very emotional, so you learned how to provide effective support and comfort to others)?

The way your parents interacted with you has had an impact on your behavior and attitudes, although the impact is not always straightforward. One study found a correlation between self-reports of mothers' aggressive communication style and those of their college-aged children, but did not find such a relationship between fathers' communication style and those of their children.[60] Another study found that seventh graders' responses were similar to their mothers' views on openness in sharing thoughts and feelings and to their fathers' views on conformity and authority. By the eleventh grade, however, children's views on openness matched their fathers', whereas their views on conformity matched their mothers'.[61] Students' views on sex and alcohol use were not found to correlate with their parents' attitudes, but the more open the communication in the family was about sex and alcohol, the more likely students were to engage in safe behavior.[62] The exact effects of your parents' communication style on you, and of yours on your children, are obviously unclear; however, it is clear there are effects. Many of the interpersonal communication skills and principles covered throughout this text can be applied to enhance interactions with your parents and your own children, whether you are using good listening skills, providing confirming responses, managing conflict constructively, being other-oriented, or clarifying perceptions.

### Siblings

Making generalizations about communication between siblings is difficult, because so many factors influence the nature of the relationship, most notably the sexes and ages of the siblings. Just as your relationship with your parents changes over time, so do your relationships with your siblings. During childhood, sibling rivalry often occurs as children vie for their parents' love or compete with one another. This rivalry can last throughout the siblings' lifetime. Sibling rivalry is only one issue that leads to conflict among children in the same family. However, there is a positive side to sibling relationships. Siblings can often provide warmth and support to each other, both as children and as adults. One study found that young adults were more likely to turn to their siblings than to their parents to discuss such things as their dating experiences and life problems.[63] In addition, young adults preferred talking to a same-sex sibling about sexual matters to talking to any other family member.[64] The authors of this study found that such disclosures occurred because there was less fear of evoking disappointment or disapproval from a sibling than from a parent.

## Becoming Other-Oriented

### Intimacy and Power in Relationships

*D*ifferences in partners' perceptions of their relationship often spur conflicts. You might see your relationship as more intimate than your partner does and thus behave in a way your partner feels is inappropriate. Your partner might feel more attracted to you than you are to him or her and thus request more of your time than you are willing to give. Although partners' perceptions will al-ways differ, one way to minimize any detrimental impact is to recognize and understand these differences. Being other-oriented can enhance your un-derstanding of your partner's percep-tions and thus your understanding of your partner's communication and behaviors.

Two important dimensions exam-ined in this chapter are intimacy/attraction and power. See if you can identify some of the differences in your perceptions and those of some of your relational partners. For each of the two dimensions, put an X at the point on each line that you think represents a partner's perception of the relationship, and an O on the line at the point that represents how you see the relationship. After marking each scale, write down one reason that you believe your perceptions dif-fer from those of the other person.

If possible (and if you are comfort-able doing so), show your responses to the three people whose perceptions you recorded. Ask them to share with you their actual perception and discuss whether you were accurate or not.

**Intimacy**

| | | |
|---|---|---|
| Friend | Very Intimate | Not at all intimate |
| Current/Past Romantic Partner | Very Intimate | Not at all intimate |
| Father or Mother | Very Intimate | Not at all intimate |

**Power**

| | | |
|---|---|---|
| Friend | Partner dominates | I dominate |
| Current/Past Romantic Partner | Partner dominates | I dominate |
| Father or Mother | Partner dominates | I dominate |

Often children's first playmates are their brothers and sisters. Children gain valu-able psychosocial skills through interactions with siblings that translate into how they interact with friends and peers. Some learn parenting skills when there is such a large age difference between siblings that the older ones play a nurturing role.

Children without siblings may be somewhat at a disadvantage in that they miss the opportunity to practice and develop certain interpersonal skills. One study of first-through sixth-graders found that only children weren't any different than those with siblings in terms of the number or quality of friends; however, only children were less well liked, more aggressive, and victimized by their peers.[65] The researchers suggest these problems reflect only children's difficulty in managing interpersonal conflict. If you have effective conflict management skills, perhaps they were nurtured as you were forced to work through sibling squabbles in your childhood. How your parents re-sponded to sibling conflicts is also likely to have influenced your conflict management skills as well as your relationships with your siblings.

# Summary

An interpersonal relationship can be viewed as a system—a set of interconnected elements in which a change in one element affects all the others. Viewing a relationship as a process acknowledges that it is constantly changing. Relationships of circumstance occur because surrounding conditions cause you to interact with someone. In contrast, you create relationships of choice when you intentionally seek to establish a relationship you could otherwise avoid.

Interpersonal intimacy reflects the degree to which interpersonal relationships confirm and show acceptance of the partners' sense of self. Our relationships vary in their level of intimacy, and intimacy affects communication. Interpersonal attraction, the degree to which you want to form or maintain a relationship, is a factor contributing to intimacy.

Before you interact with a stranger or during your first interactions, you might experience short-term initial attraction, but as a relationship develops you form more long-term maintenance attraction. Elements that influence feelings of attraction include physical appeal, proximity, similarity, complementary needs, relationship potential, reciprocation of liking, as well as credibility, competence, and charisma.

Your ability to influence other people in the direction you desire—interpersonal power—is an important factor in the development and success of relationships. Power derives from individuals' needs, is possessed by both partners, exists in all interactions and relationships, is circumstantial, and is negotiated in the relationship. The pattern of power in relationships can be complementary (one partner dominates and the other submits), symmetrical (both have the same amount of power, which is competitive when both are strong, or submissive when both are weak), or parallel (changing from situation to situation).

Power is negotiated by first assessing needs, assessing how a relationship meets those needs, identifying how power affects interpersonal conflicts, and finally by directly discussing power issues.

Relationships with friends, lovers, and family represent the most important interpersonal relationships we experience. Friends (people we like and who like us) play an important part in our lives by providing support, helping us manage the mundane and cope with stress, shaping our personality, and providing material help. Our friendships change as we move from childhood through adolescence to adulthood and then to old age. A variety of factors influence our friendships with those who differ from us in age, sex, culture, race, and ethnicity. These relationships require a special sensitivity to how the differences affect our partners and these relationships.

Romantic relationships differ from friendships because lovers expect more, talk more about the relationship, and are more passionate, more intimate, and more committed. Our relationships with lovers vary according to three dimensions (passion, intimacy, and commitment) that make up the triangular theory of love. Love can be categorized as eros, ludis, storge, mania, pragma, or agape.

Communication among family members includes interactions between husbands and wives, between parents and their children, and among siblings. Married couples can be categorized as traditional (being interdependent, sharing, and compassionate), independent (allowing for individual space but exhibiting sharing and compassion), separate (supporting marriage but putting the individual above the couple), or mixed (in which the two partners display different styles). The way parents interact with their children strongly affects the development of their children's interpersonal communication skills. As children grow up, their relationships with their parents often change a great deal. The communication skills covered in this text are as applicable to parents dealing with children as they are to any relationship. Siblings often support each other by discussing such issues as dating or negative experiences without having to worry about disapproval or disappointment (which their parents might display in discussing such matters).

# For Discussion and Review

## Focus on Critical Thinking

1. Imagine that you wanted to increase an acquaintance's attraction toward you. Formulate strategies to accomplish this using each of the elements that contribute to attraction described in the chapter.

2. Under what circumstances is the exercise of power in a relationship appropriate? Inappropriate?

3. How do your friendships with same-age friends differ from friendships you have with anyone substantially older or younger than you?

4. What types of love are most likely to characterize the different types of relationships found in a family?

## Focus on Ethics

5. Under what circumstances is it appropriate for a person to use the power he or she has over another person to satisfy personal goals?

6. Under what conditions is it ethical or unethical to seek an intimate relationship with (a) a coworker, (b) a subordinate, or (c) a supervisor you feel attracted to?

7. What ethical responsibilities do you have toward a person you consider your best friend?

# For Your Journal

1. Monitor a face-to-face conversation between two or three of your friends for at least four minutes; you should simply be a quiet observer. Write down the ways in which your friends attempted to gain or concede power during the interaction. Include examples of the language they used and the nonverbal cues they exchanged.

2. Think about three relationships you have now or have had: a close romantic relationship (or a very close relationship with someone of the opposite sex); a very close friendship; and your relationship with the family member with whom you are closest. Describe two characteristics common to these three relationships (for example, perhaps they all provide support, involve similar levels of disclosure or intimacy, or involve complementary power). Describe two characteristics that distinguish each relationship from the other two (for example, maybe you are most open with the close friend or receive the most support from the family member). What generalizations about your relationships can you draw from these comparisons?

# Learning with Others

1. Create two lists of names: people you regard as casual friends and those you regard as close friends. Identify what attracts you to the people on your list. Compare your ideas of what attracts you to casual friends and close friends with the ideas of other students. How does your list fit with the categories of attraction identified in the text? What's different? What's the same?

2. Write down all the qualities you can think of that you associate with someone you would call your "friend." Now write down the qualities you associate with someone you would call your "lover." Get together in groups of four or five students, and compare your lists. What qualities have you listed that nobody else has? Why do you think you included that quality in your list? What qualities did everyone in the group list? To what degree are the qualities defined by your culture? In what way are the qualities for friends the same as for lovers? In what ways are they different?

3. Some people develop relationships of choice with their family members. In groups of five or six, identify someone who has developed such a relationship with (a) a sibling, (b) a parent, and (c) another relative. Discuss why some students have developed friendships with these family members and why other students have not. Explore how these relationships are likely to change over the next ten to twenty years.

http://www.solvedating.com/  Do you believe that people can be "soulmates"? Here's a web site devoted to finding your soulmate, including a calculator to determine how many people you have to meet to insure that you find your soulmate.

http//:www.quizstop.com  This site contains a variety of five-question quizzes about your personal thoughts and feelings, such as whether you can remain friends with someone of the opposite sex. (Remember, this is just for fun—the assessment and advice should not be taken too seriously.)

http://members.aol.com/sfenelli/report.htm  This site, created for an English-as-a-Second-Language class, discusses differences in marital practices between the United States and other countries.

http://lovetests.adoringyou.com/luvtests1.html  This site lets you assess which of six types of love discussed in this chapter describes your own romantic relationships.

# 10 Developing Interpersonal Relationships

## OBJECTIVES

1. Explain the stages of relational escalation.

2. Explain the stages of relational de-escalation and define post-intimacy relationships.

3. Describe two theories that explain how relationships develop.

4. Describe the skills and strategies used primarily during the initiation stage of a relationship.

5. Describe the skills and strategies used in both initiating and escalating relationships.

6. Describe the skills and strategies used in escalating and maintaining relationships.

## OUTLINE

Stages of Interpersonal Relationships

Theories of Interpersonal Relationship Development

Strategies and Skills for Developing Interpersonal Relationships

*You can't stay in your corner of the forest waiting for others to come to you. You have to go to them sometimes.*

Winnie the Pooh

---

**Scenario 1:** Josh and Nona are strangers standing at a bus stop.

*Josh:* Hi. I noticed your T-shirt says Michigan Tech. Are you a student there?

*Nona:* Huh, oh, no, I picked this up at a T-shirt clearance sale. I just thought it looked cool—I liked the husky on it. Are you from Michigan Tech?

*Josh:* My family used to vacation near there and we've visited the campus.

*Nona:* Where exactly is it?

*Josh:* It's in Houghton, Michigan, which is way up in northern Michigan. Have you ever been in northern Michigan?

*Nona:* No, but I've been in lower Michigan. I went skiing there once with some friends from school.

**Scenario 2: Several months later:**

*Nona:* Hey Josh, I was thinking that maybe you'd like to go home with me over break and meet my family and friends. How about it?

*Josh:* Wow. It's really nice that you'd like me to meet your family and all, but I really don't think I'd be very comfortable doing that.

*Nona:* Oh. Okay, I guess. I just wanted them to meet you, but if you don't want to . . .

*Josh:* Don't be angry. I just think it's a little early for us to be meeting each other's families. Maybe we can make the trip another time.

**Scenario 3: A couple months later:**

*Josh:* Nona, where do you want to go to eat?

*Nona:* I'm not really up for going out, but you go ahead. I'll see you tomorrow.

*Josh:* What's wrong?

*Nona:* I don't know, Josh. I'm just feeling the need to cool things in our relationship right now. I think I just need something different from a relationship.

*Josh:* Oh. I'm sorry if I haven't been able to give you what you want. I guess I've been feeling a little distant in our relationship too.

*Nona:* I do like you, Josh, and I really value your friendship. You've really become like a big brother to me.

The three scenarios that start this chapter provide a snapshot of how communication changes as relationships develop. In the first scenario, Josh and Nona are following a getting-acquainted ritual and sharing safe information as they initiate a relationship. The communication in scenario 2 is much more relaxed and personal, reflecting an interaction between two individuals who have gotten to know each other well. In the final scenario, the communication signals problems in the relationship that lead Josh and Nona to discuss a de-escalation of the relationship. These snapshots reflect some of the stages that people experience as their relationships move toward and away from intimacy. While Josh and Nona's relationship is a romantically intimate one, remember that the term *intimacy* is not used in this book to refer to sexual activity but rather to describe any close relationship in which each partner confirms the other's sense of self.

This chapter begins with a model and description of the typical stages through which interpersonal relationships progress. Next, we discuss two theories that offer explanations of why we move from one stage to another. Finally, the chapter presents three sets of skills and strategies for initiating, escalating, and maintaining interpersonal relationships.

## *S*tages of Interpersonal Relationships

A lthough researchers use different terms and different numbers of stages, all agree that **relational development** does proceed in discernible stages. Understanding these stages is important to your studies because interpersonal communication is affected by the stage of the relationship. Individuals in an intimate stage discuss topics and display nonverbal behaviors that do not appear in the early stages of a relationship. We use interpersonal communication to move a relationship forward as we proceed from being strangers to acquaintances to friends. Outsiders usually can tell what stage a relationship is in by observing the interpersonal communication.

You can think of the stages, from first meeting to intimacy, as the floors in a high-rise building. Relational development is like an elevator that stops at every floor. As you get to each floor, you might get off and wander around for a while before taking the elevator to the next floor (see Figure 10.1). Each time you get on, you don't know how many floors up the elevator will take you, or how long you will stay at any given floor. In fact, sometimes you never get back on the elevator, electing instead to stay at a particular stage of relational development. But, if you fall head over heels in love, you might want to move quickly from floor to floor toward intimacy. Part of the time you share this elevator with your partner, and the two of you make decisions about how far up you will go on the elevator, how long to stay at each floor, and when and whether to ride the elevator down.

Just as there are lights on a panel to let you know the elevator has moved from one floor to another, markers, or turning points, signal a move from one stage to another in a relationship. **Turning points** are specific events or interactions that are associated with positive or negative changes in a relationship.[1] A first meeting, first date, first kiss, first sex, saying "I love you" for the first time, meeting a partner's family, going away together somewhere, making up after a conflict, moving in together, providing help in a crisis, or providing a favor or gift might all be turning points that indicate a relationship is moving forward. One pair of researchers found that 55 percent of the time, these turning points inspired a discussion about the nature of the relationship.[2] Such discussion helps the partners reach mutual agreement about the definition of the relationship.

Turning points can be divided into two types. **Causal turning points** are events that directly affect the relationship. Finding out that your romantic partner has

---

**relational development.** The movement of a relationship from one stage to another, either toward or away from greater intimacy.

**turning point.** Specific event or interaction associated with positive or negative changes in a relationship.

**causal turning point.** An event that brings about a change in a relationship.

FIGURE *10.1*

Model of Relational Stages

| Escalation | | | | | | De-Escalation |
|---|---|---|---|---|---|---|
| Intimacy | | | | | | Turmoil or Stagnation |
| Intensification | | | | | | Deintensification |
| Exploration | | | | DOWN | | Individualization |
| Initiation | | UP | | | | Separation |
| Preinteraction Awareness | | | | | | Postinteraction Effects |

cheated on you might cause you to terminate the relationship. Because the event causes a change in the relationship, it is a causal turning point. On the other hand, receiving and accepting an invitation from a friend to visit his or her family for the first time is a **reflective turning point,** because it signals that a change has occurred in the definition of the relationship. The invitation and acceptance don't cause a change, but reflect a change in how you and your friend perceive the relationship.

## Relational Escalation

**Relational escalation** is the movement of a relationship toward greater intimacy. This movement usually goes through a series of discernible stages: preinteraction awareness, initiation, exploration, intensification, and intimacy. Movement from one stage to another represents an increase in the amount of intimacy between two people. Each stage is accompanied by specific communication patterns, turning points, and relational expectations.

**reflective turning point.** An event that signals that a change has occurred in the way a relationship is defined.

**relational escalation.** Movement of a relationship toward intimacy through five stages: preinteraction awareness, initiation, exploration, intensification, and intimacy.

### Preinteraction Awareness

As you can see in the model in Figure 10.1, the first floor is the *preinteraction awareness stage.* At this stage, you might observe someone or even talk with others about him or her without having any direct interaction. Gaining information about others without directly interacting with them is a *passive strategy.*[3] Through your passive observations, you form an initial impression. You might not move beyond the preinteraction awareness stage if that impression is not favorable or the circumstances aren't right.

### Initiation

If you are attracted to the other person and the circumstances are right, you might proceed to the *initiation stage,* one of the first turning points in a relationship. In this stage, the interaction typically is routine; you might ask each other various standard questions during the first four minutes of conversation,[4] sticking to safe and superficial topics, and presenting a "public self" to the other person. Your partner is now riding on the elevator with you, and any decision about whether the elevator should go up, down, or nowhere is a mutual one for the rest of the ride. The relationship could remain at this stage if you don't share any further information about yourselves other than what occurs during the initiation ritual.

### Exploration

If you decide to go to the next floor, *exploration,* you will begin to share more in-depth information about yourselves. But you will have little physical contact, maintain your social distance, and limit the amount of time you spend together. This stage can occur in conjunction with the initiation stage. During this stage, communication becomes easier, and a large amount of low-risk disclosure occurs.

### Intensification

If you proceed to the *intensification stage,* you will start to depend on each other for self-confirmation and engage in more risky self-disclosure. You will spend more time together, increase the variety of activities you share, adopt a more personal physical

*As couples proceed from exploration to intensification, they have more physical contact and begin sharing more activities and confidences.*

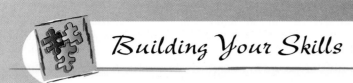

## Building Your Skills

### Graphing Your Relationship Changes

*T*hink of an interpersonal relationship that you have had for at least a year. On the graph at right, plot the development of that relationship from stage to stage, reflecting the relative amount of time you spent in each stage. You can also indicate whether you backed up to a previous stage at any point.

If possible, have your relational partner fill out a similar graph and compare your perceptions of how the relationship has developed. What differences are there and why?

You also might want to share your graph with those of classmates to compare how different relationships develop. What can you tell from the graphs about the nature of their relationships?

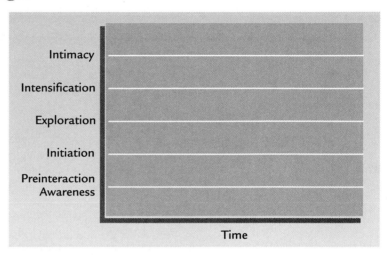

distance, engage in more physical contact, and personalize your language. Also, you may discuss and redefine the relationship often in this stage, perhaps putting a turning-point label on yourselves, such as "going steady," "good buddies," or "best friends." Other turning points associated with this stage include decisions to date each other exclusively, to become roommates, or to spend time with each other's families.

### Intimacy

The "top floor" in the relational high-rise is the *intimacy stage.* In this stage the two partners turn to each other for confirmation and acceptance of their self-concept. Their communication is highly personalized and synchronized. They talk about anything and everything. There is a free flow of information and intimate self-disclosure. There is a commitment to maintaining the relationship that might even be formalized through marriage or some other agreement. The partners share an understanding of each other's language and nonverbal cues and have a great deal of physical contact. They use fewer words to communicate effectively, and they have a clearer definition of their roles and of the relationship. Reaching this stage takes time—time to build trust, time to share personal information, time to observe each other in various situations, and time to build a commitment and emotional bond.

### Relational De-Escalation

**Relational de-escalation** is the movement that occurs when a relationship decreases in intimacy. Our model identifies five stages in this process: turmoil or stagnation, deintensification, individualization, separation, and postinteraction. These stages can be observed when an intimate relationship becomes less so or comes to an end. The

**relational de-escalation.** Movement of a relationship away from intimacy through five stages: turmoil or stagnation, deintensification, individualization, separation, and postinteraction.

process of ending a relationship is not as simple as going down the same elevator you came up on: It is not a reversal of the relationship formation process. Relational de-escalation can also involve only one or two of the stages. For example, a relationship might move from being one between good friends to a more casual friendship.[5] A **post-intimacy relationship** occurs when partners de-escalate from the intimate stage but still maintain a relationship. A couple might decide they like each other as friends but no longer want a romantic or exclusive relationship; thus, they de-escalate and maintain the relationship at the intensification or exploratory stage.

### Turmoil or Stagnation

When an intimate relationship is not going well, it usually enters the stage of either *turmoil* or *stagnation*. Turmoil involves an increase in conflict, as one or both partners tend to find more faults in the other. The definition of the relationship seems to lose its clarity, and mutual acceptance declines. The communication climate is tense and exchanges are difficult.

Stagnation occurs when the relationship loses its vitality and the partners become complacent. Communication and physical contact between the partners decrease; they spend less time together, but do not necessarily fight. Partners in a stagnating relationship tend to go through the motions of an intimate relationship without the commitment; they simply follow their established relational routines.

As with the up elevator, individuals can stop at this point on the down elevator and decide to quit descending. The relationship can remain in turmoil or stagnate for a long time, or the individuals can repair, redefine, or revitalize the relationship and return to intimacy.

### Deintensification

If the turmoil or stagnation continues, however, the individuals might move to the *deintensification stage,* decreasing their interactions; increasing their physical, emotional, and psychological distance; and decreasing their dependence on the other for self-confirmation. They might discuss the definition of their relationship, question its future, and assess each partner's level of satisfaction or dissatisfaction. The relationship can be repaired and the individuals can move back to intensification and intimacy, but that is more difficult to accomplish now.

### Individualization

On the next floor down, the *individualization stage,* the partners tend to define their lives more as individuals and less as a couple. Neither views the other as a partner or significant other anymore. Interactions are limited. The perspective changes from "we" and "us" to "you" and "me," and property is defined in terms of "mine" or "yours" rather than "ours." Both partners turn to others for confirmation of their self-concepts.

### Separation

In the *separation stage,* individuals make an intentional decision to eliminate or minimize further interpersonal interaction. If they share custody of children, attend mutual family gatherings, or work in the same office, the nature of their interactions will change. They will divide property, resources, and friends. Early interactions in this stage are often tense and difficult, especially if the relationship has been intimate. For relationships that never went beyond exploration or intensification, however, the negotiation is often relatively painless.

For former intimates, one of the awkward things about separating is their extensive personal knowledge about one another. Their talk is limited to superficial things,

**post-intimacy relationship.** A formerly intimate relationship that is maintained at a less intimate stage.

although they still know a lot about each other. This tends to make the interactions fairly uncomfortable. Over time, of course, each partner knows less about who the other person has become. For example, even after spending just a few years away from your high school friends, you might have difficulty interacting with them because your knowledge of one another is out of date.

### Postinteraction Effects

Although interaction may cease altogether, the effect of the relationship is not over. The relational-stages high-rise is like something out of the old TV series *Twilight Zone:* Once you enter it, you can never leave it. The bottom floor on the down elevator, where you remain, is the *postinteraction stage.* This floor represents the lasting effects the relationship has on your self, and therefore on your other interactions and relationships. Noted relationship scholar Steve Duck claims that in this final stage of terminating relationships, we engage in "grave-dressing."[6] We create a public statement for people who ask why we broke up and also come to grips with losing the relationship. Sometimes our sense of self gets battered during the final stages of a relationship, and we have to work hard to regain a healthy sense of self.

Of course, we are all aware of people who hop on an express elevator to get out of a relationship, bypassing all the normal stages of decline. One study found that of the various ways to terminate a relationship, abandoned partners most dislike the quick exit without discussion.[7]

## Theories of Interpersonal Relationship Development

The model of relational stages provides a description of the stages you can expect to experience as you move through interpersonal relationships. However, it doesn't really provide an explanation of what motivates people to move from one stage to another. Think about some of your closer relationships. How did you move from being acquaintances to being close friends? The earlier description of attraction theories provides a partial answer to this question by offering explanations of what evokes your interest in another person. However, the theories don't adequately explain why you might stay at one stage, back down from a stage, or move forward to the next. Steve Duck suggests we go through a process of "filtering" whereby at each stage of relational development we apply criteria that a potential close friend must meet.[8] In essence, a move from one stage to another toward intimacy means that a person has passed through another, finer screen or filter. These screens represent decision points in which we make some assessment of the relationship and decide how we want to proceed. We can choose to either escalate, maintain, or de-escalate the relationship. Two theories reflect the kind of decision making that might be taking place: social exchange theory and dialectical theory (or dialectics).

### Social Exchange Theory

Social exchange theory is an economic model of human behavior that has been used to explain how people arrive at decisions in a variety of situations. **Social exchange theory** posits that people seek the greatest amount of reward with the least amount of cost.[9] You've probably been in a difficult relationship where you have asked yourself, "Is this relationship really worth it?" What you are asking is whether the rewards you are gaining from the relationship are worth the trouble or expense necessary to sustain

**social exchange theory.** A theory that claims people make relationship decisions by assessing and comparing the costs and rewards.

the relationship (the costs). Students frequently tell us about breaking up from long-distance relationships because the expense (driving time, telephone calls, missing activities where they live, and so on) ends up being greater than the rewards of the intermittent contact. For others, the rewards associated with long-distance relationships remain greater than the costs, and those relationships continue to prosper.

*Immediate and Forecasted Rewards and Costs*   Relationships can be evaluated in terms of immediate, forecasted, and cumulative rewards and costs.[10] **Immediate rewards and costs** occur in a relationship in the present moment. You can think about your current relationships and assess their present value. **Forecasted rewards and costs** are based on projection or prediction. We make guesses about the potential of a relationship or its future outlook (what communication scholar Michael Sunnafrank calls its *predicted outcome value*).[11] When you meet someone, you go through an initial assessment about whether a relationship with this person would be rewarding. You use forecasting to decide whether to remain in existing relationships during troubled times (when costs escalate or rewards deteriorate). However, you don't immediately abandon long-term relationships at the first sign of trouble (low immediate rewards/high immediate costs) if you believe that things will improve (forecasted rewards).

*Cumulative Rewards and Costs*   Another reason people remain in relationships during periods of low immediate rewards has to do with cumulative rewards and costs. **Cumulative rewards and costs** represent the total rewards and costs accrued over the duration of the relationship. Just as when you have more income than expenses, you put your extra money in savings, so you build up a relational savings account of the extra rewards. You can draw on that savings account during times when the relationship is not paying off well. You hold on to a relationship because you have invested a lot in it and have gotten a lot out of it. However, just as your savings account can run out of money, cumulative rewards can lose value, and at that point you might decide to terminate the relationship.

*Magnitude and Ratio*   You can also consider rewards and costs in terms of their magnitude and ratio. Suppose you have two friends, Kelsey and Moira. Kelsey makes you feel good about yourself, is helpful, and is lots of fun (rewards) but she is very needy and demanding (costs). Moira is lots of fun and helpful, but she is also needy. Which friendship would you pursue more? You might be inclined to pursue the relationship with Kelsey, because she is helpful, fun, and makes you feel good, whereas Moira is only fun and helpful. The magnitude of the rewards from the relationship with Kelsey is greater than that of the rewards of the relationship with Moira. However, you might pursue a relationship with Moira because that relationship has a better ratio of rewards to costs (two rewards to one cost, compared to Kelsey's three rewards to two costs). You might think that further developing a relationship with Moira might result in increased rewards with the same costs. However, at some point relationships seem to achieve a maximum return for the investment—that is, a point where no matter how much you invest, either the reward does not increase further or the costs increase significantly. Suppose your only shared interest with Moira is movies. Once a week you spend some very satisfying time together, seeing and talking over a new film. You decide to spend more time with her (cost) and find awkward dead spots in the conversation because there isn't really anything else of mutual interest to talk about (reward). In terms of your relationship with Moira, this means that having fun with her and getting her help is the only reward you will gain, regardless of

**immediate rewards and costs.**
Rewards and costs that are associated with a relationship at the present moment.

**forecasted rewards and costs.**
Rewards and costs that an individual assumes will occur, based on projection and prediction.

**cumulative rewards and costs.**
The total rewards and costs accrued during a relationship.

how much you invest in the relationship. Finding that point where you maximize your rewards while minimizing costs is one challenge of relational development.

*Expected Rewards and Costs*   People seem to construct templates in their minds for what relationships should be like. **Expected rewards and costs** represent expectations and ideals about how rewarding a relationship should be relative to its costs. We have a mental model of the ideal friend, the ideal lover, the ideal coworker, and so on. We use the expected costs and rewards associated with these ideals to assess current relationships. We might abandon a relationship if we don't think it matches or has the potential to match our ideal. In essence, we set standards or criteria for our relationships by which we assess the desirability of a given relationship. Like Duck's filtering process, ideal images allow you to sort through relationships and focus on those that come closest to or exceed your ideal. The major difficulty associated with such comparisons rests in setting reasonable standards or ideals. For example, some parents adopt a philosophy of never arguing in front of their children. As the children become adults, they may have an expectation that happy marriages are ones without conflicts and thus they may evaluate their own marriages as unsuccessful because they do not achieve this ideal. If you find that you are continually unable to find relationships that measure up to your ideals, you may need to reassess your standards.

Finally, we compare our current relationships to the rewards and costs we forecast for other potential relationships. We reduce our time spent with one friend when we believe we can have a more rewarding relationship with another person. Communication researchers Gerald Miller and Malcolm Parks have proposed that we will move quickly to terminate a relationship if it falls below our expectations and we think we have an opportunity to develop a new relationship that has the potential to exceed all of our expectations.[12] We try to spend the most time with those relationships that have the best relative outcomes. All these comparisons work in concert with one another. We compare our current relationships to previous ones, to the ideal, and to potential ones.

A recent research study used social exchange principles to examine whether couples maintained friendships after dissolving their romantic relationship.[13] In this study couples who continued to provide each other with rewards and/or resources (love, status, services, information, goods, or money) continued to maintain a friendship. Those couples for which there were costs or barriers (lack of support by family or friends for a friendship, involvement in a new romance, or use of neglect to end the romance) had lower-quality friendships.

## Dialectical Theory

**Dialectical theory** looks at the human condition in terms of sets of opposing forces. When applying dialectical theory to interpersonal relationships, we can identify forces pulling us toward intimacy and opposing forces pulling us toward independence.

### Three Dialectical Tensions

Researcher Leslie Baxter has identified three dialectical tensions that have been widely used in interpersonal research.[14]

*Connectedness versus Autonomy*   We desire to connect with others and to become interdependent at the same time we have a desire to remain autonomous and independent. In one study of married couples, the desire to be both connected and autonomous was found to be the most frequently occurring of the dialectical tensions.[15]

**expected rewards and costs.** An expectation of how much reward we should get from a given relationship in comparison to its costs.

**dialectical theory.** A theory that relational development occurs in conjunction with various tensions that exist in all relationships, particularly connectedness versus autonomy, predictability versus novelty, and openness versus closedness.

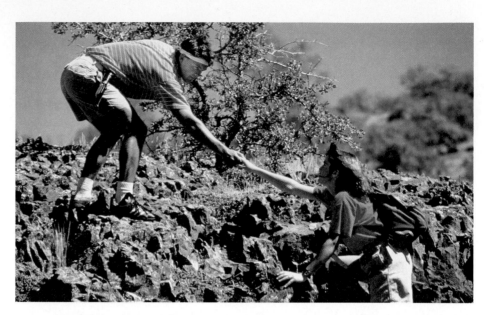

*W*hen a couple commits to a relationship, they must find a new balance between autonomy and connectedness.

***Predictability versus Novelty (Certainty versus Uncertainty)*** Knowing what to expect and being able to predict the world around us helps reduce the tension that occurs from uncertainty. At the same time, we get bored by constant repetition and routine and therefore are attracted to novelty and the unexpected. This might explain why people relish horror movies, where the unexpected jumps out at them. Fright becomes pleasurable because it meets a need for the unexpected.

***Openness versus Closedness*** We wish to disclose information to others and to hear those we are attracted to disclose to us. One ideal we seem to have in relationships is the ability to be totally open with our partner. However, we also value our privacy and feel a desire to hold back information. This tension was identified in the study of married couples mentioned earlier as the most important of the three tensions, although it did not occur as often as the other two tensions.[16] Research conducted by Mark Redmond found that the number-one way that people adapt content in interactions is to hold back or modify information.[17]

According to the dialectical theory, each pair of tensions is present in every relationship, but the impact of each changes as a relationship progresses. Movement in relationships can be seen as a shift that occurs in the relative pull of one tension. For example, when you begin developing a new friendship, one issue you have to address is whether you want to give up some of your autonomy (freedom to do your own things) in order to spend time with this other person (connectedness). Notice how this is similar to social exchange theory in that you weigh costs (giving up autonomy) against rewards (becoming connected).

### Dialectical Tensions and Relational Development

Both forces of autonomy and forces of connectedness can be found even in close relationships.[18] Even though long-married couples have usually settled the issue of interdependence versus independence, dialectical theory asserts (and research supports) that tension is still present from these forces. Generally, such tension diminishes as we become more intimate; however, many an engagement has been called off at the last minute because of the inability of the bride or groom to resolve this tension. This tension represents the challenge faced by individuals forming close relationships who are faced with maintaining their own identities while at the same time, melding their identity with that of another person.

One study of married couples found that dialectical tensions existed both at the individual level (for example, the wife or the husband trying to decide whether to be open or closed) and at the relational level (partners differing in terms of desires for autonomy, openness, or novelty).[19] In addition, the study found that extreme closedness related to greater autonomy—which makes sense, since those couples who share less information may also be likely to share less time together.

Movement in relationships can be seen as occurring because some element of tension has been resolved or overcome.[20] For example, during the initial stages of a relationship, you are restrained in your self-disclosures (closedness). As long as you remain closed, the relationship can only progress so far. You are confronted with the question of whether you should share information and increase the level of intimacy in the relationship. Thus, a tension exists until you make your decision. Once you have decided, some of the tension is relieved. If you decide on more openness, the reduction in tension is accompanied by a change in the relationship.

## *S*trategies and Skills for Developing Interpersonal Relationships

So far, this chapter has focused on the nature of relational development. Now, the focus shifts to discussing specific strategies and skills for starting, escalating, and maintaining interpersonal relationships. The lists provided are neither fail-safe nor complete—they are offered primarily to stimulate consideration of your own thoughts and behaviors as you develop new relationships.

*W*e can learn the skills that can help us reduce the interpersonal tensions that most of us feel at the start of a relationship.

When you meet someone that you initially like, how do you go about fostering a relationship? Once you have established a relationship, how do you ensure that it remains healthy and at the level of intimacy with which you are most comfortable? The following three sections provide strategies you can use to address these questions. The first section discusses skills and strategies used primarily in initiating interaction. The next section covers skills and strategies used in both the initial stage and the later stages of relational development. The final section focuses on skills used in either maintaining a relationship or moving it toward more intimacy once it has been established.

### Skills and Strategies Used Primarily During the Initiation Stage

In the opening scenarios, Josh used the "free" information that was available on Nona's T-shirt as a way to open a conversation with her. You can use readily available information to begin conversations and initiate relationships. In the initiation stage of relational development, people generally follow a script that helps both parties reduce their level of anxiety about interacting with a stranger. They also stick to safe topics and disclose only descriptive information about themselves as they begin to build the foundations for a potential relationship. The following sections explain some of the principles to follow as you interact with others for the first time.

### Observe and Act on Approachability Cues

Subway riders in New York learn to avoid eye contact because it is a signal of approachability. Other ways we can signal approachability include turning toward another person, smiling, being animated (versus sitting very still), taking an open body posture, winking, and waving. In the absence of these cues, we generally conclude that a person wants to be left alone.

Sometimes circumstances prevent us from exchanging approachability cues. The seating arrangements in your class, for example, might hamper the use of nonverbal cues. So instead, you may try to develop some sensitivity to the way other people respond to your greetings. Saying "Hello" lets people know that you are approachable, and it tests approachability. If the other person responds with a warm smile and a few words, such as "Have you finished today's assignment yet?" then the door might be open for further interaction. But if the person gives you a silent half smile and hurries on, you can take this as a signal that the door is closed.

DRABBLE reprinted by permission of United Feature Syndicate, Inc.

## Identify and Use Conversation Starters

Like Nona in the opening scenario of this chapter, we all are sources of a certain amount of "free" information that others can easily observe. You can use that information as a starting point for a conversation. When Josh noted that Nona was wearing a Michigan Tech T-shirt, he asked whether Nona was a student there. You can apply the same approach. If someone is walking a dog of the same breed as your childhood pet, you can open a conversation by offering an observation about some peculiarity of the breed. If someone is carrying a book from a class you took last semester, ask him or her how the course is going. For example, "Hi; isn't that book you're carrying the one for the dreaded Dr. Bellfinger's class? I really had to work my tail off in that class."

## Follow Initiation Norms

Many of the initial interactions in a relationship are almost ritualistic, or at least scripted. In the United States, when two strangers meet for the first time, they typically follow this pattern of conversation:[21]

*Greetings:* Say "Hello," "Hi," or "Howdy."

*Introductions:* Exchange names and pleasantries.

*Topic 1:* Discuss the present situation or weather.

*Topic 2:* Discuss current or past residences (where they live, hometown, and so on).

*Topic 3:* Determine whether they know people in common.

*Topic 4:* Discuss their educational backgrounds or occupations.

*Topic 5:* Discuss general topics such as TV shows, movies, music, family, sports, books, and/or travel.

*Discuss further meeting (optional):* Say something like "Let's get together sometime."

*Exchange pleasantries:* "Nice to meet you," "Hope to see you again," and so on.

*Close conversation:* Indicate the intent to end the conversation with such statements as "See you later," "Got to go to class now," or "Give me a call."

*Goodbyes:* Make final statements, say "Bye," and move in different directions.

Following the script provides some comfort and security because both partners can thus reduce the level of uncertainty. If you deviate too much from this script, you might undermine your partner's sense of security and discourage him or her from pursuing a relationship. For example, after an initial greeting, how would you react to a stranger who deviated from the script by saying, "Nice to meet you, too. Did you know that television is becoming the vast wasteland of American intellect, draining the very life blood of our youth?" Most of us would be a bit leery of jumping directly into a discussion of such an issue with a person we had just met.

As you follow the script, however, you should take advantage of opportunities to expand and develop the conversation in safe ways. Listen for details about the person's background and interests that you can inquire about, and share information about your own interests.

## Ask Questions

The very act of asking questions can enhance your partner's attraction toward you.[22] Asking questions shows your interest in the other person in an indirect way and promotes reciprocity of liking. Asking questions can also provide you with information about the other person, helping reduce uncertainty and improving your ability to adapt to your partner. However, accomplishing these benefits requires the ability to ask questions without "interrogating" the other person, to ask open questions that invite elaboration and discussion, and to ask meaningful follow-up, or probing, questions. Starting with impersonal, specific questions, often about the circumstance or surroundings, encourages a response by reducing a person's reluctance to answer; for example (while standing in a movie line) "Have you heard any reviews of this movie?" After the initial question, asking more open and encompassing questions helps to facilitate the conversation: "What did they have to say?" The Building Your Skills box lists a number of sample questions.

Once you've asked an initial question, be flexible and ask follow-up questions related to the answer you get. Be open and provide information about yourself that is relevant to the questions. Usually the other person will also ask you questions. If the other person gives short responses without any reciprocal questions, that may be a signal that he or she is not particularly interested in interacting. If so, you're probably better off not pursing the interaction any further.

You might ask a question that you believe is safe and appropriate, such as "What does your father do for a living?" to which the stranger gives an unexpected response: "I haven't heard from him since I was 5." Unknowingly, you may have evoked uncomfortable feelings and memories. Some questions should obviously be avoided because of their inappropriateness in an initial interaction; however, almost any seemingly simple question can sometimes evoke a negative reaction. Having little information about a stranger on which to base your communication decisions means you need to monitor the interaction carefully. Recognize that the experiences and feelings evoked by your questions differ from person to person. A question that is easy and comfortable for you to answer may not be for others. Be sensitive to how the other person responds to your questions, and be prepared to adapt your comments appropriately. Other-oriented communication skills can help you manage sensitive situations. Put yourself in the other person's shoes. If you hadn't seen your father since you were five, what would you most like your conversation partner to say next?

### Don't Expect Too Much from the Initial Interaction

Initial interactions do not necessarily determine the future of a relationship. In movies, initial interactions between the hero and the heroine are often brusque and unfriendly, but after sharing traumatic experiences, they eventually find love. Although real life does not usually work this way, keep in mind that the scripted nature of an initial interaction limits the opportunity for you and your partner to achieve an in-depth understanding of each other. Relax and arrange another meeting if you feel the spark of attraction. It will probably take a few interactions before you can make a sound cost-benefit analysis of the relationship.

Initiating conversation is only one step in the process of developing an interpersonal relationship. Next we examine ways to escalate a relationship once it gets started.

### Skills and Strategies Used in Both Initiating and Escalating Relationships

"No kidding! I love chocolate-covered strawberries too." "It's nice to be able to talk to someone else who's a fan of *Trading Spaces.*" Statements like these two emphasize commonalties in order to encourage the listener to like the speaker (this is called "affinity seeking"). We sometimes make these types of statements when we are first

# Building Your Skills

## Questions to Keep the Conversation Going During a Date

How would you feel if, on a first date, you were asked these questions? Think about other questions that could be asked after you read through this list.

1. Have you ever been here (the restaurant or other setting the two of you are in) before? (Discuss aspects of the facility such as food, amenities, and so forth.)

2. Do you live in (name of town or city)? How long have you lived in the area? How do you like it here? (This can lead into a discussion of area politics and other local issues.)

3. Have you visited the local (park, library, shopping center)? (Talk about the special attractions of your town.)

4. Did you grow up here? (If the answer is no): Where did you live before this? What was it like there? How does this area compare with that one?

5. Does the rest of your family live nearby? (Parents, grandparents, aunts, uncles?)

6. What do you like most about the area?

7. What kind of movies do you like? What is the worst movie you ever saw? Who is your favorite actor/actress?

8. What is your favorite TV show? What is your least favorite?

9. Did you catch the Academy Awards (or that new show, or the game, etc.) last night?

10. What kind of music do you enjoy? Who is your favorite performer/group/band? Who do you think is the hottest this year? Do you think they still will be next year?

11. What is your favorite type of reading matter? Who is your favorite author? What's the best book you've read recently? Do you subscribe to magazines?

12. Do you belong to any local clubs or organizations?

13. Are you a morning person, or do you find yourself at your peak later in the day?

14. What kind of career are you interested in? Or What are your career goals?

15. What do you like to do in your spare time? (hobbies, interests)?

16. How did you get involved in your hobby? What do you like most about it?

*Source:* Tim Arends, retrieved on December 20, 2000 from http://dating.about.com/people/dating/gi/dynamic/offsite. htm?site=http%3A%2F%2Fwww.life-n-leisure.com%2Fdating%2F articles%2Fquestions.htm Used by permission of the author.

getting to know someone, but similar statements are also used when trying to escalate a relationship. Trying to increase someone's attraction toward us is just one strategy that is common to both the initiation and escalation stages of interpersonal relationships. Other skills and strategies include appropriately self-disclosing, gathering information to reduce uncertainties, monitoring your perceptions, listening actively and responding confirmingly, and socially decentering and adapting. Let's look more closely at each of these ways to initiate and escalate relationships.

### Communicate Attraction

When we are attracted to people, we use both indirect and direct strategies to communicate our liking through nonverbal and verbal cues. *Nonverbal immediacy* refers to nonverbal cues we display when we are attracted to someone. For instance, we tend to reduce the physical distance between us; increase our eye contact and use of touch; lean forward; keep an open body orientation; and smile. We also use the courtship readiness behaviors, preening behaviors, positional cues, and appeals to invitation described in Chapter 7.

*In social situations, we learn to present ourselves in a positive way using both nonverbal and verbal cues.*

We also indirectly communicate our attraction verbally. We use informal and personal language, addressing the person by his or her first name and often referring to "you and I," and "we." We ask questions to show interest, probe for details when our partner shares information, listen responsively, and refer to information shared in past interactions. All these behaviors confirm that we value what the other person is saying.

We can also directly communicate our attraction verbally. Most of us don't do this very often. But think about how you feel when a friend tells you that he or she likes you. It raises your self-esteem; you feel valued. You can make others feel that way by communicating your liking for them, although in the early stages of relational development, there are social mores against doing so. We verbally communicate liking in more subtle ways as well. We might tell someone that we like a particular trait or ability, such as the way she tells jokes, or the way he handled an irritating customer. Or we might compliment someone's outfit, hairstyle, or jewelry. Each of these messages communicates attraction for the other person and is likely to elicit a positive response from him or her.

We also use **affinity-seeking strategies** to get people to like us. Table 10.1 summarizes strategies identified by the research team of Robert Bell and John Daly.[23] Deciding to display nonverbal immediacy cues or to verbally confirm the other person are not only ways we communicate our attraction toward other people, they are also ways of getting other people to like us. Other affinity-seeking strategies include establishing mutual trust, being polite, showing concern and caring, and involving people in our activities. Apparently, these strategies do work. Bell and Daly found that individuals who seemed to use many affinity-seeking strategies were perceived as likeable, socially successful, and satisfied with their lives.[24]

**affinity-seeking strategies.**
Strategies for getting other people to like you.

**TABLE *10.1* Affinity-Seeking Strategies**

| | Strategies | Examples |
|---|---|---|
| 1. Control | Present yourself as in control, independent, free-thinking; show that you have the ability to reward the other person. | • "I'm planning on going to grad school, and after that I'm going to Japan to teach English."<br>• "You can borrow my notes for the class you missed if you'd like." |
| 2. Visibility | Look and dress attractively; present yourself as an interesting, energetic, and enthusiastic person; increase your visibility to the other person. | • "Wow, that was a great show about Chinese acrobats. I do gymnastics too. Would you like to come watch me next week in our dual meet?" |
| 3. Mutual Trust | Present yourself as honest and reliable; display trustworthy behaviors; show that you trust the other person by self-disclosing. | • "That guy you're having problems with called me and asked about you. I told him I didn't have anything to say."<br>• "I've never told anyone this, but I've always hoped I could find my birth parents." |
| 4. Politeness | Follow appropriate conversational rules; let the other person assume control of the interaction. | • "I'm sorry. I interrupted. I thought you were done. Please, go on."<br>• "No, you're not boring me at all; it's very interesting. Please tell me more about it." |
| 5. Concern and Caring | Show interest in and ask questions about the other person; listen; show support and be sensitive; help the other person accomplish something or feel good about himself or herself. | • "How is your mother doing after her operation?"<br>• "I'd like to help out at the benefit you're chairing this weekend."<br>• "That must have been really hard for you, growing up under those conditions." |
| 6. Other-Involvement | Put a positive spin on activities you share; draw the other person into your activities; display nonverbal immediacy and involvement with the other person. | • "This is a great party. I'm glad you came."<br>• "A group of us are going to get a midnight snack; how about coming along?" |
| 7. Self-Involvement | Try to arrange for encounters and interactions; engage in behaviors that encourage the other to form a closer relationship. | • "Oh hi! I knew your class ended at two, so I thought I'd try to catch you."<br>• "It would really be fun to go camping together this summer; I have this favorite place." |
| 8. Commonalities | Point out similarities between yourself and the other person; try to establish equality (balanced power); present yourself as comfortable and at ease around the other person. | • "I've got that computer game too. Don't you love the robots?"<br>• "Let's both work on the project together. We're a great team."<br>• "It's so easy to talk to you. I really feel comfortable around you." |

*Source:* Adapted from R. A. Bell and J. A. Daly, "The Affinity Seeking Function of Communication," *Communication Monographs,* 51 (1984): 91–115.

## Building Your Skills

### Affinity-Seeking Observation

Go somewhere where you can observe strangers interacting, such as at a party or a student center. Without violating anybody's privacy, see if you can observe affinity-seeking behaviors or hear what is being said that communicates attraction between people. Which of the affinity-seeking strategies seem to be used the most? The least? How do people seem to respond to the affinity-seeking behaviors of their partners?

### Be Open and Self-Disclose Appropriately

Disclosing information about yourself allows the other person to make an informed decision about whether to continue the relationship. Remember, both of you need to be in a position to make such a decision. You may have found out what you want to know and decided that you have a lot in common with the other person, but he or she may not have reached that same point. However, be careful not to violate the script or cultural expectations about what is appropriate to disclose in an initial conversation. You have probably had the experience of someone you have just met tell you his or her problems. Such disclosures usually alienate the other, rather than advancing the relationship.

In Chapter 2 we pointed out that self-disclosure is a critical element for movement toward intimacy. People cannot form truly intimate relationships without mutual self-disclosure. Restricting the amount of self-disclosure is one way to control the development of a relationship. If a relationship is moving too fast, you might choose to reduce how much you are self-disclosing, as a way to slow the progression of the relationship. The level of self-disclosure needs to be appropriate to the level of development, and both partners must be sensitive to the timing of the disclosures. Failing to disclose or disclosing the wrong thing at the wrong time can damage a relationship.

### Gather Information to Reduce Uncertainty

Meeting strangers and starting relationships is rarely easy. We all seem to share a fear of the unknown, which includes interactions with strangers whose behavior we cannot predict. The research team of Charles Berger, Richard Calabrese, and James Bradac developed a theory to explain relational development.[25] Their **uncertainty reduction** theory is based on one basic assumption: We like to have control and predictability in our lives; therefore, when we are faced with uncertainty, we are driven to gain information to reduce that uncertainty. Reducing uncertainty requires using a number of skills we have already covered, but primarily depends on effective perception and active listening. You need to gather as much information as you can about your partner to increase predictability and reduce anxiety.

Usually we reduce uncertainty by gathering either cognitive or behavioral information about others.[26] Cognitive information relates to thoughts, attitudes, and opinions. Behavioral information relates to reactions and remarks in various situations. As you have seen, you gather some of this information during the preinteraction stage of a relationship through observations and conversations with others who know the person. Later, you can observe the other's behaviors directly in your own interactions

**uncertainty reduction theory.**
A theory that claims people seek out information in order to reduce uncertainty, thus providing control and predictability.

# *applying theory and research*

## *Initiation Stage: Male-Initiated versus Female-Initiated Date Requests*

According to custom in the United States, men are expected to take the initiative in asking women out. While certain taboos or negative impressions have been associated with women initiating dates, more women seem to be taking this initiative. Communication scholars Paul Mongeau, Jerold Hale, Kristin Johnson, and Jacqueline Hillis examined male-initiated versus female-initiated date requests. For one part of their study, they created four written scenarios describing a male asking a female out, a male or a female initiating the date request after hints from the other, and a female asking a male out. Over four hundred student participants evaluated the females and males in these scenarios. In comparison to the woman who waited for the man to ask her out, the woman who directly asked the man out was seen as more active, flexible, truthful, and extroverted, more of a feminist, more so-cially liberal, and less physically attractive (though no pictures were provided). Female students perceived the female initiator as more likeable and tactful than did the males.

### *Applying the Research to Your Life*

What is your view of a woman who asks a man out for a first date?

To what degree does your view differ if the woman asks the man to (a) go to a movie, (b) come over to her apartment for dinner, or (c) go to a party with her.

(Male students answer these questions):

Has a woman ever asked you out on a first date?

How was your attitude toward her affected by her request?

(Female students answer these questions):

Have you ever asked a man out for a first date?

How do you think the man's attitude toward you was affected by your request?

If you haven't initiated a date with a man, how do you think a man would react if you did?

Survey five or six of your male and female friends and collect their answers to the above questions. How similar are their responses? To what degree do males and females agree or disagree?

*Source:* P. A. Mongeau, J. L. Hale, K. L. Johnson, and J. D. Hillis. "Who's Wooing Whom? An Investigation of Female Initiated Dating," in P. J. Kalbleisch (Ed.), *Interpersonal Communication: Evolving Interpersonal Relationships* (Hillsdale, NJ: Lawrence Erlbaum, 1993, pp. 51–68).

with him or her, and also ask direct questions. Usually people gather behavioral information through observation and cognitive information through interactions.

We are particularly motivated to gain information early in a relationship when uncertainty is greatest, and when we are trying to evaluate the relationship's predicted outcome value.[27] We also are likely to seek out information if others behave in an unexpected way.[28] If your close friend who watches *South Park* every night suddenly begins reading during that time slot, you will probably ask why. Whether the friend shares with you what is going on will depend on how comfortable he or she is in revealing information about himself or herself.

## Monitor Your Perceptions

You need to be aware of your perceptual biases that affect your reactions to your partner. Such biases might inhibit the growth of a relationship because of an inaccurate inference. Effective perception can enhance your ability to understand and adapt to your partner as a relationship escalates. Perception checking helps you reach a more accurate understanding of your partner, and thus provides you with better information

## Building Your Skills

### Anxiety Level and Familiarity

*W*rite down at least ten different social situations you can recall having been in, such as attending weddings, funerals, or ball games; going to your grandmother's for dinner; visiting your best friend's parents for the first time; or meeting your new roommate. Next to each one, indicate how nervous you felt in that situation. Use a scale from 1 to 10, with 1 being calm and cool and 10 being highly apprehensive. After you have rated each situation, go back and rate each one on how familiar or unfamiliar the situation was. Again use a scale of 1 to 10, with 1 being very familiar and 10 being very unfamiliar.

According to uncertainty reduction theory, there should be a strong correlation between your level of anxiety and the level of familiarity. Which situations caused the most anxiety? To what degree did your unfamiliarity with the situation affect your level of anxiety? What were you most uncertain about in each situation? In which situations were you most comfortable and why? Did you feel uncomfortable in some circumstances even though the situation was familiar? Why?

---

about whether to continue the relationship. Directly asking your partner for explanations about things you have perceived can potentially lead to more effective relationship management. For example, suppose you are interacting with Miguel, whom you don't know very well. During the conversation, every time you start to talk about a mutual friend, Sandra, Miguel changes the subject. One interpretation of this observation is that Miguel is rude and impolite, and if you assume this is the case, you might decide to abandon the relationship. Or you might ask Miguel about your perception. The explanation might be that he and Sandra recently had a fight and he prefers not to talk about her. A hasty inference in this case might have precluded the development of a potentially satisfying relationship.

### Listen Actively and Respond Confirmingly

Listening skills are also crucial for developing and maintaining relationships. Listening clues you in to others' needs, wants, and values, and it enables you to respond to them in appropriate ways. In the initial stages of a relationship, partners share a great deal of information. The amount of information tapers off in the later stages and as a relationship continues over time. This tapering off creates the illusion that you don't have to listen as much or as well as you did early on. But listening is a way to demonstrate ongoing interest in another person. Even in long-term relationships, you do not know everything your partner has to say. It is still important to stop, look, and listen—to put down the newspaper or turn off the radio when your close friend begins talking to you.

You also need to listen actively and provide confirming responses. In Chapter 5 we discuss the notions of confirming and disconfirming responses. Using confirming responses increases your partner's sense of self-worth and communicates the value you place on him or her. In addition, if you can develop an awareness of the biases that prevent you from responding with empathy, you can deliberately work to overcome them as you ask questions and paraphrase your partner's messages.

### Socially Decenter and Adopt an Other-Oriented Perspective

The skills covered in Chapter 4 for social decentering, empathizing, and adapting to others enhance the initiation, escalation, and maintenance of relationships. Social decentering helps you better understand your partner, which provides you with a basis for choosing the most effective strategies for accomplishing your communication goals. We have been discussing the notion of "appropriateness" of your behaviors to the effective advancement and maintenance of your relationships. Determining appropriateness depends on your ability to read the situation and your partner, and then to adapt or choose the best behaviors. Essentially, you can consider either what your partner is thinking now or what he or she will think in response to your actions—put yourself in your partner's shoes. For example, suppose you recently met someone to whom you are attracted and you are trying to decide whether to tell this person about a very intimate relationship you had, which just ended. Put yourself in the other person's shoes. Would you want someone you just met to tell you about his or her recent breakup? What information do you have that can help you determine this person's reaction? As relationships become more intimate, you receive more and more information that can improve decentering and adaptation.

Gaining information about your partners is one way you will be able to make decisions about how to help them in distressing situations. One pair of researchers, Ruth Ann Clark and Jesse Delia, studied how people wanted to be treated by their friends in response to six different distressing situations.[29] There was wide variation in how people wanted their friends to approach the six issues. Clark and Delia found that people did not have a strong desire to talk about the situations. When people were distressed, they wanted to be the ones to decide whether to bring up the issue or not. Clark and Delia also found that people wanted their friends to keep attempts at comforting short. This means that rather than a formulaic approach to distressed friends, you should use your ability to socially decenter and adapt to each one's particular needs. The abilities to provide comfort, social support, and ego support are qualities associated with being a best friend.[30]

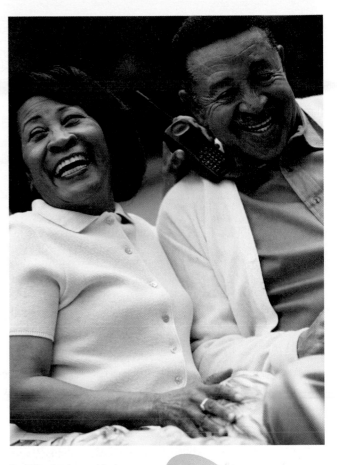

*W*ell-adjusted couples display support and affection for each other through positive nonverbal cues.

## Skills and Strategies Specific to Escalating and Maintaining Relationships

Certain skills and strategies can be used to further escalate a relationship or to keep a relationship at a given stage. These include a willingness to express your emotions, openness to relationship talk, tolerance of your partner's flaws and failures, the ability to manage conflict cooperatively, and finally, skill in gaining compliance. The use of the entire range of skills and strategies covered in these sections can help you develop and maintain strong and satisfying relationships.

### Express Emotions

Expressing emotions is a particular form of self-disclosure and is a skill that can be improved, as discussed in Chapter 6. Many of us are embarrassed about expressing our feelings, yet sharing feelings at the appropriate time during the development of a relationship is one way to continue its escalation. Conversely, sharing the wrong feelings at the wrong time can have a detrimental effect.

There are two ways we share feelings with our partners. The first is to disclose information about our past or current emotional states that do not relate to our partner, such as sadness about the death of a family member, or fear about what we will do after we graduate. The second way is to directly express our emotional reactions to our partner, such as feelings of attraction to, love for, or disappointment in our partner. As relationships become more intimate, we have a greater expectation that our partner will disclose emotions openly. The amount of risk associated with such emotional disclosures varies from person to person. Most of us are comfortable sharing positive emotions such as happiness and joy but are more reserved about sharing negative emotions such as fear or disappointment. We may think expressing negative emotions makes us appear weak or vulnerable. However, in a study of forty-six committed, romantic couples, researchers found that the number-one problem was the inability to talk about negative feelings.[31] For example, partners often made the following types of observations: "When she gets upset, she stops talking"; "He never lets me know when he's upset with something he doesn't like"; and "He just silently pouts." We generally want to know how our partners in intimate relationships are feeling, even if those feelings are negative.

However, a constant barrage of negative expressions can also alienate a partner. Research has found that marital satisfaction rises with the number of positive feelings the partners disclose, not with the number of negative ones.[32] A balance has to be found that includes expressing both positive and negative emotions at the right time in a constructive and confirming manner.

### Engage in Relationship Talk

**Relationship talk** is talk about the nature, quality, direction, or definition of a relationship. Relationship talk is generally considered inappropriate in the early stages of a relationship. A relationship might be terminated prematurely if one partner tries to talk about it too early. Willingness to talk about the relationship is one way to implicitly signal your partner about your level of interest and commitment to the relationship. As relationships move toward greater intimacy, however, the amount of direct relationship talk increases. As the relationship escalates, we should be prepared to discuss our thoughts and feelings about it. In more intimate relationships, relationship talk helps the partners resolve differences in their perceptions of the relationship that might be contributing to conflict and dissatisfaction. Unwillingness to talk about the relationship in an intimate relationship can ultimately drive a partner away.

### Be Tolerant and Show Restraint

The most satisfying relationships are those in which both partners refrain from continually disagreeing, criticizing, and making negative comments to each other. Both

**relationship talk.** Talk about the nature, quality, direction, or definition of a relationship.

## Becoming Other-Oriented

### Adapting Relational Strategies and Skills to Your Partner

*B*esides presenting a model of the stages of relational development, this chapter discusses a variety of skills and strategies you can use to initiate, escalate, and maintain interpersonal relationships. Your decisions about what strategies to implement should be adapted to the anticipated reactions of your partner. In addition, to be effective, you must understand what is appropriate for a given stage of development, and then adapt the strategy or strategies accordingly. Below is a list of some of the skills and strategies covered in this chapter, to which your partner is likely to have some reaction. Think about a friend whom you know fairly well, but who isn't your best friend. Briefly assess how comfortable and skilled you are at using each strategy, what you think your friend's reaction would be to its use, and how you can adapt the strategy to fit the level of intimacy that exists in your relationship.

| Skill/Strategy | How would I feel about using this skill/strategy? | How would my friend react/feel if I used this skill/strategy? | How should the skill/strategy be adapted to be appropriate to the relationship stage? |
|---|---|---|---|
| Communicating Attraction | _____ | _____ | _____ |
| Being Open and Self-Disclosing | _____ | _____ | _____ |
| Listening Actively and Confirmingly | _____ | _____ | _____ |
| Expressing Emotions | _____ | _____ | _____ |
| Talking About the Relationship | _____ | _____ | _____ |
| Being Tolerant and Showing Restraint | _____ | _____ | _____ |
| Managing Conflict Cooperatively | _____ | _____ | _____ |

individuals learn to accept the other and do not feel compelled to continually point out flaws or failures. One study found that well-adjusted couples focus their complaints on specific behaviors, whereas maladjusted couples complain about each other's personal characteristics. Well-adjusted couples are also kinder and more positive, and have more humor in their interactions. They tend to agree with each other's complaints, whereas the partners in maladjusted relationships launch countercomplaints.[33] In addition, happy couples, when compared to unhappy couples, display more affection through positive nonverbal cues, display more supportive behaviors, and make more attempts to avoid conflict.[34]

Maintaining a relationship requires tolerance. You must learn to accept your partners for who they are and put up with some things you dislike. When couples lose their tolerance, they begin focusing on and criticizing characteristics that they used to accept. Then relationships begin to deteriorate.

### Manage Conflict Cooperatively

Conflicts are inevitable in interpersonal relationships. As relationships develop, the individuals share more personal information and spend more time together, so the likelihood for conflict increases. The key to successful relational development and maintenance is not to avoid conflict altogether, but rather to manage it effectively. As we discussed in Chapter 8, a cooperative management style can actually transform conflict into an experience that strengthens a relationship. It can clarify the definition of a relationship, increase the exchange of information, and create a cooperative atmosphere for problem solving.

### Seek Compliance

The final skill for escalating and maintaining relationships might seem somewhat contrary to the ones we have been discussing. Strictly speaking, **compliance gaining** in-

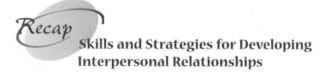

### Recap

## Skills and Strategies for Developing Interpersonal Relationships

**Skills and Strategies Used Primarily During the Initiation Stage**

Observe and Act on Approachability Cues

Identify and Use Conversation Starters

Follow Initiation Norms

Ask Questions

Don't Expect Too Much from the Initial Interaction

**Skills and Strategies Used in Both Initiating and Escalating Relationships**

Communicate Attraction

Be Open and Self-Disclose Appropriately

Gather Information to Reduce Uncertainty

Monitor Your Perceptions

Listen Actively and Respond Confirmingly

Socially Decenter and Adopt an Other-Oriented Perspective

**Skills and Strategies Specific to Escalating and Maintaining Relationships**

Express Emotions

Engage in Relationship Talk

Be Tolerant and Show Restraint

Manage Conflict Cooperatively

Seek Compliance

**compliance gaining.** The use of persuasive strategies to accomplish personal goals.

volves the use of persuasive strategies to accomplish your personal goals—that is, to get your own way. We are not urging you to force your will on others. We are, however, suggesting that it is sometimes ethical and moral to persuade others to go your way. In an ideal situation, the resulting actions will fulfill both partners' goals.

You need compliance-gaining strategies if you encounter resistance to fulfilling your goal. For example, suppose you want to go out to a movie and you need to borrow money from one of your friends to pay for it. You may simply ask, "Can I borrow eight dollars so I can go to a movie?" If your friend says, "Sure," the interaction is completed. If your friend says, "No, you haven't paid me back from last time," however, you will probably use some compliance-gaining strategy.

Compliance-gaining strategies are responsive to the ongoing, transactive nature of interpersonal relationships.[35] We plot strategies that develop over a number of interactions and modify them in accordance with others' responses. For example, before you ask to borrow money from your friend, you might first do a few favors for her during the day. Then if your friend says no, you might remind her that she owes you for all you've done for her. If she still says no, you might offer to help her over the weekend with her class project. The type of relationship you have established with the other person will affect your strategy selection. Often we face little resistance to our requests from our partners, so we have no need for any compliance-gaining strategy.

# *S*ummary

As relationships escalate toward intimacy or de-escalate away from it, they go through identifiable stages. Each stage is marked by turning points, differences in self-disclosure, and specific verbal and nonverbal communication patterns. Escalating relationships move through preinteraction awareness, initiation, exploration, intensification, and intimacy. Relationships that are becoming less intimate go through turmoil or stagnation, deintensification, individualization, separation, and postinteraction effects. The de-escalation of a romantic relationship does not mean that the relationship necessarily ends; sometimes couples are able to maintain effective post-intimacy relationships.

Two theories that explain relationship development are social exchange theory and dialectical theory. Social exchange theory posits that we make decisions about becoming more or less intimate on the basis of the rewards and costs that we perceive to be associated with the relationship. Decisions are made on the basis of forecasted and cumulative rewards and costs as well as comparisons with previous, potential, and ideal relationships. Dialectical theory sees our decisions being based on resolution of competing forces in our lives, particularly connectedness versus autonomy, predictability versus novelty, and openness ver-

sus closedness. As we address these forces, we move either toward or away from intimacy in our relationships.

A variety of strategies and skills can be applied to the initiation, escalation, and maintenance of interpersonal relationships. Certain skills and strategies are used primarily during the initiation of a relationship, including observing and acting on approachability cues, identifying and using conversation starters, following initiation norms, asking questions, and controlling expectations. Another set of skills and strategies is applicable to both the initiation of a relationship and the escalation of relationships toward greater intimacy. These include communicating attraction, being open and appropriately self-disclosing, reducing uncertainty, monitoring perceptions, listening actively and responding confirmingly, and socially decentering and adopting an other-oriented perspective. The final set of skills and strategies covered in this section are used primarily for moving a relationship toward intimacy or for maintaining existing relationships. This set includes expressing emotions, engaging in talk about the relationship, being tolerant and showing restraint, managing conflict cooperatively, and seeking compliance. All of these skills and strategies can be learned and enhanced to help you more effectively manage your interpersonal relationships.

# *F*or Discussion and Review

## Focus on Critical Thinking

1. Trace two of your own close relationships—one with a friend of the same sex, and one with a friend of the opposite sex—through the applicable stages of relational escalation and de-escalation. What differences and similarities do you find at each stage? How can you explain them?

2. Explain how social exchange theory relates to dialectical theory.

3. Of all the skills for developing interpersonal relationships, which three are the most important? Why? Which three are the least important? Why?

## Focus on Ethics

4. If two people have agreed to maintain a relationship below the highest level in the model of relational stages (the intimacy stage), is it ethical for one of the people to nonetheless continually try to move the relationship to the intimacy stage?

5. Assuming you were very skilled and adept at using strategies for developing interpersonal relationships, how ethical would it be for you to use those skills to satisfy your interpersonal needs in a given relationship, knowing that your partner was less skilled at getting his or her own needs met?

6. You are in a romantic relationship that has become physically intimate. How ethical is it for you to say, "I love you" if you really aren't sure you do? If your partner says "I love you," should you say, " I love you, too," even if you don't mean it?

# *F*or Your Journal

1. Use the various stages in the relational development model to analyze the progression of the most intimate relationship that you have had that has come to an end (either a friendship or a romantic relationship). Identify specific turning points that occurred during each of the stages.

2. For three or four days at the end of the day, assess which of the interpersonal skills and strategies for developing relationships you used in your interactions that day. Do you find a consistent pattern in your use of particular skills and strategies? What skills and strategies do you seem to use the most? What skills and strategies could you have used to manage your interactions more effectively?

# *L*earning with Others

1. In class, divide up into at least five pairs of students. Each pair should choose a particular stage of relational development without telling the rest of the class. Then each pair should spend two minutes role-playing a discussion of plans for the upcoming weekend in a way that communicates the stage they have chosen. The rest of the class should write down what stage they think each pair is portraying. After all the pairs have finished their dialogues, score each others' responses. Which stage was easiest to portray and identify? Which stage was most difficult? How easy is it to see differences in communication behavior at various stages?

2. In small groups, brainstorm some of the turning points that each of you has experienced in important relationships. Identify the relational stages that the turning points led to. Which stages crop up most often? Least often? What does the frequency tell you about those stages?

3. Divide into groups of four or five students. Each member of the group should describe the most successful conversation starter he or she has experienced or used. What made it successful? What did the person like about it? What was the outcome? Next, each group member should describe the worst conversation starter that he or she has experienced or used. What made it the worst? What was the outcome?

http://www.familydigest.com/stories/marriage_stages.cfm
This site offers a discussion of the relationship stages
experienced by couples after getting married.

http://www.nwmissouri.edu/nwcourses/martin/general/
socialpsyc/sld008.htm  Check out these slides for more
information on social exchange theory.

http://www.afirstlook.com/links.cfm?expand=2  For more
information on dialectical theory, check out this site.

http://www.ivillage.com/relationships/  While this site is
designed primarily for women, men can learn from it too.
It offers a variety of suggestions, quizzes, and articles related
to relationships, romance, and love.

## CHAPTER 11

# Managing Relationship Challenges

## OBJECTIVES

1. Describe the process by which failure events are addressed.

2. Explain the impact of distance on interpersonal relationships.

3. Identify the types of relationships that challenge social norms.

4. Describe the types of deception and their impact on interpersonal relationships.

5. Explain how messages can be hurtful.

6. Describe aggressive and argumentative communication.

7. Discuss potential responses to relational problems.

8. Identify some of the causes of relational de-escalation and termination.

9. Describe a model of how relationships end.

10. Discuss strategies for ending relationships.

11. Describe steps to promote post-dissolution recovery.

## OUTLINE

*Love begins with a smile, grows with a kiss,
and ends with a teardrop.*

Anonymous

*Charise:* I heard you went to the new Tom Hanks movie last night.

*Simon:* Yeah, it was pretty good.

*Charise:* I thought we agreed to go see it together?

*Simon:* Oh, sorry. I forgot; besides, you were busy anyway.

*Charise:* Don't lie. You didn't forget—you just didn't want to go with me.

*Simon:* Hey, wait a minute. It's no big deal. It was just a movie.

*Charise:* Who'd you go with?

*Simon:* A gang of us from work went.

*Charise:* Who?

*Simon:* Just some people from work.

*Charise:* You're a liar! I heard it was just you and some bimbo.

Throughout this book you have read about various factors that can impede effective interpersonal communication: language misunderstandings, biased perceptions, incorrect interpretation of nonverbal cues, weak listening skills, destructive conflict styles, and inappropriate self-disclosures. All of these factors can have a negative effect on interpersonal relationships. The above exchange between Charise and Simon reflects another set of issues that are covered in this chapter. Simon has obviously broken a promise he made to Charise about seeing a movie together, which places a strain on the relationship. Simon compounds the problem by being deceptive, but Charise calls him on it in an aggressive manner. Unlike the specific conflicts that you read about in Chapter 8, the challenges covered in this chapter reflect larger, more systemic, relational issues. Interpersonal communication also has a dark side, in that it can be used in ways that are detrimental to others. These include being deceitful, as Simon is, saying things that hurt other people's feelings, like Charise does, and being verbally aggressive or argumentative. These relationship challenges and the darker aspects of interpersonal communication can contribute to relational de-escalation and termination, which are the focus of the last section of this chapter.

# Relationship Challenges

The movement toward an intimate relationship doesn't always go smoothly. You've read about a variety of potential difficulties in the previous chapters. Chapter 10 identified some of the skills and strategies that can be utilized in the day-to-day management of relationships—but what happens when you encounter the unexpected? Any relationship can be challenged by one partner's failure to meet the other's expectations (a failure event); by attempts to maintain a relationship over long distances; or by social biases against certain types of relationships. Overcoming each of these challenges requires strong resolve and commitment by the relationship partners.

## Failure Events

Your roommate agrees to clean up the apartment over the weekend, and then fails to do so. Your friend says he'll meet you at the restaurant at 7:00, but doesn't show up until 8:00. Some very personal information that you shared with only one other person is suddenly common knowledge among all your other friends. Your fiancée is seen out on a date with your best friend. These **failure events** are violations of understandings that exist between people in relationships. Such understandings can be implicit or explicit. For example, when dating, you might believe that you are involved in an exclusive relationship without ever having talked about this arrangement with your partner (an implicit understanding); or, you and your partner might have agreed to date exclusively (an explicit understanding). Although failing to fulfill an implicit expectation is more likely to be forgiven than failing to fulfill an explicit expectation, it also may lead to an explicit agreement.

Failure events vary in their severity and impact on relationships. You would probably be frustrated by but continue your relationship with the messy roommate described above; on the other hand, your fiancée's transgression might end the relationship. One form of failure event you've probably heard about is the relational transgression of sexual infidelity. However, relational transgression can also include nonsexual involvement with others, deception, flirting, betraying a trust, breaking a promise, continued attachment to former partners, or failing to return affection.[1]

Effective management of a failure event can lead to a clearer understanding and greater appreciation of the relationship. Failure events follow a specific pattern of interaction in which a number of decisions must be made. The first decision is whether a failure event has actually occurred. Had both parties agreed to a specific rule or expectation? Did both parties understand the rule? Was the rule appropriate or acceptable? After answering these questions, both parties must decide whether to discuss the failure.[2] Many times we ignore minor failures or focus on establishing explicit rules.

The decision to complain to or reproach a partner should be motivated by a desire to clarify relational expectations or to avoid the failure event in the future by modifying the partner's behaviors.[3] A **reproach** is a message that a failure event has occurred. Reproaches are usually direct statements, but they can also be conveyed indirectly through hints or nonverbal messages. If you are upset that a close friend forgot your birthday, you might act cold and distant. Reproaches range from *aggravating* (threatening and severe) to *mitigating* (mild). For example, if your friend forgets to return a book she borrowed, you might offer a mitigating reproach such as, "Hey, Sally, I was wondering if you were done with that book I loaned you?" On the other hand, "Remind me to never loan you a book again, Sally; you are obviously irresponsible" is an aggravating reproach. What would you say to each reproach if you were Sally? To

**failure events.** Violations of understandings between people in relationships.

**reproach.** A message that a failure event has occurred.

## Building Your Skills

### Responding to Failure Events

For each of the following failure events, suggest an aggravating reproach and a mitigating reproach.

- Your best friend borrowed two of your CDs without asking and lost them.

- Your roommate has been making long-distance phone calls on your cell phone without permission.

- A person you are dating says he or she can't get together with you because he or she needs to study, but then you hear that the person was seen at a party.

- A friend is supposed to pick you up from work at 5:00 but doesn't show up.

Now suppose you are the person who caused each of the above failure events. What accounts could you give that would be the least infuriating to the other person? What accounts would be the most infuriating?

---

which reproach would you be more likely to apologize? Which would you be more likely to ignore?

The nature of the reproach affects the response, or the **account.**[4] Accounts can also be self-initiated, simply because a person knows he or she has failed to live up to an expectation. Relationship scholar Frank Fincham postulated that self-initiated accounts are more likely to evoke a favorable reaction from a partner than are accounts given in response to reproaches.[5] In one episode of the *Bernie Mac Show,* the three kids know they have been caught taking advantage of a new maid. To avoid punishment, they decide to admit their wrong-doing before they are reproached. However, in this instance, their strategy doesn't work, because Bernie Mac realizes they are trying to con him. Following are the typical types of accounts people offer:

- *Apologies* include admission that the failure event occurred, acceptance of responsibility, and expression of regret.

- *Excuses* include admission that the failure event occurred, coupled with a contention that nothing could have been done to prevent the failure; that it was due to unforeseen circumstances.

- *Justifications* involve accepting responsibility for the event but redefining the event as not a failure.

- *Denials* are statements that the failure event never took place.

- *Absence of an account* or *silence* involves ignoring the reproaches or refusing to address them.

In providing an account to another person, you should examine your culpability. You should adopt an other-oriented perspective by considering the reproacher's objectives, desires, and feelings so that you can understand his or her reason for the reproach. Regardless of the legitimacy of the reproach, the person's feelings and reactions are real, and you must determine the most effective manner to address them. Sometimes simply admitting your failure and making a genuine effort to correct it is the best response.

Once they receive an account, reproachers must decide whether they find the account acceptable and consider the issue resolved. When accounts are rejected, account

**account.** A response to a reproach.

givers often provide another account. However, rejection of accounts can escalate the failure event into an interpersonal conflict. Management of the conflict requires the skills and strategies discussed in Chapter 8.

### Physical Separation and Distance

The mobility of today's population means that we are often moving away from people with whom we have formed interpersonal relationships. Periodically, our romantic relationships, friendships, and family relationships are subjected to physical separation and distance. In addition, more and more people are meeting and developing long-distance relationships through computer-mediated communication (discussed in Chapter 12). Distance creates another challenge to maintaining relationships. Long-distance relationships vary in terms of expected length of separation, length of time between face-to-face visits, and the actual distance between the partners.

Sometimes people experience only temporary separation, such as when one partner is on a vacation, an extended trip, or studying abroad. Even though the separation is a temporary condition, it still requires adjustment and management by the partners. On the other hand, permanent physical separation produces different expectations, interactions, and relational management strategies. One of the authors of this book lives in Iowa and the other two live in Texas. This is a permanent condition, although we usually see each other face-to-face at least once a year. Fortunately, despite the distance, we are able to maintain our friendship and working relationship through e-mail and telephone calls.

How often partners are able to get together face-to-face also determines the impact of the physical distance. One study suggests that people who are in long-distance romantic relationships but who are able to get together at least once a week can maintain relationships similar to those between people who are geographically close.[6] Think about your own experience of being in a long-distance relationship: Was it the number of miles between you or the frequency of getting together that has the most impact? (Of course, usually the more miles between people, the less frequent their visits.) There are times when partners are relatively close geographically, but are limited in how often they can get together. The infrequency of face-to-face interactions might have an artificially positive effect on the partners, because they might work harder to be on their good behavior when they do get together.[7] This good behavior is probably one reason partners in romantic long-distance relationships report as much satisfaction and closeness as those who are geographically close.[8] Another reason for this reported satisfaction is that it is apparently easier to maintain an idealized image of a romantic relationship when you don't spend as much time with your partner.[9] Researchers Laura Stafford and James Reske found that couples in long-distance premarital relationships had less communication but surprisingly greater satisfaction and higher expectation for the likelihood of marriage than those in *proximal*, or geographically close, relationships.[10] Couples who are apart have fewer facts about their partners to get in their way. What happens when long-distance couples get together is unclear, but the idealized image is probably altered. Another explanation for the survival of long-distance relationships is that participants report feeling "moral commitment"; they feel they "ought" to continue the relationship.[11]

Social exchange theory (analysis of rewards and costs) offers one way to analyze the survival of long-distance relationships. Distance introduces added costs to maintaining a relationship, including actual monetary costs such as long-distance phone charges and expenses involved in commuting (for gasoline, airline tickets, food), as well as the expenditure of time spent commuting to see a partner and the disruption of normal routines (leaving less time available for other activities). These costs are weighed against the benefits or rewards of the relationship. The rewards depend on what you are seeking in the relationship. Obviously, if you are looking for a relationship that meets physical needs and need for affection, a permanent long-distance relationship would probably be unsatisfactory. On the other hand, if your need is for a confidant, and you don't require face-to-face interactions, a long-distance arrangement might be acceptable.[12]

Tensions sometimes arise when one person is trying to maintain both long-distance relationships and proximal relationships.[13] For example, the autonomy that a long-distance relationship affords provides more time for proximal relationships with others. Visits by long-distance partners can put strains on proximal partners if the two sets of friends don't get along, or if they vie for the mutual friend's time together during those visits.[14]

Social exchange theory predicts that we maintain long-distance relationships when we feel the rewards exceed the costs; however, if we consider the costs to be too high, we are likely to end such relationships. Usually, the costs continue to escalate while the rewards diminish, causing the relationship to simply fade away. However, individuals in some long-distance relationships may perceive the costs as investments rather than losses and thus sustain their commitment to the relationship.[15] Some relationships continue for a lifetime, even with little face-to-face time, because the interactions that do occur are rewarding. In these relationships, the partners' satisfaction is based primarily on the communication that they have together, since activities and face-to-face interactions are limited.

Maintaining communication is probably the most important factor in sustaining strong relationships, even over long distances. The more open and honest you can keep the communication, the more similar your long-distance relationships will be to proximal ones. Partners in romantic long-distance relationships, should try their best to reduce the impact of idealization if they seriously want to determine the viability of the relationship and reduce potential disappointments when they are no longer physically separated. Finally, your long-distance relationships will benefit from determining the needs the relationship meets and being honest with yourself and your partner about the resulting relational definition. For example, if you have been maintaining a long-distance romantic relationship and discover that what you value are the meaningful conversations and not the time spent face-to-face, you might need to redefine and renegotiate the relationship.

## Relationships That Challenge Social Norms

Each culture establishes certain norms about what are appropriate and inappropriate relationships, based on social values, biases, and prejudices. Among the types of relationships often discouraged are those between people of different races, religions, or ethnicity. In addition, many societies have social mores against romantic relationships between individuals who differ significantly in age or who are of the same sex. When social norms are violated, partners face social pressure to conform or risk being ostracized. Fortunately, the norms can be changed, and in the United States the number of relational restrictions have decreased in the last thirty years; nonetheless, developing any of these types of relationships poses challenges.

Partners in intercultural relationships face the challenge of communicating and interacting effectively, as discussed in Chapter 4. In addition, like partners in interracial relationships, they also may confront bias against their very relationship. Movies

# *Understanding Diversity*

## The Colors of Love

*K*imberly Hohman writes a regular column for about.com on issues of race, often drawing on her own experiences in an interracial marriage to a white man. She also wrote a book intended as a guide for blacks involved in interracial relationships. The following story of an interracial couple is excerpted from that book.

### Tracey and Scott's Story

Tracey used to think of herself as "SOUL SISTER NUMBER 1" (with capital letters). Not only would she never have considered dating interracially, she was "completely against interracial dating." . . .

Tracey's notions about interracial dating began to change after she met Scott, though it did take a lot of convincing. Tracey and Scott met in college. If you ask her, it took three whole meetings before he even remembered her name. He claims it was only two. Either way, it didn't take long before the two of them became buddies. They quickly realized that despite differing skin colors, they had a great deal in common.

"I was very interested in social politics and Scott and I had a mutual love for debate. Our friendship began with simply sharing our views and opinions about the world and life."

That friendship grew, over months and eventually a year, to a point where Tracey stopped seeing Scott as a white man and started focusing on him as just a man.

"Over time, we found ourselves agreeing on issues, and not only on the issues of race. When affirmative action policies were challenged at my university, he understood both the opposing and supporting views. I found myself trying to stump him when it came to race issues. 'What do you know about W. E. B. DuBois? What could you know about Marcus Garvey?' Months passed, then almost a year went by. We started sharing our poetry and other essays. Suddenly I wasn't just dealing with a white man, I was dealing with a man. How could this be, from the girl who practically caused a riot in a mall because a brother walked into a store with a white girl? My friends and family were shocked, and so was I. What was happening to me?"

What was happening was that Tracey was falling in love, though she was reluctant to admit it. And even as she and Scott made the decision to turn their friendship into something more, Tracey still found herself facing those demons from her past.

"I truly had to confront some of my personal prejudices about race when I started dating Scott. I also realized some issues that I had about how I defined beauty. I considered myself to be attractive, but I never thought someone outside my race (other than black men) would also find me attractive. It took a while for me to become romantically close to Scott because I had all these screwy ideas about interracial dating before I met him."

Yet, according to Tracey, the more she got to know Scott, the less bearing race had on her perceptions of him.

"Each time race could potentially become an issue, it was not an issue, and then it became a non-issue." . . .

Though there was some initial questioning from both families, the couple now enjoys close relationships with them. And while Tracey and Scott have had a few bumps in the road in their interracial relationship, Tracey finds that they're more like any other couple than they are different.

"We still live one day at a time, handling the prejudice we face as it comes, but honestly, Scott taking out the trash and me balancing the checkbook are usually greater issues."

She still recommends that couples enter into a relationship with their eyes open. "I think for interracial couples, there has to be a conscious decision to count up the costs—so to speak—to evaluate the real challenges that face interracial couples (and you as an individual couple) to determine truthfully and honestly if both people are willing to confront the inevitable/potential struggles together for the sake of the relationship."

*Source:* From *The Colors of Love: The Black Person's Guide to Interracial Relationships,* © 2002 by Kimberly Hohman (pp. 24–27). Used with permission of Lawrence Hill Books.

such as *South Pacific, West Side Story, Guess Who's Coming to Dinner, Remember the Titans, Jungle Fever,* and *Snow Falling on Cedars* have explored the difficulty partners in intercultural and interracial relationships have communicating with each other, as well as the negative responses they face from those around them.

One aspect of many of these relationships is the clash between out-groups and in-groups. One's racial or ethnic group is one's **in-group;** those who are not part of this group are part of an **out-group.** People can be considered part of an in-group whenever they view themselves as such; cliques and gangs are examples of such in-groups. If you have a friend or romantic partner from a different racial or ethnic group, you must adapt your behavior to what is, to you, an out-group when you are with your partner's in-group. A white person invited home for dinner by a Latino friend may be seen as an "outsider" by the family. This can create discomfort and uncertainty until the outsider gains acceptance by that family by adapting his or her communication to this other group. However, the outsider who totally abandons his or her own cultural heritage in order to adapt to another group is usually viewed suspiciously. A variety of racist terms are used to label individuals who try to act as though they are members of another culture.

One model of relational development, based on interviews with romantic couples, suggests that interracial couples (and probably intercultural couples as well) go through four stages: (1) awareness of racial differences balanced against attraction between the individuals; (2) coping with their racial difference and the responses they get as a couple; (3) the emergence of their own identity as a couple (similar to the third culture concept discussed in Chapter 4); and (4) maintenance of the relationship.[16] To succeed, interracial couples need to develop communication strategies for coping with negative social reactions to their relationships.[17] In addition, interracial couples can reframe their relationship in a positive light by recognizing the value of such a unique relationship. Sometimes interracial couples may be inclined to ignore their racial difference, but (like any difference between two people in a relationship) racial and cultural differences often need to be discussed so that the partners can genuinely understand and appreciate each other.

Unlike the other relationships that we've been discussing, homosexual relationships are not relationships between two people who are different, but relationships between two people who are similar. Gay and lesbian relationships often face strong social hostility, which may be one reason gays and lesbians seek social networks that confirm their relationships and allow them to be forthright about them.[18] Many individuals hide their homosexual relationships from others for fear of the reactions and rejection they may face. Despite the social stigma that these are "abnormal" relationships, gay and lesbian couples engage in the same kinds of relational maintenance activities as heterosexual couples.[19]

Besides relationships among gays and lesbians, there are also nonsexual relationships between heterosexuals and homosexuals. Such a relationship has served as the foundation for the friendship portrayed on the TV show *Will and Grace.* An individual's sexual orientation shouldn't be a factor in whether you form a friendship, any more than a person's race, ethnicity, or age should be—but it often is. Straight people are referred to as *homophobic* when they fear interaction and friendship with gays and lesbians. While you might not find a person's sexual orientation to be a problem, a study published in 2000 by Tim Mottet found that heterosexual respondents reported that even if they had a lot in common with someone identified as homosexual, they were more inclined to forgo a friendship with that person and restrict themselves to relationships with heterosexuals.[20] This tendency was significantly stronger for the male respondents than for the females.

*C*ouples who choose to establish relationships outside of a culture's norms face challenges and social pressures.

**in-group.** One's racial or ethnic group.

**out-group.** A race, culture, religion, or ethnic group different from one's own.

## Building Your Skills

### Friends with a Difference

Think of someone you know or imagine yourself in a friendship with someone from each of the following groups: (a) someone at least ten years older than you are; (b) someone from a country where people speak a different language than you do;

(c) someone of a different sexual orientation; (d) someone of a different race; (e) someone of a different religion.

1. With which of these people is communication easiest? Why?

2. With which of these people is communication hardest? Why?

3. How do your family and friends react to this relationship? Why?

4. How have your differences affected your interpersonal communication in each friendship?

5. How does this friendship compare to friendships with those who are similar to you?

Knowing that others are likely to avoid developing friendships with them might lead gays and lesbians to hide their sexual orientation. The desire to be able to form nonsexual friendships has to be weighed against the risks of being open and self-disclosing. This scenario creates a paradox, because interactions with homosexuals positively influence the attitudes heterosexuals have toward them.[21] Regardless of your own sexual orientation, take some time to consider your attitudes and openness to forming relationships with all people, no matter how they differ from you.

### Recap

### Relationship Challenges

| | |
|---|---|
| **Failure Events** | Violations of understandings between people in relationships. |
| **Reproach** | Message by a partner that a failure event has occurred. |
| **Account** | A response to a reproach. |
| **Physical Separation and Distance** | Add costs and challenges to the maintenance of a relationship. |
| **Relationships That Challenge Social Norms** | Include relationships between those who differ in age, race, religion, ethnicity, or sexual orientation. |

## The Dark Side of Interpersonal Communication

Interpersonal communication that is used in damaging, unethical ways represents the "dark side" of interpersonal communication. Throughout the text, we have focused primarily on how interpersonal communication can be used for developing fulfilling relationships, for managing conflict cooperatively, for improving relationships, and for helping you meet your interpersonal needs. However, interpersonal communication can also be used to hurt people, to deceive them, and in aggressive, selfish, and argumentative ways. Regrettably, the dark side of interpersonal communication is more prevalent than you might think; for example, studies focusing on deception have found that it is pervasive in interpersonal interactions.[22]

## Deception

You wake up to discover you've overslept, but because an absence would hurt your grade, you come to class late and tell the instructor that you had car trouble. Your roommate is going on a date wearing an outfit that you think is nice—but not on her; when asked what you think, you say, "I've always liked that outfit," omitting the fact that you don't think it suits her. You're involved in an intimate relationship but find you no longer have strong feelings toward your partner. Your partner asks, "Do you still love me?" and you answer, "Yes." You are developing a close physical relationship with someone but are unwilling to disclose the extent of your previous sexual relationships.

Each of these scenarios represents a situation in which there is deception, but the impact and seriousness of the deceptions differ. One way to assess the seriousness is to ask yourself, "What would happen if the other person found out I was deceitful?" Your instructor and your roommate might be upset, but deceiving them would probably not have the same impact as falsely declaring your love or not disclosing your sexual activity to a partner.

One of the unique characteristics of symbolic, human communication is that we can falsify information or intentionally mislead listeners who assume we are being truthful and honest. You can deceive either by omission (leaving out information to create an erroneous impression) or by commission (knowingly presenting fabricated or false information).

### Deception by Omission (Concealment)

**Deception by omission (concealment)** involves intentionally holding back some of the information another person has requested or that you are expected to share. For example, your parents ask where you were last night, and you reply that you went to the movies. While that is true, you don't tell your parents that you also went to a party at a friend's house afterwards. You have not "lied," but you have been deceptive. Determining whether an omission is deceptive depends on the intention of the deceiver. What was your reason for omitting the information about the party? Were you attempting to avoid your parents' response, or did you simply forget?

We can also present information and leave out information in such a way as to intentionally mislead the listener. For example, telling your roommate "I've always liked that outfit" is intended to create the impression that you think the outfit is attractive on her. This deception provides you some protection if you are later called to task by your roommate for not saying the outfit looked bad. You can reply, "I never said it looked good on you." Despite your claim, your roommate would know your intention was to deceive. These types of omissions are sometimes called "half-truths," because the statements themselves are truthful, but they are not the complete truth.

Another form of deception by omission demonstrates how deceptions can be failure events. You may fail to share information that you know you should provide to another person because of relational expectations. For example, knowing that your best friend's fiancée has been having an affair but not telling your friend about it is deception by omission. Your friend's discovery that you didn't share the information is likely to create a conflict, because he will no doubt believe you owed it to him to share your "secret." Deception by omission can undermine decision making; for example, not disclosing sexual history prevents one's partner from making informed decisions about

**deception by omission (concealment).** Intentionally holding back some of the information another person has requested or that you are expected to share.

*H*ow will the mother react if she finds out her daughter's lies are lies of commission and not of omission?

the level of risk he or she might be encountering.[23] While omitting information usually is not considered as grievous as falsifying information,[24] when the omitted information is important, omission is viewed as just as deceptive as falsifying.[25]

### Deception by Commission

**Deception by commission** is the deliberate presentation of false information[26]—lying. Among the types of deception by commission are white lies, exaggeration or embellishment, and baldfaced lies. **White lies** typically involve only a slight degree of falsification that has a minimal consequence. Calling these deceptions "white lies" seems to make us feel a little less guilty. Telling someone you were at the library studying when you really fell asleep in your room would probably be considered a white lie. Sometimes we use **exaggeration**—"stretching the truth" or embellishing the facts. Telling someone you were at the library for a couple of hours when it was only twenty minutes is an exaggeration, and a lie. Most of us have stories that we've told over and over that continue to become more embellished as we tell them. The old TV show *Get Smart* included a regular routine in which Maxwell Smart would begin telling an exaggerated story to which everyone would respond skeptically, leading him to reduce his exaggeration with the tag line "Would you believe . . . ?" and to repeat the cycle until they believed him.

### Baldfaced Lies

**Baldfaced lies** are outright falsifications of information intended to deceive the listener. Baldfaced lies have more impact on the behavior of those who hear them than other kinds of deception by commission, which means the impact is more serious than the other forms of deception. There is little doubt about the intentions of a baldfaced liar. The emotional impact of such deception is related to the importance of the relationship, the importance of the information, and the importance of honesty to the people involved (see Applying Theory and Research for more details).[27] The potential impacts explain why we are less likely to lie to our best friends than we are to strangers.[28]

While there are a variety of reasons people are deceptive,[29] those reasons can be placed into two general categories: altruistic and self-serving. Altruistic motivation is a common reason we lie to a close friend. Our concerns about hurting other people may lead us to lie to protect them—for example, not telling a roommate her outfit is unbecoming. On the other hand, we might deceive others because we either gain personally through the deception or avoid some undesirable consequence. Not being truthful with the instructor about why you were late to class is an attempt to avoid a negative consequence. In general, we lie more to strangers and acquaintances than to friends, and those lies are more likely to be for personal gain or exploitation, whereas relatively more of our lies to friends are altruistic or other-centered.[30] The two categories of altruistic and self-serving lies include a number of specific reasons for deception.

1. *To gain resources.* Deception might help us acquire material resources, such as money or property. We may also use deception to achieve intangible goals, such as fostering a relationship or bolstering our self-esteem.

2. *To avoid harm or loss of resources.* Deception may be used to prevent another person's negative reaction or to protect resources. For example, if an angry friend suspected you had broken her computer, you might lie if you were afraid

**deception by commission.** The deliberate presentation of false information.

**white lies.** Deception by commission involving only a slight degree of falsification that has a minimal consequence.

**exaggeration.** Deception by commission involving "stretching the truth" or embellishing the facts.

**baldfaced lie.** Deception by commission involving outright falsification of information intended to deceive the listener.

she would damage something of yours in retaliation. Or you might avoid having to give up your free time by lying to a friend about not being able to help her move over the weekend.

3. *To protect one's self image.* Most people attempt to present or maintain a certain image that they think others will find desirable, and people will lie if they fear their actions undermine that image. For instance, you might always be late for appointments, but you don't want people to think you are habitually late, so you lie about what made you late.

4. *For entertainment.* Teasing can be a form of deception if we tell other people things that aren't true. "I heard that Billy has a crush on you—not!" The reason for this kind of deception is to laugh at the other person's reaction. *The Jamie Kennedy Experiment, Punk'd,* and *Jackass* are television programs that often involve the use of deception to create entertainment.

5. *To protect another person's resources, self-image, or safety.* If we believe that certain information is harmful to another person, we might choose to keep it secret or to falsify it. In lying to protect friends from what we view as "harmful truths," we need to be honest with ourselves about whether the lies are really for their benefit. Is saying "I love you" when you don't really love someone a way to avoid hurting the person—or is it a way to avoid facing conflict and threats to your resources?

While at times deception seems to be acceptable because of the benefits it provides, deception can also cause harm, and there are also fundamental ethical questions about dishonesty. Harm can either be the direct result of the deception, or can result when deception is detected or uncovered. Here are some of the more obvious ways deception can be harmful:

1. *Leading to incorrect decisions or actions.* If false information is used in decision making, then a person may take the wrong course of action; for example, telling your roommate that he is supposed to meet his girlfriend (whom you don't like) at 8:00 in the student union, when you know she expects to meet him at 7:00, will obviously cause your friend to do the wrong thing.

2. *Harming relationships.* Obviously, lying to your roommate about when to meet his girlfriend may have a negative impact on his relationship with his girlfriend— but it could also have a negative impact on your roommate's relationship with

## applying theory and research

### When Lies Are Uncovered

*W*hat happens when you find out your best friend has lied to you? Do you end the relationship? Do you ignore the lie? Do you accept an apology and continue the relationship? These kinds of questions led Steve McCornack and Timothy Levine to investigate the emotional impact and the impact on the relationship of detecting a partner's deception. Student participants were asked to think of a recent situation in which they discovered their relational partner had lied. They then completed a number of scales that assessed such things as how intimate the relationship was, the respondents' inclination to be generally suspicious, the importance of the topic the person lied about, the importance attributed to the act of lying, and the level of emotional response. In addition, respondents indicated whether the relationship was a friendship or a romance and the current state of the relationship and gave an open-ended explanation of why the relationship had ended, if it had.

The level of emotional response was related to the type of relational involvement, the importance of the information, and the importance attributed to the act of lying. Examining the impact of the lying on respondents' relationships was more challenging. Only 24 percent of the respondents reported that their relationships had terminated since the lie occurred, which meant that at least when the study was conducted, students were maintaining relationships despite discovering the lie. Nonetheless, the more important the information that was lied about, the greater the likelihood that the relationship had ended. The researchers coded the open-ended explanations of the forty-six students whose relationships had terminated and found that 51.6 percent of them reported breaking up because of what was lied about, 32.3 percent because of the act of lying itself (which resulted in loss of trust), and the remaining 16.1 percent because of a combination of the two.

On one hand, this study suggests that lying about important information can have a serious impact on close relationships, even leading to their termination. On the other hand, the majority of us continue our relationships even after discovering our partner has lied.

### *A*PPLYING
#### the Research to Your Life

Consider your own experiences of lying. Examine the grid below and think about four times when you were caught telling a lie that fit into one of each of the four quadrants: a lie about something unimportant, in a casual relationship and in an intimate one; a lie about something important, in a casual relationship and an intimate one. What was the impact of the lie in each case?

|  | **Casual Relationship** | **Intimate Relationship** |
|---|---|---|
| **Unimportant Lie** | Impact? | Impact? |
| **Important Lie** | Impact? | Impact? |

Now think about a time when you caught someone else lying to you. What impact did each lie have on you and on the relationship? To what degree do your responses match those found in McCornack and Levine's study?

*Source:* Steven A. McCornack and Timothy R. Levine, "When Lies Are Uncovered: Emotional and Relational Outcomes of Discovered Deception," *Communication Monographs,* 57 (June 1990): 119–38.

you. Thus, another significant impact of deception is harming relationships, perhaps even leading to their termination.

3. *Loss of trust.* Part of the harm to a relationship that results from lying is the development of suspicion and the erosion of trust. Trust is a fundamental element of relationships, and once deception has been detected in a relationship, it may be hard for partners to regain trust.[31] Repeated deception and detection may result in someone's being labeled a liar, with the result that anything the person says is assumed to be untrue.

4. *Harming innocent bystanders.* Lies often have a ripple effect, whereby other people (innocent bystanders) are harmed by the lie. Your roommate's girlfriend will be indirectly affected by your misreport of the time for meeting. If she lashes out angrily at your roommate for being late, she will have to apologize and defend herself to your roommate, and he may be wary of her for a while afterwards. This might also cause her to be short-tempered with other people, who then become additional unwitting victims of your deception.

5. *Additional harm.* Among other negative consequences of deception listed by students in response to a survey by communication scholars Dan O'Hair and Michael Cody were punishment, embarrassment, guilty conscience, and a damaged reputation.[32]

Deception occurs in all our relationships. We are both instigators and recipients of deception. Ethically, we should strive for honest relationships, and it would be nice to believe we could be totally honest all the time. However, we know that honesty can be harmful too, so we are faced with weighing the harms of honesty against the harms of deception. The survival of our interpersonal relationships depends upon our ability to effectively manage the challenge of deception.

### Communication That Hurts Feelings

When people discover that they have been deceived, they usually feel betrayed, foolish, angry, and/or hurt. But deception is only one way in which we hurt people's feelings. As we discussed earlier, the truth can hurt, too. One of the more powerful aspects of language is that it can be used to cause emotional pain. Think of the last time someone said something that hurt your feelings. What hurt you about what was said? Students answered a similar question in a study by communication scholar Anita Vangelisti, and based on their responses, Vangelisti produced the following list of topics or contexts for hurtful messages:[33]

| | |
|---|---|
| *Romantic Relations* | "I don't want to see you anymore." |
| | "I've never loved you." |
| *Personality Traits* | "You have no sense of humor at all." |
| | "You are a dull person." |
| *Nonromantic Relations* | "You're not a very good friend." |
| | "You're a rotten brother." |
| *Physical Appearance* | "You need to lose weight." |
| | "That haircut is awful." |
| *Abilities/Intelligence* | "You're obviously not very bright." |
| | "You're a terrible player." |
| *Time* | "You never seem to want to get together anymore." |
| *Self-Worth* | "I don't care about you anymore." |
| | "You're worthless." |
| *Sexual Behavior* | "You're a slut." |
| | "You've only got one thing on your mind." |
| *Ethnicity/Religion* | "Get lost, you Bible-beater." |
| | "Did you hear the one about . . ." |

*W*hat we say and how we say it can hurt other people's feelings, especially those of family members or romantic partners.

Disconfirming responses (discussed in Chapter 5) are one type of message that hurts listeners by undermining their sense of self-esteem, even when that is not the speaker's intention. When we receive a hurtful message, such as a disconfirming response, we try to determine the speaker's intention. The intention affects how hurt we feel.[34] A heartfelt apology can help alleviate another person's hurt when we have said something casually that has an effect that we didn't really intend: "I'm sorry, I didn't mean it like it sounded." In some instances, speakers can minimize the impact by claiming they were "just kidding." Researchers Stacy Young and Amy Bippus found that as the perceived intentionality of hurtful messages increased, so did the reported emotional pain.[35] In addition, they found that in general, humorously phrased hurtful messages were found to be less hurtful than non-humorously phrased comments. However, humorous messages were found to hurt more than nonhumorous messages when they were about abilities or intelligence, de-escalating the relationship, or about a person's hopes or plans. Apparently, there are some issues, like our abilities or dreams, about which kidding is more hurtful than straightforward comments.

Research by Anita Vangelisti and Linda Crumley identified three general categories of reactions to messages that hurt.[36] The first category, **active verbal responses,** includes reactive statements made by the hurt person, such as counterattacks, self-defense statements, sarcastic comments, and demands for explanations. The second category includes crying, conceding, or apologizing, which are considered **acquiescent responses.** Finally, **invulnerable responses** such as ignoring the message, laughing, or being silent are attempts to show that the message did not hurt.

Among their other findings on hurtful messages, Vangelisti and Crumley found that people are more hurt by messages from family members than from nonfamily members and that romantic relationships are more damaged by hurtful messages than either family or nonromantic, nonfamily relationships.[37] Vangelisti has found that, in general, informative messages that evoke pain ("I've been cheating on you" or "I don't love you anymore") have a more negative impact than an accusation or comment about one's abilities.[38] She speculates that people can defend themselves against accusations or point to times when they have shown ability, but it's more difficult to dismiss negative informative messages.

**active verbal responses.** Reactive statements made in response to a hurtful message.

**acquiescent responses.** Crying, conceding, or apologizing in response to a hurtful message.

**invulnerable responses.** Ignoring, laughing, or being silent in response to a hurtful message.

You need to be cognizant of your emotional reactions to others' messages and to the emotions your messages evoke in others. Hurtful messages are probably unavoidable in interpersonal relationships, but how you respond to and manage the impact of those messages affects the level of satisfaction and happiness you feel in your relationships. When you are the recipient of a hurtful message, you should let the speaker know that your feelings are hurt and ask the person to clarify the reasons for making such a statement. The speaker might not realize that the message was hurtful. The speaker may have intended to address some conflict or problem but did so awkwardly or poorly. When the message is intentional, we might need to employ healthy ways of managing the pain. Being told by a romantic partner that he or she wants to end the relationship is going to hurt, and there may be little we can do to avoid the breakup. We might seek comfort from friends as we work through the painful feelings or we might seek professional counseling. Many times the issues are less traumatic and we can easily manage the hurt on our own.

A strong other-orientation is needed if you are to monitor the impact of your messages on other people. You might unknowingly send a message that hurts another person, but by closely monitoring responses to your messages, you will be able to tell when your messages are hurtful. In these instances, you can apologize for any pain you have caused, clarify your intent, and correct your message. On the other hand, the message might be intentional, even if the pain is not. Generally, your understanding of the other person can help you select the best strategy for presenting a hurtful message.

Timing is another factor to consider when delivering a hurtful message; there are better and worse times. In one episode of *Friends,* Rachel wanted to fire an employee her friend Phoebe was dating, while Phoebe wanted to break up with him. Neither friend wanted to be the second person giving the guy bad news because of the added pain they felt the timing of their message would create.

How much comfort and support you ought to provide depends on the recipient of the message, the depth of the relationship, and the reason for the message. Most of us dislike hurting other people's feelings and may use white lies, understate the issue, provide rationalizations, or use indirect strategies in an attempt to convey the message while minimizing pain. Hurt may be avoided for a while, but usually other emotions are aroused that might be just as undesirable. Such indirect strategies can create uncertainty, anxiety, fear, and friction because the other person is unclear about what you are communicating.

## Aggressive and Argumentative Communication

### Aggressive Communication
"I can't believe you kept me waiting! You're scum, that's what you are. You're an insensitive creep who doesn't care about me. You only care about yourself because you're a lazy fool." Have you been on the receiving end of such a verbally aggressive stream of words? If so, you know it hurts when people put you down; they are being verbally aggressive. **Aggressive communication** is communication in which a speaker demands his or her own way, attacks another person's self-concept, or uses words to cause pain. A verbally aggressive person vehemently attacks the very essence of the listener.

Why are some people verbally aggressive? There are several possible reasons.[39] Some people may simply be disposed to being aggressive (the communibiological view); others have learned that being aggressive gets them what they want. Verbally aggressive people often use hurtful language as a way of gaining or maintaining power over others.[40] As long as they continue to get what they want and are reinforced for

**aggressive communication.** Communication in which a speaker makes demands, attacks another person's self-concept, or uses words to cause pain.

*Building Your Skills*

## Assessing Your Verbal Aggressiveness

$\mathcal{T}$he following questionaire is designed to assess your verbal aggressiveness. Use one of the numbers from the following scale to indicate the extent of your agreement with each statement.

1 = Almost never true
2 = Rarely true
3 = Occasionally true
4 = Often true
5 = Almost always true

### How Verbally Aggressive Are You?

_____ 1. I am extremely careful to avoid attacking individuals' intelligence when I attack their ideas.

_____ 2. When individuals are very stubborn, I use insults to soften the stubbornness.

_____ 3. I try very hard to avoid having other people feel bad about themselves when I try to influence them.

_____ 4. When people refuse without good reason to do a task I know is important, I tell them they are unreasonable.

_____ 5. When others do things I regard as stupid, I try to be extremely gentle with them.

_____ 6. If individuals I am trying to influence really deserve it, I attack their character.

_____ 7. When people behave in ways that are in very poor taste, I insult them in order to shock them into proper behavior

_____ 8. I try to make people feel good about themselves even when their ideas are stupid.

_____ 9. When people simply will not budge on a matter of importance, I lose my temper and say rather strong things to them.

_____ 10. When people criticize my shortcomings, I take it in good humor and do not try to get back at them.

_____ 11. When individuals insult me, I get a lot of pleasure out of really telling them off.

_____ 12. When I strongly dislike an individual, I try not to show it in what I say or how I say it.

_____ 13. I like poking fun at people who do things that are very stupid in order to stimulate their intelligence.

_____ 14. When I attack a person's ideas, I try not to damage his or her self-concept.

_____ 15. When I try to influence people, I make a great effort not to offend them.

_____ 16. When people do things that are mean or cruel, I attack their character in order to help correct their behavior.

_____ 17. I refuse to participate in arguments when they involve personal attacks.

_____ 18. When nothing seems to work in trying to influence others, I yell and scream in order to get some movement from them.

_____ 19. When I am not able to refute others' positions, I try to make them feel defensive in order to weaken their positions.

_____ 20. When an argument shifts to personal attacks, I try very hard to change the subject.

### How to Compute Your Verbal Aggressiveness Score:

*Step 1:* Add the numbers you assigned to items 2, 4, 6, 7, 9, 11, 13, 16, 18, 19.

*Step 2:* Add the numbers you assigned to items 1, 3, 5, 8, 10, 12, 14, 15, 17, 20.

*Step 3:* Subtract the total in step 2 from 60.

*Step 4:* Add the total in step 1 to the number you obtained from step 3.

### What the Scores Mean:

*Score*

59–100: You are highly verbally aggressive.

39–58:  You are moderately verbally aggressive.

20–38:  You are rarely verbally aggressive.

### Questions for Reflection:

1. Does your score seem to fit your understanding of yourself?

2. Ask others who will be honest with you about their perceptions of your verbal aggressiveness. Do their perceptions fit your score on this test?

3. If you are highly verbally aggressive, what are some alternative ways of communicating your ideas without being aggressive?

*Source:* Dominic Infante and C. J. Wigley, "Verbal Aggressiveness: An Interpersonal Model and Measure," *Communication Monographs,* 53 (1986): 61–69. Used by permission of Taylor & Francis Ltd. http://www.tandf.co.uk/journals/titles/03637751.html

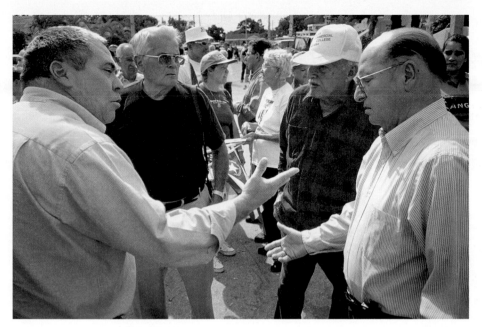

*V*erbal aggression is contagious; it escalates as each partner reciprocates aggressive behavior.

their verbal aggressiveness, they continue to use it. Still other people are verbally aggressive as a way of expressing bottled-up emotions and frustrations. Some verbally aggressive people say they lash out because they are merely sticking up for their own rights. And finally, verbal aggressiveness is contagious. When one person is verbally aggressive, others are likely to reciprocate.[41]

What should you do if you are a victim of verbal aggressiveness? The simple and obvious answer is to avoid relationships with people who are verbally aggressive. Using constructive strategies to let the aggressor know he or she is valued may help if the verbal aggression is tied to low self-esteem. But if a person has a long-held pattern of being verbally aggressive, don't expect a few positive comments or compliments to bring about quick or dramatic changes in the aggressive person. Often what you need to do is to be appropriately assertive—to stand up for your rights without infringing on the rights of the other person.

### Argumentative Communication

Roger was always ready to argue. If you said it was hot, he would argue that it was not as hot as it was last summer. If you ventured an opinion about politics, Roger would seem to delight in taking the opposite point of view and defending his ideas with gusto. People like Roger seem to enjoy a good argument. Ross, on the other hand, is just the opposite—he avoids arguing, generally tends to agree with others, and rarely, if ever, stands up for his own ideas. Are you more like Roger or Ross?

Research on the characteristic of being argumentative suggests that it's not always a bad thing to be forthright and argue your point. People who have good argumentative skills appear to have less violent marriages; they use words instead of their fists to express themselves.[42] People who are argumentative are also more skilled in developing counterarguments when someone is trying to persuade them.[43] Being argumentative is different from being verbally aggressive. Whereas the verbally aggressive person makes his or her negative comments a personal attack, the argumentative person sticks to the issues at hand and bases the argument on evidence and reasoning.

# Building Your Skills

## Assessing Your Argumentativeness

Test your level of argumentativeness by taking the following test developed by communication researchers Dominic Infante and Andrew Rancer.

### Instructions

This questionnaire contains statements about controversial issues. Indicate how often each statement is true for you according to the following scale:

1 = Almost never true
2 = Rarely true
3 = Occasionally true
4 = Often true
5 = Almost always true

_____ 1. While in an argument, I worry that the person I am arguing with will form a negative impression of me.

_____ 2. Arguing over controversial issues improves my intelligence.

_____ 3. I enjoy avoiding arguments.

_____ 4. I am energetic and enthusiastic when I argue.

_____ 5. Once I finish an argument, I promise myself that I will not get into another.

_____ 6. Arguing with a person creates more problems for me than it solves.

_____ 7. I have a pleasant, good feeling when I win a point in an argument.

_____ 8. When I finish arguing with someone, I feel nervous and upset.

_____ 9. I enjoy a good argument over a controversial issue.

_____ 10. I get an unpleasant feeling when I realize I am about to get into an argument.

_____ 11. I enjoy defending my point of view on an issue.

_____ 12. I am happy when I keep an argument from happening.

_____ 13. I do not like to miss the opportunity to argue a controversial issue.

_____ 14. I prefer being with people who rarely disagree with me.

_____ 15. I consider an argument an exciting intellectual challenge.

_____ 16. I find myself unable to think of effective points during an argument.

_____ 17. I feel refreshed and satisfied after an argument on a controversial issue.

_____ 18. I have the ability to do well in an argument.

_____ 19. I try to avoid getting into arguments

_____ 20. I feel excitement when I expect that a conversation I am in is leading to an argument.

### Scoring

1. Add the numbers you assigned to items 2, 4, 7, 9, 11, 13, 15, 17, 18, and 20.

2. Add 60 to the sum obtained in step 1.

3. Add the numbers you assigned to items 1, 3, 5, 6, 8, 10, 12, 14, 16, and 19.

4. To compute your argumentativeness score, subtract the total obtained in step 3 from the total obtained in step 2.

### Interpreting Your Score

Scores between 73 and 100 indicate high argumentativeness.

Scores between 56 and 72 indicate moderate argumentativeness.

Scores between 20 and 55 indicate low argumentativeness.

_Source:_ "A Conceptualization and Measure of Argumentativeness," by Dominic Infante and Andrew Rancer, _Journal of Personality Assessment,_ 1982, Vol. 46, pp. 72–80. Copyright © 1982 Lawrence Erlbaum Associates, Inc. Reprinted by permission of Lawrence Erlbaum Associates, Inc. and the authors.

Researchers who study arguments suggest that to argue is a natural and normal part of our conversations with others. We use language to express our disagreements and to negotiate resolutions to the disagreements.[44] Most cultures have rules that govern the way people argue. Among North Americans, when there is a disagreement, both parties express their points and the reasons for the disagreement. An argumentative person is one who seems to enjoy making rational arguments to prove his or her point.

You might be wondering why being argumentative is being discussed as a dark side of interpersonal communication. The reason is that **argumentativeness**—incessantly challenging other people's views and being perceived as *always* arguing—is detrimental to relationships. In addition, arguments can easily be perceived as personal attacks on others or as unhealthy exchanges. Furthermore, to be excessively argumentative, coupled with not being a good listener, lowers your credibility. We don't suggest you shy away from all arguments and just agree with people who challenge your ideas. We do suggest that you avoid adopting a communication style of constantly disagreeing and arguing. The test in the Building Your Skills box will help you assess your level of argumentativeness.

When you do find yourself in disagreement with someone, argue so that you don't demean the other person or undermine his or her self-worth. State your point tactfully. Don't interrupt; let the other person finish his or her statements while you listen. Monitor your voice level and avoid emotional attacks to help maintain a controlled emotional climate. As you read in Chapter 6, the words you use can help foster a supportive climate or engender a defensive climate. Acting like you've got all the answers or are always right will evoke defensiveness.

*Recap*

## The Dark Side of Interpersonal Communication

| | |
|---|---|
| **Deception** | The use of communication to deceive through false or misleading information. |
| **Deception by Omission** | Holding back information so as to leave an incorrect impression with a listener. |
| **Deception by Commission** | Deliberately presenting false information in such forms as white lies, exaggeration, or baldfaced lies. |
| **Communication That Hurts Feelings** | We can cause pain to others either intentionally or unintentionally, by such means as asserting undesirable information or criticizing traits or abilities. |
| **Aggressive Communication** | Communication in which speakers demand their own way, attack other people's self-concepts, or use words to cause pain. |
| **Argumentativeness** | The tendency to argue constantly, which undermines effective listening and credibility. |

**argumentativeness.** The tendency to argue constantly, which undermines effective listening and credibility.

## De-Escalation and Termination of Relationships

The inability to effectively manage relational challenges or the dark side of interpersonal communication can contribute to the de-escalation or even termination of a relationship. For example, how likely would you be to continue a relationship after discovering that your partner had deceived you? We noted earlier that deception might lead to the termination of a relationship, depending on the nature of the deception (how important the information was). Once a deception has been uncovered, relationships are more likely to be terminated when the offender can be avoided and there is lack of overall communication.[45]

Part of effective relationship management involves being sensitive to cues that signal relational problems or change. As Understanding Diversity: Gender and Ending Relationships indicates, women usually sense trouble in a relationship earlier than men do—but what exactly do they sense? Because each stage in a relationship has unique communication qualities, specific verbal and nonverbal cues can tip us off when a relationship begins to de-escalate.[46] There is a decrease in touching and physical contact (including less sexual activity), physical proximity, eye contact, smiling, vocal variety in the voice, and ease of interaction. In addition, there is a decrease in the amount of time spent together, an increase in time between interactions, and more separation of possessions. The interactions become less personal, and so does the language the partners use. Couples use fewer intimate terms; they use present tense less and passive language more often; they make fewer references to their future in the relationship; they use more qualified language ("maybe," "whatever," "we'll see"); make fewer evaluative statements; and spend less time discussing any given topic. They fight more, and they disclose less. If one person becomes less open about discussing atti-

## *Understanding Diversity*

### Gender and Ending Relationships

Men and women differ when it comes to dating and marital breakups. Women tend to be stronger monitors of the relationship, so they usually detect trouble before men do. Women's sensitivity to the health of the relationship may be one factor that makes them more likely to initiate the termination of a relationship as well.[47] However, some men who want out of a relationship engage in behaviors that women find totally unacceptable so that their partners are then motivated to break up with them. This allows each partner to feel as if he or she was the one who initiated the breakup and therefore lets them both "save face."

Relationship-ending problems are sometimes associated with behaviors that appear early in a relationship. Marriages in which the men avoid interaction by stonewalling and responding defensively to complaints are more likely to end in divorce.[48]

In one study of divorce, men tended to see the later part of the process as more difficult, whereas the women said the period before the decision to divorce was more difficult. In addition, two-thirds of the women were likely to discuss marital problems with their children as compared to only one-fourth of the men; and men were twice as likely to say that no one helped them cope with the worst part of the process.[49]

tudes, feelings, thoughts, and other personal issues, he or she is probably signaling a desire to terminate, or at least to redefine the relationship.

John Gottman, who studied couples relationships for over twenty years, identified four categories of communication behavior that indicate increasing problems in a marriage.[50] These behaviors undermine effective communication between couples and can lead to the end of the relationship. The first warning sign is criticism or attacks on someone's personality. The second sign is the display of contempt through insults and psychological abuse. The third sign is defensive behavior such as denying responsibility, making excuses, whining, and countercomplaining. The final communication behavior that undermines a marriage is stonewalling, in which the partners withdraw, quit responding to each other, and become minimally engaged in the relationship. Among the four, stonewalling is the single best predictor of divorce. If all four signs are consistently present, there is a 94 percent chance the couple will eventually divorce.[51] Most couples experience some of these behaviors, but happy couples develop effective communication patterns to overcome them.

### Responses to Relational Problems

When you pick up signals of relational problems, you have three choices: you can wait and see what happens; make a decision to redefine or end the relationship; or try to repair the relationship. Repairing the relationship involves applying all the maintenance skills we talked about earlier. Some of the strategies for dealing with conflict that you learned in Chapter 8 will also help you. Underlying the success of any repair effort, however, is the degree to which both partners want to keep the relationship going. The nature of the problem, the stage of the relationship, and the commitment and motivation of the partners all affect the success of repair efforts. There is no single quick solution to relational problems because so many factors influence each one. You need to focus on the specific concerns, needs, and issues that underlie the problem; then adapt specific strategies to resolve it. Professional counseling may be an important option.

The likelihood of creating a post-intimacy relationship depends on several factors.[52] For gay and lesbian couples, the strongest factors are whether the partners are part of a family-like network with mutual friends, the uniqueness of the relationship, and the degree to which the partners still like each other. For opposite-sex romantic couples, the factors are the degree to which the partners still like each other, how much they hope to renew the romantic relationship, and their expectations or previous experience in maintaining a post-intimacy relationship. Think about your own relationships, whether romantic or not. What factors led you to continue contact even though the relationship was no longer intimate? How did you feel about maintaining the non-intimate relationship? How did you feel about those you did not maintain?

What if it is your partner who wants to end the relationship? There is no pat answer for addressing this situation. If a friend stops calling or visiting, should you just assume the relationship is over and leave it alone, or should you call and ask what's up? People lose contact for a myriad of reasons. Sometimes it is beneficial to ask an individual directly if he or she is breaking off the relationship, although such direct requests place your self-concept on the line. How should you react if your friend confirms a desire to end the relationship? If possible, try to have a focused discussion on what has contributed to his or her decision. You might get information you need to repair the relationship. Or you might gain information that will help you in future relationships.

## The Decision to End a Relationship

If you do choose to change the level of intimacy in a relationship, consider your goals. Do you want to continue the relationship at a less intimate level, or terminate it altogether? Do you care enough about the other person to want to preserve his or her self-esteem? Are you aware of the costs of ending the relationship? There is no one correct or best way to end a relationship. Ending relationships is also not something you can practice. But you *can* practice the effective relational management skills of decentering and empathy, adaptation, and compliance gaining. These skills will also help you in ending relationships.

We rely on our social networks for support and self-confirmation when an intimate relationship comes to an end. Advice about how to handle the loss of a close relationship is plentiful, but basically each person must find a way to compensate for the loss of intimacy and companionship. The loss of an important relationship hurts, but it need not put us out of commission if we make the most of our friends and family.

De-escalation or termination of a relationship is not inherently bad. Not all relationships are meant to endure. Ending a relationship can be a healthy move if the relationship is harmful, or if it no longer provides confirmation of the self or satisfies interpersonal needs; ending a relationship also can open the door to new ones. Sometimes we choose not to end a relationship, but rather to de-escalate to a less intimate stage where there is a better balance between benefits and costs.

Breaking up an intimate relationship is hard because of the degree to which we become dependent on the other person to confirm our sense of self. When a relationship ends, we may feel as if we need to redefine who we are. The most satisfying breakups are those that confirm both partners' worth rather than degrade it. "I just can't be what you want me to be"; "I'll always love you but ..."; or "You're a very special person, but I need other things in life" are all examples of statements intended to protect the other person's self-esteem.

The process of ending a relationship is considerably different when only one party wants out of the relationship than it is when both parties agree to the breakup.[53] In **bilateral dissolutions,** both parties are predisposed to ending the relationship; they simply need to sort out details such as agreeing on timing, dividing possessions, and defining conditions for contact after the breakup. In a **unilateral dissolution,** the person who wants to end the relationship must use compliance-gaining strategies to get his or her partner to agree to the dissolution. Sometimes, however, people simply walk out of a relationship.

## How Relationships End

A declining relationship usually follows one of several paths. Sometimes a relationship loses energy slowly, like a dying battery. Instead of a single event causing the breakup, the relationship **fades away**—the two partners just drift further and further apart. They spend less time together, let more time go by between interactions, and stop disclosing much about themselves. You've probably had a number of friendships that ended this way—perhaps long-distance relationships. Long-distance relationships require a great deal of effort to maintain, so a move can easily decrease the level of intimacy.

Some relationships end in sudden death.[54] As the name suggests, **sudden death** is the abrupt and unplanned ending of a relationship. One partner might move away or actually die; more frequently, however, a single precipitating event such as infidelity, breaking a confidence, a major conflict, or some other major role violation precipitates the breakup. Sudden death is like taking an express elevator from the top floor to ground level.

**bilateral dissolution.** The ending of a relationship agreed to by both parties.

**unilateral dissolution.** The ending of a relationship even though one party wants it to continue.

**fading away.** Ending a relationship by slowly drifting apart.

**sudden death.** The abrupt and unplanned ending of a relationship.

## Understanding Diversity

### Empathy and Sexual Orientation

*I* once volunteered as a crisis phone counselor in a large metropolitan area. We were trained to use effective counseling skills, such as empathy, in relating to the callers' crises. One night, a call came in from a very distressed and depressed man about his breakup with his homosexual partner, with whom he had a long-term intimate relationship. At first I was uncomfortable dealing with the situation. Despite extensive training and role-playing, I wondered how I, as a heterosexual male, could empathize with or relate to this caller. However, I continued to ask questions about how he felt, what he saw as his needs, and his perception of the problems. The more we talked, the more empathic I became, because I realized that his description was very familiar. I had been divorced some four years earlier, and this caller's descriptions of his feelings matched the feelings I experienced during that time. I was able to talk about some of the feelings I had experienced, and this seemed to help him understand his own situation. I realized that though the sex of our partners was different, the overriding issue was the loss of an intimate relationship. I grew a little wiser that night.

—Mark V. Redmond

In between fading away and sudden death lies incrementalism. **Incrementalism** is the process by which conflicts and problems continue to accumulate in a relationship until they reach a critical mass that leads to the breakup; the relationship becomes intolerable or, from a social exchange perspective, too costly. "I just got to a point where it wasn't worth it anymore," and "It got to the point where all we did was fight all the time" are typical statements about incremental endings.

### Reasons for De-Escalating and Terminating Relationships

When a relationship comes to an end, we often ask ourselves, "What happened?" "Why did the relationship come to an end?"[55] We engage in this "postmortem" regardless of whether we or our partner initiated the breakup. If our partner initiated the breakup and did not provide adequate explanations, we are left to wonder and guess about what happened. We may continue behaviors that undermine future relationships because we failed to understand how we contributed to the termination of the present relationship.

According to researcher Michael Cody, students' assessments of what caused their intimate heterosexual relationships to break up can be put into three categories.[56] As Table 11.1 shows, "faults" were cited as the number-one cause. These are personality traits or behaviors in one partner that the other partner dislikes. The number-two cause, "unwillingness to compromise," represents a variety of failings on the part of one or both partners, including failure to put enough effort into the relationship, a decrease in effort, or failure to make concessions for the good of the relationship. The final cause, "feeling constrained," reflects one partner's desire to be free of the commitments and constraints of a relationship. But a variety of other elements can contribute to the breakup of both romantic and nonromantic relationships, including loss of interest in the other person, desire for independence, and conflicting attitudes about issues affecting the relationship, such as sexual conduct, marriage, and infidelity.

**incrementalism.** The process by which conflicts and problems finally reach a critical mass and cause a relationship to end.

TABLE *11.1*    **Reasons Given for Breakups**

| | |
|---|---|
| **Faults** | I realized that he/she had too many personality faults. |
| | He/she behaved in ways that embarrassed me. |
| | His/her behaviors were more to blame for the breakup than anything else. |
| **Unwillingness to Compromise** | I realized he/she was unwilling to make enough contributions to the relationship. |
| | I felt that he/she no longer behaved toward me as romantically as he/she once did. |
| | I felt that he/she took me for granted. |
| | I felt that he/she wasn't willing to compromise for the good of the relationship. |
| **Feeling Constrained** | I felt that the relationship was beginning to constrain me, and I felt a lack of freedom. |
| | Although I still cared for him/her, I wanted to start dating other people. |
| | Although this relationship was a good one, I started to get bored with it. |
| | He/she made too many contributions, and I started to feel suffocated. |

*Source:* Adapted from M. J. Cody, "A Typology of Disengagement Strategies and an Examination of the Role Intimacy, Reactions to Inequity and Relational Problems Play in Strategy Selection," *Communication Monographs,* 49(3), 1982, 162.

Just as there are behavioral rules for making and maintaining friends, there are behaviors that, if you pursue them, will almost certainly cost you a friendship. Listed in order of offensiveness, they are as follows.[57]

1. Acting jealous or being critical of your relationship

2. Discussing with others what your friend said in confidence

3. Not volunteering help in time of need

4. Not trusting or confiding in your friend

5. Criticizing your friend in public

6. Not showing positive regard for your friend

7. Not standing up for your friend in his or her absence

8. Not being tolerant of your friend's other friends

9. Not showing emotional support

10. Nagging your friend

In Chapter 10 you read how relationships intensify or sometimes become less intense in predictable stages. Relationship dissolution is also not a single event but a process. Love relationships usually end more abruptly and with more emotional intensity than friendships do. When one researcher asked individuals to identify why

$\mathcal{P}$artners may experience one of three types of relationship termination: fading away—where the partners drift slowly apart; sudden death—where separation is immediate; or incrementalism—where the conflicts gradually build until the couple reaches the breaking point.

their friendships with a friend of the same sex ended, first on the list was physical separation,[58] which was discussed earlier. Second, respondents reported that new friends replaced old friends as circumstances changed. Third, people often just grow to dislike a characteristic of the friend's behavior or personality. And finally, one friend's dating activity or romantic relationships can interfere with and contribute to the decay of a friendship. It should come as no surprise that casual friendships are more likely to end than are those between close or intimate friends. Close friendships are better able to withstand change, uncertainty, and separation.

## A Model of Ending Relationships

Steve Duck developed a model to show stages in the ending of a relationship.[59] As Figure 11.1 on page 340 shows, first one partner reaches some threshold of dissatisfaction that prompts him or her to consider ending the relationship. Having passed this threshold, the person enters an **intrapsychic phase,** in which he or she privately evaluates the partner's behaviors, often focusing on the reasons in Table 11.1 to justify withdrawing. Social Exchange Theory predicts that in this phase we would assess the relationship's costs and rewards and would be inclined to terminate a relationship that was no longer "profitable."[60] We might still remain in an unprofitable relationship if there was a reservoir of profits to offset the current costs. However, as with a savings account, there is only so much we can withdraw before we have to close the account or end the relationship. We might also remain in an unprofitable relationship if we predicted that the relationship would become profitable again.

From time to time we all become frustrated with a relationship—and for some of us the frustration may become severe enough that we consider terminating, but never proceed further than this phase. However, we might "leak" our thoughts and feelings through our communication, displaying such emotions as hostility, anxiety, stress, or guilt. We might decide to confide to a third party about our dissatisfaction. We might consider various strategies for ending the relationship.

**intrapsychic phase.** The first phase in relationship termination, when an individual engages in an internal evaluation of the partner.

FIGURE *11.1*

A Model of Ending Relationships.

*Source:* S. Duck, "A Typography of Relationship Disengagement and Dissolution," from *Personal Relationships, 4: Dissolving Relationships,* edited by S. Duck (Academic Press: London), p. 16.

At some point we might decide to move from our private internal contemplations about the relationship to confronting our partner. This is the **dyadic phase** in the model. If our partner feels challenged and intimidated by our desire to end the relationship, we might have to justify our thoughts and feelings. Our partner might also criticize our behavior and identify our failings. He or she might raise issues that cause us to reevaluate the relationship, our partner, and the costs of dissolving the relationship. We might decide instead to work on improving and repairing the relationship.

If we decide to end the relationship, we enter the **social phase** and begin making the information public. Sometimes a person's social network will mobilize to preserve the relationship. Friends might act as mediators, encouraging reconciliation and suggesting ways to repair the relationship. Of course, friends can also reinforce a decision to separate. Rumors and stories about what happened and what is happening can fuel bad feelings and hasten the end of the relationship.

In the **grave-dressing phase,** one or both partners may attempt to "place flowers on the grave" of their relationship to cover up the hurt and pain associated with its death. They need a public story that they can share with others about what happened: "We still love each other; we just decided we needed more in our lives." Such a story often places blame on the other partner: "I knew he had his faults, but he thought he could change, and he just wasn't able to." During this phase, our friends encourage us to get back into social activities; they might even try to fix us up with dates. Most importantly, we go through an internal stage in which we try to accept the end of the relationship and let go of feelings of guilt, failure, and blame.

### Strategies for Ending Relationships

When the vitality in long marriages fades away over a period of years, the individuals move slowly through the de-escalation stages before finally divorcing. Relationships that haven't lasted as long are far more likely to end abruptly. As you saw in Chapter 10, the further up in the relational high-rise you go on the elevator, the longer the ride down.

**dyadic phase.** The second phase in relationship termination, when the individual discusses termination with the partner.

**social phase.** The third phase in relationship termination, when members of the social network around both parties are informed of and become involved in the termination process.

**grave-dressing phase.** The final phase in relationship termination, when the partners generate public explanations and move past the relationship.

But no matter what stage a relationship is in, partners use both direct and indirect strategies when they wish to end it. **Indirect termination strategies** represent attempts to break up a relationship without explicitly stating the desire to do so. **Direct termination strategies** involve explicit statements. The strategy that a person chooses will depend on the level of intimacy in the relationship, the level of desire to help the partner save face, the degree of urgency about terminating the relationship, and the person's interpersonal skills.

### Indirect Termination Strategies

Relationship scholar Leslie Baxter identified three strategies that people use to indirectly disengage: withdrawal, pseudo-de-escalation, and cost escalation. *Withdrawal* involves reducing the amount of contact and interaction without any explanation.[61] This strategy is the most dissatisfying for the other partner.[62] Withdrawal represents an attempt to avoid a confrontation and to save face.

In *pseudo-de-escalation,* one partner claims that he or she wants to redefine the relationship at a lower level of intimacy, but in reality, he or she wants to end the relationship. Statements such as "Let's just be friends" or "I think of you as more of a sister" may be sincere, or they may reflect an unspoken desire to disengage completely. When both parties want to end the relationship, they sometimes use mutual pseudo-de-escalation and enter into a false agreement to reduce the level of intimacy as they move to disengagement.

*Cost escalation* is an attempt to increase the costs associated with the relationship in order to encourage the other person to terminate it. A dissatisfied partner may ask for an inordinate amount of the other person's time, pick fights, criticize the other person, or violate relational rules. As Understanding Diversity: Gender and Ending Relationships (page 334) indicates, men apparently use this strategy more often than women do.

### Direct Termination Strategies

Baxter also identified four direct strategies that people use to terminate relationships: negative identity management, justification, de-escalation, and positive tone.[63] *Negative identity management* is a direct statement of the desire to terminate the relationship. It does not take into account the other's feelings, and it may even include criticisms. "I want out of our relationship," "I just can't stand to be around you anymore,"

**indirect termination strategies.**
Attempts to break up a relationship without explicitly stating the desire to do so.

**direct termination strategies.**
Explicit statements of a desire to break up a relationship.

and "I'm no longer happy in this relationship and I want to date other people" are examples of negative identity management.

*Justification* is a clear statement of the desire to end the relationship, accompanied by an honest explanation of the reasons. Justification statements may hurt the other person's feelings: "I've found someone else that I want to spend more time with who makes me happy" and "I feel as if I've grown a great deal and you haven't." But a person who uses justification does not fault the other person, and he or she makes some attempt to protect both parties' sense of self. One researcher found that most people on the receiving end can tolerate this strategy best.[64]

*De-escalation* is an honest statement of a desire to redefine the relationship at a lower level of intimacy or to move toward ending the relationship. One partner might ask for a trial separation so that both people can explore other opportunities and gain a clearer understanding of their needs:[65] "Neither of us seems to be too happy with the relationship right now, so I think we should cool it for a while and see what happens."

*Positive tone* is the direct strategy that is most sensitive to the other person's sense of self. This strategy can seem almost contradictory, because the initiator tries to affirm the other's personal qualities and worth while nevertheless calling a halt to the relationship. "I love you; I just can't live with you"; "I'm really sorry I've got to break off the relationship"; and "You really are a wonderful person, you're just not the one for me" are examples of positive tone statements.

## Recap

### Strategies for Ending Relationships

|  | Term | Explanation |
|---|---|---|
| **How Relationships End** | Fading away | The relationship dissolves slowly as intimacy declines. |
|  | Sudden death | The relationship ends abruptly, usually in response to some precipitating event. |
|  | Incrementalism | Relational conflicts and problems accumulate until they become intolerable and the relationship ends. |
| **Indirect Termination Strategies** | Withdrawal | Reducing the amount of contact, without any explanation. |
|  | Pseudo-de-escalation | Claiming a desire for less intimacy, when you really want out. |
|  | Cost escalation | Increasing relational costs to encourage the other to end the relationship. |
| **Direct Termination Strategies** | Negative identity management | Directly stating a desire to end the relationship, without concern for the other person's feelings. |
|  | Justification | Directly stating a desire to end the relationship, with an explanation of the reasons. |
|  | De-escalation | Directly stating a desire to lower the level of intimacy or move toward termination. |
|  | Positive tone | Directly stating a desire to end the relationship, while affirming the other person's value. |

## Strategies for Post-Dissolution Recovery

Our identities are often tied to our relationships, and the more intimate the relationship, the more our identity is likely to be threatened if the relationship ends. Letting go of a close relationship is not easy, and the accompanying grief and pain can be debilitating. However, maintaining positive self-esteem and being able to nurture other relationships requires engaging in effective post-dissolution recovery. Relationship researcher Ann Weber created a list of strategies to help address the grief and loss of nonmarital breakups.[66] The following strategies are adapted from her list:

1. *Express your emotions.* You need to vent your feelings, if not to your "ex," then to a sympathetic listener, in a journal, or in some other forum. (There are even web sites where you can share your story.)

2. *Figure out what happened.* Understanding what occurred in the relationship is one way to get a handle on your current emotions. You need to accept the reasons for the breakup and work toward acceptance.

3. *Realize, don't idealize.* We sometimes view the end of a relationship as the death of a dream. In order to deal with a loss more realistically, Weber suggests mentally reviewing your partner's flaws.

4. *Prepare to feel better.* You might be surprised to find yourself feeling relief and joy. Finding the humor and irony in the breakup can help you cope with the grief. There's often a funny side to most situations; we need to be able to joke and laugh about the situation with our friends.

5. *Expect to heal.* Some of the hardest words to accept from others are "It will get better." Although we may not want to believe it, we do recover from injuries, and breakups are a type of injury.

6. *Talk to others.* Isolation is usually not a very healthy way to handle grief. Friends expect to provide comfort by listening to you discuss your feelings. The more open and honest you can be in sharing your thoughts and feelings, the faster

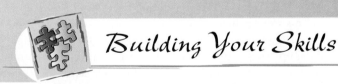

## *Building Your Skills*

### Assessing Your Past Relationships

Identify two relationships that you ended and two relationships that the other person ended. In each case, try to determine which of the indirect or direct strategies were used. What differences were there in how the relationships ended? What effects do you think the choice of strategy had on you and your partner?

What strategies did you use to recover from the breakup? Which was the most helpful? Which the least? What other strategies for recovery have you used that helped?

Survey your friends to find out how they have ended close relationships and how they recovered from the termination of a close relationship. Try to identify the termination and recovery strategies they seem to have used.

## Becoming Other-Oriented

### Considering Emotional Reactions

This chapter has covered various interpersonal situations in which emotion is a key element. Strong emotions are evoked by failure events, deception, aggressiveness, and relational termination. Emotional reactions can't be avoided, but there are various ways of managing the emotions. While each of us responds emotionally in different ways, social decentering and being other-oriented can help us appreciate another person's emotional state. Reflect on each of the following scenarios as you answer the accompanying questions. Compare your responses to those of your classmates or your friends.

● Jane and Jeremy have been dating for two years, and Jane thought that after they graduated from college this spring they would get married. Two months before graduation, Jeremy tells Jane that he isn't ready to settle down and thinks they should break up. What emotions do you think Jane experiences?

● Sierra's best friend since high school, Regina, is a lesbian. Over the years, Sierra has made derogatory remarks about gays and lesbians, so Regina feared revealing her sexual orientation; she always played along whenever the conversation turned to men, dating, or homosexuals. Sierra finds out through some mutual friends about Regina's sexual orientation. What emotions do you think Sierra experiences? What emotions do you think Regina would experience if Sierra confronted her?

● Jorge waits on tables at a restaurant to help pay for his college education. One night toward the end of a long and demanding shift, he approaches a man and a woman to take their order. The man says, "It's about time you got your f***ing a** over here. You look like a pretty sorry excuse for a waiter. Is there someone else who can wait on us—I don't like people like you serving me my food." What emotions is Jorge likely to experience? (Bonus questions: What might the customer be feeling? Why might he be acting the way he is? And finally, what would be the best way for Jorge to respond?)

you will heal. Don't be afraid to be direct in explaining to friends what you want or need from them; they can't read your mind.

7. *Get some perspective.* This strategy involves a little bit of wallowing in your misery by reading stories, seeing movies, or listening to songs about other people's experiences in breaking up. These can help you put your own situation into perspective. This approach was the focus of an episode of the TV series *The Gilmore Girls* in which Lorelai tried to help her stoic daughter, Rory, address a recent breakup by spending a day "wallowing" while watching such movies as *Love Story, The Champ, An Affair to Remember,* and *Old Yeller.*

8. *Be ready for further punishment, or maybe reward.* Weber suggests that once you've gone through the above strategies, it's time to explore potential relationships. Learn from your past experiences, hang on to pleasant memories, and move forward.

Facing the end of a relationship that has meant a great deal to us is one of the more difficult experiences we face in our social lives. The more intimate and involved we become, the more heartbreaking the end. But as the advice above suggests, there is life after the breakup of a relationship, and it is important to go through a recovery cycle that includes accepting the breakup, accepting the pain, realizing that you still have value and worth, and then moving on. Of course, all of this is easy to say and much more difficult to accomplish—which is one reason we should not isolate ourselves but lean on other interpersonal relationships and family members to help us cope. Regretably, relationships do come to an end, but just as we develop skills in initiating relationships, we can develop the ability to cope effectively with their termination.

# *S*ummary

The development and maintenance of an interpersonal relationship often depends on the ability to handle relationship challenges and the dark side of interpersonal communication. The inability to effectively manage these perils can mean the end of the relationship. Sometimes partners violate each other's expectations, which leads to failure events. Such violations may evoke a reproach, whereby the failure is pointed out. In response, the violator may offer an account in the form of an apology, excuse, justification, denial, or silence. Whether the account is accepted determines the likelihood of the failure event escalating into a conflict. Physical separation and distance is another challenge that many relationships seem to face. Long-distance relationships lend themselves to the maintenance of ideal images and good behavior during face-to-face interactions, creating general relationship satisfaction. However, long-distance relationships sometimes incur greater costs, which lead to their de-escalation. Communication is a critical element to the successful maintenance of long-distance relationships. Social norms can pose a challenge to relationships between individuals who differ in race, religion, ethnicity, or age. Relationships with and between gays and lesbians also face social disapproval. Development of such relationships requires an appreciation and acceptance of people's differences and willingness to face the social pressure to conform.

The dark side of interpersonal communication refers to the ways in which communication can be harmful or detrimental. Deception varies in intent and severity and can be accomplished either by omission (leaving out information) or by commission (providing false information). Deception by commission includes white lies, exaggeration, and baldfaced lies. People lie to gain resources, avoid harm, protect their self-image, for entertainment, and to protect others. The consequences of deception include promoting incorrect decisions, causing harm to the relationship, loss of trust, and causing harm to others.

Messages are sometimes hurtful, either by intention or accident. We are hurt when others (particularly family members and romantic partners) make negative comments about such things as the relationship or our personality, appearance, abilities, or dreams. People respond to such messages by either defending themselves, conceding the issue, or ignoring the message. Verbally aggressive communication involves making demands while attacking the other person's self-concept. Aggressive communication often begets aggressive reactions, which may be one reason such communication occurs in situations where one partner is abusive. Being argumentative isn't detrimental in and of itself, but it becomes so when it is an individual's dominant style. Being labeled as argumentative usually means an individual is seen as an ineffective listener with low credibility.

People can react to relational problems by either ignoring them, trying to address and repair them, or choosing to redefine or end the relationship. In a bilateral dissolution, both parties want to end the relationship, whereas in a unilateral dissolution one person wants to end the relationship and the other wants to maintain it. Relationships typically end in one of three ways: by fading away, through sudden death, or incrementally.

In general, relationships seem to end when the costs exceed the rewards over some period of time. Reasons for ending a relationship fall into three categories: faults, unwillingness to compromise, and feeling constrained.

One model of how relationships end identified four phases: the intrapsychic phase, dyadic phase, social phase, and grave-dressing phase. First, we internally assess the value of the relationship and consider termination; then we discuss it with our partner; we proceed by announcing the termination and interacting with friends and family; and finally, we come to grips with the consequences of separation.

Partners can use direct or indirect strategies to bring a relationship to an end. Indirect strategies to terminate a relationship include withdrawal, pseudo-de-escalation, and cost escalation. Among the direct strategies for ending a relationship are negative identity management, justification, de-escalation, and positive tone. Strategies for post-dissolution recovery include expressing emotions, figuring out what happened, talking to others, and getting some perspective.

# *For* Discussion and Review

## Focus on Critical Thinking

1. James was supposed to help clean up the apartment Saturday, but he was gone all day. His roommate reproached him when he returned. Create three accounts that James could provide that differ in terms of how likely they are to make the situation worse.

2. What factors would influence your reaction to the discovery that another person had deceived you?

3. How do you know when it is time to get out of a relationship?

## Focus on Ethics

4. Jack and Jill are in an exclusive romantic relationship, but because they attend different schools, they are living 300 miles apart. Things have not been going very smoothly recently, and Jill decided to go out with a guy at school a few times without telling Jack. Is Jill's behavior ethical?

5. Under what circumstances is it okay to be deceptive?

6. Under what circumstances is it ethical for a person in an intimate relationship to use sudden death withdrawal as a strategy for ending a relationship? Under what circumstances would this behavior be unethical?

# *For* Your Journal

1. Rank order the following four relationships in terms of how comfortable you would be with them: (1) a romantic relationship with someone of a different race; (2) a romantic relationship with someone of a different religion; (3) a romantic relationship with someone significantly older than you are; and (4) a close friendship with someone of a different sexual orientation. What affects your comfort level with each relationship?

2. Think about a close relationship you had that you ended. What strategy did you first use? How well did

this strategy work? What was your partner's reaction to this strategy? How did you feel using this strategy? What other strategies were used, if any? What were the reactions to those? If you had it to do over again, what other strategy might you have chosen to use? How do you think your partner would have reacted to that strategy? Why? If you can't think of any relationship that you have ended, think of one that your partner ended, and adapt the questions accordingly.

# *Learning* with Others

1. In a group of three or four students, generate a list of failure events that you have experienced and rank them in terms of their severity. What makes some failure events more injurious than others? Discuss how violators responded to these failure events.

2. Get together with two or three other students and identify long-distance relationships that each of you have experienced, including those with friends, lovers, and family. Discuss which relationships have continued and why. Discuss which relationships have ended and why.

3. Working in groups of four or five students, use your own experiences to develop an answer to the following question: Do the reasons for breaking up a relationship change as the relationship becomes more intimate? To answer this question, start with casual relationships and identify reasons that people end those relationships. Next, talk about friendships, and discuss reasons for ending them. And finally, talk about intimate relationships and the reasons they break up. What are the similarities and differences among these different types of relationships and the reasons they break up?

http://www.soc.ucsb.edu/sexinfo/?article=communication& refid=010  The site run by graduate students in Sociology at the University of California—Santa Barbara has information on a variety of relational and sexual topics. This link provides information on long-distance relationships.

http://www.canoe.ca/LifewiseHeartVal00/lies.html  This web site has a humorous list of lies men and women tell each other.

http://quiz.ivillage.com/relationships/tests/breaktest.htm  Here's a quick and simple breakup quiz that is supposed to help you decide whether it's time to move on.

http://quiz.ivillage.com/relationships/tests/breakup.htm  Here's a post-breakup quiz for women to find out if you are over the "ex."

http://breakup-songs.com/  This site offers a ranking of the top 250 breakup songs, best lyrics from breakup songs, and lists of breakup songs sorted by decade.

http://dateable.com/advicecorner/advice/Romance/ Breaking_Up/index.shtml  Here are a variety of articles on breaking up and divorce, many providing advice.

# 12 Interpersonal Relationships at Home, on the Internet, and at Work

## OBJECTIVES

1. Define the term *family* and describe four types of families.

2. Briefly describe the circumplex model of family interaction.

3. Identify and describe ways of improving family communication.

4. Distinguish among the different types of computer-mediated communication.

5. Compare face-to-face communication with computer-mediated communication.

6. Describe principles for using computer-mediated communication to initiate relationships.

7. Describe principles for using computer-mediated communication to maintain existing relationships.

8. Describe the impact of workplace friendships and romances.

9. Describe principles of upward, downward, horizontal, and outward communication.

## OUTLINE

Interpersonal Relationships at Home

Interpersonal Relationships on the Internet

Interpersonal Relationships at Work

*People who have good relationships at home*
*are more effective in the marketplace.*

Zig Ziglar

Debbie logs on to her AOL e-mail account and a chirpy voice says, "You've got mail!" The first message is from her dad:

> It was great seeing you this weekend. Your mom and I always appreciate it anytime you can get home during the semester. As to your changing majors, I want you to know that whatever decision you make is okay with me. Don't worry about having to stay an extra semester to finish up—the world will still be here when you graduate. That communication course you're taking on how to interact with people sounds like a lot of fun—maybe I could take one like it too. Well, I've got to get back to work. Just wanted you to know how nice it was to have you home for a couple days. Write when you get a chance, Love Dad.

Debbie clicks on the Reply button and writes her dad a quick response. Next she opens an e-mail from Tyrone, one of her coworkers:

> Man, you picked a great weekend not to work. Harry went ballistic with all the employees—he yelled his head off, accusing everyone of being lazy and good for nothing before storming out. It was quite the scene. He came back a couple hours later and apologized, but everyone still felt tense. Be prepared when you come in today. How was your visit with your folks? I haven't seen my family all term. I'm looking forward to break so I can fill up on my mom's baking. See you at work, Ty.

Suddenly a small box appears on the screen with an Instant Message from Maria:

*Maria:* What's up girl?

*Debbie:* Not much, just got back into town.

*Maria:* Whoa, I forgot. You missed a big blowup at work.

*Debbie:* Yea, Tyrone e-mailed me about it.

*Maria:* Tyrone? I didn't know you two were an item—cooooooooooool.

*Debbie:* We're just friends, you jerk : - )

Computer-mediated communication is quickly becoming another tool to use in interacting with friends and families. The interactions just described illustrate three specific contexts that are the focus of this chapter: the family, cyberspace, and the workplace. Each of these contexts has unique characteristics and demands that involve particular forms of interpersonal communication. Family relationships and those at work are typically relationships of circumstance—relationships that are created not by choice, but because of the situation. In Chapter 9 you read about how these relationships can become relationships of choice when people become friends or develop more intimate relationships with family members or coworkers.

E-mail messages convey information about the nature of the relationships among the correspondents. The opening e-mails show that Debbie has formed friendships with at least two of her coworkers, Maria and Tyrone. Debbie's father expresses his feelings about her weekend visit and confirms his support for the decisions she's making. Tyrone's e-mail contains information about work, includes personal disclosures, and lets Debbie know he values her friendship. Maria's comments reflect an easy and relaxed interactive style typical of close friends. In each instance, computer-mediated communication supplements face-to-face relationships. It is also possible to develop and maintain relationships over the Internet without ever meeting face to face.

## Interpersonal Relationships at Home

Families have changed since your parents were children. In the 1950s a majority of American families were like the Cleavers from the TV sitcom *Leave It to Beaver*; almost two-thirds consisted of a working father, stay-at-home mother, and at least two biological children. Today, according to the U.S. Bureau of the Census, less than 7 percent of all American families fit that description. Divorce, single-parent families, mothers with careers outside the home, the longer wait to start families, the move from an agrarian to an industrial society, and increasing mobility all have dramatically altered the very nature of American families. Communication within the family has changed too. The way family members interact with one another has been altered by a variety of social influences. Most research on family communication tends to be descriptive; it describes how different types of families interact. We can offer suggestions on how to improve or enhance communication in families, but *there is no single best way to communicate in families.* Each family faces unique challenges for understanding and improving communication.

Our discussion in this chapter focuses on the American family. Like many other entities covered in this book, families are dynamic and changing. Because the members of a family get older, roles and relationships change over time. In addition, families add members and lose others. As new children are born, or as a member moves out of the home, the dynamics of the family changes. Ultimately, what is true of a family at one moment of time may not hold true later. By now you have already experienced the kinds of change that takes place in families as you have become older and gone from being very dependent on your parents to becoming more independent. As you get older, you may discover that your relationship with your parents changes still more if you begin providing care for them. As you consider your own family experiences and apply the principles we discuss in this chapter, remember above all to continually monitor your family relationships and adapt accordingly.

## Family Defined

You might think that because families are basic to human existence, there's no need for a formal definition of a family—but definitions have been attempted, and there has been considerable controversy as to what constitutes a family. Traditional definitions of a family focus on the roles of husbands, wives, and children who all live together under one roof. Here is one definition written by sociologist George Murdock in 1949:

> The family is a social group characterized by common residence, economic cooperation, and reproduction. It includes adults of both sexes, at least two of whom maintain a socially approved sexual relationship, and one or more children, of one's own or adopted, of the sexually cohabitating adults.[1]

More recently, sociologists Gilbert Nass and Gerald McDonald defined a family as

> a social group having specified roles and statuses (e.g., husband, wife, father, mother, son, daughter) with ties of blood, marriage, or adoption who usually share a common residence and cooperate economically.[2]

Other definitions of a family deemphasize the traditional role of mother, father, and children, placing more emphasis on interpersonal relationships and personal commitment. In 1982, the New York State Supreme Court ruled that it is legal for a man to adopt his homosexual lover as a son. The court stated,

> The best description of a family is a continuing relationship of love and care, and an assumption of responsibility for some other person. Certainly, that is present."[3]

So should a homosexual couple be considered a family? In a survey conducted a few years after the New York State Supreme Court ruling, more than 30 percent of unmarried couples believed that homosexual couples should have the same legal rights as married couples. Art Bochner's definition of a family echoes this relational emphasis. For him, the family is

> an organized, naturally occurring relational interaction system, usually occupying a common living space over an extended time period, and possessing a confluence of interpersonal images which evolve through the exchange of messages over time.[4]

For our purposes in this chapter, we synthesize these perspectives to define the **family** as a self-defined unit made up of any number of persons who live or have lived in relationship with one another over time in a common living space, and who are usually, but not always, united by marriage and kinship.

## Family Types

Virginia Satir, a well-known expert in family therapy, has identified four types of families: natural, blended, single-parent, and extended.[5] The traditional family—a mother and father and their biological children—is often considered to be the **natural family,** or nuclear family. But because changes in culture, values, economics, and other factors have rendered this family type no longer typical, the traditional family is sometimes called an *idealized natural family.*

An increasingly common family type today is the **blended family.** This family type consists of two adults and their children. But because of divorce, separation,

**family.** Unit made up of any number of persons who live or have lived in relationship with one another over time in a common living space and who are usually, but not always, united by marriage and kinship.

**natural family.** Mother, father, and their biological children.

**blended family.** Two adults and their children. Because of divorce, separation, death, or adoption, the children may be the offspring of other parents, or of just one of the adults who is raising them.

death, or adoption, the children may be the offspring of other biological parents or of just one of the adults who is raising them.

The **single-parent family** is self-explanatory. This type of family has one parent and at least one child. Divorce, unmarried parents, separation, desertion, and death make single-parent families the fastest growing type of family unit in the United States today.

The **extended family** typically refers to the relatives—aunts, uncles, cousins, or grandparents—who are part of the family unit. Some extended families also include individuals who are not related by marriage or kinship but are treated like family. These surrogate family members may even be called Mom, Dad, Aunt, or Uncle to honor them as part of the family circle.

In addition to Satir's categories, at least one other can encompass any of her definitions. The family in which you were raised—no matter what type it is—is your **family of origin.** It is in your family of origin that you learned the rules and skills of interpersonal communication and developed your basic assumptions about relationships. You may have had more than one family of origin if you come from a blended family; following divorce, separation, or death of a parent, you may have been reared in more than one family of origin.

Families come in all sizes and forms. A gay or lesbian couple may decide to live together and form a family and raise a child or children. At the heart of our definition of a family is the concept that it includes people who live in relationship with one another. A family is a family if the people in it think of themselves as a family.

## A Model of Family Interaction

Regardless of the type of family you have, communication plays a major role in determining the quality of family life. As shown in Figure 12.1, one research team found that over 86 percent of the families who reported family difficulty and stress said that communication was the key source of the problem.[6] Virginia Satir thinks good family communication is so important that she calls it "the largest single factor determining the kinds of relationships [we make] with others."[7] Psychologist Howard Markman found that the more pos-

**single-parent family.** One parent raising one or more children.

**extended family.** Relatives such as aunts, uncles, cousins, or grandparents and/or unrelated persons who are part of a family unit.

**family of origin.** Family in which a person is raised.

FIGURE *12.1*

Sources of Family Difficulties

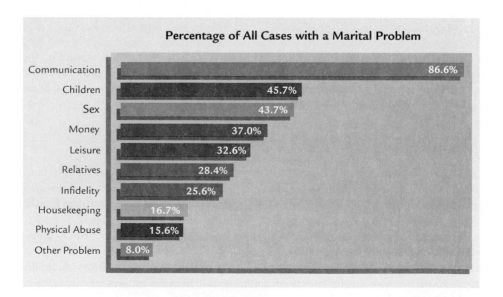

**Percentage of All Cases with a Marital Problem**

| | |
|---|---|
| Communication | 86.6% |
| Children | 45.7% |
| Sex | 43.7% |
| Money | 37.0% |
| Leisure | 32.6% |
| Relatives | 28.4% |
| Infidelity | 25.6% |
| Housekeeping | 16.7% |
| Physical Abuse | 15.6% |
| Other Problem | 8.0% |

# *Building Your Skills*

## Identifying Your Family System

Choose the statement from each set of four that best describes the behavior typical of your family.

### Level of Cohesion

1A. There is little closeness in my family. We are all pretty independent of each other. None of us have any real strong feelings of attachment to the family, and once the kids get to move out, there's not much drive to stay connected with the family.

1B. There is some closeness in my family and some interdependence, but not much—mainly we each do our own thing. The family usually gets together just for special occasions.

1C. My family is connected to each other, but we also have our independence. We get together at times besides just the holidays. There are feelings of loyalty to the family and we are pretty close to each other.

1D. My family is very close-knit and tight. We depend a lot on each other. We are always doing things together. There is nothing family members wouldn't do for each other. My family members feel a need for each other.

### Level of Adaptability

2A. Family members come and go to the dinner table as they see fit. There are few rules about how to behave at the dinner table. My parents don't have a particular role at dinner.

2B. There are a few rules that govern dinner table behavior. My mom and dad are about equal in terms of who says what the kids should do, but the kids get a lot of say in what happens and how things are done. Both parents play a similar role.

2C. In my family, usually my mom [dad] makes most of the decisions, and my dad [mom] goes along with that. The kids get to have some input about what happens. We usually get together for dinner and have a set of rules to follow.

2D. Only one parent in my family makes the decisions and the other parent follows along. There are a lot of rules about how the kids should behave. At dinner, there are a number of rules that we follow and roles that we play—who clears the dishes, asking for things, etc.

Look at the circumplex model in Figure 12.2 and determine where the statement you chose from the first set fits along the Cohesion continuum; then locate your choice from the second set on the Adaptability continuum. Draw a vertical line down from the point you marked on the Cohesion continuum; draw a horizontal line to the right from the point you marked on the Adaptability continuum. Where the lines intersect gives a rough idea of what your family might be like in terms of its cohesion and adaptability. What communication behaviors might be typical for your family type? How does your family compare to the typical type?

---

itively premarital couples rated their communication with their partner, the more satisfied they were with their marriage relationships more than five and one-half years later.[8]

Another team of researchers developed a model called the **circumplex model of family interaction** to explain the dynamics of both effective function and dysfunction within family systems.[9] The model's three basic dimensions, as indicated in Figure 12.2 on page 354, are adaptability, cohesion, and communication. Complete the Building Your Skills questions about family systems to find out how these dimensions apply to your family. **Adaptability,** which ranges from chaotic to rigid, is the family's ability to modify and respond to changes in its own power structure and roles. For some families, tradition, stability, and historical perspective are important to a sense of comfort and well-being. Other families that are less tradition-bound are better able to adapt to new circumstances.

The term **cohesion** refers to the emotional bonding and feelings of togetherness that families experience. Family cohesion ranges from excessively tight, or enmeshed,

**circumplex model of family interaction.** Model of the relationships among family adaptability, cohesion, and communication.

**adaptability.** A family's ability to modify and respond to changes in the family's power structure and roles.

**cohesion.** The emotional bonding and feelings of togetherness that families experience.

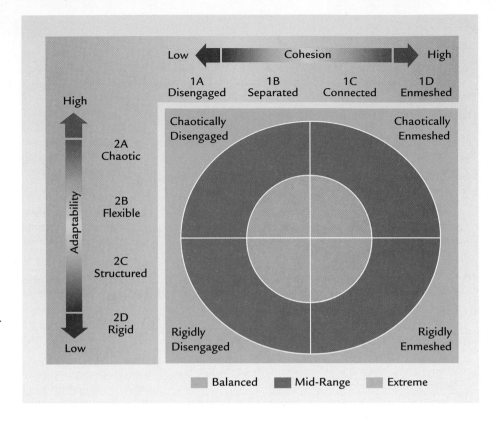

FIGURE *12.2*

A Circumplex Model of Family Systems.
*Source:* Adapted from David H. L. Olson, Candyce S. Russell, and Douglas H. Sprenkle (Eds.), *Circumplex Model: Systemic Assessment and Treatment of Families* (New York: Haworth Press, 1989). Used by permission.

to disengaged. Because family systems are dynamic, families usually move back and forth along the continuum from disengaged to enmeshed.

The third key element in the model—and the most critical one—is communication. It is not labeled in Figure 12.2 because *everything* in the model is influenced by communication. Through communication families can adapt to change (or not) and maintain either enmeshed or disengaged relationships or something in-between. Communication determines how cohesive and adaptable families are. Communication keeps the family operating as a system.

The circumplex model helps explain relationships among family cohesiveness, adaptability, and communication at different stages of family development. In general, families with balanced levels of cohesion and adaptability function better across the entire family life cycle than do those at the extremes of these dimensions. A balanced family has a moderate amount of cohesion and adaptability—represented by the center circle on the model. Balanced families can often better adapt to changing circumstances and manage stressful periods, such as the children's adolescence. Not surprisingly, these balanced families usually have better communication skills.

As we have already emphasized, however, research suggests that *there is no single best way to be a family.* At some stages of family life, the ideal of the balanced family may not apply. Older couples, for example, seem to operate more effectively when there is more rigid structure and a lower level of cohesiveness. Families with younger children seem to function well with high levels of both cohesion and adaptability. Only one thing is constant as we go through family life: Effective communication skills play an important role in helping families change their levels of cohesiveness or adaptability. These skills include active listening, problem solving, empathy, and being supportive. Dysfunctional families—those that are unable to adapt or alter their levels of

*U*se what you know about the circumplex model and the cues you see in this photo to describe the relationships in this family.

cohesion—invariably display poor communication skills. Family members blame others for problems, criticize one another, and listen poorly.

### Improving Family Communication

Wouldn't it be fantastic if you could learn special techniques guaranteed to enrich your family life? But, alas, there are no sure-fire prescriptions for transforming your

## *Building Your Skills*

### The Circumplex Model Applied to TV and Movie Families

One way to test your understanding of the circumplex model of family systems is to see if you can identify families that match the characteristics of family types identified in the model. See if you can think of families portrayed on TV or in the movies that fit each of the four following extreme family types:

| Family Type | TV or Movie Family |
| --- | --- |
| Chaotically Disengaged | |
| Chaotically Enmeshed | |
| Rigidly Disengaged | |
| Rigidly Enmeshed | |

Is any one of the extreme types portrayed more than others? If so, why do you suppose that type is portrayed more? Which of the types is portrayed the least? Why do you suppose that is? Examine any differences in how you and other students classified the same families. Try to determine why people's views differ.

family system into one that a TV sitcom family would envy. Instead, we can pass on some skills and principles that researchers have either observed in healthy families or applied successfully to improve dysfunctional ones.

Virginia Satir found that in healthy families, "the members' sense of self-worth is high; communication is direct, clear, specific, and honest; rules are flexible, humane, and subject to change; and the family's links to society are open and hopeful."[10] In such families, she notes, people listen actively; they look *at* one another, not *through* one another or at the floor; they treat children as people; they touch one another affectionately regardless of age; and they openly discuss disappointments, fears, hurts, angers, and criticism, as well as joys and achievements.[11]

In a recent study, John Caughlin identified ten factors that were associated with families that had good communication.[12] Those factors, in order of impact, are openness, maintaining structural stability, expression of affection, emotional/instrumental support, mind-reading (knowing what others are thinking and feeling), politeness, discipline (clear rules and consequences), humor/sarcasm, regular routine interaction, and avoidance of personal and hurtful topics. After reviewing several research studies, family communication scholars Kathleen Galvin and Bernard Brommel identified eight qualities exhibited by functional families: interactions are patterned and understood; there is more compassion and less cruelty; problems are addressed to the person who created them—other family members are not scapegoated; there is self-restraint; boundaries about safe territories and roles are clear; life includes joy and humor; misperceptions are minimal; and positive interactions outweigh negative ones.[13] Of the qualities identified in these two studies, how many are present in your family? Which qualities do you think your family could use more of?

Not all of the qualities identified in the above lists specifically involve communication, though all are certainly affected by and affect communication. The following sections explore some of the skills and strategies you can follow to improve your family communication.

### Take Time to Talk About Relationships and Feelings

Healthy families talk.[14] The quantity of communication depends on family members' needs, expectations, personalities, careers, and activities. But the talking extends beyond idle chatter to focus on issues that help the family adapt to change and maintain a sense of cohesiveness.

Often, because of the crush of everyday responsibilities and tasks, family members may lapse into talking only about the task-oriented, mundane aspects of making life work: house cleaning, grocery shopping, errand running, and other uninspiring topics. Healthy families communicate about much more: their relationships, how they are feeling, and how others are feeling. They make time to converse, no matter how busy they are. They have an other-orientation in these conversations, instead of focusing on themselves. In addition, they enjoy each other and don't take themselves too seriously.[15]

### Listen Actively and Clarify the Meaning of Messages

Because talking about relationships is important in healthy families, it is not surprising that effective listening is also important. In the often stressful context of family life, good listening skills are essential.

Good listening requires an other-orientation. In Chapter 5, we presented fundamental skills for listening and responding to messages. Family members will communicate with greater accuracy if they learn to stop, look, and listen. Stop: minimize mental and outside distractions; don't try to carry on a conversation over a TV blaring, a video game bleeping, or a stereo's distracting rhythmic pulse. Look: Constantly monitor the rich meaning in nonverbal messages; remember that the face and voice are prime sources for revealing emotional meaning; body posture and gestures provide clues about the intensity of an emotion. Listen: Focus on both details and major ideas. Asking appropriate follow-up questions and reflecting content and feelings are other vital skills for clarifying the meaning of messages. And remember the importance of checking your perceptions of the meaning of nonverbal messages.

### Support and Encourage One Another

A smoothly functioning family can be a supportive, encouraging sanctuary from everyday stresses. Through communication, people can let others know that they support and value them. Satir suggests that many, if not most, sources of dysfunction in families are related to feelings of low self-worth.[16] Healthy families take time to nurture one another, express confirming messages, and take a genuine interest in each person's unique contributions to the family. Researchers have found that supportive messages—those that offer praise, approval, help, and affection—can lead to higher self-esteem in children, more conformity to the wishes of the parent, higher moral standards, and less aggressive and antisocial behavior.[17] Jane Howard, who traveled extensively in search of a "good family," found that "good" families have a sense of valuing and supporting each other.[18]

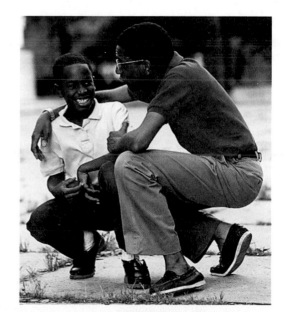

### Use Productive Strategies for Managing Conflict, Stress, and Change

The inability to manage conflict and stress in a family may be a contributing factor to family violence. In the United States in 2001, women experienced an estimated 588,490 rapes, assaults, and robberies at the hands of current or former lovers or husbands.[19] In 1998, about 160,000 men were the victims of a violent crime by an intimate partner.[20] The last National Incidence Study on Child Abuse estimated that 614,100 children were physically abused, 300,200 were sexually abused, and 532,200 were emotionally abused in the year covered by the study.[21] Abuse and violence are the extreme examples of what happens when people fail to resolve conflicts in a collaborative manner. Husbands and wives must learn to manage conflict in constructive ways and to manage their conflicts with their children similarly.

John Gottman has developed a set of suggestions for handling conflict between couples, some of which apply equally well to parent–child and sibling conflicts.[22]

*W*ise parents use support and encouragement rather than coercion as a primary strategy for shaping their children's behavior. The challenge is to find a middle ground that tempers support with appropriate control.

## *applying theory and research*

### *Family Rituals*

Family rituals are patterned interactions that take on special meaning or symbolic significance to family members. For instance, your family might have a ritual of gathering on Sunday night to watch TV and eat popcorn, playing a game of touch football before Thanksgiving dinner, or taking a trip each summer to visit your grandparents. Each family establishes its own set of rituals, drawing on the rituals experienced by the parents as children or creating new ones. Blended families present a unique challenge, because each of the parents brings his or her own established family rituals to the newly formed family. Rituals can play an important role in establishing a new family identity; however, children in blended families can be frustrated, confused, and angry if rituals they used to follow are abandoned because their new stepparents don't want to follow them.

Dawn Braithwaite, Leslie Baxter, and Anneliese Harper interviewed twenty stepparents and thirty-three stepchildren about family rituals that either ended, continued, were adapted, or were created from scratch when the blended family was formed. The researchers found that several children in single-parent situations had special rituals (like talking about their day while fixing dinner with their mom or dad) that were no longer possible when they became part of a blended family.

Sometimes the new spouse could not or did not want to continue or participate in the previously established ritual. And sometimes the circumstances prevented continuation of the ritual— as when a divorced father moved away and could no longer take his children for weekend outings on his boat. Stepchildren reported more of a sense of loss about ended rituals than did the stepparents.

Some rituals were imported into the blended family unchanged, because the ritual previously existed in both families— for example, going to a worship service on Saturday or Sunday. Some rituals were so important that acceptance as a family member required participation: going to Grandma's for Thanksgiving dinner, going out for birthday dinners, and the like. Participation in such rituals was one way a stepparent or child might gain acceptance by the other family members. Sometimes the rituals were adapted to fit the new family circumstances—for instance, continuing to take a summer vacation in July, but changing the destination. Several respondents reported that adapting the old rituals was an important part of adjusting to the new family and showed respect for other family members. Again, stepchildren seemed to find this harder to do than the stepparents.

Attempts to impose new rituals often failed because the attempts created conflict and ignored the values of certain family members. New rituals were accepted when all members were involved in their development and when both the old and new family values were recognized and respected.

### Applying the Research to Your Life

While you may or may not be from a blended family, you certainly have been exposed to various family rituals. Make a list of your family rituals (remember, these can include simple routines or traditions such as calling home every Sunday night). Which of these rituals is most important to you? Why? How have the rituals changed as you've grown up? What rituals are no longer practiced in your family? Why not? What rituals would you like to continue when you start your own family? How will you adapt to the rituals that your spouse may bring into the family? Compare your list with those of other classmates and discuss the similarities and differences.

*Source:* Dawn O. Braithwaite, Leslie A. Baxter, and Anneliese M. Harper, "The Role of Rituals in the Management of Dialectical Tensions of 'Old' and 'New' in Blended Families," *Communication Studies,* 49 (Summer 1998): 105–20.

Many of his suggestions reflect recommendations made in Chapter 8 on managing conflict. Gottman suggests picking your battles carefully, scheduling the discussion, employing a structure (build an agenda, persuade and argue, resolve), and moderating your emotions. In dealing with your partner, acknowledge his or her viewpoint before presenting your own, trust your partner, communicate nondefensively, and provide comfort and positive reinforcement. Conflict might be tempered by enhancing the romance and finding enjoyment in the relationship. He further suggests taking stock of the relationship and knowing when to seek help or to end the relationship.

No list of do's and don'ts will help you manage all differences in a family relationship. The suggestions offered here provide only a starting point. As we have emphasized, you will need to adapt these skills and suggestions to the context of your unique family system. But research consistently shows that listening skills and empathy are strong predictors of family satisfaction.

## Recap

### How to Improve Family Relationships

**Take time to talk about relationships and feelings.**

● Be other-oriented in your focus.

● Don't take yourself too seriously.

**Listen and clarify the meaning of messages.**

● Stop, look, and listen.

● Check your interpretation of messages.

**Support and encourage one another.**

● Use confirming messages.

● Be selective in disclosing your feelings.

**Use productive strategies for managing conflict, stress, and change.**

● Watch for communication warning signs.

● Learn to renegotiate role conflicts.

# Interpersonal Relationships on the Internet

Interactions among friends and family members have been dramatically altered by the introduction of the personal computer and computer-mediated communication. **Computer-mediated communication (CMC)** was initially seen as a tool for accessing information, but it has quickly become an integral tool for human interaction. People have moved from using independent computers for word processing to using networked computers that allow them to send and receive messages and documents. As the technology has been introduced to the home, more and more families use the Internet to keep in contact. E-mail and instant messaging provide useful communication tools for maintaining interpersonal relationships with friends, family members, and lovers. Chat rooms and discussion groups give people the ability to meet strangers and develop new interpersonal relationships. Thus, CMC allows you to meet two interpersonal goals: to make contact with strangers and thus initiate and develop new relationships and to maintain existing relationships. These two goals affect your Internet interactions differently.

**computer-mediated communication (CMC).** Communication between and among people through the medium of computers (includes e-mail, chat rooms, bulletin boards, and newsgroups).

## Comparing Face-to-Face (FtF) Communication and Computer-Mediated Communication (CMC)

There are advantages and disadvantages to both face-to-face (FtF) communication and computer-mediated communication (CMC). In FtF communication people obtain a lot of information by seeing how other people behave, how they react, and how they look. However, such visual information has a down side when we have biased reactions to what we see (reacting to a person's age, sex, race, or physical size). Such attributes may not be readily apparent in CMC, and we might engage in fruitful and fulfilling chat with someone online whom we might have avoided if we had seen what he or she looked like first. Besides minimizing the use of nonverbal cues, CMC has interesting characteristics related to the importance of the written word, how much time delay there is between the interactants' messages, the occurrence of deception, and ease with which communication partners can simply disappear.

### Nonverbal Cues

CMC is more limited in its use of nonverbal cues than FtF communication—for instance, completely ignoring touch and smell and limiting one's ability to use visual and aural cues. Thus, words and graphics become more important in CMC than in FtF communication because you must rely solely on them to carry nonverbal messages. In FtF communication you can hear people's voices, see their facial expressions, and watch their body movements. These provide the context by which you attribute meaning to the words people speak. In CMC such cues are limited or nonexistent, which means that words are taken at their face value. There are some basic things users do to add emotion to their messages, including CAPITALIZING THE MESSAGE (which is considered "yelling"), making letters **bold,** or using emoticons: combinations of symbols used to represent some emotion—smiley faces : - ), frowning faces with glasses 8-( , and so on). Despite these efforts, the ability to tease or make sarcastic remarks is limited in CMC, because there is no tone of voice in the written message, which means the author must usually write out an accompanying interpretation—for example, "Boy, am I insulted by that or what?! (just kidding)."

CMC researchers Lisa Tidwell and Joseph Walther think that the lack of nonverbal communication cues in CMC might be one reason they found CMC partners using direct communication strategies like disclosure or asking questions to reduce their uncertainties more than partners in similar FtF interactions.[23] In face-to-face interaction we can tell a person's sex, race, and relative age, which lead to the formation of a certain impression. The lack of nonverbal cues to provide this information necessitates the more direct strategies and open discussions that occur online.

### The Role of the Written Word

The reliance on the written word also affects Internet interactions. One online scholar suggests that a person's typing ability and writing skills affect the quality of any relationship that is developed.[24] The ability to encode thoughts quickly and accurately into written words is not a skill everyone has. Not only do writing skills affect your ability to express yourself and manage relationships, they also affect how you are perceived by others. Look at the following two e-mail messages and think about the impressions you form of the two authors.

*GigoloMan:* "Hey, babe, whad's up? no what im thnking now we shuld do?"

*GentleJim:* "Hi. Boy, have I been swamped with work lately. How's your day been?"

What's your impression of the two e-mailers? What affected your impression? The first example is filled with grammar and spelling errors that might create a negative impression because the author is not particularly skilled at writing. The second author uses correct grammar and spelling, which is more likely to produce a positive impression. The user name or nickname (also called a "nick" among CMC users) that is listed for each author also affects our impression.[25] "GigoloMan" sends a clear but politically incorrect message to those who see his moniker. The selection of words has a strong impact on the impression others draw about us from the Internet.

### Response Time

It takes longer to formulate a typewritten response than a spoken or nonverbal one. The amount of delay (which is similar to silence in FtF interactions) can have an impact on the interpretation of the message's meaning. In chat sessions, participants expect to see a response to their posting very quickly. This is one reason chat sessions often involve very short and concise messages that can be written and sent rapidly. Most chat sessions involve a rapid succession of short messages that foster a sense of synchronicity and interaction. By the time a long message gets written and sent, it is often no longer germane to the discussion. The exception to this is when people are in private or small-group chat sessions, where they ask questions to which a longer, more developed response is expected.

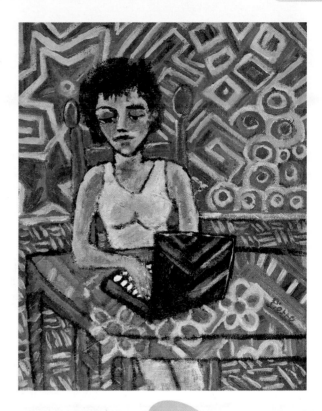

*C*omputer-mediated communication has made it easy for us to have access to family, friends, coworkers, and even complete strangers. The key to success is to apply the same skills that you would in a face-to-face relationship.

E-mailing someone allows you time to compose your message and craft it more carefully than you might in a FtF interaction. You can take time to consider your message and delete it before sending if you don't feel you have worded the message the way you want. Even in chat sessions, you might finish typing a line and then decide to delete it and write something else. In FtF interactions, people can think about what they want to say; but once having spoken, they cannot take their words back. As a sender of Internet messages, you have more control over what you say and the impression you create; as the receiver of Internet messages, realize that the other person has had the chance to shape his or her message carefully for its greatest impact on you. Such deliberation is one reason you must be cautious about accepting the validity of Internet messages—deception is relatively easy.

### Challenges of Computer-Mediated Communication

The use of CMC as a surrogate for face-to-face encounters creates some unique and intriguing challenges. One overriding rule that you should follow when communicating on the Internet is to follow all the rules you would normally follow in face-to-face interactions.[26] For example, in getting acquainted with someone, don't disclose too much too soon. Be a good "listener," and confirm the statements made by your Internet partners. Be other-oriented by considering how your Internet partners will react to what you have written: What is their context for interpreting your messages? What do they know about you? What do you know about them?

The kind of information you provide and acquire through CMC has a direct impact on impression formation and relational attraction. Even though you are not able to use many of the usual nonverbal cues from which you draw impressions of other people (for example, their physical looks), you still form impressions about those with whom you interact. Prominent Internet researcher Joseph Walther has found that the impressions people developed about other people on the Internet became more similar to the impressions formed in face-to-face interactions the more users interacted.[27]

Initially, those in face-to-face interactions are likely to form a more detailed and comprehensive impression than those interacting through CMC; however, the impressions formed in CMC have been found to be stronger or more extreme.[28] This finding may reflect the fact that there are fewer cues in CMC on which to focus; thus, greater emphasis may be placed on those cues, resulting in more stereotyping. This might be one reason that often one of the first questions you're asked when you join a chat room is "A/S/L" for age, sex, and location. That small amount of information serves as the categorical foundation for impressions.

### Ease of Deception

The detection of deception in face-to-face encounters is aided by nonverbal cues. A 50-year-old white male (named Sam) could not claim to be a 20-year-old Chinese female (Samantha) without a major makeover. However, online such deception is almost as easy as typing. We say "almost," because you can assess the content of the written message for clues to deceit. Sam writing as Samantha might talk about how much "she" enjoyed watching the Beatles live on *The Ed Sullivan Show* (they appeared in 1964 and 1965) when she was growing up. This might alert a communication partner to the fact that Samantha would have to be older than 20, and is probably not from China.

One survey of 191 students at one college found that 40 percent had lied on the Internet: 15 percent about their age, 8 percent about their weight, 6 percent about appearance, 6 percent about marital status, and 3 percent about what sex they were.[29] College student respondents in another study reported the most common indicator of deception was someone's implausible statement or bragging.[30] The criteria for detecting deception apparently change as the Internet relationship becomes more intimate. As friendships develop over the Internet, to detect deception people come to depend on the personal knowledge and impressions of their partners acquired over the course of their correspondence.[31] Interestingly, this study also found that those who reported lying most were the ones most likely to suspect other users of lying.[32]

The ease with which someone can create a false persona means that you need to be cautious in forming relationships with Internet strangers.

### Ease of Disappearance

Besides the potential for developing relationships with people who falsely present themselves, another aspect of Internet relationships is that a person can simply disappear or assume another nick without your ever knowing. Unless the person is using a site-specific user name, such as "iastate.edu" or "swt.edu," which represent university locations, you may have no way of knowing where they reside, much less their names. The use of an AOL, MSN, or Hotmail address means you are virtually in the dark about the people with whom you interact. People can simply change their e-mail addresses, and you are totally cut off. Disappearing is more difficult or at least impractical in face-to-face relationships; disappearing from interactions with a classmate with whom you've had a relationship would necessitate dropping the course and maybe even dropping out of school.

## Types of Computer-Mediated Communication

E-mail, chat rooms, instant messaging, bulletin boards, listservs, and mailing lists are among the ways we use personal computers to connect with other people. Sometimes we direct our comments to a particular person (e-mail and instant messaging); at other times we simply put our ideas out for anybody to read (bulletin boards, listservs, and chat rooms). Some forms allow us to have an active conversation with someone (chat rooms and instant messaging), while others allow us to post our ideas for others to read and respond to at a later time (e-mail and bulletin boards). This last distinction refers to *synchronicity*—whether individuals are engaging in an interaction simultaneously or with some period of delay between the message being sent and the message being read. Each form of computer-mediated communication can be used in different ways to establish and maintain interpersonal relationships.

### Synchronous Interaction

In defining interpersonal communication in Chapter 1, we noted that it involves mutual influence, meaning that the participants are influencing each other at the same time. In the cyber world, a **synchronous interaction** involves both participants actively engaging in the interaction at the same time. Face-to-face interactions are, by their very nature, synchronous. Only some Internet interactions are synchronous, such as group or private chat sessions.

*Chat Rooms*    Chat rooms (also referred to as *Internet relay chat,* or *IRC*), where people are actively involved in sending and receiving messages, are more similar to face-to-face interactions than is e-mail. Discussion groups or public chat rooms often involve many people engaging in a kind of group discussion. However, one intriguing aspect of public chat rooms is that even though ten or twelve people might be chatting at one time, the participants often pair up and simply respond to their partner's comments, ignoring the rest. Although this "selective" chatting may at first be confusing, chatters usually develop a knack for being able to discern relevant comments. Typed statements often start with the name of the person for whom the message is intended. Such "interpersonal" dyadic exchanges often draw in the other chat room members, because everything that is written is open to public viewing. In this way it's like sitting in a small group in which you are talking with just one other member, but the other group members can still hear your conversation. Chatters often move to a "private room" where only those who are invited can participate. This allows chatters the privacy to carry on uninterrupted and confidential conversations.

Technology already has been developed that lets users go beyond the limitations of using only written words. Several chat rooms now allow audio links and take on the feeling of a large telephone party line. The introduction of spoken instead of written messages on the Internet adds nonverbal information for listeners. Just like the telephone, audio chat rooms provide information that gives you hints about the person's age, sex, and ethnicity (through accents). In addition, people can use the full range of vocal cues discussed in Chapter 7: pitch, tone, rate, volume, and silence. There are also visual chat rooms and teleconferencing that let you actually see the person with whom you are interacting. The use of video feed on the Internet makes this type of interaction more like face-to-face interactions. Note that the ability to post visual images does not guarantee that people won't post surrogate images rather than actual ones.

*Instant Messaging*    Instant messaging is similar to interacting in a private chat room. Most Internet providers allow their members to create a "friends and family" list. When any of the "buddies" you've put on your list are logged on to the Internet, you are notified. You can then send them a message and engage them in an "instant" exchange of messages. Instant messaging approximates a personal conversation or a small-group discussion if you are connected with several people at the same time. One disadvantage

**synchronous interaction.**
Interaction in which participants are actively engaging at the same time.

Allison Barrows/Universal Press Syndicate.

of instant messaging is that you might be involved in some other activity when someone contacts you. This creates a "listening" problem for you, because you might try to continue your other computer activity while still instant-messaging, thus dividing your attention and causing delays or disconfirming responses to your partners. Handling this situation is similar to handling the same dilemma in a face-to-face situation: you either tell your partner you can't talk right now, or you postpone your other activity.

### Asynchronous Interactions

Most Internet interactions are **asynchronous,** meaning that the participants are not necessarily logged on at the same time but rather send and receive posted messages. Bulletin boards, discussion forums, and e-mail represent asynchronous interactions. They are interactions to the degree that the participants post responses to what they have read. On bulletin boards a thread about a particular subject can continue for days or weeks.

**E-Mail**    E-mail is not really a form of interpersonal communication, although it can be used to develop and maintain relationships. The speed with which people can send and receive letters through e-mail makes it seem a lot more interactive than letters sent through the postal service. One emerging Internet norm is that you are expected to respond as soon as possible to your e-mail; failure to do so sometimes evokes resentment from correspondents.

**Bulletin Boards, Mailing Lists, and Listservs**    Electronic bulletin boards are similar to traditional bulletin boards: You can post a message electronically that can be read by anyone who happens along, and readers can leave a response. Because the message is essentially displayed in public, you don't know who will read it or respond. Threads develop when an issue evokes a number of postings; the postings resemble a conversation when people read and respond sequentially to each other's messages over a period of time. The anonymity associated with postings, however, sometimes leads to heated exchanges that erupt into "flaming," in which posters attack one another on a personal level (ego conflicts).

Mailing lists and listservs represent a blend of e-mails and bulletin boards; there is a defined and often known list of individuals who receive the same electronic message. The list of recipients can be created by one individual (a mailing list), or interested participants can subscribe to it (a listserv). Instructors who send out class announcements to students by way of the Internet are using a mailing list. Recipients often have the choice of responding only to the originator or to the entire list of readers. Listservs

**asynchronous interaction.** Interaction in which participants send and receive messages from each other with delays between reception and response.

are usually created around some interest or topic, and many have interesting names; for instance, one listserv for communication research is called CRTNET; interpersonal communication instructors can subscribe to a listserv called EMPATHY; and the EPA has a listserv for New England called GREENBYTES-NE. Depending on the size of the list or the number of members on the listserv, you may or may not get to know the members as individuals. The more frequently a specific individual posts messages, the more likely it is that you form an impression of that person. When the impressions are positive, you may be motivated to exchange personal e-mails and develop more personal relationships.

## Using Computer-Mediated Communication to Initiate New Relationships

By now it's commonplace for people to form personal relationships over the Internet. In a study of discussion groups reported in 1996, over 60 percent of the survey respondents reported forming personal relationships with someone they met on the Internet.[33] Further analyses of these relationships revealed an almost equal number of mixed-sex (55 percent) and same-sex relationships (45 percent), and only 8 percent were considered romantic. Over half of the respondents reported communicating with their friend at least once a week. Interestingly, this study found women were more likely to form personal relationships in these groups than men (72 percent of the female respondents, as compared to 55 percent of the males). In 1999 and 2000, researchers conducted a national telephone survey of youth (10- to 17-year-olds) who used the Internet at least once a month and asked about their use of the Internet during the previous year. The results indicated that 55 percent of respondents used CMC with people they hadn't known face-to face; 39 percent had used it more than once with the same person; 25 percent reported forming a casual online friendship, 14 percent a close online friendship, and 2 percent a romantic relationship; and 7 percent reported actually meeting face-to-face with an Internet partner.[34] Most met in chat rooms (59 percent); 30 percent met through instant messaging or e-mail (having made connections on the recommendation of a friend or family member); 5 percent met in gaming sites; and 6 percent met in some other way. Most were relationships with someone of the opposite sex. Undoubtedly, the number of young people who establish relationships online has increased since this survey was conducted. Survey results published in 2001, based on the responses of 191 students at one southeastern U.S. college, revealed that almost 60 percent met someone new online, and 25 percent of those developed into friendships; 7 percent of respondents became emotionally involved, 16 percent met face-to-face, and 2 percent ended up living together.[35] If you haven't already formed an online relationship, the chances are that you will in the future. How should you act? What skills do you need to successfully manage online relationships? In general, the same principles and skills you read about in the last three chapters apply to the Internet. For example, similar strategies are used in the opening and closing of FtF and computer-mediated interactions.[36] However, there are some unique issues you should understand as you enter the world of CMC relationships.

### Choose the Right Chat Room
One way we normally make friends is by engaging in activities that allow us to meet people with similar interests. You probably have made friends with people who are members of your church, softball team, or math class. An attraction to those who share similar interests can be the basis for starting Internet relationships. Finding people with similar interests on the Internet is relatively easy, because chat rooms are

# Building Your Skills

## Some Hypotheses About How Text Influences Internet Relationships

The following are some hypotheses about how online text relationships work and their pros and cons, taken from a list created by Professor John Suler of Rider University. As you read the list, decide whether you think each hypothesis is valid, and think about how your own experiences might support or challenge its validity. After you read the list, generate your own hypotheses about how text affects interpersonal interactions and the development of relationships over the Internet.

1. Text talk is a sophisticated, expressive art form. People vary greatly in their ability to express themselves via text. While it can be learned, some people are naturally good at it.

2. Some people are more sensitive in detecting the meaning and mood expressed "between the lines" of text communication. There is a special type of interpersonal empathy that is unique to text relationships.

3. Humor, and especially sarcasm, is difficult to express in text relationships.

4. Receiving no reply in a text relationship tends to result in projections as to why the person did not reply.

5. A person's ambivalence about intimacy may be expressed in text communication, which is a paradoxical blend of allowing people to be honest and to feel close, while also maintaining their distance.

6. People who are very verbal and expressive offline may not be in an online relationship, and vice versa.

7. People who lack FtF verbal skills may prefer text relationships.

8. Lacking FtF cues, text communication disinhibits people, encouraging them to be more open and honest than usual, or encouraging them to act out inappropriately.

9. The lack of touch and body contact can significantly reduce the experience of intimacy in text relationships.

10. The ability to delay responding in e-mail and message boards can enhance self-control, self-reflection, and the assimilation of experiences in the relationship.

11. During emotional points in an asynchronous text relationship, people sometimes respond immediately without taking advantage of the time delay.

12. The easy and continuous opportunity to send a message to the other person can create a comforting feeling that the connection to that person is "always there" or even that the other is "always present." Feelings of separation may be eased.

13. In an ongoing text relationship, the people involved develop their own private "language" of abbreviations, symbols, and phrasings.

14. A person's writing style and message format reflects his or her personality. Changes in style and format reflect changes in mood and thinking.

15. Despite conscious attempts to present oneself exactly as one wishes, hidden elements of one's personality unconsciously surface in text communication.

16. As a way to avoid "saying their goodbyes," online relationships and groups may tend to "fizzle out" by people gradually sending fewer and fewer messages.

*Source:* Suler, J. (2002). "Hypotheses about Online Text Relationships." In *The Psychology of Cyberspace,* www.rider.edu/suler/psycyber/basicfeat.html (article originally published 1996).

often organized according to topics and interest groups. There are chat rooms or discussion groups for almost every sport, activity, and interest that you can imagine—and if there isn't one, you can create your own. There are also general social chat rooms that are very unstructured, where unfortunately the main goal of some of the male participants is to hit on the females. Women who enter such rooms should realize that they are likely to be exposed to indelicate and suggestive messages.

### Accept the Slower Pace of Relational Development

As mentioned earlier, the development of impressions is slower with CMC than FtF interactions. This means that the process of forming interpersonal relationships is also likely to be slower. The major reason for this difference is that almost all information on the Internet must be put into text, whereas FtF interactions use a variety of nonverbal channels. Early researchers doubted that true interpersonal relationships could be formed online, but subsequent research has found that the kind of effects that occur quickly in FtF interactions also occur on the Internet—they just require more time.[37] CMC users can self-disclose honestly and openly with each other, to the point of forming truly intimate relationships. One advantage of the text-only medium is a reduction in our perceptual biases about a person's physical attractiveness.[38] At some point in Internet relationships, the users usually provide a physical description of themselves (people seem to want to know the other person's sex, age, and location at the very beginning); eventually they may exchange photographs and even arrange to meet in person.

### Apply Strong Verbal Skills

Sending someone a hug and a kiss over the Internet does not provide the same kind of satisfaction as it does in person. Among the conversational skills used in FtF interactions are verbal and nonverbal expressiveness (including being articulate), listening and nonverbal sensitivity, humor, effective question asking, and responsiveness. These skills have their parallels in CMC, but for the most part are dependent on the ability to express yourself in writing. The reliance on verbal strategies is demonstrated by a study that found that e-mail pen pals apparently compensated for the lack of nonverbal feedback by increasing the use of personal questions.[39] Thus, good question-asking skills are advantageous on the Internet.

The most skilled Internet communicators know CMC shorthand, incorporate emoticons and other devices to enhance their text, and adapt to their partners. As a listener/respondent, you can't use eye contact, head nodding, and "uh-huhs" to let the person know you are attentive and interested. You must write responses that show you are listening. This reflects another advantage of the Internet over FtF interactions— you have a record of what was sent by your partner. So instead of not hearing what he or she said because your mind was wandering, you can simply review what was written if your concentration faltered during a chat session. It's a good idea to hang on to e-mail so you can look through previous correspondence if you are afraid you have forgotten some information your partner shared.

## Using Computer-Mediated Communication to Maintain Existing Relationships

A recent study found that the major use of home e-mail was for relationship maintenance.[40] This included using e-mail as a way to keep in touch with family and friends. E-mail is simple, quick, cheap, convenient, efficient, and provides a sense of interaction. For ongoing relationships, e-mail provides a kind of freedom from time zone and schedule conflicts, allowing users to send messages at their convenience. Survey respondents reported that e-mail made it easier to share ideas, express opinions, and provide information with friends and family all over the world.[41] As of May 2002, the Internet provider America Online handled 390 million e-mails and 3.1 billion instant messages daily. Multiply this by the number of providers and add the growth that is occurring, and you get a glimpse of how important this medium is to interpersonal relationship maintenance. We use e-mail, instant messaging, chat rooms, and discussion groups as a way of interacting with our friends and family. The expansion of CMC has begun to produce a virtual community, **computer-supported social networks (CSSN)**.[42] The development of social networks is enhanced by the ability of users to create buddy lists. These lists result in personal networks of friends with whom you can exchange group-addressed e-mails or create group chat sessions.

### Communicate!

The very act of sending regular e-mails or engaging in chat sessions is probably the primary way the Internet helps maintain relationships. Maintaining an active line of communication with people is one of the best ways to preserve the relationship. Interest in the other person and commitment to the relationship is reflected in the very act of communicating. However, the amount of communication that is needed is defined by the people in the relationship. You might have one friend whom you e-mail daily and another whom you e-mail two or three times a year. Are these relationships different? Is one less intimate than the other? The answers are not really cut and dried. You might feel as close to both people, but the daily interactions create a sense of interdependence that is probably not found in the other relationship. Daily interactions mean you are both informed about each other's activities and probably providing daily support and confirmation.

Increases or decreases in how much you communicate with someone provide one way to signal your level of interest and commitment to the relationship. You establish expectations about how often you e-mail a particular person, and deviations from those expectations signal a potential change in the relationship. A change in the amount of communication represents a turning point in the relationship's development (as discussed in Chapter 10). You might become concerned about the status of a relationship if you have exchanged daily e-mails with a friend and then notice that he or she only responds every couple of days. This might prompt you to engage in a direct strategy and inquire about the status of the person and the relationship.

The Internet might actually result in increased communication among friends and lovers who are separated by distance. Information technologist Patricia Wallace speculates that the ease with which people can send each other e-mail greeting cards results in increased communication.[43] People are creative in the way they use the Internet to make contact and interact. One of the authors' sons still manages to play games over the Internet with a school friend who has moved away. Wallace tells a story in her book, *The Psychology of the Internet,* of one couple who use the Internet to keep in contact when the husband is away on business trips and who link up with other people to play bridge online.[44]

### Use Relational Maintenance Strategies

Keeping in contact with someone is one way to maintain the relationship and show your interest. You can also use a variety of the other strategies discussed in Chapter 10. In your e-mails you should appropriately disclose information about yourself. Remember that self-disclosure is related to relational development. Don't disclose too much if you are not interested in escalating the relationship; however, not disclosing anything might create stagnation and de-escalation.

Some of your disclosures might include sharing your emotions. Having limited nonverbal cues means that your partner depends on your verbalizing your feelings. You can describe the feelings you have about events in your life and you can also express your feelings toward your partner.

Engaging in relational talk is another way to maintain your relationships over the Internet. Relationship talk and expressing feelings are fruitful when done within the

**computer-supported social network (CSSN).** A virtual community created by networking among individuals through CMC.

norms appropriate to the relational stage. The Internet can seduce you into being too open about your feelings and thoughts about your relationships, as compared to face-to-face discussions. Just as you need to show restraint in face-to-face disclosures, you need to do the same in CMC.

Dependence on verbal messages means that you need to monitor your perceptions to ensure that you have accurately interpreted your partner's messages. Asking for clarification, expressing misunderstanding, or paraphrasing what you think your partner means are good ways to enhance the accuracy of messages. Such strategies help maintain relationships because they reduce the impact of conflicts and stress associated with misunderstanding. Apply the principles of listening discussed in Chapter 5 to your behavior during online relational interactions. Empathic listening on the Internet involves writing to let your partners know that you are sensitive to and understand their feelings. You can write messages that show you are involved and engaged in the discussion of their situation. The use of confirming responses that show you understand their feelings will help maintain a positive relationship.

### Be Other-Oriented and Adapt

The way you write to your partner depends on your relationship and what you know about your partner. Throughout this text we have emphasized trying to look at interactions from your partner's perspective—to socially decenter and to empathize. This principle is no less applicable to the maintenance of Internet relationships. As you acquire more and more knowledge about your partner through both your FtF and CMC interactions, apply that knowledge by adapting your communication. If anything, CMC provides you more time to take into consideration what you know about another person and create appropriate messages.

### Using CMC to Initiate and Maintain Relationships

#### Initiating Relationships

| | |
|---|---|
| ● Choose the right chat room. | Interact in places where you are likely to find other people who share your interests. |
| ● Accept the slower pace of relational development. | The process of forming trust and getting to know another person online will probably be slower than in FtF relationships. |
| ● Apply strong verbal skills. | CMC favors those who have the ability to express themselves well in a written and graphic mode. |

#### Maintaining Relationships

| | |
|---|---|
| ● Communicate. | The very act of regularly sending messages to another person is one way to help maintain the relationship. |
| ● Use relational maintenance strategies. | Appropriate self-disclosing, sharing feelings, and engaging in relationship talk are among the strategies that can be used. |
| ● Be other-oriented and adapt. | Use the knowledge you gain about other people through CMC to adapt your communication. |

# Interpersonal Relationships at Work

Organizations look for employees who can relate effectively to other people—bosses, subordinates, peers, and clients. All the skills you have been studying throughout this text can improve your effectiveness in organizational relationships.

Your interactions in the workplace typically vary according to their degree of task versus social orientation. This variation is the source of both personal satisfaction and conflict. After you graduate, the workplace becomes a major source for developing interpersonal relationships. You make friends with the people with whom you work. You will socialize both on and off the job with various people from the organization. Conflicts arise when job-related decisions affect personal relationships, and vice versa. As a manager, you might become friends with some of your subordinates, but if the work performance of one of those subordinates falls below a satisfactory level, the friendship could interfere with your ability to address that problem. Many companies used to have policies prohibiting socializing among employees; however, such policies created strong dissatisfaction and discontent. Organizational policies that nurture relationships among employees build camaraderie and a supportive work atmosphere.[45]

## Workplace Friendships

Friendships at work are like any other relationships in terms of their dimensions and development. One study, in which coworkers were extensively interviewed, identified three distinct transitions: acquaintance to friend, friend to close friend, and close friend to "almost best" friend.[46] Interestingly, the researchers found respondents hesitant to refer to a coworker as "best" friend, opting instead for "best friend at work" or "very close." The initial development of workplace friendships occurred for a variety of reasons, such as proximity, sharing tasks, sharing a similar life event, or perceiving similar interests.[47] As the relationships developed, the changes identified in this study were similar to those typically found in any developing friendship—easier and more flexible communication, increased self-disclosing, more frequent interactions, more socializing, and increased discussion of both work problems and nonwork topics.[48]

Workplace friendships might be limited to a particular context: perhaps you have a lunch buddy, or you develop a friendship with someone working on a shared project, in which case the relationship ends when the project is completed. Outside of the workplace, friendships often find us associating with other people who are similar in age, status, and the like; however, workplace friendships often involve people who differ in age or status.[49] For example, you may find yourself becoming friends with a supervisor or subordinate who is considerably older or younger than you. Having a friend who is of the opposite sex may be more likely at work than it is outside of work, where such relationships might be expected to become romantic or might threaten existing intimate relationships. Results of a recent study indicated that men felt that socializing outside of the workplace was more important to their friendships with male coworkers than to friendships with female coworkers.[50]

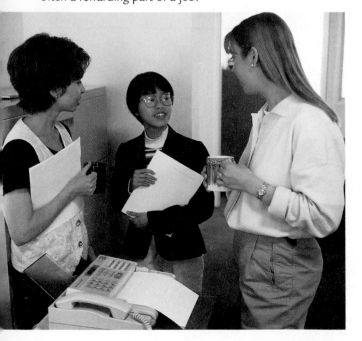

Interpersonal communication skills help in interactions with coworkers. Developing satisfying interpersonal relationships in an organization is often a rewarding part of a job.

In addition, as their workplace relationships became more intimate, same-sex friends continued and expanded their relationships outside of the workplace; however, cross-sex relationships continued to be defined specifically as "workplace friendships." Workplace friendships enhance an organization's communication network by increasing the flow and openness of information. Just as outside friendships provide us with support and resources, so do workplace friendships. Workplace friends are in a position to understand and appreciate our organizational complaints and related frustrations. Friends help friends, and in an organization that can mean lending a hand, providing information, being an ally, or providing material support.

## Workplace Romances

The workplace actually provides an opportune arena for the development of intimate relationships because of the convenience and exposure to a wide pool of potential partners. Many people find their future spouses in the workplace. In a recent survey of managers and executives, 13 percent reported meeting their future spouses at work.[51] Some companies even hire married couples because they see a value in having both partners working for the same company. On the other hand, some companies have policies prohibiting dating a coworker—but how can a policy prevent people from becoming attracted? In the workplace you interact with people in a safe and defined context that affords the opportunity to learn about others and share information about yourself. Trust evolves, similarities are discovered, attraction develops, and the interactions move toward more intimacy. In general, dating in the workplace is not particularly problematic when those involved work in different units or when there are no direct job-related power issues. Dating among members of the same unit can be a problem if it interferes with the ability of the individuals to perform their jobs. If you are involved in such a situation, your interactions with your partner at work need to remain professional. Coworkers sometimes are uncomfortable around romantic partners and may worry about inappropriate sharing of information, unequal work distribution, or other potential problems.

The most significant problems in workplace romances occur when the relationship is between a boss and his or her employee. The employee might feel coerced into the romantic relationship, which constitutes sexual harassment. Even if the superior does not threaten or show favoritism to the subordinate, the subordinate could believe that rejecting the superior's advances would be professionally detrimental. This type of sexual harassment is usually referred to as **quid pro quo,** a Latin phrase that basically means "You do something for me and I'll do something for you." A supervisor who says or implies, "Have sex with me or your job will be in jeopardy" or "If you want this promotion you should have sex with me," is obviously using his or her power as a boss to gain sexual favors in exchange for something the employee wants. To avoid these situations, organizations often develop extensive policies about these types of relationships. You should learn the policies of any organization that employs you and assert your rights if you find yourself being sexually harassed.

## Upward Communication:
## Talking with Your Boss

"Please place your suggestions in the suggestion box," announces the boss. The suggestion box is the symbol for upward communication. **Upward communication** involves the flow of communication from subordinates up to superiors. Although today's organizational emphasis on quality encourages communication from lower

**quid pro quo.** Latin phrase that can be used to describe a type of sexual harassment. The phrase roughly means "You do something for me and I'll do something for you."

**upward communication.** Communication that flows from subordinates to superiors.

$\mathcal{W}$orkplace satisfaction is related to the quality of the communication between boss and employees.

levels to higher levels, effective upward communication is still far from the norm. Many employees fear that their candid comments will not be well received. Others may wonder, "Why bother?" If managers offer no incentive for sharing information up the line, it is unlikely that their subordinates will make the effort. In 1952, an organizational researcher discovered that subordinates were more satisfied in their jobs when they felt their immediate supervisor had influence on decisions made at higher levels.[52] This is called the Pelz effect, after its discoverer, Donald Pelz. Subsequent research by organizational communication scholar Fred Japlin found when subordinates perceived their supervisors as supportive, the Pelz effect was particularly strong in creating a sense of openness and satisfaction.[53]

If there is little upward communication, the organization may be in a precarious situation. Those lower down in the organization are often the ones who make contact with the customer, make the product, or work most closely with the development and delivery of the product or service; they hear feedback about the product's virtues and problems. If supervisors remain unaware of these problems, productivity or quality may suffer. In addition, if employees have no opportunities to share problems and complaints with their boss, their frustration level may be dangerously high. Upward communication helps managers to deal quickly with problems and to hear suggestions for improving processes and procedures. One pair of researchers suggests that subordinates can "manage up" by being sensitive to the needs of supervisors.[54] If you know what your boss's most important goals are, along with his or her strengths, weaknesses, and preferred working style, you will be in a good position to establish a more meaningful relationship that will benefit both of you.

If you are a manager yourself, encourage your subordinates to share both good news and bad. Be visible and cultivate their trust by developing a system that elicits feedback and comments. Use a suggestion box (paper or electronic), informal discussions, or more formal meetings and presentations. Making time for these exchanges will pay off in the long run.

### Downward Communication:
### Talking with Your Subordinates

The owner of the local movie theater tells the manager that she plans on changing the theater format to specialize in international and independent films. During a weekly meeting, the manager tells the shift supervisors of the impending change. Your supervisor then tells you and the rest of the crew working Friday nights about the new format. This sequence of interactions represents **downward communication,** the flow of information from those higher up in an organization to those of lower rank. It can happen via memo, phone call, newsletter, poster, or e-mail or, of course, face-to-face. Most downward communication consists of instruction about how to do a job, rationales for doing things, statements about organizational policies and procedures, feedback about job performance, and information that helps develop the mission or vision of the organization.[55]

What is the best way to communicate with employees—in writing or face to face? It depends on the situation. Often it's best to communicate orally, with a written follow-up. If you need immediate employee action, face-to-face communication followed by a written reminder is the most effective (sending only a written memo is the least effective).[56] On the other hand, if you are communicating about long-term actions, a written message is the most effective. Certain situations, such as reprimanding an employee or settling a dispute, are best handled in face-to-face interactions rather than through the use of any written messages.[57] The best managers take care to develop and send ethical, other-oriented messages. Then they follow up to ensure that the receiver understood the message and that it achieved its intended effect. Managers need to be especially other-oriented when they are sharing sensitive information or broaching personal topics.

As mentioned earlier, behaviors by supervisors that involve using power against subordinates for sexual favors constitute sexual harassment. However, supervisors also have a responsibility to eliminate a second type of sexual harassment that represents another dark side of interpersonal communication: a hostile environment. An employee in a **hostile environment** feels his or her rights are being violated because of working conditions or offensive behavior on the part of other workers. Telling lewd or obscene stories or jokes about members of the opposite sex, using degrading terms to describe women or men, or displaying risqué photographs of nude or seminude people can contribute to a hostile working environment. A supervisor who either creates or fails to change work situations that are threatening to a subordinate is a party to sexual harassment. Jokes are not innocent and pictures are not "all in fun" if they make an employee feel degraded. Supervisors must adopt an other-oriented approach with respect to this issue; it is the receiver, not the sender, of the message who determines whether the behavior is hostile. Court cases have been won by defendants who were able to prove that a supervisor tolerated a hostile work environment, even if the supervisor did not directly participate in the offensive behavior. Wise supervisors do not wait for a problem to occur. They take a proactive approach, offering all workers seminars on how to avoid engaging in sexually offensive behavior and explicitly discussing what workers should do if they become the victims of sexual harassment.

## Horizontal Communication:
## Talking with Your Colleagues

You poke your head into your coworker's office and say, "Did you hear about the possible merger between Byteware and Datamass?" Or while you are tossing pizza dough at the Pizza Palace, one of your fellow workers asks how much pepperoni to put on a Super Duper Supreme. Both situations illustrate horizontal communication. **Horizontal communication** refers to communication among coworkers at the same level within an organization. In larger organizations you may talk with other workers in different departments or divisions who perform similar jobs at a similar level; that, too,

**downward communication.** Communication that flows from superiors to subordinates.

**hostile environment.** Type of sexual harassment in which an employee's rights are threatened through offensive working conditions or behavior on the part of other workers.

**horizontal communication.** Communication among colleagues or coworkers at the same level within an organization.

# *Understanding Diversity*

## An Office-Speak Primer

"*Dysfunctional communication*" typically occurs when men minimize legitimate concerns expressed by women, according to management and organization expert Kathleen Reardon. But women contribute to this pattern with behavior that makes them vulnerable, she contends in her book *They Don't Get It, Do They?*

Consider the following approach taken by Janet, a 40-year-old manager for a food products company, who has learned of an informal meeting that took place without her. She was the only committee member not told about the meeting, where important decisions were made.

*Janet:* I felt left out of the planning of this project, Fred. The meeting was held without my knowledge.

*Fred:* Now Janet, let's not make this a personal thing. Frank, Bill, and I happened to run into each other, so we got some work done.

*Janet:* But I am on the planning team. You could have run it by me.

*Fred:* You shouldn't waste your energy on this, Janet. It's nothing. Don't feel bad.

*Janet:* It's happened several times.

*Fred:* Getting a little paranoid, aren't we?

*Janet:* I just want to be kept informed.

*Fred:* OK, Janet. OK. It's no big deal.

Janet erred, according to Reardon, by focusing on her own emotional state rather than the infraction of her colleagues. Reardon contends Janet would have been better off asking herself two questions:

1. What is the problem?

2. What do I want?

By stating the answers to these questions in a simple and direct way, Janet would have been more forceful and received more respect, Reardon said. She believes the following would have been the best approach:

*Janet:* Fred, no more meetings without me.

If Fred tries to defend his position or suggest she is paranoid, Janet should stop him.

*Janet:* None of that is relevant, Fred. No personal attacks intended or necessary. I'm on the team. I should be at the meetings. It's simple.

*Source:* Meg Sullivan, *University of Southern California Chronicle,* April 17, 1995, vol. 14, no. 28.

---

is horizontal communication. Most often you communicate with your colleagues to coordinate job tasks, share plans and information, solve problems, make sure you understand job procedures, manage conflict, or get a bit of emotional support on the job.[58]

Information travels through a workplace the way gossip travels through "the grapevine." And sometimes errors creep into workplace information that is spread this way. Although grapevine errors can cause problems for an organization, most continue to encourage coworker communication because it enhances teamwork and allows the work group to develop a certain degree of independence. Some organizations even try to formalize horizontal communication by forming *quality circles,* or groups of employees who meet together on a regular basis. These groups usually talk about such issues as how to improve the quality of services or products, reduce mistakes, lower costs, improve safety, or develop better ways of working together. This active participation in the work process encourages workers to do a better job. Moreover, the training they receive to participate in these groups—in group problem solving, decision-making skills, listening, relating, speaking, and managing conflict—applies to other areas of their work as well.

## Outward Communication:
## Talking with Your Customers

"Attention, K-Mart shoppers: Submarine sandwiches are now a blue-light special, on sale for one dollar each for the next fifteen minutes." This is one kind of communication with customers. But in addition to pitching to their customers, today's organizations are also asking customers what they think about the quality of the goods and services the organization produces. Increasingly, successful organizations are those that are other-oriented; they focus on the needs of those they serve through **outward communication.** They are spending time and money to find out what the *customer* perceives as quality, rather than relying solely on the judgments of their corporate executives. And they are training their staffs to develop more empathy, better listening skills, and more awareness of nonverbal messages from customers.

**outward communication.** Communication that flows to those outside an organization (such as customers).

## Becoming Other-Oriented

### At Home, Online, and at Work

*T*hroughout this text we have advocated taking an other-oriented approach to interpersonal communication. There are times when taking an other-oriented perspective or being empathic could be disadvantageous, if you ignore your own needs, values, or priorities. Look at the following situations and consider how being other-centered might be counterproductive or lead to poor decisions. How can you be other-centered and still make good decisions in each situation?

- You receive a call from the middle school principle that your seventh-grade son is being suspended for two days for fighting with another student. Because you are other-centered, you understand the following about your son: He is very self-conscious about being overweight, and the other kids make fun of him for it. He has been struggling with his studies because he has a hard time concentrating and reading material. He has low self-esteem and does not feel that other kids like him.

- You have developed an online friendship with someone of the opposite sex whom you have never met. You have been exchanging e-mails and instant messaging for over a year and have become very close. You are considering flying out to meet this person. Based on information presented by your friend and your own impressions, you have concluded the following: Your cyberpal is very lonely; is an only child whose parents divorced when he or she was ten; was laid off from work two weeks ago; places a lot of importance on the relationship with you; depends on you for self-confirmation; has lots of self-doubt and appreciates your support and kind words.

- You are a manager and one of your subordinates is increasingly late to work, misses deadlines and appointments, and is turning in poor work. Taking an other-centered approach, you come to realize this employee is facing a divorce, has a child who was recently arrested, and is suffering from panic attacks.

# *S*ummary

Interpersonal interactions occur in a variety of contexts. Communication principles and skills can be applied to interpersonal relationships at home, on the Internet, and at work.

A family unit is made up of any number of people who live in relationship with one another over time in a common living space and are usually, but not always, united by marriage and kinship. One model for describing families considers family cohesion and adaptability and the role of communication in affecting family members' roles and relationships. The term *cohesion* refers to the emotional bonding and the feeling of closeness that families experience. The term *family adaptability* refers to the flexibility of family members in responding to changes in family roles, rules, and relationships.

There is no one best way to be a family. However, several skills and strategies can enhance the quality of family life: Take time to talk with other family members about relationship issues; listen to others; support and encourage one another; use productive strategies for managing conflict and stress.

A new context for interpersonal relationships is cyberspace, or the Internet. You can initiate and develop new relationships totally through computer-mediated communication (CMC) or you can use the Internet as a tool for maintaining existing relationships. CMC includes bulletin boards, e-mail, chat rooms (IRC—Internet relay chat), and instant messaging. Compared to face-to-face (FtF) communication, CMC offers fewer nonverbal cues, requires more reliance on the written word, can be either synchronous or asynchronous, and allows posters to be deceptive or even to simply disappear.

In initiating new relationships over the Internet, you need to participate in the right kind of a chat room, generally one that reflects your interests. Follow the same rules in developing a new relationship over the Internet as you would in person, realizing that the process is generally slower through CMC. People with strong verbal skills have an advantage in using the Internet for initiating and developing interpersonal relationships. Information that would be transmitted in other ways in FtF interactions must be put into written form for Internet interactions. The very act of keeping up with communication through the Internet helps maintain existing relationships. The amount of CMC and changes in the amount provide some indication of a person's interest in and commitment to the relationship. CMC can be used as a tool for implementing the various relational maintenance strategies discussed in Chapter 10. Being other-centered in your cyberinteractions will help you adapt your messages and responses to maintain your interpersonal relationships most effectively.

Relationships at work can involve both a task and a social dimension. Forming friendships at work is one way people meet social needs and often helps produce a positive work atmosphere. The challenge of workplace interpersonal relationships is maximizing the satisfaction derived from such relationships while minimizing any negative impact on work performance. Relationships are often defined by the organization, especially in terms of power.

In most organizations, communication flows up, down, horizontally, and out to customers. Through upward communication you can share ideas and strategies for improving the work process; you can also enhance your relationship with your boss. Downward communication involves making contact with those who work for you. Decide whether you will send messages in writing, in person, or through mediated channels. Horizontal communication concerns the communication you have with your colleagues on your level throughout the organization; most of the time, however, horizontal communication occurs with those who work in your immediate vicinity. Most organizations are encouraging better communication with customers and clients. Contacting those outside the organization who receive the organization's goods and services is an important way to ensure that what the organization offers is of high quality.

# For Discussion and Review

## Focus on Critical Thinking

1. Do you think the institution of the family is deteriorating, or is it just changing? Support your answer.

2. Despite the availability of relatively cheap interactive web cams for Internet use, people don't seem to be turning to them as much as they are to text-only interactions. Why might this be the case? Which would you use if you had a choice of the two? Why?

3. Jerry is president of Southwest Technical Computing. He has a sense that his managers are not tapping the wealth of ideas and suggestions that lower-level employees might have for improving productivity. What specific strategies could Jerry implement to improve upward communication?

## Focus on Ethics

4. Is it ethical to withhold honest thoughts and feelings from other family members? Should family members always "tell it like it is"? Should parents encourage their children to "tell everything" they know and feel?

5. In chat sessions on the Internet, is it really wrong to present false information about yourself just for fun when you know you will never meet the other people with whom you are interacting? Under what circumstances is presenting yourself over the Internet as someone of a different sex, age, race, or ethnicity ethical? When is it unethical?

6. Clayton has e-mail service at work, but not at home. His brother has e-mail service at his home. Is it ethical for Clayton to use the computer at work on company time to send and receive e-mail messages from his brother three or four times a week?

# For Your Journal

1. Select two TV situation comedies or dramas that revolve around a family. One program could be one that is still broadcast in reruns, such as *Leave It to Beaver, All in the Family,* or *The Brady Bunch,* and the other show could be a more contemporary program. Describe the communication patterns in the TV programs that you observe. Draw on the principles and skills presented in this chapter as you describe the family communication patterns. Discuss which of your TV families seems to do the most effective job of communicating with one another.

2. Log on to a social chat room and then onto a topic-specific chat room. You don't have to post any messages; just be a "lurker" and watch what happens. What do people do to compensate for the lack of nonverbal cues? What do you notice about the messages themselves (for example, how long are they, what is the vocabulary like, how is the grammar, what jargon or slang is used)? How do the two sites compare in terms of language? Focus on a couple of the posters on each site. What is your impression of these posters on the basis of what you observe?

3. Consider an organization in which you are or were an employee. What was your communication like with your boss? How open was your boss in sharing information with you (downward communication)? How open was your boss to communication from you (upward communication)? How did this flow of information with your boss affect your job satisfaction? How did it affect your job performance? How open was communication with your peers? What kinds of information did you and your peers discuss? How did your communication with your peers affect your satisfaction and performance?

# Learning with Others

Indicate whether you agree or disagree with the following statements. Then break into small groups and try to get group members to agree or disagree unanimously with each statement. Try to find reasons for differences of opinion. If your group cannot reach agreement or disagreement, you may change the wording in any statement to promote unanimity.

## Agree–Disagree Statements About Families

_____ 1. Most family members know how to communicate effectively; they just don't take the time to practice what they know.

_____ 2. Family conflict is a symptom rather than a cause of deteriorating family relationships.

_____ 3. Family conflict is harmful to family harmony, and all conflict should be avoided at all costs.

_____ 4. Most family conflict occurs because we don't understand the other family member; we fail to communicate effectively.

_____ 5. Families function best if there is one central leader of the family.

_____ 6. Ineffective communication is the single most important cause of family conflict, divorce, and family tension.

_____ 7. Nonverbal communication (facial expression, eye contact, tone of voice, posture, and so on) is more important than verbal communication; what you do is more important than what you say.

_____ 8. It is sometimes necessary to ignore the feelings of others in order to reach a family decision.

_____ 9. The best way to love your marriage partner is to care more for your partner than you care for yourself.

_____ 10. Generally speaking, the quality of family life is deteriorating today.

_____ 11. There is one best approach or set of rules and principles that will ensure an effectively functioning family.

## Internet Study Group

Find three or four other students in your class with whom you feel comfortable and confident. Arrange times when you can all log on to the Internet to do instant messaging, send e-mails copied to all the other group members, or create a chat room for your group. Share information with one another about assignments, examinations, or papers for this class. Discuss among yourselves through the Internet what is expected for the assignments, share any information each of you has that might help the others prepare better, and ask questions to help clarify information. If you are preparing for an exam, each of you might pose practice questions to the others, or each take a turn explaining some concept.

## Workplace Interviews

Divide into teams of two or three people. Each team will interview a businessperson or supervisor in a nonprofit organization such as a hospital or school about the workplace issues covered in this chapter. Ask such questions as

- What do you do to enhance upward communication among the people you supervise?

- How do your interpersonal relationships with coworkers affect your job?

Afterward, discuss your results with other groups and see what general conclusions you can reach.

http://www.emode.com/tests/tvfamily/ Although it requires you to register before you can access it, this site has a large number of fun quizzes, including one that tells you what TV family most resembles your own.

http://www.pewinternet.org/reports/toc.asp?Report=47 Pew Report on the Internet, Community, and Long-Distance Relationships

http://www.rider.edu/~suler/psycyber/psycyber.html This site is maintained by a professor at Rider University and has a number of interesting articles on cyber-relationships.

http://editorial.careers.msn.com/worklife/workplace_issues/ This site offers a variety of work-related articles and suggestions, covering issues like workplace friendships, office romance, and sexual harassment.

http://www.workrelationships.com/site/quiz/ This quiz should help you to understand behaviors that can create a hostile work environment or that are sexually harassing.

# Notes

## Chapter 1

1. E. T. Klemmer and F. W. Snyder, "Measurement of Time Spent Communicating." *Journal of Communication,* 20 (June 1972): 142.

2. E. E. Graham and C. K. Shue, "Reflections on the Past, Directions for the Future: A Template for the Study and Instruction of Interpersonal Communication," *Communication Research Reports,* 17 (Fall 2000): 337–48.

3. F. E. X. Dance and C. Larson, *Speech Communication: Concepts and Behavior* (New York: Holt, Rinehart and Winston, 1972).

4. Dance and Larson, *Speech Communication.*

5. For an excellent overview of interpersonal communication research, see M. E. Roloff and L. Anastasiou, "Interpersonal Communication Research," in *Communication Yearbook 24* (Mahwah, NJ: Erlbaum, 2000), 51–71.

6. J. T. Masterson, S. A. Beebe, N. H. Watson, *Invitation to Effective Speech Communication* (Glenview, IL: Scott, Foresman, 1989).

7. L. M. Webb and M. E. Thompson-Hayes, "Do Popular Collegiate Textbooks in Interpersonal Communication Reflect a Common Theory Base? A Telling Content Analysis," *Communication Education,* 51 (April 2002): 210–24.

8. M. Buber, *I and Thou* (New York: Scribners, 1958); Also see M. Buber, *Between Man and Man* (New York: Macmillan, 1965). For a detailed discussion of perspectives on interpersonal communication and relationship development, see G. H. Stamp, "A Qualitatively Constructed Interpersonal Communication Model: A Grounded Theory Analysis," *Human Communication Research,* 25, (June 1999): 531–47; J. P. Dillard, D. H. Solomon, and M. T. Palmer, "Structuring the Concept of Relational Communication," *Communication Monographs,* 66 (March 1999): 49–65.

9. Buber, *I and Thou.*

10. D. Yankelovich, *The Magic of Dialogue: Transforming Conflict into Cooperation* (New York: Simon & Schuster, 1999); for an excellent discussion of dialogue, also see S. W. Littlejohn and K. Domenici, *Engaging Communication in Conflict: Systemic Practice* (Thousand Oaks, CA: Sage, 2001), 25–51.

11. Buber, *I and Thou.*

12. V. Satir, *Peoplemaking* (Palo Alto, CA: Science and Behavior Books, 1972); J. B. Miller and P. A. deWinstanley, "The Role of Interpersonal Competence in Memory for Conversation," *Personality and Social Psychology Bulletin,* 28 (January 2002): 78–89.

13. K. E. Davis and M. Todd, "Assessing Friendship: Prototypes, Paradigm Cases, and Relationship Description," in *Understanding Personal Relationships,* edited by S. W. Duck and D. Perlman (London: Sage, 1985); B. Wellman, "From Social Support to Social Network," in *Social Support. Theory, Research and Applications,* edited by I. G. Sarason and B. R. Sarason (Dordrecht, Netherlands: Nijhoff, 1985); R. Hopper, M. L. Knapp, and L. Scott, "Couples' Personal Idioms: Exploring Intimate Talk," *Journal of Communication,* 31 (1981): 23–33; S. Pendell, "Affection in Interpersonal Relationships: Not Just 'A Fond or Tender Feeling,'" in *Communication Yearbook 26,* edited by W. B. Gudykunst (Mahwah, NJ: Erlbaum, 2002): 71–115.

14. M. Argyle and M. Hendershot, *The Anatomy of Relationships* (London: Penguin Books, 1985), 14.

15. See J. L. Winsor, D. B. Curtis, and R. D. Stephens, "National Preferences in Business and Communication Education: A Survey Update," *Journal of the Association for Communication Administration,* 3 (September 1997), 174; *The Wall Street Journal,* September, 9, 2002: 1A.

16. M. Argyle, *The Psychology of Happiness* (London: Routledge, 1987).

17. J. J. Lynch, *The Broken Heart: The Medical Consequences of Loneliness* (New York: Basic Books, 1977).

18. R. Korbin and G. Hendershot, "Do Family Ties Reduce Mortality: Evidence from the United States 1968," *Journal of Marriage and the Family,* 39 (1977): 737–45.

19. D. P. Phillips, "Deathday and Birthday: An Unexpected Connection," in *Statistics: A Guide to the Unknown,* edited by J. M. Tanur (San Francisco: Holden Day, 1972).

20. M. Argyle, *The Psychology of Happiness* (London: Routledge, 2001).

21. For a comprehensive overview of the history of the study of interpersonal communication, see M. L. Knapp, J. A. Daly, K. F. Albada, and G. R. Miller, "Background and Current Trends in the Study of Interpersonal Communication," in *Handbook of Interpersonal Communication,* edited by M. L. Knapp and J. A. Daly (Thousand Oaks, CA: Sage, 2002), 3–20.

22. Among the first scholars to identify a link between the sender of a message and message context was Kurt Lewin in K. Lewin, *A Dynamic Theory of Personality* (New York: McGraw-Hill, 1935).

23. See V. E. Cronen, W. B. Pearce, and L. M. Harris, "The Coordinated Management of Meaning: A Theory of Communication," in *Human Communication Theory: Comparative Essays,* edited by F. E. X. Dance (New York: Harper & Row, 1982), 61–89.

24. L. C. Tidwell and J. B. Walther, "Computer-Mediated Communication Effects on Disclosure, Impressions, and Interpersonal Evaluations: Getting to Know One Another a Bit at a Time," *Human Communication Research,* 28 (July 2002): 317–48.

25. A. Harmon, "Online Dating Sheds Its Stigma at Losers.com," *The New York Times,* June 29, 2003, p. 1.

26. For an excellent discussion of the effects of computer-mediated communication and interpersonal communication, see J. B. Walther, "Interpersonal Effects in Computer-Mediated Interaction: A Relational Perspective," *Communication Research,* 19 (1992): 52–90; J. B. Walther, "Relational Aspects of Computer-Mediated Communication:

Experimental and Longitudinal Observations," *Organization Science,* 6 (1995): 186–203; J. B. Walther, J. F. Anderson, and D. Park. "Interpersonal Effects in Computer-Mediated Interaction: A Meta-Analysis of Social and Anti-Social Communication, *Communication Research,* 21 (1994): 460–87; N. Negroponte, *Being Digital* (New York: Knopf, 1995); J. B. Walther and L. Tidwell, "When Is Mediated Communication Not Interpersonal?" in K. Galvin and P. Cooper, *Making Connections* (Los Angeles, CA: Roxbury Press, 1996); P. Wallace, *The Psychology of the Internet* (Cambridge, England: Cambridge University Press, 1999).

27. J. B. Walther and J. K. Burgoon, "Relational Communication in Computer-Mediated Interaction," *Human Communication Research,* 19 (1992): 50–88.

28. Tidwell and Walther, 2002.

29. L. K. Trevino, R. L. Draft, and R. H. Lengel, "Understanding Managers' Media Choices: A Symbolic Interactionist Perspective," in *Organizations and Communication Technology,* edited by J. Fulk and C. Steinfield (Newbury Park, CA: Sage, 1990), 71–74.

30. Tidwell and Walther, 2002.

31. Walther and Tidwell, 1996.

32. I. Reed, "The World Is Here," in *Writin' Is Fighting* (New York: Atheneum, 1988).

33. See D. Barnlund, *Interpersonal Communication: Survey and Studies* (Boston: Houghton Mifflin, 1968).

34. O. Wiio, *Wiio's Laws—and Some Others* (Espoo, Finland: WelinGoos, 1978).

35. S. B. Shimanoff, *Communication Rules: Theory and Research* (Beverly Hills: Sage, 1980).

36. M. Argyle, M. Hendershot, and A. Furnham, "The Rules of Social Relationships," *British Journal of Social Psychology,* 24 (1985): 125–39.

37. T. Watzlawick, J. Bavelas, and D. Jackson, *The Pragmatics of Human Communication* (New York: Norton, 1967).

38. See J. C. McCroskey and M. [J.] Beatty, "The Communibiological Perspective: Implications for Communication in Instruction," *Communication Education,* 49 (January 2000): 1–6; M. J. Beatty and J. C. McCroskey, "Theory,

Scientific Evidence, and the Communibiological Paradigm: Reflections on Misguided Criticism," *Communication Education,* 49, (January 2000): 36–44. Also see J. C. McCroskey, J. A. Daly, M. M. Martin, and M. J. Beatty, (eds.), *Communication and Personality: Trait Perspectives* (Cresskil, NJ: Hampton Press, 1998); and M. J. Beatty, A. D. Heisel, A. E. Hall, T. R. Levine, and B. H. La France, "What Can We Learn from the Study of Twins about Genetic and Environmental Influences on Interpersonal Affiliation, Aggressiveness, and Social Anxiety? A Meta-Analytic Study," *Communication Monographs,* 69 (March 2002): 1–18.

39. See J. Ayres and T. S. Hopf, "The Long-Term Effect of Visualization in the Classroom: A Brief Research Report," *Communication Education,* 39 (1990): 75–78; and J. Ayres and T. S. Hopf, "Visualization: A Means of Reducing Speech Anxiety," *Communication Education,* 34 (1985): 318–23.

40. For a discussion of criticism of the communibiological approach, see C. M. Condit, "Culture and Biology in Human Communication: Toward a Multi-Causal Model," *Communication Education,* 49, (January 2000): 7–24.

41. S. R. Wilson and C. M. Sabee, "Explicating Communicative Competence as a Theoretical Term," in *Handbook of Communication and Social Interaction Skills,* edited by J. O. Greene and B. R. Burleson (Mahwah, NJ: Erlbaum, 2003), 3–50.

42. M. J. Collier, "Researching Cultural Identity: Reconciling Interpretive and Postcolonial Approaches," in *Communication and Identity Across Cultures,* edited by D. Tanno and A. Gonzalez (Thousand Oaks, CA: Sage, 1998), 142. Also see S. DeTurk, "Intercultural Empathy: Myth, Competency, or Possibility for Alliance Building?" *Communication Education,* 50 (October 2001): 374–84.

43. Miller and deWinstanley.

44. M. Argyle, *The Psychology of Interpersonal Behavior* (London: Penguin, 1983).

45. M. V. Redmond, "Adaptation in Everyday Interactions," paper presented at the annual meeting of the National Communication Association (November, 1997).

46. C. H. Adams, "Prosocial Bias in Theories of Interpersonal Communica-

tion Competence: Must Good Communication Be Nice? In *Communication and Community,* edited by G. Shepherd and E. W. Rothenbuhler (Mahwah, NJ: Erlbaum, 2001), 37–52.

47. M. Argyle is widely acknowledged as the first scholar to suggest a systematic approach to apply learning theory to the development of social skills, including interpersonal communication skills. See Argyle, *The Psychology of Interpersonal Behavior.*

**Chapter 2**

1. K. Horney, *Neurosis and Human Growth* (New York: Norton, 1950), 17.

2. E. Goffman, *The Presentation of Self in Everyday Life* (Garden City, NY: Doubleday, Anchor Books, 1959). Also see E. Goffman, *Frame Analysis: An Essay on the Organization of Experience* (Cambridge, MA: Harvard University Press, 1974).

3. Goffman, *Frame Analysis,* 508.

4. C. H. Cooley, *Human Nature and the Social Order* (New York: Scribners, 1902).

5. G. H. Mead, *Mind, Self, and Society* (Chicago: University of Chicago Press, 1934).

6. H. S. Sullivan, *The Interpersonal Theory of Psychiatry* (New York: Norton, 1953).

7. J. T. Masterson, *Speech Communication in Traditional and Contemporary Marriages* (doctoral dissertation, University of Denver, 1977). Also see S. A. Beebe and J. T. Masterson, *Family Talk: Interpersonal Communication in the Family* (New York: Random House, 1986), 91–100.

8. For an excellent discussion of the role of gender and communication, see J. C. Pearson, L. H. Turner, and W. Todd-Mancillas, *Gender and Communication,* 3d ed. (Dubuque, IA: William C. Brown, 1995). Also see D. K. Ivy and P. Backlund, *Exploring Genderspeak* (New York: McGraw-Hill, 2004).

9. Pearson, Turner, and Todd-Mancillas, *Gender and Communication;* Ivy and Backlund, *Exploring Genderspeak.*

10. Mead, *Mind, Self, and Society.*

11. D. G. Ancona, "Groups in Organizations: Extending Laboratory Models," in *Annual Review of Personality and Social Psychology: Group and*

*Intergroup Processes,* edited by C. Hendrick (Beverly Hills, CA: Sage, 1987), 207–31. Also see D. G. Ancona and D. E. Caldwell, "Beyond Task and Maintenance: Defining External Functions in Groups," *Group and Organizational Studies,* 13 (1988): 468–94.

12. S. L. Bem, "The Measurement of Psychological Androgyny," *Journal of Consulting and Clinical Psychology,* 42 (1974): 155–62.

13. L. A. Lefton, *Psychology* (Boston: Allyn & Bacon, 2000).

14. J. C. McCroskey and M. J. Beatty, "The Communibiological Perspective: Implications for Communication Instruction," *Communication Education,* 49 (January 2000): 1–28.

15. C. M. Condit, "Culture and Biology in Human Communication: Toward a Multi-Causal Model," *Communication Education,* 49 (January 2000): 7–24.

16. P. Zimbardo, *Shyness: What It Is, What to Do About It* (Reading, MA: Addison-Wesley, 1977).

17. S. Booth-Butterfield, "Instructional Interventions for Situational Anxiety and Avoidance," *Communication Education,* 37 (1988): 214–23.

18. J. C. McCroskey and V. P. Richmond, *Fundamentals of Human Communication: An Interpersonal Perspective* (Prospect Heights, IL: Waveland Press, 1996).

19. Booth-Butterfield, "Instructional Interventions."

20. Zimbardo, *Shyness.*

21. E. Sahlstein and M. Allen, "Sex Differences in Self-Esteem: A Meta-Analytic Assessment," in *Interpersonal Communication Research: Advances Through Meta-Analysis,* edited by M. Allen, R. W. Preiss, B. M. Gayle, and N. A. Burrell (Mahwah, NJ: Erlbaum, 2002), 59–72; K. Dindia, "Self-Disclosure Research: Knowledge Through Meta-Analysis," in *Interpersonal Communication Research: Advances Through Meta-Analysis,* edited by M. Allen, R. W. Preiss, B. M. Gayle, and N. A. Burrell (Mahwah, NJ: Erlbaum, 2002), 169–85.

22. E. Berne, *Games People Play* (New York: Grove Press, 1964).

23. S. Ting Toomey, J. G. Oetzel, and K. Yee-Jung, "Self-Construal Types and Conflict Management Styles," *Communi-cation Reports,* 14 (Summer 2001): 87–104.

24. Ting Toomey, Oetzel, and Yee-Jung, "Self-Construal Types."

25. L. Armstrong, *It's Not About the Bike: My Journey Back to Life* (New York: Putnam's, 2000), 146.

26. K. Sugarman, "Tennis and Positive Self-Talk," *WorldWide Tennis Ladder* (August 2000): http://www.sportsladders.com/tennis/tips/artcl-selftalk.asp

27. J. Ayres and T. S. Hopf, "The Long-Term Effect of Visualization in the Classroom: A Brief Research Report," *Communication Education,* 39 (1990): 75–78.

28. J. Canfield and M. V. Hansen (Eds.), *Chicken Soup for the Soul* (Deerfield Beach, FL: Health Communications, 1995).

29. F. E. X. Dance and C. Larson, *The Functions of Human Communication* (New York: Holt, Rinehart and Winston, 1976), 141.

30. Our discussion of decentering specific-other and generalized other perspective is from M. V. Redmond, "The Functions of Empathy (Decentering) in Human Relations," *Human Relations,* 42 (1993): 593–606. Also see M. V. Redmond, "A Multidimensional Theory and Measure of Social Decentering," *Journal of Research in Personality* (1995).

31. H. Brody. *The Placebo Response: How You Can Release Your Body's Inner Pharmacy for Better Health* (New York: HarperCollins, 2000). Also see H. Brody, "Tapping the Power of the Placebo," *Newsweek,* August 14, 2000, 68.

32. A. A. Milne, "Pooh Does a Good Deed," in *Pooh Sleepytime Stories* (New York: Golden Press, 1979), 44.

33. *Looking Out/Looking In,* edited by R. B. Adler and N. Towne (Fort Worth, TX: Harcourt Brace Jovanovich, 1993). Also see C. R. Berger, "Self Conception and Social Information Processing," in *Personality and Interpersonal Communication,* edited by J. C. McCroskey and J. A. Daly (1986): 275–303.

34. A. A. Milne, "Owl Finds a Home," in *Pooh Sleepytime Stories* (New York: Golden Press, 1979), 28.

35. D. E. Hamachek, *Encounters with the Self* (New York: Holt, Rinehart and Winston, 1982); Berger, "Self-Conception."

36. W. C. Schutz, *FIRO: A Three-Dimensional Theory of Interpersonal Behavior* (New York: Holt, Rinehart and Winston, 1958).

37. McCroskey and Beatty, "Communibiological Perspective."

38. See J. C. McCroskey and V. P. Richmond, *Fundamentals of Human Communication.*

39. Dindia, "Self-Disclosure Research."

40. I. Altman and D. A. Taylor, *Social Penetration: The Development of Interpersonal Relationships* (New York: Holt, Rinehart and Winston, 1973).

41. W. B. Gudykunst and T. Nishida, "Social Penetration in Japanese and American Close Friendships," in *Communication Yearbook 7,* edited by R. N. Bostrom (Beverly Hills, CA: Sage, 1963), 592–611.

42. J. C. Korn, "Friendship Formation and Development in Two Cultures: Universal Constructs in the United States and Korea," in *Interpersonal Communication in Friend and Mate Relationships,* edited by A. M. Nicotera (Albany: State University of New York Press, 1993), 61–78.

43. J. Luft, *Group Process: An Introduction to Group Dynamics* (Palo Alto, CA: Mayfield, 1970).

44. Dindia, "Self-Disclosure Research."

45. Dindia, "Self-Disclosure Research."

46. J. Powell, *Why Am I Afraid To Tell You Who I Am?* (Niles, IL: Argus Communications, 1969), 12.

47. Powell, *Why Am I Afraid.*

48. L. C. Tidwell and J. B. Walther, "Computer-Mediated Communication Effects on Disclosure, Impressions, and Interpersonal Evaluations: Getting to Know One Another a Bit at a Time," *Human Communication Research,* 28, (July 2002): 317–48.

49. M. Argyle, M. Henderson, and A. Furnham, "The Rules of Social Relationships," *British Journal of Social Psychology,* 24 (1985): 125–39.

50. A. L. Vangelisti, J. P. Caughlin, and L. Timmerman, "Criteria for Revealing Family Secrets," *Communication Monographs,* 68 (March 2001): 1–27.

51. A. P. Bochner, "On the Efficacy of Openness in Close Relationships," in

*Communication Yearbook 5,* edited by
M. Burgoon (New Brunswick, NJ:
Transaction Books, 1982), 109–24.

**Chapter 3**

1. C. R. Berger, "Self-Conception and
Social Information Processing," in *Personality and Interpersonal Communication,* edited by J. C. McCroskey and J. A.
Daly (Newbury Park, CA: Sage, 1987),
275–304.

2. P. R. Hinton, *The Psychology of
Interpersonal Perception* (New York:
Routledge, 1993).

3. D. W. Miller, "Looking Askance
at Eyewitness Testimony," *Chronicle of
Higher Education,* February 25, 2000:
A19–20.

4. P. Watz1awick, J. Bevelas, and D.
Jackson, *The Pragmatics of Human Communication* (New York: Norton, 1967).

5. A. L. Sillars, "Attribution and
Communication: Are People Naive
Scientists or Just Naive?" in *Social Cognition and Communication,* edited by
M. E. Roloff and C. R. Berger (Beverly
Hills: Sage, 1982), 73–106.

6. Watzlawick et al., *The Pragmatics
of Human Communication.*

7. R. D. Laing, H. Phillipson, and
A. R. Lee, *Interpersonal Perception*
(New York: Springer, 1966).

8. C. R. Berger and J. J. Bradac,
*Language and Social Knowledge*
(Baltimore: Edward Arnold, 1982).

9. S. Asch, "Forming Impressions of
Personality," *Journal of Abnormal and
Social Psychology,* 41 (1946): 258–290.

10. D. M. Wegner and R. R.
Vallacher, *Implicit Psychology: An
Introduction to Social Cognition* (New
York: Oxford University Press, 1977).

11. S. Bruner and R. Tagiuri, "The
Perception of People," in *Handbook of
Social Psychology,* edited by G. Lindzey
(Cambridge, MA: Addison-Wesley,
1954).

12. A. L. Sillars, "Attributions and
Communication in Roommate Conflicts,"
*Communication Monographs,* 47 (1980):
180–200.

13. D. A. Infante and A. S. Rancer,
"Argumentativeness and Verbal Aggressiveness: A Review of Recent Theory and
Research," in *Communication Yearbook
19,* edited by B. R. Burleson (Thousand
Oaks, CA: Sage, 1996), 319–52.

14. D. Hample, "The Life Space of
Personalized Conflicts," in *Communication Yearbook 23,* edited by M. E. Roloff
(Thousand Oaks, CA: Sage, 1999),
171–208.

15. G. A. Kelly, *The Psychology of
Personal Constructs* (New York: Norton,
1995).

16. F. Heider, *The Psychology of
Interpersonal Relations* (New York:
Wiley, 1958). Also see E. E. Jones and
K. E. Davis, "From Acts to Dispositions:
The Attribution Process in Person Perception," in *Advances in Experimental
Social Psychology,* vol. 2, edited by L.
Berkowitz (New York: Academic Press,
1965).

17. G. A. Kelly, *The Psychology of
Personal Constructs* (New York: Norton,
1955).

18. A. L. Vangelisti and S. L. Young,
"When Words Hurt: The Effects of Perceived Intentionality on Interpersonal
Relationships," *Journal of Social and Personal Relationships,* 17 (2000): 393–424.

19. G. W. F. Hegel, *Phenomenology of
Mind* (Germany: Wurzburg & Bamburg,
1807).

20. R. Nisbett and L. Ross, *Human
Inference: Strategies and Shortcomings of
Social Judgment* (Englewood Cliffs, NJ:
Prentice Hall, 1980).

21. Nisbett and Ross, *Human
Inference.*

22. E. E. Jones and R. Nisbett, "The
Actor and the Observer: Divergent Perceptions of the Causes of Behavior," in
*Attribution: Perceiving the Causes of
Behavior,* edited by E. E. Jones et al.
(Morristown, NJ: General Learning
Press, 1972), 79–94; D. E. Kanouse and
L. R. Hanson, Jr., "Negativity in Evaluations," in Jones et al., *Attribution,* 47–62.

23. F. T. McAndrew, A. Akande,
R. Bridgstock, L. Mealey, S. C. Gordon,
J. E. Scheib, B. E. Akande-Adetoun, F.
Odewale, A. Morakinyo, P. Nyahete, and
G. Mubvakure, "A Multicultural Study
of Stereotyping in English-Speaking
Countries," *The Journal of Social
Psychology,* 140 (2000): 487–502.

24. Nisbett and Ross, *Human
Inference.*

25. Asch, "Forming Impressions of
Personality."

26. P. Brown and S. C. Levinson,
*Politeness: Some Universals in Language
Use* (Cambridge, England: Cambridge
University Press, 1987).

27. E. Goffman, *The Presentation of
Self in Everyday Life* (New York:
Doubleday, 1959).

28. K. Floyd, "Attributions for
Nonverbal Expressions of Liking and
Disliking: The Extended Self-Serving
Bias," *Western Journal of Communication,*
64 (Fall 2000): 388.

29. Floyd, "Attributions for Nonverbal
Expressions of Liking and Disliking."

30. Goffman, *The Presentation of Self
in Everyday Life.*

31. Brown and Levinson, *Politeness.*

32. Floyd, "Attributions for Nonverbal
Expressions of Liking and Disliking."

33. M. V. Redmond, "The Functions
of Empathy (Decentering) in Human
Relations," *Human Relations,* 42(4),
(1993): 593–606

**Chapter 4**

1. M. E. Ryan, "Another Way to
Teach Migrant Students," *Los Angeles
Times,* March 31, 1991, B20, as cited by
M. W. Lustig and J. Koester, *Intercultural
Competence: Interpersonal Communication Across Cultures* (Boston: Allyn &
Bacon, 2003), 11.

2. Lustig and Koester, *Intercultural
Competence,* 8.

3. G. Chen and W. J. Starosta, "A
Review of the Concept of Intercultural
Sensitivity," *Human Communication,* 1,
(1997): 7.

4. Lustig and Koester, *Intercultural
Competence,* 10.

5. *Newsweek,* July 12, 1999, 51.

6. U.S. Bureau of the Census,
*Statistical Abstract of the United States:
1996,* 116th ed. (Washington, DC:
1996) as cited by Lustig and Koester,
*Intercultural Competence,* 8.

7. U.S. Bureau of the Census, *Report 1999,* as reported in R. E. Schmid,
*Austin-American Statesman,* September
17, 1999, A20.

8. U.S. Bureau of the Census,
*Report 1999,* A20.

9. "One Nation, One Language?"
*U.S. News & World Report,* September
25, 1995, 40, cited by Lustig and
Koester, *Intercultural Competence,* 10.

10. J. Malone, "Racial Categories in
2000 Census Reflect Diversity," *Austin-American Statesman,* March 11, 2000,
A10.

11. United States Census Bureau. Retrieved December 10, 2002 from http://www.prb.org/AmeristatTemplate

12. United States Census Bureau. Retrieved December 10, 2002 from http://www.prb.org/AmeristatTemplate

13. J. Scott, "Foreign Born in U.S. at Record High," *The New York Times*, February 7, 2002: A18.

14. Scott, "Foreign Born in U.S."

15. C. H. Dodd and J. R. Baldwin, "Family Culture and Relationship Differences as a Source of Intercultural Communication," in *Readings in Cultural Contexts,* edited by J. Martin, T. Nakayama, and L. Flores (Mountain View, CA: Mayfield, 1998), 335–44.

16. G. Smith (Ed.), *Communication and Culture* (New York: Holt, Rinehart and Winston, 1966).

17. G. Hofstede, *Culture's Consequences: International Differences in Work-Related Values* (Beverly Hills, CA: Sage, 1980).

18. J. Harwood, J. McKee, and M. C. Lin, "Younger and Older Adults' Schematic Representations of Intergenerational Communication," *Communication Monographs,* 67 (March 2000): 20–41.

19. P. Cateora and J. Hess, *International Marketing* (Homewood, IL: Irwin, 1979), 89; as discussed by L. A. Samovar and R. E. Porter, *Communication Between Cultures* (Belmont, CA: Wadsworth, 2001), 52.

20. Hofstede, *Culture's Consequences.*

21. For an extensive summary and critique of Hofstede's research, see M. W. Lustig and J. Koester, *Intercultural Competence,* 111.

22. Hofstede, *Culture's Consequences;* also see G. Hofstede, "Cultural Dimensions in Management and Planning," *Asia Pacific Journal of Management* (January 1984): 81–98.

23. For an extensive review of communication gender differences see L. H. Turner, K. Dindia, and J. C. Pearson, "An Investigation of Female/Male Verbal Behaviors in Same-Sex and Mixed-Sex Conversations," *Communication Reports,* 8 (Summer 1995): 86–96.

24. An excellent analysis and application of gender communication research has been compiled by A. Cornyn-Selby, "Are You from Another Planet or What?" presented at the Joint Service Family Readiness Matters Conference, July 14, 1999, Phoenix, Arizona.

25. See D. K. Ivy and P. Backlund, *Exploring GenderSpeak: Personal Effectiveness in Gender Communication* (New York: McGraw-Hill, 2000).

26. Hofstede, "Cultural Dimensions in Management and Planning."

27. C. R. Berger and R. J. Calabrese, "Some Explorations in Initial Interactions and Beyond: Toward a Developmental Theory of Interpersonal Communication," *Human Communication Research,* 1 (1975): 99–112.

28. For an excellent comprehensive discussion of uncertainty reduction theory, see R. West and L. H. Turner, *Introducing Communication Theory: Analysis and Application* (Mountain View, CA: Mayfield, 2000), 132–46.

29. G. Hofstede, *Cultures and Organizations: Software of the Mind* (London: McGraw-Hill, 1997).

30. Hofstede, *Culture's Consequences.*

31. W. B. Gudykunst, *Bridging Differences: Effective Intergroup Communication* (Newbury Park, CA: Sage, 1998), 45.

32. Gudykunst, *Bridging Differences.*

33. E. T. Hall, *Beyond Culture* (Garden City, NY: Doubleday, 1976).

34. Samovar and Porter, *Communication Between Cultures,* 234.

35. M. V. Redmond and J. M. Bunyi, "The Relationship of Intercultural Communication Competence with Stress and the Handling of Stress as Reported by International Students," *International Journal of Intercultural Relations,* 17 (1993): 235–54; R. Brislen, *Cross-Cultural Encounters: Face-to-Face Interaction* (New York: Pergamon Press, 1981).

36. W. G. Sumner, *Folkways* (Boston: Ginn, 1906), as cited by James W. Neuliep, *Intercultural Communication: A Contextual Approach* (Boston: Houghton Mifflin, 2000), 160.

37. Lustig and Koester, *Intercultural Competence.*

38. J. W. Neuliep and J. C. McCroskey, "The Development of a U.S. and Generalized Ethnocentrism Scale," *Communication Research Reports,* 14 (1997): 385–398.

39. R. E. Axtell, *Do's and Taboos of Hosting International Visitors* (New York: John Wiley & Sons, 1989), 118.

40. F. T. McAndrew, A. Akande, R. Bridgstock, L. Mealey, S. C. Gordon, J. E. Scheib, B. E. Akande-Adetoun, F. Odewale, A. Morakinyo, P. Nyahete, and G. Mubvakure, "A Multicultural Study of Stereotyping in English-Speaking Countries," *The Journal of Social Psychology,* 140 (2000): 487–502.

41. Kluckhohn and Murry, 1953 as quoted by J. S. Caputo, H. C. Hazel, and C. McMahon, *Interpersonal Communication* (Boston: Allyn & Bacon, 1994), 304.

42. S. Kamekar, M. B. Kolsawalla, and T. Mazareth, "Occupational Prestige as a Function of Occupant's Gender," *Journal of Applied Social Psychology,* 19 (1988): 681–88.

43. Eleanor Roosevelt, as cited by Lustig and Koester, *Intercultural Competence.*

44. B. H. Spitzberg and W. R. Cupach, "Interpersonal Skills," in *Handbook of Interpersonal Communication,* edited by M. L. Knapp and J. A. Daly (Thousand Oaks, CA: Sage, 2002): 564–611.

45. S. A. Myers and R. L. Knox, "The Relationship Between College Student Information Seeking Behaviors and Perceived Instructor Verbal Responses," *Communication Education,* 50 (2001): 343–56; J. R. Baldwin and S. K. Hunt, "Information-Seeking Behavior in Intercultural and Intergroup Communication," *Human Communication Research,* 28 (April 2002): 272–86.

46. For an excellent discussion of world view and the implications for intercultural communication, see C. H. Dodd, *Dynamics of Intercultural Communication* (New York: McGraw-Hill, 1998).

47. Dodd, *Dynamics,* 75.

48. W. B. Gudykunst, "Similarities and Differences in Perceptions of Initial Intracultural and Intercultural Encounters," *Southern Speech Communication Journal,* 49 (1983): 49–65; W. B. Gudykunst, "Theorizing in Intercultural Communication: An Introduction." In *Intercultural Communication Theory: Current Perspectives,* edited by W. B. Gudykunst (Beverly Hills, CA: Sage, 1983), 13–20; W. B. Gudykunst, "A Model of Uncertainty Reduction in Intercultural Encounters," *Journal of Language and Social Psychology,* 4 (1985): 79–97; W. B. Gudykunst, E. Chua, and A. Gray,

"Cultural Dissimilarities and Uncertainty Reduction Processes," in *Communication Yearbook 10,* edited by M. L. McLaughlin (Beverly Hills, Sage, 1987), 456–69; W. B. Gudykunst and T. Nishida, "Individual and Cultural Influences on Uncertainty Reduction," *Communication Monographs,* 51 (1984): 23–36; W. B. Gudykunst and Y. Kim, *Communicating with Strangers: An Approach to Intercultural Communication* (New York: McGraw-Hill, 1997); W. B. Gudykunst, S.-M. Yang, and T. Nishida, "Cultural Differences in Self-Consciousness and Self-Monitoring," *Communication Monographs,* 14 (1987): 7–14; Baldwin and Hunt, "Information-Seeking Behavior."

49. J. T. Wood, *Communication Mosaics: A New Introduction to the Field of Communication* (Belmont, CA: Wadsworth, 2001), 207; C. C. Innman, "Men's Friendships: Closeness in the Doing," in Julia T. Wood (Ed.), *Gendered Relationships* (Mountain View, CA: Mayfield), 95–110.

50. R. Berger and R. J. Calabrese, "Some Explorations in Initial Interactions and Beyond," *Human Communication Research,* 1 (1975): 99–125.

51. B. J. Broome, "Building Shared Meaning: Implications of a Relational Approach to Empathy for Teaching Intercultural Communication," *Communication Education,* 40 (1991): 235–249.

52. F. L. Casmir, "Foundations for the Study of Intercultural Communication Based on a Third-Culture Building Model," *International Journal of Intercultural Relations,* 23 (1999): 91–116; also see S. DeTurk, "Intercultural Empathy: Myth, Competency, or Possibility for Alliance Building?" *Communication Education,* 50 (October 2001): 374–84.

53. F. L. Casmir and N. C. Asuncion-Lande, "Intercultural Communication Revisited: Conceptualization, Paradigm Building, and Methodological Approaches," in *Communication Yearbook,* edited by J. A. Anderson, vol. 12 (Newbury Park, CA: Sage, 1989), 278–309.

54. Broome, "Building Shared Meaning."

55. Gudykunst and Kim, *Communicating with Strangers;* Gudykunst, *Bridging Differences.*

56. L. B. Szalay and G. H. Fisher, "Communication Overseas," in *Toward Internationalism: Readings in Cross-Cultural Communication,* edited by E. C. Smith and L. E Luce (Rowley, MA: Newbury House, 1979). Also see Paul E. King and Chris R. Sawyer, "Mindfulness, Mindlessness and Communication Instruction," *Communication Education,* 47 (October 1998): 326–36.

57. P. Brown and S. Levinson, *Politeness: Some Universals in Language Usage* (Cambridge, England: Cambridge University Press, 1987).

58. C. S. Lewis, *The Abolition of Man* (New York: Macmillan Publishing Company, 1947).

59. DeTurk, "Intercultural Empathy."

60. M. V. Redmond, "The Functions of Empathy (Decentering) in Human Relations," *Human Relations,* 42 (1993): 593–606. Also see M. V. Redmond, "A Multidimensional Theory and Measure of Social Decentering," *Journal of Research in Personality,* 29 (1995): 35–58; for an excellent discussion of the role of emotions in establishing empathy, see D. Goleman, *Emotional Intelligence* (New York: Bantam, 1995).

61. See H. Giles, A. Mulack, J. J. Bradac, and P. Johnson, "Speech Accommodation Theory: The First Decade and Beyond," in *Communication Yearbook,* edited by M. L. McLaughlin, vol. 10 (Newbury Park, CA: Sage, 1987), 13–48. For an excellent summary and application of accommodation theory, see R. West and L. H. Turner, *Introducing Communication Theory: Analysis and Application* (Mountain View, CA: Mayfield, 2000).

62. M. J. Bennett, "Overcoming the Golden Rule: Sympathy and Empathy," in *Communication Yearbook 3,* edited by D. Nimmo (Beverly Hills, CA: Sage, 1979), 407–22.

63. Bennett, "Overcoming the Golden Rule."

64. L. J. Carrell, "Diversity in the Communication Curriculum: Impact on Student Empathy" *Communication Education,* 46 (October 1997): 234–44.

65. Adapted from 3M Diversity Seminar, Austin, Texas, 1994.

**Chapter 5**

1. H. J. M. Nouwen, *Bread for the Journey* (San Francisco: HarperCollins, 1997), entry for March 11.

2. Nowen, *Bread for the Journey,* March 11.

3. "The Most Valued Workplace Skills," *The Wall Street Journal,* September 9, 2002: 1A.

4. L. Barker et al., "An Investigation of Proportional Time Spent in Various Communication Activities of College Students," *Journal of Applied Communication Research,* 8 (1981): 101–09.

5. Adapted from the International Listening Association's definition of listening, which may be found on their web site at http://www.listen.org

6. L. A. Januskik, "Listening and Cognitive Processing: Is There a Difference?" paper presented at the annual conference of the National Communication Association (November 2002), New Orleans, LA. Januskik suggests that it's important to include a behavioral component, such as responding to a message, in any definition of listening.

7. K. W. Watson, L. L. Barker, and J. B. Weaver, *The Listener Style Inventory* (New Orleans: SPECTRA, 1995).

8. S. L. Sargent and J. B. Weaver, "Correlates Between Communication Apprehension and Listening Style Preferences," *Communication Research Reports,* 14 (1997): 74–78.

9. M. D. Kirtley and J. M. Honeycutt, "Listening Styles and Their Correspondence with Second Guessing," *Communication Research Reports,* 13 (1996): 174–82.

10. Sargent and Weaver, "Correlates Between Communication Apprehension."

11. W. Winter, A. J. Ferreira, and N. Bowers, "Decision-Making in Married and Unrelated Couples," *Family Process,* 12 (1973): 83–94.

12. O. E. Rankis, "The Effects of Message Structure, Sexual Gender, and Verbal Organizing Ability upon Learning Message Information," doctoral dissertation, Ohio University, 1981; C. H. Weaver, *Human Listening. Process and Behavior* (New York: Bobbs-Merrill, 1972); R. D. Halley, "Distractibility of Males and Females in Competing Aural Message Situations. A Research Note," *Human Communication Research,* 2 (1975): 79–82. Our discussion of gender-based differences and listening is also based on a discussion by S. A. Beebe and J. T. Masterson, *Family Talk: Interper-*

sonal Communication in the Family (New York: Random House, 1986); J. Lurito, "Listening and Gender," paper presented to the Radiological Society of North America, Chicago (2000) as cited by L. Tanner, "Listening Study Finds Difference in the Sexes," Austin-American Statesman, (November 29, 2000), p. A11.

13. J. Stauffer, R. Frost, and W. Rybolt, "The Attention Factor in Recalling Network News," Journal of Communication, 33(1), (1983): 29–37.

14. This discussion is based on A. Vangelisti, M. Knapp, and J. Daly, "Conversational Narcissism," Communication Monographs, 57 (1990): 251–74.

15. J. Thurber, "The Secret Life of Walter Mitty," in Literature for Composition, 3d ed., edited by S. Barnet et al. (Glenview, IL: Scott, Foresman, 1992), 43.

16. R. Montgomery, Listening Made Easy (New York: Amacon, 1981); O. Hargie, C. Sanders, and D. Dickson, Social Skills in Interpersonal Communication (London: Routledge, 1994); O. Hargie (Ed.), The Handbook of Communication Skills (London: Routledge, 1997). Also see S. W. Littlejohn and K. Domenic, Engaging Communication in Conflict: Systemic Practice (Thousand Oaks, CA: Sage, 2001), 105–08.

17. R. G. Owens, "Handling Strong Emotions," in O. Hargie (Ed.), A Handbook of Communication Skills (London: Croom Helm/New York University Press, 1986).

18. K. B. Staples, "Black Men and Public Space," in Literature for Composition, 3rd ed., edited by S. Barnet et al. (Glenview, IL: Scott, Foresman, 1992), 73.

19. R. G. Nichols, "Factors in Listening Comprehension," Speech Monographs, 15 (1948): 154–63; G. M. Goldhaber and C. H. Weaver, "Listener Comprehension of Compressed Speech When the Difficulty, Rate of Presentation, and Sex of the Listener Are Varied," Speech Monographs, 35 (1968): 20–25.

20. ABC News, 20/20, January 12, 1998, featuring the research of communication researcher Kittie Watson.

21. M. V. Redmond, "The Functions of Empathy (Decentering) in Human Relations," Human Relations, 42 (1993): 593–606.

22. M. Fitch-Hauser, L. A. Barker, and A. Hughes, "Receiver Apprehension and Listening Comprehension: A Linear or Curvilinear Relationship?" Southern Communication Journal (1988): 62–71; P. Schrodt and L. R. Wheeless, "Aggressive Communication and Informational Reception Apprehension: The Influence of Listening Anxiety and Intellectual Inflexibility on Trait Argumentativeness and Verbal Aggressiveness," Communication Quarterly, 49 (Winter 2001): 53–69.

23. D. Carnegie, How to Win Friends and Influence People (New York: Holiday House, 1937).

24. K. Ruyter and M. G. M. Wetzels, "The Impact of Perceived Listening Behavior in Voice-to-Voice Service Encounters," Journal of Service Research, 2 (February 2000): 276–84.

25. J. Harrigan, "Listeners' Body Movements and Speaking Turns," Communication Research, 12 (1985): 233–50.

26. S. Strong et al., "Nonverbal Behavior and Perceived Counselor Characteristics," Journal of Counseling Psychology, 18 (1971): 554–61.

27. See R. G. Nichols and L. A. Stevens, "Listening to People," Harvard Business Review, 35 (September–October 1957): 85–92.

28. C. W. Ellison and I. J. Fireston, "Development of Interpersonal Trust as a Function of Self-Esteem, Target Status and Target Style," Journal of Personality and Social Psychology, 29 (1974): 655–63.

29. D. Goleman, Emotional Intelligence (New York: Bantam, 1995).

30. Goleman, Emotional Intelligence.

31. O. Hargie, C. Sanders, and D. Dickson, Social Skills in Interpersonal Communication (London: Routledge, 1994); O. Hargie (Ed.), Handbook.

32. J. B. Weaver and M. B. Kirtley, "Listening Styles and Empathy," The Southern Communication Journal, 60 (1995): 131–40.

33. C. Rogers, Client-Centered Therapy (Boston: Houghton Mifflin, 1951).

34. J. Gottman and J. DeClaire, The Relationship Cure (New York: Crown, 2001), 198–201.

35. Hargie, Sanders, and Dickson, Social Skills; R. Boulton, People Skills (New York: Simon & Schuster, 1981).

36. E. Sieburg and C. Larson, "Dimensions of Interpersonal Response," paper delivered at the annual conference of the International Communication Association, Phoenix, Arizona, April 1971.

37. S. DeTurk, "Intercultural Empathy: Myth, Competency, or Possibility for Alliance Building?" Communication Education, 50 (October 2001): 374–84.

38. Boulton, People Skills. We also acknowledge others who have presented excellent applications of listening and responding skills in interpersonal and group contexts: D. A. Romig and L. J. Romig, Structured Teamwork Guide (Austin, TX: Performance Resources, 1990); S. Deep and L. Sussman, Smart Moves (Reading: MA. Addison-Wesley, 1990); P. R. Scholtes, The Team Handbook (Madison, WI: Joiner Associates, 1992); Hargie, Sanders, and Dickson, Social Skills; Littlejohn and Domenici, Engaging Communication in Conflict.

39. S. Gilbert, "Self-Disclosure, Intimacy, and Communication in Families," Family Coordinator, 25 (1976).

## Chapter 6

1. B. Spitzberg and J. P. Dillard, "Social Skills and Communication," in Interpersonal Communication Research: Advances Through Meta-Analysis, edited by M. Allen, R. W. Preiss, B. M. Gayle, and N. Burrell (Mahwah, NJ: Erlbaum, 2002), 89–107.

2. C. K. Ogden and I. A. Richards, The Meaning of Meaning (London: Kegan, Paul Trench, Trubner, 1923).

3. C. F. Hockett. A Course in Modern Linguistics (New York: Macmillan, 1958).

4. See G. H. Mead, Mind, Self and Society (Chicago: University of Chicago Press, 1934); H. Blumer, Symbolic Interactionism: Perspective and Method (Englewood Cliffs, NJ: Prentice Hall, 1969).

5. D. Tannen, You Just Don't Understand: Women and Men in Conversations (New York: Morrow, 1990).

6. R. Edwards, "The Effects of Gender, Gender Role, and Values on the Interpretation of Messages," Journal of Language and Social Psychology, 17 (1998): 52–71.

7. The American Heritage Dictionary of the English Language (Boston: Houghton Mifflin, 1969), 1162.

8. A. Korzybski, *Science and Sanity* (Lancaster, PA: Science Press, 1941).

9. G. Gusdorff, *Speaking* (Evanston, IL: Northwestern University Press, 1965), 9.

10. A. Ellis, *A New Guide to Rational Living* (North Hollywood, CA: Wilshire Books, 1977); also see W. Glaser, *Choice Theory* (New York: HarperCollins, 1998).

11. C. Peterson, M. E. P. Seligman, and G. E. Vaillant, "Pessimistic Explanatory Style Is a Risk Factor for Physical Illness: A 35-Year Longitudinal Study," *Journal of Personality and Social Psychology,* 55 (1988): 23–27.

12. E. K. Heussenstaunn, "Bumper Stickers and Cops," *Transaction,* 35 (1971): 32–33.

13. B. L. Whorf, "Science and Linguistics," in *Language, Thought and Reality,* edited by J. B. Carroll (Cambridge, MA: MIT Press, 1956), 207. This discussion of the Sapir-Whorf hypothesis is based on D. Crystal, *The Cambridge Encyclopedia of Language* (Cambridge, England: Cambridge University Press, 1997).

14. We thank one of our anonymous reviewers for this example.

15. S. Martelle, "We Have a New Vocabulary After Sept. 11," *Austin-American Statesman,* November 19, 2001: E5.

16. W. Johnson, *People in Quandaries* (New York: Harper & Row).

17. A fascinating article, "The Melting of a Mighty Myth" in *Newsweek* (July 22, 1991) explores the topic of Eskimos' words for snow.

18. R. L. Howe, *The Miracle of Dialogue* (New York: The Seabury Press, 1963), 23–24.

19. H. S. O'Donnell, "Sexism in Language," *Elementary English,* 50 (1973): 1067-72.

20. See D. K. Ivy and P. Backlund, *Exploring Genderspeak* (New York: McGraw-Hill, 2004).

21. *Newsweek,* November 20, 1995, 81.

22. We acknowledge and appreciate D. K. Ivy's contribution to this section on biased language. For an expanded discussion on this topic, see D. K. Ivy and P. Backlund, *Genderspeak* (New York: McGraw-Hill, 2004).

23. J. S. Seiter, J. Larsen, and J. Skinner, "'Handicapped' or 'Handi-

capable'? The Effects of Language about Persons with Disabilities on Perceptions of Source Credibility and Persuasiveness," *Communication Reports,* 11(1) (1998): 21–31.

24. D. O. Braithwaite and C. A. Braithwaite, "Understanding Communication of Persons with Disabilities as Cultural Communication," in *Intercultural Communication: A Reader,* 8th ed., edited by L. A. Samovar and R. E. Porter (Belmont, CA: Wadsworth, 1997): 154–64.

25. D. Yankelovich, *The Magic of Dialogue: Transforming Conflict into Cooperation* (New York: Simon & Schuster, 1999).

26. J. R. Gibb, "Defensive Communication," *Journal of Communication,* 11 (1961): 141–48. Also see R. Boulton, *People Skills* (New York: Simon & Schuster, 1979), 14–26; O. Hargie, C. Sanders, and D. Dickson, *Social Skills in Interpersonal Communication* (London: Routledge, 1994); O. Hargie (Ed.), *The Handbook of Communication Skills* (London: Routledge, 1997); S. W. Littlejohn and K. Domenici, *Engaging Communication in Conflict* (Thousand Oaks, CA: Sage, 2001).

27. C. Rogers, *On Becoming a Person: A Therapist's View of Psychotherapy* (Boston: Houghton Mifflin, 1961); C. Rogers, *A Way of Being* (Boston: Houghton Mifflin, 1980); C. Rogers, "Comments on the Issue of Equality in Psychotherapy," *Journal of Humanistic Psychology,* 27 (1987): 38–39.

28. B. R. Burleson, "Comforting Messages: Features, Functions, and Outcomes," in *Strategic Interpersonal Communication,* edited by J. A. Daly and J. M. Wiemann (Hillsdale, NJ: Erlbaum, 1994), 135–61.

29. B. M. Gayle and R. W. Preiss, "An Overview of Interactional Processes in Interpersonal Communication," in *Interpersonal Communication Research: Advances Through Meta-Analysis,* edited by M. Allen, R. W. Preiss, B. M. Gayle, and N. Burrell (Mahwah, NJ: Erlbaum, 2002), 213–26.

30. M. Allen, "A Synthesis and Extension of Constructivist Comforting Research," in *Interpersonal Communication Research: Advances Through Meta-Analysis,* edited by M. Allen, R. W. Preiss, B. M. Gayle, and N. Burrell (Mahwah, NJ: Erlbaum, 2002), 237–45.

31. D. J. Dolin and M. Booth-Butterfield, "Reach Out and Touch Someone: Analysis of Nonverbal Comforting Responses," *Communication Quarterly,* 41 (1993): 383–93.

32. A. M. Bippus, "Human Usages in Comforting Episodes: Factors Predicting Outcomes," *Western Journal of Communication,* 54 (Fall 2000): 359–84; A. M. Bippus, "Recipients' Criteria for Evaluating the Skillfulness of Comforting Communication and the Outcomes of Comforting Interactions," *Communication Monographs,* 68 (September 2001): 301–13.

33. Our prescriptions for assertiveness are based on a discussion by R. Boulton, *People Skills.* Also see J. S. St. Lawrence, "Situational Context: Effects on Perceptions of Assertive and Unassertive Behavior," *Behavior Therapy,* 16 (1985): 51–62; D. Borisoff and D. A. Victor, *Conflict Management: A Communication Skills Approach* (Boston: Allyn & Bacon, 1999).

34. D. Cloven and M. E. Roloff, "The Chilling Effect of Aggressive Potential on the Expression of Complaints in Intimate Relationships," *Communication Monographs,* 60 (1993):199–219.

**Chapter 7**

1. A. Mehrabian, *Nonverbal Communication* (Chicago: Aldine Atherton, 1972), 108.

2. D. Lapakko, "Three Cheers for Language: A Closer Examination of a Widely Cited Study of Nonverbal Communication," *Communication Education,* 46 (1997): 63–67.

3. D. Matsumoto, J. LeRoux, C. Wilson-Cohn, J. Raroque, K. Kooken, P. Ekman, N. Yrizarry, S. Loewinger, H. Uchida, A. Yee, L. Amo, and A. Goh, "A New Test to Measure Emotion Recognition Ability: Matsumoto and Ekman's Japanese and Caucasian Brief Affect Recognition Test (JACBART)," *Journal of Nonverbal Behavior,* 24 (Fall 2000): 179–209; J. K. Burgoon and A. E. Bacue, "Nonverbal Communication Skills," in *Handbook of Communication and Social Interaction Skills,* edited by J. O. Greene and B. R. Burleson (Mahwah, NJ: Erlbaum, 2003), 179–219.

4. M. Zuckerman, D. DePaulo, and R. Rosenthal, "Verbal and Nonverbal Communication of Deception,"

*Advances in Experimental Social Psychology,* 14 (1981): 1–59.

5. P. Ekman and W. V. Friesen, "The Repertoire of Nonverbal Behavior: Categories, Origins, Usage and Coding," *Semiotica,* 1 (1969): 49–98.

6. E. Hess, *The Tell-Tale Eye* (New York: Van Nostrand Reinhold, 1975).

7. P. Ekman, "Communication Through Nonverbal Behavior: A Source of Information About an Interpersonal Relationship," in *Affect Cognition and Personality,* edited by S. S. Tomkins and C. E. Izard (New York: Springer, 1965).

8. J. K. Burgoon, L. A. Stern, and L. Dillman, *Interpersonal Adaptation: Dyadic Interaction Patterns* (Cambridge, England: Cambridge University Press, 1995).

9. A. S. E. Hubbard, "Interpersonal Coordination in Interactions: Evaluations and Social Skills," *Communication Research Reports,* 17 (Winter 2000): 95–104.

10. R. L. Birdwhistell, *Kinesics and Context* (Philadelphia: University of Pennsylvania Press, 1970).

11. N. Zunin and M. Zunin, *Contact: The First Four Minutes* (New York: Signet, 1976).

12. J. H. Bert and K. Piner, "Social Relationships and the Lack of Social Relations," in *Personal Relationships and Social Support,* edited by S. W. Duck with R. C. Silver (London: Sage, 1989).

13. S. M. Jones and L. K. Guerrero, "The Effects of Nonverbal Immediacy and Verbal Person Centeredness in the Emotional Support Process," *Human Communication Research,* 27 (October 2001): 567–96.

14. A. F. Koerner and M. A. Fitzpatrick, "Nonverbal Communication and Marital Adjustment and Satisfaction: The Role of Decoding Relationship Relevant and Relationship Irrelevant Affect," *Communication Monographs,* 69 (March 2002): 33–51.

15. Burgoon and Bacue, "Nonverbal Communication Skills."

16. B. M. DePaulo and H. S. Friedman, "Nonverbal Communication," in *The Handbook of Social Psychology,* edited by D. T. Gilbert, S. T. Fiske, and G. Lindzey (New York: McGraw-Hill, 1998).

17. M. Argyle, *Bodily Communication* (New York: Methuen, 1988).

18. W. G. Woodal and J. K. Burgoon, "The Effects of Nonverbal Synchrony on Message Comprehension and Persuasiveness," *Journal of Nonverbal Behavior,* 5 (1981): 207–23.

19. Argyle, *Bodily Communication.*

20. P. Ekman and W. V Friesen, "Constants Across Cultures in the Face and Emotion," *Journal of Personality and Social Psychology,* 17 (1971): 124–29; Argyle, *Bodily Communication,* 157; I. Eibl-Eibesfeldt, "Similarities and Differences Between Cultures in Expressive Movements," in *Nonverbal Communication,* edited by R. A. Hinde (Cambridge, England: Royal Society & Cambridge University Press, 1972); P. Collett, "History and Study of Expressive Action," in *Historical Social Psychology,* edited by K. Gergen and M. Gergen (Hillsdale, NJ: Erlbaum, 1984); E. T. Hall, *The Silent Language* (Garden City, NY: Doubleday, 1959); R. Shuter, "Gaze Behavior in Interracial and Intraracial Interaction," *International and Intercultural Communication Annual,* 5 (1979): 48–55; R. Shuter, "Proxemics and Tactility in Latin America," *Journal of Communication,* 26 (1976): 46–52; E. T. Hall, *The Hidden Dimension* (New York: Doubleday, 1966). For an excellent discussion of world view and the implications for intercultural communication, see C. H. Dodd, *Dynamics of Intercultural Communication* (Dubuque, IA: Brown & Benchmark, 1995); G. W. Beattie, *Talk: An Analysis of Speech and Non-Verbal Behavior in Conversation* (Milton Keynes: Open University Press, 1983); O. Hargie, C. Sanders, and D. Dickson, *Social Skills in Interpersonal Communication* (London: Routledge, 1994); O. Hargie (Ed.), *The Handbook of Communication Skills* (London: Routledge, 1997).

21. K. N. Blurton-Jones and G. M. Leach, "Behavior of Children and Their Mothers at Separation and Parting," in *Ethological Studies of Child Behavior,* edited by N. Blurton-Jones (Cambridge, England: Cambridge University Press, 1972).

22. This example originally appeared in Collett, "History and Study of Expressive Action."

23. R. Birdwhistell, *Kinesics and Context.* Also see D. G. Leathers, *Successful*

*Nonverbal Communications and Applications* (Boston: Allyn & Bacon, 1998).

24. A. E. Scheflen, "Quasi-Courtship Behavior in Psychotherapy," *Psychiatry,* 28 (1965): 245–57.

25. M. Moore, "Interpreting Nonverbal Messages," *Journal of Ethology and Sociology* (Summer 1994); also see D. Knox and K. Wilson, "Dating Behaviors of University Students," *Family Relations,* 30 (1981): 255–58.

26. M. Reece and R. Whitman, "Expressive Movements, Warmth, and Verbal Reinforcement," *Journal of Abnormal and Social Psychology,* 64 (1962): 234–36.

27. A. Mehrabian, *Silent Messages* (Belmont, CA: Wadsworth, 1972), 108.

28. Ekman and Friesen, "The Repertoire of Nonverbal Behavior."

29. A. T. Dittman, "The Body Movement–Speech Rhythm Relationship as a Cue to Speech Encoding," in *Studies in Dyadic Communication,* edited by A. W. Siegman and B. Pope (New York: Pergamon, 1972).

30. A. A. Cohen and R. P. Harrison, "Intentionality in the Use of Hand Illustrators in Face-to-Face Communication Situations," *Journal of Personality and Social Psychology,* 28 (1973): 276–79.

31. C. Darwin, *Expression of Emotions in Man and Animals* (Chicago: University of Chicago Press, 1965). Originally published 1872.

32. A. Mehrabian and M. Williams, "Nonverbal Concomitants of Perceived and Intended Persuasiveness," *Journal of Personality and Social Psychology,* 13 (1969): 37–58.

33. M. Argyle, E. Alkema, and R. Gilmour, "The Communication of Friendly and Hostile Attitudes by Verbal and Nonverbal Signals," *European Journal of Social Psychology,* 1 (1972): 385–402.

34. D. Morris, *People Watching* (London: Vantage Press, 2002), 104.

35. A. Kendon, "Some Functions of Gaze-Direction in Social Interaction," *Acta Psychologica,* 26 (1967): 22–63.

36. S. W. Duck, *Understanding Relationships* (New York: Guilford Press, 1991), 54.

37. M. Knapp and J. A. Hall, *Nonverbal Communication in Human*

*Interaction* (Fort Worth, TX: Harcourt Brace, 1997), 313.

38. P. Ekman, W. V. Friesen, and S. S. Tomkins, "Facial Affect Scoring Technique: A First Validity Study," *Semiotica*, 3 (1971): 37–58; P. Ekman and W. V. Friesen, *Unmasking the Face* (Englewood Cliffs, NJ: Prentice Hall, 1975).

39. Associated Press, "Frowning Outlawed in Meeting Code of Conduct," Retrieved May 7, 2003 from www.Boston.com

40. Ekman and Friesen, *Unmasking the Face*; Ekman, Friesen, and Tomkins, "Facial Affect Scoring Technique."

41. Ekman and Friesen, *Unmasking the Face*; Ekman, Friesen, and Tomkins, "Facial Affect Scoring Technique."

42. A. Buck, R. E. Miller, and C. F. William, "Sex, Personality, and Physiological Variables in the Communication of Affect via Facial Expression," *Journal of Personality and Social Psychology*, 30 (1974): 587–89

43. Ekman and Friesen, *Unmasking the Face*.

44. J. Schwartz, "NASA Official Says He Held Out Hope in Final Moments," *The New York Times*, February 15, 2003: A14.

45. Ekman and Friesen, *Unmasking the Face*.

46. G. J. McHugo, "Emotional Reactions to a Political Leader's Expressive Displays," *Journal of Personality and Social Psychology*, 49 (1985); 513–29.

47. D. LaPlante and N. Ambady, "Multiple Messages: Facial Recognition Advantage for Compound Expressions," *Journal of Nonverbal Behavior*, 24 (Fall 2000): 211–25.

48. J. Elliott, "If You're Happy and You Know It, You're a Buddhist," *The Sunday Times* [London], May 25, 2003: 1.14.

49. "The Crying-Baby Translator," *The New York Times Magazine*, December 15, 2002: 78.

50. R. Davitz, *The Communication of Emotional Meaning*, (New York: McGraw-Hill, 1964).

51. K. K. Sereno and G. J. Hawkins, "The Effect of Variations in Speakers' Nonfluency upon Audience Ratings of

Attitude Toward the Speech Topic and Speakers' Credibility," *Speech Monographs*, 34 (1967): 58–74; G. R. Miller and M. A. Hewgill, "The Effect of Variations in Nonfluency on Audience Ratings of Source Credibility," *Quarterly Journal of Speech*, 50 (1964): 36–44; Mehrabian and Williams, "Nonverbal Concomitants of Perceived and Intended Persuasiveness."

52. R. L. Street, R. M. Brady, and W. B. Putman, "The Influence of Speech Rate Stereotypes and Rate Similarity on Listeners' Evaluations of Speakers," *Journal of Language and Social Psychology*, 2 (1983): 37–56.

53. T. Bruneau, "Communicative Silences: Forms and Functions," *Journal of Communication*, 23 (1973): 17–46.

54. S. J. Baker, "The Theory of Silence," *Journal of General Psychology*, 53 (1955): 145–67.

55. E. T. Hall, *The Hidden Dimension* (Garden City, NY: Doubleday, 1966).

56. R. Sommer, "Studies in Personal Space," *Sociometry*, 22 (1959): 247–60.

57. Sommer, "Studies in Personal Space."

58. See B. Stenzor, "The Spatial Factor in Face-to-Face Discussion Groups," *Journal of Abnormal and Social Psychology*, 45 (1950): 552–55.

59. A. Montague, *Touching: The Human Significance of the Skin* (New York: Harper & Row, 1978).

60. Montague, *Touching*.

61. N. M. Henley, *Body Politics: Power, Sex, and Nonverbal Communication* (Englewood Cliffs, NJ: Prentice Hall, 1977).

62. J. Kelly, "Dress as Non-Verbal Communication," paper presented to the annual conference of the American Association for Public Opinion Research, May 1969.

63. J. C. Valentine, V. Blankenship, H. Cooper, and E. S. Sullins, "Interpersonal Expectancy Effects and the Preference for Consistency," *Representative Research in Social Psychology*, 25 (2001): 26–33.

64. J. Lefkowitz, R. Blake, and J. Mouton, "Status Factors in Pedestrian Violation of Traffic Signals," *Journal of Abnormal and Social Psychology*, 51 (1970): 4–6.

65. J. T. Molloy, *Dress for Success* (New York: Warner Books, 1975); J. T. Molloy, *The Woman's Dress for Success Book* (Chicago: Follett, 1977).

66. Mehrabian, *Nonverbal Communication*.

67. L. Hinkle, "Nonverbal Immediacy Communication Behaviors and Liking in Marital Relationships," *Communication Research Reports*, 16(1), (1999): 81–90.

68. For an excellent review of gender and nonverbal cues, see J. Pearson, L. Turner, and W. Todd-Mancillas, *Gender and Communication* (Dubuque, IA: William C. Brown, 1991); D. K. Ivy and P. Backlund, *Exploring GenderSpeak: Personal Effectiveness in Gender Communication* (New York: McGraw-Hill, 1994). Also see D. G. Leathers, *Successful Nonverbal Communication: Principles and Applications* (Boston: Allyn & Bacon, 1997).

69. J. K. Burgoon and B. A. Le Poire, "Nonverbal Cues and Interpersonal Judgments: Participant and Observer Perceptions of Intimacy, Dominance, Composure, and Formality," *Communication Monographs*, 66 (1999): 105–24.

70. Jones and Guerrero, "The Effects of Nonverbal Immediacy"; also see D. J. Dolin and M. Booth-Butterfield, "Reach Out and Touch Someone: Analysis of Nonverbal Comforting Responses, *Communication Quarterly*, 41 (1993): 383–93.

71. Argyle, *Bodily Communication*.

72. K. J. Tusing and J. P. Dillard, "The Sounds of Dominance: Vocal Precursors of Perceived Dominance During Interpersonal Influence," *Human Communication Research*, 26 (January 2000): 148–71.

73. Mehrabian, *Nonverbal Communication*.

74. Argyle, *Bodily Communication*.

75. Burgoon, Stern, and Dillman, *Interpersonal Adaptation*.

76. B. A. Le Poire and S. M. Yoshimura, "The Effects of Expectancies and Actual Communication on Nonverbal Adaptation and Communication Outcomes: A Test of Interaction Adaptation Theory," *Communication Monographs*, 66 (1999): 1–30.

77. Burgoon and Bacue, "Nonverbal Communication Skills."

78. See Birdwhistell, *Kinesics and Context*.

79. E. Hatfield, J. T. Cacioppo, and R. L. Rapson, *Emotional Contagion* (New York: Cambridge University Press, 1994).

80. Hubbard, "Interpersonal Coordination in Interactions."

81. For an excellent summary of deception and nonverbal communication, see Leathers, *Successful Nonverbal Communication*, 253–74. Also see P. Ekman, M. O' Sullivan, W. V. Friesen, and K. R. Scherer, "Invited Article: Face, Voice, and Body in Detecting Deceit," *Journal of Nonverbal Behavior*, 15 (1991): 125–35; P. Ekman and W. Friesen, "Detecting Deception from the Body and Face," *Journal of Personality and Social Psychology*, 29 (1974): 288–98; M. Millar and K. Millar, "Detection of Deception in Familiar and Unfamiliar Persons: The Effects of Information Restriction," *Journal of Nonverbal Behavior*, 19 (1995): 69–84; D. B. Buller, J. K. Burgoon, A. Buslig, and J. F. Roiger, "Interpersonal Deception: VIII. Further Analysis of the Nonverbal Correlates of Equivocation from the Bavelas et al. (1990) Research," *Journal of Language & Social Psychology*, 13 (1994): 396–417.

82. Adapted from Leathers, *Successful Nonverbal Communication*, with supporting research from Ekman and Friesen, "Detecting Deception from the Face and Body"; M. Zuckerman, B. M. DePaulo, and R. Rosenthal, "Verbal and Nonverbal Communication of Deception," in L. Berkowitz (Ed.), *Advances in Experimental Social Psychology*, vol. 14 (New York: Academic Press, 1981), 1–60.

83. A. Vrij, K. Edward, K. P. Roberts, and R. Bull, "Detecting Deceit Via Analysis of Verbal and Nonverbal Behavior," *Journal of Nonverbal Communication*, 24 (Winter 2000): 239–63; also see Burgoon and Bacue, "Nonverbal Communication Skills."

84. H. S. Park, T. R. Levine, S. A. McCornack, K. Morrison, and M. Ferrara, "How People Really Detect Lies," *Communication Monographs*, 69 (June 2002): 144–57.

**Chapter 8**

1. Our definition of conflict is adapted from W. Wilmot and J. Hocker, *Interpersonal Conflict* (New York: McGraw-Hill, 2000).

2. D. Cramer, "Relationship Satisfaction and Conflict Style in Romantic Relationships," *Journal of Psychology*, 134 (2000): 337–41.

3. For a review of literature about violence in relationships, see L. N. Olson and T. D. Golish, "Topics of Conflict and Patterns of Aggression in Romantic Relationships," *Southern Communication Journal*, 67 (Winter 2002): 180–200.

4. D. J. Canary, W. R. Cupach, and R. T. Serpe, "A Competence-Based Approach to Examining Interpersonal Conflict: Test of a Longitudinal Model," *Communication Research*, 29 (February 2001): 79–104.

5. J. W. Keltner, *Mediation: Toward a Civilized System of Dispute Resolution* (Annandale VA: Speech Communication Association, 1987); also see Wilmot and Hocker, *Interpersonal Conflict*.

6. R. Dumlao and R. A. Botta, "Family Communication Patterns and the Conflict Styles Young Adults Use with Their Fathers," *Communication Quarterly*, 48 (Spring 2000): 174–89. Also see W. Aquilino, "From Adolescent to Young Adult: A Prospective Study of Parent-Child Relations During the Transition to Adulthood," *Journal of Marriage and the Family*, 59 (1997): 670–86.

7. R. J. Doolittle, *Orientations of Communication and Conflict* (Chicago: Science Research Associates, 1976), 7–9.

8. D. Canary, W. Cupach, and S. Messman, *Relationship Conflict* (Thousand Oaks, CA: Sage, 1995); J. Gottman, *What Predicts Divorce? The Relationship Between Marital Process and Marital Outcomes* (Hillsdale, NJ: Erlbaum, 1994).

9. S. A. Lloyd, "Conflict in Premarital Relationships: Differential Perceptions of Males and Females," *Family Relations*, 36 (1987): 290–94.

10. E. H. Mudd, H. E. Mitchell, and J. W. Bullard, "Areas of Marital Conflict in Successfully Functioning and Unsuccessfully Functioning Families," *Journal of Health and Human Behavior*, 3 (1962): 88–93; N. R. Vines, "Adult Unfolding and Marital Conflict," *Journal of Marital and Family Therapy*, 5 (1979): 5–14.

11. B. A. Fisher, "Decision Emergence: Phases in Group Decision Making," *Speech Monographs*, 37 (1970): 60.

12. G. R. Miller and M. Steinberg, *Between People: A New Analysis of Interpersonal Communication* (Chicago: Science Research Associates, 1975), 264.

13. C. M. Hoppe, "Interpersonal Aggression as a Function of Subject's Sex Role Identification, Opponent's Sex, and Degree of Provocation," *Journal of Personality*, 47 (1979): 317–29.

14. W. Wilmot and J. Hocker, *Interpersonal Conflict* (New York: McGraw-Hill, 2000); also see S. W. Littlejohn and K. Domenici, *Engaging Communication in Conflict: Systemic Practice* (Thousand Oaks, CA: Sage, 2001).

15. J. M. Olsen, *The Process of Social Organization* (New York: Holt, Rinehart and Winston, 1978).

16. B. M. Gayle, R. W. Preiss, and M. Allen, "A Meta-Analytic Interpretation of Intimate and Nonintimate Interpersonal Conflict," in *Interpersonal Communication Research: Advances Through Meta-Analysis*, edited by M. Allen, R. W. Preiss, B. M. Gayle, and N. Burrell (Mahwah, NJ: Erlbaum, 2002), 345–70.

17. Olsen, *The Process of Social Organization*.

18. S. Ting-Toomey, "A Face Negotiation Theory," in *Theories in Intercultural Communication*, edited by Y. Kim and W. Gudykunst (Newbury Park, CA: Sage, 1988).

19. Ting-Toomey, "A Face Negotiation Theory."

20. Wilmot and Hocker, *Interpersonal Conflict*, 15–16.

21. A. C. Filley, *Interpersonal Conflict Resolution* (Glenview, IL: Scott Foresman, 1975); R. H. Turner, "Conflict and Harmony," *Family Interaction* (New York: Wiley, 1970); K. Galvin and B. J. Brommel, *Family Communication: Cohesion and Change* (New York: Addison Wesley Longman, 2000).

22. Olson and Golish, "Topics of Conflict and Patterns of Aggression in Romantic Relationships."

23. Wilmot and Hocker, *Interpersonal Conflict*, 10.

24. Adapted from D. W. Johnson, *Reaching Out: Interpersonal Effectiveness and Self-Actualization* (Boston: Allyn & Bacon, 2000), 314.

25. M. Deutsch, *The Resolution of Conflict* (New Haven, CT: Yale University Press, 1973).

26. V. Satir, *Peoplemaking* (Palo Alto: Science and Behavior Books, 1972).

27. R. Kilmann and K. Thomas, "Interpersonal Conflict-Handling Behavior as Reflections of Jungian Personality Dimensions," *Psychological Reports,* 37 (1975): 971–80; K. W. Thomas and R. H. Kilmann, *Thomas-Kilmann Conflict Mode Instrument* (Tuxedo, NY: XICOM, 1974).

28. A. Buysse. A. De Clercq, L. Verhofstadt, E. Heene, H. Roeyers, and P. Van Oost, "Dealing with Relational Conflict: A Picture in Milliseconds," *Journal of Social and Personal Relationships,* 17 (2000): 574–79.

29. J. T. Tedeschi, "Threats and Promises," in *The Structure of Conflict,* edited by R. Swingle (New York: Academic Press, 1970).

30. R. Fisher and W. Ury, *Getting to Yes: Negotiating Agreement Without Giving In* (Boston: Houghton Mifflin, 1988). Also see D. Yankelovich, *The Magic of Dialogue: Transforming Conflict into Cooperation* (New York: Simon & Schuster, 1999).

31. Our discussion of the advantages and disadvantages of using different conflict management styles is based on material in Wilmot and Hocker, *Interpersonal Conflict.*

32. L. Powell and M. Hickson, "Power Imbalance and Anticipation of Conflict Resolution: Positive and Negative Attributes of Perceptual Recall," *Communication Research Reports,* 17 (Spring 2000): 181–90.

33. D. Cramer, "Linking Conflict Management Behaviors and Relational Satisfaction: The Intervening Role of Conflict Outcome Satisfaction," *Journal of Social and Personal Relationships,* 19 (2000): 425–32.

34. D. A. Cai and E. L. Fink, "Conflict Style Differences Between Individualists and Collectivists," *Communication Monographs,* 69 (March 2002): 67–87.

35. M. E. Roloff, L. L. Putnam, and L. Anastasiou, "Negotiation Skills," in *Handbook of Communication and Social Interaction Skills,* edited by J. O. Greene and B. R. Burleson (Mahwah, NJ: Erlbaum, 2003), 801–33.

36. This section on negotiation, including each of the suggested win–lose and win–win strategies, is adapted from Roloff, Putnam, and Anastasiou, "Negotiation Skills."

37. R. Fisher and W. L. Ury, *Getting to Yes: Negotiating Agreement without Giving In* (Boston: Houghton Mifflin, 1981).

38. Fisher and Ury, *Getting to Yes.*

39. Roloff, Putnam, and Anastasiou, "Negotiation Skills."

40. D. Wallis, "Negotiator at Large," *The New York Times Magazine,* January 26, 2003, 13.

41. Roloff, Putnam, and Anastasiou, "Negotiation Skills."

42. Our discussion of conflict management skills is based on several excellent discussions of conflict management prescriptions. We acknowledge Fisher and Ury, *Getting to Yes*; R. Boulton, *People Skills* (New York: Simon & Schuster, 1979); D. A. Romig and L. J. Romig, *Structured Teamwork® Guide* (Austin, TX: Performance Resources, 1990); O. Hargie, C. Saunders, and D. Dickson, *Social Skills in Interpersonal Communication* (London: Routledge, 1994); S. Deep and L. Sussman, *Smart Moves* (Reading, MA: Addison-Wesley, 1990); Wilmot and Hocker, *Interpersonal Conflict*; M. D. Davis, E. L. Eshelman, and M. McKay, *The Relaxation and Stress Reduction Workbook* (Oakland, CA: New Harbinger Publications, 1982); W. A. Donohue and R. Kolt, *Managing Interpersonal Conflict* (Newbury Park: CA: Sage, 1992); O. Hargie (Ed.), *The Handbook of Communication Skills* (London: Routledge, 1997); Littlejohn and Domenici, *Engaging Communication in Conflict;* and M. W. Isenhart and M. Spangle, *Collaborative Approaches to Resolving Conflict* (Thousand Oaks, CA: Sage, 2000).

43. Boulton, *People Skills,* 217.

44. For additional strategies on managing emotion, see J. Gottman, *Why Marriages Succeed and Fail: And How You Can Make Yours Last* (New York: Simon & Schuster, 1994); J. Gottman, *The Seven Principles for Making Marriage Work* (New York: Crown, 1999). Also see D. W. Johnson, *Reaching Out.*

45. A. Ellis, *A New Guide to Rational Living* (North Hollywood, CA: Wilshire Books, 1977).

46. Fisher and Ury, *Getting to Yes*; Boulton, *People Skills*; Romig and Romig, *Structured Teamwork® Guide*; T. Gordon, *Leader Effectiveness Training (L.E.T): The No-Lose Way to Release the Productive Potential of People* (New York: Wyden Books, 1977).

47. S. Deep and L. Susman, *Smart Moves* (New York: Addison-Wesley, 1990).

48. J. Gottman, *What Predicts Divorce? The Relationship Between Marital Process and Marital Outcomes* (Hillsdale, NJ: Erlbaum, 1994).

49. M. Morris, J. Nadler, T. Kurtzberg, and L. Thompson, "Schmooze or Lose: Social Friction and Lubrication in E-Mail Negotiations," *Group Dynamics: Theory, Research and Practice,* 6 (2002): 89–100.

50. Ellis, *A New Guide to Rational Living.*

51. S. R. Covey, *The Seven Habits of Highly Effective People* (New York: Simon & Schuster, 1989), 235.

52. C. Pavitt and B. Kemp, "Contextual and Relational Factors in Interpersonal Negotiation Strategy Choice," *Communication Quarterly,* 47(2), (1999): 133–50.

53. Fisher and Ury, *Getting to Yes.*

54. E. Goffman, *Interaction Rituals: Essays on Face-to-Face Interaction* (Garden City, NY: Doubleday, 1967).

55. S. Ting-Toomey, "Face and Facework: An Introduction," in S. Ting-Toomey (Ed.), *The Challenge of Facework* (Albany, NY: SUNY Press, 1994), 1–14; S. Ting-Toomey, "Managing Intercultural Conflicts Effectively," in *Intercultural Communication: A Reader,* edited by L. A. Samovar and R. E. Porter (Belmont, CA: Wadsworth, 1994), 360–72. Also see S. Ting-Toomey and L. Chung, "Cross-Cultural Interpersonal Communication: Theoretical Trends and Research Directions," in *Communication in Personal Relationships Across Cultures,* edited by W. B. Gudykunst, S. Ting-Toomey, and T. Nishida (Thousand Oaks, CA: Sage, 1996), 237–61; M. W. Isenhart and M. Spangle, *Collaborative Approaches to Resolving Conflict,* 19–20.

56. J. W. Pfeiffer and J. E. Jones (Eds.), *A Handbook of Structured Experiences for Human Relations Training,* vol. 2 (La Jolla, CA: University Associates, 1974), 62–76.

## Chapter 9

1. L. von Bertalanffy, "Der Organismus als physikalisches System betrachtet," *Die Naturwissenschaften,* 28 (1940), 521–31.

2. R. A. Mackey, M. A. Diemer, and B. A. O'Brien, "Psychological Intimacy in Lasting Relationships of Heterosexual and Same-Gender Couples," *Sex Roles,* 43 (2000): 201–27.

3. F. E. Millar and L. E. Rogers, "A Relational Approach to Interpersonal Communication," in *Explorations in Interpersonal Communication,* edited by G. R. Miller (Newbury Park, CA: Sage, 1976), 87–103.

4. K. Chow, "Social Support and Subjective Well-Being Among Hong Kong Chinese Young Adults," *Journal of Genetic Psychology,* 160 (September 1999): 319–31.

5. I. Altman and D. Taylor, *Social Penetration: The Development of Interpersonal Relationships* (New York: Holt, Rinehart, and Winston, 1973).

6. L. K. Knobloch and D. H. Solomon, "Information Seeking Beyond Initial Interaction: Negotiating Relational Uncertainty within Close Relationships," *Human Communication Research,* 28 (April 2002): 243–57.

7. W. Stoebe, "Self-Esteem and Interpersonal Attraction," in *Theory and Practice in Interpersonal Attraction,* edited by S. Duck (London: Academic Press, 1977).

8. S. Sprecher, "Insiders' Perspectives on Reasons for Attraction to a Close Other," *Social Psychology Quarterly,* 61 (1998): 287–300.

9. Sprecher, "Insiders' Perspectives."

10. S. W. Duck, *Personal Relationships and Personal Constructs: A Study of Friendship Formation* (New York: Wiley, 1993).

11. Sprecher, "Insiders' Perspectives."

12. Sprecher, "Insiders' Perspectives."

13. M. Sunnafrank, "Interpersonal Attraction and Attitude Similarity: A Communication Based Assessment," in *Communication Yearbook, 14,* edited by J. A. Anderson (Newbury Park, CA: Sage, 1991), 451–83.

14. Sunnafrank, "Interpersonal Attraction and Attitude Similarity."

15. Sprecher, "Insiders' Perspectives."

16. W. Schutz, *Interpersonal Underworld* (Palo Alto, CA: Science and Behavior Books, 1966).

17. M. Sunnafrank, "Predicted Outcome Value During Initial Interaction: A Reformulation of Uncertainty Reduction Theory," *Human Communication Research,* 13 (1986): 3–33.

18. Sunnafrank, "Predicted Outcome Value During Initial Interaction."

19. Sprecher, "Insiders' Perspectives."

20. M. V. Redmond and D. A. Vrchota, "The Effects of Varying Lengths of Initial Interaction on Attraction and Uncertainty Reduction," paper presented at the annual meeting of the National Communication Association, New Orleans (1994).

21. S. Sprecher and D. Felmlee, "The Balance of Power in Romantic Heterosexual Couples over Time from 'His' and 'Her' Perspectives," *Sex Roles,* 37 (1997): 361–79.

22. Sprecher and Felmlee, "The Balance of Power in Romantic Heterosexual Couples."

23. F. E. Millar and L. E. Rogers, "Relational Dimensions of Interpersonal Dynamics," in *Interpersonal Processes: New Directions in Communication Research,* edited by M. E. Roloff and G. R. Miller (Newbury Park, CA: Sage, 1987), 117–39.

24. J. R. P. French and B. H. Raven, "The Bases of Social Power," in *Group Dynamics,* edited by J. D. Cartwright and A. Zander (Evanston, IL: Row, Peterson, 1962), 607–22.

25. M. G. Lawler and G. S. Risch, "Time, Sex and Money: The First Five Years of Marriage," *America,* 184 (2001): 16–20.

26. J. M. Honeycutt and J. M. Wiemann, "Analysis of Functions of Talk and Reports of Imagined Interactions (IIs) During Engagement and Marriage," *Human Communication Research,* 25 (1999): 399–419.

27. For an excellent review of the nature of friendship, see M. Argyle, *The Psychology of Interpersonal Behavior* (London: Penguin, 1983).

28. A. M. Nicotera, "The Importance of Communication in Interpersonal Relationships," in *Interpersonal Communication in Friend and Mate Relationships,* edited by A. M. Nicotera and

Associates (Albany: State University of New York Press, 1993), 3–12.

29. Nicotera, "The Importance of Communication in Interpersonal Relationships."

30. J. Yerby, N. Buerkel-Rothfuss, and A. P. Bochner, *Understanding Family Communication* (Needham Heights, MA: Allyn & Bacon, 1998).

31. M. Argyle, *The Social Psychology of Everyday Life* (London: Routledge, 1991).

32. Nicotera, "The Importance of Communication in Interpersonal Relationships."

33. Argyle, *The Social Psychology of Everyday Life.*

34. Argyle, *The Social Psychology of Everyday Life,* 49.

35. P. Marsh, *Eye to Eye: How People Interact* (Topfield, MA: Salem House, 1988).

36. W. J. Dickens and D. Perlman, "Friendship over the Life-Cycle," in *Personal Relationships,* vol. 2. *Developing Personal Relationships,* edited by S. W. Duck and R. Gilmour (London: Academic Press, 1981).

37. R. L. Selman, "Toward a Structural Analysis of Developing Interpersonal Relations Concepts: Research with Normal and Disturbed Preadolescent Boys," in *Minnesota Symposia on Child Psychology,* vol. 10, edited by A. D. Pick (Minneapolis: University of Minnesota Press, 1976).

38. Dickens and Perlman, "Friendship over the Life-Cycle."

39. M. Dainton, E. Zelley, and E. Langan, "Maintaining Friendships Throughout the Lifespan," in *Maintaining Relationships Through Communication,* edited by D. J. Canary and M. Dainton (Mahwah, NJ: Erlbaum, 2003), 79–102.

40. C. Buress and J. Pearson, "Interpersonal Rituals in Marriage and Adult Friendship," *Communication Monographs,* 64 (1997): 25–46.

41. H. J. Markman, F. Floyd, and F. Dickson, "Towards a Model for the Prediction of Primary Prevention of Marital and Family Distress and Dissolution," in *Personal Relationships,* vol. 4. *Dissolving Personal Relationships,* edited by S. W. Duck and R. Gilmour (London: Academic Press, 1982).

42. S. H. Mathews, *Friendships Through the Life Course: Oral Biographies in Old Age* (Beverly Hills, CA: Sage, 1986).

43. S. J. Holladay and K. S. Kerns, "Do Age Differences Matter in Close and Casual Relationships? A Comparison of Age Discrepant and Age Peer Friendships," *Communication Reports,* 12 (1999): 101–14.

44. M. J. Collier, "Communication Competence Problematics in Ethnic Relationships," *Communication Monographs,* 63, (1996): 314–35.

45. Collier, "Communication Competence."

46. H. M. Reeder, "'I like you . . . as a friend': The Role of Attraction in Cross-Sex Friendship," *Journal of Social and Personal Relationships,* 17 (2000): 329–48.

47. L. Rubin, *Just Friends: The Role of Friendship in Our Lives* (New York: Harper & Row, 1985).

48. J. D. Cunningham and J. K. Antill, "Love in Developing Romantic Relationships," in *Personal Relationships, 2: Developing Personal Relationships,* edited by S. W. Duck and R. Gilmour (London: Academic Press, 1981).

49. Z. Rubin, *Liking and Loving: An Invitation to Social Psychology* (New York: Holt, Rinehart and Winston, 1973).

50. A. Aron and E. N. Aron, "Love," in *Perspectives on Close Relationships,* edited by A. Weber and J. Harvey (Boston: Allyn & Bacon, 1994).

51. L. A. Kurdek, "Relationship Outcomes and Their Predictors: Longitudinal Evidence from Heterosexual Married, Gay Cohabiting, and Lesbian Cohabiting Couples," *Journal of Marriage and Family,* 60 (1998): 553–68.

52. R. J. Sternberg, "A Triangular Theory of Love," *Psychological Review,* 93 (1986): 119–35.

53. C. Hendrick and S. S. Hendrick, "Research on Love: Does It Measure Up?" *Journal of Personality and Social Psychology,* 56 (1989): 784–94.

54. R. Lemieux and J. L. Hale, "Intimacy, Passion, and Commitment in Young Romantic Relationships: Successfully Measuring the Triangular Theory of Love," *Psychological Reports,* 85 (1999): 497–504.

55. J. A. Lee, "A Typology of Styles of Loving," *Personality and Social Psychology,* Bulletin 3 (1977): 173–82.

56. M. A. Fitzpatrick, *Between Husbands and Wives: Communication in Marriage* (Newbury Park, CA: Sage, 1988).

57. D. L. Kelly, "Relational Expectancy Fulfillment as an Explanatory Variable in Distinguishing Couple Types," *Human Communication Research,* 25 (1999): 420–42.

58. Kelly, "Relational Expectancy Fulfillment."

59. Fitzpatrick, *Between Husbands and Wives.*

60. M. M. Martin and C. M. Andersen, "Aggressive Communication Traits: How Similar Are Young Adults and Their Parents in Argumentativeness, Assertiveness, and Verbal Aggressiveness?" *Western Journal of Communication,* 61 (1997): 299–314.

61. L. D. Ritchie and M. A. Fitzpatrick, "Family Communication Patterns: Measuring Intrapersonal Perceptions of Interpersonal Relationships," *Communication Research,* 17 (1990): 523–44.

62. M. Booth-Butterfield and R. Sidelinger, "The Influence of Family Communication on the College-Aged Child: Openness, Attitudes and Actions About Sex and Alcohol," *Communication Quarterly,* 46 (1998): 295–308.

63. L. K. Guerrero and W. A. Afifi, "Some Things Are Better Left Unsaid: Topic Avoidance in Family Relationships," *Communication Quarterly,* 43 (1995): 276–96.

64. Guerrero and Afifi, "Some Things Are Better Left Unsaid."

65. K. Kitzmann, R. Cohen, and R. L. Lockwood, "Are Only Children Missing Out? Comparison of the Peer-Related Social Competence of Only Children and Siblings," *Journal of Social and Personal Relationships,* 19 (2002): 299–316.

**Chapter 10**

1. L. A. Baxter and C. Bullis, "Turning Points in Developing Romantic Relationships," *Communication Research,* 12 (1986): 469–93.

2. Baxter and Bullis, "Turning Points."

3. C. R. Berger and J. J. Bradac, *Language and Social Knowledge: Uncertainty and Interpersonal Relations* (Baltimore: Edward Arnold, 1982).

4. W. Douglas, "Question Asking in Same and Opposite Sex Initial Interactions: The Effects of Anticipated Future Interactions," *Human Communication Research,* 14 (1987): 230–45.

5. S. W. Duck, "A Topography of Relationship Disengagement and Dissolution," in *Personal Relationships 4: Dissolving Personal Relationships,* edited by S. W. Duck (London: Academic Press, 1982), 1–29.

6. Duck, "A Topography of Relationship Disengagement and Dissolution."

7. D. DeStephen, "Integrating Relational Termination into a General Model of Communication Competence," paper presented at the annual meeting of the National Communication Association, Denver (1985).

8. S. Duck, "Interpersonal Communication in Developing Relationships," in *Explorations in Interpersonal Communication,* edited by G. R. Miller (Newbury Park, CA: Sage, 1976), 127–47.

9. J. W. Thibaut and H. H. Kelley, *The Social Psychology of Groups* (New York: Wiley, 1959).

10. I. Atlman and D. A. Taylor, *Social Penetration: The Development of Interpersonal Relationships* (New York: Holt, Rinehart and Winston, 1973).

11. S. Sunnafrank, "Predicted Outcome Value During Initial Interactions," *Human Communication Research,* 13 (1986): 3–33.

12. G. R. Miller and M. R. Parks, "Communicating in Dissolving Relationships," in *Personal Relationships 4: Dissolving Personal Relationships,* edited by S. W. Duck (London: Academic Press, 1982), 127–54.

13. A. L. Busboom, D. M. Collins, M. D. Givertz, and L. A. Levin, "Can We Still Be Friends? Resources and Barriers to Friendship Quality after Romantic Relationship Dissolution," *Personal Relationships,* 9 (2002): 215–23.

14. L. A. Baxter, "Dialectical Contradictions in Relationship Development," in *Handbook of Personal Relationships,* edited by S. W. Duck (Chichester, England: Wiley, 1988), 257–73; L. A. Baxter and B. M. Montomery, "Rethinking Communication in

Personal Relationships from a Dialectical Perspective," in *Handbook of Personal Relationships,* 2nd ed., edited by S. W. Duck (Chichester, England: Wiley, 1997), 325–49.

15. D. R. Pawlowski, "Dialectical Tensions in Marital Partners' Accounts of Their Relationships," *Communication Quarterly,* 46 (1998): 396–416.

16. Pawlowski, "Dialectical Tensions."

17. M. V. Redmond, "Content Adaptation in Everyday Interactions," paper presented at the annual meeting of the National Communication Association, Chicago (1997).

18. L. A. Baxter, "Interpersonal Communication as Dialogue: A Response to the 'Social Approaches' Forum," *Communication Theory,* 2 (1992): 330–38.

19. A. Hoppe-Nagao and S. Ting-Toomey, "Relational Dialectics and Management Strategies in Marital Couples," *Southern Communication Journal,* 67 (Winter 2002): 142–59.

20. Baxter, "Interpersonal Communication as Dialogue."

21. Adapted from K. Kellerman et al., "The Conversation MOP: Scenes in the Stream of Discourse," *Discourse Processes,* 12 (1989): 27–61.

22. A. E. Lindsey and W. R. Zahaki, "Perceptions of Men and Women Departing from Conversational Sex Role Stereotypes During Initial Interaction," in *Sex Differences and Similarities in Communication,* edited by D. J. Canary and K. Dindia (Mahwah, NJ: Erlbaum, 1998): 393–412.

23. R. A. Bell and J. A. Daly, "The Affinity Seeking Function of Communication," *Communication Monographs,* 51 (1984): 91–115.

24. Bell and Daly, "The Affinity Seeking Function of Communication."

25. C. R. Berger and R. J. Calabrese, "Some Explorations in Initial Interaction and Beyond: Toward a Developmental Theory of Interpersonal Communication," *Human Communication Research,* 1, (1975): 99–112; C. R. Berger and J. J. Bradac, *Language and Social Knowledge: Uncertainty in Interpersonal Relations* (Baltimore: Edward Arnold, 1982).

26. Berger and Bradac, *Language and Social Knowledge.*

27. Sunnafrank, "Predicted Outcome Value During Initial Interactions"; and "Interpersonal Attraction and Attitude Similarity," in *Communication Yearbook 14,* edited by J. A. Anderson (Newbury Park, CA: Sage, 1991), 451–83.

28. Berger and Bradac, *Language and Social Knowledge.*

29. R. A. Clark and J. G. Delia, "Individuals' Preferences for Friends' Approaches to Providing Support in Distressing Situations," *Communication Reports,* 10 (1997): 115–21.

30. S. A. Westmyer and S. A. Myers, "Communication Skills and Social Support Messages Across Friendship Levels," *Communication Research Reports,* 13 (1996): 191–97.

31. A. L. Vangelisti, "Communication Problems in Committed Relationships: An Attributional Analysis," in *Attributions, Accounts, and Close Relationships,* edited by J. H. Harvey, T. L. Orbuch, and A. L. Weber, (New York: Springer Verlag, 1992), 144–64.

32. G. Levinger, and D. J. Senn, "Disclosure of Feelings in Marriage," *Merrill-Palmer Quarterly* 12, (1967): 237–49. A. Bochner, "On the Efficacy of Openness in Close Relationships," in *Communication Yearbook 5,* edited by M. Burgoon (New Brunswick, NJ: Transaction Books, 1982), 109–24.

33. J. K. Alberts, "An Analysis of Couples' Conversational Complaints," *Communication Monographs,* 55 (1988): 184–97.

34. M. A. Fitzpatrick and D. M. Badzinski, "All in the Family: Interpersonal Communication in Kin Relationships," in *Handbook of Interpersonal Communication,* edited by M. L. Knapp and G. R. Miller (Beverly Hills, CA: Sage, 1985), 687–736.

35. G. R. Miller and F. Boster, "Persuasion in Personal Relationship," in *A Handbook of Personal Relationships,* edited by S. Duck (New York: Wiley, 1988): 275–88; M. G. Garko, "Perspectives and Conceptualizations of Compliance and Compliance Gaining," *Communication Quarterly,* 38, no. 2 (1990): 138–57.

## Chapter 11

1. S. Metts, "Relational Transgressions," in *The Dark Side of Interpersonal Communication,* edited by

W. R. Cupach and B. H. Spitzberg (Hillsdale, NJ: Erlbaum, 1994), 217–39.

2. F. D. Fincham, "The Account Episode in Close Relationships," in *Explaining One's Self to Others: Reason-Giving in a Social Context,* edited by M. L. McClaughlin, M. J. Cody, and S. J Read (Hillsdale, NJ: Erlbaum, 1992), 167–82.

3. G. Makoul and M. E. Roloff, "The Role of Efficacy and Outcome Expectations in the Decision to Withhold Relational Complaints," *Communication Research,* 25 (1998): 25–30.

4. M. L. McLaughlin, M. J. Cody, and H. D. O'Hair, "The Management of Failure Events: Some Contextual Determinants of Accounting Behavior," *Human Communication Research,* 9 (1983): 208–24.

5. Fincham, "The Account Episode in Close Relationships."

6. M. Dainton and B. Aylor, "A Relational Uncertainty Analysis of Jealousy, Trust, and Maintenance in Long-Distance Versus Geographically Close Relationships," *Communication Quarterly,* 49 (Spring 2001), 172–88.

7. Dainton and Aylor, "A Relational Uncertainty Analysis."

8. G. T. Guldner and C . H. Swensen, "Time Spent Together and Relationship Quality: Long-Distance Relationships as a Test Case," *Journal of Social and Personal Relationships,* 12 (1995): 313–20; A. J. Johnson, "Examining the Maintenance of Friendships: Are There Differences Between Geographically Close and Long-Distance Friends?" *Communication Quarterly,* 49 (Fall 2001): 424–35.

9. L. Stafford and J. R. Reske, "Idealization and Communication in Long-Distance Premarital Relationships," *Family Relations,* 39 (July, 1990): 274–79.

10. Stafford and Reske, "Idealization and Communication in Long-Distance Premarital Relationships."

11. J. Lyndon, T. Pierce, and S. O'Regan, "Coping with Moral Commitment to Long-Distance Dating Relationships," *Journal of Personality and Social Psychology,* 73 (1997): 104–13.

12. B. Le and C. R. Agnew, "Need Fulfillment and Emotional Experience in Interdependent Romantic Relationships," *Journal of Social and Personal Relationships,* 18 (2001): 423–40.

13. E. M. Sahlstein and T. Truong, "Proximal and Long-Distance Relations: A Web of Contradictions," paper presented at the annual meeting of the National Communication Association (2002).

14. Sahlstein and Truong, "Proximal and Long-Distance Relations."

15. Lyndon, Pierce, and O'Regan, "Coping with Moral Commitment to Long-Distance Dating Relationships."

16. A. Foeman and T. Nance, "Building New Cultures, Reframing Old Images: Success Strategies of Interracial Couples," *The Howard Journal of Communications,* 13 (2002): 237–49.

17. Foeman and Nance, "Building New Cultures, Reframing Old Images."

18. S. M. Haas and L. Stafford, "An Initial Examination of Maintenance Behaviors in Gay and Lesbian Relationships," *Journal of Social and Personal Relationships,* 15 (1998): 846–55.

19. Haas and Stafford, "An Initial Examination of Maintenance Behaviors in Gay and Lesbian Relationships."

20. T. P. Mottet, "The Role of Sexual Orientation in Predicting Outcome Value and Anticipated Communication Behaviors," *Communication Quarterly,* 48 (Summer 2000): 223–39.

21. Mottet, "The Role of Sexual Orientation in Predicting Outcome Value and Anticipated Communication Behaviors."

22. D. O'Hair and W. Cody, "Deception," in *The Dark Side of Interpersonal Communication,* edited by W. R. Cupach and B. H. Spitzberg (Hillsdale, NJ: Erlbaum, 1994), 181–213.

23. A. E. Lucchetti, "Deception in Disclosing One's Sexual History: Safe-Sex Avoidance or Ignorance?" *Communication Quarterly,* 47 (1999): 300–14.

24. O'Hair and Cody, "Deception."

25. T. R. Levine, K. J. K Asada, and L. L. Massi Lindsey, "The Relative Impact of Violation Type and Lie Severity on Judgments of Message Deceitfulness," paper presented at the annual meeting of the National Communication Association (2002).

26. M. V. Redmond, *Human Communication: Theories and Applications* (Boston, MA: Houghton Mifflin, 2000).

27. S. A. McCornack and T. R. Levine, "When Lies Are Uncovered: Emotional and Relational Outcomes of Discovered Deception," *Communication Monographs,* 57 (1990): 119–38.

28. D. A. DePaulo and B. M. Kashy, "Everyday Lies in Close and Casual Relationships." *Journal of Personality and Social Psychology,* 74, (1998): 63–80.

29. D. B. Buller and J. K. Burgoon, "Deception: Strategic and Nonstrategic Communication," in *Strategic Interpersonal Communication,* edited by J. A. Daly and J. M. Wiemann (Hillsdale, NJ: Erlbaum, 1994), 191–223; O'Hair and Cody, "Deception."

30. DePaulo and Kashy, "Everyday Lies in Close and Casual Relationships."

31. O'Hair and Cody, "Deception."

32. O'Hair and Cody, "Deception."

33. A. L. Vangelisti, "Messages That Hurt" in *The Dark Side of Interpersonal Communication,* edited by W. R. Cupach and B. H. Spitzberg (Hillsdale, NJ: Erlbaum, 1994), 181–213

34. Vangelisti, "Messages That Hurt."

35. S. L. Young and A. M. Bippus, "Does It Make a Difference If They Hurt You in a Funny Way? Humorously and Non-Humorously Phrased Hurtful Messages in Personal Relationships," *Communication Quarterly,* 49 (Winter 2001): 35–52.

36. A. L. Vangelisti and L. P. Crumley, "Reactions to Messages That Hurt: The Influence of Relational Contexts," *Communication Monographs,* 65 (1998): 173–96.

37. Vangelisti and Crumley, "Reaction to Messages That Hurt."

38. Vangelisti, "Messages That Hurt."

39. See D. A. Infante and C. J. Wigley, "Verbal Aggressiveness: An Interpersonal Model and Measure," *Communication Monographs,* 53 (1986): 61–69; D. A. Infante and W. I. Gorden, "Superior and Subordinate Communication Profiles: Implications for Independent-Mindedness and Upward Effectiveness," *Central States Speech Journal,* 38 (1987): 73–80; D. A. Infante, B. L. Riddle, C. L. Horvath, and S. A. Tumlin, "Verbal Aggressiveness: Messages and Reasons," *Communication Quarterly,* 40 (1992): 116–26; D. E. Ifert and L. Bearden, "The Influence of Argumentativeness and Verbal Aggression on Responses to Refused Requests," *Communication Reports,* 11, (1998): 145–54; also see M. J. Beatty, K. M. Valencic, J. E. Rudd, and J. A. Dobos, "A 'Dark Side' of Communication Avoidance: Indirect Interpersonal Aggressiveness," *Communication Research Reports,* 16(2), (1999): 103–09.

40. Infante and Wigley, "Verbal Aggressiveness."

41. Infante et al., "Verbal Aggressiveness: Messages and Reasons."

42. D. Kazoleas, "The Impact of Argumentativeness on Resistance to Persuasion," *Human Communication Research,* 20 (September 1993): 118–37.

43. F. H. van Eemeren and R. Grootendorst, *Argumentation, Communication and Fallacies: A Pragma-Dialectical Perspective* (Hillsdale, NJ: Erlbaum, 1992); F. H. van Eemeren, S. Jackson, and S. Jacobs, *Reconstructing Argumentative Discourse* (Tuscaloosa: University of Alabama Press, 1993).

44. D. A. Infante, *Arguing Constructively* (Prospect Heights, IL: Waveland Press, 1988).

45. S. A. Jang, S. W. Smith, and T. R. Levine, "To Stay or to Leave? The Role of Attachment Styles in Communication Patterns and Potential Termination of Romantic Relationships Following Discovery of Deception," *Communication Monographs,* 69 (2002): 236–52.

46. G. R. Miller and M. R. Parks, "Communication in Dissolving Relationships," in *Personal Relationships 4: Dissolving Personal Relationships,* edited by S. W. Duck (London: Academic Press, 1982), 127–54.

47. S. W. Duck, *Understanding Relationships* (New York: Guilford Press, 1991).

48. J. M. Gottman and S. Carrere, "Why Can't Men and Women Get Along? Developmental Roots and Marital Inequities," in *Communication and Relational Maintenance,* edited by D. J. Canary and L. Stafford (San Diego: Academic Press, 1991): 203–29.

49. G. O. Hagestad and M. A. Smyer, "Dissolving Long-Term Relationships: Patterns of Divorcing in Middle Age," in Duck, *Personal Relationships 4: Dissolving Personal Relationships,* edited by S. Duck (London: Academic Press, 1982), 155–88.

50. J. Gottman with N. Silver, *Why Marriages Succeed or Fail* (New York: Simon and Schuster, 1994).

51. Gottman and Silver, *Why Marriages Succeed or Fail.*

52. P. J. Lannutti and K. A. Cameron, "Beyond the Breakup: Heterosexual and Homosexual Post-Dissolution Relationships," *Communication Quarterly,* 50 (Spring 2002): 153–70.

53. Miller and Parks, "Communication in Dissolving Relationships."

54. S. W. Duck, "A Topography of Relationship Disengagement and Dissolution," in *Personal Relationships 4: Dissolving Personal Relationships,* edited by S. W. Duck (London: Academic Press, 1982), 1–29.

55. A. Weber, "Loving, Leaving, and Letting Go: Coping with Nonmarital Breakups," in *The Dark Side of Close Relationships,* edited by B. H. Spitzberg and W. R. Cupach (Mahwah, NJ: Erlbaum, 1998), 267–306.

56. M. J. Cody, "A Typology of Disengagement Strategies and an Examination of the Role Intimacy, Reactions to Inequity and Relational Problems Play in Strategy Selection," *Communication Monographs,* 49, (1982): 148–70.

57. M. Argyle and M. Henderson, *The Anatomy of Relationships* (New York: Guilford Press, 1991).

58. Duck, *Understanding Relationships.*

59. Duck, "A Typography."

60. Miller and Parks, "Communication in Dissolving Relationships."

61. L. A. Baxter, "Accomplishing Relationship Disengagement," in *Understanding Personal Relationships: An Interdisciplinary Approach,* edited by S. Duck and D. Perlman (Beverly Hills, CA: Sage, 1984): 243–65.

62. D. DeStephen, "Integrating Relational Termination into a General Model of Communication Competence," paper presented at the annual meeting of the Speech Communication Association, Denver (1985).

63. Baxter, "Accomplishing Relationship Disengagement."

64. DeStephen, "Integrating Relational Termination."

65. Cody, "A Typology of Disengagement Strategies."

66. A. Weber, "Loving, Leaving, and Letting Go."

**Chapter 12**

1. G. P. Murdock, *Social Structure* (New York: Free Press, 1965). Originally published in 1949.

2. G. D. Nass and G. W. McDonald, *Marriage and the Family* (New York: Random House, 1982), 5.

3. *The Miami Herald,* July 9, 1982, 12A.

4. A. P. Bochner, "Conceptual Frontiers in the Study of Communication in Families: An Introduction to the Literature," *Human Communication Research,* 2, (Summer 1976): 382.

5. V. Satir, *Peoplemaking* (Palo Alto, CA: Science and Behavior Books, 1972).

6. D. E. Beck and M. A. Jones, *Progress on Family Problems: A Nationwide Study of Clients' and Counselors' Views on Family Agency Services* (New York: Family Service Association of America, 1973).

7. Satir, *Peoplemaking.*

8. H. J. Markman, "Prediction of Mental Distress: A 5-Year Follow-Up," *Journal of Consulting and Clinical Psychology,* 49, (1981): 760–62.

9. D. H. L. Olson, H. L. McCubbin, H. L. Barnes, A. S. Larsen, M. J. Muxem, and M. A. Wilson, *Families: What Makes Them Work* (Beverly Hills, CA: Sage, 1983).

10. V. Satir, *The New Peoplemaking* (Mountain View, CA: Science and Behavior Books, 1988), 4.

11. Satir, *Peoplemaking,* 13–14.

12. J. P. Caughlin, "Family Communication Standards: What Counts as Excellent Family Communication and How Are Such Standards Associated with Family Satisfaction?" *Human Communication Research,* 29 (January 2003): 5–40.

13. K. M. Galvin and B. J. Brommel, *Family Communication: Cohesion and Change,* 5th ed. (New York: Longman, 2000).

14. J. Stachowiak, "Functional and Dysfunctional Families," in *Helping Families to Change,* edited by V. Satir, J. Stachowiak, and H. A. Taschman (New York: Jason Aronson, 1975).

15. A. Bockner and E. Eisenberg, "Family Process: Systems in Perspectives," in *Handbook of Communication Science,* edited by C. Berger and S. Chaffee (Beverly Hills: Sage, 1987).

16. Satir, *The New Peoplemaking.*

17. P. Noller and M. A. Fitzpatrick, *Communication in Family Relationships* (Englewood Cliff, NJ: Prentice Hall, 1993), 202.

18. J. Howard, *Families* (New York: Simon & Schuster, 1978), 286–91.

19. U. S. Department of Justice, Bureau of Justice Statistics. Retrieved March 2003 from www.ojp.usdoj.gov/bjs/

20. U. S. Department of Justice, Bureau of Justice Statistics. Retrieved May 2000 from www.ojp.usdoj.gov/bjs/

21. U. S. Department of Health and Human Services, Administration for Child Abuse and Neglect Information, *Executive Summary of The Third National Incidence Study of Child Abuse and Neglect* (1996). Retrieved October 31, 2003 from http://www.calib.com/nccanch/pubs/statinfo/nis3.cfm#national

22. J. Gottman with N. Silver, *Why Marriages Succeed or Fail* (New York: Simon and Schuster, 1994).

23. L. C. Tidwell and J. B. Walther, "Computer-Mediated Communication Effects on Disclosure, Impressions, and Interpersonal Evaluations, *Human Communication Research,* 28 (July 2002): 317–48.

24. J. Shuler, "E-Mail Communication and Relationships," in *The Psychology of Cyberspace,* www.rider.edu/users/suler/psycyber/psycyber.html (August 1998).

25. P. Wallace, *The Psychology of the Internet* (New York: Cambridge University Press, 1999).

26. N. L. Buerkel-Rothfuss, "Rule-Breaking in Cyberspace Relationships: Netiquette Vs. Interpersonal Competence," paper presented at the annual meeting of the National Communication Association, Chicago (November, 1999).

27. J. B. Walther, "Impression Formation in Computer-Mediated Interaction," *Western Journal of Communication,* 57 (1993): 381–98.

28. J. T. Hancock and P. J. Dunham, "Impression Formation in Computer-Mediated Communication Revisited," *Communication Research,* 28 (June 2001): 325–47.

29. D. Knox, V. Daniels, L. Sturdivant, and M. E. Zusman, "College Student Use of the Internet for Mate Selection," *College Student Journal,* 35 (March 2001): 158.

30. K. M. Cornetto, "Suspicion in Cyberspace: Deception and Detection in the Context of Internet Relay Chat Rooms," paper presented at the annual meeting of the National Communication Association, Chicago (November, 1999).

31. Cornetto, "Suspicion in Cyberspace."

32. Cornetto, "Suspicion in Cyberspace."

33. M. R. Parks and K. Floyd, "Making Friends in Cyberspace," *Journal of Communication,* 46 (1996): 80–97.

34. J. Wolak, K. J. Mitchell, and D. Finkelhor, "Close Online Relationships in a National Sample of Adolescents," *Adolescence,* 37 (Fall 2002): 441–55.

35. Knox, Daniels, Sturdivant, and Zusman, "College Student Use of the Internet for Mate Selection."

36. E. S. Rintel and J. Pittam, "Strangers in a Strange Land: Interaction Management on Internet Relay Chat," *Human Communication Research,* 23 (1997): 477–506.

37. J. B. Walther, J. F. Anderson, and D. W. Park, "Interpersonal Effects in Computer-Mediated Interaction: A Meta-Analysis of Social and Antisocial Communication," *Communication Research,* 21 (1994): 460–87.

38. Walther et al. "Interpersonal Effects."

39. L. Pratt, R. L. Wiseman, M. J. Cody, and P. F. Wendt, "Interrogative Strategies and Information Exchange in Computer-Mediated Communication," *Communication Quarterly,* 47 (1999): 46–66.

40. L. Stafford, S. L. Kline, and J. Dimmick, "Home E-Mail: Relational Maintenance and Gratification Opportunities," *Journal of Broadcasting & Electronic Media,* 43 (1999): 659–69.

41. Stafford et al., "Home E-Mail."

42. B. Wellman, J. Salaff, D. Dimitrova, L. Garton, M. Gulia, and C. Haythornthwaite, "Computer Networks as Social Networks: Collaborative Work, Telework, and Virtual Community," *Annual Review of Sociology,* 22 (1996): 213–38.

43. Wallace, *The Psychology of the Internet.*

44. Wallace, *The Psychology of the Internet.*

45. See reviews in C. Conrad, *Strategic Organizational Communication: Toward the Twenty-First Century,* 3d ed. (Fort Worth, TX: Harcourt Brace, 1994); and T. D. Daniels, B. K. Spicer, and M. J. Papa, *Perspectives on Organizational Communication,* 4th ed. (Dubuque, IA: Brown & Benchmark, 1997).

46. P. M. Sias and D. J. Cahill, "From Coworkers to Friends: The Development of Peer Friendships in the Workplace," *Western Journal of Communication,* 62 (1998): 273–99.

47. Sias and Cahill, "From Coworkers to Friends."

48. Sias and Cahill, "From Coworkers to Friends."

49. E. M. Berman, J. P. West, and M. N. Richter, Jr., "Workplace Relations: Friendship Patterns and Consequences (According to Managers)," *Public Administration Review,* 62 (2002): 217–30.

50. P. Sias, G. Smith, and T. Avdeyeva, "Sex and Sex-Composition Differences and Similarities in Peer Workplace Friendship Development," *Communication Studies,* 54 (Fall 2003): 322–40.

51. American Management Association, "Workplace Dating" [AMA online news release], February, 2003. Retrieved July, 2004 from: http://www.amanet.org/press/amanews/workplace_dating.htm

52. F. Japlin, "Superior's Upward Influence, Satisfaction, and Openness in Superior-Subordinate Communication: A Reexamination of the 'Pelz Effect,'" *Human Communication Research,* 6 (1980): 210–20.

53. Japlin, "Superior's Upward Influence."

54. J. Gabarro and J. Kotter, "Managing Your Boss," *Harvard Business Review,* 58 (1980): 92–100.

55. D. Katz and R. Kahn, *The Social Psychology of Organizations* (New York: Wiley, 1966).

56. D. A. Level, Jr. "Communication Effectiveness: Methods and Situation," *Journal of Business Communication,* 10 (Fall 1972): 19–25.

57. Level, "Communication Effectiveness: Methods and Situation."

58. R. W. Pace and D. F. Faules, *Organizational Communication* (Englewood Cliffs, NJ: Prentice Hall, 1994).

# Glossary

## A

**accommodation.** Managing conflict by giving in to the demands of others.

**account.** A response to a reproach.

**acculturation.** Process through which an individual acquires new approaches, beliefs, and values by coming into contact with other cultures.

**acquiescent responses.** Crying, conceding, or apologizing in response to a hurtful message.

**action-oriented listener.** Listener who prefers information that is well-organized, brief, and error-free.

**active listening.** Interactive process of responding mentally, verbally, and nonverbally to a speaker's message.

**active perception.** Perception that occurs because you seek out specific information through intentional observation and questioning.

**active verbal responses.** Reactive statements made in response to a hurtful message.

**adapt.** To adjust one's behavior in accord with what someone else does. We can adapt based on the individual, the relationship, and the situation.

**adapt predictively.** To modify or change behavior in anticipation of an event.

**adapt reactively.** To modify or change behavior after an event.

**adaptability.** A family's ability to modify and respond to changes in the family's power structure and roles.

**adaptors.** Nonverbal behaviors that satisfy a personal need and help a person adapt or respond to the immediate situation.

**affect display.** Nonverbal behavior that communicates emotions.

**affinity-seeking strategies.** Strategies for getting other people to like you.

**agape.** Selfless love based on giving of yourself for others.

**aggressive.** Expressing one's interests while denying the rights of others by blaming, judging, and evaluating other people.

**aggressive communication.** Communication in which a speaker makes demands, attacks another person's self-concept, or uses words to cause pain.

**allness.** Tendency to use language to make unqualified, often untrue generalizations.

**androgynous role.** Gender role that includes both masculine and feminine qualities.

**argumentativeness.** The tendency to argue constantly, which undermines effective listening and credibility.

**arousal.** Feelings of interest and excitement communicated by such nonverbal cues as vocal expression, facial expressions, and gestures.

**assertive.** Able to pursue one's own best interests without denying a partner's rights.

**assertiveness.** Tendency to make requests, ask for information, and generally pursue your own rights and best interests.

**asynchronous interaction.** Interaction in which participants send and receive messages from each other with delays between reception and response.

**attending.** Focusing on a particular sound or message.

**attitude.** Learned predisposition to respond to a person, object, or idea in a favorable or unfavorable way.

**attribution theory.** Theory that explains how you generate explanations for people's behaviors.

**avoidance.** Managing conflict by backing off and trying to side-step it.

## B

**backchannel cues.** Nonverbal cues, typically vocal cues, that signal your wish to begin or end a conversation.

**baldfaced lie.** Deception by commission involving outright falsification of information intended to deceive the listener.

**BATNA.** Best Alternative to a Negotiated Agreement; a solution to a conflict that can be achieved without negotiation.

**belief.** Way in which you structure your understanding of reality—what is true and what is false.

**bilateral dissolution.** The ending of a relationship agreed to by both parties.

**blended family.** Two adults and their children. Because of divorce, separation, death, or adoption, the children may be the offspring of other parents, or of just one of the adults who is raising them.

**bypassing.** Confusion caused by the same words' meaning different things to different people.

## C

**causal attribution theory.** Theory of attribution that is based on determining whether a person's actions are caused by circumstance, a stimulus, or the person.

**causal turning point.** An event that brings about a change in a relationship.

**channel.** Pathway through which messages are sent.

**circumplex model of family interaction.** Model of the relationships among family adaptability, cohesion, and communication.

**closure.** The filling in of missing information.

**co-culture.** A microculture; a distinct cultural group that exists within a larger cultural context (such as the gay and lesbian culture).

**coercive power.** Power based on the use of sanctions or punishments to influence others.

**cohesion.** The emotional bonding and feelings of togetherness that families experience.

**collaboration.** Use of other-oriented strategies to manage a conflict so as to achieve a positive solution for all involved.

**communibiological approach.** Theoretical perspective that suggests people's communication behavior can be predicted based on personal traits and characteristics that result from their genetic or biological background.

**communication.** Process of acting on information.

**communication accommodation theory.** Theory that all people adapt their behavior to others to some extent.

**communication apprehension.** Fear or anxiety associated with either real or anticipated communication with other people.

**communication style.** Identifiable or habitual way in which you communicate to other people.

**competition.** A conflict management style that stresses winning a conflict at the expense of the other person involved.

**competitive symmetric relationship.** Relationship in which both partners vie for control or dominance of the other.

**complementary needs.** Needs that match, such that one partner contributes something to the relationship the other partner needs.

**complementary relationship.** Relationship in which power is divided unevenly, with one partner dominating and the other person submitting.

**compliance gaining.** The use of persuasive strategies to accomplish personal goals.

**compromise.** To attempt to find the middle ground in a conflict.

**computer-mediated communication (CMC).** Communication between and among people through the medium of computers (includes e-mail, chat rooms, bulletin boards, and newsgroups).

**computer-supported social network (CSSN).** A virtual community created by networking among individuals through CMC.

**confirming response.** Statement that causes another person to value him- or herself more.

**conflict style.** The consistent pattern or approach you use to manage disagreement with others.

**connotative meaning.** Personal and subjective meaning of a word.

**construct.** A bipolar quality that you associate with people as you conceptualize them.

**constructive conflict.** Conflict that helps build new insights and establishes new patterns in a relationship.

**content.** New information, ideas, or suggested actions that a speaker wishes to share.

**content-oriented listener.** Listener who is more comfortable listening to complex, detailed information than are those with other listening styles.

**context.** Physical and psychological environment for communication.

**conversational narcissism.** Focusing on personal agendas and being self-absorbed rather than focusing on the needs and ideas of others.

**critical listening.** Listening to evaluate and assess the quality, appropriateness, value, or importance of information.

**cultural context.** Information not explicitly communicated through language but through environmental or nonverbal cues.

**cultural element.** Category of things and ideas that identify the most profound aspects of cultural influence (such as schools, governments, music, theater, language).

**cultural values.** What a given group of people values or appreciates.

**culture.** Learned system of knowledge, behavior, attitudes, beliefs, values, and norms that is shared by a group of people.

**culture shock.** Feeling of stress and anxiety a person experiences when encountering a culture different from his or her own.

**cumulative rewards and costs.** The total rewards and costs accrued during a relationship.

# D

**deception by commission.** The deliberate presentation of false information.

**deception by omission (concealment).** Intentionally holding back some of the information another person has requested or that you are expected to share.

**decode.** To interpret ideas, feelings, and thoughts that have been translated into a code.

**denotative meaning.** Restrictive or literal meaning of a word.

**dependent relationship.** A relationship in which one partner has a greater need for the other to meet his or her needs.

**destructive conflict.** Conflict that dismantles rather than strengthens relationships.

**dialectical theory.** A theory that relational development occurs in conjunction with various tensions that exist in all relationships, particularly connectedness versus autonomy, predictability versus novelty, and openness versus closedness.

**direct perception checking.** Asking for confirmation from the observed person of an interpretation or a perception about him or her.

**direct termination strategies.** Explicit statements of a desire to break up a relationship.

**disconfirming response.** Statement that causes another person to value himself or herself less.

**dominance.** Power, status, and control communicated by such nonverbal cues as a relaxed posture, greater personal space, and protected personal space.

**downward communication.** Communication that flows from superiors to subordinates.

**dyadic effect.** The reciprocal nature of self-disclosure: "You disclose to me, and I'll disclose to you."

**dyadic phase.** The second phase in relationship termination, when the individual discusses termination with the partner.

# E

**ego conflict.** Conflict that is based on personal issues; conflicting partners attack each other's self-esteem.

**egocentric communicator.** A person who creates messages without giving much thought to the person who is listening; a person who is self-focused and self-absorbed.

**elaborated code.** Conversation that uses many words and various ways of describing an idea or concept to communicate its meaning.

**emblems.** Nonverbal cues that have specific, generally understood meanings in a given culture and may substitute for a word or phrase.

**emotional contagion theory.** Theory that emotional expression is contagious; people can "catch" emotions just by observing each other's emotional expressions.

**emotional noise.** Form of communication interference caused by emotional arousal.

**empathy.** An emotional reaction that is similar to the reaction being experienced by another person; empathizing is feeling what others are feeling, rather than just acknowledging that they are feeling a certain way.

**encode.** To translate ideas, feelings, and thoughts into a code.

**enculturation.** Process of communicating a group's culture from generation to generation.

**episode.** Sequence of interaction between individuals, during which the message of one person influences the message of another.

**eros.** Sexual, erotic love based on the pursuit of physical beauty and pleasure.

**ethics.** The beliefs, values, and moral principles by which people determine what is right or wrong.

**ethnocentrism.** Belief that your cultural traditions and assumptions are superior to those of others.

**exaggeration.** Deception by commission involving "stretching the truth" or embellishing the facts.

**expectancy violation theory.** Theory that you interpret the messages of others based on how you expect others to behave.

**expected rewards and costs.** An expectation of how much reward we should get from a given relationship in comparison to its costs.

**expert power.** Power based on a person's knowledge and experience.

**expressive conflict.** Conflict that focuses on issues about the quality of the relationship and managing interpersonal tension and hostility.

**extended family.** Relatives such as aunts, uncles, cousins, or grandparents and/or unrelated persons who are part of a family unit.

# F

**face.** A person's positive perception of himself or herself in interactions with others; also, self-image or self-respect that you and your partner seek to maintain.

**facework.** Using communication to maintain your own positive self-perception (self-face) or to support, reinforce, or challenge someone else's self-perception (other-face).

**fact.** Something that has been directly observed to be true and thus has been proven to be true.

**fading away.** Ending a relationship by slowly drifting apart.

**failure events.** Violations of understandings between people in relationships.

**family.** Unit made up of any number of persons who live or have lived in relationship with one another over time in a common living space and who are usually, but not always, united by marriage and kinship.

**family of origin.** Family in which a person is raised.

**feedback.** Response to a message.

**feminine culture.** Culture that emphasizes relationships, caring for the less fortunate, and overall quality of life.

**forecasted rewards and costs.** Rewards and costs that an individual assumes will occur, based on projection and prediction.

**fundamental attribution error.** Attributing another person's behavior to internal, controllable causes rather than to external, uncontrollable causes.

# G

**generalized-other perspective.** A perspective that uses observed or imagined information about many people, or people in general, to predict a person's behavior.

**grave-dressing phase.** The final phase in relationship termination, when the partners generate public explanations and move past the relationship.

**gunny-sacking.** Dredging up old problems and issues from the past, like pulling them out of an old bag or gunny sack, to use against your partner.

# H

**halo effect.** Attributing a variety of positive qualities to those you like.

**hearing.** Physiological process of decoding sounds.

**high-context culture.** Culture that derives much information from nonverbal and environmental cues.

**horizontal communication.** Communication among colleagues or coworkers at the same level within an organization

**horn effect.** Attributing a variety of negative qualities to those you dislike.

**hostile environment.** Type of sexual harassment in which an employee's rights are threatened through offensive working conditions or behavior on the part of other workers.

**human communication.** Process of making sense out of the world and attempting to share that sense with others by creating meaning through the use of verbal and nonverbal messages.

# I

**"I" language.** Statements that use the word "I" to express how a speaker is feeling.

**illustrators.** Nonverbal behaviors that accompany a verbal message and either contradict, accent, or complement it.

**immediacy.** Feelings of liking, pleasure, and closeness communicated by such nonverbal cues as eye contact, forward lean, touch, and open body orientation.

**immediate rewards and costs.** Rewards and costs that are associated with a relationship at the present moment.

**impersonal communication.** Communication that occurs when we treat people as objects, or when we respond to their roles rather than to who they are as unique persons.

**implicit personality theory.** Your unique set of beliefs and hypotheses about what people are like.

**impression.** A collection of perceptions about others that you maintain and use to interpret their behaviors.

**impression formation theory.** Theory that explains how you develop perceptions about people and how you maintain and use those perceptions to interpret their behaviors.

**in-group.** One's racial or ethnic group.

**incrementalism.** The process by which conflicts and problems finally reach a critical mass and cause a relationship to end.

**independent couples.** Married partners who exhibit sharing and companionship and are psychologically interdependent but allow each other individual space.

**indexing.** Avoiding generalizations by using statements that separate one situation, person, or example from another.

**indirect perception checking.** Seeking additional information to confirm or refute interpretations you are making through passive perception such as observing and listening.

**indirect termination strategies.** Attempts to break up a relationship without explicitly stating the desire to do so.

**inference.** Conclusion based on speculation.

**information triage.** Process of evaluating information to sort good information from less useful or valid information.

**instrumental conflict.** Conflict that centers on achieving a particular goal or task and less on relational issues.

**interaction adaptation theory.** Theory suggesting that people interact with others by adapting to what others are doing.

**interactional synchrony.** The mirroring of each other's nonverbal behavior by communication partners.

**intercultural communication.** Communication between or among people who have different cultural traditions.

**interdependent.** Dependent on each other; one person's actions affect the other person.

**interdependent relationship.** A relationship in which each person has a similar amount of power over the other.

**interpersonal attraction.** The degree to which you are motivated to form or maintain an interpersonal relationship.

**interpersonal communication.** A distinctive, transactual form of mutual influence, usually for the purpose of managing relationships.

**interpersonal conflict.** Expressed struggle that occurs when people cannot agree on a way to meet their needs or goals.

**interpersonal intimacy.** The degree to which a person's sense of self is accepted and confirmed by another person in a relationship.

**interpersonal perception.** Selecting, organizing, and interpreting your observations of other people.

**interpersonal power.** Ability in an interpersonal relationship to influence another person in the direction one desires.

**interpersonal relationship.** A connection between two people that is based on their interpersonal communication.

**intimate space.** Zone of personal space most often used for very personal or intimate interactions, ranging from 0 to $1^1/2$ feet from the individual.

**intrapersonal communication.** Communication within yourself; self-talk; thinking.

**intrapsychic phase.** The first phase in relationship termination, when an individual engages in an internal evaluation of the partner.

**invulnerable responses.** Ignoring, laughing, or being silent in response to a hurtful message.

## J

**jargon.** Another name for restricted code: specialized terms or abbreviations whose meanings are known only to members of a specific group.

**Johari Window model.** Model of self-disclosure that reflects the movement of information about yourself from Blind and Unknown quadrants to Hidden and Open ones.

## K

**kinesics.** Study of human movement and gesture.

**knowledge.** Information that enhances understanding of others; one of the elements necessary to becoming a competent communicator.

## L

**legitimate power.** Power that that is based on respect for a person's position.

**life position.** Your feelings of regard for yourself and others, as reflected in your sense of worth and self-esteem.

**linguistic determinism.** Theory that describes how use of language determines or influences thoughts and perceptions.

**linguistic relativity.** The theory that each language includes some unique features that are not found in other languages.

**listening.** Selecting, attending to, creating meaning from, remembering, and responding to verbal and nonverbal messages.

**listening style.** Preferred way of making sense out of spoken messages.

**long-term maintenance attraction.** A liking or positive feeling that motivates you to sustain a relationship.

**looking-glass self.** Concept that suggests you learn who you are based on your interactions with others, who reflect your self back to you.

**low-context culture.** Culture that derives much information from the words of a message and less information from nonverbal and environmental cues.

**ludis.** Game-playing love based on the enjoyment of another.

## M

**malapropism.** Confusion of one word or phrase for another that sounds similar to it.

**mania.** Obsessive love driven by mutual needs.

**masculine culture.** Culture that emphasizes achievement, assertiveness, heroism, and material wealth.

**mass communication.** Communication that occurs when one person issues the same message to many people at once; the creator of the message is usually not present, and there is virtually no opportunity for listeners to respond to the speaker.

**material self.** Your concept of self as reflected in a total of all the tangible things you own.

**mediated interpersonal communication.** Communication with others established or maintained through media (such as e-mail, telephones, or faxes) rather than through face-to-face encounters.

**message.** Written, spoken, and unspoken elements of communication to which people assign meaning.

**mindful.** Aware of cultural differences and the connection between thoughts and deeds in one's interactions with someone from a background different from one's own.

**mixed couples.** Married couples in which the husband and wife each adopt a different perspective (traditional, independent, separate) on the marriage.

**motivation.** Internal state of readiness to respond to something; an element of interpersonal competence.

## N

**natural family.** Mother, father, and their biological children.

**need for affection.** Interpersonal need to give and receive love, personal support, warmth, and intimacy.

**need for control.** Interpersonal need for some degree of domination in our relationships, as well as the need to be controlled.

**need for inclusion.** Interpersonal need to be included and to include others in social activities.

**negotiation.** A communication process in which individuals or groups exchange proposals and interact with each other to create understanding and agreement, or to achieve a goal.

**noise.** Anything literal or psychological that interferes with accurate reception of the communication of the message.

**nonverbal communication.** Behavior other than written or spoken language that creates meaning for someone.

## O

**other-oriented communicator.** One who considers the thoughts, feelings, and perspectives of communication partners while maintaining his or her own integrity.

**out-group.** A race, culture, religion, or ethnic group different from one's own.

**outward communication.** Communication that flows to those outside an organization (such as customers).

## P

**parallel relationship.** Relationship in which power shifts back and forth between the partners, depending on the situation.

**paraphrase.** A verbal summary of the key ideas of your partner's message that helps you check the accuracy of your understanding.

**passive perception.** Perception that occurs because your senses are in operation.

**people-oriented listener.** Listener who is comfortable with and skilled at listening to people's feelings and emotions.

**perception.** Experiencing your world and making sense out of what you experience.

**perception checking.** Asking someone whether your interpretation of his or her nonverbal behavior is accurate.

**personal space.** Zone of personal space most often used for conversation, ranging from 1½ to 4 feet from the individual.

**personality.** Set of enduring internal predispositions and behavioral characteristics that describe how people react to their environment.

**physical attraction.** The degree to which you find another person's physical appearance appealing.

**polarization.** Describing and evaluating what you observe in terms of extremes such as good or bad, old or new, beautiful or ugly.

**post-intimacy relationship.** A formerly intimate relationship that is maintained at a less intimate stage.

**pragma.** Practical love based on mutual benefits.

**predicted outcome value theory.** Theory that people are most attracted to those relationships that potentially have greater rewards or benefits than costs.

**prejudice.** A judgment or opinion of someone formed before you know all of the facts or the background of that person.

**primacy effect.** Placing heavy emphasis on the first pieces of information that you observe about another, to form an impression.

**proxemics.** Study of how close or far away from people and objects people position themselves.

**proximity.** Physical nearness to another.

**pseudoconflict.** Conflict triggered by a lack of understanding and miscommunication.

**psychology.** Study of how thinking influences behavior.

**public communication.** Communication that occurs when a speaker addresses an audience in person.

**public space.** Zone of interactions most often used by public speakers or anyone speaking to many people, ranging beyond 12 feet from the individual.

**punctuation.** Making sense out of stimuli by grouping, dividing, organizing, separating, and categorizing information.

## Q

**quid pro quo.** Latin phrase that can be used to describe a type of sexual harassment. The phrase roughly means "You do something for me and I'll do something for you."

## R

**receiver.** Person who decodes a message and attempts to make sense of what the source has encoded.

**recency effect.** Placing heavy emphasis on the most recent information that you observe about another, to form or modify an impression.

**reciprocation of liking.** We like people who like us.

**referent.** Thing that a symbol represents.

**referent power.** Power that comes from our attraction to another person, or the charisma a person possesses.

**reflective turning point.** An event that signals that a change has occurred in the way a relationship is defined.

**reframing.** Process of redefining events and experiences from a different point of view.

**regulators.** Nonverbal messages that help to control the interaction or flow of communication between people.

**relational de-escalation.** Movement of a relationship away from intimacy through five stages: turmoil or stagnation, deintensification, individualization, separation, and postinteraction.

**relational development.** The movement of a relationship from one stage to another, either toward or away from greater intimacy.

**relational empathy.** Essence of a relationship that permits varying degrees of understanding, rather than requiring complete comprehension of another's culture or emotions.

**relational escalation.** Movement of a relationship toward intimacy through five stages: preinteraction awareness, initiation, exploration, intensification, and intimacy.

**relationship.** An ongoing connection made with another person through interpersonal communication.

**relationship dimension.** The implied aspect of a communication message, which conveys information about emotions, attitudes, power, and control.

**relationship of choice.** Interpersonal relationship you choose to initiate, maintain, and terminate.

**relationship of circumstance.** Interpersonal relationship that exists because of life circumstances (who your family members are, where you work or study, and so on).

**relationship talk.** Talk about the nature, quality, direction, or definition of a relationship.

**remembering.** Recalling information.

**reproach.** A message that a failure event has occurred.

**responding.** Confirming your understanding of a message.

**responsiveness.** Tendency to be sensitive to the needs of others, including being sympathetic to others' feelings and placing the feelings of others above your own feelings.

**restricted code.** A set of words that have particular meaning to a person, group, or culture.

**reward power.** Power based on a person's ability to satisfy our needs.

**rule.** A followable prescription that indicates what behavior is obligated, preferred, or prohibited in certain communication situations or contexts.

## S

**Sapir-Whorf hypothesis.** Based on the principles of linguistic determinism and linguistic relativity, the hypothesis that language shapes our thoughts and culture, and our culture and thoughts affect the language we use to describe our world.

**second-guessing.** Questioning the ideas and assumptions underlying a message; assessing whether the message is true or false.

**selecting.** Sorting through various sounds competing for your attention.

**selective exposure.** Principle that suggests people tend to place themselves in situations that are consistent with their self-concept and self-esteem.

**selective perception.** Directing your attention to specific stimuli and consequently ignoring other stimuli.

**self.** Sum total of who a person is; a person's central inner force.

**self-awareness.** A person's conscious understanding of who he or she is.

**self-concept.** A person's subjective description of who he or she is.

**self-disclosure.** Purposefully providing information to others that they would not learn if you did not tell them.

**self-fulfilling prophecy.** A prediction about your future actions that is likely to come true because you believe that it will come true.

**self-reflexiveness.** Human ability to think about what you are doing while you are doing it.

**self-serving bias.** The tendency to perceive our own behavior as more positive than others' behavior.

**self-worth (self-esteem).** Your evaluation of your worth or value based on your perception of such things as your skills, abilities, talents, and appearance.

**separate couples.** Married partners who support the notion of marriage and family but stress the individual over the couple.

**short-term initial attraction.** Degree to which you sense a potential for an interpersonal relationship.

**shyness.** Behavioral tendency not to talk or interact with other people.

**similarity.** Having comparable personalities, values, upbringing, personal experiences, attitudes, and interests.

**simple conflict.** Conflict that stems from different ideas, definitions, perceptions, or goals.

**single-parent family.** One parent raising one or more children.

**skill.** Behavior that improves the effectiveness or quality of communication with others.

**small-group communication.** Communication that occurs when a group of from three to fifteen people meet to interact with a common purpose and mutually influence one another.

**social comparison.** Process of comparing yourself to others who are similar to you to measure your worth and value.

**social decentering.** Cognitive process in which we take into account another person's thoughts, feelings, values, background, and perspectives.

**social exchange theory.** A theory that claims people make relationship decisions by assessing and comparing the costs and rewards.

**social information-processing theory.** Theory that explains how people use information they receive from others via e-mail and other electronic media to develop relationships with others.

**social learning theory.** Theory of human behavior that suggests we can learn how to adapt and adjust our behavior toward others; how we behave is not solely dependent on our genetic or biological makeup.

**social penetration model.** Model of self-disclosure and relational development that reflects both depth and breadth of shared information.

**social phase.** The third phase in relationship termination, when members of the social network around both parties are informed of and become involved in the termination process.

**social self.** Your concept of self as reflected in your social interactions with others.

**social space.** Zone of personal space most often used for group interactions, ranging from 4 to 12 feet from the individual.

**source.** Originator of a thought or emotion, who puts it into a code that can be understood by a receiver.

**specific-other perspective.** A perspective that uses information that one can observe or imagine about another person to predict that person's behavior.

**spiritual self.** Your concept of self based on your thoughts and introspections about your values, moral standards, and beliefs.

**standpoint theory.** The theory that a person's social position, power, or cultural background influences how the person perceives the behavior of others; where you stand makes a difference in what you see.

**static evaluation.** A pronouncement that does not take the possibility of change into consideration.

**stereotype.** To attribute a set of qualities to a person because of the person's membership in some category; to place a person or group of persons into an inflexible, all-encompassing category.

**storge.** Solid love found in friendships and family, based on trust and caring.

**submissive symmetric relationship.** Relationship in which neither partner wants to take control or make decisions.

**sudden death.** The abrupt and unplanned ending of a relationship.

**superimpose.** To place a familiar structure on information you select.

**symbol.** Word, sound, or visual image that represents a thought, concept, object, or experience.

**symbolic interaction theory.** The theory that people make sense of the world on the basis of their interactions with other people; also, theory that members of a society are bound together through common use of symbols.

**symmetric relationship.** Relationship in which both partners attempt to have the same level of power.

**sympathy.** Acknowledgment that someone may be feeling bad; compassion toward someone.

**synchronous interaction.** Interaction in which participants are actively engaging at the same time.

**system.** A set of interconnected elements in which a change in one element affects all the other elements.

**T**

**territoriality.** Study of how animals and humans use space and objects to communicate occupancy or ownership of space.

**third culture.** Common ground established when people from separate cultures create a third, "new," more comprehensive and inclusive culture.

**thought.** Mental process of creating an image, sound, concept, or experience triggered by a referent or symbol.

**time-oriented listener.** Listener who likes messages delivered succinctly.

**traditional couples.** Married partners who are interdependent and who exhibit a lot of sharing and companionship.

**triangular theory of love.** Theory that suggests that all loving relationships can be described according to three dimensions: intimacy, commitment, and passion.

**turning point.** Specific event or interaction associated with positive or negative changes in a relationship.

**U**

**uncertainty reduction theory.** A theory that claims people seek out information in order to reduce uncertainty, thus providing control and predictability.

**understanding.** Assigning meaning to sounds.

**unilateral dissolution.** The ending of a relationship even though one party wants it to continue.

**upward communication.** Communication that flows from subordinates to superiors.

**V**

**value.** Enduring concept of good and bad, right and wrong.

**visualization.** Technique of imagining that you are performing a particular task in a certain way. Positive visualization can enhance your self-esteem.

**W**

**white lies.** Deception by commission involving only a slight degree of falsification that has a minimal consequence.

**willingness to communicate.** General term for an individual's tendency to be shy or apprehensive about communicating with others.

**word picture.** Short statement or story that illustrates or describes an emotion; word pictures often use a simile (a comparison using the word *like* or *as*) to clarify the image.

**world view.** Culturally acquired perspective for interpreting experiences; perception shared by a culture or group of people about key beliefs and issues, such as death, God, and the meaning of life, which influences interaction with others.

# Index